CRITICAL SURVEY
OF
SHORT FICTION

CRITICAL SURVEY
OF
SHORT FICTION

Authors

A–Dah

3

1981

Edited by
FRANK N. MAGILL

Academic Director
WALTON BEACHAM

SALEM PRESS
Englewood Cliffs, N. J.

LIBRARY OF CONGRESS CATALOG CARD NUMBER: 81-51697

Complete Set: ISBN 0-89356-210-7
Volume 3:   ISBN 0-89356-213-0

LIST OF AUTHORS IN VOLUME 3

CHINUA ACHEBE

Born: Ogidi, Nigeria; November 16, 1930

Principal short fiction
The Sacrificial Egg and Other Short Stores 1962; *Girls at War*, 1972.

Other literary forms
Chinua Achebe's best-known work is the novel *No Longer at Ease*, which has become a modern African classic. The book is the second in a trilogy about change, conflict, and personal struggle to find the "New Africa"; the first is *Things Fall Apart* (1958). *No Longer at East* was published in 1962 and *Arrow of God* in 1964. Achebe has also published a collection of poems, *Beware Soul Brother* (1971).

Influence
Achebe is a rare and compelling artist who would have succeeded at any given period of literature written in English, as well as one of the founders of his own country's literature. The next generation of African writers will be indebted to men like Achebe because the current generation of African writers is fighting out all those questions of literary patriotism that preoccupy a colonial literature. The United States and Australia and Canada all had to free themselves from the puzzled comments of London reviewers and the disinterest of London publishers; English critics' comments toward new development in the Colonies were sometimes downright hostile. The next generation of African writers will see those questions relegated to literary histories and be able to build upon not only the achievements of Achebe but also upon the critical and theoretical positions won at the expense of so much squabbling and bad temper and offensive polemics, all of which seem so banal now, but which are in reality so important in pointing the way for a young literature. Achebe's book of literary and polemical pieces, *Morning Yet on Creation Day* (1975), is devoted to just such questions and problems.

Story characteristics
Achebe's stories are all very realistic, and although some depend heavily on viewpoint to create both effect and theme, most would have been called "slice-of-life" stories if they had been published a generation ago. Achebe has a painter's eye and an ear for the way English is spoken in Africa both by whites and "been-tos" (people who have been to Europe), as well as by those who really know English only a little better than the pidgin-speakers beloved of the Hollywood moviemakers. The best story, "Girls at War," is a sincere, earnest examination of a man's feelings which confronts the reader

strongly and straightforwardly, without any subtleties or nuances or intellec-
tualizing, without tricks of voice or viewpoint, and it is a tribute both to
Achebe's selection of material and also to the force and power of his theme
that it works so well.

Biography

Chinua Achebe, christened at birth Albert Chinualumogu, was born in
Ogidi in Eastern Nigeria on November 16, 1930, near the Niger River. His
family was Christian in a village divided between Christians and "The Others."
Achebe's great-grandfather served as the model for Okonkwo, the protagonist
of *Things Fall Apart*. Because he was an Ibo and a Christian, Achebe grew
up conscious of how he differed not only from other Africans, but also from
other Nigerians. Achebe was one of the first graduates of University College
at Ibadan in 1953. In 1954, he was made Talks Producer of the Nigerian
Broadcasting Service and in 1958 became the founding editor of Heinemann's
African Writers Series; this position and the publication, in that series, of
Things Fall Apart, account for his vast influence among writers of his and the
following generation. When a civil war began in Nigeria in 1966 with the
massacre of Achebe's fellow tribesmen in the northern part of the country,
Achebe returned to the east, hoping to establish in the new country of Biafra
a publishing house with other young Ibo writers. One of this band was the
poet Christopher Okigbo, killed later that year in action against federal forces.
After Biafra's defeat in the civil war, a defeat which meant for many of his
compatriots imprisonment in camps and "re-education," Achebe began to
make a living as a teacher and does so today. He is married and the father
of two children.

Analysis

Chinua Achebe's "Vengeful Creditor" is a story that seems to be about
what a misconceived government decree guaranteeing free education to all
can lead to, including some rather comic developments. It appears to be a
story about class struggle and then, as the reader sees layer after layer of
meaning stripped away and one theme leading directly to another, it seems
to be—and is—about something really quite different than either education
or the class system.

Mr. and Mrs. Emenike are part of the Nigerian upper class: he is a Parlia-
mentary Secretary, and he and his wife own a Mercedes and a Fiat and employ
servants from the still-uneducated masses, most of them from the village of
their birth, to which the Emenikes return periodically to shower patronage
and largesse upon the populace. At the beginning of the story, the free-
education bill has caused a mass desertion of servants, even those of college
ages, all of whom wish to go back to their villages and qualify. Apparently
many others have the same idea, for the turnout for free schooling is double

what the government statisticians had predicted. We see Emenike and his running buddies at the cabinet meeting at which it is decided to make everyone pay, after all, for the army might have to be called out if new taxes are announced to pay the unexpected costs of the program.

The Emenikes, finding themselves with this "servant problem," return to their native village and ask Martha, a village woman known to them, if her daughter Vero would come to be their baby-nurse for the princely sum of five pounds per year. Martha has led a rather sad life. She was educated at a Christian school whose reason for being was the education of African girls up to the standards expected of the wives of native pastors. The woman in charge of her school, however, by way of furthering her own romantic aspirations, persuaded Martha to marry a carpenter being trained at an industrial school managed by a white man. Carpentry never came into its own, however, at least not as much as preaching and teaching, and Martha had besides a "bad-luck marriage" which eventually left her a widow with no money and several children to support, although she was a Standard Three (beginning of high school) reader and her classmates were all married to prosperous teachers and bishops.

The withdrawal of the free-education decree has cast Martha's daughter, Vero, back onto the streets. When Mr. Emenike says that one does not need education to be great, Martha knows he is patronizing her; she knows exactly what the fate of an uneducated person usually is, but she needs the money. Mr. Emenike rounds out his recruiting pitch by saying he thinks there is plenty of time for the ten-year-old girl to go to school. Martha says, "I read Standard Three in those days and I said they will all go to college. Now they will not even have the little I had thirty years ago." Vero turns out to be quick, industrious, and creative, but there also begins to be a connection between her charge's maturing and her own chance of an education. Finally, as she comes to realize the child will be in charge until hopes of an education are past her, she tries to poison him by making him drink a bottle of red ink.

Mrs. Emenike, one of the least sympathetic Africans in any short story ever written by an African, beats Vero unmercifully. They drive back to the village where they were all born and pull her out of the car. Martha hears from Vero that she has been fired and sees the blood on her daughter and drags her to the Emenikes. Called one who taught her daughter murder, she retorts to Mrs. Emenike that she is not a murderer. Mr. Emenike, trying to break up this confrontation, says, "It's the work of the devil. . . . I have always known that the craze for education in this country will one day ruin all of us. Now even children will commit murder in order to go to school."

"Uncle Ben's Choice" is a ghost story or magical story that involves the element of human choice. A succubus-and-goddess known as the Mami-Wota, capable of many disguises, is both a seducer and betrayer. She makes it possible for a young girl who offers herself to a man to guarantee not only sexual relations but success, wealth, riches, and whatever material things the man desires. The only condition is that the Mami-Wota will prevent the man from marrying her.

"Uncle Ben's Choice" is a monologue told by Uncle Ben in a tone that is skeptical, but at the same time sincere and ingenuous. Uncle Ben is a clerk determined not to marry whose passions are scotch and a brand-new phonograph and his bicycle. His affluence brings him to the attention of the Mami-Wota because he not only lives better than the average African, but is also much more concerned with the material rewards of life than even his fellow native clerks.

A "light" girl who is Roman Catholic falls for him and he tries to stay out of her way; but he comes home one night after some heavy drinking and falls into bed only to find a naked woman there already. He thinks at first that it is the girl who has been making a play for him; then he feels her hair and it feels European. He jumps out of bed and the woman calls to him in the voice of the girl who has a crush on him. He is suspicious now and strikes a match, making the most fateful decision of his life: to abjure wealth gotten from being the exclusive property of the Mami-Wota, her lover and her slave. "Uncle Ben's Choice" is about the innate morality of men in society. Uncle Ben honors his society by suppressing his own urges and fantasies in favor of remaining a part of his family, clan, and tribe, whose rewards he values more than riches.

"Girls at War" is a story about the war between the seceding state of Biafra and Nigeria, and both the theme and the plot are foreshadowed in the spare sentence introducing the principal characters. "The first time their paths crossed nothing happened." The second time they meet, however, is at a checkpoint at Akwa, when the girl, Gladys, stops Reginald Nwankwo's car to inspect it. He falls back on the dignity of his office and person, but this fails to impress her, which secretly delights and impresses him. He sees her as "a beautiful girl in a breasty blue jersey, khaki jeans and canvas shoes with the new-style hair plait which gave a girl a defiant look." Before, in the earlier stages of the war, he had sneered at the militia girls, particularly after seeing a group recruited from a high-school marching under the banner WE ARE IMPREGNABLE. Now he begins to respect them because of the mature attitude and bearing of Gladys, who seems both patriotic and savvy, knowing and yet naïve.

The third time they meet, "things had got very bad. Death and starvation [had] long chased out the headiness of the early days. . . ." He is coming back to Owerri after using his influence as an official to obtain some food, unfortunately under the eyes of a starving crowd who mock and taunt him. He is somewhat of an idealist and this embarrasses him, but he has decided that in "such a situation one could do nothing at all for crowds; at best one could try to be of some use to one's immediate neighbors." Gladys is walking along in a crowd and he picks her up, but not because he recognizes her. She has changed: she is wearing make-up, a wig, and new clothes and is now a bureaucrat and no doubt corrupt. She reminds him that she was the one who searched him so long ago; he had admired her then, but now he just wants her, and as soon as they get into town he takes her into an air-raid bunker after Nigerian planes fly over, strafing.

Later, they go to a party where in the midst of Biafran starvation there is scotch and Courvoisier and real bread, but a white Red Cross man who has lost a friend in an air crash tells them all that they stink and that any girl there will roll into bed for a fish or a dollar. He is slapped by an African officer who, all the girls think, is a hero, including Gladys, who begins to appear to the protagonist—and to the reader—as the banal, improvident child she really is. Finally, Gladys goes home and to bed with the protagonist, who is shocked by the coarseness of her language. He has his pleasure and writes her off. Then he begins to think she is nothing but a mirror reflecting a "rotten, maggoty society" and that she, like a dirty mirror, only needs some cleaning. He begins to believe she is under some terrible influence. He decides to try to help her; he gives her food and money and they drive off together to her house. He is determined to see who is there and who her friends are, to get to the bottom of her life of waste and callousness.

On the way he picks up a soldier who has lost part of one leg. Before, he would not have picked up a mere private, not only sweaty but also an inconvenience with his crutches and his talk of war. Then there is another air raid. He pushes past Gladys, who stops to go back to help the crippled soldier out, and terrified, goes into the treeline where a near-miss knocks him senseless. When he awakens, he finds the driver sobbing and bloody and his car a wreck. "He saw the remains of his car smoking and the entangled remains of the girl and the soldier. And he let out a pierceing cry and fell down again." With Gladys' horrible death, the protagonist understands the potential for nobility within the heart and soul of even the most banal and superficial of human beings. "Girls at War" confirms Achebe's faith in humanity, and in Africa.

Major publications other than short fiction

NOVELS: *Things Fall Apart*, 1958; *No Longer at Ease*, 1962; *Arrow of God*, 1964; *A Man of the People*, 1966.

POETRY: *Beware Soul Brother*, 1971.

NONFICTION: *Morning Yet on Creation Day*, 1975.

Bibliography

Carroll, David. *Chinua Achebe.*
Killam, G. D. *The Novels of Chinua Achebe.*

John Carr

JOSEPH ADDISON

Born: Milston, Wiltshire, England; May 1, 1672
Died: Holland House, near London, England; June 17, 1719

Principal short fiction

The Tatler, 1709-1711 (with Richard Steele); *The Spectator*, 1711-1712, 1714 (with Richard Steele); *The Guardian*, 1713 (with Richard Steele); *The Free-Holder, or Political Essays*, 1715-1716.

Other literary forms

Joseph Addison first gained a literary reputation as a poet, writing at Oxford imitation classical poems in Latin, and later, heroic verse in praise of the English war against Louis XIV. His patriotic verse brought him to the attention of the Whig politicians and writers of the Kit-Cat Club. The politicians helped Addison's career in government and the writers, especially Richard Steele, helped Addison's literary career by introducing him to the theater, political pamphleteering, and periodical journalism. His modern reputation rests mainly upon essays he contributed to *The Tatler*, *The Spectator*, and other periodical papers.

Influence

With Richard Steele, Addison established the periodical essay as a popular, respectable, and permanent genre. (Addison contributed fewer numbers than Steele to *The Tatler* and *The Guardian*, an equal share to *The Spectator*, and all to *The Free-Holder, or Political Essays*, 1715-1716.) Unlike the expository essayist, the periodical essayist employs humor, fantasy, storytelling, and other imaginative devices to render delightful the philosophical ideas and moral lessons which he seeks to teach. For Addison, a fictitious tale or an exemplary story was usually only a way to vary an unchanging didactic purpose; therefore, many of Addison's essays use no device of short fiction at all. What characterizes all Addison essays, however, is an easy and graceful style. Although they are usually anthologized to display the attitudes or values of Augustan London, Addison's essays are unfailingly polished pieces; he gave a poet's care to his prose.

Story characteristics

Addison's essays employ the range of fictional devices available to the eighteenth century writer: the fable, the letter, the character, the allegory, and others. His best pieces, however, fall into two groups: first, there are the comic or satiric sketches of the important social types of Queen Anne's London, the beaux and the belles, the country squires and the amateur poets; second, there are the Oriental tales which surround moral and religious truths with the exotic decor of the Arabian Nights.

Biography

After attending Magdalen College, Oxford, Joseph Addison determined on a career in public service. Thanks to influential politicians, he received a pension which enabled him to tour Europe (1699-1703) and learn at firsthand about the countries with which he might one day have to deal as a diplomat. After the success of his poem "The Campaign" (1704), celebrating the victory at Blenheim over the French, Addison was appointed a Commissioner of Appeals. He held a series of increasingly important secretaryships until 1710 when a change of administration cost him his position. For the next three years, Addison lived solely as a man of letters, writing hundreds of essays for several different papers and bringing a tragedy, *Cato* (1713), to the stage. The accession of George I in 1714 brought Addison back into government service but he retired in 1718 after a brief tenure as secretary of state.

Analysis

Joseph Addison's essays should not be read as profound pieces; they are meant as vehicles of instruction with two particular intentions in mind. First, he wished to introduce his readers to the great minds of both classical and contemporary cultures: Homer, Marcus Tullius Cicero, John Milton, and Blaise Pascal, to name a few. In *Spectator* 10 he wrote, "It was said of *Socrates*, that he brought Philosophy down from Heaven, to inhabit among Men; and I shall be ambitious to have it said of me, that I have brought Philosophy out of Closets and Libraries, Schools and Colleges, to dwell in Clubs and Assemblies, at Tea-Tables, and in Coffee-Houses."

Second, Addison wished to recommend to his readers a golden mean in politics, manners, morality, and religion. Between 1688 and 1714, England experienced great social change, and Addison championed a middle way between the extreme positions that revolutionary change readily engendered. In politics he advocated constitutional monarchy as a median between Stuart absolutism and Puritan commonwealth; in manners he recommended an educated urbanity between aristocratic hauteur and middle-class utilitarianism; in morality he stressed a gentlemanly Christianity as the mean between libertinism and asceticism; and in religion he argued for a rational faith between superstition and atheism. In sum, Addison offered to his contemporaries the model of the cultured, self-disciplined and pious Roman citizen of antiquity.

If Addison's essays offered in their own time to cultivate the readers' sensibilities and ideas, they interest modern readers mainly for their mode of expression. When Addison moves from straightforward exposition into imaginative presentation, his modest and moral thinking takes on life. Through the accumulation of vivid detail or through humor and dramatization, Addison at his best dresses (to use the favorite metaphor of the age) his thought in attractive garb. Serious presentations of moral or religious truth wear the gossamer veils of allegory (a traditional device for presenting a religious truth) or the exotic trappings of the Oriental tale (a genre then recently made popular by translations of the Arabian Nights stories). Comic or satiric exposure of silly fashions and social opinions wears the bright dress of the character sketch and dramatic scene.

Most often Addison employs an allegory or an Oriental tale of paragraph length to illustrate the moral of the expository essay. On several occasions, however, the vision or the tale becomes the whole piece; Addison pays as much attention to the artistic presentation of the setting and events as he does to a clear expression of the lesson. *Tatler* 119, on the world revealed by the microscope, *Tatler* 161, on the blessings of Liberty, and *Spectators* 584-585, about Shalum and Hilpa, are four of Addison's better full-essay efforts in these genres. His best effort, *Spectator* 159, combines allegory and the Oriental tale: "The Vision of Mizrah" tells of the dream granted to a young prince as he sits fasting and meditating on a hill outside Baghdad.

"The Vision of Mizrah" is a completely realized story in which the moral lesson emerges from the events and scenes of the tale. Addison accounts for the tale realistically: supposedly it comes from a manuscript that was purchased in Cairo. The manuscript is Mizrah's first-person account of the marvelous happenings which occurred when he went to spend a holy day in meditation on the "Vanity of humane life" and on the notion that "Man is but a Shadow and Life a Dream." Enraptured by the melodies of a shepherd playing upon a pipe, Mizrah soon discovers that the shepherd is actually a "genius" (or genie) known to haunt this hillside.

The genius offers Mizrah a scene representing the plight of human existence, a vision that Addison sublimely describes with vivid and complete detail. Mizrah sees a valley of which the hills on either side are hidden in fog; through the valley flows a sea and across the sea stands a bridge. The genius explains that the fog-shrouded hills are the beginning and the end of time hidden from man's sight. The valley is the Vale of Misery in which man must live, the bridge is the span of human life, and the sea is the eternity into which all men will be swept. Mizrah is most fascinated by the bridge, which the genius tells him was originally built of a thousand sturdy arches but which has now only seventy ruined sections. Mizrah watches the multitude of humanity as it attempts to cross the bridge but plunges into the water below.

When Mizrah despairs at this inevitable destruction of man, the genius comforts him with a vision of the land to which the sea of eternity carries them: it "appeared to me a vast Ocean planted with innumerable islands, that were covered with Fruits and Flowers, and interwoven with a thousand little shining Seas that ran among them." These islands are the "Mansions of good Men after Death" filled with all the delightful sights and harmonious sounds that men call by the name of Paradise. Having comforted Mizrah, the genius withdraws. Skillfully, Addison works the transition from the marvelous to the mundane: "I turned again to the vision which I had been so long contemplating, but instead of the rolling Tide, the Arched Bridge, and the happy Islands, I saw nothing but the long Hollow Valley of *Bagdat*, with Oxen, Sheep, and Camels, grazing upon the sides of it."

When Addison turns his attention from religious or moral truth to the condition of society, his favorite device is the character sketch. The traditional Theophrastian character described a social type by heaping generalized qualities of appearance and thought upon him in a somewhat helter-skelter manner. Addison, while depicting a type, describes by giving localizing and particularizing characteristics, and by presenting them in dramatic situation.

Some of Addison's best *Tatler*s are elaborated sketches. *Tatler* 155 on the Political Upholsterer, *Tatler* 158 on Tom Folio the Scholar, and *Tatler* 165 on Sir Timothy Tittle the critic all achieve success by creating dramatic situations in which a particularized individual exposes his own ridiculousness and that of those who think like him. *Tatler* 163's account of Ned Softly, the modish poet, shows how deftly Addison could let character and action suggest rather than state the thesis of the essay.

In *Tatler* 163, the narrator Isaac Bickerstaff tells how the young poet-about-town Ned Softly cornered him in a coffeehouse and demanded Bickerstaff's opinion of his latest work, "To Mira on Her Incomparable Poem." More in love with his own verse than with the young lady to whom it is written, Ned Softly insists on reading the poem line by line, commenting on his literary skill, and demanding Bickerstaff's reaction. Not wishing to offend, Bickerstaff replies neutrally or ambiguously; Softly, of course, interprets all remarks to his own advantage. With exquisite skill Addison lets the would-be poet reveal the superficiality of his art and the pretentiousness of his claims:

> But now we come to the last, which sums up the whole matter. "For ah! it wounds me like his dart."
> Pray, how do you like that *ah*! doth it make not a pretty figure in the place? *Ah*!—it looks as if I felt the dart, and cried out at being pricked with it.
> "For ah! it wounds me like his dart."
> My friend Dick Easy, (continued he) assured me, he would rather have written that *ah*! than to have been the author of the *Aeneid*.

Bickerstaff hardly gets a word in edgewise, but that is part of Addison's point and method. *Tatler* 163 is the stuff of which the comedy of manners is made: revelation of social character by dialogue and dramatization. *Tatler*s like these indicate how, in the eighteenth century, fiction was gradually adopting one of the stage's most delightful methods of representation.

The possibility of dramatized presentation of particularized social types seems to underlie Addison's and Steele's conception of the Spectator Club from which *Spectator* essays supposedly come. Addison described Mr. Spectator in the first issue of the new series as an eccentric character who observes the whole London world from the Haymarket to the Exchange, but who is so shy that he never speaks in public. Richard Steele described the other members of the club in the second *Spectator*: the country squire Roger de Coverley, the merchant Sir Andrew Freeport, the witty rake Will Honeycomb, and others. Such varied and particularized types, arranged in the dramatic situation of the club, certainly gave Addison and Steele the same material with which later authors would build the novel. Addison and Steele, however, left undeveloped most of the literary possibilities of their material with the one exception of Roger de Coverley, whom they made one of the most memorable characters of English literature.

Like most other things in *The Spectator*, the character of Sir Roger de Coverley had a didactic purpose. He was intended to represent the class of country squires who constituted a powerful economic and political force in England, a force which Addison and Steele judged reactionary and unchanging. In a long series of essays (*Spectator*s 106-130), Mr. Spectator visited Sir Roger's country seat and had an opportunity to comment on various aspects of the squire's life: his relationship with servants and tenants, his ability to manage an estate, and his administration of justice in the country. From all these episodes, Mr. Spectator was to have drawn some useful lessons for other men of property and responsibility.

The Sir Roger whom they intended to tease and use as a vehicle for giving advice, however, took on a life of his own and became lovable. The reader learned through Mr. Spectator how Sir Roger behaved at church, how a "perverse widow" threw him over, and how the values and principles of his ancestors shaped him. The reader also learned little things about Sir Roger: what he liked to eat, the jokes he liked to make concerning Mr. Spectator's familiarity with chickens and ducks, instances of his generosity to tenants. The new attitude is especially evident in the later *Spectator*s when Sir Roger comes back to the city. Mr. Spectator describes him less to teach a lesson and more for the sheer fun of showing off a friend whom he loves.

Two things testify to the reality Sir Roger assumed in the imaginations of author and readers alike. Before Addison and Steele ended the *Spectator*, Addison wrote a moving account of the club's learning that Sir Roger had died; he could not let the series end without rounding off Sir Rogers' life. Since the eighteenth century, the essays in which Sir Roger appears have often been removed from the numbered sequence of essays that masks their continuity and printed together as "The de Coverley papers."

Major publications other than short fiction

PLAYS: *Rosamond*, 1707; *Cato*, 1713; *The Drummer, or The Haunted House*, 1716.

POETRY: *Letter from Italy*, 1701; *The Campaign*, 1704.

NONFICTION: *Remarks Upon Italy*, 1705; *Dialogues Upon the Usefulness of Ancient Medals*, 1721.

Bibliography

Beljame, Alexandre. *Men of Letters and the English Public in the Eighteenth Century, 1660-1744: Dryden, Addison, Pope.*
Johnson, Samuel. "Life of Addison," in *Lives of the English Poets.*
Kay, Donald. *Short Fiction in* The Spectator.
Smithers, Peter. *The Life of Joseph Addison.*

Robert M. Otten

SHMUEL YOSEF AGNON

Born: Buczaz, Galicia; July 17, 1888
Died: Jerusalem, Israel; February 17, 1970

Principal short fiction

Book of Deeds, 1932; *Tehila and Other Israeli Tales*, 1956; *A Whole Loaf*, 1957; *Two Tales: Betrothed & Edo and Enam*, 1966; *Twenty-One Stories*, 1970.

Other literary forms

Although it is for Shmuel Yosef Agnon's more than two hundred short stories that he has gained world renown, his complete works, filling twelve volumes, contain three novels: *In the Heart of Seas* (1948), *The Bridal Canopy* (1931), and *A Guest for the Night* (1968). In collaboration with Martin Buber he collected Hasidic tales; in 1948, *Days of Awe*, a compilation of learned commentaries on the holidays, appeared. He founded and coedited a journal in Berlin. In 1916 he was copublisher of a book of Polish legends.

Influence

Agnon's work has been translated into sixteen languages, and he is universally recognized as a master stylist. His classical prose, polished to lapidary elegance through innumerable revisions, evokes the ordered harmony of a vanished world. In the early stories of his Galician past, the language validates the piety and coherence; in the later stories, set in the modern world, it serves as an implicit protest against radical disorder and moral chaos.

Story characteristics

In a subdued, elegiac tone, Agnon's narrative voice tells of bereavement or loss. The typical situation is a failed quest. The protagonist, unable to fulfill an obligation or to complete a task, finds himself blocked by incomprehensible events. The plots derive from ordinary happenings: an attempt to mail some letters, or to find lodgings, or to summon a doctor for a sick father, or to get to the bedside of a dying mother. The disoriented protagonist is prevented by a series of bizarre obstacles from achieving his quest. These tales invite exegesis as religious parables through their imagery and their linguistic allusions.

Biography

Shmuel Yosef Agnon derived his pen name from the novella "Agunot," which he published in 1909. He was born Shmuel Yosef Czaczkes, the eldest of the five children of Shalom Mordecai and Esther Czaczkes. From his father, an ordained rabbi and merchant with whom he studied Talmudic commentaries, he learned Hebrew scholarship; from his mother, he gained an appreciation of German literature. He had no formal education beyond six years in private hadarim and a short period at the Baron Hirsch School, although he was given honorary doctorates by the Jewish Theological Seminary (1936) and the Hebrew University of Jerusalem (1959). In 1903, he had his first poems published. At eighteen he moved to Lvov to work on a newspaper. In 1908, he became the first secretary of the Jewish court in Jaffa, Palestine. After two years in Jerusalem, he moved to Berlin, where he taught, wrote, and met his future publisher. Salmon Schocken tried from 1916 to 1928 to have his friend's stories printed, and gave him an annual stipend so he could continue writing. Finally he had to found his own publishing firm, which moved to Tel Aviv in 1938; he opened a New York branch in 1945. Agnon married Esther Marx on May 6, 1919. His library of some four thousand volumes was burned in 1924; his seven-hundred-page manuscript of a novel called *Eternal Life* was lost in the fire. Agnon returned to Jerusalem in 1924. From 1950 to 1970, he was president of the society for the publication of ancient manuscripts; fellow of the Bar-Ilan University; recipient of the Bialik Prize for Literature in 1934 and again in 1950 and the Ussishkin Prize in 1950. In 1966 he was awarded the Nobel Prize for Literature.

Analysis

In his earliest stories, Shmuel Yosef Agnon established his genre, the medieval ethical tale, through his titles, his rhetorical devices, his use of anonymous type figures, and his narrative stance. In 1925 he published a cycle of fourteen legends, the most frequently anthologized of which is the "Fable of the Goat." The figures are flat and unindividuated, a nameless father and his son. The mode of narration is traditional. The pose of transmitting, orally, a story that has been handed down from previous tellers is established by the passive voice of the opening sentence: "The tale is told of an old man who groaned from his heart." The diction is folkloric in its simplicity, the syntax in its parataxis. Clauses are linked by coordinating rather than subordinating conjunctions; the sentences are compound rather than complex. Events are strung together in the same fashion, one simply following after the other, naïvely oblivious of cause and effect. Magical happenings are taken for granted.

Having set up the folkloric frame through these devices, Agnon persuades his reader to accept the enchantment on the same terms. The old man is cured of his unspecified ailment by the milk of a goat which periodically disappears. When the son offers to follow her by means of a cord tied to her tail, she leads him through a cave to the land of Israel. Desiring his father to follow him there, the son inserts a note in her ear. He assumes that his father will stroke the goat on its return, and that, when it flicks its ears, the message will fall out. The father, however, assumes that his son has been killed, and has the goat that led him to his death slaughtered; not until it is being flayed does he discover the note. Not only has he deprived himself of joining his son in the Holy Land, because from that time on the cave was sealed which had afforded access, but he has also slain the source of the milk "which had the taste of Paradise."

The meaning is conveyed stylistically, and the characters indicate their spiritual states by biblical allusions. The son shows that he has attained salvation through a simple leap of faith, by speaking in the language of The Song of Solomon. He sees "pleasant fruits" (4:13); "a well of living waters" (4:15); and "a fountain of gardens" (4:15). He says that he will sit beneath a tree "Until the day break, and the shadows flee" (4:6). This love song between God and Israel is traditionally recited just before the Sabbath evening prayers. When he asks the passers-by where he is, he says, "I charge you . . . ." (2:7). They tell him he is close to Safed, a town which from the sixteenth century has been famous as the center of Jewish mysticism. He sees "men like angels, wrapped in white shawls" going to pray. They are carrying myrtle branches, a Midrashic symbol for a student of the Torah. When he writes his note, it is with ink made from gallnuts, with which the Torah scrolls are inscribed.

The son urges his father to the same simple faith. He writes him not to ask questions but just to hold onto the cord "Then shalt thou walk in thy way safely" (Proverbs 3:23). The father cannot read this message, however, because it is concealed from him by his own spiritual condition. His speeches echo the dirges of fathers over sons in the Bible; like David mourning Absalom, he laments, "would God I had died for thee" (II Samuel 18:33). Like Jacob grieving for Joseph, he cries "an evil beast hath devoured him; Joseph is without doubt rent in pieces," (Genesis 37:33). His lack of faith leads him to slay his one hope of redemption. When he finds the note telling him how to attain salvation "with one bound," it is, of course, too late. With the realization that he has condemned himself to live out his life in exile, the tale closes, intensified by the ironic contrast with the believing son from whom he has by his own actions forever separated himself. The closing words quote The Psalm of the Sabbath, the son "shall bear fruit in his old age; full of sap and richness" (92:14); that he will live "tranquil and secure" refers to Jeremiah's prophecy of the end of Exile (30:10).

The goat, whose milk is as sweet as honey, personifies the traditional epithet of Israel as "the land of milk and honey." By drinking the hope of returning to Zion, the old man heals the bitterness of his life. The concealed message sent out from the Holy Land, inscribed like a Torah scroll and promising redemption, reinforces the personification and turns it into a symbol; the words of the Torah are said to be "like milk and honey." The skeptic who deprives himself of this sustenance kills his only link with salvation. The theme, succinctly rendered in three and a half pages through subtle adjustments of biblical overtones, requires an extended explication of those allusions to readers who no longer study the Bible, and that irony is also part of the point of this brief fable.

"The Kerchief" shows the changed narrative stance in Agnon's next period, when he turned from the impersonal rendering of folkloric material to the lyrical rendition of subjective experience. The story uses the dual perspective of memoir: the child's initiation is framed by the adult's remembrance. The narrator recalls how he had given his mother's kerchief to a beggar on the day of his bar mitzvah; this induction into the adult congregation occurs on his thirteenth birthday. (The story is divided into thirteen episodes, and the first edition was privately issued in thirteen copies.) "The Kerchief" was composed as a bar mitzvah present for Gideon Schocken, the son of Agnon's patron. The tale of how a boy becomes a man opens and closes with the same tableau of the mother's waiting at the window. The two scenes are informed by this difference, that at the beginning she is waiting for her husband's return and at the end she is waiting for her son's.

The time scheme relates the events to the liturgical calendar and mythicizes them. The narrator says that the week of his father's absence was like Tisha B'ab, a midsummer period of mourning for the destruction of both the first and the second Temples on the ninth of Ab. At this lowest ebb of the year, legend says, the Messiah will be born; he will be found as a ragged pauper, binding his wounds outside the city gates. This event is introduced in a dream of the narrator, who falls asleep thinking of the Messiah's advent and then dreams that a bird has carried him to Rome. There, among a group of poor men, sits a man binding his wounds. The boy averts his eyes from so much suffering. A few days after this dream, his father returns from his trip with presents for the family. His mother opens her gift, a kerchief, and strokes it lovingly, gazing silently at her husband. Because she wears it only on holidays, it becomes associated with family harmony. After she lights the Sabbath candles, the narrator imagines that angels' wings cause it to flutter. He feels a blessing flow into him as she silently strokes his head.

All these elements subtly converge in the climax of the story. On the day of his bar mitzvah, his mother has bound her kerchief around his neck. On his way home from the service he encounters a ragged beggar sitting on a pile of stones, tending his open sores; he seems to be the same figure the narrator saw in his dream. Now, having just been initiated into manhood, he does not avert his gaze, and his exchanged glance with the beggar is described with the same phrase used earlier for his parents' looks when the kerchief was first given. With a rush of feeling, the narrator hands him the kerchief, and the beggar bandages his feet and vanishes. The narrator stands for a moment before the now-empty pile of stones which seem to dazzle, and feels the sun stroke his neck in blessing. Wondering how he can explain the loss of her kerchief, he turns homeward to find her waiting at the window with such affectionate acceptance that his apologies are unnecessary.

The twenty stories in the *Book of Deeds* are ironically entitled. The first-person protagonists share an inability to act effectively. Their failed missions, most of them lapses in ritual observance, induce a pervasive anxiety. They are menaced by uncanny figures who seem to be externalizations of their own psyches. "A Whole Loaf" has been the most frequently reprinted of these ambiguous tales. Set in present-day Jerusalem on the weekend before Purim, the story, like its indecisive narrator, circles back upon itself, concluding with the same passage with which it began. The speaker, having made no preparations for the Sabbath, must go out to eat since his family is abroad. It is required to bless a braided white bread in honor of the Sabbath. He is intercepted by Dr. Yekutiel Ne'eman (both of whose names are epithets for Moses, who, according to legend, died on that day, the 7th of Adar). The narrator is asked to mail some registered letters for him. The Hebrew word for "registered" is "ahrayut," which means "obligation." Thus he has been allegorically charged with the responsibility of carrying out the Mosaic commandments. The narrator is prevented from entering the post office by Mr. Gressler. An arsonist whose name is derived from the German word for "hateful" (graesslich), he had set fire to a textile shop to get the insurance and the narrator's entire library had gone up in flames. The narrator is both attracted to and repelled by Gressler. Shortly after he enters Gressler's carriage, it overturns; both men are spilled into the street and grapple in the dust. Bruised and dirtied, the narrator cleans himself off, makes sure that he has not lost the letters, and decides that he had better appease his hunger before mailing them. Entering a restaurant, he orders "a whole loaf." Many times the waiter seems to be approaching him with trays of food, but these are always for some other customer. He begins to reproach himself for having ordered a whole loaf, when he would have been satisfied with just a single slice. He sees a child eating the saffron-flavored bread his mother used to bake for Purim and longs for a mouthful. The clock strikes, reminding him that the post office will soon close, so he jumps up, knocking down the waiter who is finally bringing his order. He is asked to wait; everyone leaves, locking him in for the night. A mouse begins gnawing on the bones and he fears that it will soon start gnawing him.

In the morning the cleaners ask who this fellow is lying on the littered floor, and the waiter identifies him as the one who had asked for a whole loaf. He heads home in a hunger sweat in dirty clothes, with a parched throat and heavy legs. Again he cleans himself and sets out once more on his quest for spiritual sustenance. The story closes in "t'shuvah," which means "return," as it returns to its initial paragraph. The narrator, although he has twice fallen, arises again to seek his tradition (symbolized by the whole hallah and the whole family). Although he is besmirched by life, he cleanses his sins (which is the second meaning of "t'shuvah," repentance). As he is locked in the empty restaurant, his soul is locked in this world for a time. Soon his body and bones will be gnawed away in death, so he must make preparations for the world to come. There is a rabbinic saying that the Sabbath is a foretaste of Paradise, so man must prepare himself. Although it is Sunday when the story ends, and the post office is closed, he plans to fulfill his commitment. Alienated though he is, he still hungers for the whole loaf of life, even though he has not yet been granted even a crumb.

Major publications other than short fiction
NOVELS: *The Bridal Canopy*, 1931; *In the Heart of Seas*, 1935; *A Guest for the Night*, 1968.

Bibliography
Band, Arnold J. *Nostalgia and Nightmare: A Study in the Fiction of S. Y. Agnon.*
Hochman, Baruch. *The Fiction of S. Y. Agnon.*

Ruth Rosenberg

CONRAD AIKEN

Born: Savannah, Georgia; August 5, 1889
Died: Savannah, Georgia; August 17, 1973

Principal short fiction
Bring! Bring! and Other Stories, 1925; *Costumes by Eros*, 1928; *Among the Lost People*, 1934; *Short Stories*, 1950; *Collected Short Stories*, 1960; *Collected Short Stories of Conrad Aiken*, 1966.

Other literary forms
Best-known as a poet, Conrad Aiken published dozens of volumes of poetry from 1914 until his death in 1973. He also published novels, essays, criticism, and a play. In addition, he edited a considerable number of anthologies of poetry.

Influence
As a short-story writer best-known for his frequently anthologized "Silent Snow, Secret Snow," Aiken has not had as much influence on the short story as he has had on poetry. Indeed, with the exception of "Silent Snow, Secret Snow," his stories are relatively unknown.

Story characteristics
Aiken's stories are clearly in the modern mode as it was practiced by such writers as Anton Chekhov, Katherine Mansfield, and James Joyce. His stories concentrate on a single incident, but one which is designed to capture both the past and the future. Influenced also by Edgar Allan Poe and Sigmund Freud, Aiken incorporates into his stories the interior world of his characters by making use of careful probings of the subconscious, including various kinds of dream structures.

Biography
When Conrad Aiken was eleven, his father killed his mother and then committed suicide. This incident could very well have influenced the subject matter of a great number of his stories, where one step more may take a character to an immense abyss of madness or death. Graduating from Harvard University in 1911, Aiken became a member of the famous Harvard group which included T. S. Eliot, Robert Benchley, and Van Wyck Brooks. He published his first volume of poems in 1914. A contributing editor of *The Dial* from 1917 to 1919, Aiken later worked as London correspondent for *The New Yorker*. Through the course of his career he was the recipient of many awards, including the Pulitzer Prize in 1930 for *Selected Poems* (1929), the National Book Award in 1954 for *Collected Poems* (1953), and the Bollingen Prize in

Poetry in 1956. He died in 1973 at the age of eighty-four.

Analysis

In "Silent Snow, Secret Snow," a story once included in almost every anthology of short fiction, Aiken describes a young boy's alienation and withdrawal from his world. The story begins one morning in December when Paul Hasleman, aged twelve, thinks of the postman, whom the boy hears every morning. The progress of the postman as he turns the corner at the top of the hill and makes his way down the street with a double knock at each door is familiar to the boy, and, as he slowly awakens, he begins to listen for the sounds of heavy boots on the cobblestones of the street as they come around the corner. When the sounds come on this morning, however, they are closer than the corner and muffled and faint. Paul understands at once: "Nothing could have been simpler—there had been snow during the night, such as all winter he had been longing for." With his eyes still closed, Paul imagines the snow—how it sounds and how it will obliterate the familiar sights of the street— but when he opens his eyes and turns toward the window, he sees only the bright morning sun. The miracle of snow has not transformed anything.

The moment and his feelings about the snow, however, remain with him, and later in the classroom as his geography teacher, Miss Buell, twirls the globe with her finger and talks about the tropics, Paul finds himself looking at the arctic areas, which are colored white on the globe. He recalls the morning and the moment when he had a sense of falling snow, and immediately he undergoes the same experience of seeing and hearing the snow fall.

As the days go by, Paul finds himself between two worlds—the real one and a secret one of peace and remoteness. His parents become increasingly concerned by his "daydreaming," inattentive manner, but more and more he is drawn into the incomprehensible beauty of the world of silent snow. His secret sense of possession and of being protected insulates him both from the world of the classroom where Deidre, with the freckles on the back of her neck in a constellation exactly like the Big Dipper, waves her brown flickering hand and from the world at home where his parents' concern and questions have become an increasingly difficult matter with which to cope.

Aiken's presentation of the escalation of Paul's withdrawal is skillfully detailed through the use of symbols. The outside world becomes for Paul fragmented: scraps of dirty newspapers in a drain with the word Eczema as name and an address in Fort Worth, Texas, lost twigs from parent trees, bits of broken egg shells, the footprints of a dog who long ago "had made a mistake" and walked on the river of wet cement which in time had frozen into rock, the wound in an elm tree. In the company of his parents Paul neither sees them nor feels their presence. His mother is a voice asking questions, his father a pair of brown slippers. These images cluster together in such a way as to foreshadow the inevitable and relentless progress of Dr. Howells down the street to Paul's house, a visit which replicates the progress of the postman.

The doctor, called by the parents because their concern has now grown into alarm over Paul's behavior, examines the boy, and, as the examination and questioning by the adults accelerate, Paul finds the situation unbearable. He retreats further into his secret world where he sees snow now slowly filling the spaces in the room—highest in the corners, under the sofa—the snow's voice a whisper, a promise of peace, cold and restful. Reassured by the presence of the snow and seduced by its whisperings and promises, Paul begins to laugh and to taunt the adults with little hints. He believes they are trying to corner him, and there is something malicious in his behavior:

> He laughed a third time—but this time, happening to glance upward toward his mother's face, he was appalled at the effect his laughter seemed to have upon her. Her mouth had opened in an expression of horror. . . . This was too bad! Unfortunate! He had known it would cause pain, of course—but he hadn't expected it to be quite as bad as this. . . .

The hints, however, explain nothing to the adults, and, continuing to feel cornered, Paul pleads a headache and tries to escape to bed. His mother follows him, but it is too late. "The darkness was coming in long white waves," and "the snow was laughing; it spoke from all sides at once." His mother's presence in the room is alien, hostile, and brutal. He is filled with loathing, and he exorcises her: "Mother! Mother! Go away! I hate you!" With this effort, everything is solved, "everything became all right." His withdrawal is now complete. All contact with the real world is lost, and he gives himself over to a "vast moving screen of snow—but even now it said peace, it said remoteness, it said cold, it said sleep." Paul's withdrawal is, as the snow tells him, a going inward rather than an opening outward: "it is a flower becoming a seed," it is a movement toward complete solipsism and a closure of his life.

"Strange Moonlight," another story of a young boy's difficulty in dealing with the realities of life and death, could be a prelude to "Silent Snow, Secret Snow." In "Strange Moonlight" a young boy filches a copy of Poe's tales from his mother's bookshelf and in consequence spends a "delirious night in inferno." The next day the boy wins a gold medal at school which he later carries in his pocket, keeping it a secret from his mother and father. The desire to keep a secret recalls Paul's need to keep from his parents his first hallucination of snow. The gold medal is "above all a secret," something to be kept concealed; it is like a particularly beautiful trinket to be carried unmentioned in his trouser pocket.

The week's events include a visit to a friend's house where the boy meets Caroline Lee, an extraordinarily strange and beautiful child with large pale eyes. Both Caroline Lee and the house in which she lives with its long, dark, and winding stairways excite and fascinate him. Within a few days, however, the boy learns that Caroline Lee is dead of scarlet fever. He is stunned: ". . .how did it happen that he, who was so profoundly concerned, had not been consulted, had not been invited to come and talk with her, and now found himself so utterly and hopelessly and forever excluded—from the house as from her?" This becomes a thing he cannot understand.

The same night he is confronted with another disturbing mystery. He overhears an intimate conversation between his father and mother. Filled with horror, the boy begins at once to imagine a conversation with Caroline Lee in which she comes back from the grave to talk with him. The next day his father unexpectedly takes the family to the beach, and the boy wanders away and finds a snug, secret hiding place on a lonely hot sand dune. He lies there surrounded by tall whispering grass, and Caroline's imagined visit of the night before becomes real for him. Rather than ending in unreality as one would expect, however, Aiken unexplicably brings the boy back to reality without resolving any of the problems set up in the story. He thus leaves a gap between the protagonist's conflicts with sexuality, reality, and unreality and their final resolution.

In another story, however, "Your Obituary, Well Written," Aiken presents a young man identified only as Mr. Grant who confronts a similar circumstance. Told in the first person by the protagonist, Mr. Grant, the story repeats what is basically the same pattern of events. Although supposedly a portrait of Katherine Mansfield to whom Aiken is strongly indebted for the forms his stories take, the character of Reiner Wilson is also strongly reminiscent of Caroline Lee, the little girl in "Strange Moonlight." The narrator says of Reiner Wilson: "I was struck by the astonishing frailty of her appearance, an otherworld fragility, almost a transparent spiritual quality—as if she were already a disembodied soul." Knowing from the first that she is not only married but also fatally ill, he manages to see her one time and fall in love with her, and then he almost simultaneously withdraws. "At bottom, however, it was a kind of terror that kept me away. . . . The complications and the miseries, if we did allow the meetings to go further might well be fatal to both of us."

The same conflicts which Paul, the child in "Silent Snow, Secret Snow," experienced are again faced by the man who is not able to resolve the riddles of sex and love, life and death. The narrator never sees Reiner again, and at her death he is left on a park bench under a Judas tree wanting to weep, but unable to: "but Reiner Wilson, the dark-haired little girl with whom I had fallen in love was dead, and it seemed to me that I too was dead." Another similarity between "Silent Snow, Secret Snow" and "Your Obituary, Well Written" is Aiken's use of a natural element as major metaphor. In "Your Obituary, Well Written," rain functions in the same manner that snow does in "Silent Snow, Secret Snow." During Grant's one meeting alone with Reiner Wilson, the room had suddenly darkened and rain fell, sounding to him as though it were inside the room. The sensations the man feels in response to the rain are similar to those Paul feels in response to the snow. Grant tells Reiner about a time when as a boy he went swimming and it began to rain:

> The water was smooth—there was no sound of waves—and all about me arose a delicious *seething*. . . . there was something sinister in it, and also something divinely soothing. . . . I don't believe I was ever happier in my life. It was as if I had gone into another world.

Reiner calls Grant "the man who loves rain," and her estimate of him is correct. Unable to open up himself, unable to make himself vulnerable and live in the real world, he is at the end of the story as withdrawn from reality as is Paul who chooses the silent and secret snow.

Besides dealing with various subconscious desires projected by means of hallucinating visions, many of Aiken's stories reflect preoccupations of the times in which the stories were written. Chief among these themes is the changing roles of women and sexual mores of the 1920's. In most of Aiken's stories, these conflicts are presented through the male point of view.

"Thistledown," a first-person narrative told by a man who is married and living with his wife, opens with private musings of the narrator, wherein he associates a young woman named Coralyn with thistledown which is being swept in every direction by the wind but which is ultimately doomed for extinction. Coralyn had been his wife's secretary, and, attracted to her, Phillip, the narrator, became bent on seduction. Far from being 'frighteningly unworldly," Coralyn is a "new woman" who has had numerous lovers. He finds her cynical and detached, she finds him an old-fashioned and sentimental fool. The affair is brief. Coralyn leaves, and as the years pass she is in and out of his life, until she disappears altogether, leaving him bitter, disappointed, and angry. The irony that marks "Thistledown" is characteristic of the stories in which Aiken examines the conventional sexual mores, holding a double-faced mirror to reflect the double standard by which men and women are judged.

In "A Conversation," this theme of double standards is examined within the framework of a conversation between two men, probably professors, taking place on a train in a sleeping car. The conversation is overheard by a visiting lecturer at the University who occupies the adjacent sleeping car. The lecturer is tired of "being polite to fools" and wants desperately to go to sleep; but the conversation he overhears keeps him awake, as do clock bells that ring marking every quarter hour. The conversation concerns the fiancée of one of the men, and the other is trying to convince his friend that the woman is not as innocent as she looks; indeed, she has been "manhandled." The engaged man keeps trying to protect his own views of the woman: her central idealism, her essential holiness—views that attach themselves to all women who are not prostitutes. By the end of the story, however, the point is made; the engagement will not last, and the woman will be put aside like a used razor or a cork that has been tampered with, images used earlier in the story. The clock bells do not ask a question; they simply continue to toll. In the end, the men cannot accept a female sexuality which is not exclusively directed toward a husband although there is never a question about their own sexual behavior.

Major publications other than short fiction
NOVELS: *Blue Voyage*, 1927; *Great Circle*, 1933; *King Coffin*, 1935; *A Heart for the Gods of Mexico*, 1939; *Conversation; or Pilgrim's Progress*, 1940.

POETRY: *Senlin: A Biography and Other Poems*, 1918; *Priapus and the Pool*, 1922; *Preludes for Memnon*, 1931; *Landscape West of Eden*, 1934; *The Soldier, a Poem*, 1944; *The Kid*, 1947; *A Letter from Li Po and Other Poems*, 1955; *The Morning Song of Lord Zero*, 1963.

NONFICTION: *Skepticisms, Notes on Contemporary Poetry*, 1919; *A Reviewer's ABC*, 1958.

Bibliography
Hoffman, Frederick J. *Conrad Aiken*.
Martin, Jay. *Conrad Aiken: A Life of His Art*.

Mary Rohrberger

PEDRO ANTONIO DE ALARCÓN

Born: Guadix, Spain; March 10, 1833
Died: Madrid, Spain; July 20, 1891

Principal short fiction

Historietas nacionales (*Stories of the Nation*), *Cuentos amatorios* (*Tales of Love*), and *Narraciones inverosímiles* (*Improbable Narratives*), 1881-1882 (a three volume collection).

Other literary forms

Having served his apprenticeship in journalism, Pedro Antonio de Alarcón did all the kinds of writing that were normal in that *métier*: sketches of daily life (*cuadros de costumbres*), book reviews, theater criticism, political reporting, and even editorial writing, for he served as editor of several journals in his younger years. His ambition, however, was to be a literary man, and the short stories he published in various journals were the part of his youthful journalistic activity that he took most seriously. They are also the work which first earned him a reputation as a writer. Trading on that reputation, he published his first novel at the age of twenty-two, and attracted still more attention with a controversial play when he was only twenty-four. He served as a war correspondent during the fighting in North Africa between Morocco and Spain in 1859-1860, and published his war articles as a book in 1861. In the edition he prepared of his complete works, Alarcón included a volume of literary criticism, a volume of travel pieces, a volume of *cuadros de costumbres*, and a volume of occasional short poems, all culled from his years as a journalist. His true claim to literary importance, however, resided in his six novels and his more than three dozen short stories.

Influence

Alarcón lacked the energy and power to be an important and influential author, either among his contemporaries or for posterity. He did not impose himself on his times, as did his rival Benito Pérez Galdós, nor did he influence literary trends by the passion of his advocacy, as did Emilia Pardo Bazán. Yet in two respects Alarcón affected Spanish literature significantly. He is the true originator of the modern short story in Spain, importing into Spanish culture the kind of work, in this new form, which he admired among such French practitioners as Honoré de Balzac and Théophile Gautier. Alarcón's predecessors and contemporaries practiced only two kinds of short composition: the literary sketch, or *cuadro de costumbres*, which described aspects of daily life, and the legend or fantastic tale, which reworked traditional and well-known subject matter. Alarcón recognized the French short story, with its careful plot, vivid characterization, and disciplined structure, as a new art form, and he introduced it into Spain a generation after it had become established in France. His second achievement, accomplished with the publication in 1874 of his most famous novel, *El sombrero de tres picos* (*The Three-Cornered Hat*), was to reintroduce into Spanish fiction the values of comic invention and gently ironic style, absent in so successful a blend since Cervantes.

Story characteristics

The considerable variety of Alarcón's short stories—in subject matter, tone, technique, and even length—is attributable to the fact that the stories are spread across the approximately thirty years of his active literary career. His early stories, written in his twenties, are marked by the influence of Romanticism which shaped his formative years: the stories are relatively long, tend to deal with the more violent passions, are sometimes improbable or fantastic in plot, and are marked technically by florid rhetoric and frequent authorial intrusion and digression. His later stories tend to be shorter, more sober and disciplined in diction, and more concerned with the ordinary emotional and psychological realities of human conduct. There, however, are two common threads which persist through all the variety of topic and manner during his career and which do define his particular short-story imagination. First, almost every Alarcón story focuses on some event or development, usually placed near the end of the narrative, which is intended to take the reader by surprise because it does not flow logically from previously narrated events. Second, the effect of this unexpected element is to give the entire narrative an ironic twist. Alarcón's creative imagination as a short-story writer was consistently attracted to material which could take on that pattern of ironic surprise. He showed little interest in building a story around an unusual character, or a striking concept, or a political or social ideal. His stories always seemed designed, in the first instance, to produce the reaction of surprise and to inspire an ironic vision of human affairs.

Biography

Pedro Antonio de Alarcón was the fourth of ten children born to a once-prosperous family come upon hard times. Neither his family's circumstances nor the impoverished environment of Guadix, in southern Spain, served his educational needs well. He had to get his high school diploma in Granada, and once he settled, in his late teens, on a vocation as a man of letters, he knew he would have to leave Guadix in order to establish a career. By the age of twenty-two, he had managed to place himself in Madrid, the active center of Spain's literary life, having previously had some experience as editor of provincial periodicals, having published a first novel, and having contributed stories and sketches to several of the best-known literary journals in the capital. Thus, success came very quickly for this precocious youngster, and between 1855 and 1860 (when he left Madrid to report on the war in North Africa), he made his name prominent by a flood of articles, poems, stories, and sketches, out of which he culled enough material to provide a three-volume book publication, in 1859, called *Cuentos, artículos y novelas (Tales, Articles and Novels)*—a remarkably productive record for a youth of twenty-six.

His work as a war correspondent marked a change of direction for Alarcón which lasted through the decade of the 1860's. He became deeply involved in politics, was elected to the legislature, and gradually shifted his posture from the revolutionary anticlericalism of his youth to a more moderate outlook, evolving finally to a quite conservative and traditionalist attitude. Meanwhile, he wrote very little and published but one volume, a collection of short stories, throughout the decade of the 1860's. His successful marriage and political defeat combined to reawaken his literary ambitions in the 1870's, during which decade he published three novels, more short stories, and a variety of travel and occasional pieces; won election to the Royal Academy; and attained his greatest eminence as a man of letters. The decade of the 1880's was a period of decline for Alarcón, who preferred to live quietly and privately with his family, publishing little except a collected edition of his works, one more novel, and an account of the origin of his various publications which amounted to an informal literary autobiography. He took no interest whatsoever in politics during that decade and was reported by occasional visitors to his home to be tired, overweight, and ill—in essence, a spent force. Toward the end of the decade, he suffered a series of strokes and died in 1891, at fifty-eight, a prematurely old man, disappointed and depressed.

Analysis

Pedro Antonio de Alarcón developed an impressive variety of narrative techniques over the course of his career by which he could entice his reader into an intriguing story and still reserve for him the kind of surprise he found to be essential to the short-story genre. The most famous story of his younger years, "El Clavo" ("The Nail"), first published in 1853 when he was only twenty, illustrates how early he learned the skills of the artful storyteller. To entice the reader into this rather wildly romantic tale of ungovernable passions, Alarcón used two separate narrative voices, recounting three apparently separate incidents, each involving a different woman of mystery.

The reader's curiosity is promptly piqued, wondering where the connection is which unites the narrator's account of the woman who rejected his love; his friend Zarco's account of the woman with whom he fell in love and whom he made pregnant, but who failed to appear for their planned wedding; and finally, the discovery the two friends make together, in the town graveyard, of a skull with a nail driven through it, strongly suggesting the murder of a husband by his wife. Since Zarco is a judge, he sets out to bring the murderess to justice, with the help of his friend Felipe, who is the narrator of the story. Eventually, a tense trial scene reveals that all three women of mystery are one and the same person. Zarco holds true to his judicial calling, suppresses his personal passion, and sees his beloved condemned to death for murder. The final twist to the story comes, however, as she mounts the scaffold to be executed: Zarco, unable to resist his passion for her, has obtained a pardon and comes bearing it to save her at the last moment, whereupon she falls in a faint at his feet and is discovered moments later to be dead. There are several improbabilities and unbelievable coincidences in this intricate plot, but Alarcón manages by his narrative skill to make it an exciting, unpredictable, and spellbinding tale, illustrating the cruel ironies of fate which prevent the consummation of true love.

Similar techniques, which control the narrative point of view and permit the surprise effect at the end, can be seen in other tales of the early period in Alarcón's career. In contrast to the somber drama of "The Nail," for example, one finds a lighthearted comic tale of thwarted love in "El Abrazo de Vergara" ("The Embrace at Vergara"), in which the victim tells his own story in the first person. Thus, the reader can know only what is known by the narrator, who attempts the seduction of a pretty young traveling companion in a stagecoach, thinking she is a foreigner because she says nothing. Just when he thinks he has succeeded, however, the stagecoach stops, the young lady gets out, is greeted by her husband, and says a cheery farewell to her victim in perfect Spanish. As a final ironic twist, the author intervenes at the very end to tease the reader, who must doubtless be disappointed because the title suggests the story is about a political alliance, known popularly as "the embrace at Vergara."

In a completely different vein, the story "La Buenaventura" ("The Prophecy") tells of a gypsy who persuades a dangerous outlaw to let him go free by offering to tell his fortune. Although it is a third-person narrative, the perspective through which the reader receives the narrative is constantly that of the gypsy, so that the unexpected fulfillment of the gypsy's prophecy at the end is not only a surprise to the gypsy but to the reader as well. This story has been almost as popular an anthology piece as "The Nail" among Alarcón's stories.

If the earliest stories bear the imprint of Alarcón's Romantic origins as a writer, his later stories of the 1860's and 1870's clearly demonstrate an altered sensibility. Improbable plots and extravagant diction have vanished, and the focus of interest is more psychological than sentimental, more realistic than fantastic, just as the prose is more concise and restrained. "La Comendadora" ("The Nun"), published in 1868 and probably Alarcón's most admired short story, exemplifies fully Alarcón's manner as a storyteller. The title character is a member of a religious order called *Comendadoras de Santiago* and an attractive woman of thirty whose fate is suggested by the story's subtitle, "The

Story of a Woman Who Had No Love Affairs." She had been forced into a
religious order by her iron-willed mother while still a young girl so that the
family fortune could be passed on intact to her brother. The brother died
young, however, and the *Comendadora* is now on leave from her convent to
help her aged mother care for the brother's spoiled son, who represents the
future of the family name and fortune.

Into this emotionally charged atmosphere intrudes the single event which
makes up this story: the little boy, having overheard two artists working in
the family palace speak of his aunt's admirably statuesque beauty, suddenly
demands to see his aunt naked so that he can understand what the artists
meant. To enforce his demand he throws a tantrum, screaming and frothing
at the mouth until his fearful grandmother, anxious above all for the future
of the family name, orders her daughter to comply because, as she explains,
it is God's will. Soon, thereafter, the grandmother wishes to comfort her
daughter but finds that the *Comendadora* has left the palace. A note explains
that, for the first and only time in her life, she has acted without her mother's
advice and has returned to her convent with the intention of never leaving
it again. A short time later the *Comendadora* dies. Her mother dies soon
thereafter, and the young Count dies in battle some years later without having
had time to leave an heir.

The most striking feature of this impressive story is that Alarcón tells it in
the sparest possible prose, offering no insight into, or comment on, the state
of the *Comendadora*'s feelings or thoughts. The reader is left to imagine and
interpret her comportment without any help from the author—a restraint of
which the youthful Alarcón would have been incapable. The story nevertheless has the standard pattern of the unexpected event and the ironic vision
of life to be found in all of Alarcón's short fiction. In this instance, a profound
psychological illumination is what is accomplished by the familiar pattern,
which is perhaps why this story is thought to be Alarcón's most modern
composition as well as his most finished short story, artistically.

In his mature storytelling, Alarcón continued to cultivate his delightful
sense of the comic side by side with his sensitivity for the tragic aspects of
human destiny such as he portrayed in "The Nun." Two well-known stories
of the 1870's illustrate this vein at its best. "La última calaverada" ("The Last
Escapade"), published in 1874, is a *tour de force* of the first-person technique,
in which the narrator first states, as a general principle, that every rake who
reforms does so as a result of a fiasco or failure, then proceeds to entertain
his audience of friends with the story of his own last escapade—the incident
which persuaded him to give up his pursuit of other women and remain faithful
to his wife. The surprise in the story, carefully prepared, is that the narrator,
on his way to his amorous rendezvous, loses his way in the darkness, is thrown
from his horse, then allows the horse to have his way, with the result that he
ends up unknowingly back at his own villa. His wife's passionate greeting

convinces him that it is foolish to imagine one will find a superior pleasure with other women. Thus, his little accident ends his career as a dedicated *calavera*, justifying the ironic subtitle of the story: "novela alegre, pero moral"—a risqué yet moral narrative.

Three years later, in 1877, Alarcón published one of his few tales with a rural setting, "El libro talonario" ("The Stub-Book"), which has proved to be one of his most popular and most frequently anthologized compositions. The story concerns an instance of the pride and ingenuity with which the gardeners of the Andalusian village of Rota, near Cádiz, take care of their celebrated tomato and pumpkin crop. The hero of the story plans to take forty of his best pumpkins to market in Cádiz and cuts them from their stalks the night before in preparation, but finds in the morning that they have been stolen. He goes to the market in Cádiz and is able to identify his own produce to the satisfaction of the police, because he has saved the stem cut from the top of each *calabaza*, and can show that each stem fits exactly on the top of one of them. Just as the authenticity of a receipt from the tax collector can be verified because it will fit the one stub in the tax collector's book from which it was torn, so the story's hero has ingeniously devised a "stub-book" of his own for authenticating his produce. The thief is thus caught and the hero congratulated.

Alarcón's short-story output was not prolific, but it has the distinction of inaugurating the genre for Spanish literature. Alarcón seemed to have an instinctive understanding of the genre as soon as he discovered it among the French writers he admired, and he demonstrated his devotion to the form by writing short stories throughout his career rather than merely during his apprentice years as a learning device. It was also by instinct, and not by conscious technique, that his stories all turned out to have the common pattern of a surprise ending and a final ironic perspective. For Alarcón, that pattern constituted the essence of the short story as a genre. The common pattern is hardly obtrusive, even for the reader who has recognized it, for the stories possess a rich variety in every other respect: theme, setting, tone, technique, structure, character types, and plot. Some of the stories are weak or contrived, a few are trivial, but there are at least a dozen of high enough quality to earn Pedro Antonio de Alarcón a significant place in the history of the European short story.

Major publications other than short fiction

NOVELS: *El final de Norma*, 1855 (*The Final Aria of Norma*); *El sombrero de tres picos*, 1874 (*The Three-Cornered Hat*); *El escándalo*, 1875 (*Scandal*); *El niño de la bola*, 1880 (*The Religious Statue of the Globe*); *El Capitán Veneno*, 1881 (*Captain Poison*); *La pródiga*, 1882 (*The Prodigal Woman*).

PLAY: *El hijo pródigo*, 1857.

NONFICTION: *De Madrid a Nápoles pasando por París, Ginebra, etc.*, 1861;

Cosas que fueron, 1871; *Juicios literarios y artisticos*, 1883; *Historia de mis libros*, 1885 (*History of My Books*).

Bibliography
DeCoster, Cyrus. *Pedro Antonio de Alarcón.*
Montesinos, José F. *Pedro Antonio de Alarcón.*
Ocano, Armando. *Alarcón.*

Murray Sachs

SHOLOM ALEICHEM
(Solomon Rabinowitz)

Born: Pereyaslav, Russia; March 2, 1859
Died: New York, New York; May 13, 1916

Principal short fiction

Jewish Children, 1920; *The Old Country*, 1946; *Inside Kasrilevke*, 1948; *Tevye's Daughters*, 1949; *Selected Stories of Sholom Aleichem*, 1956; *Stories and Satires*, 1959; *The Adventures of Mottel, the Cantor's Son*, 1961; *Old Country Tales*, 1966; *Some Laughter, Some Tears*, 1968; *The Adventures of Menachem-Mendl*, 1969; *The Best of Sholom Aleichem*, 1979.

Other literary forms

Sholom Aleichem's complete works, estimated at forty volumes, of which twenty-eight have been printed so far, consist of plays, novels, essays, children's stories, a festival cycle which was customarily read aloud at the holidays to family gatherings, translations, and journalism. His *Fiddler on the Roof* opened September 22, 1964, on Broadway, as a musical, and is still delighting audiences all over the world; it was later filmed in Hollywood. His play *Gy-Ma-Na-Sia* was shown on NET. His comedy *It's Hard to Be a Jew* made Paul Muni famous (then known as Muni Weisenfreund). Maurice Schwartz's production of *Tobias the Milkman* founded the Jewish Art Theater. In 1953, an off-Broadway production of *The World of Sholom Aleichem* was so successful it ran for many years.

Influence

Aleichem attained an immediate success with his first writings, and his reputation was already securely established when he was in his early twenties. He was acclaimed not only by Jewish critics, but also by such literary notables as Count Leo Tolstoy, Maxim Gorki, and Mark Twain, who welcomed him to America by saying, "I've wanted to meet you, because I'm told that I'm the American Sholom Aleichem." He toured Europe and Russia giving readings to standing-room-only crowds. His works have been translated into all languages, including Japanese and Esperanto. They are even more popular today than they were during his lifetime. Since his death, the Russian translations alone have sold three million copies.

Story characteristics

Aleichem's stories are monologues in which the effaced author presents himself as a listener so that the effect is one of the flow of living speech being improvised. This vernacular flavor makes them seem transcribed from actual talk. This pose gave Aleichem access to the authentic folk voice, which he preserved just as it was being extinguished. He invented several conventions for rendering it: the railroad stories, the petitions for advice, the exchange of letters. It is the language itself, as speech act, that is significant. Although the subject is poverty and suffering, the tone is humorous and benevolent. In spite of the tragedies they endure, the characters remain resiliently hopeful, filled with messianic expectations. Out of this dissonance comes the comedy, a "laughter out of tears."

Biography

Voronkov, where Sholom Aleichem spent his early childhood, was later fictionalized as "Kasrilevke." His father, Menachem Nahum, an educated merchant, lost his fortune and had to become an innkeeper. His mother died of cholera in 1872, and was replaced by a shrewish stepmother who cursed at the twelve children; Sholom's first book was a dictionary of her invectives. His second was a Yiddish version of *Robinson Crusoe*. In 1877 he tutored the thirteen-year-old daughter of a wealthy landowner, and in 1880 he was elected "Crown Rabbi" of Lubny. In 1883 he married Olga Loyev, his former pupil, and published his first short story, "Two Stones," about their romance. Inheriting his father-in-law's estate in 1885, he moved to Kiev, where he finished six novels and numerous stories by 1890. Through the annuals he founded, he became the patron of Yiddish writers. Losing his wealth on the stock exchange, he had to flee the country; he returned to Odessa after his mother-in-law had settled his debts. After the pogroms of 1905, he emigrated to America. Unable to support his large family in New York, he had to tour Europe giving readings. He collapsed with tuberculosis in 1908. His many friends organized an international jubilee and collected the money to buy back the copyrights of his books so that he would finally earn some royalties. He began his autobiography in 1913. When he died on May 13, 1916, hundreds of thousands of mourners came to pay him honor. The *New York Times* printed his last testament as "a great ethical will," and it was read into the Congressional Record. Although since his death selections from his prodigious output have been reprinted, only twenty-eight volumes out of forty have yet been published. A special building housing his works, in Hebrew translation, is located in Tel Aviv, Israel.

Analysis

It is nearly impossible to summarize the plot of one of Sholom Aleichem's stories. There is no linear, causally enchained sequence in his fiction. The type of plot to which we have become accustomed in Western fiction—that which moves through clearly defined stages to a predetermined end—is not readily found in Aleichem's work. The reason for this lies in the milieu which is embodied there. Logic and the laws of cause and effect require a stable, orderly world to function. The world of the Russian pale at the close of the nineteenth century was a turbulent chaos of pogroms, revolution, wars, cholera epidemics, starvation, overcrowding, and perpetual hunger.

Except for the few years when he was able to be a patron of letters and to pay his fellow Yiddish writers well for their contributions to his annual, in which he attempted to establish a canon, Aleichem himself was continually in debt. His prodigious output was due to his need to provide for his many dependents. These pressures, the outward instability, and the haste in which he was forced to compose contributed to the absurdist, surrealistic situations he depicted. His plots, rather than moving from explication to complication to resolution, begin in complication and accumulate further complications with ever-increasing momentum to the pitch of madness, and then abruptly stop without having been resolved; the story is simply interrupted. One can say that a typical Aleichem plot is a succession of calamities and misfortune, followed by disaster, followed by tragedy.

Aleichem's reputation is nevertheless that of one of the world's greatest humorists. In England, he was compared to Charles Dickens; in America, to Mark Twain. How could he fashion comedy from such dark materials? The answer lies in the authorial stratagems he evolved. He invented a persona, Sholom Aleichem, who is present not as a speaker but only as a listener, to whom others tell their stories. Thus, the act of speech itself is foregrounded, not the events that are related. The linguistic surface predominates. Its exuberance and charm, its wit, its pleasure in homely proverbs and folk wisdom, and its eccentric digressions shield the pain and provide a compensatory pleasure.

This quality is exemplified in the nine Tevye stories. The first published in 1894 and the last in 1914, they appeared separately over the period of twenty years. They have, however, enough structural similarity to be read as a family chronicle. What gives them their coherence is the voice of Tevye. Each episode begins with Tevye's meeting Sholom Aleichem somewhere. After greeting him, he recapitulates what has happened to him since their last encounter and then relates his most recent catastrophe. Each story closes with farewells and the promise of more to come at future meetings.

The events related are a series of disasters: loss, early death, revolution, apostasy, suicide, pogroms, and exile. These are so successfully distanced by the mode of narration that they are perceived as comedy. It is Tevye's humane, sardonic voice we hear, quarreling with God about how He runs the universe, using His Own Word against Him with such vigorous audacity and such mangling of the texts that one cannot help laughing. The monologue form focuses our attention on Tevye's moral resiliency and on his defiant debate with an invisible antagonist. It subordinates the tragic fates of the seven dowryless daughters by keeping these at the periphery. In the foreground is the poor milkman who is their father, with his rickety wagon drawn by a starving horse, punctuating his speech with lines from the prayer book. For example, when he wishes to indicate that no more need be said on any subject, he announces: "Here ends the service for the first Sabbath before Passover." It is his way of saying, "period." He tells how Tzeitl has refused a match with the rich butcher, not because he is widowed and has several children her own age, but because she is already engaged, secretly, to a poor tailor. So she marries Motel and is left with orphans when he dies of tuberculosis. The next daughter, Hodel, marries a revolutionary who is arrested soon after the wedding; Hodel follows him into exile. The third daughter, Chava, is converted by a priest in order to marry a gentile. According to religious law, Tevye must declare her dead, so he tells his wife Golde that they must "sit shiva" for her (observe the customary period of mourning for the deceased).

The next time they meet, Tevye tells Sholom Aleichem that the reason his hair has turned white is because of what has happened to Schprintze. He says, "God wanted to favor his chosen people, so a fresh calamity descended upon us." The irony of having been especially elected to endure the privilege of suffering permeates these stories.

One of Tevye's customers summering in Boiberik asks his advice about her spendthrift son. Having inherited a million rubles he has lived in idleness. Tevye complies: "I sat down with him, told him stories, cited examples, plied him with quotations and drummed proverbs into his ears." Here in this self-description is the essence of Tevye's mode of speech.

Aarontchick is invited for blintzes on Shavuos. When Tevye wants Golde to bring in another platter-full, he says it, as he does everything, in liturgical metaphors. "What are you standing there for, Golde? Repeat the same verse over again. Today is Shavuos and we have to say the same prayer twice."

Schprintze and the handsome idler fall in love. Tevye, always ready with a quotation, sums it up from the Psalms. "Don't we say in the Psalms: 'Put your trust in God?'—Have faith in Him and He will see to it that you stagger under a load of trouble and keep on reciting: 'This too is for the best.'"

Tevye is summoned to the widow's. He thinks that it is to arrange the details of the wedding. He is asked "How much will this affair cost us?" He answers that it depends on what sort of a ceremony they have in mind. It turns out that they want to buy him off and end the engagement.

Mother and son leave without saying good-bye and still owing for their milk and cheese. Schprintze wastes away from sorrow. One night as Tevye is driving home, "sunk in meditation, asking questions of the Almighty and answering them myself," he sees a crowd gathered at the pond. Schprintze has drowned herself.

Beilke marries a war-profiteer so that she can provide for her father's old age, but he loses his fortune and they are forced to flee to America. Tevye's wife dies and he is driven into exile by Russian peasants, but he remains good-humored and spiritually indestructible. That dignity and self-respect can be sustained under such extreme conditions is the secret of the immense popularity of these stories. It is the narrative strategy that permits this revelation. The monologue form allows an impoverished milkman to reveal the humaneness of his character and the grandeur of his soul without any authorial intervention.

Another way of presenting a speaking voice without mediation is the epistolary form. In 1892, Aleichem began the Menachem-Mendl letters which he continued to publish until 1913. This correspondence constitutes another famous short-story cycle. The hero's name has become synonymous with a "luftmensch," someone who builds castles in the air. He is the archetype of Bernard Malamud's luckless businessmen, like Salzman, whose office is "in his socks," and Sussman, whose enterprises are negotiated "in the air." He is the prototype of Saul Bellow's Tommy Wilhelm who loses his last cent on the stock exchange under the influence of a confidence man. He is also the projection of the author's own financial disaster at the Odessa stock exchange and his subsequent bankruptcy.

Each comic episode follows the same repetitive pattern. The husband writes from the city, feverishly detailing his latest scheme for getting rich. His skeptical wife responds from the village, urging him, with innumerable quotations from her mother's inexhaustible store of proverbs, to come home. His next letter always confirms his mother-in-law's forecasts with its news of his most recent disaster. His inevitable failures, however, have taught him nothing about economic realities because he has already flung himself enthusiastically into yet another doomed enterprise. The comedy derives from the repetition of this formula. He is flat, neither aging nor changing; rigid, driven by a single obsessive notion; he is the eternal loser whose hopes are never dimmed.

Menachem-Mendl fails as an investor. He fails as a currency speculator. He fails as a broker in houses, and forests, and oil. He fails as a writer, as a matchmaker, and as an insurance agent; but his irrepressible flow of rhetoric never fails. As he says: "the most important thing is language, the gift of speech." He can "talk against time; talk at random; talk glibly; talk himself out of breath; talk you into things; talk in circles." In the pleasure of verbalizing his experiences, relishing his own eloquence, he compensates for them. The comic effect derives precisely from this overvaluation of language. The limited protagonist deludes himself that he has masked the facts in high-flown words; the reader penetrates this verbal screen.

To be successful, comedy must sustain a rapid pace. If the events move slowly enough for us to think about them, their essential sadness is exposed. Thus, Menachem-Mendl is kept rushing. He is presented as always in a hurry. His gestures indicate frenzy, accelerated to a dizzying pace. The irony that his busyness is stasis, that his frantic activity is inert because he is speeding only to another dead end, contributes to the comic effect.

Both in these early works and in his later short-story cycles, such as The

Railway Tales, the Children's Stories, the Festival Stories, and the Kasrilevke cycles, Aleichem shows his unparalleled mastery of the extended monologue which he employs with such virtuosity.

Major publications other than short fiction

NOVELS: *Natasha*, 1884; *Sender Blank and His Household*, 1888; *Stempenyu*, 1889; *Yosele Nightingale*, 1890; *The Times of the Messiah*, 1898; *The Deluge* (*In the Storm*), 1906-1908; *Wandering Stars*, 1909-1911; *Marienbad*, 1911; *The Bloody Jest*, 1912-1913.

PLAYS: *Yakenhoz*, 1894; *Scattered and Dispersed*, 1905; *Stempenyu*, 1907; *The Gold Diggers* (*The Treasure*), 1908; *It's Hard To Be a Jew*, 1912; *The Grand Prize*, 1915; *The World of Sholom Aleichem*, 1953; *Fiddler on the Roof*, 1964.

NONFICTION: Articles on education, 1879-1881; Satirical essays, 1883; *Letters Stolen from the Postoffice*, 1883-1884; *Kontor Gesheft*, 1885; *Menachem-Mendl Letters*, 1892-1913; Zionist propaganda pamphlets, 1890's; *The Great Fair: Scenes from My Childhood*, 1916.

Bibliography

Butwin, Joseph *and* Francis Butwin. *Sholom Aleichem*.
Gittleman, Sol. *Sholom Aleichem*.
Samuel, Maurice. *The World of Sholom Aleichem*.
Waife-Goldberg, Marie. *My Father, Sholom Aleichem*.
Zborowski *and* Herzog. *Life Is with People*.

Ruth Rosenberg

NELSON ALGREN

Born: Detroit, Michigan; March 28, 1909
Died: Sag Harbor, New York; May 9, 1981

Principal short fiction
The Neon Wilderness, 1946; *The Last Carousel*, 1973.

Other literary forms
Nelson Algren is probably best known for films made from his novels *The Man with the Golden Arm* (1949) and *A Walk on the Wild Side* (1955), but his work ranges through those violent novels and short stories to Hemingwayesque essays, verse, work on the avant-garde "little magazine" *Anvil*, sketches on life in major cities, travel sketches, journalistic reporting, and other factual and fictional pieces about places and people who have "a weakness."

Influence
Although Algren wrote about drug addicts, drunks, pimps, and prostitutes before they became familiar characters in films, television series, and best-sellers, his influence has not been great. Rather, he himself has been influenced by writers such as Stephen Crane and Ernest Hemingway, as well as those in the socially concerned traditions of realism and naturalism. His loosely constructed, rhapsodic prose, similar in style to that of Thomas Wolfe, has given way to newer mannerisms of the post-Hemingway period; and his often sketchy stories, frequently hung on the *objet trouvée* of a powerful vernacular statement rather than the final surprise of the O. Henry story, have been followed by stories of a modern type which also may be sketchy, but in a different manner. His stories are characterized by a concern with the lower classes and a grotesque and surreal element found today in numerous stories, ranging from those of Jorge Luis Borges and Isaac Bashevis Singer to those of avant-garde American writers.

Story characteristics
The social commentary and protest of Algren's naturalistic and somewhat rhapsodic longer novels and the stories related to them has now passed out of fashion. His work, however, exhibits a nightmarish quality which has recently become more popular; and his combination of the banal and the bizarre, the naturalist's slice of life and the fantasist's flight of fancy, keeps a good deal of his "socially significant" work from becoming dated. His combination of closely observed detail and loose structure has become more recognizable in the recent development of the modern American story.

Biography

Born in Detroit, the descendant of Nels Ahlgren, a Swedish Jew who changed his name to Isaac ben Abraham, Nelson Algren was brought up under the "El" on Chicago's poor West Side and was the "bard of the stumblebum" of the Polish community there in the Depression. He took a degree in journalism at the University of Illinois but found it difficult to get a job after graduating. He drifted to the South and to Texas, where he wrote his first short story, "So Help Me," in an abandoned filling station outside Rio Hondo. This story led to his first novel, *Somebody in Boots* (1935). Algren's novel *The Man with the Golden Arm* reached the top of the best-seller list and won the National Book Award for 1949. He also received praise for his 1955 novel, *A Walk on the Wild Side*. Algren has gone on to write pieces for magazines and to give interesting interviews on life and literature, but the fame he achieved for his earlier novels has dimmed.

Analysis

Included in the collection *The Neon Wilderness*, the story "Design for Departure" contains the title phrase and sets the tone of the collection. The story contains some heavy-handed Christian symbolism, which can be seen in the names of the main characters, Mary and Christy. Mary closely resembles the protagonist of Stephen Crane's novel *Maggie: A Girl of the Streets* (1893); however, her world of "Kleenex, fifty-cent horse (betting) tickets, and cigarette snipes" is more a collage than a slice of gutter life. Mary is a shell of a person in her job wrapping bacon and a passive victim of a rape by a deaf man named Christiano, which seems to effect her no more than the moral problems of engaging in a badger game with Ryan, the proprietor of The Jungle (a club), or the subsequent arrest and jail term of her boyfriend Christy. When Christy is released from jail, he finds Mary on the game and on drugs, and she warns him off: she is diseased. At her request, he gives her a fatal overdose. The character of Mary is so void of emotion or response to her life that it is difficult for the reader to feel anything for her. Although there are some bright passages of real-life dialogue in the story, they tend to contribute to the self-conscious tone of the story rather than elevate its quality.

A less self-conscious and more successful story is "The Face on the Barroom Floor," a sketch that introduces one of the prototypes of *A Walk on the Wild Side*. Algren renders the bloody, senseless fight in the story marvelously. Although he does not seem to understand the psychology of the prizefighter, he effectively describes the brutal poundings of the fight. He creates a similar appeal through vivid description in "He Swung and He Missed." The little guy beaten to a pulp in the ring stands for the victim of "The System"; however, Algren occasionally succeeds in making him more than a symbol.

Algren's material is most successful when he records in journalistic manner—rather than manipulates as a writer of fiction—the real-life language and insights of his characters. Where "Design for Departure" is ambitious and basically fails, "How the Devil Came Down Division Street" succeeds because Algren has taken the Gothic and grotesque elements of an experience and set it down quickly and skillfully. Roman Orlov, trying to "drown the worm" that gnaws at his vitals, sits in the Polonia bar and stumblingly relates his bizarre and drunken tale of how his family's apartment was haunted. By the end of his story his character is clearly revealed: what the lack of hope and even the lack of a bed have made of him; how the consolations of religion are to the very poor only impediments to survival; and how that survival involves the acceptance of extraordinary circumstances which would be farcical if they were not so painful. The reader is moved to understand that for some people "there is no place to go but the taverns." With astonishment, one finds the answer to the question on which the whole story is built: "Does the devil live in a double-shot? Or is he the one who gnaws, all night, within?" In this story we feel Algren has realized his ideal, to identify himself with his subjects.

There is even more power of sympathy and understanding in "A Bottle of Milk for Mother," the tale of the "final difficulty" of Bruno "Lefty" Bicek. When a street-smart but doomed Polish boxer is charged with the robbery and murder of an old man in a shabby tenement hallway, fierce and unrelenting police interrogation leaves him in despair: "I knew I'd never get to be twenty-one." Kojaz, the wily cop, is also sensitively handled—the story should be read in connection with "The Captain Has Bad Dreams" and "The Captain Is Impaled"—as he inexorably pries from Lefty's grip what still another story calls "Poor Man's Pennies," the transparent alibis and compulsive lies of the downtrodden.

Among the "essential innocents" in Algren's work are the "born incompetents" (such as Gladys and Rudy in "Poor Man's Pennies"), the cops and robbers, the stumblebums, and the prostitutes. In "Please Don't Talk About Me When I'm Gone," the crowd draws back to let Rose be pushed into a paddy wagon, and she reflects: "My whole life it's the first time anyone made room for me." In "Is Your Name Joe?"—all her johns are Joe—another prostitute delivers a raving monologue which has a certain garish and surreal quality, reflecting the details in the world of the ex-con and ex-hookers described in the remarkable story entitled "Decline & Fall in Dingdong-Daddyland." It is this surreal quality which salvages the stereotypes of *The Man with the Golden Arm*, the stories in *The Neon Wilderness*, and the best of the later stories ("The Face on the Barroom Floor," "The Captain Is Impaled," "Home to Shawneetown," and "Decline & Fall in Dingdong-Daddyland").

There is in Algren a strain of the surreal and grotesque that links him with William Burroughs and writers who moved from depictions of the weird world of drug addicts to a harsh and often horrifying view of the "real" world from which they are desperately trying to escape. That, not his social realism (in which he is surpassed by Frank Norris, Theodore Dreiser, and many others) or his "poetic" prose (in which Thomas Wolfe, William Faulkner, and others leave him far behind), makes Algren's work more than a mere document of American social protest or a clear precursor of other writers and gives it its own value.

Major publications other than short fiction

NOVELS: *Somebody in Boots*, 1935; *Never Come Morning*, 1942; *The Man with the Golden Arm*, 1949; *A Walk on the Wild Side*, 1955.

NONFICTION: *Chicago: City on the Make*, 1951; *Who Lost an American?*, 1962; *Conversations with Nelson Algren*, 1963 (with H. E. F. Donohue); *Notes from a Sea Diary*, 1965.

Bibliography

Cox, Martha Heasley and Wayne Chatterton. *Nelson Algren*.
Eisinger, Chester E. *Fiction of the Forties*.
Geismar, Maxwell. *American Modern: From Rebellion to Conformity*.
McCollum, Kenneth G. *Nelson Algren: A Checklist*.

Leonard R. N. Ashley

HANS CHRISTIAN ANDERSEN

Born: Odense, Denmark; April 2, 1805
Died: Copenhagen, Denmark; August 4, 1875

Principal short fiction
Eventyr, 1835-1872 (*Tales*); *It's Perfectly True and Other Stories*, 1938; *Andersen's Fairy Tales*, 1948; *The Complete Andersen*, 1949; *Fairy Tales*, 1950-1958; *Hans Andersen's Fairy Tales*, 1953; *The Complete Fairy Tales and Stories*, 1974.

Other literary forms
Hans Christian Andersen's first publication was a poem in 1828, and his first prose work, a fantasy of a nightly journey titled *Fodreise fra Holmena Canal til østpynten af Amager* (1829, *A Journey on Foot from Holman's Canal to the East Point of Amager*), was an immediate success. He wrote six novels, of which *Improvisatoren* (1835, *The Improvisatore*) securely established his fame and continues in print in the United States. His nine travel books began with *En digters bazar* (1842, *A Poet's Bazaar*) and mainly concern his European travels. Other works are *Billebog uden billeder* (1840, *Tales the Moon Can Tell*) and *Syv digte* (translated 1855, *Seven Poems*). His autobiographies are *Levnedsbogen, 1805-1831* (1926), discovered fifty years after his death; *Mit Livs Eventyr* (1847, *The Story of My Life*); and the revised *The Fairy Tale of My Life* (1855). Other publications include his correspondence, diaries, notebooks and draft material, drawings, sketches, paper cuttings, and plays.

Influence
Andersen became the foremost Danish writer of his time and remains best-known for his fairy tales and stories, which have been translated into more than one hundred languages. Outside the English-speaking world, he is a famous creative writer of great appeal to adults; but in Britain and America he is known chiefly as a children's writer, partly because bad translations make his style seem childish.

Story characteristics
Although he is frequently paired with the brothers Grimm, who collected folk tales, only twelve of Andersen's tales are based on traditional stories; the remaining 144 are purely his own invention, written in a style influenced by the primitive folk tales. Approximately thirty of his tales, published between 1835 and 1850, are best known and available as separate books. These include "The Fir Tree," "The Ice Maiden," "The Nightingale," "The Emperor's New Clothes," "Thumbelina," "The Ugly Duckling," "The Snow

Queen," "The Steadfast Tin Soldier," "The Little Match Girl," "The Little Mermaid," and "The Princess and the Pea." The tales contain levels of abstraction which mystify children; many include witty, clever, and humorous observations delivered in companionable, colloquial style, which frequently show a lack of clear moral judgment. Many are set in a fantasy world or contain elements of magic; others feature animals, trees, and plants as main characters; in some, inanimate things may become animated. Usually a child as protagonist, without expressing surprise at nature's unusual sentience, traverses the realistic and alternate worlds with equal aplomb—for nothing is impossible to a child.

Biography

The son of a shoemaker, who died when Hans Christian Andersen was eleven, and an illiterate servant mother, Andersen from his early childhood loved to invent tales, poems, and plays and to make intricate paper cuttings; he loved to recite his creations to any possible listener. Later he yearned to be a *Digter*, a creative writer of divine inspiration, and to be an actor. In 1819 he journeyed to Copenhagen where he lived through hard times but developed a talent for attracting benefactors. Among these was Jonas Collin, whose home became Andersen's "Home of Homes," as he called it, who acted as a foster father, and whose son Edvard became a close friend. Through Jonas' influence and a grant from the king, Andersen attended grammar school (1822-1827) and struggled with a difficult headmaster as well as with Latin and Greek. Andersen never married, although he was attracted to several women, among them the singer Jenny Lind. Although he was very tall and ungainly in appearance, with large feet, a large nose, and small eyes, and although he was sentimental and exceptionally concerned with himself, his fears and doubts, Andersen enjoyed the company of Europe's leading professionals and nobility, including kings and queens; in later life many honors were bestowed upon him. His last nine years he lived at the home of the Moritz Melchiors, just outside Copenhagen, and he died there on August 4, 1875.

Analysis

Following publication of his *Nye eventyr* (1844, *New Tales*), Hans Christian Andersen explained in a letter that he wanted his tales to be read on two levels, offering something for the minds of adults as well as appealing to children. Three examples of such adult tales, "The Snow Queen," "The Shadow," and "The Nightingale," demonstrate how, as Andersen said, in writing from his own breast instead of retelling old tales he had now found out how to write fairy tales.

Composed of seven stories, "The Snow Queen" begins with a mirror into which people can look and see the good become small and mean and the bad appear at its very worst. Andersen could remember, in later years, that his father had maintained that "There is no other devil than the one we have in our hearts"; and this provides a clue to the plot and theme of "The Snow Queen." Only when the demon's followers confront heaven with the mirror does it shatter into fragments, but unfortunately those fragments enter the hearts of many people.

The second story introduces Little Kay and Gerda who love each other and the summer's flowers until a fragment of the evil mirror lodges in Little Kay's eye and another pierces his heart. Having formerly declared that if the Snow Queen visited he would melt her on the stove, Kay now views snowflakes through a magnifying glass and pronounces them more beautiful than flowers. He protests against the grandmother's tales with a *but* for the logic of each one, and, apparently arrived at adolescence, transfers loyalty from the innocent Gerda to the knowing Snow Queen. He follows the visiting Queen out of town and into the snowy expanses of the distant sky.

The journey from adolescence to maturity becomes for Gerda her quest for the missing Kay, her true love and future mate. Fearing the river has taken Kay, she offers it her new red shoes; but a boat she steps into drifts away from shore and, riding the river's current, she travels far before being pulled ashore and detained by a woman "learned in magic." Gerda here forgets her search for Kay until the sight of a rose reminds her. In one of the story's most abstract passages, she then asks the tiger lilies, convolvulus, snowdrop, hyacinth, buttercup, and narcissus where he might be; but each tells a highly fanciful tale concerned with its own identity. The narcissus, for example, alludes to the Echo and Narcissus myth in saying "I can see myself" and fails to aid Gerda. Barefoot, Gerda runs out of the garden and finds that autumn has arrived.

A crow believes he has seen Kay and contrives a visit with the Prince and Princess, who forgive the invasion of their palatial privacy and then outfit Gerda to continue her search. All her newly acquired equipage attracts a "little robber girl," a perplexing mixture of amorality and good intentions, who threatens Gerda with her knife but provides a reindeer to carry Gerda to Spitsbergen, where the wood pigeons have reported having seen Kay. At one stop, the reindeer begs a Finnish wise woman to give Gerda the strength to conquer all, but the woman points out the great power that Gerda has already evidenced and adds, "We must not tell her what power she has. It is in her heart, because she is such a sweet innocent child." She sends Gerda and the reindeer on their way, with Gerda riding without boots or mittens. Eventually the reindeer deposits her by a red-berry bush in freezing icebound Finmark, from which she walks to the Snow Queen's Palace.

Here she finds a second mirror, a frozen lake broken into fragments but actually the throne of the Snow Queen which the Queen calls "The Mirror of Reason." Little Kay works diligently to form the fragments into the word

"Eternity," for which accomplishment the Snow Queen has said he can be his own master and have the whole world and a new pair of skates. Gerda's love, when she sheds tears of joy at finding Kay, melts the ice in his heart and the mirror within his breast; and Kay, himself bursting into tears at recovering Gerda and her love, finds that the fragments magically form themselves into the word "Eternity." The two young people find many changes on their return journey, but much the same at home, where they now realize they are grown up. The grandmother's Bible verse tells them about the kingdom of heaven for those with hearts of children, and they now understand the meaning of the hymn, "Where roses deck the flowery vale,/There Infant Jesus, thee we hail!" The flowers of love, not the mirror of reason, make Kay and Gerda inheritors of the kingdom of heaven, the Snow Queen's elusive eternity.

Only the style makes such stories children's stories, for "The Snow Queen," with devices such as the snowflake seen under a microscope, obviously attacks empiricism; at the same time, the story offers the symbol of the foot, important to folklore; and the journey of Gerda through obstacles and a final illumination comprises a "journey of the hero" as delineated by the mythologist Joseph Campbell. So also Andersen's "The Shadow" presents an alter-ego with psychic dimensions well beyond the ken of children.

The setting with which "The Shadow" begins reflects Andersen's diary entries from his trip to Naples in June, 1846, when he found the sun too hot for venturing out of doors and began writing the story. With the hot sun directly overhead, the shadow disappears except in morning and evening and begins to assume a life of its own. Its activities, closely observed by its owner, the "learned man from a cold country," lead him to joke about its going in to the house opposite to learn the identity of a lovely maiden. The shadow fails to return, but the learned man soon grows a new shadow. Many years later, once more at home, the original shadow visits him but has now become so corporeal that it has acquired flesh and clothes. Further, it divulges, it has become wealthy and plans to marry. Its three-week visit in the house opposite, it now reveals, placed it close to the lovely maiden Poetry, in whose anteroom the shadow read all the poetry and prose ever written. If the learned man had been there, he would not have remained a human being, but it was there that the shadow became one. Emerging thence he went about under cover of a pastry cook's gown for some time before growing into his present affluence.

Later, the learned man's writings of the good, the true, and the beautiful fail to provide him an income; only after he has suffered long and become so thin that people tell him he looks like a shadow does he accede to the shadow's request that he become a traveling companion. Shadow and master have now exchanged places, but the king's daughter notices that the new master cannot cast a shadow. To this accusation he replies that the person who is always at his side is his shadow. When the new master cannot answer her scientific inquiries, he defers to the shadow, whose knowledge impresses the princess. Clearly, she reasons, to have such a learned servant the master must be the most learned man on earth.

Against the upcoming marriage of princess and shadow, the learned man protests and threatens to reveal the truth. "Not a soul would believe you," says the shadow; and with his new status as fiancé he has the learned man cast into prison. The princess agrees that it would be a charity to deliver the learned man from his delusions and has him promptly executed.

That Poetry would make a human being divine or "more than human" gives poetry the identity of Psyche, whose statue by Thorvaldsen Andersen had admired in 1833 in the Danish sculptor's studio. (Also, Andersen in 1861 wrote a story called "The Psyche.") In "The Shadow," the human qualities with which Poetry's presence infuses the shadow function for him as a soul. Thereafter his incubation under the pastry cook's gown provides him a proper maturation from which, still as shadow, he looks into people's lives, spies on their evils and their intimacies, and acquires power over them. This phase of his existence explains the acquisition of wealth, but as the shadow grows human and powerful the learned man declines.

The shadow, the other self of the learned man, reflects the psychic stress Andersen suffered in his relationship with Edvard Collin. What Andersen desired between himself and Collin has been recognized by scholars as the *Blütbruderschaft* that D. H. Lawrence wrote about—a close relationship with another male. Collin persisted, however, in fending off all Andersen's attempts at informality, even in regard to the use of language; and in the story the shadow is obviously Collin, whose separate identity thrives at the expense of the learned man's—Andersen's—psyche. Writing in his diary of the distress and illness brought on by a letter from Edvard Collin, Andersen contemplated suicide and pleaded "he must use the language of a friend"(1834); so also the story's shadow rejects such language and commits the learned man to prison and to death. The problem of language appears twice in the story, although various translations diminish its effect. The shadow's newly acquired affluence, on his first visit to his former master, provides him with the daring to suggest that the learned man speak "less familiarly," and to say "sir," or—in other translations—to replace "you' with "thee" and "thou." Frequently argued between Andersen and Collin as the question of *"Du"* versus *"De,"* the problem reappears in the story when the learned man asks the shadow, because of their childhood together, to pledge themselves to address each other as *"Du."* (In some translations, this reads merely "to drink to our good fellowship" and "call each other by our names.") In the shadow's reply, Andersen improved upon Edvard's objection by having the shadow cite the feel of gray paper or the scraping of a nail on a pane of glass as similar to the sound of *"Du"* spoken by the learned man.

Such touches of individuality made Andersen's writing succeed, as evidenced by a tale he borrowed from a Spanish source, the tale of "The Emperor's New Clothes," which he said he read in a German translation from Prince don Juan Manuel (1282-c. 1349). Andersen's version improved upon the original in several respects, including his theme of pretense of understanding as well as ridicule of snobbery and his ending with the objection of the child—an ending which Andersen added after the original manuscript had been sent to the publisher.

Andersen's talent for universalizing the appeal of a story and for capitalizing on personal experiences appears time and again throughout his many tales. Because of his grotesque appearance, which interfered with his longed-for stage career, Andersen knew personally the anguish of "The Ugly Duckling," but his success as a writer made him a beautiful swan. His extreme sensitivity he wrote into "The Princess and the Pea," detailing the adventures of a princess who could feel a pea through twenty mattresses. Andersen in this story borrowed from a folk tale in which the little girl understands the test she is being put to because a dog or cat aids her by relaying the information, but Andersen contrived that her sensitivity alone would suffice. Nevertheless some translators could not accept the idea of her feeling a single pea and changed the text to read three peas and the title to read "The Real Princess."

Andersen's stories thus objectify psychic conditions, and among these his frequent association with nobility enabled him to depict with humor the qualities of egotism, arrogance, and subservience found at court. In "The Snow Queen" the crow describes court ladies and attendants standing around, and the nearer the door they stand the greater is their haughtiness; the footman's boy is too proud to be looked at. The princess is so clever she has read all the newspapers in the world and forgotten them again.

One of Andersen's best depictions of court life and, at the same time, one of his best satires is "The Nightingale," which he wrote in honor of Jenny Lind, the singer known as the Swedish Nightingale. The story's theme contrasts the artificial manners and preferences of the court with the natural song of the nightingale and the ways of simple folk. Far from the palace of the Emperor of China where bells on the flowers in the garden tinkle to attract attention to the flowers, the nightingale sings in the woods by the deep sea, so that a poor fisherman listens to it each day and travelers returning home write about it. The Emperor discovers his nightingale from reading about it in a book, but his gentleman-in-waiting knows nothing about it because it has never been presented at court. Inquiring throughout the court, he finds only a little girl in the kitchen who has heard it and who helps him find it. Brought to the court, it must sing on a golden perch, and, when acclaimed successful, it has its own cage and can walk out twice a day and once in the night with twelve footmen, each one holding a ribbon tied around its leg. When the Emperor of Japan sends as a gift an artificial nightingale studded with diamonds, rubies, and sapphires, the two birds cannot sing together and the real nightingale flies away in chagrin. The court throng honors the mechanical bird with jewels and gold as gifts, and the Master of Music writes twenty-five volumes about it. The mechanical bird earns the title of Chief Imperial Singer-of-the-Bed-Chamber, and in rank it stands number one on the left side, for even an Emperor's heart is on the left side.

Eventually the mechanical bird breaks down, and the watchmaker cannot assure repair with the same admirable tune. Five years later the Emperor becomes ill, and his successor is proclaimed. Then, with Death sitting on his chest and wearing his golden crown, he calls upon the mechanical bird to sing. While it sits mute, the nightingale appears at the window and sings Death away and brings new life to the Emperor. With the generosity of a true heroine, it advises the king not to destroy the mechanical bird, which did all the good it could; however, it reminds the Emperor, a little singing bird sings to the fisherman and the peasant and must continue to go and to return. Although it loves the Emperor's heart more than his crown, the crown has an odor of sanctity also. The nightingale will return, but the Emperor must keep its secret that a little bird tells him everything.

Andersen's comment comparing the heart and the crown of the emperor may be his finest on the attraction of the great, an attraction which he felt all his life. Early in 1874, after visiting a Count in South Zealand, he wrote to Mrs. Melchior that no fairy tales occur to him any more. If he walks in the garden, he said, Thumbelina has ended her journey on the water lily; the wind and the Old Oak Tree have already told him their tales and have nothing more to tell him. It is, he wrote, as if he had filled out the entire circle with fairy-tale radii close to one another. On his seventieth birthday, April 2, 1875, the royal carriage was sent to fetch him to the castle, and the king bestowed another decoration. It was his last birthday celebration, for in a few months Andersen had filled out the circle of his life.

Major publications other than short fiction

NOVELS: *Improvisatoren*, 1835 (*The Improvisatore*); *O. T.*, 1836; *Kun en Spillemand*, 1837 (*Only a Fiddler*); *De To Baronesser*, 1848 (*The Two Baronesses*); *At være eller ikke være*, 1857 (*To Be or Not To Be*); *Lykke-Peer*, 1870 (*Lucky Peer*).

PLAYS: *Kjærlighed paa Nicolai Taarn, eller Hvad siger Parterret*, 1829 (*Love on St. Nicholas Tower: Or, What Says the Pit*), *Agnete og havmanden*, 1833 (*Agnete and the Merman*); *Mulatten*, 1840 (*The Mulatto*).

POETRY: *Digte*, 1830-1833 (*Collected Poems*).

NONFICTION: *Rambles in the Romantic Regions of Saxon Switzerland*, 1831; *Billebog uden billeder*, 1840 (*Tales the Moon Can Tell*); *En digters bazar*, 1842 (*A Poet's Bazaar*); *I Sverrig*, 1851 (*In Sweden*); *I Spanien*, 1863 (*In Spain*); *Et besøg i Portugal 1866* (*A Visit to Portugal 1866*).

Bibliography
Brandes, Georg. *Creative Spirits of the Nineteenth Century*.
Bredsdorff, Elias. "A Critical Guide to the Literature on Hans Christian Andersen," in *Scandinavica*. VI, No. 2 (1967), pp. 108-125.
───────── . *Hans Christian Andersen: The Story of His Life and Work 1805-75*.
Spink, Reginald. *Hans Christian Andersen and His World*.

Grace Eckley

SHERWOOD ANDERSON

Born: Camden, Ohio; September 13, 1876
Died: Colón, Panama; March 8, 1941

Principal short fiction

Winesburg, Ohio, 1919 ; *The Triumph of the Egg,* 1921; *Horses and Men,* 1923; *Death in the Woods and Other Stories,* 1933; *The Sherwood Anderson Reader,* 1947.

Other literary forms

Sherwood Anderson published seven novels, three memoirs seeking to explain his philosophy and art, one book of poems, dramatizations of *Winesburg, Ohio,* and three other stories. His memoirs are termed "fanciful," but offer important insights into his fictions. Anderson was a prolific article writer and for a time owned and edited the Republican and Democratic newspapers in Marion, Virginia. In 1921, he received a two-thousand-dollar literary prize from *The Dial* magazine. While employed as a copywriter, he also wrote many successful advertisements.

Influence

Anderson exerted a formative influence on writers such as Ernest Hemingway, William Faulkner, and John Steinbeck, some of whom later rejected him, Hemingway going so far as to burlesque the novel *Dark Laughter* (1925) in his *The Torrents of Spring* (1926). Anderson was a protomodernist who was originally praised by literary rebels, then generally accepted as an innovator in the field of the short story, then attacked by the Left in the 1930's as confused and even fascistic. In the 1950's, he began to be reassessed as an important American writer. Today he is viewed as an influence upon writers such as Carson McCullers, Bernard Malamud, Flannery O'Connor, and Saul Bellow. In his short stories, Anderson elevated nostalgia for small-town America to elegiac proportions; he employed his watered-down version of Depth psychology in motivating his protagonists and was straightforward about their sexuality; and he sentimentalized and at times glamorized neurotics and psychotics.

Story characteristics

Anderson's characters are denizens of Midwestern towns (usually Ohio) who do not fit into the social mainstream. They have become isolated because of ill-fortune in love, youthful inexperience, lack of education, poverty, provincialism, or stupidity, which traps them in mechanistic outlooks that aggravate their alienation. The stories are often first-person narratives told with a bittersweet voice compounded with an element of weirdness. The language is simple and direct, with an effective use of repetition and a striving to be suggestive about familiar situations. There is rarely reference to scientific, musical, artistic, political, social, or even literary aspects of the larger culture in Anderson's stories, a glaring omission in works portraying education-hungry nineteenth century Americans.

Biography

Sherwood Anderson was the third of seven children of a father who was an itinerant harness maker and house painter and a mother of either German or Italian descent. His father was a Civil War veteran (a Southerner who fought with the Union), locally famed as a storyteller. His elder brother, Karl, became a prominent painter who later introduced Sherwood to Chicago's Bohemia, which gained him access to the literary world. Declining fortunes caused the family to move repeatedly until they settled in Clyde, Ohio (the model for Winesburg), a village just south of Lake Erie. The young Anderson experienced a desultory schooling but led an otherwise normal childhood. After army service in Cuba during the Spanish-American War (he saw no combat), he acquired a further year of schooling at Wittenberg Academy in Springfield, Ohio, but remained undereducated throughout his life. Jobs as advertising copywriter gave him a first taste of writing, and he went on to a successful business career. In 1912, the central psychological event of his life occurred; he suffered a nervous breakdown, which led him to walk out of his paint factory in Elyria, Ohio. He moved to Chicago, where he began to meet writers such as Floyd Dell, Carl Sandburg, and Ben Hecht, a group collectively known as the Chicago Renaissance. A significant nonliterary contact was Dr. Trigant Burrow of Baltimore, who operated a Freudian therapeutic camp in Lake Chateaugay, New York, during the summers of 1915 and 1916. It should be noted, however, that Anderson ultimately rejected scientific probing of the psyche, for he typically believed that the human mind is static and incapable of meaningful change for the better. Publication of *Winesburg, Ohio* catapulted him into first prominence and he traveled to Europe in 1921, where he became acquainted with Gertrude Stein, Ernest Hemingway, and James Joyce. In 1923, while living in New Orleans, he shared an apartment with William Faulkner. Anderson married and divorced four times. His first wife gave him three children. His second wife, Tennessee Mitchell, had been a lover to Edgar Lee Masters, author of the *Spoon River Anthology* (1915). His last wife, Eleanor Copenhaver, had an interest in the Southern labor movement which drew Anderson somewhat out of his social primitivism, and, for a time in the 1930's, he became a favorite of Communists and Socialists. His death, in Colón, Panama Canal Zone, while on a voyage to South America, was notable for its unique circumstances: he died of peritonitis caused by a toothpick accidentally swallowed while eating hors d'œuvres.

Analysis

Sherwood Anderson's best-known and most important work is the American classic, *Winesburg, Ohio*. It is a collection of associated short stories set in the mythical town of Winesburg in the latter part of the nineteenth century. The stories catalog Anderson's negative reaction to the transformation of Ohio from a largely agricultural to an industrial society which culminated about the time he was growing up in the village of Clyde in the 1880's. Its twenty-five stories are vignettes of the town doctor; the voluble baseball coach; the still attractive but aging-with-loneliness high school teacher; the prosperous and harsh farmer-turned-religious fanatic; the dirt laborer; the hotel keeper, the banker's daughter, and her adolescent suitors; the Presbyterian minister struggling with temptation; the town drunk; the town rough; the town homosexual; and the town halfwit. The comparison to Edgar Lee Masters' *Spoon River Anthology* is obvious: both works purport to reveal the secret lives of small-town Americans living in the Middle West, and ironically both owe their popular success to the elegiac recording of this era, which most Americans insist upon viewing idyllically. Anderson's work, however, differs by more directly relating sexuality to the bizarre behavior of many of his characters and by employing a coherent theme.

That theme is an exploration of psychological "grotesques"—the casualties of economic progress—and how these grotesques participate in the maturing of George Willard, the teenage reporter for the *Winesburg Eagle*, who at the end of the book departs for a bigger city to become a journalist. By then his sometimes callous ambition to get ahead has been tempered by a sense of what Anderson chooses to call "sophistication," the title of the penultimate story. The achievement of George's sophistication gives *Winesburg, Ohio* its artistic movement but makes it problematic for many critics and thoughtful Americans.

The prefacing story defines grotesques. A dying old writer hires a carpenter to build up his bed so that he can observe the trees outside without getting out of it (while living in Chicago in 1915 Anderson had his own bed similarly raised so that he could observe the Loop). After the carpenter leaves, the writer returns to his project—the writing of "The Book of the Grotesque," which grieves over the notion that in the beginning of the world there were a great many thoughts but no such thing as a "truth." Men turned these thoughts into many beautiful truths such as the truth of passion, wealth, poverty, profligacy, carelessness, and others; a person could then appropriate a single one of these truths and try to live by it. It was thus that he or she would become a grotesque—a personality dominated by an overriding concern which in time squeezed out other facets of life.

This epistemological fable, which involves a triple-reduction, raises at least two invalidating questions: first, can there be "thoughts" without the truth to establish the self-differentiating process which generates thought, and second, if universals are denied and all truths have equal value (they are *all* beautiful), then why should a person be condemned for choosing only one of these pluralistic "truths"? Needless to say, these questions are not answered in *Winesburg, Ohio*, (or anywhere else in Anderson's works), and it does not ever occcur to Anderson to raise them. The stories in *Winesburg, Ohio* nevertheless do grapple with Anderson's intended theme, and a story such as "Hands" clearly illustrates what he means by a grotesque. The hands belong to Wing Biddlebaum, formerly Adolph Myers, a teacher in a Pennsylvania village who was beaten and run out of town for caressing boys. Anderson is delicately oblique about Wing's homosexuality, for the thrust of the story demonstrates how a single traumatic event can forever after rule a person's life—Wing is now a fretful recluse whose only human contact occurs when George Willard visits him occasionally. Even so George puzzles over Wing's expressive hands, but never fathoms the reason for his suffering diffidence. "Hands," besides giving first flesh to the word grotesque, makes the reader understand that a character's volition is not necessarily the factor which traps him into such an ideological straightjacket; sympathy can therefore be more readily extended.

"The Philosopher" provides a more subtle illustration of a grotesque and introduces the idea that a grotesque need not be pitiable or tragic; in fact, he can be wildly humorous as demonstrated at the beginning of the story with the philosopher's description:

> Doctor Parcival, the philosopher, was a large man with a drooping mouth covered by a yellow moustache . . . he wore a dirty white waistcoat out of whose pocket protuded a number of black cigars . . . there was something strange about his eyes: the lid of his left eye twitched; it fell down and it snapped up; it was exactly as though the lid of the eye were a window shade and someone stood inside playing with the cord.

It is George Willard's misfortune that Dr. Parcival likes him and uses him as a sounding board for his wacky pomposity. He wishes to convince the boy of the advisability of adopting a line of conduct that he himself is unable to define but amply illustrates with many "parables" which add up to the belief (as George begins to suspect) that all men are despicable. He tells George that his father died in an insane asylum, and then he continues on about a Dr. Cronin from Chicago who may have been murdered by several men, one of whom could have been yours truly, Dr. Parcival. He announces that he actually arrived in Winesburg to write a book. About to launch on the subject of the book, he is sidetracked into the story of his brother who worked for the railroad as part of a roving paint crew (which painted everything orange), and on payday the brother would place his money on the kitchen table— daring any member of the family to touch it. The brother, while drunk, is run over by the rail car housing the other members of his crew.

One day George drops into Dr. Parcival's office for his customary morning visit and discovers him quaking with fear. Earlier a little girl had been thrown from her buggy, and the doctor had inexplicably refused to heed a passerby's call (perhaps because he is not a medical doctor). Other doctors, however, arrived on the scene, and no one noticed Dr. Parcival's absence. Not realizing this, the doctor shouts to George that he knows human nature and that soon a hanging party will be formed to hang him from a lamppost as punishment for his callous refusal to attend to the dying child. When his certainty dissipates, he whimpers to George, "If not now, sometime." He begs George to take him seriously and asks him to finish his book if something should happen to him; to this end he informs George of the subject of the book, which is: everyone in the world is Christ and they are all crucified.

Many critics have singled out one or another story as the best in *Winesburg, Ohio*; frequently mentioned are "The Untold Lie," "Hands," and "Sophistication." Aside from the fact that this may be an unfair exercise, however, because the stories in *Winesburg, Ohio* were written to stand together, these choices bring out the accusation that much of Anderson's work has a "set-up" quality—a facile solemnity which makes his fictions manifest. "The Philosopher" may be the best story because Dr. Parcival's grotesqueness eludes overt labeling; its finely timed humor reveals Anderson's ability to spoof his literary weaknesses, and the story captures one of those character types who, like Joe Welling of "A Man of Ideas," is readily observable and remembered, but proves irritatingly elusive when set down.

Anderson exhibits a particular interest in the distorting effect that religious mania has upon the personality, and several stories in *Winesburg, Ohio* attack or ridicule examples of conspicuous religiosity. "Godliness," a tetralogy with a Gothic flavor, follows the life of Jesse Bentley, a wealthy, progressive farmer who poisons the life of several generations of his relatives with his relentless harshness until he becomes inflamed by Old Testament stories and conceives the idea of replicating an act of animal sacrifice. Because of this behavior, he succeeds in terrifying his fifteen-year-old grandson, the only person he loves, who flees from him never to be heard from again, thus breaking the grandfather's spirit.

Two stories, "The Strength of God" and "The Teacher," are juxtaposed to mock cleverly a less extravagant example of piety. The Reverend Curtis Hartman espies Kate Swift, the worldly high school teacher, reading in bed and smoking a cigarette. The sight affronts and preoccupies him severely and plunges him into a prolonged moral struggle which is resolved when one night he observes her kneeling naked by her bed praying. He smashes the window through which he has been watching her and runs into George Willard's office shouting that Kate Swift is an instrument of God bearing a message of truth. Kate remains entirely oblivious of the Reverend, for she is preoccupied with George, in whom she has detected a spark of literary genius worthy of her cultivation. Her praying episode—an act of desperation which the Reverend mistook for a return to faith—was the result of her realization, while in George's arms, that her altruism had turned physical.

It is exposure to these disparate egoisms, the death of his mother and a poignant evening with Helen White, the banker's daughter, which are gathered into the components of George's "sophistication," the achievement of which causes him to leave town. George's departure, however, has a decidedly ambivalent meaning. Anderson as well as other writers before and after him have shown that American small-town life can be less than idyllic, but *Winesburg, Ohio* is problematic because it is not simply another example of "the revolt from the village." In the story "Paper Pills," the narrator states that apples picked from Winesburg orchards will be eaten in city apartments that are filled with books, magazines, furniture, and people. A few rejected apples, however, which have gathered all their sweetness in one corner and are delicious to eat, remain on the trees and are eaten by those who are not discouraged by their lack of cosmetic appeal. Thus the neuroses of Anderson's grotesques are sentimentalized and become part of his increasingly strident polemic against rationality, the idea of progress, mechanization, scientific innovation, urban culture, and other expressions of social potency. Anderson never wonders why pastorals are not written by pastors but rather by metropolitans whose consciousnesses are heightened by the advantages of urban life; his own version of a pastoral, *Winesburg, Ohio*, was itself written in Chicago.

Anderson published three other collections of short stories in his lifetime, and other stories which had appeared in various magazines were posthumously gathered by Paul Rosenfeld in *The Sherwood Anderson Reader*. These are anthologies with no common theme or recurring characters, although some, such as *Horses and Men*, portray a particular milieu such as the racing world or rustic life. Many of the stories, and nearly all of those singled out by the critics for their high quality, are first-person narratives. They are told in a rambling, reminiscent vein and are often preferred to those in *Winesburg, Ohio* because they lack a staged gravity. The grotesques are there, but less as syndromes than as atmospheric effects. The Gothic nature of the later stories becomes more pronounced, and violence, desolation, and decay gain ascendancy in his best story, "Death in the Woods," from the collection of the same name. This work also has another dimension: it is considered "to be among that wide and interesting mass of creative literature written about literature", for as the narrator tells the story of the elderly drudge who freezes to death while taking a shortcut through the snowy woods, he explains that as a young man he worked on the farm of a German who kept a bound servant like the young Mrs. Grimes. He recalls the circular track that her dogs made about her body while growing bold enough to get at her bag of meat when he himself has an encounter with dogs on a moonlit winter night.

When the woman's body is found and identified, the townspeople turn against her ruffian husband and son and force them out of town, and their dwelling is visited by the narrator after it becomes an abandoned and vandalized hulk.

Because Mrs. Grimes is such an unobtrusive and inarticulate character, the narrator is forced to tell her story, as well as how he gained each aspect of the story, until the reader's interest is awakened by the uncovering of the narrator's mental operations. This process leads the narrator to ponder further how literature itself is written and guides him to the final expansion: consciousness of his own creative processes. The transfer of interest from the uncanny circumstances of Mrs. Grimes's death to this awareness of human creativity lends some credibility to Sherwood Anderson's epitaph, "Life, Not Death, Is the Great Adventure."

"The Man Who Became a Woman," from *Horses and Men*, is another critic's choice. A young horse groom is sneaking a drink at a bar and imagines that his image on the counter mirror is that of a young girl. He becomes involved in an appalling barroom brawl (its horror contradicts the popular image of brawls in our Westerns), and later, while sleeping nude on top of a pile of horse blankets, he is nearly raped by two drunken black grooms who mistake him for a slim young woman. The several strong foci in this long story tend to cancel one another out, and its built-in narrative devices for explaining the reason for the telling of the story succeed only in giving it a disconnected feel, although it is the equal of "Death in the Woods" in Gothic details.

"I Am a Fool," also from *Horses and Men*, is Anderson's most popular story. Here a young horse groom describes a humiliation caused less by his own gaucheness with the opposite sex than by the gulf of social class and education which separates him from the girl. The story re-creates the universe of adolescent romance so well presented in *Winesburg, Ohio* and brings a knowing smile from all manner of readers.

In "The Egg" (from *The Triumph of the Egg*), a husband-and-wife team of entrepreneurs try their hand at chicken-raising and running a restaurant. They fail at both, and the cause in both instances is an egg. This is a mildly humorous spoof on the American penchant for quick-success schemes, which nevertheless does not explain the praise the story has been given.

"The Corn Planting" (from *The Sherwood Anderson Reader*) is Anderson without histrionics. An elderly farm couple are told that their city-dwelling son has been killed in an automobile accident. In response, the pair rig a planting machine and set about planting corn in the middle of the night while still in their nightgowns. At this concluding point, a generous reader would marvel at this poignant and internally opportune description of a rite of rejuvenation. An obdurate one would mutter Karl Marx's dictum on the idiocy of rural life (not quite apropos since Marx was referring to European peasants, not technologically advanced American farmers); but this reader shall remark that the story itself functions within its confines and breezily add that Anderson's favorite appellation (and the title of one of his short stories) was An Ohio Pagan.

Major publications other than short fiction

NOVELS: *Windy McPherson's Son*, 1916; *Marching Men*, 1917; *Poor White*, 1920; *Many Marriages*, 1923; *Dark Laughter*, 1925; *Beyond Desire*, 1932; *Kit Brandon*, 1936.

PLAY: *Winesburg and Others*, 1937.

POETRY: *Mid-American Chants*, 1918; *A New Testament*, 1927.

NONFICTION: *A Story Teller's Story*, 1924; *Tar: A Midwest Childhood*, 1926; *Sherwood Anderson's Notebook*, 1926; *Hello Towns!*, 1929; *Perhaps Women*, 1931; *Puzzled America*, 1935; *Home Town*, 1940; *Sherwood Anderson's Memoirs*, 1942.

Bibliography

Anderson, Margaret. *My Thirty Year's War*.

Burbank, Rex. *Sherwood Anderson*.

Chase, Cleveland B. *Sherwood Anderson*.

Howe, Irving. *Sherwood Anderson*.

Sutton, William A. *The Road to Winesburg: A Mosaic of the Imaginative Life of Sherwood Anderson*.

Weber, Brom. *University of Minnesota Pamphlet #43*.

Julian Grajewski

ISAAC ASIMOV

Born: Petrovici, Russia; January 2, 1920

Principal short fiction

I, Robot, 1950; *Foundation*, 1951; *Foundation and Empire*, 1952; *Second Foundation*, 1953; *The Martian Way*, 1955; *Earth Is Room Enough*, 1957; *Nine Tomorrows*, 1959; *The Rest of the Robots*, 1964; *Asimov's Mysteries*, 1968; *Nightfall and Other Stories*, 1969; *The Early Asimov*, 1972; *Tales of the Black Widowers*, 1974; *Buy Jupiter and Other Stories*, 1975; *More Tales of the Black Widowers*, 1976; *The Bicentennial Man and Other Stories*, 1976.

Other literary forms

A prolific writer by any standard, with more than two hundred books published by 1979, Isaac Asimov has written on a variety of subjects, among them history, literature, mythology, sex, and humor, although he is best known for popularizations of science and science fiction. An award winner for his *The Foundation* Trilogy (1961) and the novel *The Gods Themselves* (1972), he has also published two mystery novels, a novelization of the film *Fantastic Voyage* and a scenario, "Waterclap," which was never filmed.

Influence

One of the major writers to introduce authentic science into science fiction at the time of World War II, Asimov defends scientific extrapolation and speculation as the major justification for science fiction as a distinct branch of literature. His robot stories posited the "Three Laws of Robotics" which, along with their assertion of the subordination of machine to man, became a permanent addition to the literature. *The Foundation* Trilogy, received as "novels" the decade after their original publication, introduced into galaxy-spanning "space opera" a humans-only civilization and a concentration on politics and decisionmaking in preference to slam-bang action. Asimov's idealization of scientific ways of thinking helped achieve a kind of respectability for a literature best known before him for spectacle, sensationalism, and oversimplification.

Story characteristics

Although a number of Asimov's stories are characterized by reliance on surprise endings, extending from puns to logical extensions of a single point of technological extrapolation, his most characteristic work has a serious edge to it. Exploiting the resources of science fiction to teach lessons in science and social acceptance of technology, his stories often revolve around puzzles or mysteries, the solutions to which may be mechanical, but the effects of which are at least potentially profound.

Biography

Brought to the United States when he was three, Isaac Asimov was reared in New York by his Jewish parents and taught to take education seriously, especially science. A child prodigy, he was graduated from high school at fifteen and went on to earn his B. S., M. A., and Ph. D. in chemistry at Columbia University, with a brief interruption for noncombatant military service at the end of World War II. Although he failed to achieve his dream, and that of his parents, to become a doctor, he did join the faculty of the medical school at Boston University, where he became an Associate Professor of Biochemistry before turning to full-time writing. A science-fiction fan since his early teens, he published his first story at eighteen. After nineteen books of fiction in the 1950's, however, he concentrated much more heavily on nonfiction. He has been married twice, to Gertrude Blugerman from 1942 to 1973, with whom he had two children, and to psychiatrist Janet Jeppson since 1973. Asimov rarely travels, spending most of his time in New York.

Analysis

A naïve, untutored writer by his own admission, Isaac Asimov learned the art of commercial fiction by observing the ways of other science-fiction writers before him, with considerable assistance from John W. Campbell, Jr., editor of *Astounding Science Fiction*. Although the diction of pulp writers, for whom every action, however mundane, must have a powerful thrust, colored much of his earlier work, he soon developed a lucid style of his own, spare by comparison with the verbosity of others, which was spawned by the meager word rates for which they worked. Melodramatic action is not absent from his fiction, but confrontations are more commonly conversational than physical. Characters are seldom memorable, nor are there many purple passages of description for their own sake; everything is subordinated to the story, itself often an excuse for problem-solving to show scientific thinking in action.

Although his first popularity came in the 1930's and 1940's, Asimov's best work was published in the 1950's. In addition to most of his novels, many of his best stories were written then, including "The Ugly Little Boy" (1958), which concerns a Neanderthal child snatched into the present, and the consequences of his nonscientific governess' forming an attachment to him. This is one of several stories in which the results of science and technology and devotion to them are cast in a negative or at least ambivalent light, contrary to the view Asimov usually maintains.

Other stories from this period include "Franchise," in which a single voter decides those few issues computers cannot handle; "What If?," in which a newly married couple catches a glimpse of how their lives might have been; and "Profession," in which trends in accelerated education are taken to an extreme. Three stories concern societies so technologically sophisticated that what the reader takes for granted must be rediscovered: writing in "Someday," mathematics in "The Feeling of Power," and walking outdoors in "It's Such a Beautiful Day." "The Last Question" extrapolates computer capabilities in the far future to a new Creation in the face of the heat death of the universe, while "Dreaming Is a Private Thing" concerns a new entertainment form which bears a certain resemblance to traditional storytelling.

Spanning his career, Asimov's robot stories generally involve an apparent violation of one or more of the "Three Laws of Robotics" which Campbell derived from his earliest variations on the theme. Their classical formulation is as follows:

1. A robot may not injure a human being or, through inaction, allow a human being to come to harm.
2. A robot must obey orders given it by human beings except where such orders would conflict with the First Law.
3. A robot must protect its own existence as long as such protection does not conflict with the First or Second Laws.

While this formulation was an attempt to dispel what Asimov called the "Frankenstein complex," it was also a set of orders to be tested by dozens of stories. The best of the robot stories may well be "Liar!," in which a confrontation between robot and human produces an unusually emotional story, in which the fear of machines is not trivialized away. "Liar!" introduces one of Asimov's few memorable characters, Susan Calvin, chief robopsychologist for U. S. Robots, whose presence between "chapters" of *I, Robot* unifies to some extent that first collection of Asimov's short fiction. Usually placid, preferring robots to men, an argument for which Asimov has considerable sympathy, Calvin is shown here in an uncharacteristic early lapse from the type of the dispassionate spinster into that of "the woman scorned."

The story begins with a puzzle, an attempt to discover why an experimental robot, RB-34 (Herbie), is equipped with telepathy. Trying to solve this puzzle, however, Calvin and her colleagues are sidetracked into the age-old problem of human vanity, which ultimately relegates the original puzzle and the robot to the scrapheap. Aware of the threat of harming them psychologically if he tells the truth, Herbie feeds the pride of the administrator, Alfred Lanning, in his mathematics, along with the ambition of Peter Bogert to replace his superior, and the desire of Calvin to believe that another colleague, Milton Ashe, returns her affection, when he is in fact engaged to another.

As the conflict between Bogert and Lanning escalates, each trying to solve the original puzzle, Herbie is asked to choose between them. Present at the confrontation, Calvin vindictively convinces the robot that however it answers will be injurious to a human being, forcing it to break down. Since Herbie is a conscious being, more interested in romantic novels than in technical treatises, Calvin's act is not simply the shutting down of a machine, but also an act of some malevolence, particularly satisfying to her, and the whole story underlines the human fear of being harmed, or at least superseded, by machines.

Asimov's next published story, "Nightfall," is still his best in the opinion of many readers, who have frequently voted it the best science-fiction story of all time, although it shows its age and the author's, since he was barely twenty-one when he wrote it. Written to order for Campbell, it begins with a quote from Ralph Waldo Emerson's *Nature* (1836) which Campbell and Asimov in turn have reinterpreted: "If the stars should appear one night in a thousand years, how would men believe and adore, and preserve for many generations the remembrance of the city of God." Asimov fulfilled Campbell's demand that the event, taken as an astronomical possibility, would drive men mad, but this conclusion is partly counterbalanced by the author's faith in the power of science to explain, without completely succumbing to, awe and superstition.

With the Emerson quote as an epigraph, "Nightfall" was committed to an inevitable, rather than a surprise, ending. From the start, the catastrophe is imminent, predicted by astronomers who have no idea of what is really in store. Aton 77, director of the university observatory where the action takes place, reluctantly permits a newspaper columnist, Theremon 762, to stay and observe, thus setting the stage for a story which is almost all exposition. Sheerin 501, a psychologist, becomes Theremon's major interlocutor, explaining both the physical and behavioral theory behind the predictions which the media and the populace have ridiculed.

Astronomical observation, gravitational theory, and archaeological findings have confirmed the garbled scriptural account of the Cultists' *Book of Revelations* that civilization on the planet Lagash must fall and rise every two millennia. Lit by six suns, Lagash is never in darkness, never aware of a larger universe, except when another world, a normally invisible "moon," eclipses the only sun then in the sky, an event which happens every 2049 years. In hopes of overcoming the anticipated mass insanity, the scientists have prepared a Hideout in which some three hundred people may be able to ride out the half-day of darkness and preserve some vestige of scientific civilization.

While Sheerin is explaining all this and glibly countering commonsense objections, a Cultist breaks in to threaten the "solarscopes," a mob sets out from the city to attack the observatory, and the eclipse indeed begins. Amid flickering torches, the scientists withstand the vandals' charge that they have desecrated the scriptures by "proving" them only natural phenomena. They then speculate ironically about a larger universe, even an Earthlike situation presumed inimical to life, but neither they nor the Cultists are prepared for the truth of "thirty thousand mighty suns" or the gibbering madness which demands light, even if everything must be burned down in order to obtain it.

Other than the astronomical configuration—a highly unlikely and inherently unstable situation—and its consequences, there is nothing "alien" in the story, which is about potential human reactions. The diction is heavily influenced by 1930's pulp style, some pieces of the puzzle are not rationally convincing, and the story leaves loose ends untied, but it is dramatically convincing, like H. G. Wells's inversion of a similar dictum in "The Country of the Blind." Although Asimov's moral survives, that people can, through scientific observations and reasoning, do something to improve their state, it is largely overshadowed by the effectiveness of the ending. However well-prepared for and rationalized away, the concluding vision of "Nightfall" evokes exactly that quasimystical awe and wonder Asimov is usually constrained to avoid.

Relying more on single "impossibilities," correlated extrapolation and reasoning from present-day knowledge, Asimov's best fiction generally stems from the 1950's. The best example of his positive attitude toward future expansion by man and his knowledge, "The Martian Way" illustrates the conviction expressed by most of his novels and much of science fiction that the future lies "out there" in space beyond the "cradle" for man provided by Earth, its history and prehistory. A "space story" to be sure, "The Martian Way" also concerns political conflict, which is resolved not by drawn blasters at fifty paces, but rather by reason and ingenuity, based on a setting and assumptions alien to Earthmen both at the time of writing and at the time period in which the novella is set.

There are a puzzle and a solution, of course, but they are an excuse on which to hang the story. The rise of a demagogic Earth politician, Hilder (modeled on Senator Joseph McCarthy, but echoing Hitler by name), threatens the human colony on Mars which depends on Earth for water, not only for drinking, washing, and industry, but also as reaction mass for its spaceships. Among those who will be affected, Marlo Esteban Rioz and Ted Long are Scavengers, who snag empty shells of ships blasting off from Earth and guide them to Martian smelters. Although Rioz is the experienced "Spacer," the "Grounder" Long has a better grasp of "the Martian way," which means not tying one's future to Earth, rather facing outward to the rest of the Solar System and beyond.

Campaigning against "Wasters," Hilder parallels past profligacy toward oil and other resources with the present Martian use of water from Earth's oceans. The Martian colonists recognize the spuriousness of that charge, but they also recognize its emotional impact on Earth. The solution is a marriage of scientific elegance and technological brute force, breathtaking in context even to the Spacers themselves, who set off on a year's journey to bring back an asteroid-sized fragment of ice from Saturn's rings. How they do it is chronicled

by the story, along with the euphoria of floating in space, the political wrangling with Earth, and the challenges of colonizing the new frontier.

Throughout the narrative resonates the claim by Long that Martians, not
Earthmen, will colonize the Universe. The fundamental difference lies less
with the planet of one's birth than with the direction in which one looks to
the future. Scientifically more astute and less burdened by racial prejudices,
Martians work in teams rather than as individual heroes. Although there are
distinct echoes of the legendary American West, the situation on Mars is
more radically discontinuous with its predecessors on Earth. The arrival of
an independent water supply is just the excuse they need to cut at last the
umbilical cord to Earth and the past.

If "The Martian Way" points toward Asimov's novels, most of which take
place off Earth, even beyond the Solar System, "The Dead Past" is more
typical of the extrapolation Asimov defends in his critical writings as "social
science fiction." The novella begins harmlessly enough with a professor of
Ancient History being denied access to government-controlled chronoscopy,
which would let him see at firsthand the ancient city of Carthage. Although
time-viewing is the central science fiction, the focus of the story switches to
"the closed society," as Professor Potterly seeks to subvert governmental
controls. Scientists in this near-future society have bartered their freedom of
inquiry for recognition, security, and financial support. This position is defended by a young physics professor named Foster, whose future depends on
his staying within the bounds of his discipline and of the controls which have
evolved from governmental support of research.

The point is exaggerated, as is the conspiracy of silence surrounding chronoscopy, but the satirical edge is honed by the subsequent activity of the two
academics and Foster's cooperative Uncle Ralph, a degreeless, prestigeless,
but well-paid science writer. With his help and the shortcut supplied by his
specialty, "neutrinics," Foster reinvents the chronoscope at a fraction of its
earlier cost and difficulty, and the conspirators give out the secret to the
world. In contrast to Foster's newly gained fanaticism, Potterly has begun to
have doubts, in part because of his own wife's nostalgic obsessions. In a
melodramatic confrontation with the FBI, they discover that the chronoscope's operating limits are between one hundred and twenty-five years and
one second ago, making privacy in the present a thing of the past. Either a
whole new utopian society will have to evolve, a doubtful supposition, or the
government's suppression of information will turn out, in retrospect, to have
been for the good. Although the story has flaws and its fantasy is almost
certainly unrealizable, the satire is engaging and the ending is a thoughtful
variation on the theme that there may indeed be some knowledge not worth
pursuing.

Asimov's fiction usually has a makeshift quality about it, his characterizations are often featureless, and his propensity for suprise endings and mel-

odramatic diction and situations may irritate some readers. Nevertheless, his exploitation of scientific thought and rationality, his emphasis on the puzzle-solving which makes up a good deal of science, and his generally good-humored lucidity have made him, along with Robert A. Heinlein and Arthur C. Clarke, one of the cornerstones of modern science fiction.

Major publications other than short fiction

NOVELS: *Pebble in the Sky*, 1950; *The Stars Like Dust*, 1951; *The Currents of Space*, 1952; *The Caves of Steel*, 1954; *The End of Eternity*, 1955; *The Naked Sun*, 1957; *The Death-Dealers*, 1958 (also known as *A Whiff of Death*); *Fantastic Voyage*, 1966; *The Gods Themselves*, 1972; *Murder at the ABA*, 1976.

NONFICTION: *The Chemicals of Life*, 1954; *Realm of Nummbers*, 1959; *The Wellsprings of Life*, 1960; *Planets for Man*, 1964; *The New Intelligent Man's Guide to Science*, 1965; *Asimov's Guide to the Bible*, 1968; *Asimov's Guide to Shakespeare*, 1970; *Asimov's Biographical Encyclopedia of Science and Technology*, 1964; *Earth: Our Crowded Spaceship*, 1974; *Science Past—Science Future*, 1975; *Extraterrestrial Civilizations*, 1979; *In Memory Yet Green*, 1979 (autobiography); *In Joy Still Felt*, 1980.

Bibliography

Goble, Neil. *Asimov Analyzed.*
Miller, Marjorie. *Isaac Asimov: A Checklist of Works Published in the United States.*
Moore, Maxine. "Asimov, Calvin and Moses," in *Voices for the Future.* Edited by Thomas D. Clareson. I (1979).
Moskowitz, Sam. "Isaac Asimov," in *Seekers of Tomorrow: Masters of Modern Science Fiction.*
Olander, Joseph and Martin Harry Greenberg, eds. *Isaac Asimov.*
Patrench, Joseph. *The Science Fiction of Isaac Asimov.*

David N. Samuelson

MIGUEL ÁNGEL ASTURIAS

Born: Guatemala City, Guatemala; October 19, 1899

Principal short fiction

Leyendas de Guatemala, 1930 (*Legends of Guatemala*); *Week-end en Guatemala*, 1956 (*Weekend in Guatemala*); *El espejo de Lida Sal*, 1967 (*Lida Sal's Looking Glass*).

Other literary forms

Miguel Ángel Asturias' first published works are translations of Mayan Indian lore whose influence is strongly present in his own writings. His novel *El señor Presidente* (1946, *Mr. President*) is a subjective account of the Estrada Cabrera dictatorship in Guatemala, and a trilogy of novels which deals with the imperialistic excesses of the United Fruit Company. His five dramas have been called an entirely new experiment in theater because of their use of intense visual images to appeal to the audience's subconscious. Asturias is also a poet and an essayist.

Influence

One of the first to take cultural elements of native origin as inspirational, Asturias portrayed the richly layered reality of his country from inside the minds of those for whom the word and nature were still magic. This technique, along with the use of colloquial language to poetic effect, have now become important features of Latin American "new fiction." Asturias is the first Latin American novelist to win the Nobel Prize for Literature (1967).

Story characteristics

Asturias' tales have been characterized as stories-poems-dreams that evoke indigenous myths and magic. His prose employs unexpected associations and the free-flow of images. Some of his stories are legends that tell the origin of a popular custom or object. Others, while employing the same surrealist techniques, are more overtly protest literature.

Biography

Miguel Ángel Asturias' first two decades were lived under the shadow of the nefarious Estrada Cabrera. After the latter's overthrow, Asturias earned a law degree, wrote a prize-winning thesis on the sociocultural problems of the Indian, and founded a popular university. Later he studied Mayan writings at the Sorbonne. He joined the diplomatic corps but was exiled from his country after American intervention helped to overthrow Guatemala's freely elected government. Later, his citizenship was restored, and he ended his career as Ambassador to France. In 1966 he received the Lenin Peace Prize, and the Nobel Prize followed in 1967.

Analysis

It is likely that, in general terms, Miguel Ángel Asturias is most known for his literature of social denunciation. Indeed, there are those who would claim that his receipt of the Nobel Prize was primarily due to fiction attacking political oppression in Latin America and particularly the deleterious influence of American capitalism. Nevertheless, Asturias is notably prominent in Latin American literature for what one may loosely call a highly "poeticized" fiction; that is, a fictional texture that proposes the dissolution of conventional distinctions between poetic and prosaic registers. Nowhere is this aspect of his writing more apparent than in his first book of short fiction, *Leyendas de Guatemala* (*Legends of Guatemala*).

Like many Latin American writers, Asturias spent his culturally formative years in France. This French experience was doubly significant. Not only was it the opportunity to enter into contact with the most important writers, artists, and intellects of the ebullient *entreguerre* period in Paris. It was also the transition from a feudal Latin American society of his youth to the free-wheeling, liberal if not libertine society of postwar Europe. The result for many writers like Asturias is the fascinating conjunction of traditional, autochthonous, and folkloric—and even mythic—Latin American material and themes and a mode of literary discourse shaped by surrealism and the other vanguard modernist tendencies of the 1920's and 1930's in the "sophisticated" centers of the West. Surrealism maintained a prominent interest in the primitive and the antirational, and had as one of its primary goals the demythification of the primacy of so-called high culture in Western society. Thus it is only natural to find a continuity among the intellectuals of the 1920's and 1930's of the interest in Latin American materials that dates back to early anthropological and archaeological studies of the nineteenth century.

In the case of Asturias, what is particularly significant is his opportunity to work in Paris with Georges Raynaud, who was engaged at that time in preparing a scholarly translation of the *Popol Vuh*, the sacred texts of the Quiché Indians of Guatemala. That is, Asturias, in moving from Guatemala to Paris, exchanged a context of the oppression of indigenous culture for one of scholarly and intellectual interest in the cultural accomplishments of the native population of his own country. In the *Legends of Guatemala*, Asturias attempts to stand as a mediator between the Western and Quiché cultures. It is a mediation consisting of both linguistic and cultural "translations" of indigenous materials into cultural idioms or codes of twentieth century literary discourse. This means not ethnographic or folklortistic transcription of indigenous legends, nor does it mean the re-creation of indigenous narratives and their rearticulation in terms of homologous modern myths. Rather, it means the semantic reformulation of indigenous materials in terms of the linguistic and cultural symbologies of the modern writer. The representation in Spanish, either directly or indirectly, of indigenous myths can never be only a translation. The rhetorics, styles, and modes of writing of a modern Western language such as Spanish, although they may be influenced by the poetic attempts to incorporate the modalities of an indigenous language such as Quiché, can never be the anthropologically faithful or scientific re-creation of the original materials because of the enormous distance that separates the two linguistic and cultural systems.

The so-called poetic language of Asturias in the *Legends of Guatemala* or in the novel *Hombres de maíz* (1949, *Men of Corn*) is not, therefore, a translation into Spanish of Quiché materials. Nor is it the attempt to write in Spanish as though one were in reality writing in Quiché. Rather, it is the attempt to attain an independent discourse that, on the one hand, will suggest the melding of the two cultures into an idealized sociohistoric reality and, on the other hand, will attest to the role of the artist and writer as the mediating bridge between two cultures which deplorable but all-too-present circumstances keep separate by a virtually unbreachable abyss.

The influence of surrealism in Latin American literature has meant not merely the recovery of the subconscious and the unconscious as it has in European culture. More significantly, it has meant the recovery of indigenous cultures and the aspects of those cultures that may be seen as prerational or authentically mythic. The discovery by the Latin American of his subconscious reality is, therefore, not simply a psychological discovery; it is the discovery of those mediating cultural elements—usually indigenous but often creole— which were repressed by nineteenth century liberal and Europeanizing ideologies.

"Leyenda del sombrerón" ("Legend of the Big Hat") is an excellent example of the elaboration in a fictional text of the aforementioned principles. Superficially, it reminds one of those nineteenth century narratives by such writers as Peru's Ricardo Palma or Colombia's Tomás Carrasquilla—narratives that represent an ironic, urbane retelling of traditional or legendary material of a quasi-documentary nature, lightly fictionalized by a somewhat patronizing narrator who claims to have either discovered his material in an out-of-the-way corner of a dusty library or heard it on the lips of gossipy washerwomen and garrulous mule drivers. These narratives were part of the Romantic and prerealist fiction of Latin America and represented that area's version of local color and the discovery of an idealized past and an idealized *Volkspoesie*.

Asturias' story is like these antecedents in that it deals with quasi- or pseudo-legendary material: the origin of the devil's big hat. The legend as Asturias tells it concerns a monastery built by the Spanish conquerors of Central America, a monastery inhabited by devout monks, specifically by one monk who spends his time in appropriately devotional readings and meditation. One day, the monk's exemplary otherworldliness is broken by a ball that comes flying through the window, the lost toy of an Indian boy playing outside the walls of the monastery. At first, the monk is entranced by this unknown object which he takes in his hands, imagining that so must have been the earth in the hands of the Creator. Thus distracted from his saintly preoccupations, the monk begins to play with the ball with almost childish joy. A few days later, however, the child's mother comes to the door of the monastery to ask that her son be given religious instruction; it seems that he has been heartbroken since the loss of his ball in the area of the monastery, a ball claimed popularly to be the very image of the devil. Suddenly possessed by a violent rage, the monk runs to his cell, picks up the ball, and hurls it beyond the walls of the monastery. Flying through the air, the ball assumes the form of the black hat of the devil. The story ends with: "And thus is born to the world the big hat."

The superficial resemblance of Asturias' text with its nineteenth century ironic predecessors is borne out by an overt narrator who obliquely addresses himself to the reader. This narrator assumes the function of telling the reader what happened and sharing with him the unusual, surprising, and notable event. Thus, the text is characterized by a number of rhetorical ploys to be seen as markers of this conventional form of ironic storytelling: the explicit allusions to the recovery of the story from antiquarian sources, the fact that the event narrated concerns a remote time and place that because of its strangeness for the reader makes the story all the more notable, the heavy-handed condescension toward the simplicity of manner and ingenuous behavior of the participants—the monk, the Indian child, and his humble mother, and, finally, the explicit allusions to the fact that someone is telling a story. These allusions take the form of phatic formulas such as "Let us continue," "Let us go on," "And thus it happened," "And thus it was," as well as frequent references to the noteworthiness of the event being related, toward confirming the value of the narrative as narrative and as a form of privileged discourse.

Nevertheless, it must be stressed that all of these features are only superficial characteristics of nineteenth century ironic, local-color literature. Indeed, the fact that they are superficial echoes in Asturias' text becomes a wholly different sort of irony, an irony at the expense of a reader willing to take them as indicative of peasant superstitions recounted in a straightforward fashion by a narrator slightly amused at folk superstitions. In order to understand the way in which Asturias' story is much more than such a retelling of a local superstition, it is necessary to keep in mind the presence of two systems of cultural reference in the text. In the first place, it is necessary to recall the enormous sociocultural impact of the activities of religious orders in Latin America during the Colonial period. The conquest was accompanied by religious orders charged with the establishment in the New World of Christianity and the conversion of the indigenous population. In the case of the area known today as Guatemala, this imperative meant the wholesale destruction of the artifacts of indigenous culture, so that today less than a half dozen of the Quiché codices are the survivors of the Christian priests' destructive zeal. It would be no exaggeration to say that, as a consequence, the sort of monastery described with much detail in Asturias' text dominated the daily lives of the conquered indigenous peoples.

Second, it is important to remember that ballplaying enjoyed a ritual and religious status in Quiché culture. Indeed, one of the cultural contributions of the Quichés to their conquerors was the ball, an artifact of leisure. Thus, in Asturias' text, the encounter between the priest and the ball—and through the ball, between the former and indigenous culture—may be a circumstancial occurrence. In terms, however, of the cultural system represented on the one hand by the pious monk and the fortress-like monastery he occupies and the system represented by the Indian boy's ball are posited by the story as antagonic forces. The ball becomes a token in a pattern of cultural invasion and expulsion. In the event narrated, the cultural space of the monk is "penetrated" or "invaded" by the alien object, just as the cultural space of the Quichés had been invaded by the Spanish conquerors and their representatives of an alien religion. The indigenous culture, however, cannot displace the invading culture. The priest's almost hysterical realization of the "diabolical" meaning of the ball with which he has played with such childish abandon is the acknowledgment that the ball is much more than a child's toy. In casting the ball away from the monastery, he is expelling indigenous culture from the fortress of Christianity and reaffirming the primacy and the dominion of the latter. The miraculous transformation of the ball into the devil's hat is not really a fantastic but a phenomenological circumstance. At issue is not a superstitious belief in such occurrences (although an antirational ideology may well affirm them), but rather the perception of the symbolic importance of the object the priest flings away from him with words that recall the "Vade retro, Satanas" commonplace.

It is significant that the narrator of Asturias' story does not end his description of the monk's expulsion from his sanctuary of the artifact of indigenous culture with an explanation of the meaning of that gesture, particularly since, in the opening segments of the text, he takes great pains to describe the setting of the religious community concerned and the monk's initial distraction with the child's stray toy; yet, it is the abrupt end of the text that most confirms the significance of the symbolic interplay between the cultures here described. By not appending an explanatory conclusion, the narrator runs the risk of his reader's taking the event at face value—that is, as a miraculous or fantastic event, the authenticity of which is maintained by conventional and ingenuous superstition. Nevertheless, to the extent that the conventions of serious twentieth century literature preclude the telling of superstitious material for shock effect, the reader is obliged, when confronted with such material, to attribute to it some profound, if only vaguely perceived, semiological value. Such is the case with the encounter between the monk and the ball.

The reader need not endorse the overwhelming significance here implied of the religious community on the one hand and the ritual value of the child's ball on the other to appreciate how the story concerns conflicting antagonic forces. In terms of the most elemental cultural values in the story one sees the ball interpreted in a conflicting manner by the monk: he sees it first as a symbol of God's creation and it is only with the appearance of the peasant woman and her casual reference to the ball as the image of the devil that he suddenly becomes enraged with its offending presence. It crosses the monk's mind initially that the ball may be bewitched; nevertheless, he sees in it something less worldly that his books cannot explain. In giving himself over to its humble simplicity, he is, to a certain extent, escaping the treacheries of a bookish culture. Thus there is a subsystem of oppositions whereby on the larger level of the narrative there is a contrast between the monk and the ball, between Christian and indigenous sociocultural values, and there is in the monk's own world a contrast between signs of the devil and signs of God's grace. Before he realizes that the ball is the symbol of the devil, to the extent that it is an artifact of the culture which Christianity is dedicated to eradicating, he considers the errant toy a sign of God's simple grace against the potential treachery of the books with which he surrounds himself. The opposition between grace and evil which the monk perceives in his cell with the appearance of the ball is projected onto the larger plane of the opposition between two alien cultures.

In the world evoked by Asturias' story, there is an impenetrable barrier between two cultures given objective representation by the walls of the monastery. Asturias' text is nevertheless a mediator between these two cultures in the sense that they are brought together as opposing and interdependent elements in a narrative system. Without either one, there would be no story. It is because both are necessary in order that this narrative may exist that the text then becomes a form of mediation between the two of them, confirming the unique status of the text as a form of unifying cultural discourse. Asturias' text is unquestionably ideological, but not in the sense of sociopolitical denunciation. Rather, it is ideological by virtue of the implied conception of the praxis of narrative art as a form of mediation between two cultures often condemned to an oppressor/oppressed relationship. Writing such as that of Asturias provides the attempt at mediation with a coherence and purpose that is singularly distinctive.

Major publications other than short fiction

NOVELS: *El señor Presidente*, 1946 (*Mr. President*); *Hombres de maíz*, 1949 (*Men of Corn*); *Viento fuerte*, 1950 (*Strong Wind*); *El papa verde*, 1954 (*The Green Pope*); *Los ojos de los enterrados*, 1960 (*The Eyes of the Interred*); *El alhajadito*, 1961 (*The Bejeweled Boy*); *Mulata de tal*, 1963 (*Mulatta So-and-So*); *Maladrón*, 1969 (*Bad Thief*).

PLAYS: *Soluna*, 1955 (*Sunmoon*); *La audiencia de los confines*, 1957 (*Tribunal of the Frontiers*); *Chantaje*, 1964 (*Blackmail*); *Dique seco*, 1964 (*Dry Dock*).

POETRY: *Poesía: Sien de alondra*, 1949 (*Lark's Temple*); *Ejercicios poéticos en forma de soneto sobre temas de Horacio*, 1951 (*Poetic Exercises in Sonnet Form on Themes of Horace*); *Clarivigilia primaveral*, 1965 (*Watch in the Spring Light*).

NONFICTION: *Rumania, su nueva imagen*, 1964 (*Romania, Its New Image*); *Comiendo en Hungría*, 1969 (*Eating in Hungary*, with Pablo Neruda); *Hector Poléo*, 1969; *Latino América y otros ensayos*, 1970 (*Latin America and Other Essays*); *El novelista en la universidad*, 1971 (*The Novelist in the University*); *América, fábula de fábulas*, 1972 (*America, Tale of Tales*); *Novela y novelistas: reunión de Malaga*, 1972 (*Novel and Novelists: Meeting in Malaga*).

Bibliography

Bellini, Guiseppe. *La narrativo de Miguel Ángel Asturias*.

Callan, Richard J. *Miguel Ángel Asturias*.

Essays on Miguel Ángel Asturias: A Survey of Recent Criticism, in Latin American Center Essay Series 5.

Menton, Seymour. "Miguel Ángel Asturias," in Narrativa y crítica de nuestra América. Edited by Joaquín Roy.

David W. Foster

ST. AUGUSTINE
Aurelius Augustinus

Born: Tagaste, Numidia, North Africa; 354
Died: Hippo (now Bône, Algeria); August 28, 430

Principal work
Confessions, 397-401; *The City of God*, 413-426.

Influence
Augustine was a father of the Church, rhetorician, psychologist, opponent of the Manichaean, Donatist, and Pelagian heresies, and author of a vast number of works, including two extraordinarily influential masterpieces, the *Confessions* (thirteen books) and *The City of God* (twenty-two books). Augustine is, after St. Paul, the most important Christian writer.

Story characteristics
Augustine recounted the story of himself and the story of the world, both autobiography and history, teleologically viewed.

Biography
The eldest of the three children of a pagan father, Patricius, and a dominant Christian mother, Monica (afterwards St. Monica), Augustine (Aurelius Augustinus) was educated in a Christian fashion; but, as he tells the reader, his passions and his omnivorous intellect led him into moral incontinence, philosophical substitutes, and religious alternatives—Manichaeaism, a kind of Pyrrhonism, and finally Neoplatonism—before his conversion, largely through the influence of St. Ambrose of Milan, in 386, and baptism on Easter Saturday in 387. His subsequent withdrawal into a monastic life contrasted with his earlier public and rhetorical prominence in Carthage, Rome, and Milan. He was soon, however, almost dragooned into the priesthood by admiring Christians at Hippo and then into the See of Hippo, where his administrative and polemical efforts continued in the turbulent last days before the fall of Rome (410) and the besieging of Hippo by the Vandals in the year of his own death (430).

Analysis
Augustine is the most effective and affecting of the Church Fathers: his intellectual power, rhetorical skills, and passionately candid nature combine to present to the modern reader a man addressing other men, or as he would have expressed it, a sinner preaching to other sinners. The Manichaean (dualistic struggle between light and darkness), Donatist (extremists arguing that the efficacy of the sacraments was dependent upon the personal sanctity of

the celebrants), and Pelagian (too confident a view of the nature of man's free will) heresies occupied large parts of his career, but the two central events in his life are his conversion, described in the *Confessions*, and the fall of Rome, the impetus for the philosophical/theological reflections, *The City of God*. Although Augustine used the term "confessions" in the sense of "praises" rather than simply "admittings" or "revealings," the frank description of his failings and the beauty of his personal God-given conversion have led others to write their confessions.

Confessions differs from other contemporary spiritual autobiographies in two basic ways: first, in the extraordinary candor of the egocentric author and, second, in the stress on one's conversion being not a static, permanent resting place, but rather a miraculous shift in status still fraught with temptation, dangers, and doubts. As a forty-year-old priest, Augustine wrote about the young man he had been from the perspective of the Christian leader he currently was. The mistakes which he had made, the temptations to which he had succumbed, and the grace which he had received are presented in the form of a prayer to God, a heuristic device as well as a spiritual offering. Although the ideas in *Confessions* are often demanding on the reader, they are presented in the midst of such vivid detail and with such dramatic passion that, even at first reading, the student is captivated by the book. Augustine's just sense of his own self-importance allowed him to see his own emotional experience as representative of the turbulence in the souls of his contemporaries. Since those turmoils were not unique to the fourth century alone, Augustine's spiritual progress has had an attraction and significance for readers throughout the subsequent fifteen centuries.

Confessions itself is largely chronological. The first of the thirteen books takes the reader up through Augustine's fifteenth year, and in its opening paragraph articulates a central theme of his theology: "Thou madest us for Thyself, and our heart is restless until it repose in Thee." Both the idea of God as the only satisfying object of the soul's delight and the idea that emotional delight is at the heart of man's being recur throughout *Confessions*, for it is a text both free from the aridities of intellectual autobiography and loaded with the richness of a life drawn equally from the experiences of heart and head. In the opening book, the two most vivid illustrations are, first, that of the not-so-innocent infant who is envious of a sibling rival, whose innocence is the direct result of its physical, not volitional weakness, and in whose moral imperfection one sees the fruits of Adam's original sin, a central Christian doctrine for Augustine; and second, that of his school days, when he feared corporal punishment, disliked Greek, hated grammar, arithmetic, and other rote studies, but fell in love with the story of the wooden horse and burning Troy, even to the point of weeping for Dido when he was unmoved by his own sinfulness. In Book II, Augustine denies that his retelling of these sinful days is done for current pleasure; he argues instead that the contrast between his past carnality and his present understanding of God's grace will lead him to love God all the more. The reader of these revelations may indeed suspect that, in the return to his past transgressions, Augustine is garnering a vicarious and repeated pleasure, although he explicitly denies this in his opening paragraph.

The most celebrated vignette in this book, and perhaps in the entire work, is that of the gratuitous stealing of the unwanted pears: "it was foul and I loved it." There is no more striking example of the psychology of adolescent criminality in literature (and the images and rhythm of Augustine's description of this episode seem to have caught in the mind of James Augustine Joyce when his Stephen Dedalus chose art over the priesthood on the beach in *A Portrait of the Artist as a Young Man*, 1916). Book III describes Augustine's life in Carthage, filled with its lustfulness and its involvement with the Manichaean heresy, and describes the distress both of these vices caused his mother Monica. Students of T. S. Eliot will note the opening sentence of the book and its influence upon the poet of *The Waste Land* (1922), "To Carthage I came, where there sang all around me in my ears a cauldron of unholy loves." Book IV takes him to the age of twenty-eight; besides presenting one of the best indictments of sophistic rhetoric—"In those years I taught rhetoric and overcome by cupidity, made sale of a loquacity to overcome by"—it provides the reader with a most poignant analysis of friendship and the laceration produced by the death of a friend.

In Book V, Augustine meets in Carthage with the chief Manichaean spokesman, Faustus, whose limitations free the author from the snares of that heresy; later, he hears his first sermons by Ambrose in Milan. Students of Augustine's prose artistry, however, will be drawn in this book to the image of the deceived Monica, in tears as her son secretly leaves Carthage for Rome; the description parallels the central image of the weeping and wept-for Dido of Book I. Book VI carries Augustine forward as he profits from discussion with his friends Alypius and Nebridius about good and evil. Although there is an aspect of Epicureanism in his own arguments and in his own life, Augustine quickly takes another woman to replace his concubine and the mother of his son, Adeodatus, while the concubine is reluctantly dismissed as an impediment to a prospective marriage for Augustine. Book VII shows Augustine still wrestling with the problem of the origin of evil and the nature of free will. Although he is led by his study of the Platonists to look for ultimate truth in a spiritual nonmaterial mode, the *Epistles* of St. Paul, no longer self-contradictory to him but rather luminously consistent, ultimately provide the truth.

Book VIII leads Augustine to hear of the conversion of Victorinus, a most prominent Roman rhetorician; then, still wrestling with doubts, particularly about his incontinent behavior, he and his friend Alypius go into the garden in which by miraculous direction he is converted. Just as St. Anthony had been told by a voice to pick up and read a particular passage of Scripture, so Augustine is directed to Romans 13.13.14: "Not in rioting and drunkenness, not in chambering and wantonness, not in strife and envying: but put ye on the Lord Jesus Christ, and make not provision for the flesh." The loyal Alypius, similarly moved, points out that the passage continues, "Him that is weak in the faith receive." Both are converted and first tell Monica, whose greatest hope is now realized.

Although Augustine is everywhere and at all times in the center of the stage of *Confessions*, his natural sense for the dramatic gives the reader vignettes of other people: friends, mentors, and, of course, Monica. His artistry in this central garden episode is at its height, for not only does it provide a garden to replace the orchard of the stolen pears (Book II), but it also provides the graphic, contrasting, and probably symbolic detail of the exact place within the garden of the conversion, "under a certain fig-tree." Book IX has Augustine renounce his career as a rhetorician, commit his life to the service of God, prepare for baptism (along with his friend Alypius and his son Adeodatus), and set out to return to Africa. Monica, however, dies in her fifty-sixth year at Ostia (with her son now the symbolically significant age of thirty-three). Augustine provides the reader with a hagiographical description of the life of his mother, and *Confessions* seems to come to a proper and expected end.

Book X, however, powerfully demonstrates that his conversion does not cause calmness, for many of the old temptations return to besiege the new Christian, especially those in the forms of sexual desire and greediness. In this same book, Augustine discusses the nature of memory which, for all its retention of images drawn from the evil days, serves to provide a sequence of experiences which holds together the uniqueness of the individual and without which individuality, so precious to Augustine, would disappear. More modern writers as disparate as Alfred Tennyson, James Joyce, and Marcel Proust have also shared this perception, and Augustine's protoapplication of the sense in this chapter begins a long literary tradition which flows sometimes directly through such diverse writers as St. Ignatius of Loyola, John Donne, Joris Karl Huysmans, and Joyce. The increase in a wide-ranging and detailed analysis of the psyche again makes Augustine the foremost pre-twentieth century analyst of the depth and breadth of human emotions. Book X brings the reader closest to a personal and contemporary Augustine, a man as real and relevant today as he had been fifteen centuries ago. Books XI, XII, and XIII offer a Christian's reading of the opening chapters of Genesis and are of interest chiefly to students of exegesis, hermeneutics (especially the hexameral tradition), and particularly of John Milton and his *Paradise Lost* (1667).

Augustine's masterpiece, *The City of God*, written over the sixteen years following the sack of Rome (410), has been called one of the two books (the other is Vergil's *Aeneid*, c. 29-19 B. C.) whose knowledge is required by a

Christian scholar in the European tradition. It is a carefully designed work: the opening five books are concerned with those who are religious because the gods will give them happiness on this earth; five subsequent books are devoted to those who worship the gods in the hope of everlasting happiness; and the last twelve books are divided into three groups of four books each, dealing, respectively, with the origin of the two cities, "one of God, the other of the world," the history of the two cities, and their futures. Augustine's chief motivation in writing *The City of God* was that of defending the Church against the widespread accusation made by articulate Roman aristocrats that the fall of Rome was the result fundamentally of the influence of Christianity. The basic image in the work which refutes this pagan argument is that of two communities, one bent on earthly satisfaction and therefore doomed to ultimate perdition, and the other devoted to the spiritual standards of Christ and therefore destined for salvation. Augustine calls these communities "Cities." The "city of the world," sometimes called the "city of men," is composed of those who love the wrong things, and the "City of God" is made up of those who by loving God rise above self-love. These two contrasting communities are clearly differentiated although they are invisible; they are, in another metaphor, the sheep and the goats who will be separated on the last day.

The City of God is hardly as autobiographical as *Confessions*, but, in the midst of its carefully developed arguments, there are revelations of Augustine's particular enthusiasms—especially for oddities of nature and for the beauty of the world—expressed in many asides. Whatever our delight in his interest in magnetism, Pygmies, miraculous cures (as he assures the reader that the age of miracles is not over), and other such diversions, the work excels because of Augustine's mastery of both the scriptures and the classics, with a judicious juxtaposition of the two literatures to the advantage of the former. Even pagans and skeptics who were not prepared to accept the supremacy of St. Matthew and St. Paul to Vergil found pleasure in the wide-ranging recollection of classical literature. Some readers are offended by Augustine's heavy sarcasm levied against the myths of Roman moral supremacy such as those espoused by Lucrece, but the excessive sarcasm (and it is scarcely up to the level of St. Jerome's virulence) is part of his larger tactic of contrasting the Roman love of earthly fame with the Christian thirst for heavenly glory. Finally, it should be noted that Augustine, whose own style if not spirit was imbued with Marcus Tillius Cicero and other classical rhetoricians, waged a lifelong war with his pagan enemies; he nevertheless continued to respect, if not love, them as himself. Indeed, near the end of *The City of God*, he admits that the ancients in their brilliance and power of argumentation (albeit in the cause of erroneous positions) are not being recognized justly by apologists, thus demonstrating that the rich tension between the sincere Catholic bishop and the former rhetorician remained to the very end of Augustine's life.

Bibliography
Battenhouse, Roy W. *Companion to the Study of St. Augustine.*
Brown, Peter. *Augustine of Hippo: A Biography.*
Burnaby, John. *Amor Dei: A Study of the Religion of St. Augustine.*
Cochrane, Charles N. *Christianity and Classical Culture.*
Dodds, Eric R. *Pagan and Christian in an Age of Anxiety.*
Marrou, H. I. *History of Education in the Ancient World.*
Portalie, E. *A Guide to the Thought of St. Augustine.*

Rosemary Barton Tobin

JANE AUSTEN

Born: Steventon, Hampshire, England; December 16, 1775
Died: Winchester, England; July 18, 1817

Principal short fiction

Minor Works (Volume VI of the *Oxford Illustrated Jane Austen*, 1954).

Other literary forms

Jane Austen's best works are her six novels.

Influence

Although she was not widely recognized in her own day, Austen did enjoy the appreciation of discriminating readers whose contemporary esteem has since become the critical consensus. The scrupulous accuracy, complex irony, and serious moral speculation of Austen's novels of middle-class life provided the groundwork for the "great tradition" of the nineteenth century novel. Austen's short fiction, written before she turned seventeen, is experimental work in which the beginning writer mocks the absurdities and limitations of the sentimental novel popular at the end of the eighteenth century and tentatively explores the possibilities of themes and literary techniques that she will later develop in her mature work.

Story characteristics

Most of Austen's short works poke fun at the conventions of the sentimental fiction for which readers hungered at the end of the eighteenth century. By slightly exaggerating the sensibility of a heroine, the refinement of a hero, the effusiveness of their conversations, and the unlikelihood of their adventures, Austen makes plain the absurdity of the world view purveyed by sentimental novels.

Biography

Jane Austen's life was outwardly uneventful. The youngest of seven children of a Hampshire clergyman, she never married but lived at home with her lively, literary family at Steventon, Bath, Southampton, Chawton, and finally Winchester, the sorts of country towns and watering places she depicts in her fiction.

Analysis

With unsurpassed charm and subtlety, Jane Austen's novels of country life present and appraise the manners, morals, and relationships of Regency England's prosperous middle class. In choosing to depict on what she called her "bits of ivory" the segment of the world she knew best, Jane Austen steered the course of the English novel away from the melodramatic implausibilities that dominated popular fiction at the turn of the nineteenth century. Sir Walter Scott, who recognized the importance of Austen's choice, also praised her for the literary finesse that made such a choice workable, "the exquisite touch which renders commonplace things and characters interesting from the truth of the description and the sentiment."

Although the subject of Jane Austen's novels was contemporary life, it was contemporary literature with its various excesses and deficiencies which inspired her earliest attempts at fiction. In the short pieces collected as her Juvenilia—tales, miniature novels, and epistolary narratives—Austen applies the conventions of sentimental fiction, which she and her family read avidly but critically, with rigorous consistency and pushes them to their logical extremes to demonstrate that such standards produce slipshod literature and convey a false view of the world.

Austen's juvenile fiction differs from the novels in its audience as well as in its subject matter. The young author wrote these short pieces for the private amusement of her family, and as an experienced novelist never contemplated revising and publishing them. Consequently the reader familiar with the decorous elegance of the public prose sees a new side of Jane Austen in the short fiction which, like her letters, voices a tough candor and a blunt humor that the novels mute: remarks such as "Damme Elfrida *you* may be married but *I* wont" seldom make their way from the nursery of Austen's short fiction to the drawing rooms of her adult novels.

Many of the apprentice pieces are literary parodies and burlesques poking fun at the distinctive features of the novel of sensibility: the high-flown language, incredible coincidences, instant friendships, immoderate loves, unaccountable lapses of memory, and sudden recognitions. For example, *Evelyn* amusingly points out the dangers of the cult of sensibility's much-vaunted "sympathetic imagination" unallied with judgment by portraying a village full of utterly and undiscriminatingly benevolent people. *The Beautifull Cassandra* achieves its comic effect by yoking two shortcomings of the popular novel: absurd, unmotivated action included to engage readers and trivial details supplied to convince them. A typical effusion from *Frederic and Elfrida* demonstrates the emptiness of the sentimental novel's stock praises and the egocentricity of its refined protagonists:

> Lovely & too charming Fair one, notwithstanding your forbidding Squint, your greasy tresses & your swelling Back, which are more frightfull than imagination can paint or pen describe, I cannot refrain from expressing my raptures, at the engaging Qualities of your Mind, which so amply atone for the Horror, with which your first appearance must ever inspire the unwary visitor.
>
> Your sentiments so nobly expressed on the different excellencies of Indian & English Muslins, & the judicious preference you give the former, have excited in me an admiration

of which I alone can give an adequate idea, by assuring you it is nearly equal to what I feel for myself.

Perhaps the most wide-ranging and successful of the literary burlesques is *Love and Freindship* (1922), in which Laura, a paragon of sensibility, relates her adventures through a series of letters. Here, Jane Austen lampoons most of the conventions of the sentimental novel and its popular successor, the Gothic romance: the convoluted plots, star-crossed loves, cruel families, and in particular the transports of emotion that, in the world of sensibility, are the index of personal excellence. At the climax of this story containing enough harrowing incident for a triple-decker novel, Laura and her bosom friend Sophia discover "two Gentlemen most elegantly attired but weltering in their blood" who turn out to be their husbands. The heroines react in the prescribed manner:

> Sophia shreiked & fainted on the Ground—I screamed and instantly ran mad—. We remained thus mutually deprived of our Senses some minutes, & on regaining them were deprived of them again—. For an Hour & a Quarter did we continue in this unfortunate situation—Sophia fainting every moment & I running Mad as often. At length a Groan from the hapless Edward (who alone retained any share of Life) restored us to ourselves—. Had we before imagined that either of them lived, we should have been more sparing of our Greif—. . . .

Sophia, in fact, literally dies of the sensibility that has engendered her "shreiks and faints," though not before warning Laura of the medical risks that she now, too late, knows attend on swoons: "Run mad as often as you chuse," Sophia concludes, "but do not faint." These last words undercut many a sentimental deathbed.

In *Love and Freindship*, Jane Austen's satire points out the weaknesses of the literary fashion of sensibility but extends its criticism to include the code of behavior as well. Sensibility as embodied by Laura and Sophia, who meddle, lie, and even steal with perfect complacency, is ethically bankrupt as well as absurdly unrealistic. In several of the juvenile pieces, among them *The Three Sisters*, *Lesley Castle*, and *Catherine*, literary parody gives way to concern with the social and moral themes that pervade the mature novels; but the most sophisticated example of Austen's "serious" short fiction is *Lady Susan* (1871, 1925), an epistolary narrative written after the juvenilia but before the versions we now possess of the six novels.

Lady Susan is unique among Jane Austen's works for several reasons. Lady Susan Vernon, the beautiful and brilliant main character, is Austen's only aristocratic protagonist, and her only *femme fatale*. Unlike the heroines of the novels, whose characters are being formed by experience and who will place themselves in society by the ultimate act of self-definition, marriage, Lady Susan possesses a character matured, even hardened, by years of social skirmishing in the Great World. Furthermore, as a titled widow she already has an established place in society, a most respectable public position she has every intention of retaining without sacrificing her private taste for amorous adventures. Whereas the heroines of the novels gradually learn what they need to know, Lady Susan knows from the start of the story exactly what she wants: "Those women are inexcusable," she observes, "who forget what is due to themselves and to the opinion of the World."

The substance of *Lady Susan* is social and romantic intrigue. Lady Susan balances the attentions of her kindly brother-in-law, her married lover, the rich and well-born fool she has marked out for her insignificant daughter, and the self-assured young man of fashion whose heart she wins for amusement and thinks of retaining as an investment, while two virtuous but worldly women, the brother-in-law's wife, Mrs. Vernon, and her mother, Lady De Courcy, do their best to frustrate her efforts. Although *Lady Susan*'s action, deftly manipulated by the protagonist until luck finally thwarts her, is interesting as pure narrative, its chief fascination is psychological revelation. Lady Susan is as honest with herself as she is false to others; and the epistolary format, often a clumsy way of presenting a story, is ideally suited to pointing up this contrast between her social roles and her true character. The letters Lady Susan's dupes and foes exchange with one another and with her show how easily she can identify and play upon the follies of "virtuous" people; Lady Susan's candid letters to her confidante Mrs. Johnson let us see how far the scheming adventuress surpasses the other characters in the quality that is the first step to true virtue: self-knowledge.

Thus, this important piece of short fiction is more than a chronological transition from Jane Austen's juvenilia to her novels; it is a moral bridge as well. In *Lady Susan*, Austen moves from the realm of literary burlesque into sustained, serious treatment of moral problems, but the conclusion she leaves us to draw is more completely ironic and hence more "literary" than any found in the later works. Never again in Jane Austen is vice so attractive and successful and virtue so unappealing.

Major publications other than short fiction
   NOVELS: *Sense and Sensibility*, 1811; *Pride and Prejudice*, 1813; *Mansfield Park*, 1814; *Emma*, 1815; *Northanger Abbey*, 1818; *Persuasion*, 1818.

Bibliography
Lascelles, Mary. *Jane Austen and Her Art.*
Laski, Marghanita. *Jane Austen and Her World.*
Litz, A. Walton. *Jane Austen: A Study of Her Artistic Development.*
Mudrick, Marvin. *Jane Austen: Irony as Defense and Discovery.*

                                                                                                Peter W. Graham

ISAAC BABEL

Born: Odessa, the Ukraine, Russia; 1894
Died: The Soviet Union; 1939-1941?

Principal short fiction
Red Cavalry, 1926; *Odessa Tales*, 1927; *Benya Krik, the Gangster and Other Stories*, 1948; *The Collected Stories*, 1954; *Lyubka the Cossack and Other Stories*, 1964; *You Must Know Everything: Stories, 1915-1937*, 1969.

Other literary forms
Isaac Babel was primarily a short-story writer, although he also wrote a number of screenplays, various kinds of reminiscences, newspaper articles, and biographical materials. Several novels may have been completed but there is no definitive edition of Babel's work, all Soviet editions showing some marks of censorship.

Influence
Unlike his contemporary Vladimir Nabokov, Isaac Babel remained in Russia throughout the revolution and continued to live there until his death. He was one of the writers who turned away from the nineteenth century realistic mode to modernist techniques as exemplified by writers such as James Joyce, William Faulkner, T. S. Eliot, Ezra Pound, William Butler Yeats, Franz Kafka, and Bertolt Brecht. Having been involved in the political revolution, Babel also proclaimed a liberation of the imagination, and his mastery of the short-story form contributed to its popularity in Russia during the early 1920's.

Story characteristics
Babel's stories are more like lyric poems than traditional narrative types. Making use of a Gogol-like blend of horror and mirth, his stories are surreal in their effect, with clusters of images building into patterns which then take on symbolic implications and point to theme. Plots are truncated, and stories end on an epiphany.

Biography
Born of Jewish parents who had lived in the Ukraine for several generations, Isaac Babel attended school in Nikolayev, where he excelled in the study of languages, undertaking to learn not only Russian and Hebrew, but also English, French, and German. In 1905, Babel enrolled in the Commerical School of Odessa. In 1911, unable to attend the University because of a Jewish quota, he went to the Institute of Financial and Business Studies at Kiev. In 1915, with his formal education completed, he moved to St. Petersburg, where he met Maxim Gorky, who helped him with his literary career. In 1917, Babel

joined the army and was sent to the Romanian front. Afterwards, he seems to have served with the Soviet Secret Police. Two years later he was back in military uniform during the assault on Petrograd. By 1920, he had returned to civilian life, and by 1925, he had completed the two volumes of stories on which his fame mainly rests—*Odessa Tales* (1927) and *Red Cavalry* (1926). Political pressures, however, soon made it increasingly difficult for Babel to write, and during the 1930's his voice was almost silenced. Arrested in 1939, he disappeared from sight; the manner and date of his death are unknown.

Analysis

In the *Odessa Tales*, Isaac Babel calls upon the mythos of his Jewish background, creating stories that employ characters that are larger than life and incidents both simply exaggerated and totally bizarre. In "The King," for example, Babel's brand of grotesque irony is manifest from the beginning. Rather than creating a gentle King of the Jews, Babel's king is a violent and explosive King of the Criminals. The plot, ostensibly about how Benya Krik's men prevent a police raid by burning down the police station, actually is a means of providing a subsurface where, by means of image patterns and justaposition, a more important story can be told. The conflagration is replicated in the bacchanalian rites associated with the wedding feast that Benya sets up for his sister, and the burning is of the flesh as well, both in its sexual and religious connotations.

Another of the Odessa tales that is almost a counterpart to "The King" is "Lyubka the Cossack." Whereas the former exists as an ironic variation on the theme of the King of the Jews, the latter is a variation on the figures of the Madonna, the Christ child, and Joseph, all presented with great gusto. Lyubka, rather than seeking an inn, is the proprietor of one; she is unmarried with a child. Visiting the inn and bringing gifts of cigars, silks, and cocaine, all contraband items, are three sailors of different nationalities. Tsudechkis, the Joseph figure, succeeds in weaning the child from his mother's breast, becoming thereby a surrogate father and also winning a position as manager of Lyubka's operations, consisting of smuggling, prostitution, and drink. Babel's mockery of Christian mythology here is no different from his mockery of Hebraic tradition as presented in "The King." Styles in the two stories are similar—exaggeration, hyperbole, a protagonist with heroic/mythic dimensions, and image patterns which direct underlying meaning.

The stories in the *Red Cavalry* series are composed of the same surrealistic blend. Shorter than the stories in the *Odessa Tales*, the *Red Cavalry* stories are often no more than several pages, but the literary power of these few pages is awesome. The first story in the collection, "Crossing into Poland," is typical of both theme and method. Told in the first person by an as-yet-unnamed narrator, the story is about the progress of a Cossack regiment as it crosses the Zbruch into Poland, beginning the Soviet counteroffensive of the 1920 war. The first paragraph of the story seems at first to do little more than orient a reader as to time and place, but the casual tone of the beginning of the paragraph abruptly changes when the highway from Brest to Warsaw is described as having been built by Nicholas I "upon the bones of peasants." The second paragraph is also primarily descriptive, but the image patterns about halfway through the paragraph again make a violent shift. The first part of the paragraph creates an almost idyllic picture: fields flowering crimson with poppies, a breeze playing in the yellowing rye, a peaceful stream losing itself in the pearly haze of a birch grove. Then, without transition, the peaceful scene turns into a surreal nightmare. An orange sun is given startling dimensions when we are told it "rolled down the sky like a lopped-off head." The violence and grotesque proportions of the image are replicated both in the immediate sentences that follow and in the action of the story soon to be revealed. For now the reader can smell yesterday's blood of slaughtered horses and both hear and see the struggle of the Cossacks as they crossed the Zbruch.

The movement of the Cossacks, subtly suggesting a transition perhaps from ignorance into knowledge but surely from innocence into guilt and hell, is replicated in the experience of the narrator who emerges as a character, clearly speaking in his own voice, only in the third paragraph. This paragraph begins the action of the story, which is abruptly terminated one page later. The plot recounts the experience of the narrator, who, upon reaching Novograd with his regiment, is billeted in the shack of some Jews: a pregnant woman, two who are red-haired and scraggy-necked, and one apparently asleep, huddled next to a wall with his head covered up. The shack is filthy with dirt, human excrement, and fragments of crockery used during Passover. The narrator gives an order that the place be cleaned up, and the two men, monkey-fashion, hop about to the narrator's order. The Jews provide for the narrator "a feather bed that had been disemboweled," set next to the man who is asleep.

Lying on the ripped-open mattress, the narrator falls asleep and dreams that the Commander of the Division, after pursuing the Brigade Commander, shoots him twice between the eyes. As the Brigade Commander's eyes drop to the ground, the Division Commander shouts at the wounded man "why did you turn back the brigade?" At this point the narrator awakes, feeling the pregnant woman's hands groping over his face. She tells him that he has been crying out, tossing to and fro, and pushing her father about. At this point she removes the blanket from the huddled body and reveals a dead old man whose throat has been torn out, his face cleft in two; blue blood is clotted on his beard "like a lump of lead." The Poles, she says, had cut his throat, with him begging them, "Kill me in the yard so that my daughter shan't see me die." Now the pregnant woman cries out with a sudden and terrible violence the question that ends the story: "I should like to know where in the whole world you could find another father like my father?"

Later in the *Red Cavalry* story cycle, the narrator himself is revealed as a young Jew, and consequently the ironies present in "Crossing into Poland" become more apparent; but even without explicit evidence, a reader can discern from the images, doublings, and juxtapositionings the symbolic role which the narrator plays. Entering into the home of the Jews, he enters his own nightmare, which is a replication of the nightmarish happenings around him. When he cries out to the Jews "What a filthy way to live!" his comment describes all the action in the story in its multiple layerings: the highway built upon the bones of peasants; Russian, Polish, and Jewish peasants engaged in what is a senseless and violent war; a narrator hiding from his heritage and finding it in a nightmare vision. The narrator is like a missing son; the dead father is his father; the pregnant woman is his sister/mother. Her groping hands both give him sight, restoring the eyes lost in his dream vision, and deliver him from the disemboweled mattress as from a womb. The narrator is also the dead father next to whom he lies; but the father now has no hope of delivery. The crockery used in the Passover are simply fragments, shattered like the dream of a savior son come not in the guise of deliverer but rather in the role of recorder of violence fought in the name of revolution.

"The Death of Dolgushov" is another story in the *Red Cavalry* series. The narrator, named Lyutov later in the series, is shown in this story to be different from the other members of the Red Cavalry. A bespectacled Jewish intellectual, he is estranged from the Cossacks, who cannot accept him physically or intellectually because of his own Jewish background, which represents for him a dead heritage. Although intellectually dedicated to the destruction of the old world, the narrator still cannot bring himself to kill, and thus he has conscious doubts of his own potency and subconscious doubts as to whether the revolution will accomplish its aim. Although he is with the regiment as a war correspondent rather than as a soldier, there are still occasions when he is asked to kill. "The Death of Dolgushov" records such an occasion.

Cossacks and Poles are in the midst of battle. Bullets shriek and wail as officers ride by shouting orders or curses. Finally, the regimental commander gives orders to move, an act which will leave the wounded behind. The narrator's friend, Afonka, with tears in his eyes, follows the regiment, but the narrator and a companion, Grischuk, remain behind, wandering around between walls of fire. Amidst all the death and horror, Grischuk asks: "What's the point of women slaving away. . . . What's the point of betrothals and marriages? Why do chaps make merry at wedding feasts . . .?" As if in answer, Dolgushov, the regiment's signaler, says, "Look at me." Dolgushov is leaning against a tree; his belly is torn apart and his intestines spill out over his knees. The narrator notes that he can see his heart beating, although he cannot feel Dolgushov's anguish and pain or respond to the wounded man's plea that the narrator kill him. The pattern here is the same as had been expressed earlier when Grischuk asked the questions concerning ultimate morality and meaning at a time when the narrator was in a mortal frenzy over losing his own life.

The narrator cannot bring himself to kill Dolgushov and runs away as a coward shrinking from battle. At this point, Afonka returns and, learning that Dolgushov has asked to be relieved of his pain, shoots him through the mouth. The narrator returns and with a wry smile says to Afonka: "I just couldn't do it." Now Afonka turns on the man he had called friend: "'Go away!' he said, turning pale, 'or I'll kill you! You four eyes have about as much pity for us as a cat has for a mouse. . . .'" In this indictment, Afonka underscores the distrust the Cossacks have for the Jewish intellectual. Afonka cocks his rifle pointing it at the narrator, but Grischuk interferes, telling Afonka not to be so stupid, and Afonka rides away leaving Grischuk and the narrator. "You see how it is," the narrator says; "today I've lost Afonka, the best friend I ever had. . . ." As if in response Grischuk offers the narrator a shriveled apple. "Eat this," Grischuk tells the narrator; "Go on, eat it. Please. . . ." These words end the story, leaving the reader to puzzle out the ending as it relates to the pattern of events preceding it.

Unlike "Crossing into Poland," which operates with very little plot and ends on a clear epiphany, "The Death of Dolgushov" has a linear sequence of events and an apparent climax and denouement. The appearance is deceptive, however, and a careful reading reveals that the ending of the story is not falling action leading to a resolution but rather continuously rising action leading to an epiphany. The offering of the apple is a clear biblical allusion, putting the narrator simultaneously in touch with sinning humanity and the cause of human misery. This merging of antitheses—the juxtaposition of such startling images as sinner and sinned against, the hunter and the hunted, the pursuer and the pursued, father and son, friend and enemy, Jew and Gentile, dream and reality, and the tragic and comic—is the trademark of the surrealist, as is the black humor that results from the yoking together of incongruous elements. It is by means of these juxtapositions that Babel is able in his best stories to create powerful effects in only a few pages. The ambiguities presented delineate a world complex in its structure where there are no simple answers couched in absolute terms. What Babel was saying and the manner in which he was saying it was acceptable to Russia in the early 1920's, but after 1925, the energies of the nation were directed toward reconstruction and reorganization, toward simply stated goals. In answer to the social need, Russian prose writers turned back to a realistic mode.

Babel turned back to his childhood to find subject matter for his stories, and, as he did, he turned to linear plots and more fully developed settings. The stories are longer, considerably less brilliant, and few in number. Indeed, from about 1927 to 1937, Babel's publications were so sparse that he found it necessary to try to explain to Soviet officials the reasons for his silence. Not only was he having difficulty in writing but he was also encountering difficulties in publishing what he did finish. By 1937, Stalin's purges were in full swing, and Babel consented to an interview taking place before the Union of Soviet Writers. The interview, said to be an exercise in double talk, was not published until 1964.

When Babel was arrested in 1939, all existing manuscripts were confiscated, and most have been lost. During the years from 1939 to the mid-1950's, Babel's existence and writings were erased in the Soviet Union. Since then, publication has been resumed, and some of the stories that survived have been printed. None, however, matches the brilliance and power of the works that brought him both glory and death.

Major publications other than short fiction
PLAY: *Benya Krik: A Film Novel*, 1935.

Bibliography
Alexandrova, Vera. *A History of Soviet Literature: 1917-1964.*
Falen, James E. *Isaac Babel: Russian Master of the Short Story.*
Slonim, Marc. *Modern Russian Literature from Chekhov to the Present.*

Mary Rohrberger

JAMES BALDWIN

Born: New York, New York; August 2, 1924

Principal short fiction
Going to Meet the Man, 1965.

Other literary forms
In addition to short stories, James Baldwin has published two plays, several important novels, and some of the most distinguished essays of this era.

Influence
Baldwin's work is important partly as black literature, as an extensive and sensitive account in several genres of black life. His work is also universal, however, and worthy of attention quite apart from its illumination of black experience. His debt to Henry James—especially his attention to social reality—has occasionally been identified. Many of his stories, like those of James Joyce, describe the preparation for the experience by a character of an epiphany: a sudden illumination. Baldwin is traditional in his choice of themes, such as love and alienation, but he creates unusual variations on those themes: homosexuality, bisexuality, interracial love, and the alienation of black Americans. Most critics and readers agree that his essays are superb, but there is a wide range of opinion about the merits of his fiction. Despite that disagreement, his work has sold well for about a quarter of a century and has appeared in many anthologies.

Story characteristics
Baldwin's stories are convincing portraits of social and psychological reality, albeit of parts of that reality unknown to many Americans. The stories also have a moral dimension that deals not only with the plight of blacks but also with moral issues that have traditionally interested serious writers of fiction. His techniques are traditional, his work clear, and his prose style impressive.

Biography
James Arthur Baldwin grew up in Harlem. While he was still attending DeWitt Clinton High School in the Bronx he was a Holy Roller preacher. After high school, he did odd jobs and wrote for *The Nation* and *The New Leader*. A turning point for him was meeting Richard Wright, who encouraged him to write and helped him obtain a fellowship that provided income while he was finishing an early novel. After moving to Paris in 1948 he became acquainted with Norman Mailer and other writers. His first major work, *Go Tell It on the Mountain*, appeared in 1953 and was followed by a long list of

books. He moved back to New York in 1957 and during the 1960's his writing and speeches made him an important force in the civil rights movement. Recently he has spent most of his time in Europe. He has received such honors as a Guggenheim Fellowship and the Foreign Drama Critics' Award and has been elected to the National Institute of Arts and Letters.

Analysis

James Baldwin's "The Man Child," the only story in *Going to Meet the Man* that has no black characters, scathingly describes whites, especially their violent propensities. The central character is Eric, an eight-year-old. The story opens as he, his mother, and his father are giving a birthday party for Jamie, his father's best friend. In the next scene Eric and his father walk together and then return to the party. After a brief summary of intervening events, the story moves forward in time to a day when Jamie meets Eric, entices him into a barn, and breaks his neck. The story described thus, its ending seems to be a surprise, and it certainly is a surprise to Eric. In fact, his sudden realization that he is in grave danger is an epiphany. "The Man Child" is thus a coming-of-age story, an account of a young person's realization of the dark side of adult existence. Eric, however, has little time to think about his realization or even to generalize very much on the basis of his intimation of danger before he is badly, perhaps mortally, injured.

The story, however, contains many hints that violent action will be forthcoming. A reader can see them even though Eric cannot because Eric is the center of consciousness, a device perfected, if not invented, by Henry James. That is, Eric does not narrate the story so the story does not present his viewpoint, but he is always the focus of the action, and the story is in essence an account of his responses to that action. The difference between his perception of the events he witnesses (which is sometimes described and sometimes can be inferred from his actions) and the perception that can be had by attending carefully to the story encourages a reader to make a moral analysis and finally to make a moral judgment, just as the difference between Huck Finn's perception and the perception that one can have while reading *The Adventures of Huckleberry Finn* (1884) at first stimulates laughter and then moral evaluation. Eric's lack of perception is a function of his innocence, a quality that he has to an even larger extent than has Huck Finn, and thus he is less able to cope in a threatening world and his injury is even more execrable. If the measure of a society is its solicitude for the powerless, the miniature society formed by the three adults in this story, and perhaps by implication the larger society of which they are a part is sorely wanting.

To be more specific about the flaws in this society and in these persons, they enslave themselves and others, as is suggested very early in the story: "Eric lived with his father . . . and his mother, who had been captured by his father on some faroff unblessed, unbelievable night, who had never since burst her chains." Her husband intimidates and frightens her, and his conversation about relations between men and women indicates that he believes she exists at his sufferance only for sex and procreation. Her role becomes questionable because in the summary of events that happen between the first and last parts of the story one learns that she has lost the child she had been carrying and cannot conceive anymore. The two men enslave themselves with their notions about women, their drunkenness (which they misinterpret as male companionship), their mutual hostility, their overbearing expansiveness, in short, with their machismo. Eric's father is convinced that he is more successful in these terms. He has fathered a son, an accomplishment the significance of which to him is indicated by his "some day all this will be yours" talk with Eric between the two party scenes. Jamie's wife, showing more sense than Eric's mother, left him before he could sire a son. Jamie's violent act with Eric is his psychotic imitation of the relation of Eric's father to Eric, just as his whistling at the very end of the story is his imitation of the music he hears coming from a tavern. Eric is thus considered by the two men to be alive merely for their self-expression. His father's kind of self-expression is potentially debilitating, although still somewhat benign; Jamie's version is nearly fatal.

"Going to Meet the Man" is a companion to "The Man Child," both stories having been published for the first time in *Going to Meet the Man*. Whereas the latter story isolates whites from blacks in order to analyze their psychology, the former story is about whites in relation to blacks, even though blacks make only brief appearances in it. The whites in these stories have many of the same characteristics, but in "Going to Meet the Man" those characteristics are more obviously dangerous. These stories were written during the height of the civil rights movement, and Baldwin, by means of his rhetorical power and his exclusion of more human white types, helped advance that movement.

The main characters in "Going to Meet the Man" are a family composed of a Southern deputy sheriff, his wife, and his son, Jesse. At the beginning of the story they are skittish because of racial unrest. Demonstrations by blacks have alternated with police brutality by whites, each response escalating the conflict, which began when a black man knocked down an elderly white woman. The family is awakened late at night by a crowd of whites who have learned that the black has been caught. They all set off in a festive, although somewhat tense, mood to the place where the black is being held. After they arrive the black is burned, castrated, and mutilated—atrocities that Baldwin describes very vividly. This story, however, is not merely sensationalism or social and political rhetoric. It rises above those kinds of writing because of its psychological insights into the causes of racism and particularly of racial violence.

Baldwin's focus at first is on the deputy sheriff. As the story opens he is trying and failing to have sexual relations with his wife. He thinks that he would have an easier time with a black and "the image of a black girl caused a distant excitement in him." Thus, his conception of blacks is immediately mixed with sexuality, especially with his fear of impotence. In contrast, he thinks of his wife as a "frail sanctuary." At the approach of a car he reaches for the gun beside his bed, thereby adding a propensity for violence to his complex of psychological motives. Most of his behavior results from this amalgam of racial attitudes, sexual drives, fear of impotence, and attraction to violence. For example, he recalls torturing a black prisoner by applying a cattle prod to his testicles, and on the way to see the black captive he takes pride in his wife's attractiveness. He also frequently associates blacks with sexual vigor and fecundity. The castration scene is the most powerful rendition of this psychological syndrome.

The deputy sheriff, however, is more than a mere brute. For example, he tries to think of his relation to blacks in moral terms. Their singing of spirituals disconcerts him because he has difficulty understanding how they can be Christians like himself. He tries to reconcile this problem by believing that blacks have decided "to fight against God and go against the rules laid down in the Bible for everyone to read!" To allay the guilt that threatens to complicate his life he also believes that there are a lot of good blacks who need his protection from bad blacks. These strategies for achieving inner peace do not work, and Baldwin brilliantly describes the moral confusion of such whites:

> they had never dreamed that their privacy could contain any element of terror, could threaten, that is, to reveal itself, to the scrutiny of a judgment day, while remaining unreadable and inaccessible to themselves; nor had they dreamed that the past, while certainly refusing to be forgotten, could yet so stubbornly refuse to be remembered. They felt themselves mysteriously set at naught.

In the absence of a satisfying moral vision, violence seems the only way to achieve inner peace, and the sheriff's participation in violence allows him to have sex with his wife as the story ends. Even then, however, he has to think that he is having it as blacks would. He is their psychic prisoner, just as the black who was murdered was the white mob's physical prisoner.

Late in this story one can see that Jesse, the sheriff's eight-year-old son, is also an important character. At first he is confused by the turmoil and thinks of blacks in human terms. For example, he wonders why he has not seen his black friend Otis for several days. The mob violence, however, changes him; he undergoes a coming of age, the perversity of which is disturbing. He is the center of consciousness in the mob scene. His first reaction is the normal one for a boy: "Jesse clung to his father's neck in terror as the cry rolled over the crowd." Then he loses his innocence and it becomes clear that he will be a victim of the same psychological syndrome that afflicts his father: "he watched his mother's face . . . she was more beautiful than he had ever seen her. . . . He began to feel a joy he had never felt before." He wishes that he were the man with the knife who is about to castrate the black, whom Jesse considers "the most beautiful and terrible object he had ever seen." Then he identifies totally with his father: "at that moment Jesse loved his father more than he had ever loved him. He felt that his father had carried him through a mighty test, had revealed to him a great secret which would be the key to his life forever." For Jesse this brutality is thus a kind of initiation into adulthood, and its effect is to ensure that there will be at least one more generation capable of the kind of violence that he has just seen.

Whereas "The Man Child" has only white characters and "Going to Meet the Man" is about a conflict between whites and blacks, "Sonny's Blues" has only black characters. Although the chronology of "Sonny's Blues" is scrambled, its plot is simple. It tells the story of two brothers, one, the narrator, a respectable teacher and the other, Sonny, a former user of heroin who is jailed for that reason and then becomes a jazz musician. The story ends in a jazz nightclub, where the older brother hears Sonny play and finally understands the meaning of jazz for him. The real heart of this story is the contrast between the values of the two brothers, a contrast that becomes much less dramatic at the end.

The two brothers have similar social backgrounds, especially their status as blacks and, more specifically, as Harlem blacks. Of Harlem as a place in which to mature the narrator says, "boys exactly like the boys we once had been found themselves encircled by disaster. Some escaped the trap, most didn't. Those who got out always left something of themselves behind, as some animals amputate a leg and leave it in a trap." Even when he was very young the narrator had a sense of the danger and despair surrounding him:

> when lights fill the room, the child is filled with darkness. He knows that every time this happens he's moved just a little closer to that darkness outside. The darkness outside is what the old folks have been talking about. It's what they've come from. It's what they endure.

For example, he learns after his father's death that that seemingly hardened and stoical man had hidden the grief caused by the killing of his brother.

At first the narrator believes that Sonny's two means for coping with the darkness, heroin and music, are inextricably connected to that darkness and thus not survival mechanisms at all. He believes that heroin "filled everything, the people, the houses, the music, the dark, quicksilver barmaid, with menace; and this menace was their reality." Later, however, he realizes that jazz is a way to escape: he senses that "Sonny was at that time piano playing for his life." The narrator also has a few premonitions of the epiphany he experiences in the jazz nightclub. One occurs when he observes a group of street singers and understands that their "music seemed to soothe a poison out of them." Even with these premonitions, he does not realize that he uses the same strategy. After an argument with Sonny, during which their differences seem to be irreconcilable, his first reaction is to begin "whistling to keep from crying," and the tune is a blues. Finally the epiphany occurs, tying together all the major strands of this story. As he listens to Sonny playing jazz the narrator thinks that

> freedom lurked around us and I understood, at last, that he could help us be free if we would listen, that he would never be free until we did. Yet, there was no battle in his face now. I heard what he had gone through, and would continue to go through.

The idea in that passage is essentially what Baldwin is about. Like Sonny, he has forged an instrument of freedom by means of the fire of his troubles, and he has made that instrument available to all, white and black. His is the old story of suffering and art; his fiction is an account of trouble, but by producing it he has shown others the way to rise above suffering.

Major publications other than short fiction
    NOVELS: *Go Tell It on the Mountain*, 1953; *Giovanni's Room*, 1956; *Another Country*, 1962; *Tell Me How Long the Train's Been Gone*, 1968; *If Beale Street Could Talk*, 1974; *Just Above My Head*, 1979.
    PLAYS: *Blues for Mister Charlie*, 1964; *The Amen Corner*, 1968.
    NONFICTION: *Notes of a Native Son*, 1955; *Nobody Knows My Name: More Notes of a Native Son*, 1961; *The Fire Next Time*, 1963.

Bibliography
Eckman, Fern Maja. *The Furious Passage of James Baldwin*.
Kinnamon, Kenneth A., ed. *James Baldwin: A Collection of Critical Essays*.
Macebuh, Stanley. *James Baldwin: A Critical Study*.
O'Daniel, Therman B., ed. *James Baldwin: A Critical Evaluation*.

John Stark

J. G. BALLARD

Born: Shanghai, China; November 15, 1930

Principal short fiction

The Voices of Time, 1962; *Billenium*, 1962; *Passport to Eternity*, 1963; *The Terminal Beach*, 1964; *The Impossible Man*, 1966; Love and Napalm: Export U. S. A.*, 1969 (originally published as *The Atrocity Exhibition*); *Vermilion Sands*, 1971; *Chronopolis and Other Stories*, 1971; *The Best Short Stories of J. G. Ballard*, 1978.

Other literary forms

J. G. Ballard has been as prolific in the novel as in the short story, systematically developing a set of themes and extending his range of narrative techniques. Four of his novels, for example, deal with apocalyptic themes, each novel centering around destruction caused by one of the four elements. His recent work can be viewed as a collection of condensed novels or linked short stories.

Influence

Although Ballard writes science fiction, he has always defied the conventions of the genre, showing no interest in space travel, gadgetry, or beings from other planets. His use of new techniques and his preference for writing about the near future rather than the far future have identified him as one of the early practitioners of the New Wave in science fiction.

Story characteristics

Both his short stories and his novels deal primarily with extensive, vaguely defined catastrophes. Not a prophet of doom, Ballard is more concerned with man's adaptation to the challenge of destruction and isolation than with the causes of disaster.

Biography

James Graham Ballard grew up in China, and did not go to England until he entered Cambridge to study medicine. After two years, he left Cambridge and worked briefly for a scientific journal. Then he tried writing science fiction, which he had begun to read after he left China. What happened to him in wartime China—he experienced at first hand as a prisoner in a Japanese camp a sense of desolation and destruction that became for him symbolic of the future prospects of mankind—eventually found expression in science fiction. Ballard has since been able to support himself and his family by working full time as a writer.

Analysis

Much of J. G. Ballard's work can be considered an imaginative recasting of one dominant experience from his early years. While living with his parents in China during World War II, he was interned by the Japanese in a camp near Shanghai. Shortly after his internment the Japanese vacated the area, and eventually the Americans intervened. The camp was a world in which time had stopped, a world of abandoned machines, deserted beaches and buildings, and wide stretches of inland water. The experience left young Ballard with a landscape which in time would become an image for the state of contemporary man.

In his twenties he became an avid reader of science fiction and began writing in that genre. Stories he wrote in the early 1960's, many of which appeared originally in the British magazine *New Worlds*, revealed the pattern latent in his Asian experiences only in a fragmentary way, but evidence of its influence is easily detectable. In these stories from the 1960's, isolation and catastrophe appear in a European setting. Although the circumstances of the catastrophe are often vague and generalized, the vagueness usually serves as a means of creating suspense, and the characters are developed as persons with concerns and feelings that are conventional and readily identifiable.

In "Chronopolis," Conrad Newman, in prison awaiting his trial, seems to be more absorbed with the workings of a sundial and the power it gives him than in his imprisonment. Conrad is not misguided; no individual is allowed to measure time. Conrad, as an extended flashback makes clear, has always been curious about time, even as a child, and his curiosity has led him to reinvent ancient time-keeping devices. Although his parents, aware that the Time Police still exist, discourage his inquiries, the child Conrad persists, develops a water clock, then stumbles upon a watch that an old man had been hiding. Conrad uses it to impress his schoolmates. Eventually one of his teachers discovers his secret and undertakes the responsibility of explaining to Conrad what has happened to clocks. The city they live in, the teacher explains as he takes Conrad on a tour, once measured fifty miles in diameter and supported thirty million people. Now there are only two million people living in a band that circles the decayed center of the city. The only way to manage the old city of thirty million had been to control the activities of the inhabitants by a rigid time schedule, which in turn led to revolt and the destruction of the clocks. As the teacher talks on, Conrad spots a clock that is still working, and escapes from his teacher, who turns out to have been an agent of the Time Police.

Conrad finds that several clocks are being maintained by an old man, and with the old man's help Conrad himself becomes a mender of clocks, including the biggest one in the middle of the city, one with chimes. Months later, after the chimes ring out thirty miles away in the inhabited band that rings the city, Conrad is discovered and imprisoned. The final section of the story continues from the opening scene in prison. Conrad has been given a twenty-year sentence, but just as he was distracted during the opening scene by his sundial, his primary concern now is still to create some means of measuring time. To his surprise, a clock has already been provided for him, and he rejoices, only after two weeks beginning to note the clock's insanely irritating click.

The story can be read partly as a satire of life in a large modern city, where the resources for living and moving about seem to be strained to the utmost, and where time in all its carefully marked segments has become everyone's obsession. It can also be read as a story with a trick ending, one in which a character is punished by the very thing he wishes for. The ending, however, is more than a gimmick; it is the culmination of the progressive undercutting of what might otherwise have been taken as a Promethean effort by Conrad to give man back his awareness of time. Neither the quest for time nor the destruction of it, the structure of the story seems to suggest, is unquestionably valuable. It is characteristic of Ballard in most of his stories to develop the complexities of his themes rather than to identify with one or the other side of an issue. Such an approach is in no sense new to mainstream writing, but it is unusual in science fiction.

Ballard has written several stories as technically polished as "Chronopolis." "Billenium," for instance, describes a world so crowded that individuals are allotted cubicles with no more than four square meters of floor area. One of the more intricate stories of the period is "Thirteen for Centaurus," the title referring to thirteen astronauts supposedly on their way to Centaurus. A young man named Abel (like Conrad in "Chronopolis") precociously discovers something those around him have repressed. Abel figures out that this flight to Centaurus, which has been in progress for generations, has never left the earth. The original crew were volunteers in an experiment to test the effects of lifetime cruises, but the original arrangement required that their descendants would be conditioned to have all knowledge of their origins obliterated and never learn that they are in fact going nowhere. The obliteration requires constant psychological conditioning, for even though the "astronauts" have never seen a sun, there is an archetypal sense of a burning disk which haunts them.

Since space flights begun after this experiment have failed and mankind has abandoned the idea of space travel, the government wishes to cut expenses and free what have now in effect become prisoners. Abel's mentor, however, the psychologist Dr. Francis, wants the experiment to continue. He argues that his patients are not equipped emotionally to survive the revelation of their true condition, and furthermore, information that has been and will be obtained from the experiment might still be valuable, and might have averted the disasters of past space travel had it been available. Government officials propose a series of well-intentioned but absurd compromises, and Dr. Francis withdraws to the ship permanently. His victory is as short-lived as Conrad's, for in trying to while away the time by acquiescing to some random number of experiments devised by Abel, he finds himself Abel's victim. His prospects of escaping from Abel's experiments, which are the just rewards for his attempts to make the people on board his subjects, are no greater than Conrad's chances of escaping the prison in "Chronopolis." In positing the failure of space travel, and in revealing the trip as a sham, Ballard is close to parodying the concerns of conventional science fiction. As in "Chronopolis," he is more interested in where man's desire will lead him than in the hopes of advancement through technology. Ballard writes more in the dystopian than the utopian tradition of science fiction, but the center of his attention is on his characters and not on the pessimistic themes.

Two years after writing these stories Ballard moved even further from science fiction by abandoning traditional narrative devices. At this point the experiences of his youth latent in the earlier stories now manifest themselves fully. In the sense of abandonment and destruction that characterized "Chronopolis" it is possible to detect the influence of a period of incarceration characterized less by torture than by the absence of authority, a sort of endless interregnum. In the stories of *Vermilion Sands*, and in a story such as "The Terminal Beach," the actual images taken from Ballard's Asiatic experience—water, sand, abandoned buildings—begin to predominate.

The technique of "The Terminal Beach" could be taken as avant-garde only in a genre as conservative as science fiction in the 1960's. Action is minimal. Traven, a middle-aged former Navy pilot, has gone to Eniwetok with its ruined block houses and fused plastic figures left from atomic tests to search for the specters of his wife and child, who have been killed in an automobile accident. The time is set in the near future, presumably after World War III. The story is divided into sections each with a separate topical heading, and occasionally the sequence of events is broken by the intrusion of a different narrative source, such as the journal of a biologist who discovered Traven on the island. The climax of the story is an imaginary dialogue, set up with stage directions, between a Japanese corpse and Traven. The philosophical exchange reveals the nature of Traven's quest on Eniwetok, his hunt for the "white leviathan, zero" in a place free of the hazards of time and space, free of what Ballard has designated as "quantal flux." If Traven's objectives and the resolution of his conflicts are blurred, what does stand out sharply is an image of a ruined island.

Out of "The Terminal Beach" grew another collection titled in Britain *The Atrocity Exhibition* and in the United States *Love and Napalm: Export U. S. A.* The collection is a series of what Ballard has called "condensed novels." Since there are close links between the stories, the collection as a whole is sometimes designated as a novel. The protagonists of the stories are variously called Travis, Talbot, Tallis, Travert, or Talbert; and this character, who has also suffered the death of his wife Margaret in an auto accident, is clearly a continuation of the protagonist of "The Terminal Beach." Instead of being a military pilot wandering on Eniwetok, he is a psychiatrist in an institution in which he is sometimes mistaken for one of the psychotic patients. He creates for himself a series of imaginary sexual deviations in an attempt to cope with his wife's death, or as it is sometimes expressed, to cope with the exhaustion of affection in contemporary life. Travis constantly fuses his perceptions of his surroundings, of buildings and landscapes around him, with his perception of women, either a woman on a movie screen or a girl named Karen Novotny, endowing each with the properties of the other. What stimulates him the most is the idea of filmed atrocities, from napalming to crashes. A catalog of the new deviations he imagines would make such old-fashioned deviations as sodomy as amusing and antiquated as "pottery ducks on suburban walls."

In one characteristic excerpt, entitled "Summer Cannibals," the characters are unnamed, but from passages in surrounding stories which repeat parallel incidents, we can presume they are Travis and Karen Novotny. The man and the woman are shown alternately in the familiar Ballardian landscape of a deserted beach and in the man's apartment. Beyond the apartment is an open-air cinema projecting "immense fragments of Bardot's magnificent body" and beyond the screen what is for Travis the mysterious repository of all erotic stimulation, a multistory car park. Travis amuses himself with imaginary juxtapositions of the woman's body and the parts of the car, and disputes with himself the difference between conventional intercourse and the stimulation obtained from the angle between two walls. In one scene he imagines the woman emerging from a car wreck, blood oozing sensually on her legs and clinging to her dress, and in the next he imagines a love scene in which he pursues her from his car, "her broad hips lit by the glare of the headlamps," and then he switches off the lights and drives toward her, positioning her image against the backdrop of the cinema and the car park. The order of the two sequences, which is the reverse of what one might expect if one looked for causal connection, obscures the man's intent and responsibility for the imagined accident. It would be convenient to consider Ballard's intention in this collection satiric, but it is hard to distinguish this Travis from the Traven who wandered around Eniwetok, and Ballard has avowed his view of his earlier doomed figures as apostles of a new consciousness. What little attention the volume attracted has been vituperative. One critic designated it as horrible, boring, and pointless, and saw it as an attempt to make the novel a form of abuse.

Because Ballard seems to position himself between genres, he has no particular audience which can accept and assimilate all that he writes. He is too much an innovator to fit the mold of a science fiction writer, but neither can he be considered avant-garde. His language, from the "quantal flux" of "The Terminal Beach" to the repetitive, abstract formulations of *Love and Napalm*, with its "geometries of sensations," "geometry of aggression and desire," "algebra of pillow arrangements," "anthology of junctions," and "anthology of irritations," is still the vocabulary of science fiction. What is clear is that his imagination, however its morality may be viewed, is original, and that he has brought to the subject of desolation, incarceration, and abandonment an altogether different viewpoint.

Major publications other than short fiction
NOVELS: *The Wind from Nowhere*, 1962; *The Drowned World*, 1962; *The Drought*, 1964 (later retitled *The Burning World*); *The Crystal World*, 1966; *Crash*, 1973; *Concrete Island*, 1974; *High Rise*, 1975;. *The Unlimited Dream Company*, 1979.

Bibliography
Aldiss, Brian. "The Wounded Land: J. G. Ballard," in *SF: The Other Side of Realism*. Thomas D. Clareson, ed.
Goddard, James and David Pringle. *J. G. Ballard: The First Twenty Years*.

John Gerlach

HONORÉ DE BALZAC

Born: Tours, France; May 20, 1799
Died: Paris, France; August 18, 1850

Principal short fiction

Romans et contes philosophiques, 1831-1837; *Nouveaux contes philosophiques*, 1832; *Contes drolatiques*, 1832-1837 (*Droll Stories*).

Other literary forms

Honoré de Blazac's reputation is based mainly on the novel form, particularly on *Le Comédie Humaine* (*The Human Comedy*), a collection of some ninety-three novels written between 1829 and 1850. He was also a major journalist and essayist, and he wrote several plays, the most successful at the conclusion of his career.

Influence

Balzac exemplified the Romantic novelist in France and simultaneously introduced certain significant literary innovations leading to the establishment of realism toward the middle of the nineteenth century. He combined vision, imagination, energy, encyclopedic knowledge, and enthusiasm in his innovative study of contemporary French life. For the first time, settings were carefully analyzed and emotions, passions, and obsessions recorded and documented. Inspired in part by the scientist Geoffroy Saint-Hilaire, whose theories of evolution predate those of Charles Darwin, Balzac used techniques which influenced the realists and naturalists in France, established the serial novel as an art form, and encouraged the study of sociology well before the career of Emile Durkheim. Intending to become the "secretary of society," in his career he produced more than 150 works, almost twice as many as that other giant of nineteenth century French letters, Victor Hugo. He profoundly influenced Gustave Flaubert, Émile Zola, Marcel Proust, and the French theater. He is also generally credited with having invented the detective-story genre. In England, his literary descendants include William Makepeace Thackeray, George Moore, and Oscar Wilde; in the United States, Henry James, Theodore Dreiser, and William Faulkner; and in Italy, he is acknowledged to be one of the major influences leading to *verismo*.

Story characteristics

Like his novels, Balzac's short stories display vast enthusiasm for his characters, be they noble or base, poor or wealthy. His detailed portraits include not only the physical person and setting, but also the subject's emotions and driving passions, philosophical and religious ideas, social and political stature, and influence. More than any other author of his time, Balzac also dwells on things financial; the power of money is represented in vivid detail, with great relish, as are all the forces that act on human nature. For Balzac, life in society is a constant struggle for survival, and his work, like Zola's novels, represents an outstanding example of social Darwinism.

Balzac's topics range from the most mundane to the most mystical and supernatural, from philosophical inquiries to licentious tales. What characterizes all the stories is his style; it is flamboyant, verbose, and ostentatious; it demonstrates a sophisticated expertise regardless of the subject being treated (be it antiques, ecclesiastical politics, high finance, or painting), and it is always compelling. In essence, Balzac's style reflects his own personality, which will not be repressed and which is present even in the most "objective" of narratives. While his temperament naturally inclined toward the expansive possibilities of the novel form, his stories, however melodramatic or farfetched, are told with such assurance that the sheer weight of his personality hastens the reader's surrender to the work of art.

Biography

Honoré de Balzac grew up in a bourgeois family in Tours, then moved with them to Paris, where he completed his undistinguished education—he was apparently too much of a dreamer to perform well in classes. Working as a clerk in law and financial practices and attending the Sorbonne lectures of Victor Cousin and François Guizot in the evenings led him to develop an abhorrence for the mundane existence of the salaried working class. In 1819, he suddenly announced that he intended to become a writer, and there followed years of misery as he eked out his living in garrets and attics, existing like a hermit by extraordinary economy and by producing a flood of anonymous cheap tracts and novels. Although his family hoped that these conditions would bring Balzac back to his senses, unyielding patterns were formed instead, traits that would continue for the rest of his life. His prodigious energy, combined with a strong will, established his daily regimen of writing—often twenty hours, nonstop—which he sustained by his own blends of coffee. His penniless existence helped whet his appetite for financial success to the degree that he was often tempted to embark on the most elaborate schemes to make his fortune. It was not that his ideas, such as forming a publishing company that would produce inexpensive copies of the classics, were unsound; in fact, his notions were far ahead of his time. His sense of management, however, as well as his choice of partners and financial backers were inevitably naïve, and few, if any, of his financial ventures were to succeed.

As a result, Balzac turned to the newspapers, where he sold essays and short stories and where his real apprenticeship took place. Publishing deadlines and payment by the word encouraged him to prolific writing as a means of paying off his debts. In 1829 came his first success under his own name; this was a historical novel influenced by Sir Walter Scott, *Les Chouans* (1829,

The Chouans), which dealt with the royalist uprising in Brittany during the French Revolution. After this, his output became truly prodigious, for in addition to the normal demands of journalism, he produced ninety-three novels between 1829 and 1850. Like both Scott and Fyodor Dostoevski, he was constantly writing to satisfy his creditors; and that he managed under these circumstances to produce enduring works of art is testimony to his genius.

The year 1829 was also the date that Balzac's anonymous *La Physiologie du mariage* (*The Physiology of Marriage*) appeared; although seemingly satirical, it demonstrated the same profound empathy and understanding for women that would lead him toward numerous enduring relationships. Many were begun by correspondence, the most famous being that with the Polish Countess Hanska, whom he pursued for eighteen years. Their correspondence, published posthumously as *Lettres à Madame Hanska* (four volumes, 1967-1971, *Letters to Madame Hanska*), forms a fascinating account of Balzac's life and works. Although they married in March, 1850, by then he was in very poor health, and it was too late for her fortune to be of assistance to him in his constant financial entanglements. Balzac died, exhausted, in August of 1850.

Analysis

Honoré de Balzac's immense production and his celebrated writing schedule of some two thousand pages per year suggest an artist who gave no thought to theory or form, and of course, a glance at some of his journalistic endeavors will readily confirm these clichés. Quite early in his career, however, examples of Balzac's genius were expressed in his short fiction. "Le Chef-d'œuvre inconnu" ("The Unknown Masterpiece") was first published in newspaper form in 1831, and was later included in *The Human Comedy* under the classification of *Études philosophiques* (1831-1835, *Philosophical Studies*). The story deals with the lifelong obsession of master-painter Frenhofer to discover ideal beauty and its representation. Two admiring disciples, Franz Purbus and Nicolas Poussin, real-life artists used by Balzac to add verisimilitude to his story, come to seek advice; in exchange, they propose that the mistress of Poussin be the model for the work that Frenhofer has been trying to complete after all these years. No sooner does the master see the young woman than his inspiration permits him to complete without further delay the elusive painting. When he unveils the work for his friends, however, they are dumbfounded to see on the canvas a mass of colors and lines, but no figure. Embarrassed and wondering if Frenhofer may not be playing a joke on them, they hem and haw, examine the painting with great attention, and finally discern a foot, a beautiful, living foot, lost in the haze of colors and details. When the master, lost in ecstasy, understands the reality of his disciples' incomprehension and realizes that even his fellow artists are unable to grasp the significance of his creation, he sends them away, burns his paintings, and dies.

Balzac's story fits into the tradition of the *ars poetica*, works about the act of artistic creation. It reveals to what extent the young and busy author himself meditated on this critical topic, on the distinction between artistic theory and artistic practice, and, in this case at least, anticipated the aesthetic revolution to be launched by the Impressionists.

Completely different in tone, *Droll Stories* recalls the gross farce of François Rabelais and the bawdy dimensions of the *esprit gaulois*. Like the *fabliaux* of the late Middle Ages, they poke good-humored fun at indecency. Like Giovanni Boccaccio's *The Decameron* (1353), there is a semblance of morality, but it is spread so thin that the reader has to laugh, along with the author, at the adulterous couples, lascivious men of the Church, deceived husbands, and others that constitute the universal menagerie of the farce. Whereas the form is inspired by Geoffrey Chaucer and Boccaccio, the style Balzac adopts is very similar to that of Rabelais, and it shows tendencies that later become Balzac's trademark: long lists of synonyms and abundant technical details that in fact have little to do with the story line but which permit the author to indulge his passion for words and his delight at demonstrating his verbal dexterity. The collection is signed by the author as "de Balzac," the first use of the snobbish *particule* that Balzac used consistently thereafter, along with a family coat of arms that he either "discovered" or invented himself. The vivid and racy spirit of Rabelais, which is so close to that of Balzac himself, permeates his other works, as does the Renaissance spirit of enthusiasm and lust for life. His sheer exuberance sustained him throughout his complex career.

Another typical story is "La Grande Bretèche" ("The Grande Bretèche"), which continues the tradition of a story within a story. In this case, Dr. Bianchon, a character who recurs throughout *The Human Comedy* and for whom Balzac called as he lay dying, tells of a strange property he visited in the Vendôme, and of the provocative tale that lay behind it. A suspicious husband returns home earlier than expected and confronts his wife, asking her to open her closet door so that he can see her lover. On her affirmation that there is no one there, and that, further, if her husband should doubt her word and actually open the door to verify it, their relationship will be forever dissolved, the husband agrees; he then promptly has a worker build up a wall over the doorway, smiling with assurance at his distressed wife. Balzac here presents a fascinating study of conjugal jealousy with medieval overtones, and he anticipates scenes later exploited by Alexandre Dumas and Edgar Allan Poe.

These same melodramatic touches distinguish "Facino Cane," a story evoking the sensuality and political corruption of eighteenth century Venice (another idea borrowed by Dumas for *The Count of Monte-Cristo*, 1844), which gives Balzac full rein for his use of local color, obsessive emotions, and money as a prime motivating force in modern society. It is difficult for the modern reader to realize to what extent Balzac's treatment of money in literature was truly new. While greed has always been represented in literature, Balzac was among the first to dwell on what he termed the modern age, "la necessité de calculer."

It is important to note that Balzac made no clear distinctions between the novel and the short story, and that many of his best early works are in fact works of short fiction now scattered throughout the framework of *The Human Comedy*. The magnum opus, including its recurring characters, was first conceived of in 1834, and carried a Preface by Felix Davin, a friend of Balzac. Three years later, however, Balzac had written so much more than anticipated that the project was expanded, and by 1840, the unifying title, recalling Dante's work, was established. The finishing touches were applied in 1842, when Balzac replaced Davin's earlier preface with his own preface—a critical document and the cornerstone of his aesthetics. His extraordinary range of knowledge and precise powers of observation combined with a vigorous personality which could not resist sharing its personal views with others, make Balzac one of his century's, and one of the world's, most distinguished chroniclers of French society.

Major publications other than short fiction

NOVELS: *Les Chouans*, 1829 (*The Chouans*); *La Comédie Humaine*, 1829-1850 (*The Human Comedy*).

PLAYS: *Cromwell*, 1819; *Vautrin*, 1840; *Les Ressources de Quinola*, 1842 (*The Resources of Quinola*); *Paméla Giraud*, 1843; *Le Faiseur*, 1844 (Mercadet); *La Marâtre*, 1848 (*The Stepmother*).

NONFICTION: *La Physiologie du mariage*, 1829 (*The Physiology of Marriage*).

Bibliography

Berdèche, Maurice. *Balzac.*

Bertault, Philippe. *Balzac and The Human Comedy.*

Hemmings, F. W. J. *Balzac: An Interpretation of* La Comédie Humaine.

Hunt, Herbert J. *Balzac's* Comédie Humaine.

_____ . *Honoré de Balzac: A Biography.*

Laubriet, Pierre. *L'Intelligence de l'art chez Balzac.*

Lock, Peter W. "Point of View in Balzac's Short Stories," in *Balzac and the Nineteenth-Century.*

Rogers, Samuel. *Balzac and the Novel.*

Zweig, Stefan. *Balzac.*

Robert W. Artinian

IMAMU AMIRI BARAKA
LeRoi Jones

Born: Newark, New Jersey; October 7, 1934

Principal short fiction
Tales, 1967.

Other literary forms
More a playwright, poet, and essayist than a writer of prose fiction, Imamu Amiri Baraka has published or produced more than twenty-five plays, published more than twelve volumes of poems and seven volumes of essays, and edited some twelve anthologies.

Influence
For somewhat less than a decade Baraka was considered to be the most talented of contemporary black writers and in the forefront of the avant-garde movement in literature which had its genesis in such writers as T. S. Eliot, James Joyce, Samuel Beckett, Jean-Paul Sartre, Ezra Pound. It was during this period that he wrote his novel, *The System of Dante's Hell* (1965), and published his collection of short stories, *Tales*. It was also during the middle to late years of the 1960's that Jones identified more and more with his black heritage, changed his name to Baraka, began to associate himself more directly with black militancy, and became increasingly involved with the communal art of the black revolutionary theater.

Story characteristics
With rich images juxtaposed in seemingly chaotic ways, rhythmic patterns often functioning as incantation, startling montage effects, minimal or no plot lines, Baraka's stories often seem more like poems than ordinary prose fiction and often more surreal than based in the mundane and the experiential. Still, the total effect is of the starkly real.

Biography
Educated at Rutgers University, Howard University, Columbia University, and the New School for Social Research, Imamu Amiri Baraka (LeRoi Jones) also taught at the New School for Social Research, the University of Buffalo, Columbia University, and San Francisco State University. Married twice, he has seven children from the two marriages. He is the recipient of a John Whitney Foundation Fellowship for poetry and fiction (1962), an Obie Award (1964 for his play, *Dutchman*), a Longview Foundation Award, and a Guggenheim Fellowship (1965-1966). In the mid-1960's he founded the Black Arts

Repertory Theater in Harlem and Spirit House, a black community theater, in Newark.

Analysis

Imamu Amiri Baraka's *Tales* consists of sixteen pieces of short fiction ranging in length from two pages to more than twenty pages. Some of the pieces, such as "A Chase (Alighieri's Dream)" and "The Alternative," seem in style and method to be closely related to *The System of Dante's Hell*, with its jumble of images and surreal effects. Others, such as "Uncle Tom's Cabin: Alternative Ending," "The Death of Horatio Alger," and "Salute," follow a fairly simple plot line and present fewer difficulties. Still others, such as "Heroes Are Gang Leaders" and "Words," appear to be more like illustrated lectures than fully developed short stories. Most of the "tales," however, in spite of certain differences in technique, present themes similar to those explored by Baraka in his novel, plays, poems, and essays published during the decade of the 1960's. The black poet like his white counterpart suffers from a disassociation of sensibilities, but the black poet's alienation is even more severe since he must confront not only the greater tradition but also find his own special artistic image and authentic black voice.

The young black poet, then, is pursued not only by the literary voices of the white world but also by the voices of myriad black people who demand articulation. At first the black poet struggles to hold on to the voices of the white world. Their words seduce him. In "The Alternative" the leader, Ray McGhee, sits on his bed in the dormitory of a college that teaches white literature and whose authorities emulate white cultural values. In spite of the fact that Ray's room is filled with his black contemporaries speaking the language of the streets, Ray is trying to read William Shakespeare and William Butler Yeats. He repeats the words of a Spanish poem as incantation and imagines himself as Joyce's Stephen Dedalus; and the voices that he reads paralyze him. He is caught up in what Baraka later calls "the deathurge of this twisted society," the dead minds of a dying Europe. In this regard Ray is similar to the protagonist of *The System of Dante's Hell*: "I said my name was Stephen Dedalus. And I read Proust and mathematics and loved Eliot for his tears." The immersion in the voices of the Euro-American tradition, however, leads the black poet to hell, a narcissistic journey to the inner self, solipsistic and masturbatory. The black poet must divorce himself from Western values, free himself from inaction, and cleave to the authenticity of his black experience. In "New-Sense" the narrator makes the point:

> Having understood
> the most noble attempts of white men to make admirable sense of the
> world, now, reject them, along with any of them. And the mozarts
> are as childish as the hitlers.

Because reflect
never did shit for any of us. Express would. Express. NOW NOW
NOW NOW NOW NOW.

Blood Everywhere.
And heroes march thru smiling.

The Hamlet burden is "white bullshit." It sent Ray "sailing around the stupid
seas" with a "little brown girl waiting for him while he masturbated among
pirates . . . dying from his education. Shit."

In "The Screamers" Baraka describes an authentic black experience, a
dance to "mean honking blues." Following the lead of the strutting musicians,
their horns held high, the dancers form a line and the narrator joins them.
They dance through the lobby and down the steps of the building into the
street, halting traffic as they go. "We screamed and screamed at the clear
image of ourselves as we always should be. Ecstatic, completed, involved in
a secret communal expression." How wonderful it would be, the narrator
thinks, to make this dance line the form of a revolution, "to hucklebuck into
the fallen capitol, and let the oppressors lindy hop out." This dance line,
however, creates no such effect. Within minutes the police arrive with paddy
wagons, billy sticks, and crushing streams of water, and knives, razors, and
coke bottles used as weapons appear, and war rages in the streets.

In "Now and Then" Baraka once again speaks of the music as a revolutionary force, but this time the revolution is in the souls, the spirituality of
the musicians expressed as hallucinatory energy. As they play, the music
climbs and bombards everything, and civilizations are destroyed. Nuns whim-
per and blond babies bleed; dogs eat their mothers and television is destroyed
until there is left only: "A black way. A black life."

The most forceful and fanciful projection of the revolution that Baraka
images is presented in "Answers in Progress," the last story in the volume.
One of the shorter pieces, the story is only five and a half pages long, but the
vision is explicit, the detail graphic, the message potent. Images of waste and
dismemberment open the story as Baraka suggests that violence is the cutting
edge of the answer to the problem facing black people. Nausea accompanies
the violence, but the violence acts as a newspaper proclaiming the birth of
a new culture washed clean of the old values by the bloodbath under way.
Cassius Clay gives way to Muhammad Ali, and slain in the street is a "whipped
figure of jesus," beaten to pulpy answers. In place of Jesus are The Jazz
Messengers, Art Blakey records, and the Sun-Ra tape. The prevalence of the
music appears to have signaled spacemen, for in the middle of the revolution
spaceships land asking for Art Blakey records; and the spacemen understand
the revolution for what it is, a necessary evolution. The spacemen are "blue
winggly cats, with soft liquid sounds out of their throats for voices." And
perfect harmony exists between the blue spacemen and the black patriots—
blue, blues, music, jazz.

Baraka's imaginative mix is striking. While the Sun-Ra tape plays, blanks (whites) stagger out of department stores. The dead mayor of Newark is carried by in a black truck. Bamberger's is burning down, and dead blancos are all over. At the same time the blue spacemen with a hip walk are "hoppin' and bopadoppin' up and down" trying to find out what happened after Art Blakey and inviting the black men to talk with them and "dig what they were in to." The black people are trying to restore some order, find out what is happening elsewhere (Chicago is still burning), make evaluations, and write reports, while the tapes of the blues continue. Smokey Robinson comes on, his songs no longer of unrequited love but rather of the beauty of the whole, similar one would think to the song lyric that Baraka places about a third of the way through the story. The lyric speaks of love and brotherhood for all the people of the earth, for now the earth belongs to them and they can open their lives "to walk/tasting the sunshine/of life." Finally the revolutionaries get to the courthouse and can see the Hall of Records intact even though the top of the building has been blown off. The ironic play on the Hall of Records is tangential but significant. For the white society the Hall of Records is a library of papers, static, dead. For the black society, one must assume, the Hall of Records will be living music, a repository for the soul and spirituality, a mirror reflection of the new flag being designed: "Black heads, black hearts, and blue fiery space in the background."

Spacemen, out-of-town brothers, and the Newark revolutionaries come together on Weequahic Avenue. The narrator says he was tired as a dog and wanted to smoke some "bush," but the spacemen have something better, something that tastes like carrots. As they rest they talk about "the changing reference, of our new world" and about "how we knew it was our turn." Love is "heavy in the atmosphere" and the narrator is pleased because tomorrow he has a day off, "and I know somebody waiting for me at my house, and some kids, and some fried fish, and those carrots, and wow."

The last paragraph of the story is a single sentence: "That's the way the fifth day ended." The sentence, quiet, apparently understated in view of the events preceding it, seems anticlimactic, but is actually a further and important means to understanding. In a sense Baraka has in this story created his own version of Genesis. One must assume that by the seventh day all will be done—a new earth will be in existence with a new people, new rituals, a new relationship to the firmaments, and a new god.

"Answers in Progress" is a surreal projection of an interior state of mind created by means of juxtaposition of the apparently incongruous and absurd. The statement is both nonlinear and oblique. The story takes three or four readings before one is even reasonably sure of what is happening. The difficulties are compounded by the merging of fantasy and reality. Although there is little by way of unorthodox and unusual spellings, contractions, and word usages common in Baraka's prose and poetry, there are unusual topographical features including arrangements of lines more common to poetry than to prose and the use of various sizes and type faces. The style Baraka uses here is characteristic of most of his prose fiction. In addition, although not employed in "Answers in Progress," Baraka often makes use of a peculiar point of view which shifts from first to third person and of a narrator or persona who exists in several time frames.

It was surely the use of these techniques along with the subject matter of his prose that caused him to identify himself as one of "The Moderns" in the anthology of short fiction by that title that he edited in 1963 and in which he included three of his own prose pieces—two excerpts from *The System of Dante's Hell* and "The Screamers," later published in *Tales*. It was, also, surely the use of these techniques that caused the scholarly establishment, the critics, and reviewers (all mostly white) to place him in the contemporary avant-garde, to hail his presence, and to extol his achievements. It was also surely these techniques and devices that caused him to eschew his earlier work, describing it as a "cloud of abstraction and disjointedness, that was just whiteness" (*Black Magic Poetry*, 1967). Art, Baraka now believes, should be a part of the whole life of a community and not something limited to a reading public skilled in post-Joycean prose techniques. Consequently, Baraka's current involvement in the communal art of the black revolutionary theater is a logical movement for him, even though some critics believe the new plays mask his achievement, smother his verbal skills, and pervert his considerable literary talent.

Major publications other than short fiction

NOVEL: *The System of Dante's Hell*, 1965.

PLAYS: *Dutchman, The Slave*, 1964; *The Baptism* and *The Toilet*, 1967; *Four Black Revolutionary Plays*, 1969; *BA-RA-KA*, 1972.

NONFICTION: *Blues People: Negro Music in White America*, 1963; *Black Music*, 1968; *In Our Terribleness*, 1970.

Bibliography

Benston, Kimberly W. *Baraka: The Renegade and the Mask.*
Dace, Letitia. *LeRoi Jones: A Checklist of Works by and About Him.*
Hudson, Theodore R. *From LeRoi Jones to Amiri Baraka.*
Margolies, Edward. *Native Sons: A Critical Study of Twentieth-Century Negro American Authors.*

Mary Rohrberger

JOHN BARTH

Born: Cambridge, Maryland; May 27, 1930

Principal short fiction

Lost in the Funhouse, 1968.

Other literary forms

Except for *Lost in the Funhouse*, John Barth's fiction is in the novel form. He has also written critical articles and essays on the nature of fiction and the state of the art. Some of his material has been recorded, since several of his stories require an auditory medium to achieve their original purposes and effects.

Influence

Barth's fiction has regenerated interest in the purity of language and its self-sufficient capacity to delight. While he is always concerned with the sounds of words, he writes a fiction of ideas, of metaphysical and aesthetic exploration, in which his characters and voices assume a position if only for the joy, or necessity, of violating that position. Barth's work, with its philosophic and linguistic textures, with its interest in fiction *being part of* the fiction presented, has served to break open the conventional narrative in contemporary literature.

Story characteristics

Barth's stories display a passionate absorption and pleasure in language itself and often operate as performances. They are self-conscious constructions in which the drama is less that of conventional plot than a result of the tension of language play and tonal shifts that arise when ideas or attitudes shift. Often these ideas are in conflict, and the stories give the effect of improvisation dealing with curiosity, terror, and self-knowledge. Barth's use of humor is extensive, although he rejects the label "black humor" sometimes attached to his work.

Biography

John Barth's first artistic interest was in music, and he studied briefly at the Juilliard School of Music before entering The Johns Hopkins University in Baltimore, Maryland, in the fall of 1947. He was married to Harriette Anne Strickland in January 1950. In 1951, he received his B.A. in creative writing, and his first child, Christine, was born. Barth completed his M.A. in 1952, and began work on his Ph.D. in the aesthetics of literature. His second child, John, was born in 1952, and with his wife expecting a third child (Daniel, born in 1954), Barth abandoned work on his Ph.D. and took a teaching job at Pennsylvania State University in 1953. In 1965, he left Pennsylvania State to teach at The State University of New York at Buffalo. He is currently Alumni Centennial Professor of English and Creative Writing at The Johns Hopkins University. Barth received the National Book Award for fiction in 1973 for *Chimera* (1972). In 1974, he was elected to both the National Institute of Arts and Letters and the American Academy of Arts and Sciences.

Analysis

Although John Barth is best known for his novels, his stories "Night-Sea Journey," "Lost in the Funhouse," "Title," and "Life-Story" from his single collection of short fiction, *Lost in the Funhouse*, are frequently anthologized. The book is a sequence of related stories which operate in a cycle beginning with the anonymity of origins and concluding, like the serpent with its tail in its mouth, with the anonymity of a life's conclusion and the narrator's exhaustion of his art. Some of Barth's characters are nameless, having both a personal and a universal dimension. Others, such as those in "Echo" and "Menelaiad," take their names from mythology. Three stories, "Ambrose His Mark," "Water Message," and "Lost in the Funhouse," reveal three turning points in the life of a developing character, Ambrose: his naming as an infant; his first consciousness of *fact*, both in conflict and alliance with a romanticized truth; and a larger apprehension of life suffused with his first sexual consciousness. Barth's characters, or voices, are all natural storytellers compelled to make sense of what they experience; they become living metaphors for states of love, art, and civilization. As they quest, the author joins them so that Barth's technique often conforms with his subject matter. Only the first two Ambrose stories could be considered conventional in structure; the remaining stories are fictions which investigate each individual's experience through voice shift, idea, and the self-evident play of language.

In these stories Barth questions the meaning of love, love in relation to art, and the artist's and lover's place within civilization—not merely time-bounded culture, but art's progress through history, its aspirations and its failures. Barth's characters face the revelation that the individual facts of their lives are painful, that self-knowledge hurts and is in conflict with their original visions of the world. The characters turn to storytelling, not just to comprehend the complexities of their personal lives, but to preserve their sanity as they encounter knowledge. The creation of artifice literally kills time, and by virtue of narrative organization, even when suffering cannot be explained, life may become bearable. In "Life-Story," which spans only part of a day, the narrator speaks of himself:

> Even as she left he reached for the sleeping pills cached conveniently in his writing desk and was restrained from their administration only by his being in the process of completing

a sentence. . . . There was always another sentence to worry about.

In "Autobiography," a story written for monophonic tape, the speaker says, "Being me's no joke," and later, "I'm not what either parent or I had in mind."

The tradition underlying Barth's stories is the language itself, the very process of storytelling, not merely the genre of story. In this sense his work has much in common with experimental films and some contemporary poetry, as his characters transform their personal worlds of fact into worlds of fiction. For Barth, that is one solution of the fact of existence. The question remains: does one then become nothing more than one's story? If the body does not live, does it matter that the words might, even if they can solve nothing? The very playfulness and intrigue of Barth's language, along with its intellectual complexity, suggests that romantic disillusion may be at least temporarily combatted through the vehicle of self-examining narrative. The underlying fear is that the story might exhaust itself, that fiction might become worn out and the words have nowhere to go but back into the narrator's mind.

"Night-Sea Journey," which opens the collection, is the story of the life of a single sperm cell as it travels toward the possibility of linkage and conception upon the shores of a mythic Her. The narrator is the sperm and is quoted throughout by the authorial voice, yet the narrator addresses himself and finally the being he may become, not an audience, so the story reads as a first-person interior monologue. Being "spoken inwardly," "Night-Sea Journey" is similar to later stories in the collection which are first-person accounts by the author. This similarity effects a parallel between the struggles of the sperm cell and later struggles by the author, which, in turn, parallel the struggles of everyman in his journey through life.

At first, the narrator shares the determination of the other "swimmers" to "reach the shore" and "transmit the Heritage." His enthusiasm, however, wanes as he considers the philosophy of a friend, who has since "drowned." The friend claimed that since their ultimate destiny is to perish, the noble thing to do is to commit suicide. He considered the hero of heroes to be he who reached the shore and refused "Her." Pondering this and such questions as whether the journey is real or illusory, who or what causes the difficult passage, and whether arrival will mean anything at all, the narrator considers various possible explanations of the meaning, if any, of the journey. Here Barth parodies philosophical and religious positions familiar to the sophisticated reader. He also parodies common adolescent ramblings about the meaning of life: "Love is how we call our ignorance of what whips us." The whipping here results from the sperm's tail, causing movement toward an unknown destiny. Barth makes deliberate use of clichés and puns to ease the reader into identification with the narrator's voice, which speaks phrases we have all spoken in our most baffled or despairing moments. The humor is as adolescent as the state of the speaker's anxieties: "I have seen the best swimmers of my generation go under."

Constantly suspicious that the journey is meaningless, the speaker is finally swayed to accept his pessimistic friend's advice; he gives up and ceases to swim; however, his decision has come too late. By continuing to live he has been drawn ever nearer to the "shore" and is pulled by the force of the female element. He reaches "a motionless or hugely gliding sphere" and is about to become a link in another cycle of life and death. Before joining with Her, however, he expresses his "single hope" that he might transmit to the being he is becoming "a private legacy of awful recollection and negative resolve." The speaker declares: "You to whom, through whom I speak, do what I cannot: terminate this aimless, brutal business! Stop your hearing against Her song! Hate Love!" In spite of the speaker's desire to end all night-sea journeys, all life—"Make no more"—he cannot resist biological fate and plunges "into Her who summons, singing . . . 'Love! Love! Love!'" This conclusion and Barth's parody throughout the story of attempts to understand life suggest that the meaning of life may be nothing more than life itself. To borrow a statement from *Chimera*, one of Barth's novels, "the key to the treasure is the treasure."

"Lost in the Funhouse" appears midway in the collection. It opens with young Ambrose, perhaps the being formed through the union of the sperm with Her in "Night-Sea Journey," traveling to Ocean City, Maryland, to celebrate Independence Day. Accompanying him through this eventual initiation are his parents, an uncle, his older brother Peter, and Magda, a thirteen-year-old neighbor who is well developed for her age. Ambrose is "at that awkward age" when his voice and everything else is unpredictable. Magda is the object of his first sexual consciousness and his need to do something about it, if only barely to touch her. The story moves from painful innocence and aspects of puppy love to the stunned realization of the pain of self-knowledge. Barth uses printed devices, italics, dashes, and so on to draw attention to the storytelling technique throughout the presentation of conventional material: a sensitive boy's first encounters with the world, the mysterious "funhouse" of sexuality, illusion, and consciously realized pain.

As the story develops, Barth incorporates comments about the art of fiction into the narrative:

> He even permitted the single hair, fold, on the second joint of his thumb to brush the fabric of her skirt. Should she have sat back at that instant, his hand would have been caught under her. Plush upholstery prickles uncomfortably through gaberdine slacks in the July sun. The function of the *beginning* of a story is to introduce the principal characters, establish their initial relationship, set the scene for the main action . . . and initiate the first complication or whatever of the "rising action."

Such moments, when the voice seems to shift outside Ambrose's consciousness, actually serve to unite the teller with the tale, Barth with his protagonist, and life with art. Among other things, "Lost in the Funhouse" is a portrait of the artist as an adolescent. The developing artist, "Ambrose . . . seemed unable to forget the least detail of his life" and tries to fit everything together. Most of all, he needs to know himself, to experience his inner being, before he will have something to express.

Ambrose develops this knowledge when he becomes lost in the carnival funhouse, which, on one level, represents the mind. Just before emerging from the funhouse, he strays into an old, forgotten part of it and loses his way. Here, separated from the mainstream—the funhouse representing the world for lovers—he has fantasies of death and suicide, recalling the "negative resolve" of the sperm cell from "Night-Sea Journey." He also finds himself reliving incidents with Magda in the past, and imagining alternative futures. He begins to suffer the experience of illusion and disillusion: "Nothing was what it looked like." He finds a coin with his name on it and imagines possible lives for himself as an adult.

These experiences lead to a new fantasy: Ambrose dreams of reciting stories in the dark until he dies, while a young girl behind the plyboard panel he leans against takes down his every word, but does not speak, for she knows his genius can only bloom in isolation. This fantasy is the artistic parallel to the sperm's union with "Her" in "Night-Sea Journey." Barth thus suggests that the artist's creative force is a product of a rechanneled sexual drive. Although Ambrose "would rather be among the lovers for whom funhouses are designed," he will construct, maybe operate, his own funhouse in the world of art. His identity as artist derives from the knowledge he has gained of his isolation—the isolation of the artist, who is not "a person," but must create his self and his world, or, rather, his selves and his worlds. The difference between lovers and artists, however, may not be as definitive as it seems, for Barth's fiction implies that Ambrose's predicament may be the same as everyman's.

The final story in *Lost in the Funhouse* is "Anonymiad," the life-story of a minstrel who becomes an artist, perhaps an Ambrose grown up, as well as an alter ego for Barth himself. If translated into realistic terms, the life of the minstrel would parallel Barth's literary career. The minstrel grows up singing in a rural setting with the most lovely goatherd maiden as his mistress. Dreaming of fame, he takes his song to the city where he meets Queen Clytemnestra and becomes a court minstrel. As he becomes more musically adept, he spends more time in court intrigues than with his maiden, Merope. When King Agamemnon goes off to war, an interloper, Aegisthus, steals the Queen's love, woos Merope, and casts the minstrel on a deserted island with nine casks of wine. To each of these the minstrel gives the name and properties of one of the nine muses. For the remainder of his life the minstrel, now without his lyre, composes something new, literature, which he casts adrift in the empty wine bottles. These bottles parallel the sperm cell of "Night-Sea Journey," transmitting the Heritage.

Isolated on his island, like Ambrose in the funhouse, the minstrel is unhappy. His life has not worked out; his work has been mediocre and unacclaimed; love has failed; and later he says that his "long prose fictions of the realistical, the romantical and fantastical" are not what he meant them to be. He writes these fictions on the island to structure his life; he tans the hides of native goats and sends his manuscripts out to sea in the large urns after drinking up all the wine. Urn by urn, he writes his way through the panorama of fiction's possibilities. Then he loses interest and decides that all he has written is useless. There is one amphora left, and one goat, hard to catch, whom he names Helen. Rousing himself, he decides to write one final, brilliant piece, his "Anonymiad," which he hopes will be filled with the "pain of insight, wise and smiling in the terror of our life." Everything must be deliberated to get all this on a single skin. This is vital, as an earlier work had come floating back to shore in its urn, drenched and unreadable. After painstakingly writing this final piece, the writer sees it only as a "chronicle of minstrel misery." No more living creatures exist on the island; the writer is totally alone. In spite of these facts, however, the minstrel is content. He has sent his "strange love letter" to Merope, now his muse. He knows that "somewhere outside myself, my enciphered spirit drifted, realer than the gods, its significance as objective and undecoded as the stars." He imagines his tale "drifting age after age, while generations fight, sing, love, expire." Sadly, he thinks: "Now it passes a hairsbreadth from the unknown man or woman to whose heart, of all hearts in the world, it could speak fluentest, most balmly— but they're too preoccupied to reach out to it, and it can't reach out to them." Like the minstrel, his tale will drift and perish, but the story ends "No matter." A noontime sun "beautiful enough to break the heart" shines on the island where "a nameless minstrel wrote it." The collection of stories ends, turning back toward its *tabula rasa* of origin.

Barth, who always hoped to bring alive philosophical alternatives in his stories, reviving old themes of literature and life—literature's because they *are* life's—is able to make a progression through these short fictions, retackling the problems, not by repetition, but by constantly distilling the possibilities of technique. He has clearly opened the narrative consciousness, the academic ear, and the imagination of readers and writers alike. While he never presumes to answer one of his posed questions, his inventiveness and sincerity make his stories experiences of real substance, as well as of words. Throughout the collection, words and stories help to ease human pain and serve as a source of curious investigation and delight.

Major publications other than short fiction

NOVELS: *The Floating Opera*, 1956; *The End of the Road*, 1958; *The Sot-*

Weed Factor, 1960; *Giles Goat-Boy; Or, The Revised New Syllabus*, 1966; *Chimera*, 1972; *Letters: A Novel*, 1979.

Bibliography
Joseph, Gerhard. *John Barth.*
Morrell, David. *John Barth, An Introduction.*
Tharpe, Jac. *The Comic Sublimity of Paradox.*
Weixlmann, Joseph N. *John Barth: An Annotated Bibliography.*

James L. Green

WARREN BECK

Born: Richmond, Indiana; c. 1900

Principal short fiction

The Blue Sash and Other Stories, 1941; *The First Fish*, 1947; *The Far Whistle*, 1951; *The Rest Is Silence*, 1963.

Other literary forms

Warren Beck was an academic who taught for forty years at Lawrence University in Appleton, Wisconsin, as well as at various summer writers' conferences (including Bread Loaf); he also wrote a number of critical essays for scholarly journals over the years on William Faulkner and other topics. He began with the publication of short stories, which remained his chief medium. In addition he wrote three novels and several volumes of literary criticism, as well as one-act plays.

Influence

Beck won various writing and scholarly awards but his fiction cannot be said to have been influential. Rather, his stories were influenced from the beginning, as he says, by what he "cared about as reader, the vein of Chekhov and Joyce's *Dubliners*, Katherine Mansfield, Anderson's *Winesburg, Ohio* and some of Maupassant and Hemingway." It cannot be claimed that even his best-crafted stories approach the quality of his inspirations or even that the work of these masters of short fiction and their techniques were made familiar to American writers through the medium of Beck. He does not fit especially well into such categories as "realist" or "regionalist," and his small successes in the short story and, to a lesser extent, the novel do not qualify him as the leader of any school.

Story characteristics

Critic Jeanne Desy in *Contemporary Novelists* (1976) describes Beck's best work (his short stories) perfectly when she calls him the storyteller of "post-mediated moral crises, frequently told in the first person, often with more activity in the characters' minds than in the events." The novel *Into Thin Air* (1951), for example, is largely the meditation of an aging man who sees in the destruction of the house next door a symbol of all his own dreams vanishing into thin air and ruminates philosophically on his lost youth and a very melodramatic story of guilty love and sacrificed ambition. The stories likewise are often meditative or even melodramatic, but most often didactic; in the words of one critic, they "frequently deal with the concern of a father for the perilous innocence of his child, or some other child-like character, or for his own moral innocence."

Biography

Born in Indiana, Warren Beck has made use in his stories of its people and locales and especially of the characters one sees around a small Wisconsin university such as the one at Appleton: professors and students, football players and small-town reporters, and ordinary townspeople. His involvement in both World War I and World War II is reflected in the anti-Fascist message of his first novel, but he did not see enough action of any kind to be able to write war novels or stories. *Pause Under the Sky* (1947) features a pair of lovers held apart by the war, but they might as well have been separated by anything else besides the war, and the main subject is not any political enemy abroad but a creeping vulgarity at home. The problem that faces the "middle-aged party" in "Out of Line" is a home-front dilemma.

Years of teaching English literature and of advising would-be writers at summer conferences inevitably leave their mark: Beck's penchant is for allegory and for arranging his works to deliver a messsage which is unmistakable. He never succumbs, however, to the latest fads in short-story writing, and his work cannot be described as avant-garde or adventurous, obscure or profound. He may have "a faculty for transmuting rather ordinary situations into something subtly and absorbingly interesting," as one critic has been kind enough to say, but he deals in ordinary people who hold few surprises.

Beck is a good example of the American short-story writer who is neither imitative of European masters nor too faddish in a modern, even "antistory," vein. His work shows artistic competence, but fundamentally he has neither brilliance of technique nor strikingly original ideas. He writes occasional satire without savage indignation, melodrama without sensationalism, love stories without explicit sex scenes, and humor without rowdy laughter.

Analysis

Warren Beck began to be noticed in 1941 when *The Blue Sash and Other Stories* collected the pieces he had been publishing in "little magazines" and appropriate academic quarterlies such as *Story*, *North American Review*, and *The Writer's Forum*. They all show the influence of the editors of *Story* at the time; they are the sort of story one would expect of literary journals: serious, craftsmanlike imitations of the old masters (Guy de Maupassant, Anton Chekhov, and so on) and the new idols (such as James Joyce, Katherine Mansfield, and Ernest Hemingway). Beck's first book of stories clearly copies Hemingway's approach, Joyce's epiphanies, Thomas Wolfe's flow, and other modern formulas. "The Blue Sash" is the best of these stories, a typical "little magazine" story of the period which shows a refined sensibility and conscious craftsmanship. "Encounter on the Parnassian Slope" and "The Jap" are other stories in this uneven collection full of "sincerity of purpose." Beck's is not a great talent, and the literary influences on him are not harnessed to any real passion for storytelling. The result is fiction that is respectable and interesting, but never gripping.

"The First Fish" and "The Far Whistle" and other stories which followed are well-made and well-meaning academic fiction. Most often told in the first-person point of view, they rely heavily on allegory and stress more than people and motivations. Because Beck's novels engage in even more philosophizing and rambling, his stories are undoubtedly better than his longer works, a fact which can be seen by comparing the best story in *The Far Whistle*—"Detour in the Dark"—with any of the three novels. "Detour in the Dark" is an intelligent balance of sentiment and rumination which avoids sentimentality and too much stasis. It involves the thoughts, more than the experiences, of a father forced to spend the night in a decrepit town with his son.

When so much is slapdash, shoddy, and sentimental in modern popular fiction, it is difficult to criticize harshly Beck's lapidary and honest work; but much as academics may like Beck's stories, he is by no means a natural storyteller; he is among the college creative writers who lack the nerve and even vulgar touch of the born yarn-spinners. He ranks well among the writers who must publish or perish and who do their honest best to turn out a fine if uninspiring, workmanlike but never thrilling product.

There have been many concerned and skillful, dedicated and determined writers in the groves of academe who were (as *The Spectator* said in summing up what was wrong with Beck's *Pause Under the Sky*) "philosophizing in the . . . stream of consciousness" but not at all in the mainstream of American fiction and who, perhaps very unjustly, faded away, suffering what a poet once called the deaths of all the "little magazines" that died to make verse free. These concerned writers left behind some good (if pale) stories and a great many students who had been instructed in the arts and crafts of short fiction. Warren Beck was surely among the most dedicated members of this group.

Major publications other than short fiction
NOVELS: *Final Score*, 1944; *Pause Under the Sky*, 1947; *Into Thin Air*, 1951; *Huck Finn at Phelps Farm*, 1958.

NONFICTION: *Man in Motion: Faulkner's [Snopes] Trilogy*, 1961; *Joyce's "Dubliners": Substance, Vision, and Art*, 1969.

Bibliography
"Books Briefly Noted," in *The New Yorker*. XXVII (February 24, 1951), p. 98.
Desy, Jeanne. "Warren Beck," in *Contemporary Novelists*.
Halsband, Robert. "Review of *Pause Under the Sky*," in *Chicago Sun Book Week*. (May 18, 1947), p. 3.

                                                                Leonard R. N. Ashley

SAMUEL BECKETT

Born: Foxrock, near Dublin, Ireland; April 13, 1906

Principal short fiction
More Pricks Than Kicks, 1934; *Stories and Texts for Nothing*, 1967; *First Love and Other Shorts*, 1974; *Fizzles*, 1976.

Other literary forms
Samuel Beckett has written poetry, criticism, novels, and plays as well as short stories. Probably his most famous work is the play *Waiting for Godot* (1952), which first gained for him critical and popular attention. In recent years he has abandoned poetry and criticism for drama and fiction, which since 1945 he has written for the most part in French, subsequently translating it alone or with others into English. In 1969 he won the Nobel Prize for Literature.

Influence
Like James Joyce, Beckett expresses his enormous knowledge of languages, literature, and philosophy by means of quotations, allusions, and puns, originally sophomoric but more refined in the later works. Joyce's concern with language is also echoed in the progression of Beckett's fiction, where, as in all his work, there is a paring down, a minimizing of syntax and content, until the later stories emerge as austerely crafted articulations of despair reflecting his struggles with the central paradox, the inadequacy of language to express what must be said. He also displays a Kafkaesque precision as he details an incomprehensible world impinging on his antiheroes, who exist in ever vaguer locales as their consciousness of their inner chaos increases.

Story characteristics
Unconventional in style and plot and often difficult, Beckett's stories, like the novels and plays, usually revolve around a down-and-out tramp figure in Ireland or in unnamed places, engaged in various activities—crawling, sleeping, remaining still or silent, begging in the street, or taking pleasure in his solitude or withdrawal from "ordinary" life. A grimly humorous voice speaks, in either the first or third person, and focuses on memories, isolated acts and objects, sensations, cogitations, and language itself. Beckett's stories are published in collections and are best read together for a sense of his philosophical concern with the nature of the self and the human condition.

Biography
Reared as an upper-middle-class Anglican, and educated in Ireland, Samuel

Beckett repudiated his religion when young and studied modern languages at Trinity College, Dublin. While teaching English at the École Normale Supérieure in Paris from 1928 to 1930, he met James Joyce and became part of his avant-garde literary circle. Beckett's devotion to surrealism dates from that period. He subsequently returned to Trinity as lecturer in French, spent a few years in London, and in 1938 moved permanently to Paris. Little is known of his personal life, for he is notoriously reticent about himself and his works, responding tersely to queries from critics, whom he derides: "A very fair scholar I was too, no thought, but a great memory."

Analysis

Samuel Beckett is best known for his plays and novels; his stories are seldom anthologized separately, perhaps because together they elucidate and echo the longer works, with which they share theme, characters, and style— the minimal use of conventional literary trappings such as description, dialogue, special rhetorical effects, and traditional plotting. Presumably, their spareness gives a clearer view of the essence of things. As a Beckett narrator says of a pair of gloves: "Far from blunting the shapes [of hands] they sharpened them by simplifying."

In fact, to call them "stories" is to extend that term, for some lack even the rudimentary characteristics of the genre. "Action" is limited, settings vague, characters few—often the lone monologuist—while beginnings and endings are discerned primarily through their position in a work, for relations between elements are not so much lacking as obscure, to the reader as well as the bemused narrator. Seldom named, this figure pours forth a convoluted stream of language, digressing at length on apparent trivia—it is hard to be certain what is important, or even what *is*. His continual theme is the inability to extract meaning from an absurd world, yet the need to keep trying: "I can't go on, I must go on, I'll go on."

This speaker, when personified, is physically and psychologically grotesque, often a bum. He wears old clothes, shows symptoms of filth, and even without a total description, appears repugnant. For example, the narrator of "The End," in *Stories and Texts for Nothing*, finds a boat in a shed among rats and toads and there makes a home ("I was very snug in my box, I must say") in seclusion, darkness, and relative contentment. He summarizes his inclinations: "To contrive a little kingdom, in the midst of the universal muck, then to shit on it, that was me all over." He is fastidious if not clean, repulsive but self-aware, as he elaborates on his person with a humor not all readers will find palatable.

Before this stage of narration, however, Beckett's most traditional collection, *More Pricks Than Kicks*, appeared and received no critical notice. Narrated in the third person, its ten stories center on Belacqua, a Dubliner named after a representative of sloth in Dante's *Purgatory*. His indolence and freakish nature prefigure Beckett's other protagonists, yet Belacqua is somewhat of this world, even as the book's narrative style is still relatively conventional, although decidedly odd. In "Ding-dong," for example, "this queer customer who always looked ill and dejected" enters a pub, where "he was known, in the sense that his grotesque exterior had long ceased to alienate the curates [bartenders] and make them giggle." On the other hand, he is interested in women, twice marries, and falls ill and dies, all ordinary happenings. In another passage, the reader sees his indecision coupled with the "belief that the best thing he had to do was move constantly from place to place." The inability to do what one must, the "must" based on an inner imperative, is the quintessential dilemma for Beckett, seen again and again in all his works.

In *Stories and Texts for Nothing*, published more than twenty years later, the style is more recognizably Beckett's. Here the obscurity results from a bleakness, the less dense use of detail, found even in the book's title. It contains three stories—monologues told by less personalized Belacqua types, men expelled from their rooms by "them," unspecified "keepers"—and thirteen "texts," plotless pieces which are numbered, not titled. Apparently formless, these deal with loneliness, decay, and death, and the compulsion to speak and to go on.

The speaker in "The Expelled" begins,

> There were not many steps. I had counted them a thousand times, both going up and coming down, but the figure has gone from my mind. I have never known whether you should say one with your foot on the sidewalk, two with the following foot on the first step, and so on, or whether the sidewalk shouldn't count. At the top of the steps I fell foul of the same dilemma. In the other direction, I mean from top to bottom, it was the same, the word is not too strong. I did not know where to begin nor where to end, that's the truth of the matter. I arrived therefore at three different figures, without ever knowing which of them was right.

This passage reveals Beckett's delight in trivial detail, his humor, and the way he invests his details with significance. In fact, digressions form his text. There is for this speaker a certain tragicomic anguish at the mundane, and the reader laughs at and with him as he tries to express and come to terms with himself. His words seem impromptu and formless, as do his perambulations around the town, which he barely knows, for "I went out so little! Now and then I would go to the window, part the curtains and look out. But then I hastened back to the depths of the room, where the bed was. I felt ill at ease with all this air about me. . . ."

Such a monologue can hardly be called a plot, yet the stories and texts in this book contain little more than wanderings and meditations such as these. This is nevertheless a less bleak collection than the more nihilistic and elemental *Fizzles*, which carries Beckett's minimalizing tendency to its most recent extreme. It includes eight prose pieces, some only four pages long, written between 1960 and 1975. Only three are titled, and each is a single paragraph. From the first to the eighth there is an obvious progression, seen in the syntax, which requires greater effort by the reader trying to piece together the now-familiar images. "Fizzle One" opens conventionally enough: "He is barehead, barefoot, clothed in a singlet and tight trousers too short for him. . . ." Written in the third person, it describes a man trying to walk in a confined space. "Fizzle Three" is even more clearly in Beckett country: "Ruinstrewn land, he has trodden it all night long, I gave up, hugging the hedges, between road and ditch, on the scant grass, little slow steps, no sound . . . I gave up before birth. . . ." The following "Fizzle" starts with this last phrase and includes birth, life, death, a "he" and an "I" (the same person?) going on and staying still, while the syntax of "Fizzle Five" is even more spare, saying only what is necessary: "Closed place. All needed to be known for say is known. There is nothing but what is said. Beyond what is said there is nothing. What goes on in the arena is not said." It is a setting of dark and light, no people, not even an "I." "Fizzle Seven" describes, without pronouns, a man in a room watching the sinking sun. There is an almost painterly preoccupation with cataloging relations and motions of parts of the body: "Legs side by side broken right angles at the knees. . . . Trunk likewise dead plumb right up to top of skull seen from behind including nape clear of chairback." "Fizzle Eight" is perhaps the least accessible of Beckett's published works. The image of a skull appears through twisted syntax so that, again, barely discerned essentials convey Beckett's themes of consciousness, light and dark, a desertlike hellish void, and deformed creatures: two dwarfs appear, enacting a ritual perhaps, carrying between them "the dung litter of laughable memory." Perhaps a metaphor for the human journey, *Fizzles* adds nothing new to the Beckett canon, but carries farthest certain tendencies.

Critics and readers are puzzled but fascinated as they try to understand the significance of this writer who himself seeks to extract meaning from an ungiving universe. It is intriguing but difficult to speculate about Beckett's next work.

Major publications other than short fiction

NOVELS: *Murphy*, 1938; *Molloy*, 1951; *Malone meurt*, 1952 (*Malone Dies*); *The Unnamable*, 1953; *Watt*, 1953; *Comment c'est*, 1961 (*How It Is*).

PLAYS: *En Attendant Godot*, 1952 (*Waiting for Godot*); *Fin de partie*, 1957 (*Endgame*); *Krapp's Last Tape*, 1958; *Happy Days*, 1961; *Sans*, 1969; *Not I*, 1974.

POETRY: *Whoroscope*, 1930; *Echo's Bones and Other Precipitates*, 1935.

NONFICTION: *Proust*, 1931.

Bibliography

Cohn, Ruby. *Samuel Beckett: The Comic Gamut.*

Federman, Raymond. *Journey to Chaos: Samuel Beckett's Early Fiction.*
Kenner, Hugh. *Samuel Beckett: A Critical Study.*
Levy, E. P. *Beckett and the Voice of Species: A Study of the Prose Fiction.*
Tanner, J. F. and J. Don Vann. *Samuel Beckett: A Checklist of Criticism.*

Diana Bloom

MAX BEERBOHM

Born: London, England; August 24, 1872
Died: Rapallo, Italy; May 20, 1956

Principal short fiction

A Christmas Garland Woven by Max Beerbohm, 1912; *Seven Men*, 1919;
A Variety of Things, 1928.

Other literary forms

Max Beerbohm's eclectic published work includes biography, caricatures
and cartoons (with captions), dramatic and literary criticism, essays, letters,
plays, radio broadcasts, and verse. Although critics often see Beerbohm as
a many-sided figure, dabbling superficially in myriad literary forms, he nevertheless has a consistent comic development and outlook. The reader will find
this special style of invention, exaggeration, and parody displayed in all his
works, especially in his short fiction.

Influence

A few of Beerbohm's stories are still widely read by students, notably
"Enoch Soames," but much of his work is dated. He captures the spirit of
an age, the 1890's, which seems remote to us today. Furthermore, because
he parodies writers of the nineteenth and twentieth centuries who are now
obscure and little read themselves, the value of these parodies is somewhat
diminished. Still, Beerbohm's contribution is significant for his effect on the
styles of later writers and critics such as Thornton Wilder, W. Somerset
Maugham, Evelyn Waugh, Edmund Wilson, Truman Capote, and Muriel
Spark. His elegant and witty style has also made possible the success of
magazines that appeal to a discriminating, limited audience. The American
magazine *The New Yorker*, says Bruce McElderry, is perhaps the example
that best reflects Beerbohm's influence.

Story characteristics

Beerbohm's stories are satirical but not malicious. They have a tender comic
vein, which achieves its effect by exaggeration and wit. Most of the stories
are, in fact, sketches of personalities both real and imagined, and Beerbohm
makes them memorable through his unique gift of parody.

Biography

Sir Henry Maximilian Beerbohm was educated at Charterhouse and at
Merton College, Oxford, where he made friends with many luminaries such
as painters William Rothenstein and Aubrey Beardsley and writers Oscar
Wilde and Bernard Shaw. He contributed often to the famous magazine *The*

Yellow Book and frequently sold essays and caricatures to various other magazines. When Shaw resigned as dramatic critic of the *Saturday Review*, Beerbohm succeeded him and for twelve years was one of the English theater's most celebrated critics. In 1910 he married Florence Kahn and moved to Rapallo, Italy, where he remained until 1956. He stayed in England during both World Wars and periodically returned there to publish his books and exhibit his caricatures. He received an honorary doctorate from the University of Edinburgh in 1930 and was knighted by the British government in 1939.

Analysis

Max Beerbohm is both a product and a critic of the late nineteenth century Aesthetic movement. He emphasizes the quality of beauty in a work of art, rather than its moral implications; this beauty is perceived by the reading audience in the writer's style, his ability to choose the appropriate word. Although Beerbohm's style develops from the stunning effects of exaggeration and fantasy in the 1890's to a more measured, classical style in the 1920's, his temperament and attitude remain the same through all forms of his writing. His delicate, elegant style, balanced by humor, biting satire, and accurate parody, treats us to some of the most amusing short fiction of this century.

Beerbohm understands that his work does not include that which is called "important"; he aims more for "the perfect adjustment of means to ends," yet his writing is not merely brilliant surface. Within this approach of intelligent good sense, Beerbohm's criticism of art, artists, and life shows a subtle insight into man's behavior and the ambiguities of human nature. In his fantasy stories he captures the moods and social conventions of the society of his time; in his parodies he dissects not only the style, but also the thought of famous authors. His art, then, reveals a good measure of truth.

Seven Men is a collection of stories that blurs the distinction between fact and fiction. In a very modern way Beerbohm self-consciously introduces himself as a character in the story, reminiscing about some of his extraordinary experiences. The stories also follow different periods in Beerbohm's life. The autobiographical and realistic elements are further reinforced by the introduction of actual persons into the narrative. The two central stories, "Enoch Soames" and "'Savonarola' Brown," focus upon this relationship of life to art, and the illusions that can dominate both. Beerbohm characteristically parodies himself and his susceptibility to the manners and modes of the time; and as an author he also comments obliquely on the nature of art itself.

"Enoch Soames" begins with Max looking eagerly into Mr. Holbrook Jackson's book of the 1890's for the entry SOAMES, ENOCH. Finding it missing as he had suspected, Beerbohm tells us about his meetings with the poet and author Enoch Soames and tells us why his story *must* be written. Sprinkled throughout the sketch are the names of the masters of the 1890's: Wilde, Rothenstein, Sickert, and Beardsley. Soames patronizes the café society of this decade and tries to be as intellectually daring as the other famous artists and poets. We understand very soon, however, that the personality of the "stooping, shambling" Soames is of a different order from that of his colleagues. Max describes him as ridiculous and "dim," and Rothenstein does not remember him. Rothenstein, in fact, will not even draw him, asking, "How can one draw a man who doesn't exist?" Beerbohm reads Soames's book *Negations*, but he cannot understand what it is about. It seems to have form but no substance, like Soames himself.

Soames is well aware that people, especially reviewers, do not notice him, and what he wants more than anything else is artistic recognition, especially for posterity. While dining with Max at le Restaurant du Vingtième Siècle, Soames, who earlier confessed to Max that he was a Catholic Diabolist, says he wants to go one hundred years into the future to see the editions, commentaries, and bibliographies of himself in the British Museum. For this, he says, "I'd sell myself body and soul to the devil." The gentleman sitting next to them *is* the Devil and quickly accepts Soames's terms. Soames disappears and then returns to Beerbohm, confirming the author's suspicion that Soames's search would be fruitless. The only reference to Soames, in the phonetic language of 1897, is that he is an imaginary character in a "sumwot labud sattire" by Max Beerbohm. Soames's last words before the Devil fulfills his bargain are, "*Try* to make them know that I did exist." Later, Max sees the Devil "over-dressed as usual" and is deliberately snubbed.

It seems that Soames, and possibly Max himself, is typical of the young authors of the 1890's whose talent was imaginary or at least of little value to later generations. There are many like Soames who are only parodies of the French Symbolists or the Decadent novelists. The satire, however, succeeds at a deeper level. Beerbohm creates reflections and images that mirror the nature and the problems of art and artists. There is a fine distinction between art and life, and the author must create his own reality which may be ephemeral. Max both acknowledges and fears the Soames side of his own character, the mediocre element, the part rebuffed by the Devil. In fashioning this type of narrative, Beerbohm examines the truth of fiction and our attitudes toward it. Soames is a fiction trying to become real, and the truth of his predicament both within the circumscribed world of the story and without is problematic. Beerbohm, on the other hand, is the working storyteller trying to get inside his fiction to make it more authentic and artistic. As he says about the Café Royal in the story, "This indeed . . . is life." For Beerbohm, art and life coalesce, one imitating the other, each a part of the other's style and reality.

In "'Savonarola' Brown" Beerbohm disrupts our sensibilities by giving us a play within a story. The satire is ostensibly against the conventions of Elizabethan drama and the blank verse imitations of Algernon Charles Swinburne, Alfred, Lord Tennyson, and Robert Browning; but the formal qualities of the work make it a satire on the conventions of short fiction. Beerbohm first meets Brown at school; and then later in life, when Max is dramatic critic for the *Saturday Review*, he sees him frequently at the theater. Brown is writing a play about Savonarola, and he discusses it at length with Beerbohm over a number of years. Max argues against Brown's improvised view of how a play should end. Brown wants Savonarola to work out his own destiny, to come alive as a real character. Max says, "My dear Brown, the end of the hero *must* be logical and rational." Not believing in this kind of causality, Brown says that there is nothing to prevent a motor-omnibus from knocking him down and killing him. By a strange coincidence, one Beerbohm says playwrights ought to avoid, Brown is knocked down and killed by a bus. Beerbohm is made literary executor and attempts to publish Brown's unfinished play.

The play is disappointing to Beerbohm, but he thinks it a virtue that there is not one line that does not scan, a telling admission for a theater critic on a major magazine. Beerbohm presents us with the play itself, a lively, absurd parody involving such figures as Dante, Lucrezia Borgia, St. Francis of Assisi, Lorenzo and Cosimo de Medici, Machiavelli, and other incongruous historic characters. The play has Lucrezia plotting her revenge on Savonarola for spurning her. Lorenzo de Medici attempts to turn a mob, in which "cobblers predominate," against Savonarola. When Lucrezia enters, the mob attends her arguments also and is swayed, in a wildly comic scene, by whoever is speaking. Pope Julius settles the issue by putting both Lucrezia and Savonarola in a dungeon. A Fool ("Methinks the Fool is a fool") helps them to escape and is killed by mistake by Cesare Borgia. Brown's play ends here, and Beerbohm apologizes for forcing us to judge a work that is unfinished.

As in "Enoch Soames," Max suffers the apprehension that the play would, if completed, have merit. The story now illustrates the problem of art on two levels. As a serious play by Brown, it is ludicrous and unintentionally humorous with all the worst elements of Renaissance drama and some poor examples of twentieth century language. Savonarola's hair turns white in only three hours; of this he says, "The scandal, the incredible come down!" Being outside the events of the fiction, however, we find it a fine example of parody. Beerbohm, again, is playing with our attitudes toward art.

Although Max tries to get the play produced, no one will accept it without an ending. He finishes it, of course, having Machiavelli betray Savonarola and the now mad Lucrezia, who together take deadly nightshade to avoid capture by Pope Julius. The significance of Beerbohm's conclusion is that he acknowledges Brown as a master in that Brown's conception is greater than his own. The characters will not breathe for Max, and he begins to hate them. By finishing the play, he also accepts Brown's view of probability and coincidence. Beerbohm is changing our ideas, not only of Elizabethan blank verse, but of literature itself. We are taken into the fiction and brought back out again until we are unsure about the nature of art and its designs upon us.

One of the most unusual collections of modern short stories is *A Christmas Garland*, in which Beerbohm further comments on technique and fiction through parodies of famous authors. Some of these certainly miss the mark today because authors such as A. C. Benson, G. B. Street, and Maurice Hewlett are little known to the general public. Nevertheless, parodies of Henry James, G. K. Chesterton, Rudyard Kipling, and Joseph Conrad are still effective since many readers have a necessary familiarity with these authors. It is ironic that Beerbohm excels in a form that is significantly bound to the vagaries of time. All of Beerbohm's best qualities of observation, satire, style, and wit, however, are to be found in these parodies.

The artistic center of *A Christmas Garland Woven by Max Beerbohm* is the work of Henry James, for Beerbohm the most notable expression of imaginative fiction. In the story "The Mote in the Middle Distance, H*nry J*m*s," Beerbohm parodies the style and thought of James found in *The Wings of the Dove* (1902), with echoes of *The Turn of the Screw* (1898) and other James novels. Simply, we are taken on a journey into the minds of the two children, Keith Tantalus and his sister Eva, as they consider whether or not to peer into their Christmas stockings at the foot of their bed. We encounter a typical Jamesian situation with limited action and heightened perceptual and moral awareness. Each thought is qualified by another, reflected in the syntactically complex, broken sentences which raise James's style almost to the point of absurdity. Although the detail and word choice is obvious, a criticism of James's often pretentious and serious manner, we are compelled to evaluate the dilemma in both comic and artistic terms. We feel the sexual tension underlying the brother-and-sister relationship that is present in much of James's work, and we feel that block of moral perception which complicates human choice. The narrator says of Keith, "That his fear of what she was going to say was as nothing to his fear of what she might be going to leave unsaid." This precocious insight in a small child and the recognition of James's style of creating effect by the use of negatives triggers our humorous reaction. It seems that James goes wrong in excess, and Beerbohm makes clear the value and the flaw in this idiosyncrasy. At the same time, the sentence seems so right, so subtle in its representation, that we almost believe it is the work of James himself. Thus we have an astute criticism of James, a comment upon the act of literary creation, and a new work of art which is Beerbohm's. Beerbohm involves himself in the work of art to a greater extent—and in a different way—than he does in *Seven Men*, more effectively challenging the definition between form and content, between art and artist.

Beerbohm continues, throughout *A Christmas Garland Woven by Max Beerbohm*, to submerge himself in what Keats would call an act of "negative capability" to parody Chesterton's paradoxes, Kipling's authoritarianism, Conrad's foreign style, and many others. Ultimately, valid questions about art are raised, but there are no resolutions; only ambiguities remain. Beerbohm's achievement, then, is the creation of a style that is as complex as life. He develops a language and an image of himself in his fiction, often through self-parody, which mirrors and distorts both the real world and the imaginative one. With the self-consciousness of the modern author, he parodies with elegance and charm the forms, conventions, and ideas found in late nineteenth and early twentieth century writing. Although his purpose is always to amuse and delight, he makes the reader more aware of the nature of art and its deceptions, what John Felstiner aptly calls "the lies of art."

Major publications other than short fiction
NOVEL: *Zuleika Dobson: Or, An Oxford Love Story*, 1911.
PLAYS: *The Happy Hypocrite*, 1900; *A Social Success*, 1913.
POETRY: *Max in Verse*, 1963.
NONFICTION: *Yet Again*, 1909; *And Even Now*, 1920; *Around Theatres*, 1924; *Lytton Strachey*, 1943; *Mainly on the Air*, 1957; *Max Beerbohm: Letters to Reggie Turner*, 1964 (edited by Rupert Hart-Davies).

Bibliography
Behrman, S. N. *Portrait of Max: An Intimate Memoir of Sir Max Beerbohm.*
Cecil, David. *Max: A Biography.*
Felstiner, John. *The Lies of Art: Max Beerbohm's Parody and Caricature.*
McElderry, Bruce R. *Max Beerbohm.*
Mix, Katherine Lyon. *Max and the Americans.*
Reiwald, J. G. *Sir Max Beerbohm, Man and Writer: A Critical Analysis with Brief Life and a Bibliography.*
_____ , ed. *The Surprise of Excellence: Modern Essays on Max Beerbohm.*

James MacDonald

SAUL BELLOW

Born: LaChine, Quebec, Canada; June 10, 1915

Principal short fiction

Mosby's Memoirs and Other Stories, 1968.

Other literary forms

Saul Bellow is known primarily for his novels; he has also published a play, a book of nonfiction prose about a trip to Jerusalem, and a number of essays.

Influence

Bellow is recognized around the world as an eminent writer whose work will endure; his stature was acknowledged when he was awarded the Nobel Prize for Literature in 1976.

Story characteristics

At first glance Bellow's stories are psychological and sociological studies. Bellow, although among the most erudite of contemporary American writers of fiction, carries his learning lightly, so that the intellectual substance of his work is not immediately obvious. Similarly, the moral dimension of his fiction is unobtrusive but certainly present. He also has a characteristic, effective prose style. The presence of so many dimensions is a major reason that his fiction is important.

Biography

Saul Bellow was born in Canada but grew up in Chicago and was graduated from high school there. He spent his first two years of college at the University of Chicago and the last two at Northwestern, being graduated in 1937. That same year he began a brief interlude of graduate work in anthropology at the University of Wisconsin. A few years later he started his writing career, which has been marked by three National Book Awards—for *The Adventures of Augie March* (1953) in 1954, for *Herzog* (1964) in 1965, and for *Mr. Sammler's Planet* (1970) in 1971—and, as a culmination of three and a half decades of excellent writing, by a Nobel Prize in 1976.

Analysis

Saul Bellow's honors and reputation document but do not explain his importance, which, although it will be more clearly seen in the future when some of the main tendencies of the American fiction of this era have been fully developed, can be understood now. He is important because he has both preserved and enhanced qualities that are present in the great fictional works of the eighteenth and nineteenth centuries but which have recently been denigrated by writers who have other interests and even by critics who have sold their birthrights for a mess of turgid and irrelevant publications. In "Some Notes on Recent American Fiction" Bellow advocates a conception of literature similar to that held by Lionel Trilling and asserts that, sadly, few current writers agree with him. In particular, he decries the pervasiveness in contemporary fiction of a scorn for this era that has been too facilely arrived at and an overprotective attitude toward one's own sensibility (not one's *self*: most recent writers assume that nothing so substantial remains).

In contrast, Bellow's characters have selves and interact with a society and a culture that Bellow has created in detail after careful observation. In some of his works, especially *Mr. Sammler's Planet*, Bellow's attitude toward that society and that culture borders on scorn, but his attitude has been earned, not merely stated in response to limitations on his own sensibility. The interaction between self and society in his work occurs against the backdrop of moral ideas. This is not to say that Bellow is didactic; rather, his work is infused with his sophisticated understanding of moral, social, and intellectual issues. In addition to preserving a rich but increasingly neglected tradition, Bellow has enriched that tradition. Since the exuberant opening words of *The Adventures of Augie March*, he has also added new possibilities to the prose style of American fiction. In short, his work offers some of the benefits that readers in previous centuries sought in fiction—most notably, some ideas about how to be a person in the world—yet it also offers a technical brilliance that he keeps in rein instead of letting it control his work.

"Looking for Mr. Green" is set in Chicago during the Depression and recounts the efforts of a civil servant, George Grebe, to deliver relief checks to black residents of the South Side. This is the stuff of social protest literature, and Bellow's story does dramatize the suffering that was endemic at that time, but it is much more than didactic. Bellow avoids a single-minded attack on economic injustice and the resulting inartistic story by, among other things, using a number of contrasts and ironies. For example, two scenes set on the streets and in the tenements of Chicago are separated by a scene at Grebe's office, and in that scene a philosophical discussion between Grebe and his boss, Raynor, is interrupted by a welfare mother's tirade. The basic situation of the story is ironic, because it seems odd that anyone would have trouble delivering checks to persons who desperately need them. These persons, however, are difficult to ferret out and their neighbors will not reveal their whereabouts because they fear that Grebe is a bill collector, process-server, or other source of trouble, and because he is white. This irony vividly illustrates the degree to which the Depression has exaggerated the instinct of self-preservation and widened the gulf between black and white.

Grebe's name points out several of the contrasts in "Looking for Mr. Green." Grebes are birds known for their elaborate courtship dances, but

George Grebe is a bachelor. More important for the story, grebes live in pairs rather than in flocks and remain in their own territories, but George, because of his job, is forced into society and into territory where he is an alien, not only because he is white but also because he is the son of the last English butler in Chicago and was a professor of classics. This is not to say that he is a stranger to trouble: he "had had more than an average seasoning in hardship." Despite his troubles, Grebe is shocked by suffering, distrust, and decrepit physical settings.

Oddly enough, these conditions are for him not only a moral problem but also an epistemological one. Raynor, his supervisor, brings up this problem by asserting that "nothing looks to be real, and everything stands for something else, and that thing for another thing." In contrast, Grebe later concludes that objects "stood for themselves by agreement, . . . and when the things collapsed the agreement became visible." The physical setting and the social and economic structure in this story are rapidly deteriorating, if not collapsing. Grebe complicates his analysis by asking "but what about need?" thereby suggesting that because of the Depression the agreement itself is collapsing and perhaps with it reality. Some of the persons he meets want to hasten that collapse. The welfare mother "expressed the war of flesh and blood, perhaps turned a little crazy and certainly ugly, on the place and condition," and another person advocates an alternate agreement, a plan whereby blacks would contribute a dollar apiece every month to produce black millionaires. Grebe's finding Mr. Green indicates that he can do something about this obscure world in which appearance and reality are mixed. Near the end of the story he asserts that it "was important that there was a real Mr. Green whom they could not keep him from reaching because he seemed to come as an emissary from hostile appearances."

"The Gonzaga Manuscripts" is a subtle story that traces changes in a young man, Clarence Feiler, and puts those changes in the context of important issues pertinent to the proper functions of literature and to its relation to everyday reality. Bellow carefully delineates the psychological state of Feiler, to whom literature makes an enormous difference, and shows the impingement upon him of Spanish society, which also was the environment of the writer about whom he cares passionately, Manuel Gonzaga. These themes are developed in the context of Feiler's search in Madrid and Seville for the unpublished manuscripts of poems written by Gonzaga. Feiler learns finally that the poems are lost forever, buried with Gonzaga's patron.

When Feiler arrives in Spain he is a confirmed Gonzagan, and while searching for the manuscripts he immerses himself in Spanish society and even in Gonzaga's former milieu. Bellow meticulously paints in the Spanish background by describing the cities, religious processions, political climate, and a representative group of Spaniards. As a result of his immersion Feiler begins virtually to relive Gonzaga's poems. For example, early in the story Feiler quotes part of a poem:

> I used to welcome all
> And now I fear all.
> If it rained it was comforting
> And if it shone, comforting,
> But now my very weight is dreadful.

The story ends thus: "as the train left the mountains, the heavens seemed to split. Rain began to fall, heavy and sudden, boiling on the wide plain. He knew what to expect from that redheaded Miss Walsh at dinner." That is, the rain is not comforting, and he fears that Miss Walsh will continue to torment him.

Feiler maintains his allegiance to Gonzaga, but there is considerable evidence in the story indicating that his allegiance is misplaced. For example, Gonzaga's friends are unimpressive. His best friend, del Nido, is a babbling mediocrity who sees little need for more poetry, and Gonzaga's patron has had the poems buried with her, thus denying them to the world. Another acquaintance misunderstands Feiler's search, thinking that he is after mining stock. One of Gonzaga's main beliefs is that one needs to take a dim view of human potential; he advocates being little more than a creature and avoiding the loss of everything by not trying to become everything. Even though Feiler himself has few aspirations besides finding the lost poems, he ends in despair. In fact, Gonzaga resesmbles the writers whom Bellow castigates in "Some Notes on Recent American Fiction" because of their minimal conception of human potential and their concomitant solicitousness for their own sensibility. Bellow's essay is a defense of a view of literature that Feiler unflatteringly contrasts to Gonzaga's.

"Mosby's Memoirs" was published in 1968, two years before *Mr. Sammler's Planet,* and, like that novel, is a study in world-weariness. Mosby is writing his memoirs in Oaxaca, Mexico, where the fecund land and the earthy existence of the people contrast to his own dryness. His mind ranges back through his life, particularly to recall two friends: Ruskin, a poet who has a theoretical bend of mind, and Lustgarden, who alternates between endlessly elaborated Marxism and piratical capitalism. At the end of the story Mosby is in a tomb that, along with his inability to get enough air to breathe, suggests that he is moribund. Although *Mr. Sammler's Plant* depicts a sympathetic character fending off as best he can the horrors of contemporary life, "Mosby's Memoirs" shows the danger of rejecting one's era

Mosby's critique is conservative: he had worked for Hearst, had shaken Franco's hand, had agreed with Burnham's emphasis on managing, even to the point of admiring Nazi Germany's skill at it. Partly because Lustgarden's Marxism is not made to appear attractive either, Mosby's politics are not as unattractive as his attitude toward other persons. He is intolerant and is characterized by "acid elegance, logical tightness, factual punctiliousness, and merciless laceration in debate." Even more damaging to him is a scene at a concert in which he is described as "stone-hearted Mosby, making fun of flesh and blood, of those little humanities with their short inventories of bad and good." His attitude is also obvious in his treatment of Lustgarden in his memoirs. Rather than using as a political parable or as an occasion to demonstrate pity his friend's disastrous attempts to make money, Mosby plans to use them for comic relief, in the process eschewing his "factual punctiliousness" in order to make Lustgarden more laughable.

Although these stories were written over a fairly long time span, there are many resonances among them; for example, Grebe's immersion in squalor contrasts with Mosby's flight from it. The other three stories in *Mosby's Memoirs and Other Stories* are also solid achievements. As a result, this book is certainly one of the better collections of contemporary American short stories.

Major publications other than short fiction

NOVELS: *Dangling Man*, 1944; *The Victim*, 1947; *The Adventures of Augie March*, 1953; *Seize the Day*, 1956; *Henderson the Rain King*, 1959; *Herzog*, 1964; *Mr. Sammler's Planet*, 1970; *Humboldt's Gift*, 1975.
PLAY: *The Last Analysis*, 1964.
NONFICTION: *To Jerusalem and Back: A Personal Account*, 1976.

Bibliography

Clayton, John Jacob. *Saul Bellow: In Defense of Man.*
Cohen, Sarah Blacher. *Saul Bellow's Enigmatic Laughter.*
Detweiler, Robert. *Saul Bellow: A Critical Essay.*
Dutton, Robert P. *Saul Bellow.*
Malin, Irving, ed. *Saul Bellow and His Critics.*
_____ . *Saul Bellow's Fiction.*
Porter, M. Gilbert. *Whence the Power? The Artistry and Humanity of Saul Bellow.*
Rovit, Earl. *Saul Bellow.*
_____ . *Saul Bellow: A Collection of Critical Essays.*
Tanner, Tony. *Saul Bellow.*

John Stark

STEPHEN VINCENT BENÉT

Born: Bethlehem, Pennsylvania; July 22, 1898
Died: New York, New York; March 13, 1943

Principal short fiction

Thirteen O'Clock, 1937; *Tales Before Midnight*, 1939; *Twenty-five Short Stories*, 1943; *The Last Circle*, 1946.

Other literary forms

Stephen Vincent Benét's publications include five novels and a substantial amount of poetry. His best-known poem, *John Brown's Body* (1928), won the Pulitzer Prize in 1929. In 1944 he was posthumously awarded the Pulitzer Prize for his volume of verse *Western Star* (1943), and the same year *America*, a brief history for the U. S. Office of War Information, was published for distribution abroad. His short story "The Devil and Daniel Webster" has been made into a play, an opera, and a motion picture entitled *All That Money Can Buy*. In 1941, "Listen to the People," a poetic radio script, was published by *Life* and read over NBC prior to an address by President Roosevelt.

Influence

Benét's career stands out for its brevity, its frustrations, its diversity, and its relative richness and fertility. His ability to master various genres makes him one of the most versatile of American writers. Benét's broad appeal to Americans is the result of his focus on the American heritage of freedom. Sometime during the mid-1920's, Benét began to write original and popular stories. A typical example of this is "The Sobbin' Women," derived from the Roman legend of the Sabine women and transformed by Benét through the use of distinctly American characters. In his later stories Benét widened his historical themes to include Western and contemporary issues.

Story characteristics

In his stories Benét uses the traditional short-story structure with a definite beginning, middle, and end to depict the patriotic motif through his focus on history and folklore. Benét skillfully uses the device of narrator to establish informal immediacy and rapport with the reader. The opportunity of self-revelation or concealment which this point of view affords has significant relevance to the overall meaning of his stories.

Biography

Stephen Vincent Benét was the younger brother of William Rose Benét. He was graduated from Yale in 1919, and in the autumn of 1920 he accepted a fellowship to attend the Sorbonne in Paris. On his return to the United

States in 1923, he published *King David, The Ballad of William Sycamore, 1790-1880,* and *Jean Huguenot,* a novel. In 1926 he returned with a Guggen-heim Fellowship to France, where he worked on *John Brown's Body* (1928), a poem about the Civil War, which won the Pulitzer Prize in 1929. He was also elected to the National Institute of Arts and Letters the same year. In 1933 he became editor of the Yale Series of Younger Poets Competition, and two years later began reviewing for the New York *Herald Tribune* and *Saturday Review of Literature.* In 1936 his short story "The Devil and Daniel Webster" was awarded the O. Henry Memorial Prize for the best American short story of the year. In 1937 his story "Johnny Pye and the Fool-Killer," and in 1940 "Freedom's a Hard-Bought Thing," won similar honors. In 1938 he was elected to the American Academy of Arts and Letters, and he spent the remaining years of his life in the rejuvenation of this select body. Benét died in New York City on March 13, 1943. In 1944 he was posthumously awarded the Pulitzer Prize for his volume of poetry, *Western Star.*

Analysis

Stephen Vincent Benét achieved mastery of the short fiction form only after laborious and persistent efforts. His preference was for poetry and the freedom it offered as opposed to the restrictions of the short story. Perhaps because of this, he never experimented with short-story form and unflinchingly favored the traditional-structure stories with a definite beginning, middle, and end. Benét also skillfully employed the traditional device of the narrator to bring about a sense of immediacy and the interesting possibility of self-revelation and concealment which this perspective offered; but he was not an innovator of any new form of the short story.

Early in his career, Benét reconciled his conscience with his economic needs by writing original short stories designed to elicit popular appeal. He achieved this self-appeasement by basing his stories on material from American history and folklore and transfusing it with his vivid imagination. This reconciliation resulted in such stories as "The Devil and Daniel Webster," "Daniel Webster and the Sea Serpent," "Daniel Webster and the Ides of March," "Jacob and the Indians," "A Tooth for Paul Revere," "Freedom's a Hard-Bought Thing," and "Johnny Pye and the Fool-Killer."

The first Webster story, "The Devil and Daniel Webster," was published in 1936 in the *Saturday Evening Post,* and its tremendous success gave Benét immediate national recognition and fame. The cause of its success was deep rooted—it sparked the latent historic and cultural feelings in the American mind. Moreover, in Webster, Benét found an ideal folk hero who had all the myth surrounding his character to provide ample material for productive characterization. The basis for the conflict in the story is extremely interesting. Webster was renowned for his superb oratorical powers, and consequently he was the perfect protagonist to meet the Devil in an oratorical contest and defeat him. This symbolic contest between the representatives of good and evil had wide appeal and was complemented not only by Benét's use of local humor but also by the story's inherent universal significance. These elements of the story combined with the tones of pathos and human nobility make it more than a simple humorous fantasy—it is a classic American fable. The New England dialect of the narrator forms a striking blend with the rhythm and visual imagery drawn from several literary sources. In addition Benét's use of little-known historical characters on the jury—Simon Girty, the renegade, and Reverend John Smeet, the strangler—adds novelty and helps give the story a sustained interest. The narrator's final comment that the Devil "hasn't been seen in the state of New Hampshire from that day to this" and "I'm not talking about Massachusetts or Vermont" redeems the story from heavy didactic moralizing.

The story, however, has a moral derived from the grass roots of American tradition. It is, from one perspective, an American version of the story of Job and the Faust legend. Although the name Jabez Stone is implicitly suggestive, Stone is initially unlike Job. He is a poor man plagued by bad luck. When his troubles multiply, he sells his soul to the Devil, not for power like Faust, but for the typically American goal of material prosperity. Unlike Faust, the tug-of-war for Jabez's soul is not between God and the Devil, but between the epitome of Americanism, Daniel Webster, and Mr. Scratch. Jabez, however, is not damned like Faust, for the American virtues imbedded in Webster make him use his capacity to reason, to awaken pity from a biased jury. Webster points out that since the Devil is a foreign prince, he has no authority over an American citizen. The Devil's line of argument is clever and logical. He dates his citizenship back to the day when the first injustice was done to the Indians and when the first slave ship set sail from Africa; and when Webster permits the Devil to choose any judge and jury as long as they are American citizens, the Devil selects Judge Hathorne of the Salem witch trials and a dozen wicked men from hell. Webster uses his powers of elocution to awaken pity from the jury by reviving their sense of manhood. He recalls the simple pleasures of life that can only be enjoyed in freedom. He concedes that although errors and discrimination had taken place in America, something new had been born out of all this—a freer, more vital way of life built by everybody's efforts. Although Jabez is a mean man, he is a man and thus has some good in him. Webster then stresses the fact being a man is a matter of pride because even in hell a man's mettle could be recognized.

In his concluding statements Webster makes, through his plea for Jabez, a plea for himself and for mankind. Webster observes that the jurors were out to get Jabez, as well as condemn him, if he fought them with their own weapons. He evokes their sympathy by recalling the symbolic journeying of all men which was filled with failures and deceptions. Only real men, he stresses, can see the inherent greatness of the journey. This triggers the latent chords of manhood in the jury and their spokesman declares: "The jury has considered its verdict. We find for the defendant, Jabez Stone." The verdict is tempered by the spirit rather than the letter of the law, for the spokesman adds: "but even the damned may salute the eloquence of Mr. Webster." Resorting to a similar spirit Webster also lets the Devil go. The Devil will be back but his evil has been conquered in some of the United States by humanity, justice, and by the representative of a country that symbolizes all of mankind's positive hopes. These layers of symbolic connotations give Benét's story a depth which equals the humor.

Benét's other two Webster tales cannot measure up to the quality of "The Devil and Daniel Webster." In "Daniel Webster and the Sea Serpent," for example, Benét weaves another humorous myth, but the story has little, if any, national significance. Nevertheless, he often channeled this penchant for history into realism and achieved aesthetically laudable results.

In stories such as "The Die-Hard," "Jacob and the Indians," and "Freedom's a Hard-Bought Thing," Benét uses the historical base to portray realism. His technique in these stories is to focus on a protagonist who represents a given historical period and to make his experiences reflect the essence of that period. This type of story obviously requires a strong central character who has to be typical and yet distinct and plausible enough to sustain the reader's interest. Probably the best story of this genre is "Freedom's a Hard-Bought Thing," which won the O. Henry Memorial Award for the best short story of 1940. The story, which derives its effect from its realism and its moral, is equally notable for depicting faithfully the colorful dialect and point of view of specific ethnic groups. The story has a strong narrative core with the narrator, a Negress, telling the children the story of Cue, a plantation slave. Benét's faithful depiction of her speech patterns, rhythms, and diction helps to individualize her but does not obstruct the flow of the plot.

Cue, the protagonist of "Freedom's a Hard-Bought Thing," grows up to be a proud, strong, and affable young man. He likes his work at the plantation blacksmith shop and has no complaints about his life until his parents die in an epidemic. Soon after this, their cabin is given to new slaves, and all that remains is their burial ground. The tragedy changes Cue's complacent outlook on life, and he begins to ask himself questions. This state leads him to Aunt Rachel, a conjure woman, who diagnoses his problem as freedom sickness:

It's a sickness in your blood. . . . It's a sickness in your liver and veins. Your daddy never had it that I know of—he took after his mommy's side. His daddy was a corromante and they is bold and free, and you takes after him. It is the freedom sickness, son Cue.

Aunt Rachel then tells Cue about the underground road and how to find it. Cue then runs away but is caught and whipped. Because of his good record, however, his owners are easy on him. The failure of his attempted escape makes him ponder Aunt Rachel's advice about learning the wisdom of nature by observing her creatures. He even channels his effort toward learning to read so he may acquire some of the wisdom of the white man.

Eventually he meets a white man who tells him of freedom and the underground railroad. Yet Cue again fails to escape because he gives the last place on a boat to his girl friend Sukey. Cue is branded a runaway and all his bitterness is diverted toward Aunt Rachel because the burden of gaining freedom literally drains him. She then reassures him by reminding him of the ancient freedom of her people and the long tedious road ahead for him. Her words of wisdom solidify Cue's faith and he feels that he is bound to be a witness to freedom. Soon after this, Cue is sold to new owners and he confronts deliberate cruelty and suffering for the first time. Finally he manages to escape and through the underground railways arrives in Canada—a free man finally. Unable at first to grasp totally the ramifications of his new state, he ultimately gives himself a full name—John H. Cue—to symbolize his nascent freedom.

One of the reasons for the overwhelming impact of the story is its resemblance to biblical parables. Cue's dual strength of body and mind make him a symbol for all slaves who have struggled to attain freedom, and the dialect of his narrator, as well as the direct invocations of God, remind the reader of the King James Bible. The storyteller's name, "Aunt Rachel," recalls the Old Testament, and her specific memory of her past juxtaposed with the symbolic connotations of Cue's story makes "Freedom's a Hard-Bought Thing" a narrative of a whole people. In addition, Benét's portrayal of Cue is specific and select enough to individualize him and make the overall effect of the story extremely realistic. Details in setting, such as the bubbling pot in Aunt Rachel's cabin and her advice to Cue to study the wisdom embedded in the creatures of nature add both realism and a dash of local color. Finally Benét's sentimentalism is rewarding Cue with another Sukey at the end has a thematic justification; it represents the reevolution and continuity of the race under its newly acquired freedom.

Benét was not always an optimist and did not always stress fulfillment of hopes in his tales. Through "Johnny Pye and the Fool-Killer" he vented a subdued preoccupation to illustrate the dismal aspect of folklore. This story deals with the failure of people who do not follow the rudiments of common sense.

Johnny Pye, the protagonist, is the typical naïve youth who is initiated to the ways of the world through hard experience. Johnny, an orphan in a small town, has foster parents, a miller and his wife, who treat him like a fool because they think that is the proper way to bring up a child. When the miller tells him that he is the most foolish boy he has ever seen (Johnny being already fearful of the legendary Fool-Killer), he runs away. Johnny's life after this is a series of apprenticeships with a quack doctor who makes the mistake of returning to a town he had previously visited, and a merchant who is totally obsessed with making money. These follies make Johnny run away again to avoid entrapment in similar situations. He then meets an inventor of a perpetual motion machine, a drunken fiddler, impetuous soldiers and Indians, a Republican Congressman, a Democratic Congressman, and finally a President of the United States; the last three barrage Johnny with the notion of the omniscience of their respective parties.

On the night he wins the hand of the girl he loves, Johnny hears the dogged steps of the Fool-Killer, but he marries her anyway and accepts the President's appointment to be the postmaster in his hometown. Soon after this, Johnny encounters the Fool-Killer, an old scissors-grinder, putting an edge on a scythe. The Fool-Killer tells Johnny that it is his time. The old man, however, gives Johnny a deferral when he protests. He even agrees to give Johnny the first reprieve in history if he can answer one question: How can a man be a human being and not be a fool?

When Johnny is forty he faces the first major tragedy in his own family—his eldest son drowns. Obsessed with grief, Johnny confronts the Fool-Killer. The Fool-Killer evades him and reminds him that even though his grief cannot be healed, time will pass by, and that his present responsibilities lie in taking care of his wife and the other children. Time passes and Johnny becomes a grandfather, although his wife dies. When Johnny is ninety-two years old, he meets the Fool-Killer for the final time. Since the last meeting, Johnny has gone through a great deal and has an answer to the Fool-Killer's question. All men are basically fools although the wise and the brave account for the occasional progress. Humanity is a conglomerate of different types and qualities of men, and only a creature foolish by nature could have been ejected from the Garden of Eden or chosen to come out of the sea into dry land. Johnny realizes that he has no use for a man who has not been labeled a fool by any of his acquaintances. This answer satisfies the Fool-Killer, who offers Johnny eternal life. Johnny, after pondering the problem, declines on the grounds that his physical decay will continue with the progression of years. In addition, Johnny realizes that with his wife and friends gone, he would have no one to talk to if he decided to accept the Fool-Killer's offer. He questions the Fool-Killer to find out if he would see his friends eventually on the Day of Judgment if he decided to stay around. The Fool-Killer answers: "I can't tell you that . . . I only go so far." Johnny leaves with him, content to go that distance.

In "Johnny Pye and the Fool-Killer," Benét varies his style to suit his material. Although the story begins with a direct address to the reader—"You don't hear much about the Fool-Killer these days"—the narrator has no symbolic identity other than that specific function. He remains anonymous and blends the elements of humor, folklore, and native wisdom to enhance the total impact. He narrates the tale without serious moralizing and integrates a subtle, refined humor directed to underline the pretensions and eccentricities of the American character. The shift in tone implicit in Johnny's discovery that the "Fool-Killer" is a manifestation of time is achieved smoothly and without any abrupt recourse to philosophical discourse. The theme of the story finally comes into focus when Johnny realizes that folly is an essential and humanizing frailty. His recognition is a reflection of the vision of the "New American Adam" as a creature with distinct possibilities and human flaws. Benét's larger focus, however, is on human morality. The pathos in the final scene, tempered with hope, seems to be a fitting epitaph for Johnny and a fitting ending to an American Fable.

Benét's forte was not the short story, yet his tales will always be popular because of their typically American grass roots. Although his stories were written during a period of national and world upheavals, their patriotic blend of American history, wisdom, and folklore has a timeless quality because it captures the essence of the American spirit—freedom, justice, equality, opportunity, and plain common sense.

Major publications other than short fiction

NOVELS: *The Beginning of Wisdom*, 1921; *Young People's Pride*, 1922; *Jean Huguenot*, 1923; *Spanish Bayonet*, 1926; *James Shure's Daughter*, 1934.

PLAYS: *Nerves*, 1924 (with John Farrar); *That Awful Mrs. Eaton*, 1924 (with John Farrar); *The Devil and Daniel Webster*, 1939.

POETRY: *Five Men and Pompey*, 1915; *Young Adventure*, 1918; *Heavens and Earth*, 1920; *Tiger Joy*, 1925; *John Brown's Body*, 1928; *Ballads and Poems, 1915-1930*, 1931; *Burning City*, 1936; *The Ballad of the Duke's Mercy*, 1939; *Western Star*, 1943.

NONFICTION: *America*, 1944.

Bibliography

Fenton, Charles A. *Stephen Vincent Benét: The Life and Times of an American Man of Letters.*

Stroud, Parry. *Stephen Vincent Benét.*

Zia Hasan

DORIS BETTS

Born: Statesville, North Carolina; June 4, 1932

Principal short fiction
The Gentle Insurrection, 1954; *The Astronomer and Other Stories*, 1966; *Beasts of the Southern Wild and Other Stories*, 1973.

Other literary forms
Doris Betts has published three novels, but the short-fiction form provides a medium that enables her to deal more expressly with two of her favorite fictional interests: time and mortality.

Influence
Betts is too young a writer for her influence to be assessed as yet, but it may prove to be substantial. Noteworthy is her aggressively imagistic and philosophical mythopoetic imagination. She continues to exert an influence on young writers in the English-speaking world through her works and her teaching at the University of North Carolina, Chapel Hill.

Story characteristics
Betts's first collections were solidly realistic stories about her own part of the world, the Piedmont Upper South, and they stressed the victory of feeling and sentiment over, for example, segregation and the assumption that blacks were inferior to whites. Her later work has moved all the way into fantasy and passed through a concern with death into a consideration of the afterlife. Her most recent stories, although still rich from the point of view of diction and image, operate on several levels simultaneously.

Biography
Doris June Waugh Betts is the daughter of William Elmore and Mary Ellen Freeze Waugh. She was educated in the public schools of Statesville, North Carolina, and at the University of North Carolina at Greensboro (1950-1953) and later at Chapel Hill (1954). On July 5, 1952, she was married to Lowry Betts, a lawyer. Betts claims that her childhood experiences as an Associate Reform Presbyterian have stayed with her. "The Bible is a strong source in my writing because I grew up in a strict religious family, strongly fundamentalist. . . . Bible stories themselves are marvelous, really marvelous, background for a writer—a lot of the rhythms, to begin with, in the Bible are good for writers. And secondly, all these stories are very physical, very specific and concrete." Betts now teaches English, including writing, at the University of North Carolina at Chapel Hill. She received a Tanner Award for excellence

in undergraduate teaching in 1973, the same year that *Beasts of the Southern Wild* was nominated for a National Book Award. The state of North Carolina presented her with its Medal for Literature in 1975.

Analysis

In the first movement of Doris Betts's *The Astronomer and Other Stories*, the eponymous hero (his real name is Horton Beam) retires from the huge, noisy textile mill in North Carolina where he has spent most of his adult life. It is his last day, and they give him a gold watch as he collects his last paycheck. At last, after a lifetime of subservience to the machine, he crosses a patch of grass outside the plant in defiance of a "Keep Off the Grass" sign and mutters (under his breath) "They can all go to hell." It is important for the tone of the story and for Beam's ultimate position in life that he does not have the guts to yell it out loud or to commit any major infraction of the rules. He tells his coworkers on that last day that he is going to do nothing (one of them, by way of the author's foreshadowing, is reading a pulp science-fiction novel, *Bride of the Green Planet*). At home, his watch off, he begins looking at the books left in the house and comes across his dead son's copy of Walt Whitman's *Leaves of Grass* (1855) and sees the line ". . . heard the learned astronomer." Beam decides on impulse to become a Learned Astronomer. This is a novel (or novella) of ideas, a short allegory set in prose form, a multileveled symbolic novel in the tradition of Nathaniel Hawthorne, and, as it turns out, a consummate exercise in mythopoetic fiction—for Betts's artistry is such that it can be all these things, and in such a short space.

The next day, a young man, Fred Ridge, appears on Horton Beam's doorstep, wanting to rent a room. The Astronomer ignores him and studies his star charts all day, but the young man is still there at nightfall, so he rents him a room. The next morning he presents The Astronomer with his paramour—and the representative of the labyrinth: Eva, who has abandoned her husband and children and run off with one of her husband's used-car salesmen. These characters are not merely people but are the allegorical embodiment of ideas or forces or human options and choices. Eva, of course, reminds us of Eve by her name, but she is more like Lilith, the first (and evil) wife of Adam. Lilith, according to legend, objected to the recumbent position in sexual intercourse, preferring the superior one; when Adam tried to compel her obedience, she uttered the name of God and left. Lilith now became the destroyer of the newborn (just as, later in the short story, Eva aborts the lovechild she conceived during her affair with Fred). God is supposed to have sent three angels, Senoy, Sansenoy and Semangelof, to fetch Lilith back; she would not go, but agreed to spare newborn children if the names of the three or their likenesses on an amulet appeared above the infants. This led to the apotropaic rite formerly practiced by devout Jews in which a message in charcoal was written inside a charcoal circle on the wall of the newborn's room: "ADAM AND EVE. OUT, LILITH!" Jewish children who laughed in their sleep were supposed to have been caressed by Lilith.

The other Hebrew legend about Lilith is that she ruled as queen in Zmargad and in Sheba; another was that because she left Adam before the Fall, she was immortal, and that she not only strangled sleeping infants but also seduced men in their sleep. In this novella, The Astonomer once, at the height of his infatuation for Eva, feels that he has for a moment seen through sheet and mattress and boards and earth right down to hell, and this is certainly congruent to Eva's representing Lilith. Of course, if Lilith is a demon, then The Astronomer represents Judeo-Christian spiritual history against the forces of darkness, another reading of the allegorical content of this novella. The Astronomer at another point claims identification with Adam in that he gives names to stars. It might also be noted, however, that this allegory is not merely religious, but aesthetic; its conflict is between the artists and those involved in the quotidian burdens of life. To give the story a "middle reading," these are real people too, in a real workaday North Carolina. The car lot where Fred used to work for Eva's husband was depressing, Eva says. The progress of life annoys her; for her, the momentary pleasures of life, the feeling of slight removal from things rushing to their conclusions is part and parcel of living. She fears final things, and so, from the beginning, her adventure with Fred and her abandonment of the children can only be a momentary loop in the straight road to death through alienation and despair. She is not, perhaps, a good example of those who live recklessly by improvisation, dedicated to survival by their wits, but here, as in so many Betts stories, there are no final winners.

Eva is a sensualist. She has, like her little girl, chewed tar from the telephone poles, and she asks The Astronomer if he has ever chewed peach-tree gum or eaten wild locusts (this reference is almost biblical). Eva is pregnant with Fred's child, however, and she goes to an abortionist on the street running between the black and white communities. He makes her prostitute herself as the price of the abortion. Eva's troubles, her new sordid life, and his going down into Nighttown to find her force a conversion upon The Astronomer (and it might be remembered that in Hebrew legend, Lilith goes East, beyond Eden, to live by the Red Sea, home of the lascivious demons). It is not quite a religious experience; Betts's control does not leave her for an instant. Now The Astronomer begins to think of Fred, and now he begins to feel sexual desire for Eva as she recovers from her abortion; desire is something he has not felt for a long, long time. He comes alive; he thinks he can hear the grass growing. The telescope becomes covered with dust. After Eva recovers, both of them disappear, an ending that shocks the reader but provides a perfect conclusion to the story.

Betts has said about the story "Benson Watts Is Dead and in Virginia," that it "is a logical extension of the things that interest me most in fiction, which, as I say, are mortality and time. . . ." The premise is intriguing. It is in fact the one question that has tormented every human culture since time began: where do we go when we die? In this first-person narrative, Benson Watts, sometime schoolteacher, dies and wakes up in Virginia. He is sixty-five and survived by grandchildren, "none of whom I liked very much." He looks like John L. Lewis and teaches United States and world history in high schools all over Texas.

When he wakes up one day, he is bald, younger, forty again, dressed in Dacron trousers and a pair of shoes he has never owned. Around his neck hangs a medallion which says:

1. Dwell, then travel
2. Join forces
3. Disremember

He finds a house he immediately recognizes as the one Henry David Thoreau built by Walden Pond. Shortly thereafter Olena, a pregnant red-headed woman in a hairdresser's white uniform, appears; she is in her late twenties and has stayed alive eating persimmons. Next, as throughout the novella, animals from medieval bestiaries once read by Benson Watts begin to follow them everywhere, coming almost close enough to be seen in detail. Then the two are joined by a religious fanatic who is beaten to death in an alley by men who thought he was someone else. This is Melvin Drum, who is a connoisseur of religions and a streetcorner preacher. At this point, a welter of religious ideas, allusions, references, symbols, and speculations enter the story. Betts is writing here of Everyman Dead, and not just a meditation on the Christian heaven or purgatory, limbo or paradise.

The three have been following, at first separately and now together, the first injunction written on their discs: *Travel*. Now all three begin to travel through endless virgin forests, over pure limpid streams, deeper and deeper into a world that none of them recognizes. Now, with the exception perhaps of Benson Watts, they begin to obey the third injunction: *Disremember*. Benson Watts begins to make love to Olena. Drum disappears. They continue to drift across an empty planet thick with forests. The baby in Olena's body disappears, the first disconcerting sign: perhaps their time in this limbo is keyed to the number of years each has lived. Finally Olena dies, leaving Benson Watts alone. The novella ends with Watts closing his journal (the novella has been a sort of epistle intended for dispatch to the Void, or perhaps for the next one to come along) and waiting for an end he cannot imagine. The novella is built around a powerful idea, which accounts for most of its power, but its execution and the expert blending of philosophy with realistic rendering of the human beings involved makes it almost unique in American letters. Betts breaks new ground in her first fantasy short story and dramatizes many beliefs and attitudes toward death. The most important thing about the story, however, is that it reads almost like a biblical tale: it is authentic, human, cathartic.

"The Spies in the Herb House" is a beautiful evocation through unobtrusive prose of a happy childhood; it is based on a wickedly funny conceit: that two innocent young girls growing up in Piedmont, North Carolina, during World War II could believe that a popular graffito could stand for Fight Until Children Killed. There is not much motion in the story, in the great tradition of stories of childhood remembered, and it is rather closely autobiographical (one little girl's name is Doris), but the diction, the timing of the joke (and it is timed as expertly as any stand-up comedian's), and of course the characterization of the girls all make the story more than worthwhile. The Herb House of the story is a large, ugly wooden building in the Herb Capital of the World (Statesville, North Carolina) where elder flowers, true love, wild cherry bark, blackberry and pokeweed roots, sumac berries, ginseng, sassafras bark, catnip, balm of Gilead buds, and other herbs were stored until a few years before the story opened; the warehouse is no longer in use. It is the sort of place two tomboys like Doris and Betty Sue would break into, and they do: and discover an *X* on a box, which they mistake for a swastika (this story takes place during World War II, and Doris' playmate has boyfriends in the service who write her letters). Later the girls, who believe that they have discovered a German spy hideout, have "other dreadful discoveries to make." They see "two long glass counters against one wall. They were about as high as the glass counters which held candy at the dime store. By taking turns, by twisting our necks, we could see they were lined with velvet." Doris immediately deduces the German spies are engaged in diamond smuggling. "Why would the Germans do that?" Betty Sue asks. "Submarines cost money!" Doris says. Then they see the graffito written on the wall and deduce its meaning too and feel utterly powerless and alone. "There was so much I understood that day—valor, and patriotism, and the nature of the enemy. Even my fear was specific. The war had come to me and I did not have to go to it. I was one with all the innocent victims of history." This is not a bad discovery, however frightening, to make at any age.

Major publications other than short fiction
NOVELS: *Tall Houses in Winter*, 1957; *The Scarlet Thread*, 1965; *The River to Pickle Beach*, 1972.

Bibliography
Carr, John, ed. *Kite-Flying and Other Irrational Acts: Conversations with Twelve Southern Writers*.

John Carr

AMBROSE BIERCE

Born: Horse Cave Creek, Meigs County, Ohio; 1842
Died: Mexico; 1914(?)

Principal short fiction

Tales of Soldiers and Civilians, 1891 (republished under the title *In the Midst of Life*, 1898); *Can Such Things Be?*, 1893.

Other literary forms

As a lifelong journalist and commentator, Ambrose Bierce's output of miscellaneous work was prodigious. He was fond of vitriolic epigrams and sketches, together with miscellaneous literary criticism, epigrams, and both prose and verse aphorisms.

Influence

Having less than extensive influence, Bierce has always been regarded as one of the less amiable offbeat products of a state which has never been noted for its shortage of literary eccentrics. Although some few of his Civil War and supernatural stories have been reprinted, Bierce can hardly lay claim either to a devoted coterie of readers or to a dedicated school of followers. Recent critical attention to him has been almost entirely biographical rather than literary in its focus, and this fact alone speaks for his lack of literary influence on subsequent writing.

Story characteristics

Bierce's stories fall into two not mutually exclusive categories. The first consists of Civil War stories based upon Bierce's own experiences in that conflict. The second consists of more or less gruesome stories of the supernatural, noteworthy more for shock value than for profundity of social or psychological insight.

Biography

Ambrose Gwinett Bierce was brought up on the farm in Meigs County, Ohio, where he was born in 1842. Although information about his early life is sparse, the evidence of his stories and the fact that he quarreled with and repudiated his large family with the exception of one brother indicate an unhappy childhood and an abnormal hatred of parental figures. His only formal education consisted of one year at a military academy. He fought with the Indiana infantry in the American Civil War, was wounded at the battle of Kennesaw Mountain, and ended the conflict as a brevet major. After the war, he settled in California, where, following a brief stint as a watchman at the San Francisco mint, he drifted into literary work. He wrote for the San

Francisco *Argonaut* and *News Letter* and published his first story, "The Haunted Valley" (1871), in the *Overland Monthly*. He married and, on money received as a gift from his father-in-law, traveled abroad to England in 1872, returning to California in 1876 because of bad health. Upon his return he again became associated with the *Argonaut*. From 1879 to 1881 he took part in the Black Hills gold rush, returning in 1881 to San Francisco, having found no success as a miner. There he began, in association with the San Francisco *Wasp*, his famous column "The Prattler," transferred to William Randolph Hearst's San Francisco *Examiner* upon the *Wasp*'s failure, and continued at the *Examiner* until 1896, when Hearst sent him to Washington as a correspondent for the New York *American*. Much of Bierce's subsequently collected work appeared first in "The Prattler." Divorced in 1904, Bierce resigned from the Hearst organization in 1909 and, in a final quixotic gesture, disappeared into Mexico in the thick of the Mexican Revolution. He was never heard from again.

Analysis

Perhaps the most rewarding way to approach Ambrose Bierce's writing is to note that it was in many respects the product of two intertwined biographical factors, inseparable for purposes of analysis. The first of these reflects Bierce's thorny and irascible personality which made him, on the one hand, quarrel with practically everyone he ever knew, and on the other, a follower of romantic and often impossible causes, the last of which led to his death. The second reflects his lifelong employment as a journalist, more specifically as a writer of short columns, generally aphoristic in nature, for various newspapers. The interaction of these two often contradictory strands explains, as well as any single factor can, both the strengths and weaknesses of Bierce's writing.

Philosophically, Bierce's work is almost completely uncompromising in its iconoclasm; his view of existence is despairing, revealing only the bitterness of life within a totally fallen world promising neither present happiness nor future redemption. This "bitterness," which almost every critic has remarked in Bierce's work, is not completely fortunate. It can, and in Bierce's case often does, lead to that kind of adolescent cynicism which delights in discovering clouds in every silver lining. Too many of the insights which once seemed sterling are now fairly obviously only tinfoil. The definition of "economy" in *The Devil's Dictionary* (1911) is a case in point: "Purchasing the barrel of whiskey that you do not need for the price of the cow that you cannot afford"—an arresting idea, certainly, succinctly expressed, but by no means a profound one. In fact, it is precisely the kind of item one would expect to find on the editorial page of the morning newspaper, and perhaps remember long enough to repeat at the office. Indeed, this particular aphorism did first appear in a newspaper, with most of the other contents of *The Devil's Dic-*

tionary and, predictably, did not really survive the transformation into book form. *The Devil's Dictionary*, like much of Bierce's work, is now much more generally read about than actually read. At its best, however, Bierce's cynicism is transformed into often passionate statements of the tragedy of existence in a world in which present joys are unreal and future hopes vain, as a glance at one of Bierce's best-known stories, "An Occurrence at Owl Creek Bridge," will show.

This story, for all its apparent simplicity, has attracted uniform critical admiration and has been complimented not only by being extensively anthologized but also by having been made into an award-winning film. Purporting to be an incident from the American Civil War, the story opens with the execution by hanging of a nameless Confederate civilian. His name, Peyton Farquhar, is revealed later, as is his apparent crime: he was apprehended by Union soldiers in an attempt to destroy the railroad bridge at Owl Creek, from which he is about to be hanged. The hangman's rope breaks, however, precipitating Farquhar into the current below. He frees his bound hands and, by swimming, manages to escape both the fire of the Union riflemen who have been assembled to witness the execution and, more miraculously, the fire of their cannon. Reaching shore, Farquhar sets out for home along an unfamiliar road, and after a night-long journey in a semidelirious condition arrives at his plantation some thirty miles away. His wife greets him at the entrance, but as he reaches to clasp her in his arms he suffers what is apparently a stroke and loses his senses. He has not, it develops, suffered a stroke; the last sentence of the story tells us what has really happened. The rope had not broken at all: "Peyton Farquhar was dead; his body, with a broken neck, swung gently from side to side beneath the timbers of the Owl Creek bridge."

"An Occurrence at Owl Creek Bridge" sounds, in summary, contrived. What is it, after all, more than a tired descant on the familiar theme of the dying man whose life passes before his eyes, coupled with the familiar trick of the unexpected happy ending put in negative terms? The answer, from the perspective of one who has read the story rather than its summary, is that it is much more. For one thing, the careful reader is not left totally unprepared for the final revelation. He has been alerted to the fact that something may be amiss by Bierce's remark that Farquhar had, before his apparent death, fixed "his last thoughts upon his wife and children." Moreover, Farquhar's journey home is described in terms which become constantly less real. The unreality of the details of his homeward journey not only expresses Farquhar's growing estrangement from the world of reality, his "doom," perhaps, or— for those more at home in modern Freudianism—his "death wish," but also subtly indicates that what *seems* to be happening in the story may not in fact actually *be* happening, at least in the real world. In any event, Bierce's point is clear and reinforced within the story by a consistent movement in grammatical usage from the actual, "he was still sinking" (speaking of Farquhar's fall from the bridge into the water), toward the hypothetical, such as "doubtless," the word Bierce uses to describe Farquhar's apparent return to his plantation.

What, then, makes this story more than the predictable reverse of the typical tricky story with the illogical happy ending? The difference is to be found simply in Bierce's uncompromisingly negative view of the world. We begin in a world where every man is symbolically sentenced to death, from which his reprieve is only temporary, and we wander with him through a field of illusions which become more attractive as they escape the confines of reality. We end, reaching for a beauty and love which we sought but which was unobtainable, dead under Owl Creek Bridge. The symbolism of Owl Creek is not gratuitous: wise old owls discover that every road leads only to death.

The master image of "An Occurrence at Owl Creek Bridge" of a delusory journey leading to an ultimately horrible and horrifying revelation is central to many of Bierce's stories, one more of which is worth brief mention here. "Chickamauga," not as well known as the former story, is equally chilling and equally cunning in its artistry. It tells of a nameless young boy, "aged about six years," who with toy sword in hand wanders away from his home one day into the adjacent woods, where he successfully plays soldier until, unexpectedly frightened by a rabbit, he runs away and becomes lost. He falls asleep, and when he awakens it is nearly dusk. Still lost, his directionless night journey through the forest brings him upon a column of retreating soldiers, all horribly wounded and unable to walk, who are fleeing a battle (presumably the 1863 Battle of Chickamauga in the American Civil War, although this is never specifically stated) which has been fought in the neighborhood and of which the child, whom we later discover to be both deaf and mute, has been unaware. In a ghastly parody of military splendor, the child takes command of these horribly wounded soldiers and leads them on, waving his wooden sword. As the ghastly cavalcade limps forward, the wood mysteriously begins to brighten. The brightness is not the sun, however, but the light from a burning house, and when the little boy sees the blazing dwelling he deserts his troops and, fascinated by the flames, approaches the conflagration. Suddenly he recognizes the house as his own, and at its doorway he finds the corpse of his mother.

Again, the magic of this story vanishes in paraphrase, in which the masterfully controlled feeling of horror inevitably sounds contrived, the revelation slick rather than profound. The compelling quality of "Chickamauga" is largely a function of Bierce's style, which at once conceals and reveals what is going on. The story of a small boy who wanders off into the woods with a toy sword and who is frightened by a rabbit scarcely seems to be the kind of fictional world in which such uncompromising horrors should logically take place. Yet on a symbolic level, the story has a curiously compelling logic. The first reading of the tale leaves one with a slightly false impression of its meaning. The story does not tell us, as it seems to, and as so many fairy tales do, that it is better not to leave home and venture into the wild wood; the story's meaning is darker than this. In the world of "Chickamauga," safety is to be found neither at home nor abroad. By wandering away into the woods the boy perhaps escaped the fate of those who remained at home, and yet his symbolic journey has only brought him back to a world where death is everywhere supreme. To emphasize this point more strongly, in 1898 Bierce retitled the book of short stories in which both the above tales appeared *In the Midst of Life*. The reader, of course, is expected to complete the quotation himself: "we are in death."

Although most of Bierce's stories which are widely remembered today deal with military themes, many of his other stories are quite frankly supernatural. By and large these supernatural stories seem less likely to survive than his military ones, if only because Bierce has less sense for the implicit thematic structure of supernatural tales than he does for macabre stories about the military. His ghost stories are avowedly "shockers," without the psychological depth to be found in the works of true masters of the supernatural. They have not the profundity, for example, of Mary Shelley's *Frankenstein* (1818) or Bram Stoker's *Dracula* (1897). Nevertheless, the best of them do have a certain compelling quality simply because of the bizarre nature of the revelation of what lies at the heart of the supernatural event which Bierce relates.

"The Damned Thing" offers a convenient case in point. This is, quite simply, the story of a man who is hunted down and finally killed by some kind of animal, apparently a wildcat. We never know precisely what kind of animal it is, however, since it has one peculiar quality: it is invisible. The story is told with the last scene first. This last scene, tastelessly entitled "One Does Not Always Eat What Is on the Table," takes place at the coroner's inquest over the body of one Hugh Morgan, who has met a violent death. His friend, William Harker, explains how Morgan had acted inexplicably on a hunting trip, apparently falling into a fit. The coroner's jury agrees, at least to an extent. Their ungrammatical verdict is "We, the jury, do find that the remains come to their death at the hands of a mountain lion, but some of us thinks, all the same, they had fits." In the closing scene of the story, Morgan's diary is introduced as explanation, and in it we read of his growing awareness that he is being stalked by some kind of invisible animal. A pseudoscientific rationale is given for this invisibility. The animal is "actinic," at least according to Morgan. "Actinic" colors, we are informed, are colors that exist at either end of the spectrum and that cannot be perceived by the human eye. We have, in other words, either an infrared or an ultraviolet mountain lion. Neither choice is particularly satisfactory, and the difficlty with our willing suspension of disbelief in the tale is indicated by precisely this: the science is bad, and yet it pretends not to be. The notion of an ultraviolet mountain lion is basically more silly than chilling, and since the story has no fiber to it other than the revelation of what the mountain lion actually consists of, we cannot take it seriously. In fact, we feel vaguely victimized and resentful, as though we have been set up as the butt of some kind of pointless joke.

Yet even in this story, relatively unsuccessful as it is, we see at work the underlying preoccupations which make some of Bierce's other stories unforgettable. The attempt in a Bierce story is always to shock someone by removing him from a commonplace world and placing him—like the little boy in "Chickamauga"—in another world whose laws are recognizable, though strange. The logic of a Bierce story is often very like the logic of a nightmare, in which the reader is placed in the position of the dreamer. When we are trapped in the toils of nightmare we feel the presence of a certain inexorable logic, even though we may not, at the moment, be able to define exactly how that logic operates or of what precisely it consists. It is the feeling for the presence of this hostile and malevolent order which gives the best of Bierce's stories their perennial fascination.

Major publications other than short fiction

NONFICTION: *The Fiend's Delight*, 1872; *Nuggets and Dust Panned Out in California*, 1872; *Cobwebs from an Empty Skull*, 1873; *Black Beetles in Amber*, 1895; *Fantastic Fables*, 1899; *Shapes of Clay*, 1903; *The Cynic's Word Book*, 1906 (republished under the title *The Devil's Dictionary*, 1911).

Bibliography

Berkove, Lawrence I. *Ambrose Bierce: A Braver Man than Anybody Knew.*
De Castro, Adolphe. *Ambrose Bierce as He Really Was.*
Gaer, Joseph. *Ambrose Gwinnett Bierce, Bibliography & Biographical Data.*
Grattan, C. Hartley. *Bitter Bierce: A Mystery of American Letters.*
Grenander, M. E. *Ambrose Bierce.*
Neale, Walter. *Life of Ambrose Bierce.*

James K. Folsom

HEINRICH BÖLL

Born: Cologne, Germany; December 21, 1917

Principal short fiction

Wanderer, kommst du nach Spa . . . , 1950; *So Ward Abend und Morgan*, 1955; *Unberechenbare Gäste*, 1956; *Doktor Murkes gesammeltes Schweigen und andere Satiren*, 1958; *Der Bahnhof von Zimpren*, 1959; *Erzählungen, Hörspiele, Aufsätze*, 1962; *18 Stories*, 1966; *Children Are Civilians Too*, 1970.

Other literary forms

Besides short stories, Heinrich Böll has written many novels as well as radio plays, essays, dramas, and a few poems. He has also translated English, Irish, and American works into German.

Influence

Böll himself has stated that the most important influences on his work have been Heinrich von Kleist and Johann Peter Hebel. Other German authors who influenced him are Borchert, Stifter, Fontane, Joseph Roth, and Karl May. Non-German influences include Proust, Dostoevski, London, Hemingway, Camus, Green, Faulkner, Wolfe, Dickens, Balzac, Chesterton, Bloy, Flaubert, and Swift. Böll is one of the most popular writers in Germany today, and his works have been translated into most European languages.

Story characteristics

Böll's early stories focus on World War II and the immediate postwar years; his later ones on contemporary German society. His protagonists are ordinary, unheroic people caught in a net of events beyond their control. They feel fear and despair; they bear their fate, suffer, and die. Böll's stories often deal either with political problems such as militarism and Nazism and its aftermath, or with human failings such as greed, hypocrisy, and bigotry. They are frequently humorous or satirical, although the satire is rarely vituperative. A recurrent theme is modern man's loss of individuality. The stories usually have everyday settings.

Biography

Heinrich Böll attended high school in Cologne. After completing his studies in 1937, he worked for a secondhand bookseller in Bonn. In 1938 he was drafted into the labor service. Later he began studying German literature, but his studies were interrupted when he was drafted into the army in 1939. He served on the Western and Eastern fronts and was wounded four times. In 1942 he married Annemarie Cech, a teacher, and has three sons. During the war he deserted twice and was captured by the Americans. On his return from prisoner-of-war camp in 1945, he worked as a carpenter and for the Cologne Bureau of Statistics while resuming his studies. Since 1951 he has earned his living as a writer. In 1971 he was elected president of the International PEN Club. Böll has received numerous prizes, including the Nobel Prize for Literature in 1972.

Analysis

For Böll, commitment is the essence of art. In an essay first published in 1952 entitled "Bekenntnis zur Trümmerliteratur" ("Defence of Rubble Literature" in *Missing Persons and Other Essays*, 1977), he praises Charles Dickens for just such a commitment: Dickens wrote about the social abuses he saw in the English schools, prisons, and poorhouses, and by depicting these abuses, helped bring about change. Böll has the same goal for himself. Moreover, he definitely believes in the power of literature to change society, a rather uncommon notion in the second half of the twentieth century. In the speech "Die Sprache als Hort der Freiheit" (1958), he says that words contain enough dynamite to destroy whole worlds, and it is for this reason that dictatorships fear the printed word almost more than armed resistance, since the former often paves the way for the latter. In his stories, Böll points out what he sees as social abuses, hoping thereby to effect change. The early stories attack the senselessness and futility of war, while the postwar stories criticize what Böll sees as hypocrisy and materialism in modern society. For Böll, one of the most important attributes of a writer is an "X-ray eye" which sees beneath the surface of reality, an eye that should, however, be humane as well as keen and incorruptible. An emphasis on humaneness is typical of Böll's writings; he cares about people deeply and also feels a strong sense of moral, political, and religious responsibility as a writer. A believing Catholic, Böll has been sharply critical of the Church.

In an interview with the critic Horst Bienek in 1961, Böll said that the short story is his favorite form because it is concise and aptly suited to dealing with present-day problems. Böll's stories are themselves spare and concise; they contain precise descriptions of settings and terse dialogue stripped of everything unessential.

"Wanderer, kommst du nach Spa . . ." ("Stranger, Bear Word to the Spartans, We . . .") is typical of Böll's war stories in which the hero is a passive sufferer, and in which the action takes place behind the front lines in dingy stations, barracks, or hospitals. Böll emphasizes the brutality and desolation of war and the waste of lives. The hero is always an ordinary person, a victim of forces beyond his control. In this story, the narrator is a badly wounded young soldier who has been brought to a makeshift hospital in a Prussian high school behind the front lines. From the ambulance he is carried hurriedly by the stretcher-bearers to the school art room, passing on the way pictures of

Frederick the Great and the other Hohenzollern rulers, Hitler, and racial paradigms of Nordic officers and Rhine maidens, as well as a Parthenon frieze, Ludwig Feuerbach's Medea, and busts of Caesar, Cicero, and Marcus Aurelius. The incongruous juxtaposition of Hitler and the humanist tradition shows the distortion of values that has gone on in the school. Formerly the school was called "St. Thomas's"; now it is the "Adolf Hitler School." It is supposedly a humanistic high school, yet the values it inculcates are those of Nazism. After the school was renamed, a cross which had hung over the door was taken down, but despite a fresh coat of paint, a mark where the cross had been is still visible, an accusing sign of the destruction of values under Hitler, and also a symbol of the suffering caused by the war.

As in other stories by Böll, the narrator is alone with his suffering. At first he does not know how severely he is wounded, particularly since the art room where he is lying is ironically labeled "minor surgery." He has a premonition, however, that he is mortally wounded, a sense that grows as he glimpses the school war memorial and reflects that his name should appear there. It seems to him that he is in his old high school which he had just left three months before to go to war. Fragments of memory pass through his fevered mind, in particular the figure of Birgeler, the school janitor, whose room was a refuge from the school's strict Prussian discipline, where one could go to drink milk and sneak a smoke. Now, Birgeler's room is a morgue. Only when the narrator sees his own handwriting on the black board, a penmanship exercise he had to do, is he certain that he is in his old school. The incomplete text, the title of the story, is from the inscription on the grave of Leonidas, who in Classical Greek history was the king of Sparta when the Persians invaded Greece, and who with his men held the pass at Thermopylae to their death. The text shows the futility of war which ends only in death. The parallel is ironic, however: the men at Thermopylae Pass died defending civilized Greece from the barbarians, while in Germany it is Hitler and his regime who are themselves the barbarians. Seeing his own handwriting is especially ironic, for he soon discovers that he has lost a leg and both arms, and will never write again. Finally he recognizes the old fireman who had given him water as Birgeler and whispers "milk," a desperate yearning for nourishment and comfort.

The narrator in this story has no name and stands for the fate of youth in this period. This passive sufferer, however, is a hero, since for Böll heroism consists not in glory or victory, but in bearing one's fate and suffering. War is experienced through the eyes of the ordinary person. Birgeler, with his tired, sad face, is a humane character in the story, but is helpless to ease the wounded soldier's suffering. All he can do is try to comfort him.

"Lohengrins Tod" ("Lohengrin's Death") deals with the immediate postwar years. As in many of Böll's stories, a child is the central character. The story opens as an injured child is being carried into a hospital by unfeeling stretcher-bearers. He has been stealing coal from a train to sell for food when it suddenly stopped, causing him to fall and fracture both legs. To ease the pain, he is given an injection, and then the nurse, nun, and doctor notice how thin and undernourished he is. Gradually glimpses of his past life are revealed: his mother has been killed in the war; his father and elder brother are rarely at home, leaving Grini, as he is nicknamed, to be responsible for his two younger brothers. In his fever, a confused sequence of ideas races through his mind. He is worried about his brothers, who will be waiting for him to prepare dinner and who, because he has punished them in the past for eating up the whole week's bread ration, will not dare to eat bread when he does not return. Nobody else will care for them. His anxiety about his brothers and his wish to buy them huge mountains of bread alternate with scraps of black-market price information. Although this undernourished boy seems to have little in common with his namesake, Lohengrin, the knight of the Holy Grail, he is a hero. At his death, he is not thinking of himself, but of his brothers. He is also worried because he has not been baptized, and when the nun "baptizes" him, he dies peacefully.

Like all children in Böll's stories, Grini is an innocent victim. He has to fend for himself and his brothers in the menacing world of adults; he is old beyond his thirteen years because of the responsibility he has been forced to assume too early. His sufferings are caused by adults; he is overworked and plagued by worries. In death his face looks old, but death seems almost a welcome release from his daily sufferings.

"Die Waage der Baleks" ("The Balek Scales") also has a child as the central character. The story is a strong plea, typical of Böll, for justice. The narrator tells the story of his grandfather's childhood. His grandfather's family works in the flax sheds amid slowly lethal dust. While the parents are at work, the children are responsible for the household chores and for gathering mushrooms, herbs, and wildflowers which they sell to the Baleks who, in turn, sell them profitably to the city. All the goods must be weighed on the Balek scales, for there is a local law providing that only the Baleks are allowed to own scales. If someone were to infringe this law, he would be unable to work in the area, for the Baleks wield great influence because of their wealth. To celebrate being raised to the nobility by the emperor in 1900, the Baleks give each family the equivalent of about a quarter of a pound of coffee, and the narrator's grandfather is sent to collect the coffee for four families. While the servant is out of the room, he weighs the four packages of coffee, finding that they are five pebbles short of a pound. Distressed and angered, he walks miles to the apothecary in another town to have the pebbles weighed: the amount "short of justice" is fifty-five grams (about two ounces) on the pound. The villagers calculate just how much the Baleks have defrauded them over five generations. In the midst of the calculations, the police arrive, shooting and stabbing, and the grandfather's younger sister is killed as well as a gendarme. This village and several others rebel, but the rebellion is put down. The grandfather's family has to move away, but they never stay long in one place because they can never find justice. They try to tell their story, but there are few who listen, which implies a faint hope since at least there are some, however few, who do listen.

The relationship of the villagers to the Baleks had been like that of a trusting child to its parents. This trusting relationship, lasting for five generations, collapses in one night as the villagers realize how the Baleks have cheated them that long. Order is restored by force, and most of the villagers passively acquiesce, aware of the injustice but helpless to combat it. The grandfather's family alone vainly seeks a place where justice reigns.

"Doktor Murkes gesammeltes Schweigen" ("Murke's Collected Silences") is a good example of Böll's satire. Here Böll satirizes the mass culture industry. The story takes place in Broadcasting House where Murke is chosen to delete the word "God" from two speeches by the great Bur-Malottke. At the end of the war, Bur-Malottke, a famous cultural figure, had converted to Catholicism; now he has second thoughts and, as he put it, "suddenly felt he might be blamed for contributing to the religious overtones in radio." Instead of using the word "God" in his speeches, he wants it replaced by "that higher Being Whom we revere." This causes problems. First, the phrase has to be transposed into different grammatical cases. Second, because of its length, it adds a minute to the two speeches in which "God" appears twenty-seven times. Bur-Malottke is revising all his works to delete the word "God" and he wants the director of Broadcasting House to cut "God" from all his speeches since 1945—one hundred and twenty hours of spoken Bur-Malottke. He is a well-known figure in the world of culture, an author of numerous books of a "belletristic-philosophical-religious and art-historical nature." As a committed writer himself, Böll disapproves of this kind of art.

Bur-Malottke is a pedant for whom Murke conceives an absolute hatred as he sees through his hypocrisy and self-importance. After Bur-Malottke has taped the new phrases, Murke escapes to the coffee shop, but here, too, there is no peace. He keeps hearing the word "art" used with such reverence that it makes him wince since he has just heard it one hundred and thirty-four times in Bur-Malottke's two half-hour speeches. In this story, Böll attacks the emptiness of modern culture and the dishonesty of some of its noted figures. Wanderburn, another character, works for the broadcasting industry. He plagiarizes everything he can find, with no scruples whatsoever.

Another butt of Böll's satire is the director. He has received a letter from a listener who complains that not enough attention is given to dogs. She writes that although Hitler may have had his faults, he genuinely loved dogs and did a lot for them (a comment which shows her complete lack of perspective). Rather than ignoring this absurd letter, the director immediately orders a program on the canine soul. Murke is sickened by all this cultural hypocrisy.

For escape, he collects silent segments which he cuts from tapes and listens to at home. Only by listening to these silences can he relax and forget the pretensions and pedantry of his work at Broadcasting House.

These stories, which are typical of Böll, focus on the ordinary man who is struggling to survive in a hostile world. As a satirist, Böll is rarely caustic because of his essential humaneness and his concern for his fellow man. With his stories, Böll tries to make his readers aware of the problems of the time and make them realize the need to help those who are oppressed. There is a glimmer of hope through all the bleakness in the stories because of the author's ultimate faith in man.

Major publications other than short fiction

NOVELS: *Der Zug war pünktlich*, 1949 (*The Train Was on Time*); *Wo warst du, Adam?*, 1951 (*Adam, Where Art Thou?*); *Und sagte kein einziges Wort*, 1953 (*And Never Said a Word*); *Haus ohne Hüter*, 1954 (*The Unguarded House*); *Das Brot der frühen Jahre*, 1955 (*The Bread of Those Early Years*); *Billard um halbzehn*, 1959 (*Billiards at Half Past Nine*); *Die Ansichten eines Clowns*, 1963 (*The Clown*); *Ende einer Dienstfahrt*, 1966 (*End of a Mission*); *Gruppenbild mit Dame*, 1971 (*Group Portrait with Lady*); *Die verlorene Ehre der Katharina Blum oder Wie Gewalt enstehen und wohin sie führen kann*, 1974 (*The Lost Honor of Katharina Blum*).

PLAYS: *Ein Schluck Erde*, 1962; *Aussatz*, 1969.

NONFICTION: *Das Irische Tagebuch*, 1957 (*Irish Diary*).

Bibliography
Hoffman, Leopold. *Heinrich Böll: Einführung in Leben und Werk.*
Schwarz, Wilhelm Johannes. *Heinrich Böll: Teller of Tales.*
Stresau, Hermann. *Heinrich Böll.*
Vogt, Jochen. *Heinrich Böll.*

Jennifer Michaels

JORGE LUIS BORGES

Born: Buenos Aires, Argentina; August 24, 1899

Principal short fiction

Historia universal de la infamia, 1935 (*A Universal History of Infamy*); *El jardín de senderos que se bifurcan*, 1941; *Ficciones, 1935-1944*, 1944 (*Fictions*); *El Aleph*, 1949 (*The Aleph*); *El hacedor*, 1960 (*Dreamtigers*); *Antología personal*, 1961 (*A Personal Anthology*); *Labyrinths*, 1962; *El informe de Brodie*, 1970 (*Doctor Brodie's Report*); *El libro de arena*, 1975 (*The Book of Sand*).

Other literary forms

Jorge Luis Borges also wrote detective stories; biographies; essays on literary, philosophical, and linguistic subjects; fantasies; screenplays; and poetry.

Influence

Utilizing literary and philosophical ideas as well as events from Argentinian history, Borges has written both realistic historical fiction and exremely unrealistic, idea-packed fiction, often based on the paradoxes that fiction is closer to reality than life itself and that words are keys to meanings in experience and yet themselves enigmatic. Speculations about ideas and about language have major interest in Borges' fiction rather than developed characterization or realistic presentation of events. His more recent stories about gauchos, revolutionaries, and settlers, however, show a renewed interest in literary naturalism. His stories have reached an international readership of highly educated and sophisticated people, and they anticipated doctrines popular in the 1960's and 1970's under the general name of structuralism: that language is the ultimate datum of our reality; that human culture depends upon an original act of signifying experience by concepts but that concepts may betray experience; that word-symbols exist objectively but have various interpretations according to individual subjectivity and cultural patterns; and that storytelling, as the product of particular consciousness, mirrors that consciousness while pretending to represent wider human experience. Borges' stories have appeared in serious magazines in Europe, Latin America, and North America.

Story characteristics

The major stories of Borges involve extensive philosophical, biblical, or literary allusions, the deliberate playing with word meanings, hidden clues and puzzles, and ironic touches of humor. The plots are relatively simple and not strongly sequential since the narrator interjects ideas or opinions frequently. The situations often involve imaginary, fantastic, or archaic worlds.

Biography

Descendant of fighters for Argentinian independence, which he has used for his biographical essays and later fiction as background, Jorge Luis Borges received his early education privately. His home languages, reflecting Latin American and Scottish ancestry, were both Spanish and English. In 1914, he traveled to Europe with his parents. The outbreak of World War I stranded his family in Switzerland, which was where he continued his education. After meeting with leaders of the *ultraísmo* literary movement in Spain, he joined with friends in Argentina upon his return to found a review based on similar principles, *Prisma*, and he later edited several literary magazines, all named *Proa*. Poetry and essays were succeeded by fiction writing which he began writing to help recuperate from a head injury (1938). His public dissatisfaction with the Perón regime led to humiliations at the hands of the authorities; but *Ficciones, 1935-1944 (Fictions)* received the Prize of Honor from the Argentinian Society of Writers, and Borges' most productive period of short-story writing followed. He became Director of the National Library (1955) after the end of the Perónista period, a member of the Argentinian Academy of Letters (1955), professor of English Literature at the University of Buenos Aires (1956), and recipient of the National Prize for Literature, also in 1956. He has also received the International Publishers' Prize (1961) for his international reputation and held the Norton Lecturership at Harvard University (1967).

Analysis

Taking the idea from idealist philosophy that existence is a function of our perception of things, Jorge Luis Borges conceives that our thoughts and their presentation in language have more reality for us than actual events which, in any case, find significance only as we interpret them. Since our inner life has wide variations of feeling, reflectiveness, and content, any efforts made by literary realists to imitate the workings of the mind are likely to fail. Therefore, in his major stories, Borges does not develop characters through motivation or the interaction of motive and outside circumstances. Instead he creates private worlds in which language itself or ideas are the center of interest, thus crossing the more public essay with imaginative fiction.

In "Pierre Menard, Author of *Don Quixote*," the bookish Menard sets out to re-create Cervantes' famous novel, first by trying to relive the circumstances of Cervantes' life, although Menard really lives in the twentieth century, and second by rewriting, word for word, Cervantes' work, an effort which succeeds perfectly in duplicating the original even though, as the narrator humorously informs us, the re-creation is infinitely richer than the original. The reader is reminded that the second part of *Don Quixote* itself deliberately refers back not simply to earlier events in Part I, but the actual text and writer of that part. It reflects its own writing. "Pierre Menard, Author of *Don Quixote*" asks us to inquire whether Cervantes' novel is more real than he himself or than the life of his imitator, Menard, whose life becomes his art, and who is, after all, a character in a Borges story. Any text like that of Cervantes is altered in its meaning by accruing cultural changes to which the text itself has contributed. Recent critics have also posed the question of where the actual meaning of a text lies—in the reader, the author, the words themselves, or in its relationship with other cultural products.

Borges has pointed to the exhaustion of realistic technique in fiction by showing that any storytelling is artificial since it requires, even for an unsophisticated teller, unrealistic conventions. Direct access on the part of the reader to the "facts" supposedly underlying its presentation of events is impossible. The reader in solving puzzles about fiction is himself undergoing a discovery of the truth which the writer has had to struggle to achieve. The story "Tlön, Uqbar, Orbis Tertius" presents an imaginary country first discovered by Bioy Casares, a real friend of Borges, in a volume of a pirated edition of an American encyclopedia, this copy being unique. Despite doubts about the reality of the account, the reader is persuaded by further evidence— namely the discovery of a volume of an encyclopedia, *Orbis Tertius*, commissioned by an eccentric millionaire to describe an imaginary society—that it nevertheless has some existence. Or does it? The reader is told about the peculiarities of Tlönian society in Uqbar: the inhabitants are all idealists living entirely in their mental states which, being subjective, they cannot name. They are directed by "heresiarchs" (a learned term invented by Borges), whose title implies that they lead others into false beliefs; except in Tlön innumerable systems describing reality actually exist, thus it obviously becomes impossible for any belief to be false. Time itself cannot exist in Uqbar since in this purely mental world, both memory (past events) and expectation (future events) intermingle. Memory itself, according to the narrator, is compounded of desires. Consequently the past can be reconstructed as the individual wishes, and an infinite number of pasts can exist. A later discovery of a complete set of *Orbis Tertius* permits researchers to verify the truth of their earlier deductions about Tlön. Further paradoxical evidence comes to light when heavy metal cones from Tlön are discovered; it is not then purely mental.

The story deliberately obscures the reality of Tlön or Uqbar, which may be simply a series of mental events which can have no physical past and hence only a subjective history, or it may be a material place which an encyclopedia can represent by its descriptive language. The encyclopedia itself can only be surmised, at first, by researchers using the only yet-discovered volume. They try to understand the lives of the Tlönians even as researchers try to find meaning in our puzzling universe. Yet the narrator insists that this imaginary universe is mathematically ordered, and the labyrinth of *Orbis Tertius* has been devised to be deciphered. In a warning which had political overtones when the story appeared in the 1940's, the narrator warns that humanity generally, like the citizens of Tlön, enjoys a tidy universe of its own conceiving, forgetting over and over "that it is the rigor of chess masters, not of angels." Tlön, then, is any country where men are trying to present experience to one another, being at the mercy of the power of language, and where they construct conflicting but abstract, orderly systems of ideas which they are tempted to take as absolute visions of reality rather than as language games.

In "The Garden of the Forking Paths," a story presenting one of Borges' favorite symbols, the labyrinth, existent at various levels of reality, Yu Tsun, a spy for the Germans in Britain during World War I, must "cry out the secret name" of a British artillery station so that his superior in Berlin will be warned, and aircraft raids can be suitably directed against it. The "secret name" is a reference in the lore of the Cabala to the last of the hundred names of God, the mystical name, and the superior is, presumably, God. By chance, Tsun finds a Stephen Albert in the telephone directory, the only one who can help him transmit the required name (although the reader is not told why). Making his way to Albert's house through labyrinthine roads and pondering meanwhile on the "populous" novel of his grandfather, Hsi P'Eng, who had provided directions for making a labyrinth, Tsun soon finds himself actually caught in a garden maze at Albert's home. His host not only confuses Tsun with his grandfather, whom by chance he had known, but also has deciphered Hsi P'Eng's manuscripts, which seemed to refer to the garden maze and its forking paths but actually refer to the plot of a novel. In the novel, according to Albert, the branching plot action is not limited to one alternative in each instance, but it encompasses all alternatives. It creates diverse future actions in diverse time frames; the novel itself is the whole universe in infinite time. Yu Tsun, coming to himself from this "nightmare," suddenly realizes that he has been pursued and, pressed for "real" time, kills Albert. He reveals to the reader his encipherment of the name of the artillery station for his superior in Berlin just as his pursuer, a British agent, closes in to kill him. His own life finds its destiny in a twice-repeated phrase in his grandfather's novel: "Kill and die." The puzzle clue is that Tsun had to kill an Albert so that news of the murder might reach Berlin and provide the necessary information, for that, as it turns out, is also the name of the artillery station.

The story gathers together a number of problems which intrigue Borges. Albert has decoded a fiction, but that novel represents all of life itself. He is a real person for Tsun but merely a name, a part of a code, for someone in Berlin. The initial choice of Albert is random yet destiny has led Tsun to one who sees in him his own grandfather, and it is Tsun's destiny which is predicted by the novel. Tsun's own narrative is embedded in a frame story which asserts that someone else has discovered it in manuscript. The destiny of Tsun seems increasingly imaginary, and yet the novel is the most real thing of all and determinative of Tsun's life. Tsun must alter reality—in the form of Albert's existence—so that it becomes symbolic and provides the necessary clue for his employer. The novel does what no fiction or life can do: it encompasses all possible choices. Human thought can envisage all possibilities of action but can actualize only a limited number. Our mental world is more rich in possibilities than the real world, hence closer to God. Despite the inadequacies of language, we still seek the perfect word which will make everything clear, but the danger is that we may also destroy others to make meaning possible. Albert has found meaning in the puzzling fiction of Hsi P'Eng's novel but is fated to become a coded message at another level of reality—that of the ultimate or divine. Man himself, the maker of language, is his own enigma. The mirroring devices of the story indicate that all chance is destiny, all times are one time, human fictions are actual truth, and men use language, but it also constructs their culture.

Conflicting interpretations of experience, the inconsistencies of efforts to harmonize facts, the alternating possibilities of interpretations which beget misinterpretations, and the endless possibility of mirrorlike regress in imaginative accounts of life—all these ideas appear in "The Library of Babel." It is an endless series of hexagons, in tiers, with its books all of the same length, its pages and lines also exactly numbered although the symbols seem random. Their meaning is not clear. Some librarians think that the library is a dream although they think the symbols may have an undiscovered order. Two pages have been interpreted, but they turn out to be a language which, as the reader realizes, no human being has ever used although the researchers know its ancestry. Each book is unique, or so it is assumed, and consequently the library may be total in its meaning. The researchers, when not disappearing ominously on the staircases connecting its various levels, keep trying to find "vindications" for their theories about the books, but no one has yet discovered the super-language which could decipher all the texts, and no one expects it to be found. The reader may realize in this Babel of languages that the books cannot be real books since they are simply masses of print and paper without meaning, and the library is not even that without real books. The librarians keep trying to find significance by building theories, some of them assuming an idealist view of reality, but they have no expectations that truth will ever be found. Someone, paradoxically, must have created the order for some purpose, and, after all, the narrator tells his readers about the chaos of language in *a* language. Efforts to find meaning for the library texts by sheer chance or to find no meaning by rigorous elimination through destruction of books have produced no interpretation. Perhaps a Crimson Hexagon exists filled with all-powerful books to decode the others and even a Man of the Book who can explain everything although he may be only a book himself.

No one knows. The "impious" see this incoherence as "normal," but the narrator, who is in opposition, insists that he can justify everything by allegorical methods.

The Man of the Book may be that fount of pure language assumed in so many traditions to be God, whom the unbelievers find unreal; but the joke is on those seeking meaning in the universe since symbolic systems like allegory rely upon established correspondences between things and names for things. Language might arise from sheer accident or it might arise from selective attention to features of experience, but in any case even our ability to represent the divine as ultimate reality is dependent upon that signifying process of language which remains a puzzle to man.

The probing intensity of Borges' short stories—long on ideas and questions, concise or even sketchy in plots, and briefly characterized—has provided him with his international, intellectual readership. Despite his once insisting that every young Argentinian writer was writing about dream-tigers and labyrinths, he has found few strong disciples, Donald Barthelme being one. It is unlikely, given his strong philosophical, linguistic, and literary theoretical concerns, that he will have many literary descendants.

Major publications other than short fiction

POETRY: *Luna de enfrente*, 1925 (*Moon Across the Way*); *El otro, el mismo*, 1960 (*The Other, the Same*); *Selected Poems, 1923-1967*, 1973; *Elogio de la sombra*, 1969 (*In Praise of Darkness*); *El oro de los tigres*, 1972 (*Gold of the Tigers*).

NONFICTION: *Inquisiciones*, 1925 (*Inquisitions*); *El tamaño de mi esperanza*, 1926; *El idioma de los argentinos*, 1928; *Discusión*, 1932; *Neuva refutación del tiempo*, 1947; *Otras inquisiciones*, 1964 (*Other Inquisitions, 1937-1952*).

Bibliography
Alazraki, Jaime. *Jorge Luis Borges*.
Christ, Ronald J. *The Narrow Act: Borges' Art of Allusion*.
Irby, James E. "Introduction" to *Labyrinths*.
Stabb, Martin S. *Jorge Luis Borges*.
Sturrock, John. *Paper Tigers: The Ideal Fictions of Jorge Luis Borges*.
Updike, John. "Books: The Author as Librarian," in *The New Yorker*. (October 30, 1965), pp. 223-246.
Wheelock, Carter. *The Mythmaker: A Study of Motif and Symbol in the Short Stories of Borges*.

Roger E. Wiehe

ELIZABETH BOWEN

Born: Dublin, Ireland; June 7, 1899
Died: London, England; February 22, 1973

Principal short fiction
Encounters, 1923; *Ann Lee's and Other Stories*, 1928; *Joining Charles*, 1929; *The Cat Jumps and Other Stories*, 1934; *Look at All Those Roses*, 1941; *The Demon Lover*, 1945; *A Day in the Dark and Other Stories*, 1965.

Other literary forms
Elizabeth Bowen is as well known for her ten novels as she is for her short-story collections. She has also written books of history, travel, literary essays, personal impressions, a play, and a children's book.

Influence
In theme and technique Bowen's short fiction has been influenced by Anton Chekhov and Guy de Maupassant. She is mainly a writer in the tradition of Gustave Flaubert, especially concerning such matters as relevance and impersonality. Her short fiction is also influenced by Henry James, who shares her interest in the supernatural and in a complexity and tautness of style.

Story characteristics
On the surface Bowen's stories are realistic narratives of events in the lives of ordinary people. Through her use of impressionistic techniques, however, she selects and patterns detail that becomes transformed to carry symbolic meaning. Description often objectifies states of mind, and "ghosts" and figures in dream and hallucination represent aspects of the psyche. Sometimes her characters symbolize levels or aspects of society. She also employs alter-egos to examine aspects of human consciousness, and she utilizes myth to provide her work with archetypal dimensions.

Biography
Elizabeth Dorothea Cole Bowen received her formal education at Downe House in Kent and at the London County Council School of Art. In 1923 she married Alan Charles Cameron and lived with him in Northampton and Old Headington, Oxford. In 1935 she and her husband moved to Regent's Park, London, where Bowen became a member of the Bloomsbury group. During World War II she stayed in London, where she worked for the Ministry of Information and as an air-raid warden. In 1948 she was made a Commander of the British Empire. She was awarded an honorary Doctor of Letters by Trinity College, Dublin, in 1949. After the death of her husband in 1952, Bowen returned to live at Bowen's Court in Ireland, her family estate. In

1957 she was awarded an honorary Doctor of Letters by Oxford University. In 1960 she sold Bowen's Court and returned to Old Headington, Oxford. After a final trip to Ireland, Elizabeth Bowen died in London on February 22, 1973.

Analysis

Elizabeth Bowen's stories are set in the first half of the twentieth century in England and Ireland. Often the action takes place against a background of war. Taken together, her stories provide a chronicle of the social, political, and psychic life of England from the beginning of the century through World War II. Her characters are mainly drawn from the middle class, although upper- and lower-class characters appear as well. Although Bowen's protagonist is usually a woman, men also play important roles. By selecting significant detail and by utilizing mythic parallels, Bowen constructs stories whose settings, actions, and characters are simultaneously realistic and symbolic.

Bowen's characters exist in a world which has lost contact with meaning; traditional forms and ideas have lost meaning and vitality. Both identity and a sense of belonging are lost; "Who am I?" and "Where am I?" are typical questions asked by Bowen protagonists. Some characters merely go through the motions and rituals of daily life, experiencing pattern without meaning. Others have a vague consciousness that something is wrong; unfulfilled, they suffer from boredom, apathy, and confusion. Sometimes, such characters are driven to seek alternatives in their lives. In "Summer Night," while the Major, an example of the first type of character, goes about his evening routine, shutting up the house for the night, his wife, Emma, pretending to visit friends, leaves her traditional family for an assignation with Robinson, a man she hardly knows. He represents another type: the man who adapts to meaninglessness by utilizing power amorally to manipulate and control. Emma is disillusioned in her search for vitality and love when she discovers that Robinson wants sex and nothing else. Other characters, such as Justin, are fully conscious of the situation; they know that they "don't live" and conceive the need for a "new form" but are impotent to break through to achieve one.

Although Bowen's stories focus on those characters who seek meaning or who are in the process of breaking through, they also represent a final type— one whose thinking and feeling are unified and in harmony with existence. An example from "Summer Night" is Justin's deaf sister, Queenie. While Robinson is left alone in his house, while Emma leans drunk and crying against a telegraph pole, and while Justin goes to mail an angry letter to Robinson, Queenie lies in bed remembering a time when she sat with a young man beside the lake below the ruin of the castle now on Robinson's land: "while her hand brushed the ferns in the cracks of the stone seat emanations of kindness passed from him to her. The subtle deaf girl had made the transposition of this nothing or everything into an everything." Queenie imagines:

"Tonight it was Robinson who, guided by Queenie down leaf tunnels, took the place on the stone seat by the lake." It is Queenie's memory and imagination that creates, at least for herself, a world of love, unrealized, but realizable, by the others. Memory recalls the lost estate of man, represented here by the castle, its grounds, and its garden, as well as man's lost identity. Queenie *is* a queen. All human beings are rightfully queens and kings in Bowen's fiction. Queenie's memory reaches back to the archetypal roots of being, in harmony with life; her imagination projects this condition in the here and now and as a possibility for the future. Queenie's thinking is the true thinking Justin calls for, thinking that breaks through to a "new form," which is composed of archetypal truth transformed to suit the conditions of modern life. Throughout Bowen's fiction this kind of thought takes the form of fantasy, hallucination, and dream. Bowen's fiction itself, the expression of *her* imgagination, also exemplifies this thinking.

Toward the end of "Summer Night" it occurs to Justin that possibly Emma should have come to him rather than Robinson. In "Her Table Spread" Bowen brings together two characters much like Emma and Justin. Valeria Cuff, heiress and owner of a castle in Ireland, situated on an estuary where English ships are allowed to anchor, invites Mr. Alban, a cynical and disillusioned young man from London, to a dinner party. These characters represent opposites which concern Bowen throughout her fiction: male and female, darkness and light, thought and feeling, physical and spiritual, rational and irrational. The separation or conflict of these opposites creates a world of war; their unification creates a world of love.

Valeria's orientation is romantic, "irrational," and optimistic: "her mind was made up: she was a princess." She invites Alban to her castle, "excited" at the thought of marrying him. Alban is realistic, rational, and pessimistic: "He had failed to love. . . . He knew some spring had dried up at the root of the world." Alban is disconcerted by Valeria's erratic, impulsive behavior and by her apparent vulgarity. He has heard "she was abnormal—at twenty-five, of statuesque development, still detained in childhood." Ironically, as Alban realizes "his presence must constitute an occasion," he is "put out of" Valeria's mind when a destroyer anchors in the estuary. Valeria believes it is the same destroyer that had anchored there the previous spring at Easter when two officers, Mr. Graves and Mr. Garrett, came ashore and were entertained by friends. Valeria's expectation that the officers will come to dinner initially separates her from Alban. When the officers fail to arrive, she runs outside to signal them with a lantern. Old Mr. Rossiter, uncle to Mrs. Treye, Valeria's aunt, leads Alban to the boathouse to prevent Valeria from rowing out to the destroyer. When a bat flies against Alban's ear, he flees, and, ascending the steps back toward the castle, he hears Valeria sobbing in the dark. When he calls to her, expressing concern and sympathy, she mistakes him for Mr. Garrett. Her fantasy of love is realized as she and Alban stand together, unified in a field of light shining from the castle.

Symbolic details and analogies with pagan and Christian myth universalize the meaning of the story. Alban is associated with the destroyer, with Graves and Garrett, and with their emblems, statues of Mars and Mercury. Like the destroyer, Alban is "fixed in the dark rain, by an indifferent shore." The officers represent aspects of Alban. The name Graves suggests death; and the statue associated with Graves is Mars, god of war. Garrett is a pun on *garret*, which derives from a word meanning to defend or protect. Garrett's statue is Mercury, a god associated by the Romans with peace. Alban's link with the destroyer, with death and war, threatens the destruction of Valeria's dreams of love and peace. The Garrett aspect of Alban, however, linked with protection and peace, offers the possibility of the realization of Valeria's dreams.

Valeria is associated with two symbolic items. Among the gifts she has to offer is a leopard skin, suggesting the animal and the sensual, and a statue of Venus, goddess of love. Valeria thus offers love in both its physical and spiritual aspects. Contained in her fantasies is the expectation that love will put an end to war. She thinks: "Invasions from the water would henceforth be social, perhaps amorous," and she imagines marrying Garrett and inviting "all the Navy up the estuary" for tea; "The Navy would be unable to tear itself away." As Valeria attempts to signal the destroyer with the lantern, she thinks that Graves and Garrett will have to fight for her; instead, the battle takes place within Alban.

The pagan symbolism in "Her Table Spread" is overlaid and transformed by Christian symbolism. Valeria's castle and its grounds, like the ruins of the castle in "Summer Night," represent a lost Eden. Valeria *is* an heiress and a princess; she is an incarnation of Eve seeking her rightful role and place in a paradise of love and peace. Symbolically, she calls to Adam (Alban) to reclaim *his* inheritance—to join her in re-creating the garden. The way is expressed in Bowen's use of the second major Christian myth. Alban must undergo the experience of Christ, the second Adam, to redeem his "fallen" self; he must reject temptation and undergo crucifixion—sacrifice his ego. The trip to the boathouse is Alban's descent into hell. There he is tempted by Old Mr. Rossiter, the Devil. Rossiter offers Alban whiskey, which he refuses, and tempts him with Valeria: "She's a girl you could shape. She's got a nice income." Alban's rejection of this temptation, his refusal to *listen* to the Devil, is signified by his flight from the boathouse when a bat flies against his ear.

As Alban ascends the steps, he recognizes where he is: "Hell." this recognition is the precondition for discovering where he belongs. At this point he undergoes a symbolic crucifixion. Hearing Valeria "sobbing" in "absolute desperation," Alban clings "to a creaking tree." The sympathy Alban feels for Valeria signifies the death of Graves within him and the resurrection of

Garrett. Valeria has also experienced crucifixion. Graves and Garrett have not arrived and her lantern has gone out; she, too, is in hell. Humbled and in darkness, the two meet. Alban speaks with tenderness: "Quietly, my dear girl." Valeria speaks with concern. "Don't you remember the way?" The year before the destroyer had anchored "at Easter." Now Valeria is present at and participates in resurrection: *"Mr. Garrett has landed."* She laughs "like a princess, and magnificently justified." Standing with Valeria in the glow of light from the castle, observed by the two female guests, Alban experiences love: "such a strong tenderness reached him that, standing there in full manhood, he was for a moment not exiled. For the moment, without moving or speaking, he stood, in the dark, in a flame, as though all three said: 'My darling. . . .' "

A world of love is achieved, if only momentarily, in "Her Table Spread." In "The Demon Lover" Bowen creates a story of love denied or repressed, and its power transformed into the demonic. The stories complement each other. The first takes place at a castle in Ireland in the spring and recalls the previous Easter; the second is set in an abandoned London flat in autumn during the bombing of London in World War II and recalls a previous autumn during World War I. The action of "Her Table Spread" concludes with the coming of night. The protagonists of the first story are a young woman in search of love and a young man associated with war; those of the second are a forty-year-old married woman who has denied love and her fiancé of twenty years before, a soldier lost in action during World War I. Both female characters are "abnormal": Valeria of "Her Table Spread" caught up in fantasy, Kathleen of "The Demon Lover" subject to hallucination. Bowen utilizes elements of the Eden myth to universalize the meaning of both stories.

In "The Demon Lover" Mrs. Kathleen Drover returns to her abandoned London flat to pick up some things she had left behind when her family moved to the country to escape the bombing. In the dark flat where everything is covered with a dustlike film, she opens a door, and reflected light reveals an unstamped letter recently placed on a hall table. Since the caretaker is away and the house has been locked, there is no logical explanation for the appearance of the letter. Unnerved, Mrs. Drover takes it upstairs to her bedroom, where she reads it. The letter reminds her that today is the anniversary of the day years before when she made a promise of fidelity to a young soldier on leave from France during World War I—and that they had agreed to meet on this day "at an hour arranged." Although her "fiancé was reported missing, presumed killed," he has apparently survived and awaits the meeting. When Kathleen hears the church clock strike six, she becomes terrified, but maintains enough control to gather the items she came for and to formulate a plan to leave the house, hire a taxi, and bring the driver back with her to pick up the bundles. Meanwhile, in the basement "a door or window was being opened by someone who chose this moment to leave the house."

This statement provides a realistic solution to the problem of the letter's appearance, but a psychological interpretation offers an alternative conclusion. The London flat symbolizes Kathleen's life as Mrs. Drover, and the shock of finding the letter reveals to Kathleen the meaninglessness of this life and the falseness of her identity as Mrs. Drover. By marrying Drover, Kathleen has been "unfaithful" not only to the soldier but also to herself. It is this self which emerges as a result of the "crisis"—actually the crisis of World War II—and which has unconsciously motivated Mrs. Drover's return to the house. The fact that the letter is signed K., Kathleen's initial, suggests that she wrote the letter, which is a sign of the reemergence of her lost self. The house not only represents Kathleen's life as Mrs. Drover, but also the repressed-Kathleen aspect of her identity. The person in the basement who leaves the house at the same moment Mrs. Drover lets herself out the front door is a projection of this repressed self, the self Mrs. Drover now unknowingly goes to face.

Overlaid on the psychological meaning of the story are two additional levels of meaning, one allegorical, the other archetypal. The young Kathleen represents England, defended and protected by the soldier, who represents the generation of men who fought for the country during the first war. Kathleen's loveless and meaningless marriage to Drover represents England's betrayal of the values the war was fought to defend—a betrayal which has contributed to the creation of World War II. The letter writer asserts: "In view of the fact that nothing has changed, I shall rely upon you to keep your promise." Because Kathleen and England have betrayed themselves, because love has failed, war continues, and both the individual and the country must suffer destructive consequences.

On the archetypal level, Kathleen and the soldier are incarnations of Eve and Adam, although the soldier is an Adam transformed by war into a devil who coerces Eve to "fall," forces her to make the "sinister truth." The soldier's uniform is the sign of his transformation. His true nature, his Adamic self, is covered and denied by the clothes of war. Kathleen is unable to touch the true self of the soldier, and he is unable to reach out to her. The scene takes place at night in a garden beneath a tree. Intimidated by not being kissed and by being drawn away from, Kathleen imagines "spectral glitters in the place" of the soldier's eyes. To "verify his presence," she puts out a hand, which he takes and presses "painfully, onto one of the breast buttons of his uniform." In this way he forces her to make a vow of fidelity—a pact with the Devil. He says "I shall be with you . . . sooner or later. You won't forget that. You need do nothing but wait. Kathleen suffers the fate of Eve, feels that unnatural promise drive down between her and the rest of all human kind." When the soldier, her "fiancé," is "reported missing, presumed killed," she experiences "a complete dislocation from everything."

Compelled now to confront her fate, she gets into a taxi, which seems to be awaiting her. When the driver turns in the direction of her house without being told where to drive, Kathleen leans "forward to scratch at the glass panel that divided the driver's head from her own . . . driver and passenger, not six inches between them, remained for an eternity eye to eye." Reunited with her demon lover, Kathleen screams "freely" as the taxi accelerates "without mercy" into the "hinterland of deserted streets." The failure of love condemns Kathleen—and by implication mankind—to insanity and damnation in the modern wasteland.

In spite of the pessimistic conclusion of "The Demon Lover," Bowen's short fiction is ultimately affirmative. In a 1970 *McCall's* essay she lamented that many people, especially the young, are "adrift, psychologically . . . homeless, lost in a void." She expresses her desire to "do something that would arrest the drift, fill up the vacuum, convey the sense that there is, after all, SOMETHING . . . (For I know that there is.)" Bowen's fiction conveys the existence of this something, which some would call God, others simply the source of being. Whatever it is called, it exists within each individual and in the natural world. Its primary nature is love, expressed in acts of kindness, sympathy, understanding, and tolerance. It is the potential for unity among people and harmony with the world. This potential is mirrored in the unity and harmony of Bowen's stories. The lyric descriptive passages, the coherence of matter and form, the intense visual images, and the emotional force of her stories demonstrate Bowen's mastery of the short-story form. Her stories deserve to be recognized as among the best written in the twentieth century.

Major publications other than short fiction

NOVELS: *The Hotel*, 1927; *The Last September*, 1929; *Friends and Relations*, 1931; *To the North*, 1932; *The House in Paris*, 1936; *The Death of the Heart*, 1938; *The Heat of the Day*, 1949; *A World of Love*, 1955; *The Little Girls*, 1964; *Eva Trout*, 1968.

Bibliography
Austin, Allan E. *Elizabeth Bowen.*
Blodgett, Harriet. *Patterns of Reality: Elizabeth Bowen's Novels.*
Brooke, Jocelyn. *Elizabeth Bowen.*
Heath, William W. *Elizabeth Bowen: An Introduction to Her Novels.*
Kenney, Edwin J. *Elizabeth Bowen.*

James L. Green

PAUL BOWLES

Born: Long Island, New York; December 30, 1910

Principal short fiction

The Delicate Prey, 1950; *A Hundred Camels in the Courtyard*, 1962; *The Time of Friendship*, 1967; *Things Gone & Things Still Here*, 1977; *Collected Stories, 1939-1976*, 1979.

Other literary forms

Paul Bowles's twenty-four published books include plays, translations, autobiography, novels, and short stories, for which he is best known. His novel *The Sheltering Sky*, published in 1949, is considered a modern classic in American literature, a book-length metaphor of the modern world with the theme of sterility and disintegration of humankind's spirit.

Influence

Bowles's writing is unique in that it creates its own myths from modern situations and settings, focusing on the everyday, commonplace horrors that besiege humankind as it struggles to survive. His short stories have a timeless quality about them and have appeared in major anthologies and major magazines.

Story characteristics

Bowles's realistic, wry stories portray people in ordinary situations confronted by circumstances that suddenly go beyond their control and create a setting of psychological terror for them. In the beginning, the style is clear and terse, speaking to the reader directly and simply; as the story progresses, however, the style becomes eerily complex, pulling the reader into a horrifying quagmire as the central character becomes engulfed in a terrifying web of circumstances from which there is no release.

Biography

Paul Bowles was educated at the University of Virginia, but he left after a short period of study to go to Europe. He lived in France and published many of his poems in the "little magazines" of the 1920's, especially *Transition*. Between 1929 and 1945 he made a name for himself as a distinguished composer. With his wife, writer Jane Bowles, he lived in Mexico and New York and traveled extensively. After World War II, they made their permanent home in Tangier, Morocco. It was not until 1945 that Bowles seriously started writing short fiction, and the result was the strange and beautifully haunting story "The Scorpion," which was published in *View*. His reputation as a writer and as a composer continued to grow internationally, and he produced a collection of native North African music gathered for the Library of Congress. He continues to create short fiction and translations. A gifted linguist, he speaks several languages.

Analysis

Paul Bowles tells a tale and tells it well. He creates characters that are caught in a precise and shattering moment in their lives, and then he presents the reader with an oftentimes bizarre and wise clarification. This clarification may be horrifying, terrifying, violent, or poignant, but it is achieved and revealed at the conclusion of the story. Themes that have occupied his writing include the constantly shifting line between reality and illusion, the raw energies and strength of youth, the sadness of old age and its accompanying conflicts, and the subtle deceit and unexpected revelations of friendship. Bowles's writing has a dreamlike quality, and he allows the reader to experience and share the dream completely. About this device, Bowles has stated: "Dreams are symbolic. Dreams represent unclassified fears in which we all share collectively. That is the way my stories are. Each one is a different dream, and each reader undertakes it differently." Like his music, Bowles creates a tightly structured story—terse and intense, the words are carefully chosen like musical notes, and his attention to detail is flawless. By concentrating on the surface of the landscape—be it the human mind, a village in the mountains, or a bizarre occurrence—he allows the reader to interpret the underpinning, and by so doing, achieves a transference of identity wherein the reader's mind becomes one with that of the character. It is a difficult technique, but one which Bowles is able to employ successfully in every story he has published. The achievement of this unique literary effect has assured him of a lasting position in American literature. Bowles uses locales in which he has lived; namely, Mexico and North Africa.

The story "The Delicate Prey" is one of the best examples of psychological horror fiction written in the twentieth century by an American. It is a classic story wherein the horror is not so much what happens to the characters, but what becomes of their minds. Typical of Bowles's writing, the denouement of the story is compounded by a second horror that is as terrifying as the first. The story concerns a young boy, Driss, and his two uncles; the setting is in the desert of North Africa. On a trading journey into another village, the three encounter a stranger. They are wary of the stranger but allow him to accompany them because it is a long journey and the man has a sharp sense of humor. On the pretense of hunting, the stranger takes the two uncles out into the desert and kills them. Driss is taken, bound by rope, and stripped naked. He is molested in a manner that not only terrifies the boy but the reader as well: the stranger takes a razor, stretches the boy's penis taut and cuts it off at the base, then cuts an opening in the boy's side where the limp member is placed and covered over. The stranger turns the boy over on his stomach and sexually assaults him throughout the night despite the boy's screams of acute agony and pain. In the morning, the satisfied stranger awakes, takes the razor blade, and takes pleasure in sawing through the maimed boy's windpipe. He enjoys watching the boy bleed to death. The horror, however, is not over. The stranger is suspected of the murders in the next village. Despite his pleas of innocence, he is taken into the desert and buried up to his neck. Only his head is left above the sand. The stranger's punishment is to suffer heat, thirst, fire, visions, death—in that order. Madness overtakes him as he is dying. Bowles concludes the story with the line: "The wind blew dust along the ground into his mouth as he sang."

The reader is presented with another kind of horror in "A Distant Episode." It is the story of a brilliant professor confronted with a strange culture in North Africa. He is captured by a camped band of nomads, and he immediately tries to communicate with them, employing several different languages which he has mastered. The nomads laugh at him and then cut out his tongue. He is made into their personal toy and becomes the official clown for the group's entertainment. A most serious, civilized individual, the professor is now used as a means to make his captors laugh. The professor goes mad. In the story "Allal," a young boy exchanges personality with a snake; and in the story, "You Are Not I," a madwoman becomes her sane sister.

These stories—"The Delicate Prey," "A Distant Episode," "Allal," and "You Are Not I"—show Bowles at his creative best and his writing at its most complex level. The theme of madness interwoven with the theme of the shifting line between illusion and reality is clearly delineated in these stories. Bowles's unique ability in employing the most effective words to achieve a penetrating effect on the reader's unconscious mind is very evident. These stories have encouraged younger writers to probe more deeply into the psychological impact of a given situation upon a character's mind. These particular stories show how to create an atmosphere of terror out of ordinary circumstances, how to build and develop the atmosphere so that character, place, action, situation, and circumstances form a cohesive whole—a perfect painting, so to speak, so that the essential details are there intact, and the subtle shades and tones and hues are present yet forever open to individual interpretation.

Within the dreamlike quality of Bowles's short stories, a subtle nightmare lurks, ready to overtake the reader at any second; the reaction to that lurking nightmare depends entirely upon the myths which each reader has developed for his own self-protection. Some readers will find the nightmare more devastating than others, but all will feel it to some lasting degree, which is proof of the timeless quality of Bowles's fiction, and the universality of his themes.

Major publications other than short fiction

NOVELS: *The Sheltering Sky*, 1949; *Let It Come Down*, 1952; *The Spider's House*, 1955; *Up Above the World*, 1966.

POETRY: *Two Poems*, 1933; *Scenes*, 1968; *The Thicket of Spring*, 1972; *Next to Nothing*, 1977.

NONFICTION: *Yallah*, 1957 (photographs by Peter W. Haeberlin); *Their Heads Are Green and Their Hands Are Blue*, 1963; *Without Stopping*, 1972.

Bibliography

Stewart, Lawrence D. *Paul Bowles: The Illumination of North Africa.*
Straumann, Heinrich. *American Literature in the Twentieth Century.*

H. L. Prosser

KAY BOYLE

Born: St. Paul, Minnesota; February 19, 1903

Principal short fiction

Short Stories, 1929; *Wedding Day and Other Stories*, 1930; *First Lover and Other Stories*, 1933; *The White Horses of Vienna and Other Stories*, 1936; *The Crazy Hunter*, 1940; *Thirty Stories*, 1946; *The Smoking Mountain: Stories of Postwar Germany*, 1951; *Three Short Novels*, 1958; *Nothing Ever Breaks Except the Heart*, 1966; *Fifty Stories*, 1980.

Other literary forms

In addition to her short-story collections, Kay Boyle has published fourteen novels, four volumes of poetry, three children's books, an essay collection, and a book of memoirs. She has ghostwritten, translated, or edited eight other books. Hundreds of her stories, poems, and articles have appeared in periodicals ranging from the "little magazines" published in Paris in the 1920's to the *Saturday Evening Post* and *The New Yorker*, for which she was a correspondent from 1946 to 1953.

Influence

Boyle was very much a part of the group of expatriate writers living in Paris in the 1920's that has been labeled "the lost generation," and her work appeared in the avant-garde magazines alongside that of James Joyce, Gertrude Stein, Hart Crane, Archibald MacLeish, William Carlos Williams, and Ernest Hemingway. She won the O. Henry Award for best short story of 1935 for "The White Horses of Vienna" and in 1941 for "Defeat." She was awarded Guggenheim Fellowships in 1934 and 1961, received an honorary Doctorate of Literature from Columbia College in Chicago in 1971, and is a member of the National Institute of Arts and Letters. Despite her distinguished and prolific career, however, her work is not widely known today, and only a handful of her books remain in print.

Story characteristics

Many of Boyle's stories are carefully drawn portraits of a single, isolated situation in which not much "happens" on the surface. Rather, they unfold subtly and gradually to expose a truth—often bitter or ironic—and end more often in revelation than in resolution. Boyle is noted for her style and, in fact, has been pigeonholed by some critics as a mere virtuoso. Her skill is evident in her ability to capture an instant with photographic clarity, to describe scenes and landscapes as they reflect psychological states, and to reveal a character's stream of consciousness in complex internal monologues that rival those of Joyce and William Faulkner in their psychological authenticity.

Biography

Kay Boyle claims to have no home town, having traveled extensively with her family in the United States and Europe during her childhood. After studying architecture for two years in Cincinnati, she married a French-born engineer and went with him to France in 1923. What was to have been a summer vacation became an eighteen-year expatriation, during which Boyle lived and wrote in England, Austria, and France; was divorced; married artist Laurence Vail; and had four children. After returning to the United States in 1941, she was divorced from Vail and in 1943 married Joseph von Franckenstein, an Austrian baron displaced from his homeland by the Nazis, whom Boyle had met in France. They had two children and in 1946 returned to Europe. Until 1953 they lived in Germany, where Boyle was a correspondent for *The New Yorker* and her husband was employed by the United States Government. In 1963, shortly after they moved from Connecticut to San Francisco, Franckenstein died of cancer, having served a brief term as cultural attaché in Iran that same year. Boyle taught at San Francisco State University from 1963-1979, and she has been actively involved on the local, national, and international levels in movements protesting social injustices and violations of human rights. Her arrest and imprisonment following an anti-Vietnam war demonstration is the basis of her most recent novel, *The Underground Woman* (1975).

Analysis

In a 1963 article Kay Boyle defines what she sees as the role of the serious writer: to be "the spokesman for those who remain inarticulate around him, an aeolian harp whose sensitive strings respond to the whispers of the concerned people of his time." The short-story writer, she believes, is "a moralist in the highest sense of the word"; his role has always been "to speak briefly and clearly of the dignity and integrity of individual man." Perhaps it is through this definition that the reader may distinguish the central threads that run through the variegated fabric of Boyle's fiction and bind it into a single piece.

In the 1920's when the young expatriate artists she knew in Paris were struggling to cast off the yokes of literary convention, Boyle championed the bold and experimental in language, and her own early stories are intensely individual explorations of private experiences. Yet when the pressures of the social world came to bear so heavily on private lives in our century that they could not be ignored, Boyle began to expand the scope of her vision and vibrate to the note of the *new* times to affirm on a broader scale the same basic values—the "dignity and integrity" of the individual. From the 1930's to the present her subject matter has encompassed the rise of Nazism, the French resistance, the Allied occupation of postwar Germany, and the civil rights and anti-Vietnam war movements in America, yet she has never lost sight of the individual dramas acted out against these panoramic backdrops.

In the same article Boyle also quotes Albert Camus' statement that "a man's work is nothing but a long journey to recover through the detours of art, the two or three simple and great images which first gained access to his heart." In Boyle's journey of more than fifty years, a few central themes remain constant: a belief in the absolute essentiality of love to human well-being—whether on a personal or a global level; an awareness of the many obstacles to its attainment; and a tragic sense of loss when it fails and the gulfs between human beings stand unbridged.

"Wedding Day," the title story of her first widely circulated volume of short stories, published in 1930, is typical of her early works. It is an intense exploration of a unique private experience written in an experimental style. The action is primarily psychological, and outward events are described as they reflect states of consciousness. Yet it is representative of Boyle's best work for decades to come, both in its central concern with the failure of love and in its bold and brilliant use of language.

"The red carpet that was to spurt like a hemorrhage from pillar to post was stacked in the corner," the story begins. From the first sentence the reader senses that things are out of joint. The wedding cake is ignored as it is carried into the pantry "with its beard lying white as hoarfrost on its bosom." "This was the last lunch," Boyle writes, and the brother and sister "came in with their buttonholes drooping with violets and sat sadly down, sat down to eat." To the funereal atmosphere of this wedding day, Boyle injects tension and bitterness. The son and mother argue as to whether the daughter will be given the family's prized copper saucepans, unused for twenty years, and he mocks the decorum his mother cherishes when he commands her not to cry, pointing his finger directly at her nose "so that when she looked at him with dignity her eyes wavered and crossed" and "she sat looking proudly at him, erect as a needle staring through its one open eye." As the mother and son bicker over who wanted the wedding in the first place, the bride-to-be is conspicuously silent. Finally, as the son snatches away each slice of roast beef his mother carves until she whimpers her fear of getting none herself, he and his sister burst into laughter. He tosses his napkin over the chandelier and she follows him out of the room, leaving their mother alone "praying that this occasion at least pass off with dignity, with her heart not in her mouth but beating away in peace in its own bosom."

With the tension between children and mother clearly delineated and the exclusive camaraderie between brother and sister suggested, Boyle shifts both mood and scene and describes in almost incantatory prose the pair's idyllic jaunt through the spring afternoon in the hours remaining before the wedding:

The sun was an imposition, an imposition, for they were another race stamping an easy trail through the wilderness of Paris, possessed of the same people, but of themselves like another race. No one else could by lifting of the head only be starting life over again, and it was a wonder the whole city of Paris did not hold its breath for them, for if anyone could have begun a new race, it was these two.

The incestuous overtones are strong. "It isn't too late yet, you know," the brother repeatedly insists as they stride through the streets, take a train into the *bois*, and row to the middle of a pond. "Over them was the sky set like a tomb," and as tears flow down their cheeks, the slow rain begins to fall. There is perfect correspondence between landscape and emotion, external objects mirroring the characters' internal states. The rain underscores the pair's frustration and despair as they realize the intensity of their love and the impossibility of its fulfillment:

Everywhere, everywhere there were other countries to go to. And how were they to get from the boat with the chains that were on them, how uproot the willowing trees from their hearts, how strike the irons of spring that shackled them? What shame and shame that scorched a burning pathway to their dressing rooms! Their hearts were mourning for every Paris night and its half-hours before lunch when two straws crossed on the round table top on the marble anywhere meant I had a drink here and went on.

The inevitable wedding itself forms the final segment of the story, and the lyrical spell binding the pair is broken the instant they set foot in the house again to find their mother "tying white satin bows under the chins of the potted plants." The boy kicks down the hall the silver tray that will collect the guests' calling cards, and his mother is wearily certain "that this outburst presaged a thousand mishaps that were yet to come." The irony of the story lies not only in the reversal of expectations the title may have aroused in the reader but also in the discrepancy between different characters' perceptions of the same situation. The self-pitying matron worries only about the thousand little mishaps possible when a major disaster—the wedding itself—is imminent; but the guests arrive "in peace" and the brother delivers his sister to the altar. Boyle captures magnificently the enormous gulf between the placid surface appearance and the tumultuous inner reality of the situation as she takes the reader inside the bride's consciousness:

This was the end, the end, they thought. She turned her face to her brother and suddenly their hearts fled together and sobbed like ringdoves in their bosoms. This was the end, the end, the end, this was the end.

Down the room their feet fled in various ways, seeking an escape. To the edge of the carpet fled her feet, returned and followed reluctantly upon her brother's heels. Every piped note of the organ insisted that she go on. It isn't too late, he said. Too late, too late. The ring was given, the book was closed. The desolate, the barren sky continued to fling down dripping handfuls of fresh rain.

The mindless repetition of the phrase "the end" and the blind panic of the bride's imaginary flight have an intense psychological authenticity, and the recurrence of the brother's phrase "It isn't too late" and its perversion in "Too late, too late," along with the continuing rain, are evidence of the skill with which Boyle has woven motifs into the fabric of her story.

"Wedding Day" ends with dancing, but in an ironic counterpoint to the flight she had imagined at the altar, the bride's feet "were fleeing in a hundred ways throughout the rooms, fluttering from the punch bowl to her bedroom and back again." Through repetition and transformation of the image, Boyle underscores the fact that her path is now circumscribed. While the brother, limbered by the punch, dances about scattering calling cards, the mother, "in triumph on the arm of the General, danced lightly by" rejoicing that "no glass had yet been broken." "What a real success, what a *real* success," is her only thought as her feet float "Over the oriental prayer rugs, through the Persian forests of hemp, away and away" in another absurdly circumscribed "escape" that is yet another mockery of the escape to "other countries" that the pair had dreamed of that afternoon on the lake.

Ironies and incongruities are hallmarks of Kay Boyle's fiction. For Boyle, reality depends on perception, and the fact that different perceptions of the same situation result in disparate and often conflicting "realities" creates a disturbing world in which individuals badly in need of contact and connection collide and bounce off one another like atoms. In "Wedding Day" Boyle juxtaposes a *real* loss of love with the surface gaiety of a wedding that celebrates no love at all, but which the mother terms "a *real* success." She exposes the painful isolation of each individual and the tragedy that the only remedy— a bonding through love—is so often thwarted or destroyed.

The barriers to love are many, both natural and man-made. In some of Boyle's stories those who would love are severed by death. Sometimes, as in the case of the brother and sister in "Wedding Day," love's fulfillment is simply made impossible by the facts of life in our imperfect world, and although the reader can mourn for what has been lost, he can hardly argue about the obstacle itself—the incest taboo is nearly universal. Yet in many of her works Boyle presents a more assailable villain. In "Wedding Day" she treats unsympathetically the mother, who stands for all the petty proprieties that so often separate people. Boyle finds many barriers to human contact to be as arbitrary and immoral as the social conventions which cause Huck Finn's "conscience" to torment him as he helps his friend Jim to escape slavery, and in her fiction she quietly unleashes her fury against them. An obstacle she attacks repeatedly is a narrow-mindedness which blinds individuals to the inherent dignity and integrity of others, an egotism which in the plural becomes bigotry and chauvinism.

While Boyle and her family were living in Austria in the 1930's, she was an eyewitness as the social world began to impose itself on private lives, and she began to widen the scope of her artistic vision; yet her "political" stories have as their central concern the ways in which external events affect the individual. In one of her best-known stories, "The White Horses of Vienna," which won the O. Henry Award for best story of 1935, Boyle exposes the artificial barricades to human understanding and connection. The story explores the relationship between a Tyrolean doctor, who has injured his leg coming down the mountain after lighting a swastika fire in rebellion against the current government, and Dr. Heine, the young assistant sent from Vienna to take over his patients while he recovers. The Tyrolean doctor and his wife see immediately that Dr. Heine is a Jew.

The Tyrolean doctor is a clean-living, respected man. He had been a prisoner of war in Siberia and had studied abroad, but the many places in which he had been "had never left an evil mark." Boyle writes: "His face was as strong as rock, but it had seen so much of suffering that it had the look of being scarred, it seemed to be split in two, with one side of it given to resolve and the other to compassion." In his personal dealings it is the compassionate side that dominates. When his wife asks in a desperate whisper what they will do with "*him*," the Tyrolean doctor replies simply that they will send for his bag at the station and give him some *Apfelsaft* if he is thirsty. "It's harder on him than us," he tells her. Neither has the wife's own humanity been extinguished entirely by institutionalized bigotry, for when Dr. Heine's coat catches fire from a sterilizing lamp on the table, she wraps a piece of rug around him immediately and holds him tightly to smother the flames. Almost instinctively, she offers to try patching the burned-out place, but then she suddenly bites her lip and stands back "as if she had remembered the evil thing that stood between them."

The situation of the Tyrolean doctor, described as a "great, golden, wounded bird," is counterpointed in a story Dr. Heine tells at dinner one evening about the famous Lippizaner horses of the Spanish Riding School in Vienna, still royal, "without any royalty left to bow their heads to, still shouldering into the arena with spirits a man would give his soul for, bending their knees in homage to the empty, canopied loge where royalty no longer sat." He tells of a particular horse that the government, badly in need of money, had sold to an Indian maharaja. When the time had come for the horse to be taken away, a wound was discovered cut in his leg. After it had healed and it was again time for the horse to leave, another wound was found on its other leg. Finally the horse's blood was so poisoned that it had to be destroyed. No one knew who had caused the wounds until the horse's devoted little groom committed suicide that same day. When the after-dinner conversation is interrupted by the knocking of Heimwehr troops at the door, "men brought in from other parts of the country, billeted there to subdue the native people," the identification between the doctor and the steed is underscored. He cannot guide the troops up the mountain in search of those who have lit that evening's swastika fires because of his wounded leg.

Dr. Heine is relieved that the rest of the evening will be spent with family and friends watching one of the Tyrolean doctor's locally renowned marionette shows. After staring out the window at the burning swastikas, the "marvelously living flowers of fire springing out of the arid darkness," the "inexplicable signals given from one mountain to another in some secret gathering of power that cast him and his people out, forever out upon the waters of despair," Dr. Heine turns back, suddenly angry, and proclaims that the whole country is being ruined by politics, that it is impossible to have friends or even casual conversations on any other basis these days. "You're much wiser to make your puppets, *Herr Doktor*," he says.

Even the marionette show is political. The characters are a clown who explains he is carrying artificial flowers because he is on his way to his own funeral and wants them to be fresh when he gets there, and a handsome grasshopper, "a great, gleaming beauty" who prances about the stage with delicacy and wit to the music of Mozart. "It's really marvellous! He's as graceful as the white horses at Vienna, *Herr Doktor*," Dr. Heine calls out in delight. As the conversation continues between the clown, for some reason called "Chancellor," and the grasshopper, inexplicably addressed as "The Leader," Dr. Heine is not laughing so loudly. The Chancellor has a "ludicrous faith in the power of the Church" to support him; the Leader proclaims that the cities are full of churches, but "the country is full of God." The Leader speaks with "a wild and stirring power that sent the cold of wonder up and down one's spine," and he seems "ready to waltz away at any moment with the power of stallion life that was leaping in his limbs." As the Chancellor proclaims, "I believe in the independence of the individual," he promptly trips over his own sword and falls flat among the daisies.

At the story's conclusion, Dr. Heine is standing alone on the cold mountainside, longing to be "indoors, with the warmth of his own people, and the intellect speaking." When he sees "a small necklace of men coming to him" up the mountain, the lights they bear "coming like little beacons of hope carried to him," Dr. Heine thinks, "Come to me . . . come to me. I am a young man alone on a mountain. I am a young man alone, as my race is alone, lost here amongst them all." Yet ironically, what Dr. Heine views as "beacons of hope" are carried by the Heimwehr troops, the Tyrolean doctor's enemies. As in "Wedding Day," Boyle presents a single situation and plays off the characters' reactions to it against one another to illustrate the gaps between individuals and the relativity of truth and reality in our world.

His personal loyalties transcending his politics, Dr. Heine rushes to warn the family of the Heimwehr's approach. When the troops arrive they announce that the Austrian chancellor, Dollfuss, had been assassinated in Vienna that afternoon. They have come to arrest the doctor, whose rebel sympathies are known. "Ah, politics, politics again!" cries Dr. Heine, wringing his hands "like a woman about to cry." He runs outdoors and takes the doctor's hand as he is being carried away on a stretcher, asking what he can do to help. "You can throw me peaches and chocolate from the street," replies the Tyrolean doctor, smiling, "his cheeks scarred with the marks of laughter in the light from the hurricane lamps that the men were carrying down." His wife is not a good shot, he adds, and he missed all the oranges she had thrown him after the February slaughter. At this image of the Tyrolean doctor caged like an animal but still noble, with his spirit still unbroken, Dr. Heine is left "thinking in anguish of the snow-white horses, the Lippizaners, the relics of pride, the still unbroken vestiges of beauty bending their knees to the empty loge of royalty where there was no royalty any more."

In "The White Horses of Vienna," Boyle expresses hope, if not faith, that even in the face of divisive social forces, the basic connections of compassion between individuals might survive. In a work that is a testament to her humanity, she presents the Tyrolean doctor's plight with such sensitivity that we, like the Jewish assistant, are forced to view with understanding and empathy this proud man's search for a cause that will redeem the dignity and honor of his wounded people while at the same time abhorring the cause itself. Boyle sees and presents in all its human complexity what at first glance seems a black-and-white political issue. Boyle, however, is no pollyanna. As the social conflict that motivates this story snowballed into world war and mass genocide, she saw with a cold, realistic eye how little survived of the goodwill among men she had hoped for. In many of her stories written in the 1940's to the present day, she has examined unflinchingly and sometimes bitterly the individual tragedies played out in the shadow of the global one.

In "Winter Night," published in 1946, she draws a delicate portrait of a little girl named Felicia and a woman sent by a "sitting parent" agency to spend the evening with her in a New York apartment. The woman, in her strange accent, tells Felicia that today is an anniversary, that three years ago that night she had begun to care for another little girl who also studied ballet and whose mother, like Felicia's, had had to go away. The difference was that the other girl's mother had been sent away on a train car in which there were no seats, and she never came back, but she was able to write a little letter on a smuggled scrap of paper and slip it through the cracks on the floor of the moving train in the hope that some kind stranger would send it to its destination. The woman can only comfort herself with the thought that "They must be quietly asleep somewhere, and not crying all night because they are hungry and because they are cold."

"There is a time of apprehension which begins with the beginning of darkness, and to which only the speech of love can lend security," the story begins, as Boyle describes the dying light of a January afternoon in New York City. Felicia and the "sitting parent," both left alone, have found that security in each other. When, after midnight, Felicia's mother tiptoes in the front door, slipping the three blue foxskins from her shoulder and dropping the velvet bag on a chair, she hears only the sound of breathing in the dark living room, and no one speaks to her in greeting as she crosses to the bedroom: "And then, as startling as a slap across her delicately tinted face, she saw the woman lying sleeping on the divan, and Felicia, in her school dress still, asleep within the woman's arms." The story is not baldly didactic, but Boyle *is* moralizing. By juxtaposing the cases of the two little girls left alone by their mothers and cared for by a stranger, she shows that the failure of love is a tragic loss on an individual as well as on a global scale. Again, personal concerns merge with political and social ones, and we find the failure of love on any level to be the fundamental tragedy of life.

Some of the stories Boyle has written about the war and its aftermath are less subtle, "artistic" explorations of individual struggles as they are frankly moralistic adventure stories written for commercial magazines, and they were more popular with the public than with the critics. Yet one of her finest works was also a product of her war experiences. *The Smoking Mountain: Stories of Postwar Germany* (1951) consists of eleven stories, several originally published by *The New Yorker*, which had employed Boyle as a correspondent for the express purpose of sending "fiction out of Germany." It is prefaced by a seventy-seven-page nonfiction account of a denazification trial Boyle witnessed in Frankfurt in 1948, which reveals her immense skill as a reporter as well. The book presents a painful vision. Any hope that a renewed understanding among men might result from the catastrophic "lesson" of the war is dashed, for the point of many of the stories and certainly of the introduction is how little difference the war has made in the fundamental attitudes of the defeated but silently defiant Germans who can still say of 1943 and 1944—"the years when the gas chambers burned the brightest"—"Those were the good years for everyone."

To the present day, Boyle has continued writing in this more public vein, treating social issues in a more accessible, less experimental style than in earlier days and taking as her subjects the evils and injustices she has seen in America as well as in other countries. Boyle's imaginative vision is grounded in the concrete world. In the course of her career, her characters and concerns, chamelionlike, have taken on the shades of the times through which she has passed; yet they have never merged into the background entirely. Hers is a stereoscopic vision. At bottom, her fundamental concern is the individual drama, yet she never loses sight of the ways in which public events shape private experience. As an artist, Boyle maintains a sense of serious, personal responsibility to mankind, and she is undaunted by warnings that she sometimes treads close to the border of sentimentality. Boyle sees the serious writer as one who both reflects and attempts to transform the reality of his own times.

Major publications other than short fiction

NOVELS: *Plagued by the Nightingale*, 1931; *Year Before Last*, 1932; *Gentlemen, I Address You Privately*, 1933; *My Next Bride*, 1934; *Death of a Man*, 1936; *Monday Night*, 1938; *Primer for Combat*, 1942; *Avalanche*, 1943; *A Frenchman Must Die*, 1946; *1939*, 1948; *His Human Majesty*, 1949; *The Seagull on the Step*, 1955; *Generation Without Farewell*, 1959; *The Underground Woman*, 1975.

POETRY: *A Glad Day*, 1938; *American Citizen Naturalized in Leadville, Colorado*, 1944; *Collected Poems*, 1962; *Testament for My Students and Other Poems*, 1970.

NONFICTION: *The Long Walk at San Francisco State and Other Essays*, 1970.

Bibliography

Carpenter, Richard C. "Kay Boyle," in *College English*. XV (November, 1953).
_____ . "Kay Boyle: The Figure in the Carpet," in *Critique*. VII (Winter, 1964-1965).
Moore, Harry T. *The Age of the Modern and Other Essays*.

Sandra Whipple Spanier

BERTOLT BRECHT

Born: Augsburg, Germany; February 10, 1898
Died: East Berlin, Germany; August 17, 1956

Principal short fiction
Me-ti: Buch der Wendungen, 1935-1939 (*Mi-ti: Book of Twists and Turns*); *Kalendergeschichten*, 1949 (*Tales from the Calendar*); *Gesammelte Werke*, 1967 (Vol. V, *Collected Works*).

Other literary forms
Bertolt Brecht is best known as a dramatist, but he also wrote poetry, novels, screenplays, dramatic theory, and essays on politics and society, as well as short fiction.

Influence
British, American, Chinese, and French literatures influenced Brecht's work, in particular Upton Sinclair, George Bernard Shaw, William Shakespeare (and the Elizabethan drama in general), and Molière. Brecht also draws from the Bible and from folktales. From the middle of the 1920's, Marxist thought grows progressively stronger in his works. Outside of Germany, Brecht influenced such writers as W. H. Auden, Christopher Isherwood, Eugene Ionesco, Samuel Beckett, and Arthur Adamov, among others. His works have been widely translated. His influence as a dramatist and dramatic theorist developed toward the end of his career especially and since his death.

Story characteristics
Brecht's early stories are often anarchistic, even nihilistic. His stories written after he studied Marxism focus on social themes, and the tone of many is ironical. Brecht uses alienation effects (for which his plays are particularly noted) to prevent his readers from identifying with the protagonists and to provoke them to think. The stories frequently have historical settings or deal with great historical figures, whom Brecht demythologizes.

Biography
Bertolt Brecht began studying medicine at the University of Munich in 1917, but a year later he was called up for military service as a medical orderly. He married Marianne Zoff in 1922 and was divorced in 1927. Brecht left Munich for Berlin in 1924 and began an intensive study of economics and Marxism in 1926. After his divorce, he married the actress, Helene Weigel, one of the best interpreters of his plays. Brecht had to leave Germany in 1933 and lived mostly in Scandinavia until he came to California in 1941. In 1947,

he was called before the House UnAmerican Activities Committee and left the United States for Europe the next day. He settled in East Berlin in 1949 and formed the Berliner Ensemble acting company. He died in 1956 in East Berlin.

Analysis

Although primarily known for his dramas and theoretical writings, Bertolt Brecht also wrote many short stories which have been unjustly neglected. He began writing stories while at school and experimented with this genre all his life. In 1928 he won first prize for "The Beast" in the *Berliner Illustrierte* short-story competition. Brecht's early stories are nihilistic, often with exotic settings and scoundrels as protagonists. The later stories criticize society and expose social injustice; the protagonists are either ordinary people or great historical figures whom Brecht cuts down to size.

Brecht theorized less about the short story than he did about the drama, but he did make important contributions to the short-story form, and his stories show a stylistic mastery of the genre. In his later stories, he uses alienation effects to ensure that the reader does not identify with the protagonists. In "On Reading Books" in *Mi-ti: Book of Twists and Turns* Brecht criticizes fiction that makes the reader forget the real world and become engrossed in the work. The reader, he believed, should not be caught up in the action but should view each event in the plot critically and differentiate between appearances and facts. Books should be read so that they can be put aside from time to time for reflection. For this reason, Brecht praises the detective story since it is constructed logically and demands logical thought from the reader. Such a form is scientific, in Brecht's view: it presents the reader with facts and problems to be solved and it challenges him to think, question, and learn—the goals of all Brecht's later works.

"The Beast" is an example of how Brecht uses elements from the detective story to provoke his reader to think and observe facts, rather than be misled by appearances. The story's opening sentence states that a person's behavior is ambiguous and that this story, which has something shocking about it, will demonstrate this idea. Brecht, therefore, gives the reader clues at the outset as to how the story should be interpreted. At the beginning, a down-and-out old man comes to a film studio where a film about pogroms in Southern Russia is being made. Because he looks like the historical governor, Muratow, who incited the pogroms, he is hired and plays a scene in which Muratow receives a delegation of Jews who come to beg him to end the murders. The director criticizes the old man for playing the role like a petty official rather than like a beast, yet two Jews who were part of the real delegation are impressed because the old man's acting corresponds to what actually took place. According to the director, the historical Muratow constantly ate apples, and he refuses to believe the eyewitnesses when they cannot recall this habit. After trying the scene again unsuccessfully, the old man is replaced by a real actor, but before leaving he suggests sadistically that, instead of Muratow, the leader of the Jews should be forced to eat an apple which will stick in his throat because he is so afraid when he sees Muratow signing the Jews' death warrant. The suggestion is immediately accepted, and the story ends with the actor playing his role to the hilt. Similarity to the historical Muratow is clearly insufficient; art is needed to portray real bestiality. At the close, it turns out that the old man really is Muratow, which the reader should have guessed (almost as in a detective story) since the story can be shocking only if this is the case.

One major theme presented in this story is that of role playing. At first the old man appears to be a shy, lonely outsider with whom one should sympathize. Gradually Brecht peels away this mask, exposing the cruelty beneath, seen particularly in the suggestion about the apples which shows that the old man, far from feeling remorse for his deeds, is just as cruel as ever. More important is Brecht's attitude toward art and reality. Brecht shows ironically how art distorts reality; as the scene is rehearsed, it moves further and further away from the real historical event and becomes more dramatic and emotional. This is precisely the kind of art which Brecht criticized in his theoretical writings. Art should appeal to reason, he believed, yet the public prefers art that captivates the emotions, and this is the art that sells.

The next stories are taken from *Tales from the Calendar* which are counted among Brecht's best and are the ones which he himself prized most highly. He was greatly influenced here by almanacs which were widely read by the lower classes and whose stories combined popular appeal with practical moral lessons. Brecht learned from Johann Peter Hebel who wrote for almanacs, but whereas the usual almanac story tended to teach people to be satisfied with their fate, Brecht gives his stories a radical political purpose; his goal is to unmask corruption and make people indignant at social injustice.

"Caesar and His Legionnaire," an offshoot of Brecht's Caesar novel, uses history as an alienation effect. In his depiction of Roman society, Brecht gives the reader a yardstick by which to measure contemporary society, thus forcing the reader into a critical stance. The story's tone is dry and unemotional, and Brecht demythologizes Caesar by showing his death from a dual perspective. The first part of the story describes the last days of Caesar's life from his own perspective. Although he is at the height of his power, Caesar knows that his days are numbered. In an unsuccessful attempt to save his dictatorship, he tries to introduce democracy, but the people are too suspicious and fearful of him for it to succeed. He knows from a dream that he will be killed, but he is resigned to his death and goes to the senate where the conspirators fall upon him—a laconic description of one of the most famous assassinations in history. Caesar is portrayed not as a great tragic figure but rather as a ruthless dictator, one who has put many people in prison and who has profited financially from his own rule. He is accused of having put money into Spanish banks under false names. (This anachronistic and ironic allusion to modern, anonymous Swiss bank accounts is a good example of an alienation effect, whereby the reader's attention is drawn from the narrative to the present.) The story also shows the ephemeral nature and corrupting influence of power.

The second part of the story deals with the same events but from the point of view of Terentius Scaper, a veteran who comes to Rome with his family because he has been evicted for not paying his rent. There are ironic parallels between Scaper's attempts to save himself from financial ruin and Caesar's attempts to save his dictatorship. The veteran's daughter raises money from an old admirer, who demands favors in return; but Rarus, Caesar's secretary and the daughter's fiancé, indignantly takes this money, intending to return it. Instead, he uses the money to bribe the guards to help Caesar escape in Scaper's ox cart. Before the escape can take place, however, Rarus is murdered, and Caesar dies, unwittingly owing Scaper the three hundred sesterces.

Brecht is especially concerned here with the effect of history on the common man. Caesar has brought his downfall on himself and is resigned to his death, refusing to flee. Rarus, however, has no such choice but is murdered because he is too close to Caesar. As for Scaper, Caesar's death means financial disaster, which was also true of Caesar's reign. Although Rome is flourishing, Scaper is poor and has not benefited at all from Rome's conquests. The difference between what history means to the rich and powerful and what it means to the common man is a typical theme in Brecht's works.

"The Wounded Socrates" describes Socrates' "heroic" deeds in the battle of Delion (424 B. C.), and here Brecht, who was strongly averse to conventional forms of heroism, differentiates between real and false courage. Like many of Brecht's characters, Socrates is a teacher famous for his dialectical irony. He is a man of the people who is against speculation and for practical experience, and the story is told with a great deal of humor and irony. Against his will, Socrates has to fight in the battle which is supposedly to defend his city, but in reality, according to Brecht's Marxist theory, is a continuation of business by other means. The aristocrats and the business people profit from the war, but the ordinary people fight and suffer yet reap no rewards. Socrates wishes only to get out of the battle safely, and his fear shows his common sense, since Brecht always regards the instinct to survive as being sensible. At the outset of the fighting, Socrates runs away, inadvertently straying into a thorn field where he gets a thorn in his foot. In pain, unable to run, and with the fighting getting dangerously close, he begins to yell and also encourages other soldiers to yell, which makes the Persians so afraid that they retreat and the battle is won. Socrates, trying to save himself, thus becomes a hero.

When he is brought home in triumph, his suspicious wife is skeptical of his heroism, thinking that he must have been drunk. Socrates tries to hide his wounded foot for fear of ridicule. For this one act of "heroism" he has become famous, but as one of his students sourly remarks, he had been making valuable contributions to intellectual thought for years and had been ignored. Socrates refuses to be honored, partly because the thorn in his foot will show the real reason why he yelled, but partly because he has always preached pacifism and this new heroic role embarrasses him. Finally, refusing to lie, he confesses to his friend Alcibiades who honors him for his real courage in telling the truth in such an awkward situation. Socrates, with all his weaknesses, emerges as a great man since he has the courage to tell the truth, and he gains dignity because he has the courage to uphold his values. Marxist notions of war as business and the destructive nature of capitalism are also stressed in this story.

The theme of the chalk circle is used not only in "The Augsburg Chalk Circle" but also in the plays *Mann ist Mann* (1924-1925, *Man Is Man*) and *Der Kaukasische Kreidekreis* (1943-1945, *The Caucasian Chalk Circle*). Brecht learned about the chalk circle from a play by his friend Klabund who adapted a drama of the same name by Li Hsing-dao who lived in thirteenth century China. Brecht also drew on the biblical story of Solomon's wisdom in dealing with the two women who both claimed to be the mother of the same child.

In a sober and factual tone, Brecht begins in the style of a chronicler. The historical setting is the Thirty Years' War, and the geographical setting is Augsburg. It is a period of religious strife, yet religion appears in the story to be more concerned with plunder than with ideals. When the Catholic forces seize the city, Zingli, a rich Protestant, is murdered because he will not leave his profitable tannery. His wife is so preoccupied with saving her material things that she abandons her small child. Even later, when Anna the maid tells her that the child is safe, she refuses to acknowledge the child. Brecht focuses on the contrast between the rich capitalists represented by the Zinglis and the proletarian maid Anna. Anna, who has been badly treated by the Zinglis, is humane; even in this time of danger and panic, she looks at the child too long and is seduced by the dangerous temptation in this world to goodness, and she rescues the child.

In the second part of the story, the reader sees the sacrifices that Anna makes for the child. She takes him to her brother in the country, but the brother's position on the farm is not secure. He has married his wife, of whom he is afraid, only because she will inherit the farm, but the wife has typically petit bourgeois values, formed by religion and public opinion. Anna immediately sees that she must say that the child is hers, for her sister-in-law is not charitable. The sister-in-law becomes suspicious when Anna's husband does not come, and she taunts Anna. Anna's brother arranges a marriage for her with a deathly ill cottager named Otterer who suddenly recovers and takes Anna to live with him. Although Anna finds him repulsive, for the child's sake she endures the poverty and the loveless marriage, and the child thrives.

One day, years later, a fine lady takes the child away.

In the third part, Anna returns to Augsburg to sue for the return of "her" child. Court scenes, with their dialectical structure, are favorites with Brecht and also show his concern with justice. The judge is Ignaz Dollinger, a man of the people, known for his coarseness and learning, his wisdom and folk cunning. Playing the role of distraught mother, Mrs. Zingli accuses Anna of taking the child for money, a reflection of Mrs. Zingli's own motives for she has only been prompted to look for the child because he will inherit the tannery and thus provide her with a good standard of living. Anna, however, cares deeply for both the child's physical and mental development. Clearly Dollinger favors Anna, although he knows she is lying. To solve the case, he tells his clerk to draw a circle on the floor and put the child in the middle. Dollinger says that the woman with the strongest love will be able to pull the child out of the circle, demonstrating that she is the true mother. Mrs. Zingli pulls with all her might, but Anna lets go for fear of hurting the child. Contrary to the sources, it is not the real mother who gets the child but she who best represents his interests—Anna who has sacrificed everything for his sake. Brecht thus upholds justice by abusing the actual law. The story shows a Marxian idea of the importance of social bonds rather than ties of blood, and it pits a positive heroine of the people against the materialistic bourgeoisie.

The stories discussed in this essay typify themes in many of Brecht's works. Social criticism, an interest in the common man, the fight against injustice, a demythologization of famous historical figures, and the use of alienation effects were concerns of Brecht all his life. The early nihililst turned into the committed Marxist who looked toward the future to bring a utopia in which all social ills would be righted. A faint hint of Utopia is suggested in his last story—justice is done, unlike in most of Brecht's works. Although skeptical of actually reaching Utopia, Brecht nevertheless held it up as a measure to see the shortcomings of our own world.

Major publications other than short fiction

NOVELS: *Die Dreigroschenroman*, 1934 (*The Threepenny Novel*); *Die Geschäfte des Herrn Julius Caesar*, 1957 (*The Business Deals of Mr. Julius Caesar*).

PLAYS: *Baal*, 1922; *Im Dickicht der Städte*, 1923 (*In the Jungle of Cities*); *Mann ist Mann*, 1924-1935 (*Man Is Man*); *Die Dreigroschenoper*, 1928 (*The Threepenny Opera*); *Herr Puntila und sein Knecht Matti*, 1940 (*Mr. Puntila and his Hired Man Matti*); *Mutter Courage und ihre Kinder*, 1941 (*Mother Courage*); *Der gute Mensch von Sezuan*, 1943 (*The Good Person of Szechwan*); *Leben des Galilei*, 1943 (*Galileo*); *Der Kaukasische Kreidekreis*, 1943-1945 (*The Caucasian Chalk Circle*).

POETRY: *Bertolt Brechts Hauspostille*, 1927 (*Domestic Breviary*); *Gesammelte Werke*, 1967 (Vol. IV, *Collected Works*).

NONFICTION: *Der Messingkauf*, 1937-1951 (*The Messingkauf Dialogues*);

Kleines Organon für das Theater, 1948 (*Little Organon for the Theater*); *Ges-ammelte Werke*, 1967 (Vols. VII and VIII, *Collected Works*).

Bibliography
Demetz, Peter, ed. *Brecht: A Collection of Critical Essays.*
Dickson, Keith A. *Towards Utopia: A Study of Brecht.*
Esslin, Martin. *Bertolt Brecht: The Man and His Work.*
Gray, Ronald. *Brecht.*
Weideli, Walter. *The Art of Bertolt Brecht.*

Jennifer Michaels

PEARL S. BUCK

Born: Hillsboro, West Virginia; June 26, 1892
Died: Danby, Vermont; March 6, 1973

Principal short fiction

The First Wife and Other Stories, 1933; *Today and Forever*, 1941; *Far and Near, Stories of Japan, China, and America*, 1947; *Fourteen Stories*, 1961; *Hearts Come Home and Other Stories*, 1962; *The Good Deed*, 1969; *East and West*, 1975; *The Lovers and Other Stories*, 1977; *The Woman Who Was Changed*, 1979.

Other literary forms

Pearl S. Buck's over ninety published works include novels, plays, short stories, biographies, autobiography, nonfiction, translations, and children's books. She was awarded the Nobel Prize in Literature for her novel *The Good Earth* (1931) and for the biographies of her missionary parents, *The Exile* (1936) and *Fighting Angel* (1936). Other well-known works based on her personal experience in China include *China As I See It* (1970), *China: Past and Present* (1972), and *The Chinese Novel* (1939).

Influence

Buck was the first American woman to receive the Nobel Prize in Literature, and her realistic and insightful treatment of international subjects gives her work great popular appeal. Her stories and articles, which have appeared in many newspapers and magazines, reflect a humanitarian concern and a belief that literature should belong to the common man. Her fiction has been translated into more than thirty languages, and she is known for her charitable work throughout Asia and America.

Story characteristics

Buck's stories of China, Japan, India, Great Britain, and America emphasize the universal human characteristics of ordinary people encountering personal or cultural conflicts. Her stories of old ways of life in Asia resemble folktales. Love interest dominates many of the stories whether the settings are Eastern or Western, ancient or contemporary. Dialogue and action are principal techniques developing theme and character.

Biography

Pearl Sydenstricker Buck spent her childhood and young adult years in China with her missionary parents, where she attended American schools and studied with a Confucian tutor. Then she attended Randolph-Macon Woman's College in Virginia before returning to China, where she married John Lossing

Buck, an American agricultural expert. She received her M. A. in English literature from Cornell, and soon began publishing extensively. In 1932 she received the Pulitzer Prize for *The Good Earth* (1931). She divorced John Lossing Buck in 1935 and later that same year married Richard J. Walsh, president of the John Day publishing firm. Elected to the National Institute of Arts and Letters in 1936, she won the Nobel Prize in 1937. She founded the East and West Association, an organization working toward greater international understanding, and the Pearl Buck Foundation, an agency supporting homeless Amerasian children throughout Asia. Proceeds from her posthumous publications continue to fund the agency.

Analysis

Pearl S. Buck's best-known stories are typically those published first in large circulation magazines, then included in collections of her short fiction. "The Enemy," "Hearts Come Home," and "The Good Deed" are examples reflecting Buck's international themes. By depicting characters in exotic or potentially threatening surroundings, Buck heightens cultural contrasts and emphasizes common human characteristics. The outsiders she presents may meet a Good Samaritan figure, fall in love and marry, or achieve greater understanding of others and themselves as Buck foregrounds the power of human beings, however weak and short-sighted they may be, to transform one another intellectually and emotionally.

In her short fiction, as in her novel *The Good Earth*, universal human experiences dominate: love, marriage, birth of children, death of loved ones, threats of natural disaster, and the encroachment of new ways on old culture that create major conflicts. The stories, however, often lack the realism of the novel, and occasionally they become sentimental and didactic. Still, their color and simplicity of style enabled Buck to succeed in reaching the wide audience she felt literature should serve.

In "The Enemy," a story set in Japan during World War II, a wounded American washes up on the beach near the home of a respected Japanese surgeon, who finds both his daily activities and traditional attitudes transformed by their encounter. Before the American's appearance, Dr. Sadao Hoki and his family live according to the old Japanese ways despite his modern profession. Their home has the traditional inner and outer courts and gardens tended by servants; Dr. Hoki's father had lived with them until his death. The Hokis' marriage, too, is traditional, for although they met in America where both were students, they waited to fall in love until after their marriage had been parentally arranged in Japan. Mrs. Hoki remains respectfully silent much of the time she is in her husband's presence; she eats only after he has eaten his own meal. The narrative voice reveals that Dr. Hoki has many tender feelings for her because of her devotion to the old ways.

The exposition of the story is complete after the narrator describes Dr.

Hoki's thoughts as he stands gazing at the islands beyond his home. These were, according to his old father, "stepping stones to the future for Japan," a future for which he prepared his son with the best American education available. When Mrs. Hoki arrives to tell her husband that the meal is prepared, a figure appears in the mists along the rocky coast. As the man staggers, finally collapsing unconscious, they rush toward him, expecting to find an injured fisherman. With fear and horror, however, they discover that he is a white man, and they cannot decide at first what they should do with him.

They are unable to put the man back into the sea although they realize that for fear of the authorities they should do just that. When they move the injured man to safety, their servants leave for both political and superstitious reasons because they believe it is wrong to harbor an enemy. Only Mrs. Hoki remains to aid her husband when he discovers a bullet lodged near the wounded man's kidney. She washes the man's body, which she cannot bear for her husband to touch at first; then she manages to administer the anesthetic, although the sight of the man's wound sickens her. Her husband, on the other hand, marvels that the young man has survived this long and strives at length to remove the bullet without creating paralysis. Indeed, throughout the surgery Dr. Hoki cannot help speaking to the patient, addressing him as a friend despite his foreign appearance. They realize in the course of their ministrations that the man is an American, probably an escaped prisoner of war, for his body shows signs of abuse.

The surgery is successful, and the couple settles into a period of hope and fear as they await the patient's recovery. When soldiers appear with a summons, the doctor is terrified until he learns that he is needed to treat an ailing Japanese general. After the general begins to recover, the doctor confesses to him that he has helped a wounded American who would have surely died without his help and that now he cannot bear to execute the American after having spent so many years with Americans when he was in medical school. The general agrees to send assassins who will, within the next three days, murder the American even as he lies in the doctor's house.

Yet the days and nights pass, and the Hokis note only the American's recovery of strength and his deep gratitude toward them. Again they confront an opportunity to save him; the doctor gives him a boat, clothing, and food so that he may escape to a neighboring island and wait for a fishing boat. Days later, the doctor again confesses to the general that the American has somehow escaped, and in a strange reversal, the general realizes with considerable anxiety that he has forgotten his promise to the doctor. The general then begs the doctor not to reveal their secret to the authorities, and the doctor willingly swears to the general's loyalty before returning home to discover his servants returned and peace restored.

Remaining somehow troubled, Dr. Hoki turns to face the island "steppingstones" of progress as he recalls the ugly faces of all the white people he has ever known and ponders why he could not kill the young white enemy. This resolution to the story suggests that although no dramatic change has occurred in the lives of the Japanese family, an awakening has perhaps been achieved as they discovered that they must for human reasons help the injured American.

In "Hearts Come Home," a modern young businessman of China finally affirms the old ways of his culture. David Lin, a manager in a printing house, discovers to his surprise a young woman of simple beauty and individuality in the unlikely setting of a sophisticated modern dance in the home of a wealthy banker. The girl turns out to be the banker's daughter, visiting her father briefly before returning to school. Sensing in her a kindred spirit, Lin falls desperately in love with her because she is so different from the other sophisticated women of Shanghai.

Throughout David Lin's pursuit of Phyllis, the atmosphere, dialogue, and actions of their courtship heighten cultural contrasts between old and new in China. David spares no expense in treating her to the finest modern entertainment: they dance, drive about in the car, enjoy imported foods, and converse in a fashionable mixture of Chinese and American slang. Yet they grow distant rather than intimate; although they exchange kisses in the American fashion, David perceives Phyllis withdrawing from him, hiding her true personality more and more as the days pass.

He learns why one day when she suddenly asks him in Chinese whether he actually enjoys what they are doing, dancing in such a foreign and unrestrained style. Discovering that they share a dislike for dancing, she opens her heart to him, revealing to his pleased surprise that foreign things disgust her and that she does them only to please him.

The love for tradition that David and Phyllis share brings them close to each other in a new way. They exchange their traditional Chinese names, and before they know it they find themselves describing a Chinese marriage in which the old ways are celebrated. No longer will they kiss, wear foreign clothes, or eat foreign foods; their single-story house will have many courts and gardens filled with happy children. Yet David does not propose. He merely speaks of an arrangement which must soon be completed by their parents. Phyllis bids him a respectful goodbye according to the appropriate Chinese formula, and David leaves, peacefully contemplating their future.

"The Good Deed" portrays the impact of cultural changes on several generations, a common theme in Buck's work. Like "Hearts Come Home," this story suggests that the old ways can be valuable and satisfying. Mr. Pan, a Chinese emigrant to America, brings his aging mother to live with his wife and children in Chinatown in 1953. He discovers, however, that in saving her from the marauders destroying her native village, he has only brought her to another kind of suffering. For she sickens at the rebellion of his children, his wife's inability to speak her native tongue, and the loneliness of life in a busy city. Although Mr. Pan and his wife can supply the aged woman with excellent Chinese food and physical comforts, her spirit weakens daily.

The Pans decide in desperation that a visitor may help, and they invite Lili Yang, a young Chinese social worker, to visit old Mrs. Pan. Lili listens with interest as the old woman describes her native village, which lies in a wide valley from which the mountains rise as sharply as tiger's teeth. A gentle friendship develops between the two women, but a conflict develops when old Mrs. Pan discovers that Lili, twenty-seven years old, remains unmarried. The aged one is shocked and troubled as she concludes that Lili's parents had been remiss in their duties by failing to arrange a satisfactory marriage for their daughter before their deaths. Lili weeps for the children she has always wanted, although she tries to hide her loneliness from old Mrs. Pan.

Once Lili has returned to her work, old Mrs. Pan confronts her son with the responsibility of securing a husband for Lili. Indeed, the aged one decides that she herself will serve as Lili's parent, if her son will only supply her with a list of appropriate prospects. Such a good deed will be counted well in heaven for all concerned. Through the succeeding weeks old Mrs. Pan's life reflects her new-found purpose. With renewed energy she commands Mr. Pan to seek out unattached men of good character so that she may contact their parents, a project he finds most amusing as he recalls secretly that even he and his wife had fallen in love first, then allowed their parents to arrange a marriage later. He strives to explain to his mother that life in America is different, yet old Mrs. Pan remains determined.

Although she may do little else on her own, old Mrs. Pan stares daily out a window at the strangers passing along the street, hardly a suitable method of securing a mate for Lili, but at least a means of examining the young men of Chinatown. She develops an acquaintanceship with a young man who manages his father's pottery shop directly across the street. Learning from her son that this son of old Mr. Lim is wealthy and educated, she fixes upon him as an excellent prospect for Lili. Her son laughs at this possibility and tries to convince her that the young man will not submit to such an arrangement: he is handsome and educated, but Lili is plain and of simple virtue. At this argument, old Mrs. Pan becomes angry, reminding him that often women who lack beauty have much kinder hearts than their more attractive peers. She gives up her argument and makes plans of her own.

In order to meet the young man and perhaps at least introduce him to Lili, old Mrs. Pan waits until her son and his wife are gone and then asks one of the children to lead her across the street so that she may buy two bowls. The child dislikes her, however, and abandons her as soon as they reach the curb in front of the pottery shop. Fortunately, the young son of Mr. Lim rescues her, helping her into the shop and pleasantly conversing with her in excellent Chinese as she rests briefly. He then helps her find the bowls she seeks and they converse at greater length concerning the complexity of life in a large city. She finds herself confessing that if it had not been for Lili Yang, she would never have even looked out the window. When he asks who Lili Yang may be, she will not speak of her, for it would not be proper to discuss a virtuous young woman with a young man. Instead old Mrs. Pan goes into a lengthy speech on the virtues of women who are not beautiful. When he concludes that Lili must not be beautiful, old Mrs. Pan merely says that perhaps he will meet Lili some day and then they will discuss the matter of her beauty. Old Mrs. Pan, satisfied that she has made a point, leaves with graciousness and dignity.

Returning home with the purchased bowls, she informs her son that she has spoken with old Mr. Lim's son and found him indeed pleasant. Her son realizes immediately what she has been doing and secretly cooperates by inviting Lili to visit them again, providing Mrs. Pan with an opportunity to introduce the young people. Old Mrs. Pan, however, achieves much more satisfaction than he expects, for in taking Lili with her to buy more pottery, old Mrs. Pan meets old Mr. Lim. While Lili and young James Lim are conversing in English, she and the aged father agree quietly that perhaps a match is possible and that certainly to arrange a marriage is the best of all good deeds under heaven. Observing the young people together, they set a date to have the horoscopes of the children read and to arrange the match; the date they choose, the reader learns, is the day of Lili and James's first American-style date.

A final theme appearing late in Pearl Buck's work is the search for female identity. In several early novels, including *East Wind: West Wind* (1930) and *This Proud Heart* (1938), she presents women struggling to fulfill their potential in antagonistic cultural settings. In the novella *The Woman Who Was Changed*, Buck depicts a woman who succeeds in expressing herself in the artistic and personal spheres. A particularly contemporary concern, women's struggles appear also in Buck's autobiography, *My Several Worlds* (1954).

Major publications other than short fiction

NOVELS: *East Wind: West Wind*, 1930; *The Good Earth*, 1931; *The Mother*, 1934; *A House Divided*, 1935; *This Proud Heart*, 1938; *The Patriot*, 1939; *Dragon Seed*, 1942; *The Promise*, 1943; *Come, My Beloved*, 1953; *Command the Morning*, 1959; A Bridge for Passing, 1962; *The Goddess Abides*, 1972; *All Under Heaven*, 1973; *The Rainbow*, 1974; *Secrets of the Heart*, 1976.

Bibliography

Buck, Pearl S. and Carlos Romulo. *Friend to Friend.*
Doyle, Paul A. *Pearl S. Buck.*
Phelps, William Lyon. *Autobiography with Letters.*
Spencer, Cornelia. *The Exile's Daughter.*

Chapel Louise Petty

GEORGE WASHINGTON CABLE

Born: New Orleans, Louisiana; October 12, 1844
Died: St. Petersburg, Florida; January 31, 1925

Principal short fiction

Old Creole Days, 1879; *Madame Delphine*, 1881; *Strange True Stories of Louisiana*, 1889; *Strong Hearts*, 1899; *Posson Jone' and Pere Raphael*, 1909; *The Flower of the Chapdelaines*, 1918.

Other literary forms

George Washington Cable's published books include several novels and collections of essays in addition to his short stories. His first novel, *The Grandissimes* (1880), captured national attention and widespread praise. His essays, although less popular, delineated and criticized social, economic, and political conditions in the South.

Influence

Cable was the first literary voice of the New South. He contributed to the wave of local-color fiction about to sweep the nation, his attentive descriptions and reproduction of dialects inspiring others to look to their own environments. Cable opened literature to new areas of the human experience that became more powerfully depicted by Erskine Caldwell, Tennessee Williams, and William Faulkner.

Story characteristics

Cable's stories are an individualistic mixture of reality and romance. His characters and settings are based largely on extensive research of true accounts; Cable combined them with romantic plots, frequently melodramatic, and attained an allusive richness. Possessing a strongly developed social consciousness, Cable was rarely able to keep his social criticism out of his literature.

Biography

After the death of his father, George Washington Cable left school at the age of twelve and worked in a warehouse. During the years he should have been in college he was a Confederate soldier. Ever eager to learn, he read incessantly while in the service. After the war he was a reporter for a short time, then a clerk for a cotton firm while continuing to publish personal essays signed "Drop Shot" for the New Orleans *Picayune*. In 1873, he met Edward King, who carried copies of his stories to the editors of *Scribner's Monthly*. In October of that year Cable's first story was published, and his first novel was published the following year. Desiring to be closer to literary circles,

Cable left the South and settled his family in Northampton, Massachusetts. He loved the energetic atmosphere of the North, and much of what he wrote about the South after the move lacked the clarity and fire of his earlier work. During a return trip to the South in 1925, Cable died, leaving stories of a period which would never be again.

Analysis

By the 1880's, much of the passion that had divided the country during the Civil War had been displaced by a growing interest about life in other regions of the newly rejoined republic. No longer separated by political and economic differences, people began not only to accept cultural differences but also to express keen interest in them, and the fiction of local color was perfectly suited to these readers. Stories of the day tended to emphasize verisimilitude of detail within scenic elements: settings were often colorful extravaganzas; characters were typically drawn to emphasize peculiarities of their region or culture yet were often poorly developed; and plots were often thin.

These characteristics are reflected in George Washington Cable's stories of New Orleans: settings sparkle with picturesque detail and rich imagery; and character descriptions emphasize the cultural or regional peculiarities of speech, manner, and thought. Cable's characters are rarely developed beyond the superficial, being distanced by narrative perspective, vague in motivation, and frequently shrouded in mystery. Plots are sketchy events, lacking causal relationships and frequently relying on melodrama. Given these general characteristics, Cable's stories could be pigeonholed as merely more local color; but then much that is specifically Cable's richness would be lost. Deeper elements of Cable's unique literary perspective, however, play an important role in the total artistic impact of his stories. His New Orleans still retained much of her international flavor and embraced a unique mixture of races, clashing cultures, opposing values, old loyalties, and old hatreds; poverty and wealth coexisted; and caste systems were accepted and propagated. Cable's stongly developed social consciousness directed his writing talents to portray these elements sensitively. Thus, while preserving the picturesque, Cable probed the ramifications of racial juxtaposition and of social problems capturing more completely the spirit of his literary domain. This added dimension of circumstantial reality, born out of Cable's personality and New Orleans' uniqueness, distinguishes Cable's powerful stories from the mass of local-color fiction of his day.

Cable's first story, " 'Sieur George," reflects characteristics typical both of local-color fiction and of Cable's fiction. The standard picturesque setting, in this case an old tenement building, rises before us as the narrator masterfully describes it: "With its gray stucco peeling off in broad patches, it has the solemn look of gentility in rags, and stands, or, as it were, hangs, about the corner of two ancient streets, like a faded fop who pretends to be looking for employment." The simile of inanimate object to animate one is precise, and the images reinforce each other to create a subtle atmosphere of age and decay. Through its doors are seen "masses of cobwebbed iron . . . overhung by a creaking sign" into a courtyard "hung with many lines of wet clothes, its sides hugged by rotten staircases that seem vainly trying to clamber out of the rubbish." The neighborhood has been "long since given up to fifth-rate shops." The setting is thus vividly drawn by a composite of details each artistically contributing to a subtle atmosphere of time and ruin vital to the story's texture.

It is not unusual for Cable's characters to echo the atmosphere of the setting, giving it an organic quality that continues the link of inanimate to animate. When 'Sieur George first appeared, both he and the neighborhood were "fashionable." At the time of the story, some fifty years later, he is a reclusive "square small man" draped in a "newly repaired overcoat." No longer fashionable and usually drunk, 'Sieur George stumbles home "never careening to right or left but now forcing himself slowly forward, as if there was a high gale in front, and now scudding briskly ahead at a ridiculous little dogtrot, as if there was a tornado behind." The descriptive detail is visually vivid and continues the image of time and its erosion.

As is typical of local-color fiction, however, 'Sieur George is rather super-ficially portrayed, and this weakens the story. His actions are related to us by the omniscient narrator, whose detached perspective never allows us to experience any genuine sympathetic involvement with 'Sieur George. The reader hears about him but never knows his thoughts or feelings; conse-quently, he seems little more than a cardboard cutout. His motivations are vague, and his daily drunks continue only to be interrupted unexpectedly by surprising events. One day 'Sieur George shocks the neighborhood as he emerges from his apartment in full regimentals and marches off to the Mexican War, leaving his sister behind to become the new occupant of his rooms. Several years later, he suddenly reappears with battle scars and a tall dark companion. 'Sieur George and the stranger visit the sister weekly until her marriage to the stranger is announced by her appearance in bridal array. With the newlyweds gone, 'Sieur George returns to his rooms and drunken habits until the pattern is again interrupted when he returns home with the couple's infant. Since her mother had died and her drunken father had drowned in the river, 'Sieur George attentively raises the girl until it would violate pro-prieties for her to stay; finally, in a senseless moment, he blurts out that the only way for her to stay is for her to become his wife. She utters a mournful cry, runs to her room, and early the next morning leaves for a convent. 'Sieur George returns to drunkenness and finally becomes a penniless, homeless drifter searching the prairie "to find a night's rest in the high grass"—"and there's an end."

Not only are his motivations vague but he is also shrouded in Cable's frequent cloak of mystery. After 'Sieur George has lived in the neighborhood for about a year, "something happened that greatly changed the tenor of his life." "Hints of a duel, of a reason warped, of disinheritance, and many other unauthorized rumors, fluttered up and floated off." Soon he begins to display the "symptoms of decay" stumbling home, and "whatever remuneration he received went its way for something that left him dingy and threadbare." The artistically interwoven pictures of him recycle the images of decay and ruin, but the only thing the reader knows that 'Sieur George cares about, and strongly so, is the mysterious small hair trunk he carefully guards. Even 'Sieur George's implied heroism is dubious and unconvincing. The reader hears about him marching off to war, returning with battle scars, and bravely directing the infant to womanhood; yet each admirable event on the one hand is treated only summarily, and on the other is undercut by his return to drunkenness. He is not a great man who, in a weak moment, has fallen prey to vicious evils; neither he nor his vices have any true tragic element. Finally, he is not a tragic man inspiring our sympathy, but merely a man in a pathetic situation, and it is the feeling for his situation with which the reader is left.

It is 'Sieur George's landlord, Kookoo, who emerges most vividly from this story. Like his tenant and his building, Kookoo also shows the effects of time, for the "ancient Creole" has grown "old and wrinkled and brown." He is vividly sketched by three descriptive strokes: "He smokes cascarilla, wears velveteen and is as punctual as an executioner." Our perception of Kookoo is enhanced by the narrator's attitude toward him as a "periodically animate mummy" posessing "limited powers of conjecture." Kookoo's favorite pastimes are to eavesdrop on his tenants, watch the habits of 'Sieur George, and revel in the mystery of 'Sieur George's small hair trunk. His personality emerges through his actions, clearly motivated by nosiness and curiosity. Moreover, the reader becomes a partner to his consciousness as 'Sieur George leaves for war, taking the omniscient narrator with him. It is Kookoo, driven by a fifty-year-old curiosity and taking advantage of 'Sieur George's open door and drunken stupor, who leads the reader to the mysterious trunk and a final revelation about its owner: "The trunk was full, full, crowded down and running over full, of the tickets of the Havanna Lottery!"

The plot of " 'Sieur George" is thin, often vague, and finally melodramatic; and the climax is less than satisfying because the ramifications of compulsive gambling have not been portrayed in 'Sieur George's superficial development. It is not uncommon for Cable, with his social consciousness, to give social problems an antagonistic role, but the problem here is that neither 'Sieur George nor his vices stand out clearly enough against the images of Kookoo and Creole life; thus, their possible impact is lost in the collage. What holds the reader's attention, however, is the sustained suspense created by the adroit changes in the angle of narration. The perspective shifts back and forth between the omniscient narrator and Kookoo: the narrator, who initially dominates the reader's perspective of 'Sieur George, demonstrates a vast knowledge with a detached precision; when 'Sieur George is absent, however, the reader becomes partner with Kookoo, whose perspective is limited but allows deeper involvement. When 'Sieur George returns, so does the perspective of the omniscient narrator. Not only does the reader know both "sides" of the story, but also the suspense of Kookoo's curiosity is sustained as the narrator continues. This technique and its adroit management create a sustained suspense that holds the reader to the end. Cable's changing angles of narration, along with the scenic setting and glimpses of Creole life, are the final salvation of the story. The reader may well be disappointed by the less than satisfying climax, but reaching it is a fine experience, and the final praise of the story is that it is so well told.

In a later story, "Jean-ah Poquelin," Cable uses basically the same techniques, but much more effectively. The story begins in a time when the "newly established American Government was the most hateful thing in Louisiana—when the Creoles were still kicking at such vile innovations as the trial by jury, American dances, anti-smuggling laws, and the printing of the Governor's proclamation in English." This atmosphere of conflict is quickly followed by a sense of impending doom as the narrator centers the reader's attention on the stark details of the old Poquelin plantation: standing above the marsh, "aloof from civilization," "lifted up on pillars, grim, solid, and spiritless," "like a gigantic ammunition wagon stuck in the mud and abandoned by some retreating army." Two dead cypress trees "dotted with roosting vultures" and crawling waters filled with reptiles "to make one shudder to the ends of his days" create around the home an atmosphere of foreboding. This atmosphere is continued as the description of Jean Marie Poquelin unfolds. He was "once an opulent indigo planter, standing high in the esteem" of his friends, but is "now a hermit, alike shunned by and shunning all who had ever known him." Typically reflecting the setting's atmosphere, Jean is yet somewhat unique among local-color characters because of his multifaceted and full development.

His personality is discovered through a series of flashbacks to happier times. Jean had been "a bold, frank, impetuous, chivalric adventurer," but there was no trait for which he was better known than "his apparent fondness" for his little brother, Jacques. Jacques, thirty years Jean's junior and really a half-brother, was "a gentle studious book-loving recluse." Together "they lived upon the ancestral estate like mated birds, one always on the wing, the other always in the nest." The brothers' tranquil relationship is abruptly interrupted when Jean returns from a two-year slaving expedition apparently without Jacques, who, unable to tolerate his brother's long absence, had begged to go along. Jean remained silent on this issue, but rumor was that Jacques had returned "but he had never been seen again," and "dark suspicion" fell upon Jean as his name "became a symbol of witchery, devilish crime, and hideous nursery fictions." Rumors of blood-red windows, owls with human voices, and the ghost of the departed brother keep the plantation and Jean shrouded in mystery while children viciously taunt him in the streets, calling names and throwing dirt clods with youthful expertise, as ignorant adults blame him for all their misfortunes. Old Jean betrays his silence as latent boldness responds to this ill treatment; "rolling up his brown fist" he would "pour forth such an unholy broadside of French imprecation and invective as would all but craze" the Creole children "with delight." His actions are justified, and the reader cheers him on as he becomes personally involved in the story.

Time passes, and immigrants flood New Orleans, forcing growing pains on the city. Greedy non-Creole American land developers and displaced Creoles began to encroach on Jean's lonely home. Through Jean's reaction to these forces, the reader learns more about him and becomes more deeply involved in his plight. Hoping to stop the invaders, Jean appeals to the Governor, and, in doing so, he projects much of his personality: he stands proudly with his large black eye "bold and open like that of a war horse, and his jaw shut together with the fierceness of iron." His open-neck shirt reveals "a herculean breast, hard and grizzled," yet there is "no fierceness or defiance in his look" but rather a "peaceful and peaceable fearlessness." Jean's heroic stature is sensitively human for on his face, "not marked in one or another feature, but as it were laid softly upon the countenance like an almost imperceptible veil, was the imprint of some great grief"—faint "but once seen, there it hung." In broken English, Jean protests the invasion of his privacy, but the reader senses the futility of his attempt as he is answered by questions about the wicked rumors. His temper flares as he declares, "I mine me hown bizniss." Jean's motivations may still be vague, but the strength of his convictions as to his rights and his powerful presence inspire our respect.

Although he marches from the officials' rooms, Jean is kept ever present as he is discussed by the American and Creole developers. Old stories are retold, and Jean gains nobility as the greedy invaders callously plan how to oust him so that they can replace his home with a market. Their shallow commercialism and ignorant superstitions are illuminating foils to Jean's deep-seated desire to preserve his home. Jean's only champion, Little White, only temporarily stalls a mob determined to "chirivari" him, and ultimately they rush forward only to be met by Jean's only slave, an African mute, carting a draped coffin through the front gate. Old Jean is dead; and the crowd stands silent except for its unanimous gasp at seeing the white figure slowly walking behind the cart. The cause of so many rumors and cruelties is the "living remains—all that was left—of little Jacques Poquelin, the long-hidden brother—a leper, as white as snow." The African adjusts the weight of the coffin on his shoulders, and "without one backward glance upon the unkind human world, turning their faces toward the ridge in the depths of the swamp known as Leper's Land, they stepped into the jungle, disappeared and were never seen again."

Melodramatic touches are frequent as the story turns on Jean's selfless devotion. The climax brings the reader's compassion to a peak well supported by all that has been learned about Jean: how his friends have spoken so well of him; the knowledge of his loving relationship with Jacques; and his justifiable responses to the jeering children, Creole cruelty, and non-Creole American aggression. Although his motivations are vague until the end, and he is shrouded in mystery, the rightness of his actions and speeches assures the reader of his innate goodness.

Cable again employs a changing angle of narration, but Jean is ever the subject of other characters' thoughts and actions; thus, he is ever kept before the reader. All the elements of the story are clearly aimed at telling the story of Jean and his doomed resistance. Compassion for Jean and his brother remains strong after the conclusion of the story, one of the few in which Cable beautifully balances his romantic fiction and social criticism. The story succeeds as both; it is a haunting "ghost" story while it attacks ignorant prejudice and makes a touching plea for human compassion.

Cable was the first literary voice of the New South. Writing within the realm of local-color fiction, he enriched his stories with the circumstantial reality of local history; he preserved the beautiful detail of colorful New Orleans in impressionistic backgrounds peopled by unique characters; and he was the first writer to bring the crude patois of the Creoles accurately to print. Cable's stories are a unique blend of romantic elements and circumstantial reality drawn from his literary domain. Although many of his stories are hampered by a lack of clear direction, the cluttering, often paragraphic glimpses of different cultures are rewarding reading; and where Cable achieved a precise utility of a story's elements, the total impact is unforgettable.

Major publications other than short fiction

NOVELS: *The Grandissimes*, 1880; *The Creoles of Louisiana*, 1884; *Dr. Sevier*, 1884; *Bonaventure*, 1888; *John March, Southerner*, 1894; *The Cavalier*, 1901; *Bylow Hill*, 1902; *Kincaid's Battery*, 1908; *Gideon's Band*, 1914; *Lovers of Louisiana*, 1918.

NONFICTION: *The Silent South*, 1885; *The Negro Question*, 1890.

Bibliography
Bikle, Lucy L. C. *George W. Cable: His Life and Letters*.

Butcher, Philip. *George W. Cable*.

Cardwell, Gay A. *Twins of Genius*.

Rubin, Louis D., Jr. *George W. Cable: The Life and Times of a Southern Heretic*.

Turner, Arlin. *George W. Cable: A Biography*.

Kathy Ruth Frazier

JAMES M. CAIN

Born: Annapolis, Maryland; July 1, 1892
Died: University Park, Maryland; October 27, 1977

Principal short fiction

"Pastorale," 1928; "The Taking of Monfaucon," 1929; "The Baby in the Icebox," 1933; "Come-Back," 1934; "Dead Man," 1936; "Hip, Hip, the Hippo," 1936; "The Birthday Party," 1936; "Brush Fire," 1936; "Coal Black," 1937; "Everything but the Truth," 1937; "The Girl in the Storm," 1940; "Pay-off Girl," 1952; "Cigarette Girl," 1953; "Two O'Clock Blonde," 1953; "The Visitor," 1961.

Other literary forms

In addition to his uncollected stories appearing in magazines, James M. Cain wrote many articles from the time he was a reporter for the *Baltimore Sun* (1919-1923). He was also an editorial writer for the *New York World* (1924-1931) and editor-in-chief of the *Lorraine Cross*, the official newspaper of the A.E.F., 79th. He is principally known for his crime novels, most of which have been made into Hollywood movies. *The Postman Always Rings Twice* (1934), which has been a best seller for more than forty years, was filmed both in France and in Italy.

Influence

Cain's novels have sustained their popularity, particulary *The Postman Always Rings Twice*, which Albert Camus claimed influenced his novel *The Stranger*; critics, following this acknowledgment, have worked out the multitude of correspondences between the two works. Twelve of Cain's books have been reprinted in England; others have been translated into fifteen languages, including Danish, Portuguese, Spanish, French, and Yugoslavian.

Story characteristics

Cain does not write detective stories, but presents murders, while they are being committed, from the criminal's point of view. The perspective is cynical; the tone is tough; and there is little description to interrupt the swift and relentless pace of the action. The settings are usually urban; exposition is confined to dialogue, which is blunt, brisk, and fast-paced—Cain prided himself on eliminating even the tag lines (he said) in order not to slow down momentum. The characters are commonplace and usually one-dimensional. Cain said that his plot formula was to allow his characters to fulfill their forbidden impulses and to destroy themselves by having them gratified. He likens his plot lines to the opening of Pandora's box.

Biography

James Mallahan Cain was the oldest of five children of Rose Mallahan, a singer, and James William Cain, a professor at St. John's College in Annapolis, Maryland. His grandparents were Irish immigrants who settled in New Haven, Connecticut, where his father attended Yale University. Cain was eleven when his father became the president of Washington College. Cain enrolled there at the age of fifteen, was graduated in 1910, received a master's degree in 1917, and taught math and English for a year after giving up his ambition to become an opera singer. He was a reporter for several newspapers and taught journalism at St. John's; then for seventeen years he wrote scripts in Hollywood. His fourth marriage, to opera singer Florence Macbeth Whitwell in 1947, was a happy one, which encouraged him to write about music in four of his novels. The literary figure who exerted the single greatest influence on his career was H. L. Mencken, with whom he corresponded and who published his work in his periodical, the *American Mercury*.

Analysis

The protagonist of "Brush Fire" is one of the many men made homeless by the Depression, who drifts from place to place in search of work. James M. Cain was fascinated by the tramps he saw riding the boxcars into California. "Dead Man" is about a tramp who kills a railroad cop, while "The Girl in the Storm" is about another hobo who gets off a train during a downpour to seek refuge and finally finds sanctuary in a supermarket. In order to write accurately about the vagrants in *The Moth* (1948), Cain visited the missions in Los Angeles where tramps gathered and interviewed many of them.

Lack of exposition is typical of Cain's narrative style. The reader is immediately confronted with an action in the present; in only one of Cain's twelve novels is there any flashback to explain the protagonist's background. What mattered to Cain's readers was not his characters' appearance. Cain's editors usually had to ask him to be more explicit about what his people looked like; the most he ever gave them was a movie-star approximation: "Like Clark Gable [or some other movie star]—fill it in yourself." What mattered to Cain was a man's "presence" as expressed in action. It was probably this virile approach to storytelling that endeared him to the French existentialists and the postwar Italians, who favored such a style.

The opening scene of "Brush Fire" depicts a group of men wielding shovels against a forest fire, coughing from the smoke and cursing. They have come up from the railroad yards on the promise of money to be made; they have been fed a ration of stew in army mess kits, outfitted in denims and shoes, and taken by truckloads from Los Angeles to the hills to fight this brush fire. We do not learn the protagonist's name until well into the story when the CCC man calls out the roll; we never learn the name of his girl friend. The one introspective moment in the story expresses the protagonist's regret at leaving her:

> They parted—she to slip into the crowd unobtrusively; he to get his mess kit, for the supper line was already formed. As he watched the blue dress flit between the tents and disappear, a gulp came into his throat; it seemed to him that this girl he had held in his arms, whose name he hadn't even thought to inquire, was almost the sweetest human being he had ever met in his life.

By the end of the story he has committed murder for the sake of this nameless girl, and the man he kills in the evening is the same man whose life he had saved in the morning. The reporters who have covered both events are struck with the inherent ironies, but the protagonist, who moves unthinkingly from blind impulse, is unaware of ironies; such abstractions are foreign to him.

Cain keeps the story moving by not stopping to examine motivations; he simply carries the reader along in the rushing momentum of the story. The third shift is summoned for roll call and told to turn over their shovels to the fourth shift that is arriving. They assemble with singed hair, smoke-seared lungs, and burned feet. At the same moment that we learn the protagonist's name, we learn the antagonist's also.

> As each name was called there was a loud "Yo" so when his name, Paul Larkin, was called, he yelled "Yo" too. Then the foreman was calling a name and becoming annoyed because there was no answer. "Ike Pendleton! Ike Pendleton!"

Instantly Larkin races up the slope toward the fire where "a cloud of smoke doubled him back." He retreats, sucks in a lungful of air, then charges to where a body lay face down. The action is tersely rendered in taut, lean prose. "He tried to lift, but his lungful of air was spent: he had to breathe or die. He expelled it, inhaled, screamed at the pain of the smoke in his throat."

Critics complain that Cain's characters are so elemental that they seem stripped down to an animal vitality; in fact, it is precisely to this quality that Pendleton's survival is attributed. "He fought to his feet, reeled around with the hard, terrible vitality of some kind of animal." The men are fed and paid fifty cents an hour, and then the visitors, newspaper reporters, and photographers arrive. When they ask if there were any casualties, someone remembers that a man, whose name no one can remember, has been rescued. Paul is interviewed and has his picture taken as a crowd gathers. A girl, kicking a pebble, says, "Well, ain't *that* something to be getting his picture in the paper?" They talk, he buys her an ice-cream cone, they go for a walk, they embrace, and he brings her back to the camp without ever having exchanged names.

Later he sees Ike Pendleton, with doubled fists, cursing her, and the girl, backing away, crying. The explanation of the conflict is given by an anonymous choric figure. Cain claims that this technique of communicating information through dialogue—a mode of narration which effaces the narrator—which Ernest Hemingway is usually credited as having invented, was his invention; he says that he arrived at this method of minimal exposition independently, before he had ever read any Hemingway. Its effectiveness can be judged by the shock with which the reader realizes that the girl is Mrs. Pendleton.

The fight accelerates; Paul intervenes and tension mounts toward the inevitable conclusion. That Cain can convince the reader that such an improbable event could seem inevitable is a mark of his storytelling skill. The reader is not given time to think about it as these characters act out their basest, most primitive impulses.

> He lunged at Ike with his fist—missed. Ike struck with the knife. He fended with his left arm, felt the steel cut in. With his other hand he struck, and Ike staggered back. There was a pile of shovels beside him, almost tripping him up. He grabbed one, swung, smashed it down on Ike's head. Ike went down. He stood there, waiting for Ike to get up, with that terrible vitality he had shown this morning. Ike didn't move.

This, then, is the meaning of death, that the animal motions cease, and this is the end of the story whose meaning is embodied in its action without any philosophic implications, without any cultural pretensions, a brutal depiction of sexual and aggressive drives in men too crude to sublimate them and too hungry to repress them.

Major publications other than short fiction

NOVELS: *The Postman Always Rings Twice*, 1934; *Serenade*, 1937; *Mildred Pierce*, 1941; *Love's Lovely Counterfeit*, 1942; *Three of a Kind* (*Double Indemnity, Career in C Major, The Embezzler*), 1943; *Past All Dishonor*, 1946; *The Butterfly*, 1947; *Sinful Woman*, 1947; *The Moth*, 1948; *Jealous Woman*, 1950; *Root of His Evil*, 1951; *Galatea*, 1953; *Mignon*, 1962; *The Magician's Wife*, 1965.

PLAYS: *Crashing the Gates*, 1925; *Trial by Jury*, 1928; *Theological Interlude*, 1928; *The Will of the People*, 1929; *Citizenship*, 1929; *The Governor*, 1930; *Don't Monkey with Uncle Sam*, 1933.

NONFICTION: *Our Government*, 1930.

Bibliography

Frohock, W. M. *The Novel of Violence in America: 1920-1950.*
Madden, David. *James M. Cain.*
_____ . *Tough Guy Writers of the Thirties.*
Wilson, Edmund. *Classics and Commercials.*

Ruth Rosenberg

ERSKINE CALDWELL

Born: White Oak, Georgia; December 17, 1903

Principal short fiction

American Earth, 1931; *We Are the Living*, 1933; *Kneel to the Rising Sun*, 1935; *Southways*, 1938; *Jackpot*, 1940; *Stories of Erskine Caldwell*, 1944; *The Caldwell Caravan*, 1946; *Georgia Boy and Other Stories*, 1946; *The Complete Stories*, 1953; *Gulf Coast Stories*, 1956; *Erskine Caldwell's Men and Women*, 1961.

Other literary forms

The corpus of Erskine Caldwell's work includes twenty-four novels, social criticism, an autobiography, and several "photo-text" coffee-table books. His novel *Tobacco Road* (1932) was adapted as a play and for years held the record for the longest continuous run on Broadway.

Influence

Throughout his career, Caldwell has sold more volumes than the entire holdings of the Library of Congress. His reputation rests primarily on his short stories and novels published in the 1930's and 1940's, particularly *Tobacco Road* and *God's Little Acre* (1933), which sold millions of copies. William Faulkner once listed Caldwell as one of the five best writers of his generation, but today his literary reputation has declined considerably.

Story characteristics

Caldwell is first and foremost a Southern writer. His stories are usually brief, single-scene sketches depicting lower-class whites and blacks in the rural South, and they can be grimly violent or grotesquely comic. Unlike Faulkner, whose mythic vision of the South reaffirms the lost dignity of mankind and his ability to prevail, Caldwell strips his characters of any romantic illusions of honor and presents them in their earthy, ultrarealistic simplicity. Caldwell's prose style is direct, concrete, and unadorned.

Biography

The son of a well-known Presbyterian minister, Erskine Caldwell spent his boyhood in rural Georgia and South Carolina as his father moved from church to church. In 1920 he attended Erskine College for a year and a half; in 1923 he spent a year at the University of Virginia; and in 1924 he spent a summer at the University of Pennsylvania studying economics. After working for a brief time as a reporter for the Atlanta *Journal*, he left Georgia for Maine to devote his energies to full-time writing in 1926. Caldwell wrote nearly a hundred stories and novels before placing his first major publication with Maxwell Perkins and *Scribner's Magazine*. His novels in the 1930's, known primarily for their sexual suggestiveness and violence, firmly established him as a best-selling author. In 1937, in conjunction with the famous photographer Margaret Bourke-White, Caldwell published the remarkable *You Have Seen Their Faces*, a "photo-text" depicting the plight of the Southern poor that deserves to be ranked as one of the finest examples of that genre. Caldwell was a war correspondent in Russia in 1942 and one of the few American journalists to cover the invasion of Russia. His later work is generally not as good as his early work (Faulkner once said that it "grew toward trash"), but the serious reader would do well to pay attention to *Call It Experience* (1950), his autobiography, and *Deep South: Memory and Observation* (1969), a non-fictional study of Southern religion.

Analysis

Erskine Caldwell's reputation as a short-story writer rests mainly on the collections published in the 1930's: *American Earth* (1931), *We Are the Living* (1933), *Kneel to the Rising Sun* (1935), and *Southways* (1938). Most of these stories reflect a social protest against the racial and economic oppression in the South during the Great Depression. Along with such writers as John Steinbeck and James T. Farrell, Caldwell writes of the struggles of the poor and is therefore a favorite of Marxist critics; he is also highly regarded in the Soviet Union. Although Caldwell's fiction deals with social injustice, he is not overtly didactic or doctrinaire. He may write of the violence of racial prejudice, the hypocritical state of fundamentalist religion, or the economic agonies of sharecropping worn-out farmland, yet his first concern as a writer is always with the portrayal of individual characters rather than with lofty social issues. His ideology does not interfere with his art, and the result is a clean, stark narrative that often exhibits the ultrareal qualities of nightmare.

Good literature always bears the burden of altering our comfortable preconceptions of the world, and Caldwell's best fiction produces a disturbing effect on the reader. He is fond of placing his characters in complex situations, yet he has them react to these situations with the simple tropisms of instinct or the unthinking obedience to social custom. At the heart of one of his stories may be a profound moral point—such as a white dirt farmer's choice between defending his black friend or else permitting an unjust lynching— but Caldwell's characters face moral predicaments with the amoral reflexes of an automaton. There is rarely any evidence that Caldwell's characters grasp the seriousness of their situation. They do not experience epiphanies of self-redemption or rise to mythic patterns of suffering, but rather continue to submit, unaffected, to the agonies and absurdities of their world. For this reason, Caldwell's work was frequently banned in the 1930's as pornographic and for appearing to promote gratuitous violence.

"Saturday Afternoon," for example, is the story of an offhand killing by a mob of whites of a black named Will Maxie for supposedly talking to a white girl. The fact that Will Maxie is innocent is never in question. Everyone admits that he is a "smart Negro," always properly deferential and a hard worker, but the whites hate him anyway because he makes too much money and has no vices. Will is chained to a sweetgum tree and burned alive. Yet "Saturday Afternoon" is a compelling story, not because of its sensational violence, but rather because of the chilling indifference shown by the two central characters, Tom the town butcher and Jim his helper. The story opens in the back of the fly-ridden butcher shop as Tom is settling down for an afternoon nap on the butcher block, a slab of rump roast as a pillow. Jim bursts in and tells him that a lynching party is being formed, and they hurry out to join it. The two, however, are merely following the social instinct of herding animals rather than exercising any overt malice toward Will, and even the tone of the actual killing is casual, almost nonchalant: the local druggist sends his boy to sell cokes to the crowd, and Tom and Jim are as interested in swapping slugs of moonshine as they are in Will's death. Once the spectacle is over, they return to the butcher shop for the Saturday afternoon rush, business as usual. The violence may seem gratuitous, but Caldwell's carefully controlled tone undercuts its severity and reinforces the theme that mindless indifference to brutality can be more terrifying than purposeful evil. The moral impact of the story bypasses the consciousness of the characters but catches the reader between the eyes.

In "Kneel to the Rising Sun," the title story of Caldwell's 1935 collection, he shows that both racial oppression and economic oppression are closely linked. The central conflict in the story is between the white landowner Arch Gunnard and his two sharecroppers—Lonnie, a white, and Clem, a black. It is late afternoon and Lonnie has come to Arch's gas station to ask for extra food because he is being "short-rationed." The black tenant Clem has asked for extra rations and gotten them, but Lonnie cannot be so bold. The unspoken rules of the caste system are strong, even between a white tenant and a white landowner. As Lonnie tries to make his request, Arch calmly takes out his jackknife and cuts the tail off Lonnie's dog. Lonnie leaves hungry and emasculated, his tailless dog following behind. In the second part of the story, Lonnie awakens in the night to find his old father gone from his bed. Clem helps him with the search, and they find his father trampled to death in Arch's hog pen where, in a fit of hunger, he went looking for food. As all three men view the torn body, Clem again shows the courage that Lonnie cannot by openly accusing Arch of starving his tenants. An argument ensues, and Arch leaves to drum up a lynching party. Lonnie is torn between loyalty to Clem as a friend and loyalty to his own race. He promises to lead the mob away from Clem's hiding place, but once Arch arrives, Lonnie leads him to Clem in stunned obedience. Clem dies in a hail of buckshot, and Lonnie returns home to his wife who asks if he has brought extra food. "No," Lonnie quietly replies, "no, I ain't hungry."

The institutional enemy in Caldwell's fiction, as in much of his social criticism, is not so much racial bigotry as the economic system which fosters it, for bigotry is a byproduct of an agrarian system which beats down the poor of both races. Like the plantation system it replaced, cotton sharecropping enriches the few at the expense of the many, and the violence of Clem's death in "Kneel to the Rising Sun" is no worse than the starvation leveled on Lonnie's family. Blacks are beaten into submission, and whites are evicted from the land. As one cotton-field boss says in *You Have Seen Their Faces*, "Folks here wouldn't give a dime a dozen for white tenants. They can get twice as much work out of blacks. But they need to be trained. Beat a dog and he'll obey you. They say it's the same with blacks." Caldwell treats the same issues, although in more melodramatic fashion, in the stories "Wild Flowers" and "A Knife to Cut the Cornbread With."

Caldwell's prose style is plain and direct, and his method of narration depends entirely on concrete details and colloquial dialogue. It is not a method conducive to presenting symbolic import or psychological introspection, and Caldwell's critics often accuse him of creating flat characters. Yet Caldwell's carefully controlled manipulation of external descriptions can give rise to intense states of psychological unrest, as in one of his best stories, "The Growing Season." In the story Jesse, a cotton farmer, has been working in the fields all morning trying to keep the wire grass away from his crop. He has made little headway because twelve acres of cotton is too much for one man to work. As he breaks at midday, his eyes burning bloodshot from the sun, Jesse hears "Fiddler" rattle his chain. Jesse cannot eat, and his attention repeatedly turns to the wire grass in his cotton and the rattling of Fiddler's chain. Unable to bear the heat and the weeds and the noise of the chain any longer, he herds Fiddler into a gully and brutally kills him with his shotgun and ax. The violence done, Jesse sharpens his hoe and returns to the fields, optimistic that he can save his crop. Caldwell never specifies what kind of creature "Fiddler" is, but after several close readings, it becomes clear that he is not a dog or a mule but a human being—perhaps a retarded child or a black.

Jesse's psychological state is externalized; he is what he sees and feels, and the surreal qualities of the outer world reflect his psychosis. He rubs his knuckles in his eye sockets as the sun blinds him, he cannot eat or sleep, and even Fiddler changes color. Caldwell's characters often experience a disruption of physical appetite and sensory perception as they engage in headlong pursuit of their bizarre idiosyncrasies. Furthermore, Fiddler's death produces a cathartic effect on Jesse. Caldwell implies that the choking circumstances that beat heavily on the poor require sure action to overcome them—even if that action is a violent one.

Although Caldwell's plain prose style eschews most of the traditional literary devices, the rhetorical structure of his fiction utilizes the varied repetition of details and dialogue. In "Candy-Man Beechum," Caldwell incorporates the repetitions of colloquial black speech patterns to give the story the oral rhythms of a folk ballad in prose. The narrative line of the story is simple and episodic: Candy-Man leaves the rural swamp where he works as a sawmill hand and heads for town on a Saturday night to see his gal. The language of "Candy-Man Beechum," however, is the language of the tall tale, and the opening of the story ascribes to Candy-Man the larger-than-life qualities of the folk hero: "It was ten miles out of the Ogeechee swamps, from the sawmill to the top of the ridge, but it was just one big step to Candy-Man." At each stop on his journey to town, someone asks the question, "Where you going, Candy-Man?" and he supplies various boastful answers. These questions and answers give structure to the story in much the same way that a verse and refrain give structure to a popular ballad, and, again like a popular ballad, they move toward a tragic end. As Candy-Man nears the white folks' town, the questions become more ominous until a white-boss policeman asks the final question, "What's your hurry, Candy-Man?" Candy-Man, however, will not compromise his vitality by acquiescing to his demands and is shot down in the street; even in death he maintains his own exuberant sense of identity. Caldwell uses similar kinds of repetition to heighten the erotic effect of other stories such as "August Afternoon" and "The Medicine Man."

Caldwell is often referred to as a local color writer of the "Southern Gothic" school, but the range of his work shows him to be one of the most diverse and voluminous (and neglected) writers of this century. If the subject matter of his short fiction seems somewhat limited, it is only because Caldwell insists on writing about what he knows best by first-hand observation. He has said in an interview:

> I grew up in the Great Depression in Georgia. I know how poverty smells and feels. I was poor as to eating. Poor as to clothes. Poor as to housing. And nearly everybody else was too, and you can't know about poverty any better way. You don't like it and nobody else does but you can't help yourself. So you learn to live with it, and understand it and can appreciate how others feel about it.

It is this genuine "feel" of poverty and its accompanying themes of violence, bigotry, frustration, and absurd comedy that ensures a lengthy survival of Caldwell's best works.

Major publications other than short fiction

NOVELS: *Tobacco Road*, 1932; *God's Little Acre*, 1933; *Journeyman*, 1935; *Trouble in July*, 1940; *Miss Mamma Aimee*, 1967.

NONFICTION: *Some American People*, 1935; *You Have Seen Their Faces*, 1937 (with Margaret Bourke-White); *North of the Danube*, 1939 (with Margaret Bourke-White); *Say, Is This the U.S.A.*, 1941 (with Margaret Bourke-White); *All Out on the Road to Smolensk*, 1942 (with Margaret Bourke-White); *Call It Experience*, 1951; *Around About America*, 1964; *In Search of Bisco*, 1965; *Deep South: Memory and Observation*, 1969.

Bibliography

Beach, Joseph Warren. "Erskine Caldwell," in *American Fiction, 1920-1940*.

Cantwell, Robert. *The Humorous Side of Erskine Caldwell*.

Collins, Carvel. "Introduction," in *Erskine Caldwell's Men and Women*.

Korges, James. *Erskine Caldwell*.

Sutton, William A. *Black Like It Is/Was: Erskine Caldwell's Treatment of Racial Themes*.

Voss, Arthur. *The American Short Story*.

Robert J. McNutt

HORTENSE CALISHER

Born: New York, New York; December 20, 1911

Principal short fiction

In the Absence of Angels: Stories, 1951; *Tale for the Mirror: A Novella and Other Stories*, 1962; *Extreme Magic: A Novella and Other Stories*, 1964; *The Railway Police and The Last Trolley Ride*, 1966; *The Collected Stories of Hortense Calisher*, 1975.

Other literary forms

Hortense Calisher is predominantly known as a short-story writer, but in addition to her collections of short stories, she has published, since 1951, six novels, four novellas, and an autobiographical work, *Herself* (1972). She has also written articles and reviews for *The New Yorker*, *Harper's Magazine*, *Harper's Bazaar*, *Mademoiselle*, and the *Reporter*.

Influence

Calisher is often placed in the Jamesian tradition of finely crafted stories of the psychology of human motivations. Her work reflects her strong urban background, focusing upon the complexities of modern city life as an emblem of existence in the modern age. A number of her short stories and the autobiographical work *Herself* have been praised for their insight into the psychology of women and their contributions to women's literature.

Story characteristics

Calisher's stories are primarily depictions of the complexity of human experience presented via a poetic concern with language and imagery for communicating the subtleties of characters' insights into their experience. The stories are of ordinary people going through the processes of day-to-day existence and struggling for a type of meaning for their lives. Often her characters experience defeat and disillusionment, but generally there is an ameliorative note of self-awareness and commitment to principles of love and compassion that redeem the stories from pessimism and affirm a hope for human existence.

Biography

After graduating from Barnard College in 1932 with a B. A. in English, Hortense Calisher worked at a variety of jobs in New York, including jobs as a sales clerk, a model, and a social worker for the Department of Public Welfare. In 1935, she married Heaton Bennet Heffelfinger, an engineer, and had two children. Her first marriage ended in divorce in 1958, and in 1959

Calisher married Curtis Harnack, a writer. Calisher received a Guggenheim Fellowship in creative writing in 1952 and 1955 and was nominated for the National Book Award in 1961 for *False Entry* and in 1973 for *Herself*. In 1967 she received awards from both the National Council of Arts and the American Academy of Arts and Letters. She has taught creative writing and literature courses at a number of colleges and universities, including Barnard College, Iowa State University, Sarah Lawrence College, Brandeis University, University of Pennsylvania, Columbia University, and the State University of New York at Purchase.

Analysis

Hortense Calisher has described the short story as "an apocalypse, served in a very small cup," thus indicating her Jamesian penchant for intense psychological portrayals presented within the aesthetic confines of brevity of style and economy of emotional impact. Since "A Box of Ginger," her first published story, appeared in *The New Yorker* in 1948, critics have praised Calisher's writings for their complexity of theme, verbal intricacy, and strength and multiplicity of evocation. She has been compared to Henry James and Gustave Flaubert in her passion for precision and craftsmanship and to Marcel Proust in her motifs of the many-sided psychological levels of the intricacies of human experience.

Calisher has been described as a spokesman for the "middle ground" of the ordinary, rather than the extreme, the unusual, or the bizarre. Her most convincing characters are, by and large, observers and listeners who spectate upon the mysteries of human existence, seeking viable modes of action and belief in their own individual progressions toward the development of self-identity. The existential themes of choice and commitment and the search for meaning through self-definition are pervasive in her writings, as is the influence of phenomenology. Her short stories, in fact, can be seen as exemplifications in art of Edmund Husserl's definition of the phenomenological *epochē* as "the capacity of a single moment of experience to unfold itself into endless perspectives of reality."

The themes of Calisher's stories focus upon bonding, the need for individual lives to merge in moments of appreciation, empathy, or love to assuage the emptiness, alienation, and apparent meaninglessness of much of human existence. The progression in her writings is generally outward, toward a merging or a reconciliation based upon understanding and new insight. Her stories also assert the power of illusions over everyday life and the reluctance with which fantasy is surrendered for the stark obduracy of reality.

"In Greenwich There Are Many Gravelled Walks," a story many critics consider a modern classic, is an example of Calisher's themes of bonding and insight, both often attained against a background of psychological suffering and a sense of the amorphous character of life in the modern world. On an afternoon in early August, Peter Birge has returned to the small apartment he shares with his mother after taking her to the Greenwich sanitarium she had to frequent at intervals to discover that "his usually competent solitude had become more than he could bear." He is a victim of defeated plans; the money he had saved from his Army stint for a trip abroad will now have to be spent on his mother's psychiatric treatment. His mood is one of disheartenment and isolation. Recalling taking his mother to the sanitarium on this bright, clear summer day, he senses the irony of his own plight—anyone "might have thought the two of them were a couple, any couple, just off for a day in the country." He is aware that much insanity in the modern world passes for sanity and that beneath the seeming calm of most lives lie secrets and potential complexities known only to the participants themselves.

Peter's estrangement from his mother is complete; Greenwich has claimed her through the sanitarium as it had through the Village. In the Village, she had become a fixture, a "hanger-on" in the bars in the presence and superficial camaraderie of would-be painters, philosophers, and poets, until alcoholism and a steady routine of safe and predictable fantasy—"a buttery flow of harmless little lies and pretensions"—became all that she had subsisted on for more than twenty years. Arriving at the sanitarium was like playing out one more fantasy scene from the bars, a safe world of protection and illusion. For the son, however, no illusions are left to comfort him. "It was just that while others of his age still shared a communal wonder at what life might hold, he had long since been solitary in his knowledge of what life was."

Finding being alone unbearable, Peter is prompted by his loneliness to visit his friend, Robert Vielum, for the same reason that many others stopped by, "because there was likely to be somebody there." Robert is "a perennial taker of courses" who derives a "Ponce de Leon sustenance from the young." Buttressed by family fortunes, he has ambled his way through academics, gathering up a troupe of enchanted devotees fascinated by his adirectional philosophy of hedonism and apathy. Watching him closely, Peter discovers that Robert is very much like his mother; they are "charmers, who if they could not offer you the large strength, could still atone for the lack with so many small decencies." People are drawn to Robert as they are to Peter's mother for the exhilirating excitement of "wearing one's newest façade, in the fit company of others similarly attired."

Peter discovers that he has arrived in the midst of a homosexual love triangle; Robert has abandoned his plans to go to Morocco with Vince to go to Italy with Mario Osti, a painter. Robert is charmingly aloof, totally insensitive and unresponsive to Vince's emotional sufferings over being abandoned and rejected. A fight ensues, and Vince retreats to the bedroom as Robert's daughter, Susan, arrives to spend the summer in her father's apartment. When Mario looks out the window into the courtyard and discovers that Vince has committed suicide, Robert's carefully poised game of façades and practiced indifference is shattered by the reality of human despair.

Mario's self-protecting "I'd better get out of here!" is in direct contrast to Peter's compassion and empathy for Susan, whom he feels to be a fellow survivor of the carelessness and emptiness of the chaos of other people's lives. "I don't care about any of it, really," Susan tells him. "My parents, or any of the people they tangle with." Peter finds this a feeling with which he can empathize, and he agrees even more fully with her statement, "I should think it would be the best privilege there is, though. To care, I mean." The bond of empathy, of mutual understanding of what has been lost and what is missing and needed, is established between Peter and Susan as he realizes that they are alike in their same disillusionment with the world. The story ends on a note of muted optimism as Peter tells himself that "tomorrow he would take her for a drive—whatever the weather. There were a lot of good roads around Greenwich." If one envisions Greenwich in the story, both the sanitarium and the Village, as symbols of the sterility and insanity of most modern existence, then the journey "around Greenwich" may well be an affirmation that the two young people can avoid the dissipation of their parents' lives through the bond of caring the couple has established.

"In Greenwich There Are Many Gravelled Walks" is roundly critical of the self-destructive waste of emotional abilities most people's lives become, a viewpoint even more heavily endorsed in one of Calisher's more moralistic stories, "If You Don't Want to Live I Can't Help You." On the day that Mary Ponthus, a teacher at a New England college and a scholar of some repute, is to receive an honorary doctorate of letters, she pays a visit to her nephew, Paul, as the administratrix of her nephew's trust fund. Paul has lived off the trust fund for twenty years, and his life has become one cankered with dissipation. "Foredoomed to the dilettante," he has dabbled in painting, writing, and love affairs because "these were good ways to pass the time—and of time he had so much to pass." Now too, as Mary reflects, he is dabbling in disease. Suffering from tuberculosis, Paul both refuses and neglects to take care of himself. When Mary arrives, she finds him hungover and ill from a night of wild partying. Further, she discovers that Paul's lover of several years, Helen Bonner, has left him because of his manipulative and dissolute state. Mary wants to call the doctor, but Paul tells her that his doctor has given up on him because Paul refuses to enter a sanitarium and to care for himself properly. Paul pleads, instead, for Mary to call Helen and draw her back to him. "I can't manage," Paul says, seeing his own plight. "The best I can do is to cling to someone who can." Paul collapses, and Mary calls the doctor, who arrives to take Paul to the hospital. Paul tells the doctor, "I'm just like everyone else. I don't want to die." To which the doctor responds, "But if you don't want to live I can't help you." The thematic crux of the story is thus established. When it comes to life itself, the doctor tells Mary, there are "the ones who are willing, and the ones who will have to be dragged."

Attending the graduation ceremonies at which she will receive her honorary doctorate, Mary contemplates the doctor's words with a deep sense of despair. Surrounded by the young college students with eager, bright views of their future, she feels her own age weighing upon her and feels suddenly out of place, useless, and defeated. At a reception later, she notices that her usual enthusiasm for the quick and keen intelligence of the young has waned. A phone call to Helen to ask her to return to Paul has failed, and Mary considers giving up her own plans to devote the rest of her life to Paul. "People like Paul can be looked after quite easily out of duty" she reflects; "the agony comes only when they are looked after with hope." A young graduate student comes up to converse with Mary, and she feels a deep sense of his brilliance of mind and high ethical character. He stands in such marked contrast to Paul, who wasted all of his abilities, that Mary is drawn to him and to unlocking his potential. "I can't help it," Mary reflects, "I'm of the breed that hopes. Maybe this one wants to live." Her resurgence of faith and her renewed energies for survival and purpose reveal to her that this is the crux of the human situation. "We are all in the dark together, but those are the ones who humanize the dark." The ending is existential in upholding the "dark" puzzle of existence, but compassionate in asserting that those who will to live with strength and dignity humanize the darkness for us all.

The necessity of strengths of the heart is reiterated in "The Middle Drawer," a story of mother-daughter conflicts and their partial resolution through compassion. After her mother's death from cancer, Hester is about to begin the process of going through her mother's most personal effects locked in the middle drawer of her dresser. The gravity of exposing her mother's life to inspection for the final time causes Hester to reflect upon the course of their relationship and how flawed by failed communication their lives together were.

Hester had come to know the drawer's contents gradually, through the course of a lifetime. She had begun peering over the drawer's edge as a baby, had played with the opera glasses and string of pearls she had found inside as a child, and had received from the drawer for her wedding the delicate diamond chain that had been her father's wedding gift to her mother. It is a small brown-toned photograph in the back of the drawer, however, that most held Hester's attention as she was growing up. The photograph was of her mother, Hedwig, as a child of two, bedecked in the garments of respectable poverty as she grew up in the small town of Oberelsbach, motherless since birth and stepmothered by a woman who had been "unloving, if not unkind." Hester senses that her mother was one of a legion of lonely children "who inhabited the familiar terror-struck dark that crouched under the lash of the adult."

Life "under the lash of the adult" had created in Hedwig an emotional reserve that precluded any open demonstration of love to Hester. Over the years, "the barrier of her mother's dissatisfaction with her had risen imperceptibly" until the two women stood as strangers, with bitter hurts and buried sorrows the only communion they had known. Hester's misery is that "she was forever impelled to earn her mother's approval at the expense of her own." Always, Hester had known, there had been buried the wish to find "the final barb, the homing shaft, that would maim her mother once and for all, as she felt herself to have been maimed."

The opportunity for the barb is given to Hester when she is called home to visit her mother after her mother's sudden operation for breast cancer. Hester discovers that her mother is suffering from a deep fear of the revulsion of others and a horror at what has been done to her. She has taken to sleeping alone at night and to eating from separate utensils. It is clear to Hester that her father and her brother have not been successful in concealing their revulsion from Hedwig, thus contributing further to her isolation and anxiety.

One evening, when they are together in her mother's bedroom, Hedwig begins to discuss her operation with Hester and asks her if she would like to see the incision, which no one has seen since she left the hospital. Hester tells her mother that she would very much like to see it, and recalls intensely the times that she had stood as a child before her mother, "vulnerable and bare, helplessly awaiting the cruel exactitude of her displeasure." Her mother reveals the scar to Hester, and Hester, with infinite delicacy, draws her fingertips along the length of the scar "in a light, affirmative caress, and they stood eye to eye for an immeasurable second, on equal ground at last." Hester's discovery about her mother and herself in that moment of tender union is a freeing answer: "She was always vulnerable, Hester thought. As we all are. What she bequeathed me unwittingly, ironically, was fortitude— the fortitude of those who have had to live under the blow. But pity—that I found for myself." the opportunity for the barb of hurt and rejection has been replaced by the empathy of understanding.

The story's ending blends poignancy with realism and psychological insight, for Hester knows that, however tender the moment of communion "on equal ground," her struggle to win her mother's approval would have continued and that the scars from their troubled relationship remain in Hester's psyche. Her own life is in the middle drawer she is about to open. She has been made who she is by her mother's influence and by the fact that her own grandmother died too soon to leave the imprint of love upon Hedwig. Like her mother, she has been scarred by an absence of love that worked its way through two generations and is, even now, affecting Hester's relationship with her own daughter. She realizes that the living carry "not one tangible wound but the burden of innumerable small cicatrices imposed upon us by our beginnings; we carry them with us always, and from these, from this agony, we are not absolved." With this recognition, Hester opens the middle drawer to face and absorb whatever truth her life and her mother's life might contain.

Like many of Calisher's short stories, "The Middle Drawer" builds to a phenomenological *epochē* which reveals numerous multifaceted insights into the characters of the stories, the psychology of human motivations, and the metaphysics of human actions, especially actions springing from an ethical or a compassionate base. Calisher is not a facile optimist; she believes in strongly and portrays quite graphically the pain pervading most human lives. She does assert, however, an unwavering faith in the strength of the human will and in the necessity for commitment to ethical principles. Like Mary Ponthus in "If You Don't Want to Live I Can't Help You," Calisher affirms that we must "humanize the dark."

Major publications other than short fiction
NOVELS: *False Entry*, 1961; *Textures of Life*, 1963; *Journal from Ellipsia*, 1965; *The New Yorkers*, 1969; *Standard Dreaming*, 1972; *Eagle Eye*, 1973.
NONFICTION: *Herself*, 1972.

Bibliography
Hahn, Emily. "In Appreciation of Hortense Calisher," in *Wisconsin Studies in Contemporary Literature*. VI (Summer, 1965), pp. 243-249.
Kirby, David K. "The Princess and the Frog: The Modern American Short Story as Fairy Tale," in *Minnesota Review*. IV (Spring, 1973), pp. 145-149.

Christina Murphy

ITALO CALVINO

Born: Santiago de las Vegas, Cuba; October 15, 1923

Principal short fiction

L'entrata in guerra, 1952; *Fiabe italiane*, 1956 (*Italian Fables*); *Adam, One Afternoon*, 1957; *I racconti*, 1958 (*Short Stories*); *Le cosmicomiche*, 1965 (*Cosmicomics*); *Ti con zero*, 1967 (*t zero*).

Other literary forms

Italo Calvino's short stories and tales brought him to the attention of the Italian literary world, but he is best known for his novels. Some of the themes which are present in the short stories recur enlarged in the novels. His language, balanced between the serious and the humorous, characterizes his style. He also has written a critical study on Elio Vittorini (1968), a close friend and writer. Finally, Calvino has rewritten fables from the Italian folklore for young people and *Marcovaldo ovvero le stagioni in città* (1963), a book of vignettes rather than genuine short stories also for young readers.

Influence

Calvino was a member of the Italian resistance movement during World War II, and this experience is often evident in his works in the form of war episodes. He does not, however, overdo this theme. He also goes to Italian literature of the past; it has been said that Ludovico Ariosto, and the whole Italian Renaissance, has given life to his writings, especially by influencing his style. His prose often contains the fabulous or fantastic, the comic or humorous, the ironic or satirical, all of which account for his peculiar and delightful manner of writing; he is at times, as in his later writings, also serious.

Cesare Pavese and Vittorini, two well-known writers and contemporaries, were quick to recognize Calvino's talent in prose writing; and, no doubt, the first writer exercised some influence on him as did Joseph Conrad, whose works became the subject of Calvino's university "laurea," or doctorate. Soon, however, Calvino began to write following an independent course of his own and, indeed, one welcome for its literary freshness.

His training in doctoral research led him to a certain erudition and scholarly style evident, for example, in his annotated remarks and notes on the sources and origin of the fables; they represent a valuable contribution to that literary genre. Reality and fantasy are evoked by Calvino in most of his works, fused with an irony not devoid of the grotesque and the anguish which is found in today's world; and, in this respect, it may be said that the real influence on

Calvino has been life itself and the world one lives in as highlighted by the author's own propensities.

Story characteristics

Calvino's prose is often pleasant, even when dealing with the foibles and inequities of life. His escape into the mythical, as in *Il cavaliere inesistente* (1959, *The Non-Existent Knight*), removes what could really be tragic. At the same time, his stories and novels assert man's right to freedom, justice, and order. His predilection for fables may be an indication of his natural leanings; he does not aim to shock, as did Gabrielle D'Annunzio or Luigi Pirandello; he exposes quite simply, for example, the cheating practiced by businessmen and politicians in *La speculazione edilizia* (1963), "La nuvola di smog" ("Smog"), and other stories or novelettes.

Biography

Although Italo Calvino was born in Santiago de las Vegas, Cuba, in 1923, his Italian parents took him to the beautiful city of San Remo on the Italian Riviera when he was only two years old. To this day he considers that tourist spot his native city, even though he has lived mostly in Turin. Some reference books give San Remo as the city where he was born, although that statement is erroneous.

During World War II he took part in the partisan movement against the Nazis and Fascists, believing that man's freedom was at stake. Like many other writers, he joined the Communist Party after the war as a reaction to the previous regime; but like many of these writers, he also broke with the Communists when he realized that human rights were not any safer in a Communist regime than under Fascism or Nazism.

Calvino worked for a while in editorial companies, and at the end of the war he returned to the University of Turin to finish his thesis on Joseph Conrad and receive his degree. He received the Premio Riccione (The Riccione Literary Award) in 1947 for his first novel *Il sentiero dei nidi di ragno* (1947, *The Path to the Nest of Spiders*), on the recommendation of Pavese; his short stories, *I racconti*, received the prestigious Bagutta Prize in 1958. He directed with the late Vittorini the literary journal *Il menabò*, published by the Einaudi Company which printed his creative works; he is still on the editorial board of that magazine and of the Einaudi publishing house in Turin, where he lives.

Analysis

Italo Calvino must above all be recognized for his variety of themes, subjects, and genres of writing. His personal imprint, as evidenced in both content and style, quickly strikes the reader. His novels are not the long Italian *romanzi* to which readers are accustomed; even his longer stories are, in the end, still *racconti*: that is, they are short stories with a somewhat long narration. Therefore, he is mainly a short-story writer, even if his novels are indeed considered to be his major works; and he is a storyteller in the Italian tradition of the *Novellino* regardless of whether the length makes the story a novel, a novelette, a short story, or a simple tale.

His *Il visconte dimezzato* (1952, *The Cloven Viscount*), his masterpiece to date, is a case in point. The story later became a reality the first part of a trilogy, together with *Il barone rampante* (1957, *The Baron in the Trees*) and *The Non-Existent Knight*. These three fictions form one psychology and one underlying thematic representation as best exemplified by the first work, which deals with a viscount who happens to be cut in half by a cannon ball. The two parts of this man come to represent good and evil.

Calvino himself refers to this dichotomy by recalling Dr. Jekyll and Mr. Hyde; however, he stubbornly refutes the argument that he has set out to be a moralist: "Not at all did this theme enter my heart . . . ," writes the author, who contends that the viscount is modern man who has become his own enemy, suffering the modern dilemma of a split personality. Nevertheless, Calvino, whether he meant to or not, writes not only of *contemporary* mankind but also of mankind in general; it cannot be denied that such a "fable," or a topic of reality narrated as a fable, has immediate prototypes in *Orlando furioso* (1516-1531) by Ariosto and in *Don Quixote de la Mancha* (1605, 1615) by Cervantes, who was himself influenced by the Italian Renaissance satirical poet.

Medardo, the cloven viscount, is both the "two" Orlandos and the "two" Don Quixotes of our present day, an eternal schism of being or not being. The central problem becomes a matter of identity, as in many plays by Pirandello with which Calvino surely was acquainted (it especially brings to mind, although not in a serious or tragic vein, the split personality of Pirandello's Enrico IV who was not Enrico IV). Medardo is then two in one; the one half perforce cannot live with the other half; evil and good seldom go together within an ambivalent mind.

Calvino generally tells a simple story like that of "Il giardino incantato," in which the plot, and the characters are more poetic than dramatic. In the story, two children, Giovannino and Serenella, by accident come upon a beautiful garden with flowers, a swimming pool, a pingpong table, cakes, tea, and milk as in a fairy tale. To whom does it belong? Who is the landlord? They can only see a pale-faced boy in a room of the villa; the boy walks slowly, seriously, and furtively within that room. Giovannino and Serenella quietly walk away, and the story ends like a dream, like an anecdote of a faraway land. The diminutives of the two children's names seem to lend the story a magical touch like those of children's tales. Some critics have seen in a story such as this the practical propensity emanating from Calvino's inner soul: a simple, at times humorous, innocent characteristic that makes the author's thinking similar to a childlike psychology; yet to deny him a real seriousness of purpose, behind the screen of a satire or of a smile, would be fallacious, as other stories demonstrate.

In *Marcovaldo ovvero le stagioni in città*, a collection of about twenty short stories or delicate sketches which he began in 1952 but did not publish until 1963, the reader once again has Calvino tackling the same problems. He becomes, however, somewhat mellower with time. Devoid of bitterness, the melancholy nature of his writing lends his stories a sedate tonality, a poetical quality. Here unexpected events happen to Marcovaldo, as when he discovers beautiful mushrooms in the city only to learn that they are poisonous. The style and language are fresh, not difficult; the narrative is terse, humorous, and makes use of both dialogue and description of places and persons. When the stories are devoid of any political or social problems, the real and interesting Calvino can still be recognized. "Pesci grossi, pesci piccoli" ("Big Fish, Little Fish") is the story of these fish within a realistic background; it is pleasant in tone, nothing else. He seems to be concerned with the style, the expression of the content, but not necessarily the subject matter; he is thus functioning mainly as an artist.

Similarly, in another story, "Gli scherzi pesanti," Calvino pokes fun at something serious. It is an episode from his long story "Le notti dell' UNPA" ("UNPA Nights"), in which he tells in a light, humorous vein how during the last war two young men who belonged to UNPA, a service similar to our American air-raid wardens, frightened people one night with false air-raid alarms and made Belluomo, the young officer in charge, look ridiculous while they had a grand time. (Belluomo means *handsome man*, to add to the jest.)

In "Paese infido," a short story from the Bagutta Prize-winning collection, *Short Stories*, Calvino again uses a war theme, here about partisans in an Italian town under German occupation; this is, however, a serious tale. Tom, a stranded Italian partisan who is wounded and cannot escape, is about to be handed over to the Nazis. The townspeople are afraid to help him for fear of Nazi reprisals; yet, when all seems lost, a girl is sent by the people hiding in the countryside to him to tell him how to escape, and Tom is saved. This story has the potential germ of a play echoing Lope de Vega's *Fuenteovejuna* (c. 1619); and, although Calvino is not given to writing plays, he definitely misses here the literary realization of a dramatic situation which he could have expanded into a longer prose narrative, if not a play.

Calvino, it seems, prefers to leave that reflection to the reader, feeling satisfied with what he has done, or he simply does not have the élan or verve to develop further what is merely sketched. For this reason, all his works are short stories, even skeletal at times; this is true of other contemporary Italian writers as well; they all seem to be running against time. Calvino's claim to artistry, it may be argued against this criticism, lies in his own style, his jovial mood, his *fiabesco*, that is the fairy-tale, imaginative side of his short narrations; finally, it resides in his ability to deal with foibles, problems, dilemmas, and tragedies without unnecessary bitterness.

Major publications other than short fiction

NOVELS: *Il visconte dimezzato*,1952 (*The Cloven Viscount*); *Il barone rampante*, 1957 (*The Baron in the Trees*); *Il cavaliere inesistente*, 1959 (*The Non-Existent Knight*); *Se una notte d'inverno un viaggiatore*, 1979.

NONFICTION: *Vittorini . . .* , 1968.

Ferdinando D. Maurino

ALBERT CAMUS

Born: Mondovi, Algeria; November 7, 1913
Died: Near Sens, France; January 4, 1960

Principal short fiction
L'Exil et le Royaume, 1957 (*Exile and the Kingdom*).

Other literary forms
Albert Camus was an important novelist and playwright as well as a philosophical essayist and journalist. He translated and adapted the works of Spanish, Russian, and American writers such as Calderon de la Barca, Lope de Vega, Fyodor Dostoevski, William Faulkner, and James Thurber. During World War II, he was the anonymous editor of *Combat*, and often practiced the trade of journalism during his brief life.

Influence
Even though he is no longer identified with the existentialists, Camus remains the most palatable and popular writer of that movement. His writing is broad and vigorous and serves to flesh out esoteric philosophical and moral questions. His detractors have accused him of turning "middlebrow" after publishing *L'Etranger* (*The Stranger*) in 1942. This novel has been a model for short-story writers because of its economy and emotional compression and for making the antihero fashionable in literary circles. His work had immediate and widespread impact throughout Europe and Latin America. It gained a readership in the United States through the academic circuit. Today, Camus is no longer considered outlandish but is read as a provocative yet amiable author.

Story characteristics
Camus' stories are about protagonists who are shocked by a turn of events into self-confrontations. Because they usually strive to resolve their predicaments which occur in exotic parts of the world, the stories have the flavor of adventure yarns. They are written with a grave, distant touch, but evidence a specific and authentic concern for place and secondary characters which makes them absorbing.

Biography
Albert Camus was born of a Spanish peasant mother and an Alsatian father who was killed in World War I. He received a degree in philosophy from the University of Algiers in 1936. He had a brief membership in the Communist Party at that time. He pursued a varied career as actor, producer, journalist, and schoolteacher. He was an active participant in the French underground

during World War II and first came into national prominence after the war when it was revealed that he had been the editor of the famed clandestine newspaper *Combat*. He made many political and literary enemies after the war by chastising the Communists and his erstwhile friend and fellow writer Jean-Paul Sartre. A position as editor of a publishing house, lecture tours in the United States and South America, government posts, and the Nobel Prize for literature in 1957 followed until his untimely death in an automobile accident in 1960.

Analysis

Albert Camus published a single collection of short stories entitled *Exile and the Kingdom* near the end of his life. Its six stories are an important encapsulation of Camus' existential philosophy enveloped in his quasirealistic style and dramatized by exotic backgrounds. According to Camus' recondite views, the universe is meaningless; however, the human beings in it may become significant (or authentic) if they can acquire and maintain a clear awareness of its ultimate absurdity. Each story in *Exile and the Kingdom* unfolds a situation which brings the protagonist to an intimation of the lack of lawfulness and coherence in his or her life and depicts the protagonist's response to this traumatic realization. Some of the stories go no further than this; others move away from understatement and describe wrong-headed or perverse reactions; and the last story offers a solution which seems to step beyond mere awareness of absurdity.

Readers of Camus' novels and plays will recognize the cavalcade of alienated heroes, the metaphysical paradoxes, and Camus' own preoccupation with criminals and their police counterparts—all tendered in lucid, earnest prose which differentiates him from the strained cerebralisms of more philosophically rigorous existentialists such as Sartre. This collection of short stories also avoids the imperious eloquence and plain sententiousness which often mar Camus' longer works.

"The Adulterous Woman," first published in English in *Redbook* magazine, portrays the mounting hysteria of a housewife traveling with a husband who is almost wholly absorbed in selling wools and silks to disdainful Arabs reluctantly emerging from the wintry Algerian landscape.

Janine is pictured as tall and "thick," yet possessing a languid sensuality which attracts the desultory glances of bus passengers, pedestrians, and hotel guests. She often returns a look and in spite of the characteristic prejudices of her class against Arabs she can spontaneously admire one of that race who is striking in his slender virility. She frequently counters the ennui of the endless bus rides by basking in the adoration of her husband, Marcel. He can speak of little else but the volume of dry goods he can move, how much profit he will reckon by dispensing with the middleman, and how much he loathes his customers. He has made Janine his refuge from the sordidness and triviality of his life, however, and becomes instantly solicitous when prodded.

Thus, after another day of selling in yet another ordinary town, Janine rebels at the thought of retiring to their icy room for the customary nap before supper. She proposes to follow the hotel manager's suggestion to "climb up to the terrace around the fort to see the desert" and Marcel automatically assents. A marvelous description of the twilight desertscape is counterposed against Marcel's impatient complaint that he is cold and that there is nothing to see anyway.

That night, however, Janine slips out of bed to return to the fort. There, alone under the chilly and vast firmament, she suffers a moment of awareness—an epiphany. She feels the sap rising again in her body and she encompasses the sky full of stars stretched out over her as she lies against the cold parapet. This tryst with the night sky is her act of "adultery" which she does not share with Marcel, who is oblivious of her absence and only awakes to reach for a bottle of mineral water.

In all this, however, there is a note of disconcerting ambivalence. The distant tone of the narration raises the possibility that the reader has been "taken": is this story actually a clinical description of female hysteria revelatory only of Janine's disconsolate banality? More importantly, has Camus played a joke on us by forcing us to choose between two diversely wretched characters? Worse, is it possible that Camus, in his existential zeal, was unaware of these other interpretations of his own story?

These questions also arise in "The Guest," the best story in *Exile and the Kingdom*, also set in North Africa—specifically in the snows of the Atlas Mountains in Algeria. Daru, an Algerian schoolteacher of French extraction, has fully provisioned himself to weather an expected blizzard which has emptied his one-room schoolhouse of its Arab pupils. He is comfortably awaiting its onset when he observes two figures, one on horseback, toiling up the steep slope leading toward the school building. The man on horseback is Balducci, a gendarme dragging behind him a trussed and cowering shepherd who killed his cousin with a billhook during a squabble over a share of grain.

Balducci asks the astonished Daru to safeguard the prisoner for the night and deliver him the next morning to police headquarters at Tinguit, twenty kilometers away. He explains that the Algerian revolt is on and police manpower is stretched thinly over the plateau. When Daru protests that delivering criminals is not his job, Balducci counters by insisting bitterly that "In wartime people do all kinds of jobs." Then he leaves Daru a revolver and departs.

Daru has little physical fear of the obviously spent murderer but knows full well that he is caught in an impossible situation: delivering his charge will assure the probably lethal (in view of his isolated circumstances) enmity of the local Arab population; releasing him will make him a rebel and a traitor to his European countrymen. In the first case, his life would be in jeopardy, in the second his career and perhaps his freedom. Daru also feels morally affronted by the repugnant nature of his imposed task. The next day Daru escorts the felon to a trail juncture where he hands him a food package and a thousand francs. He gives him the choice of walking east for two hours to Tinguit and the police, or walking south across the plateau where nomads will shelter him according to their laws of hospitality.

On the way back to his schoolhouse Daru looks behind him and discerns the black dot of the Arab moving toward the police station. Arriving at the schoolhouse he reads a message chalked over his drawing of the four main rivers of France: "You handed over our brother, you will pay for this."

Thus the paradoxical title of this collection is explained. Daru, like his "guest," was born and has lived his life in this inhospitable plateau—this is his kingdom. Yet an accidental turn of events has transformed his kingdom into a place of exile. His strategy for eluding this onrushing absurdity has been unavailing; and worse, from the existential point of view, Daru will become a casualty with little time left to savor his newly acquired awareness of the meaninglessness of the universe.

"The Guest," because of its artistic virtuosity, is a landmark which forces comparisons for English-speaking readers with such pinnacles of the adventure story with moral and epistemological overtones as Jack London's "To Build a Fire" and Stephen Crane's "The Blue Hotel." Apropos of this analysis, however, "The Guest" is an excellent and mercifully succinct distillation of Camus' outlook and provides a take-off point for an important criticism of it in line with the previous discussion of "The Adulterous Woman."

At least one critic, John K. Simon, writing in *Studies in Short Fiction*, shifts the focus of attention from the unsolvable quandary facing Daru to an assertion that Daru himself is morally flawed for abandoning the Arab under the pretense of giving him a choice when it is patent that this outcast is neither morally, psychologically, nor physically (a walk to the police station is shorter than one across the plateau) able to decide on a proper course of action. Daru's obsession with solitude—as exemplified by the fact that at one point Balducci calls him "cracked," and also by the puzzling observation that Daru's hostility toward the Arab and toward his new role as policeman cannot be fully accounted for within the text—explains his abandonment of the prisoner and reinforces the suspicion that Daru does not understand social process. If all this is true, then Camus' existential message becomes irrelevant and Daru is not a victim of an indifferently cruel universe, but rather he is a man who has been consistently guilty of social omissions and blunders.

The last story in the collection, "The Growing Stone," has an overtly neopagan motif, a recurring interest of Camus which critics have attributed to his North African upbringing. D'Arrast, a French engineer descended from an aristocratic family, is chauffeured by a Brazilian named Socrates across the jungle to a seaside town where he will build much-needed jetties and roads. During the all-night drive they pass through the town of Registro, which is populated by Japanese immigrants who still dress in their kimonos. Arriving at Iguape, D'Arrast is effusively received by the town officials, who are grateful for his services. The welcome is spoiled, however, by the inexplicable belligerence of the drunken police chief, who loutishly proclaims that D'Arrast's passport is not in order. D'Arrast insists on touring the quarters where his future laborers reside; and while there he encounters a ship's cook who tells him that he survived a shipwreck after making a promise to St. George to carry a one-hundred-pound stone at the forthcoming procession.

D'Arrast also meets a "black Diana" who lures him to a ceremonial dance held the night before the procession. The poor of the town crowd into a large hut and engage in a frenetic, obscene, grotesque, and at times sinister ritual which at first nauseates D'Arrast but then bewitches him. At a certain point, D'Arrast is asked to leave. The ship's cook, contrary to his resolve to get a good night's sleep, stays on. The next day the weary cook falters while carrying the rock to the church. In an inspired moment D'Arrast wrests a cork mat from the encouraging crowd and shoulders the stone. Being young, strong, and well rested, he bears it easily; but nearing the portals of the church he veers away from them dramatically and, ignoring the enraged and mystified commands of the mob which dins "to the church," he heads for the cook's hovel and hurls the rectangular block onto the glowing fire in the center of the room, where it immediately becomes another idol.

This then is Camus' tentative answer to the problem of absurdity: in the face of the prevailing incongruity, arbitrariness, and disorganization, human beings can strive for an emotional coherence which sidesteps the question of absurdity, which Camus now views as merely an intellectual problem.

"The Renegade" depicts in the first person the psychotic state of mind of a missionary who, after mental and physical torture, surrenders morally to the Saharan heathens he has come to civilize. His tongue cut out, the renegade conducts a frenzied interior monologue as he waits to ambush the priest sent to replace him. This tour de force is Camus' revenge upon Christianity, but it can also be construed as an attack upon the paganism which is more favorably presented in "The Growing Stone."

"The Silent Men" is more mundane. Set in a French city, it narrates how a crew of coopers returning to work after a failed strike decide not to communicate with their boss in an attempt to salve their humiliation. In spite of Camus' on-again, off-again socialist sympathies, this story remains one of his few treatments of skilled craftsmen who, in this case, practice an obsolete craft.

Finally, "The Artist at Work" is notable only because it contains the only humor in the collection. It is an over-long cataloging of the distractions of wife, children, and zealous friends, all of whom drive a moderately talented painter to isolation and artistic impotence. "The Artist at Work," like the other stories in *Exile and the Kingdom*, presents themes that are central to

Camus' existential philosophy. They demonstrate the world of man's suffering solitude, humiliation, and isolation—meaningless lives in an absurd world.

Major publications other than short fiction

NOVELS: *L'Etranger*, 1942 (*The Stranger*); *La Peste*, 1947 (*The Plague*); *La Chute*, 1956 (*The Fall*).

PLAYS: *Caligula*, 1944; *Le Malentendu*, 1944 (*Cross Purposes*); *L'État de Siège*, 1948 (*State of Siege*); *Les Justes*, 1950 (*The Just Assassins*).

NONFICTION: *Le Mythe de Sisyphe*, 1942 (*The Myth of Sisyphus*); *Lettres à un ami allemand*, 1945 (*Letters to a German Friend*); *L'Homme révolté*, 1951 (*The Rebel*).

Bibliography

Breé, Germaine. *Camus*.
Cruickshank, John. *Albert Camus*.
Hanna, Thomas. *The Thought and Art of Albert Camus*.
Maquet, Albert. *Albert Camus: The Invincible Summer*.
Thody, Philip. *Albert Camus*.

Julian Grajewski

TRUMAN CAPOTE

Born: New Orleans, Louisiana; September 30, 1924

Principal short fiction

A Tree of Night and Other Stories, 1949; *Breakfast at Tiffany's: A Short Novel and Three Stories*, 1958.

Other literary forms

In addition to stories and short novels, Truman Capote has written travel sketches and various kinds of nonfiction. *Local Color* (1950) is a collection of travel essays, and *In Cold Blood* (1966), his most famous work, is a "nonfiction novel," a documented re-creation of the murder of a family in Kansas. *Answered Prayers* (1975) and "Dazzle" also combine the two forms. As yet unpublished in a collection, they have been excerpted in recent magazines. *Breakfast at Tiffany's* became a well-known film in 1961, and *In Cold Blood* was awarded an Emmy in 1967.

Influence

Capote's short stories often rely on Gothic devices, to which they add realistic settings and Freudian dimensions. Since the 1950's, Capote has concentrated on nonfiction experiments to illustrate his belief that the faithful reporting of real persons, their conversations, and their conflicts can expand the scope of the creative writer.

Story characteristics

Capote employs highly controlled prose that portrays characters who confront reflections of themselves. Haunting and evocative atmospheres, the blending of dream, reality and nightmare, and powerfully charged symbols make Capote's stories unforgettable.

Biography

Since his parents divorced when he was four years old, Truman Capote was reared by aunts and cousins in a small town in Alabama. At seventeen, he moved to New York City and worked his way up from mailroom clerk to feature writer for *The New Yorker*. "Miriam" won the O. Henry Memorial Award in 1943 and "Shut a Final Door" in 1946.

Analysis

Truman Capote's stories are best known for their mysterious, dreamlike occurrences. As his protagonists try to go about their ordinary business, they meet with unexpected obstacles—usually in the form of haunting, enigmatic strangers. Corresponding to some childhood memory or to someone the protagonist once knew, these people take on huge proportions and cause major changes in the character's life. The central figures of these stories are usually people who have left their home towns, who travel, or who live alone, for they seem most vulnerable to chance encounters. Their isolation gives them the time and their loneliness gives them the motivation to see these experiences through to their conclusions—and often with great risk.

Capote is a careful craftsman. His words are meticulously chosen for their evocative power, and, at their best, they create highly charged images and symbols. His descriptions of the seasons or weather further heighten the effects he wants to create. Snow, rain, dusk, and sunlight serve to separate the particular setting from a larger landscape, thus reinforcing the self-reflexive nature of his stories. Attics, kitchens, one-room walk-ups, and isolated apartments are typical settings that also provide sequestered settings. The atmosphere, location, characters, and events present a touching but often chilling and ominous beauty. The combination of reality and dream also produces a chilling and eerie beauty.

In "A Tree of Night," one of his finest stories, Kay is a young, attractive student returning to college after the funeral of an uncle. It is late on a winter night, bare and icy, when she boards the train from the deserted platform. Taking the only available seat, she sits opposite an odd-looking couple. The woman is in her fifties, with a huge head and a dwarfish body, while the man is mute, with marblelike eyes and an expressionless face. Although Kay is initially polite, she hopes to be left alone, but the woman wants company and conversation. Kay tries to remain distant, but the woman and man are persistent and aggressive. Without any warning, the man reaches towards Kay and strokes her cheek. Her reaction is immediate but confused: she is repelled by the boldness of the gesture while, at the same time, she is touched by the delicacy.

From this point on, Kay seems to view the man and woman as harbingers of danger. Capote's style remains realistic and his tone objective, but the couple behave as though they are part of Kay's nightmare. The woman talks endlessly, always wanting a response from her listener. She forces Kay to drink liquor with her and even grabs her wrist. As in a nightmare, Kay wants to scream and awaken the other passengers, but no sounds come out. Trying to escape from the woman's irritating voice, Kay has a reverie as she stares into the void face of the man, and suddenly his face and her uncle's dead face blend. She sees, or imagines that she sees, a shared secret and a stillness. This association of the stranger with someone from her past is deadly, preparing the reader for the end of the story.

By degrees, the man assumes control over Kay. He takes from his pocket a peach seed and fondles it gently. The woman insists that he only wants Kay to purchase it as a good-luck charm, but Kay is frightened, interpreting his action as some kind of warning. Trying to avoid the man, she leaves her seat for the observation platform and fresh air, but soon she senses someone beside her and knows that it must be the man. Now, without the distracting annoyance of the woman, Kay understands why she finds him so threatening. Unable to speak or to hear, he is like her uncle, dead, and the dead can haunt. She further recognizes him as a figure from her childhood dreams, the boogeyman, the "wizard-man," the mysterious personage that could bring alive "terrors that once, long ago, had hovered above her like haunted limbs on a tree of night." Kay's submission is unquestionable, but precisely what she submits to is left ambiguous. Together, she and the man return to their seats, and she gives him money for the peach seed. Then the woman takes possession of Kay's whole purse and, although Kay wants to shout, she does not. Finally the woman takes Kay's raincoat and pulls it "like a shroud" over her head. No longer struggling, Kay sinks into a strange passivity.

"A Tree of Night" raises many questions but provides few answers. The characters are realistically presented, but eccentric, to say the least. Kay is not wholly convincing, yet is still three-dimensional. It is rather the events themselves that appear unlikely and nightmarish, but since Capote delights in paradox, his story cannot be classified either as pure dream or simple reality. Why does Kay not protest? To what extent do she and the mute actually communicate? Is the submission of the young girl carefully planned by the couple? Are the two travelers real passengers who want to do her harm, or can they be projections from Kay's psyche? Or are they merely two unique strangers to whom Kay attributes much more power than they really have? These ambiguities are the source of both the story's weaknesses and its strengths; they enrich the encounter and abstract it, but they also leave the reader feeling baffled. Nevertheless, Capote seems to imply that human beings are extremely vulnerable to destructive instincts. Perhaps beginning with a memory or fear from deep within the psyche, one projects it and expands it until it acquires a frightening degree of reality. In fact, it may become a deadly kind of reality. Kay essentially wills herself first into isolation from other passengers and finally into submission. She returns from the observation platform accompanied by the stranger. She chooses neither to change her seat nor to scream. Eventually, she chooses not to struggle. Human beings are delicate creatures, and the power of the "wizard-man" is enough to cause Kay to sink into nightmarish and unnecessary helplessness.

The mysterious realm of dream can invade the workaday world and then consume it. This is precisely what happens in "Master Misery" when Sylvia leaves her home town of Easton to stay with married friends who live in New York City. Soon she becomes frustrated with her daily routine and her "nambypamby, bootsytotsy" friends. Hoping to earn money to find her own apartment, Sylvia overhears a conversation in the automat. As unlikely as it sounds, a certain Mr. Revercomb purchases dreams. Intrigued, Sylvia visits his Fifth

Avenue brownstone and discovers that Mr. Revercomb does indeed purchase dreams for cash. As she continues to visit his office, events take an unfortunate turn. The more Sylvia sees him, the more he seems eccentric, even unnatural. One time as she whispers her dream, Mr. Revercomb bends forward to brush her ear with his lips, apparently in a sexual approach.

Sylvia becomes so obsessed with selling her dreams that everything else in her life loses significance. She cuts off communication with her married friends, quits her office job, and rents a dingy studio apartment. Her only friend is Oreilly, a former clown whom she meets in Mr. Revercomb's waiting room. They have a great deal in common, for Oreilly used to sell his dreams also, but now Mr. Revercomb has no use for them. Although he spends most of his time drunk, Oreilly has the foresight to warn his new companion against the man he calls the Master of Misery, who is so adept at convincing people that parting with a dream is worth five dollars. He explains to Sylvia that she must not lose her independence or her private world of memory and dream, and he compares Mr. Revercomb to the demon of childhood nightmare, the ominous figure who haunted the trees, chimneys, attics, and graveyards of make-believe. Like the mute in "A Tree of Night," Revercomb is "a thief and a threat," for after he appropriates one's dreams, it is a short passage to one's subconscious and one's soul.

Sylvia's life contracts to unhappy proportions. She moves from Revercomb's waiting room back to Oreilly, her waiting companion, who commiserates with her shrinking self before consuming the liquor she buys with her dream-money. He does, however, advise her to ask Revercomb for her dreams back, provided that she gradually returns the money over a period of time. Kay agrees, for her life has become miserable and isolated, but this is a Faustian story, and what was spent cannot be retrieved. Revercomb informs Sylvia that under no circumstances would he return what she has sold and, besides, he has already used them up. Walking home in the falling snow, Sylvia acknowledges that she is no longer her own master and has no individuality; soon she will not have even Oreilly, who will go his own way. Thinking she used Revercomb, it turns out that he has used her, and now they are inseparable—until he discards her as he did Oreilly. The story concludes as Sylvia overhears footsteps following behind. There are two boys, who have followed her from the park and continue to do so. Sylvia is frightened, but like Kay in "A Tree of Night," she becomes passive and submissive, for there is "nothing left to steal."

As in much of Capote's short fiction, the individual tacitly gives a stranger enormous power. Once Sylvia abdicates full responsibility for herself and enters Revercomb's world, she becomes vulnerable and he becomes omniscient. Gradually she is emptied of friends, an orderly routine, ambition, desire, and, finally, of self-possession. The reader can never be sure who Revercomb is or what he does with dreams, but Sylvia, not the Master of

Misery, is the focus of interest. She allows him to create her misery, leaving her with no one, not even her former self.

Capote's early work especially makes use of the Gothic tradition, but because the details remain realistic and controlled, the mysterious elements are subtle and therefore even more insidious. The "wizard-man" is Capote's archetype—the mute in "A Tree of Night," Mr. Revercomb in "Master Misery," the young girl in "Miriam," Mr. Destronelli in "The Headless Hawk." This figure transforms forever the actual world of the protagonist, usually in undesirable and irreversible ways. Whether the encounter with this stranger is a final retreat into narcissism or a submission to a purely external presence may not be clarified, but the fragility of the human psyche is all too clear.

Major publications other than short fiction
NOVELS: *Other Voices, Other Rooms*, 1948; *The Grass Harp*, 1951.
NONFICTION: *Local Color*, 1950; *The Muses Are Heard*, 1956; *Observations*, 1959 (with Richard Avedon); *Selected Writings*, 1963; *In Cold Blood*, 1966; *The Thanksgiving Visitor*, 1968; *The Dogs Bark: Public People and Private Places*, 1973.

Bibliography
Malin, Irving. *New American Gothic*.
Nance, William L. *The Worlds of Truman Capote*.

Miriam Fuchs

WILLIAM CARLETON

Born: Prillisk, County Tyrone, Northern Ireland; March 4, 1794
Died: Dublin, Ireland; January 30, 1869

Principal short fiction

Pilgrimage to Patrick's Purgatory, Dennis O'Shaughnessy and Other Stories,
in *The Christian Examiner*, 1828-1831; *Father Butler, the Lough Derg Pilgrim,
Being Sketches of Irish Manners*, 1829; *Traits and Stories of the Irish Peasantry*,
1830, 1833; *The Poor Scholar and Other Tales*, 1830; *Tales of Ireland*, 1834;
Popular Tales and Legends of the Irish Peasantry, 1834; *The Fawn of Spring-
Vale, the Clarionet, and Other Tales*, 1841; *The Battle of the Factions and
Other Tales of Ireland*, 1845; *Characteristic Sketches of Ireland and the Irish*,
1845; *Parra Sastha; or the History of Paddy Go-Easy and His Wife Nancy*,
1845; *Roddy the Rover; or, the Ribbon Man*, 1845; *Art Maguire, or the Broken
Pledge*, 1847; *O'Sullivan's Love, A Legend of Edenmore*, 1847; *The Irishman
at Home*, 1849; *The Clarionet; the Dead Boxer; and Barney Branagan*, 1850;
Alley Sheridan and Other Stories, 1857; *The Double Prophecy; or, Trials of
the Heart*, 1862; *The Silver Acre and Other Tales*, 1862; *The Fair of Emyvale
and the Master and Scholar*, 1870; *The Red Haired Man's Wife*, 1889.

Other literary forms

Although William Carleton wrote some poetry and at least one play, his
reputation is based upon his short stories and novels. *Fardorougha the Miser*
(1839); *Valentine McClutchy, the Irish Agent* (1845); *The Black Prophet* (1847);
and *The Emigrants of Ahadarra* (1848), the best of his novels, dramatize the
plight of rural Irish society during the famine years of the nineteenth century.
In 1848, he was awarded a literary memorial of £200 annually for life.

Influence

Carleton was, as William Butler Yeats wrote, "the historian of the peasantry" because he wrote about his family, friends, and personal acquaintances
of his youth in County Tyrone. His many fictional tales are realistic accounts
of the Irish country people confronting major upheavals: the loss of their
language, land, and lives. Carleton, knowing the Irish language and oral
literary traditions, added a quality to his work unequaled by his contemporaries.

Story characteristics

Carleton wrote realistic, tragicomic, and satiric tales revealing the complex
nature of a changing world. His language, principally the idioms of the un-
schooled Irish which combined Irish and English, gives the stories a special
appeal. He incorporated local folklore, legends, myths, and beliefs into the
stories, increasing the overall effect; he also wrote a few fairy tales.

Biography
Born to a poor Catholic Irish-speaking rural family skilled in oral traditional literature and music, William Carleton was never formally educated; instead, he attended haphazard hedge schools along the roadside or in small buildings, operated by itinerant schoolmasters. After his conversion to Protestantism, he wrote anti-Catholic stories for the Church of Ireland magazine and worked for the Sunday School Society for a short while. He married Jane Anderson and had several children. Settling in Dublin in 1818, Carleton remained there the rest of his life. Many of his short stories and novels first appeared in Irish publications: *The Christian Examiner*, *National Magazine*, *Carlow College Magazine*, *Dublin University Magazine*, *Hibernian Magazine*, and *The Nation*. A few stories also appeared in the *Illustrated London Magazine* and the *Irish-American*.

Analysis
The most popular of William Carleton's short stories are contained in *Traits and Stories of the Irish Peasantry* (1830, 1833), read and appreciated by such diverse artists as Lord Alfred Tennyson and Edgar Allan Poe. Fairy tales, local legends, and episodes from his life and the lives of his neighbors comprise the subject matter of Carleton's short fiction. Years after he left his native province, Carleton still wrote about it; in one story, "Ned M'Keown," the characters' names are the real names of his neighbors.

Of the nineteen tales edited for the five volumes of *Traits and Stories of the Irish Peasantry*, most record an event in the community, including "Shane Fadh's Wedding," "Larry M'Farland's Wake," "The Battle of the Factions," "The Party Fight and Funeral," "Tubber Derg," "The Hedge School," "The Station," "The Midnight Mass," "The Horse Stealers," "An Essay on Irish Swearing," "Wildgoose Lodge," "Dennis O'Shaughnessy Going to Maynooth," and "Phelim O'Toole's Courtship." Carleton also describes people in such stories as "Mickey M'Rory, the Country Fiddler," "Neal Malone," "Rose Moan," "Mary Murray, the Irish Match-Maker," "Buckram-Back, the Country Dancing Master," and "Bob Pentland, the Irish Smuggler." Carleton's fairy tales, a mixture of the real with the unreal, are generally not of a fantastic nature; "The Three Tasks or The Little House Under the Hill," "Frank Martin and the Fairies," and "The Pudding Bewitched," for example, dramatize the relationship between the country people and characters from the spirit world. Carleton presents a panoramic view of his culture, colored by his own perception of people and events. "The Three Tasks or The Little House Under the Hill," "The Lough Derg Pilgrim," "Phelim O'Toole's Courtship," and "Tubber Derg" represent the range of his fiction.

"The Three Tasks or The Little House Under the Hill" is a story within a story. In the first series of the *Traits and Stories of the Irish Peasantry*, the lead story, "Ned M'Keown," introduces characters who, like Geoffrey Chaucer's pilgrims tell stories to one another as they sit around Ned's fireplace. The characters are not fictitious; but are actual people who lived in the region described, and who are recollected from the author's youth. "The Three Tasks or The Little House Under the Hill" is the tale Ned M'Keown tells to entertain his visitors on a stormy night at Kilrudden. In the story, Jack Magennis meets a dark man and a pipe-smoking talking dog who offer Jack riches if he wins a card game but servitude if he loses. Since Jack "heard of men being made up entirely by the fairies, till there was no end to their wealth," he agrees to play. When he loses, Jack asks for a year's grace so he can provide for his widowed mother. At the appointed hour, the dog appears with a green ribbon and a spyglass about his neck and Wellington boots upon his hind legs to take Jack to the dark man's castle.

At the castle, Jack is shown a long room with three hundred and sixty-five hooks, all but one holding a man's head. By nightfall, if he is to avoid decapitation, Jack must clean a stable that has not been cleaned in seven years. Unable to clean the stable, in his frustration Jack sings an Irish song and dances the hornpipe at triple time, attracting the attention of a beautiful young lady. Magically, she gets the task done and Jack's life is spared. He must accomplish two other tasks, however: catch a wild filly and rob a crane's nest high in a tree on an island. The beautiful lady helps Jack to bridle the filly and get the crane's eggs. In his haste, Jack leaves one of her toes, used to climb the tree, on the island. The master will know who has helped Jack; so she informs him that she must flee from the castle or be killed. Now in love with each other, the couple escapes on the filly's back.

Following the traditional folk motifs of the chase, the pair eludes the pursuing villain and his party. On three occasions, Jack delays their progress. From the filly's right ear, a dry stick, a pebble, and a drop of green water produce a forest, rocky roads, and finally a lake to drown the dark man. Arriving safely in Ireland, the beauty tells Jack that a cache of gold lies buried near his mother's cottage. He finds it, but forgets about the lady. Rich and famous, Jack is to marry the daughter of a nobleman. At the wedding feast, the talking dog appears and soon thereafter, a man on horseback who claims the bride-to-be was pledged to him. Then Jack, his lips touched by the dog's paw, suddenly remembers his adventures and finds his beautiful benefactor. A double wedding takes place. As Jack is to join his bride in the nuptial chamber, he is awakened by his mother from a long dream. He loses his bride but finds the gold, accounting for the Magennis wealth.

"The Three Tasks or The Little House Under the Hill" illustrates the dual nature of the fairies; some will help people and others will harm them, a characteristic of the Irish oral literary tradition. Unlike the Scots, whose fairies are usually demonic, and the English, whose fairies were banished during the Age of Enlightenment, the Irish treasure them and invent a variety of adventures between humans and the good and bad inhabitants of the woods, water, and the air. Folk beliefs, because of the cultural acceptance of a preternatural world, are naturally a part of Irish realistic tales. Such stories often have three dominant themes: the relationship of the people to their church, land, and family, as demonstrated in "The Lough Derg Pilgrim," "Phelim O'Toole's Courtship," and "Tubber Derg."

"The Lough Derg Pilgrim," first published in 1828 as "A Pilgrimage to Patrick's Purgatory" in *The Christian Examiner*, an anti-Catholic journal of the Church of Ireland, appeared under Carleton's pseudonym, Wilton. It was actually coauthored by Caesar Otway, the journal's editor and an ardent foe of Catholic Emancipation. When the tale was later published as "The Lough Derg Pilgrim," the objectionable inflamatory passages of Otway were deleted. This story, however, and the others that appeared in *The Christian Examiner*—"The Broken Oath," "Father Butler," "The Station," "The Death of a Devotee," "The Priest's Funeral," "The Brothers," "Lachlin Murray and the Blessed Candle," "The Lianhan Shee," "The Illicit Distiller, or the Force of Conscience," "History of a Chimney Sweep," "The Materialist," and "Dennis O'Shaughnessy Going to Maynooth"—branded Carleton as an anti-Catholic writer who ridiculed his people. These stories were categorized as "Sketches of the Irish Peasantry," "Popular Romish Legends," and Irish superstitions, a serious break in the Irish literary tradition which never considered its people to be peasants or its legends to be Romish and superstitious.

Eventually, Carleton outgrew the condemnation, but he has yet to assume the role that Dickens enjoys in England. The abridged edition of "The Lough Derg Pilgrim" begins with the narrator, a thinly disguised version of Carleton in his nineteenth year, describing his religious practices prior to his pilgrimage to Lough Derg (Irish for Red Lake). To prepare himself for a walk across water, the young man fasts and prays for three days. Then in a "pitch of superstitious absurdity," he places his foot on a water lily in his father's pond and sinks up to his neck. Crestfallen but undaunted, he sets out for Lough Derg within a month, dressed in a black suit and mistaken for a priest by the Catholics, who bow to him. On the road, he overtakes two women wearing gray cloaks with striped red-and-blue petticoats.

Because of the detailed description of the travelers, the inns, food served, and natural scenery, the reader becomes a listener and an onlooker to the pilgrimage. The two women talk to the "priest" in reverential tones and treat him differently, but not because of their piety. As the pilgrims converge on Lough Derg, they represent a wide variety of people, young and old, male and female, holy and unholy. Crowds of folks reach the island in Lough Derg where the chapel, or "Prison," is located. There they undergo physical pain which includes walking on sharp rocks, praying throughout an entire night and being kept awake by blows to the head by other pilgrims, and fasting. On his way home, the young pilgrim is robbed of his clothing and money by the two women, who were seasoned pilgrims there for the plunder. In "Dennis

O'Shaughnessy," Carleton documents another autobiographical journey, the country boy's preparation for the priesthood, an honor to his family and township.

Not all Irishmen had the religious fervor satirized in "The Lough Derg Pilgrim" and "Dennis O'Shaughnessy," but most of them loved Ireland. That love permeates Carleton's fiction. Poor or rich, the Irish, attached to their land, were concerned about passing on their holdings to posterity. "Phelim O'Toole's Courtship," a comic tale, demonstrates this concern. Phelim, an only child, is heir to "a snug estate of half an acre." His parents, loving and spoiling him, deny him nothing that their poverty can afford. By the age of ten, Phelim has become the village thief, liar, and troublemaker—a source of anxiety to his honest parents. At twenty, he is uneducated, unemployed, fond of women and whiskey, and a fugitive from the law. His parents think it is time for Phelim to marry and beget an heir for the half acre, which has been in the O'Toole family for three generations.

In a series of comic episodes, Phelim proposes to Bridget Doran, the priest's housekeeper. She is older than Phelim's mother but the source of money for his future adventures. Next, Phelim proposes to Sally Flattery, a thief and the daughter of a thief with whom Phelim operates. She tricks Phelim into believing that her father has been jailed and will not implicate Phelim in the crime if he takes care of her. Meanwhile, his father is preparing for a match with Peggy Donovan. After much wrangling with her father about the dowry to match the half acre, it is agreed that a marriage is to take place. On the following Sunday, the banns of marriage are announced between Phelim and Bridget, Sally, and Peggy. The congregation is amused, expecting this sort of behavior from Phelim, but the women are furious. They, along with relatives, rush over to the half acre, fighting it out with one another and the O'Tooles. Tricked by the village fool, Phelim is jailed while his matrimonial fate is being decided. Unable to lie his way out of jail, he is convicted and transported for life. His aged parents eventually lose the land and join the army of beggars, recollecting that they should have been more careful about Phelim's moral education.

In a much more somber tone, Carleton in "Tubber Derg" discusses the land and a family's connection with it, placing more emphasis on the family and the father's responsibilities for his children. This story tells of the poverty and sufferings of Owen M'Carthy and his family, a reality all too common in nineteenth century Ireland. Once a prosperous farmer and the descendant of an ancient and honest family, Owen, his wife, and their young children face eviction because they are unable to pay the inflated rent on their farm. By walking to Dublin to see the absentee landlord, Owen believes he can postpone the eviction. With much tenderness, Owen bids his family farewell, speaking in Irish and holding back tears. His trip to Dublin does not stay the eviction; Owen, derided by the servants, does speak to the landlord, who refers him to the agent. The fact that the M'Carthys had farmed the estate for more than two hundred years does not impress the landlord or the agent.

Returning to Tubber Derg (Irish for Red Well), Owen discovers that his young daughter has died and that his family is living in a neighbor's barn. Within a year they all leave home to beg in a strange part of the country where the proud M'Carthys are unknown. They are turned away from the homes of the rich and fed by poor families fortunate enough to have a roof and some food. Despite great odds, the family survives until the three eldest boys are hired out to herd cows, and the daughter works as a maid in a farm house. The two youngest children remain with their parents. From the children's earnings and the alms, within a few years, Owen can rent a small cottage, and the homeless begging days are over. Owen goes back to Tubber Derg to find a productive, small farm for rent. Both he and his wife want to lie beside their dead daughter in the ancient burial grounds of the M'Carthys.

At Tubber Derg, he visits the home of the family that befriended him after the eviction and goes on to his daughter's grave site. His sorrow turns to indignation when he sees a tombstone in the graveyard, wondering who would dare to bury upon the M'Carthy Mores of Tubber Derg. Shocked, Owen sees that it is his daughter's headstone, erected by a widow and her son out of respect for the M'Carthys who helped her in her distress. Then in a fresh burst of sorrow, Owen, speaking in Irish with the feeling and figurative language of the old Irish families, delivers his own greeting and that of his wife to their child, wishing she were part of the family again. That not being possible, Owen asks his child for her prayers before God to look with favor and compassion upon her family.

Sixteen years after leaving Tubber Derg, Owen and his family return with cattle and furnishings to begin anew their lives among old friends in their ancestral homesite. Like so many other stories, "Tubber Derg" contains frequent authorial passages criticizing the avaricious landlords and agents who rackrent the tenants, producing starvation and misery among the independent farmers. Carleton also points out that this type of land management leads to violence, for not all tenants are as meek as Owen M'Carthy. The violent reaction to eviction is best illustrated in "Wildgoose Lodge," in which murder and executions follow the evictions.

Carleton, categorized a decade ago as a minor Victorian writer, is a major Irish writer whose best work was written by 1850. In all his work he sings the praises of his people, damns their indolence, and mourns their sorrows. The simplistic solution to the woes of rural Ireland, according to Carleton, was a return of the landed gentry to harmonize the relationship of the working population between their church and family. Carleton's tales illustrate his belief that a good life is possible following great tragedies.

Major publications other than short fiction
NOVELS: *Fardorougha, the Miser*, 1839; *Valentine McClutchy, the Irish Agent*, 1845; *The Black Prophet, a Tale of Irish Famine*, 1846; *The Emigrants of Ahadarra*, 1848; *The Tithe-Proctor*, 1849; *The Squanders of Castle Squander*, 1852; *Red Hall; or, the Baronet's Daughter* 1852 (later called *The Black Baronet*, 1858); *Willy Reilly and His Dear Cooleen Bawn*, 1855; *The Evil Eye; or, The Black Spectre*, 1860; *Redmond Count O'Hanlon: The Irish Rapparee*, 1862.
PLAY: *Irish Manufacture or Bob Gawley's Project*, 1841.
POETRY: *The Midnight Hour: Retrospections*, 1828; *Taedet Me Vitae*, 1854.
NONFICTION: *The Life of William Carleton*, 1896.

Bibliography
Bell, Sam Hanna. "William Carleton and His Neighbors" in *Ulster Folklore*.
Boué, André. *William Carleton, Romancier Irlandais*.
Flanagan, Thomas J. *The Irish Novelists, 1800-1850*.
Kiely, Benedict. *Poor Scholar*.
O'Donoghue, David. *The Life of William Carleton*.
Shaw, Rose. *Carleton's Country*.
Sullivan, Eileen A., ed. *Carleton Newsletter*.

Eileen A. Sullivan

ALEJO CARPENTIER

Born: Havana, Cuba; December 26, 1904
Died: Paris, France; April 24, 1980

Principal short fiction
Guerra del tiempo, 1958 (*War of Time*, 1970).

Other literary forms
In contact with avant-garde groups in Havana and Paris, Alejo Carpentier wrote poetry as well as opera libretti and texts for other theatrical enterprises in his early years. Involved in publishing, broadcasting, and cinema for virtually all his life, he has contributed hundreds of articles of criticism on literature and the fine arts, especially music, some of which have been republished in book form. He is best known for his novels, which have been widely translated and studied. In 1977 he was awarded the Cervantes Prize for literature by the Royal Academy of Spain.

Influence
Carpentier, along with Jorge Luis Borges and Miguel Angel Asturias, is a founder and key figure of the Latin American new narrative. He is particularly noted for a fusion of realistic description and expressionism known as magic realism, which aims at capturing his own reality in its mythic and therefore universal dimensions. Carpentier is acclaimed for his treatment of time, his intricately symmetrical narrative structure, and his dense "neo-baroque" prose.

Story characteristics
As elaborately structured as a poem or a musical composition, Carpentier's stories almost always present some intriguing alternative to linear time. The underpinnings of traditional logic are thus exposed and questioned, with passive although appealing characters seen as carried along by the tide of events that engulf them.

Biography
Alejo Carpentier, the son of French and Russian parents, was educated in France as well as Cuba, studying architecture and music. A journalist during the 1920's, he became fascinated with Afro-Cuban culture, publishing his first novel, which dealt with this theme, shortly after exile for political activities. During the 1930's he moved among avant-garde coteries in Paris, including the surrealists, although he later rejected doctrinaire surrealism. His reencounter in 1939 with the Caribbean—Venezuela, Mexico, Haiti—initiated his years of finest literary production. Since 1959 he has served the Castro gov-

ernment in a wide assortment of cultural offices, and he is without question the most prestigious Cuban to lend it such support.

Analysis

Alejo Carpentier's "Semejante a la noche" ("Like the Night") is indicative of one of the prominent alternatives for sociological literature in the mid-twentieth century, an alternative that has had an enormous impact on the so-called new Latin American narrative. This is a mode of writing that is depersonalized, structurally geometric, and virtually allegorical in its thematic otherness. Unlike the social realism of the 1930's and 1940's in Latin America that shared with American and European counterparts a sentimentality and idealization that often bordered on kitsch and the trite, the committed literature represented by Carpentier's stories aspires, by eschewing all rhetoric of empathy, to a Brechtian intellectual and analytical contemplation. The goal may be to prevent contaminating the object—the verbal message and its sociopolitically definable meaning—with trivial emotional responses, but the artistic effect is equally to render ostensible "propositional" meaning less transparent and to increase the density of the symbolic texture. In short, fiction like Carpentier's, as properly ideological as it may be, is more complex and, therefore, less assimilable to reductionary meanings than are its ancestors in a literature of sociopolitical commitment.

"Like the Night" deals with the oppressively ideological myths of war. Three separate time frames and three separate nuclei of incident and event are seamlessly worked together to project a holistic image of war as an enterprise that engulfs a certain class of young men in convenient commonplaces concerning adventure, ennobling sacrifice, and righteous strife. Men subscribe to these ideological myths in a gesture of unconscious self-betrayal to the interests of power structures who use war not only as a means of conquest and subjugation, but also as an instrument for self-serving lies that provide the masses with a unifying and "noble" cause.

The three time frames are the Trojan War, the Spanish Conquest, and the French Conquest of the New World. In each case, an innocent youth prepares to embark by ship on an adventure that has been justified for him by his superiors. In each case, the explanation of the just cause is an ideological cliché that the reader associates with the particular culture at issue. "I breathe in deeply the breeze that came down from the olive tree groves, thinking how beautiful it would be to die in such a just cause, in the very cause of reason." These are the words of the young Trojan warrior. The Spanish sailor thinks: "They were millions of souls that we would win for our holy religion, thereby fulfilling Christ's mandate to his Apostles. We were soldiers of God at the same time we were soldiers of the king, and through those Indians baptized and claimed, freed of their barbarous superstitions by our work, our nation would know the prize of an unbreakable greatness that would give us happiness, riches and power over all of the kingdoms of Europe." Finally, the French legionnaire claims: "We were going to carry out a great civilizing task in those immense wooded territories that extended from the burning Gulf of Mexico to the regions of Chicagúa, teaching new skills to the nations that lived there." In each case the youth utters these self-serving commonplaces of an imperialistic ideology as he takes leave of a familiar and comforting personal reality: the familiar sounds and smells of his home town, his betrothed.

Thus, from a semiological point of view, the four segments of the story (one for each of the three settings; the last returns to close the cyclical pattern) arrange an opposition for the reader, in the persons of a series of innocent and uncritical youths, between familiar and comforting knowns and the threatening unknowns of exploration, war, and conquest explained and given importance by patriotic slogans. To be sure, the story depends on the reader's accepting for himself a greater perceptivity than that of the three overlapping narrators. That is, it is the reader who must realize that the thoughts of the youths which so stir their minds and hearts are so many political bromides by which governments seek to ennoble the ignoble slaughter and subjugation of their military campaigns.

The cyclical nature of the narrative is an important ingredient in the rhetorical demand for such a perception on the part of the reader. In the first place, the contemporary reader, aware thanks to historical interpretations and popular legends to the effect that the three campaigns described by Carpentier's story were not the heroic gestes that the protagonists believed them to be, is asked to perceive the thoughts of the youths as ideological clichés. In the second place, the repetition of a nucleus of narration—the preparations for a heroic adventure, the excitement of the hustle and bustle, the heightened emotions, and the patriotic claims for the adventure—in a variety of times and places serves to suggest, rather than its unique transcendence, its quality as commonplace.

This dual semiological strategy—the appeal to the reader's cultural knowledge and the repetition of a commonplace—is enhanced by what in the original Spanish is a subtle linguistic parody. If the reader recognizes the key thoughts of the one-in-three narrators as political commonplaces, he also recognizes the texture of the three first-person narrations as *kitschy* re-creations of the expressive style of the different periods and cultures. Thus, the text of the Trojan has a neutral "Attic" quality that stresses, in a way reminiscent of passages of Homer, the cumulative details of epic campaigns. The text of the Spanish youth abounds in the archaisms of fifteenth century Spanish, in the pithy and earthy proverbs of the peasant, and in reference to the clamorous sounds and pungent smells of late-medieval Mediterranean locales. By contrast the text of the French warrior is characterized by the *sermo gravis*, the measured periods, and the self-sufficient cultural superiority characteristic of French classicism; it is also the longest of the three narrations.

In order to confirm the demythificational, anti-ideological reading suggested to the reader by the three strategies mentioned, the conclusion is "revisionist" in that the Trojan narrator, to whom Carpentier returns in the fourth and final segment, suffers a moment of sudden critical reflection: "Now it would be the bugles, the mud, the wet bread, the arrogance of the chiefs, the blood spilled in error, the gangrene smelling of infected syrups. I was no longer so sure that my courage would increase the greatness and fortunes of the long-haired Achaeans. An old soldier going off to war as a job, with no more enthusiasm than the shearer of sheep heading for the stables, was telling anyone who cared to listen how Helen of Sparta was very happy in Troy and how when she lay with Paris her groans of pleasure reddened the cheeks of the virgins who dwell in Priamos' palace. It was said that the whole story of the sad captivity of Leda's daughter, offended and humiliated by the Trojans, was merely the propaganda of war, spread by Agamemnon with Menelaus' consent.

Thus Carpentier ensures his reader's "proper reading" of the separate but overlapping narrations. Carpentier's rhetorical strategies are not simply a clever artistic device for structural originality, although whatever aesthetic reaction that may derive from contemplating the neatness of the meshing narrations is certainly a legitimate response to the story. Rather, these strategies are elements in an overall narrative configuration in which Carpentier's story is in semiologically productive clash with the stories of the narrator participants. This irony vanishes suddenly in the closure of the text when the naïveté of the young warrior, challenged by the hardened soldier's cynicism, yields suddenly to a shock of recognition that confirms in a demythifying "reading" of the events and slogans surrounding the military preparations the demythifying reading of the individual narrations that the structure of Carpentier's text sets out to encourage in the reader. It is in this subtle and complex narrative texture that "Like the Night" is eminently paradigmatic of alternatives for Marxist and committed fiction in the new Latin American narrative that eschews the broadside approach of classical social realism.

Major publications other than short fiction

NOVELS: ¡*Ecué-Yamba-O!*, 1933; *El reino de este mundo*, 1949 (*The Kingdom of This World*, 1957); *Los pasos perdidos*, 1953 (*The Lost Steps*, 1956); *El siglo de las luces*, 1962 (*Explosion in a Cathedral*, 1963); *El recurso del metodo*, 1974 (*Reasons of State*, 1976); *Concierto barroco*, 1974 (*Baroque Concert*); *El arpa y la sombra*, 1979 (*The Harp and the Shadow*).

NONFICTION: *La música en Cuba*, 1946 (*Music in Cuba*); *Tientos y diferencias*, 1964 (*Preludes and Differences*); *Literatura y conciencia política en América Latina*, 1969 (*Literature and Political Awareness in Latin America*); *La ciudad de las columnas*, 1970 (*City of Columns*).

Bibliography
Echevarría, Roberto González. *Alejo Carpentier: The Pilgrim at Home.*
Müller-Bergh, Klaus. *Alejo Carpentier.*

David W. Foster

R. V. CASSILL

Born: Cedar Falls, Iowa; May, 17, 1919

Principal short fiction

15 X 3, 1957 (with Herbert Gold and James B. Hall); *The Father and Other Stories*, 1965; *The Happy Marriage and Other Stories*, 1966.

Other literary forms

Although widely praised for his short stories, R. V. Cassill has written primarily as a novelist throughout his career, his first novel being *The Eagle on the Coin* (1950) and his latest being *Hoyt's Child* (1976). He has also written two nonfiction books, *Writing Fiction* (1962) and *In an Iron Time: Statements and Reiterations: Essays* (1967). Most recently he has edited *The Norton Anthology of Short Fiction* (1978).

Influence

Cassill's major influence on the American literary community has been as a writer of short stories, a teacher of fiction writing, and a teacher of fiction. He taught at the Iowa Writers' Workshop, which has shaped the style and taste of many who entered the writing profession in the 1960's and 1970's. Through his students from Iowa and elsewhere, Cassill may exert a steady but muted influence for many years. Also, his editing of the Norton anthology is bound to popularize, to some extent, his preferences in fiction. Additionally, his own stories are sure to be more frequently anthologized in the future.

Story characteristics

In his introduction to *The Happy Marriage and Other Stories*, George P. Elliott says of Cassill as a short-story writer, "He gets to the horror," meaning the horror of subtle tensions and rigid chasms between human beings, particularly within families. Cassill is markedly a writer of the Midwest, setting many of his stories in Iowa, using Chicago as the El Dorado of boyhood dreams. By using the Midwest as his milieu, he concentrates on the complexity of people who, as "middle Americans," are often presumed to be comfortably dull. His stories often present the aspirations of the adolescent boy or the delusions of the adult. His imagery is vivid and heavily visual, and his expository passages are graceful, succinct, and usually ironic and revealing.

Biography

Before World War II, Ronald Verlin Cassill studied art, planning to become a professional painter, and won some regional art contests in Iowa in 1939 and 1940. He began to write fiction after serving as an army officer in the

South Pacific during the war. The beginning of his professional writing career was marked by his winning second place in the *Atlantic Monthly* "Firsts" contest of 1947. Several of his stories have been included in *The Best American Short Stories* and in *Prize Stories: The O. Henry Awards*. He earned B. A. and M. A. degrees from the University of Iowa, studied at the Sorbonne, and received a Fulbright fellowship, Rockefeller grant, and Guggenheim grant. He has taught at Iowa, the New School for Social Research, Purdue, Columbia, Harvard, and Brown.

Analysis

Writers whom R. V. Cassill especially admires are Gustave Flaubert, Henry James, D. H. Lawrence, and James Joyce. Their influence is not verifiable from the features of a given story so much as it is a cumulative force in Cassill's writing. His work often manifests the rich hues and texture of Flaubert's visual imagery, the complex internal conflicts of characters presented by Flaubert and James, the agonies of initiation from Joyce, and the energy and obsession of the characters of Lawrence. Considering his background in art, it is natural for Cassill to share the painterly qualities which all of these men, except the nearly blind Joyce, exhibited throughout their works. Cassill does not neglect color, shape, composition, and fine detail.

His stories, usually set in the Midwest, present rather common situations of youthful initiation, frustrated dreams, family conflict, and harbored delusion. The stories might be considered in terms of two broad types: those which examine the effects of youthful passions and those which reveal the destructiveness of self-delusion in adults. The most lyrical language and imagery in Cassill's short fiction appears in the stories of youthful initiation. Good examples of this type are "The Biggest Band" and "In the Central Blue," both of which present boyhood passions which are so strong that achieving them becomes the focal point of a boy's life. Given such a frame of mind, whatever happens to the boys in these stories is bound to be disappointing; either they fail to get what they want, or they succeed and find that the thing desired is not so valuable after all. Perhaps Cassill's most complex dramatic problems appear in the stories about adults such as "The Crime of Mary Lynn Yager" and "The Sunday Painter." In both of these pieces the protagonists are unable to face inadequacies within themselves.

In most of the stories of the first type, locale is crucial, as is the case with "The Biggest Band." This story, Cassill's own favorite, grows out of the small-town environment and financial straits of Davisburg, Iowa, during the Depression. The reflective first-person narrator (called Buddy in childhood) speaks as an adult about his experiences with the Corn State Southern Band, and what he knows now strikes a telling contrast to what he felt as a boy.

The plan to assemble a state-wide band to travel to Chicago and play at the 1933 World's Fair is promoted by Lothar Smith, whose nominal resemblance to Lothario (deceiver and seducer) carries over into his character. He resembles Meredith Wilson's "Music Man"; however, his ambition and musical ability far exceed those of "Professor" Harold Hill. A more important difference is that, despite all the appearances of a massive confidence game, the trip does take place, the band does play at the World's Fair, and Smith goes broke realizing his dream. Finally, he appears to have been more a grand dreamer than a self-server. In this regard he and Buddy are alike.

The vital factor in the success of Smith's plan is the imagination of the people, and it is a historical commonplace that hard times produce ardent dreamers. Of course, part of the plan is to sell instruments to people who want to make the trip but do not have an instrument and, therefore, usually cannot play one. Buddy's parents buy him a trombone that he must learn to play, he is later required to sell two "excursion tickets" in order to make the trip, and every appearance of a swindle is present. Buddy becomes so obsessed that he even suggests that his father should borrow money to buy the tickets. Buddy fails to sell the tickets, and his mother, who has known Smith since childhood, forces him to honor his initial promise. Buddy goes, the band plays at odd times and poorly, and the whole affair is a predictable failure. He does not discover what he expected, just as he fails to see the evasively nude Sally Rand; nevertheless, he learns more than he will admit, even in retrospect.

Buddy's selfish obsession with going to Chicago, like Smith's big plans, is presented negatively at first because both of them expect others to sacrifice for their personal fulfillment. In the end, however, Smith has given far more than he has taken, and Buddy feels "oddly free to do [his] best now that it didn't seem to count for anything." He narrates the story from adulthood and speaks laughingly of the band as "an altogether preposterous blunder committed against nature and a fine art," but he also admits the clean beauty of a performance given at dawn before a stadium which contained only a few janitors. He describes how he would have told the story to Mrs. Packer, who shared his dream, if she had been alive when he returned, and the story ends with a burst of images embodying youthful zeal and true art:

> From their staffs over the national pavilions the ultramarine and lemon and scarlet pennants streamed out like dyes leaking out into an oceanic current. It was only the empty sky that watched us—but my God, my God, how the drums thundered, how we blew.

"In the Central Blue" also deals with youthful obsession, this time the more common one of sex. The location is changed to Chesterfield, Nebraska, but the place is essentially similar. Also, as in "The Biggest Band," the proportions of the boy's desire exceed any gratification he might achieve. The first-person narrator says of the girl desired, "I loved her ignorantly, impurely and intermittently." Yet his desire is far more than a physical one:

But it was not a physical assault on her that I planned or needed. I was going to ravish her mind. With the aid of this powerful movie plus a few tickles and kisses afterward, I was going to wheedle her mind right away into the realm of wish and nonsense, where I was so lonely all by myself.

What he really wants is escape from the fearful self-doubt and loneliness of adolescence, but, like the World War I aviator-heroes of the movies and like all mortals, he finds himself condemned to "soaring in the central blue."

In the process of the story he discovers his identity as an uneasy inhabitant of the middle space between heaven and hell. More important than dealing with his frustrated desire to take "Hudson's blonde and titless cousin Betty" home and share kisses, tickles, and isolation is the discovery he makes about himself. Through the whim of his older brother, he is not allowed to go along in the car to take Betty home and fulfill his hopes. When he realizes what is being done to him, he puts up a fight to stay in the car and his father comes outside. His father, walking into the house with him, tells him he is too old to cry. In his frustration and his desire to be punished for his stupidity, he shouts back, "Well, I'm crying, you bastard." With obvious effort his father controls the urge to strike him, causing a discovery: "maybe for the first time, I saw him in his human dimension, bewildered and tugged in contrary directions like me." Even his father lives in the central blue of divided feelings. As in "The Biggest Band," the boy has not achieved what he was looking for, but he has found something more important in its place.

Representative of the other broad type of Cassill's stories is "The Sunday Painter," in which detail and delusion are interwoven to create a vivid, amusing, and ironic story. In this third-person narrative limited to the viewpoint of Joe Becker, businessman and unfulfilled amateur artist, there is a theme that works on at least two levels. First, Becker is self-deluded regarding his skill as a painter, thinking that "What had been so painful twenty years ago had mellowed and changed without being totally lost." Second, after months of painting works which are rendered with fine visual detail, Becker convinces himself that he has "explored art clean down to its sterile origin." Implicitly Cassill states that the sterility is not in art but in Becker himself. Quite like some artists in many forms of expression, Becker has transferred his own failings to art in general. In a comic and powerful final scene, he goes berserk and starts painting all over objects in his house, and ends up painting the babysitter from next door. She, who mocked his serious earlier efforts for lacking the bizarre, quickly comes to his defense as the neighbors pull him off her: "I don't think you should persecute him. . . . Artists have enough troubles as it is." Her misunderstanding of art mirrors his. The story can also be viewed as a satire of those writers and artists who complain that traditional approaches to art have become "sterile" and meaningless. Interpreted along these lines, the story argues that the fault lies not with art but with the complaining artists themselves. In the reference work *Contemporary Novelists of the English Language* (1972) Cassill comments, "As I grow older I love the commonplace of traditional thought and expression with a growing fervor."

"The Crime of Mary Lynn Yager" presents the problem of self-deception in more serious terms. Clarissa Carlson, who plans to marry Joe Meadow and leave Iowa with him once he finishes his degree and begins his promising business career, has the course of her life altered when one of her second-grade children drowns. Mary Lynn Yager, the girl Clarissa always disliked, drowns on a school outing at the lake. When Clarissa finds that the drowned child is Mary Lynn and not one of her "good ones," she feels a relief that leads to guilt later. The guilt which engulfs Clarissa in the story emanates from her refusal to face the unfairness of her attitude toward Mary Lynn. The third-person point of view is slanted through Clarissa's perception in order to heighten the effect of her turmoil. Even though Clarissa has convinced herself that the child was a "wrong little girl," it becomes clear that there was very little basis for this attitude. The teacher blames Mary Lynn's contrary nature for causing the accident because she cannot admit her own prejudice and thereby remove her submerged guilt. She is doomed to struggle subconsciously with both her guilt over the child's drowning and her guilt over having misjudged her. An underlying question is implanted in the story as to whether people's lives can be fated by the attitudes of others.

The unconfronted guilt makes Clarissa quarrelsome, driving off Joe, and one problem leads to another. She marries LeRoy Peterson, who blames her for his business troubles just as she had unjustly blamed Mary Lynn. With her confidence destroyed by LeRoy's accusations, she wonders "what was to blame for the decay of her life" and begins to agree with him "that it was she who had brought it on them." Their marriage degenerates to "protracted hostility" and ends when LeRoy deserts her.

After years of absence she returns to Iowa where she discovers that one of her "good children," Bobbie Tenman, is in trouble with the law. In fact, it becomes clear that he was better than Mary Lynn only in Clarissa's mind. She is relieved that he receives a suspended sentence for vandalism, feeling "In the maimed frustration of her loneliness any evasion of just punishment [is] a sign of hope." As Mary Lynn was misunderstood, so is Clarissa when she kisses Bobbie in an attempt to keep him innocent and unblemished in her mind. Bobbie's wife, who also happens to be one of Mary Lynn's sisters, discovers Clarissa and shoves her to the ground. The girl has no idea who Clarissa is but assumes the worst of her. In Clarissa's eyes "Mary Lynn's play with her teacher's life had been foul play," when the foul play actually has been in Clarissa's self-deception. At the end of the story she is still haunted by a picture of Mary Lynn which she has long since destroyed, and she envies the child her peace in death.

In his conscientious presentation of characters caught up in their passions and delusions, Cassill has given much to the short story. He develops irony by setting his characters in a common milieu, then twisting them slightly on their axis to reveal their agony and their worth.

Major publications other than short fiction

NOVELS: *The Eagle on the Coin*, 1950; *Clem Anderson*, 1961; *Pretty Leslie*, 1963; *The President*, 1964; *La Vie Passionnée of Rodney Buckthorne*, 1968; *Dr. Cobb's Game*, 1970; *The Goss Women*, 1974; *Hoyt's Child*, 1976.

NONFICTION: *Writing Fiction*, 1962; *In an Iron Time: Statements and Reiterations: Essays*, 1967.

James Curry Robison

WILLA CATHER

Born: Gore, in Back Creek Valley (near Winchester), Virginia; December 7, 1873
Died: New York, New York; April 24, 1947

Principal short fiction
The Troll Garden, 1905; *Youth and the Bright Medusa*, 1920; *Obscure Destinies*, 1932; *The Old Beauty and Others*, 1948; *Willa Cather's Collected Short Fiction: 1892-1912*, 1965; *Uncle Valentine and Other Stories: Willa Cather's Collected Short Fiction, 1915-1929*, 1973.

Other literary forms
Willa Cather is best known as a novelist, but she wrote prolifically in other forms, especially as a young woman; she had been publishing short stories for more than twenty years before she published her first novel. Although her fame rests largely on her twelve novels and a few short stories, she has a collection of poetry, three collections of essays, and hundreds of newspaper columns and magazine pieces to her credit. Only one of her books, *A Lost Lady* (1923), was filmed in Hollywood; after that one experience Cather forbade any of her work to be filmed again. She was awarded the Pulitzer Prize in 1923 (for 1922) for the novel *One of Ours*.

Influence
Several of Cather's early short stories appeared in journals for which she did editorial work, and were written at least partly to fill allotted space in those journals. Others appeared in the popular magazines of the time, such as *Woman's Home Companion*. As an editor with *McClure's Magazine* for several years, she met and encouraged many young writers. Although she wrote several "city stories," Cather was one of America's first modern writers to make the prairie immigrant experience an important and continuing subject for high-quality fiction. Since Cather allowed only a few of her short stories to be anthologized, she is known widely for those few stories while many other excellent stories have been too frequently overlooked. Cather enjoys particularly appreciative audiences in Japan and France, as well as in England, Canada, and the United States.

Story characteristics
Cather's short stories cover a broader range of subjects than do her novels, but basically her mature stories deal with the struggle of the sensitive artist in a small-minded, materialistic world and the relationship of human beings with the land and with the past. Cather's stories often reflect the tension she herself felt between the open landscape and the city, between East and West.

Biography

Willa Sibert Cather moved with her family from Virginia to Nebraska when she was only nine years old, a move that was to influence her mind and art throughout her life. As a student at the University of Nebraska, she wrote for various college magazines; she also became a regular contributor to the *Nebraska State Journal*, publishing book, theater, and concert reviews, as well as commentary on the passing scene. Even after she moved to Pittsburgh to take an editorial job, she continued to send columns home to the *Nebraska State Journal*. Later she also began contributing to the Lincoln *Courier*. She taught English in Pittsburgh (an experience that became the source for one of her most famous short stories, "Paul's Case") and then moved to New York to take a position with *McClure's Magazine*. After the publication of her first novel, *Alexander's Bridge*, in 1912, she left *McClure's Magazine* to devote full time to her creative work.

Analysis

Willa Cather was always conscious of a double urge in herself, toward art and toward the land. As long as her parents were living, she found herself torn between the Western prairie and the cultural centers of the East and Europe. That basic polarity appears again and again in her stories, some of which deal with the artist's struggle against debilitating influences, and some with both the pleasant and the difficult aspects of the prairie experience. Perhaps only in her work did Cather achieve a comfortable reconciliation of these polarities, by making the prairie experience the subject of her art.

All of Cather's work is consistently value-centered. She believed in characters who are good, artists who are true to their callings, people who can appreciate and use what is valuable from the past, and individuals who have a special relationship with the land. Her chief agony lay in what she saw as a general sellout to materialism—in the realm of art, in the prairie and desert, in the small town, in the city.

The struggle of the artist to maintain integrity against an unsympathetic environment and the forces of an exploitive materialism is explored in three stories that are particularly important in the Cather canon. Two of them, "The Sculptor's Funeral" and "Paul's Case," have been widely anthologized and are well known. The third, "Uncle Valentine," is an important later story.

"The Sculptor's Funeral" is about the return in death of a world-renowned sculptor to the pinched little prairie town from which he somehow miraculously sprang. Harvey Merrick's body arrives by train in the dead of winter, accompanied by one of his former students. There to meet the coffin are several prominent townsmen, among them a brusque, red-bearded lawyer named Jim Laird. Only he can appreciate the magnitude of Harvey Merrick's achievement. The watchers around the body chuckle and snort over poor Harvey's uselessness as a farm hand, over his inability to "make it" in the only things that count for them—money-making ventures in Sand City. Jim Laird, in a storm of self-hatred for having become the scheming lawyer these harpies wanted him to be, enters the room and blasts them mercilessly. He reminds the town elders of the young men they have ruined by drumming "nothing but money and knavery into their ears from the time they wore knickerbockers." They hated Harvey, Laird says, because he left them and rose above them, achieving in a world they were not fit to enter. He reminds them that Harvey "wouldn't have given one sunset over your marshes" for all of their material properties and possessions. Laird is too drunk the next day to attend the funeral, and it is learned that he dies some years later from a cold he caught while "driving across the Colorado mountains to defend one of Phelps's sons who had got into trouble there by cutting government timber."

Harvey Merrick is not the tragic figure of the story, for he, thanks to a timid father who sensed something special about this one son, managed to escape destruction. He became the artist he was destined to be, in spite of his unlikely beginnings. The money-grubbing first citizens of Sand City can wag their tongues feebly over his corpse, but they cannot touch him or detract from his accomplishment. If there is a tragic element in the story, it is the life of Jim Laird. Like Harvey, he went away to school full of idealistic fire; like Harvey, he wanted to be a great man and make the hometown people proud of him. Instead, he says, "I came back here to practice, and I found you didn't in the least want me to be a great man. You wanted me to be a shrewd lawyer." He became that shrewd lawyer and lost his soul in the process. The dead artist, imposing and serene in his coffin, serves as a perfect foil for Jim Laird, and the story stands as one of Cather's most powerful treatments of the conflict between artistic ideals and materialistic value systems.

"Paul's Case" presents a somewhat different view of that conflict. Paul, a high school youngster, is not a practicing artist, but he has an artistic temperament. He loves to hang around art galleries and concert halls and theaters, talking with the performers and basking in their reflected glory. It is glitter, excitement, and escape from the dripping taps in his home on Pittsburgh's Cordelia Street that Paul craves. A hopeless "case," Paul is finally taken out of high school by his widowed father because his mind is never on his studies. Forced from his usher's job at the concert hall and forbidden to associate with the actors at the theater, he loses the only things he had lived for and cared about. When he is denied those vital outlets for his aesthetic needs and sent to do dull work for a dull company, he carries out a desperate plan. One evening, instead of depositing his firm's receipts in the bank, he catches a train for New York. With swift determination, he buys elegant clothes and installs himself in a luxurious hotel suite, there to live for a few brief days the life he had always felt himself suited for. Those days are lovely and perfect, but the inevitable reckoning draws near; he learns from a newspaper that his father is en route to New York to retrieve him. Very deliberately Paul plots

his course, even buying carnations for his buttonhole. Traveling to the out-
skirts of town, he walks to an embankment above the Pennsylvania tracks.
There he carefully buries the carnations in the snow, and when the appropriate
moment comes, he leaps into the path of an oncoming train.

A sensitive youngster with limited opportunity, Paul is not an artist in the
usual sense. His distinction is that he responds to art, almost any art, with
an unusual fervor. To him, anything associated with the world of art is beautiful and inspiring, while anything associated with lower-middle-class America
is ugly and common. He is wrong about both worlds. With eyes only for the
artificial surface glitter that spangles the world of art, he never sees the realities
of hard work and struggle that define the life of every artist. Clearly, Cordelia
Street is not as bad as Paul imagines it to be; it is, in fact, a moderately nice
neighborhood where working people live and rear their families. Cordelia
Street, however, has inadvertently taught him that money is the answer to
all desires, that it can buy all the trappings that grace the world of art. Cordelia
Street's legendary heroes are the Kings of Wall Street.

In spite of his blindness, the reader's sympathies are with Paul because he
feels trapped in an aesthetic wasteland to which he cannot and will not return;
the reader realizes at the end that perhaps Paul's only escape lies in his final
choice. The Waldorf, after all, provided temporary breathing space at best.
His only real home is, as Cather tells us, in the "immense design of things."

Valentine Ramsay, the title character in "Uncle Valentine," is like Paul in
many ways: he is sensitive, charming, flighty, unpredictable, temperamental,
and intolerant of commonness. Unlike Paul, however, Valentine is a true
artist, a gifted composer; it is not the artificial shell of art that he values, but
the very heart of it. After several years abroad, he decides to return to
Greenacre, his family home in the lush Pennsylvania countryside. He feels
that perhaps at Greenacre he can shut out the world and find the peace he
needs to write music.

He and the neighbors next door, with whom he shares a special affection,
both artistic and social, have a magnificent year together, a "golden year."
They roam the fields and woods, they share music, and they increase in
aesthetic understanding. Casting a tragic shadow over this happy group, however, is the figure of Valentine's uncle, who haunts the premises like a grieving
ghost. A child prodigy, he had left home to pursue his art; but for reasons
never disclosed, he gave up his music and returned, burying himself in the
ashes of his ruined life.

As a young man, Valentine had made a bad marriage to a rich woman
whose materialistic coarseness became a constant affront to him; her very
presence beside him in a concert hall was enough to shatter his nerves and
obliterate the music he came to hear. Valentine has escaped from her, but
she is destined to destroy his peace once again. He and his neighbors discover
that she has purchased the large piece of property next to theirs, the property

they had loved and tramped through for endless days. She intends to move in soon, bringing her fortune, her brash assertiveness, and Valentine's only son. She, along with the encroaching factory smoke downriver, spells the end of the blessed life the little group of art fanciers has known at Greenacre. Valentine is forced to flee again, and we learn that he is killed while crossing a street in France.

Cather's message is clear. The important things in life—art and the sharing of its pleasures, friendships, a feeling for land and place, a reverence for the past—are too often destroyed in the name of progress. When economic concerns are given top priority, whether on the prairie or in Pennsylvania, the human spirit suffers. Happily, in a much-loved story called "Neighbor Rosicky" Cather affirms that material temptations can be successfully resisted. Valentine is defeated, but Rosicky and his values prevail.

Anton Rosicky, recognizable as another rendering of Ántonia's husband in Cather's best-known novel *My Ántonia* (1918), has instinctively established a value system that puts life and the land above every narrow-minded material concern. For example, when his entire corn crop is destroyed in the searing heat one July day, he organizes a little picnic so that the family can enjoy the few things they have left. Instead of despairing with his neighbors, Rosicky plays with his children. It is no surprise that he and his wife Mary agree without discussion as to what things they can let go. They refuse to skim the cream off their milk and sell it for butter because Mary would "rather put some colour into my children's faces than put money into the bank." Doctor Ed, who detects serious heart trouble in Rosicky, observes that "people as generous and warm-hearted and affectionate as the Rosickys never got ahead much; maybe you couldn't enjoy your life and put it into the bank, too."

"Neighbor Rosicky" is one of Cather's finest tributes to life on the Nebraska prairie, to a value system that grows out of human caring and love for the land. Rosicky had lived in cities for many years, had known hard times and good times there, but it occurred to him one lonely day in the city that he had to get to the land. He realized that "the trouble with big cities" was that "they built you in from the earth itself, cemented you away from any contact with the ground," so he made his decision and went West.

The only thing that disturbs his sleep now is the discontentment of his oldest son. Rudolph is married to a town girl, Polly, and he wants to leave the farm and seek work in the city. Rosicky understands Rudolph's restlessness and Polly's lonesomeness and looks for every opportunity to help the young couple find some recreation time in town. In spite of his efforts, however, Polly continues to dislike farm life and to find the Rosickys strange and "foreign." Then one day Rosicky suffers a heart attack near Rudolph's place. No one is there to care for him but Polly, and that day something lovely happens between the two of them: she has a revelation of his goodness that is "like an awakening to her." His warm brown hand somehow brings "her to herself," teaches her more about life than she has ever known before, offers her "some direct and untranslatable message." With this revelation comes the assurance that at last all will be well with Rudolph and Polly. They will remain on the land and Rosicky's spirit will abide with them, for Polly has caught the old man's vision. It is fitting that Rosicky's death a few months later is calmly accepted as a natural thing, and that he is buried in the earth he loved. That way there will be no strangeness, no jarring separation.

Rosicky is Cather's embodiment of all that is finest in the human character. He had been a city man, a lover of opera and the other cultural advantages of city life, but he found his peace in the simple life of a Nebraska farm. By contrast, Harvey Merrick, the sculptor, had been a country boy, a lover of the prairie landscape, but he found his peace in the art capitals of the world. Nevertheless, Merrick and Rosicky would have understood each other perfectly. One's talent lay in molding clay, the other's in molding lives.

Cather is sometimes accused of nostalgia, of denying the present and yearning for the past. What seems clear in her work, however, is not that she wants to live in the past, but that she deplores a total rejection of the values of the past. She fears a materialistic takeover of the human heart, or a shriveled view of human life. She is convinced that the desire for money and the things money can buy corrupts character, cheapens life, destroys the landscape, and enervates art. In her exploration of the conflicts engendered by a destructive materialism, in her celebration of art and the land, Willa Cather's devotion to an enduring system that spans time and space to embrace the good, the beautiful, and the true is made evident.

Major publications other than short fiction

NOVELS: *Alexander's Bridge*, 1912; *O Pioneers!*, 1913; *The Song of the Lark*, 1915; *My Ántonia*, 1918; *One of Ours*, 1922; *A Lost Lady*, 1923; *The Professor's House*, 1925; *My Mortal Enemy*, 1926; *Death Comes for the Archbishop*, 1927; *Shadows on the Rock*, 1931; *Lucy Gayheart*, 1935; *Sapphira and the Slave Girl*, 1940.

POETRY: *April Twilights*, 1903.

NONFICTION: *Not Under Forty*, 1936; *Willa Cather on Writing*, 1949; *Willa Cather in Europe*, 1956; *The Kingdom of Art: Willa Cather's First Principles and Critical Statements, 1893-1896*, 1966; *The World and the Parish: Willa Cather's Articles and Reviews, 1893-1902*, 1970.

Bibliography
Bennett, Mildred. *The World of Willa Cather*.
Bloom, Edward A. and Lillian D. Bloom. *Willa Cather's Gift of Sympathy*.
Brown, E. K. (completed by Leon Edel). *Willa Cather: A Critical Biography*.
Giannone, Richard. *Music in Willa Cather's Fiction*.
Lewis, Edith. *Willa Cather Living: A Personal Record*.

Randall, John H., III. *The Landscape and the Looking Glass*.
Sergeant, Elizabeth Shepley. *Willa Cather: A Memoir*.
Stouck, David. *Willa Cather's Imagination*.

Marilyn Arnold

CERVANTES
Miguel de Cervantes Saavedra

Born: Alcalá de Henares; September 29, 1547
Died: Madrid, Spain; April 23, 1616

Principal short fiction

Novelas Ejemplares, 1613 (*Exemplary Novels*).

Other literary forms

Miguel de Cervantes Saavedra is best known to readers in all languages as the author of *Don Quixote de la Mancha* (1605, 1615). That work was not only one of the first novels, but also the first truly modern novel (and one of the many wonders attendant upon its publication is the fact that such a book came so early in the life of the form); its influence appears in such disparate works as *Madame Bovary* (1857) and *Gravity's Rainbow* (1973). Cervantes' achievement is even more remarkable in view of the idiosyncratic nature of the book, its many and complex allusions to the history of Spain and the Jews in Spain, and the fact that most scholars believe that it did, indeed, start out as satire and only later, in Part II, complete the move from art through parody of art to art through the imitation of nature.

Cervantes' first novel, written when he was a young man, was *La Galatea* (1584). One eminent Cervantes scholar advises readers to forget the story, characters, and structure and imagine listening to it being read by skillful actors in a pleasant garden well furnished with wine and music. Cervantes' last novel, *Los Trabajos de Persiles y Sigismunda* (1617, *The Travels of Persiles and Sigismunda*), finished only days before his death, is a strange, wintry book composed in the kind of balanced, poetic, but tough Castilian that reminds one forcefully of William Shakespeare's diction in *King Lear* (1605); in fact, until the nineteenth century, its reputation was almost as great as that of *Don Quixote de la Mancha*.

In the Spain of his day, however, Cervantes was better known as a dramatist. After being freed from slavery in North Africa, he returned to Spain and wrote twenty to thirty plays for the theaters in Madrid. From 1580 to about 1587, all were produced and, as Cervantes said later, "were received without cucumbers or other things suitable for throwing." We have the titles of only nine of the plays, and Cervantes preserved only two in the collection of plays he published in 1615, which includes six *comedias* and eight *entremeses*, all written more than twenty years later. Cervantes' dramatic reputation rests on the *entremeses* (interludes between acts), which are spiritually very close to the short stories of *Exemplary Novels*. In one, "El rufian viudo," a pimp named Trampagos is mourning the death of his best girl until those in the crowd suggest he pick another from the whores gathered at the wake, which he does amidst scenes of low humor and drunken high spirits.

Cervantes had turned to drama to make money quickly, but he was unlucky enough to be competing against Lope de Vega, whose rambunctious, verbally dazzling, thoroughly anticlassical plays soon swept the stage; in fact, Lope de Vega wrote four hundred plays that have been preserved. Cervantes then turned to fiction. His later plays were less ambitious, more finely crafted, and were probably written more for art's sake. The *entremeses* are still performed today. Besides his short stories, Cervantes' other works include two volumes of poetry; the only one still read, *The Journey to Parnassus* (1614), is about meeting his fellow poets on Mt. Parnassus.

Influence

Cervantes was the first modern novelist, and, as such, his influence upon the novel has been recognized for centuries, not only by scholars but also by novelists themselves. What is not generally remembered is that another powerful novel, Mateo Alemán's *Guzmán de Alfarache* (1599, 1604), almost set not only the tone but also the philosophy of the modern novel. It was the epitome of all picaro novels; and not only was it the first, but it also sold fifty thousand copies in twenty-six editions—a very respectable sale in a modern industrial country and almost phenomenal in early-Renaissance Europe. We are fortunate that the example of *Don Quixote de la Mancha* prevailed, since *Guzmán de Alfarache* admits of no interchange between reader and writer.

Equally historic was Cervantes' collection of short stories, *Exemplary Novels*. As was usual during the Renaissance in almost all art forms, the Italians had been first with Giovanni Boccaccio's *The Decameron* (1353). Again, however, the *modern* short story was invented by Cervantes. His stories show men and women in conflict with the world and build up character through dialogue, and—in the "Colloquy of the Dogs"—they comment on both art and life in the way an artist must: through characterization and structure. As we shall see, some of his short stories were obviously "written for the market," and at least one, "The Jealous Estremaduran," was bowdlerized before being translated from manuscript version to book version; perhaps others were too. The ones that suit our taste, however, have thousands of descendants: "Man of Glass," for example, is a direct and undiluted prototype for the Kafkaesque short story; "Rinconete and Cortadillo" was the first "slice of life" fiction; and "La Gitanilla" is the first story about man in conflict with society.

Story characteristics

One of the problems in Cervantes scholarship is that we know that *The Jealous Estremaduran* as it existed in manuscript was a much better story than the one Cervantes published. The related problem is that the *Exemplary Novels* was published at the height of Cervantes' creativity, and yet half of the collection is of very poor quality. Whatever its faults or hypocrisies, however, the publication of *Exemplary Novels* in 1613 founded the modern short story and gave us examples of the surrealistic, allegorical, and realistic story that have only been equaled, never bested—especially "Man of Glass," "The Little Gypsy," "Colloquy of the Dogs," and "Rinconete and Cortadillo." As in *Don Quixote de la Mancha*, Cervantes achieves his effects with dialogue and with careful plotting and carefully motivated story development—techniques so usual today in traditional stories that one reads Cervantes as a contemporary. Later, when Cervantes moved to *mimesis*, especially of a society so rich in contrasts as Spain, dialogue proved itself the perfect approach to theme and structure. One more aspect of the stories has had a pervasive and ongoing influence on literature in the West: their expression of Cervantes' feeling that life is composed of one's visions (one's subjective life), one's deeds (the individual as both subject and object), and the world (the sum of all others' visions and deeds).

Biography

In recent years, scholars have begun to realize that the three greatest premodern Spanish writers were all of Jewish origin: they were *conversos*, in the ethnic jargon of the day—Jews converted to Christianity—and Miguel de Cervantes Saavedra was one of them. Many Jews had come to Spain with the Muslim conquerors of the Peninsula. In Spain, at first, they were well-treated and often rose to positions of importance; from the Great Pogrom of 1391 in Spain onwards, however, many had converted, nominally or in fact, to Christianity, realizing that once Spain was reconquered, they would be needed neither by the government nor the populace. All Jews still living in Spain and following Judaism were expelled in 1492, and dispersed to all parts of the Mediterranean, becoming the Sephardim. Only the *conversos* remained. The main problem for *conversos* in Certantes' lifetime was that their status as *hidalgos* might be questioned by the courts and the community. A *hidalgo* was not subject to arrest for ordinary (non-Royal) debt; Cervantes' claims must have been deficient, for he and his father and his grandfather were arrested for debt many times. It was the attitude that *conversos* were somehow second-class citizens which probably accounts for all the illegitimacies among the Cervantes girls: they were considered fair game for sexual adventurers.

Miguel was one of seven Cervantes children of Rodrigo and Leonor de Cortinas, five of them born, as he was, in the pleasant university town of Alcalá de Henares. What Cervantes studied as a youth has never been settled by Spanish scholars, and it is not believed he attended any university, but his description of student life as "amicable, fantastic, intrepid, free and easy, amorous, spendthrift, diabolical and amusing" surely owes something to his observations of Alcalá, or those made by his family. When Miguel was still rather young, the family moved to Valladolid, where after a few months

Rodrigo was thrown into the same prison where his father had been incarcerated—the son for debt, however, rather than over a matter of honor. The list of goods seized by Rodrigo's creditors is rather pitiful: a table, three benches, three chairs (two broken), eight sheets, six blankets, and two of his three books. The next move was to Córdoba, at the time one of the most impressive cities in Europe, where Juan de Cervantes, Miguel's grandfather, lived; he was prosperous, and could be counted on to help Rodrigo and his family. Miguel's education began there, at the Jesuit College of Santa Clara. There were more moves, but by 1564, the family was in Seville, where Cervantes studied at another Jesuit school. Including his final year of schooling at the City School of Madrid, Cervantes had only six years of schooling between the ages of six and twenty.

Cervantes was forced into exile in 1568, when he wounded a construction foreman while apparently defending his sister Andrea's nonexistent honor; unfortunately the incident occurred on the grounds of the royal palace in Madrid and thus involved unsheathing a blade in the presence of the King, a crime harshly punished all over Europe. A warrant for his arrest was issued on September 15, 1569, which specified that his right hand was to be cut off and that he was to be exiled for ten years. His pursuers had to give up their search for him when a rebellion broke out in Spain, and Cervantes escaped to Rome. His exact movements in Italy are a mystery, but he was there in 1570, serving Bishop Giulio Acquaviva, a friend of a cousin. Then he joined a Spanish regiment stationed in Naples, which belonged then to Spain, and went off to fight the Turks; he served aboard the galley *Marguesa* in the battle of Lepanto. Two days away from his twenty-fourth birthday, Cervantes lost his left hand in the battle and took two bullets in the chest. When he had recuperated, he and his brother Rodrigo boarded the galley *Sol* returning to Spain, only to be captured on September 26, 1574, by Moorish pirates and taken to Algiers as slaves. This episode, which lasted six years, was the watershed in Cervantes' life. He tried to escape his horrible conditions three times; amazingly, his only punishment was the severe beatings his captors administered. Finally, in October of 1580, he was ransomed by Trinitarian monks. Cervantes was thirty-three; he had been absent from Spain for twelve years.

During the next few years, Cervantes wrote *La Galatea* and twenty to thirty other plays. Finally, he landed a job as commissary for the Navy. This job was not without its perils: he was temporarily excommunicated when he seized some corn the Church had claimed, and he was thrown into prison when his banker went bankrupt and fled, leaving his depositors owing their creditors. It was while he was in jail in Seville in 1595, being punished for his banker's malfeasance, that he began *Don Quixote de la Mancha*; it was printed in January, 1605, by the bookman Robles. The fame of the book was immediate; only a month after its publication in Spain, Don Quixote and Sancho Panza were figures on a float in the Peruvian Mardi Gras parade. When the Madrid theaters were reopened in 1607, Cervantes wrote *Los Baños de Argel*, *El Gallardo Español*, *The Great Sultana*, and *Pedro de Urdemalas*. He wrote two more *comedias* and then discovered his form: the *entremes*. Two of his earlier plays, the six *comedias*, and his eight *entremeses* were now gathered into a book. *Exemplary Novels* was published in 1613 and the collection of plays in 1615. Whether in the *entremeses* he adapted himself to the traditions of the farce or tapped a fertile imagination fettered by the conventions of the longer plays is still an open question, but the one-act plays belong to what one scholar has called the period of his "supreme creativity."

Cervantes, while suffering from some undiagnosed malady thought by some modern scholars to be diabetes, finished *The Travels of Persiles and Sigismunda* just before his death on April 23, 1616, in Madrid. He was buried by his confreres in the Tertiary Order of St. Francis, and his body was taken to a nearby convent. No marker was put on his grave and its location has been lost.

Analysis

Miguel de Cervantes Saavedra's models for *Exemplary Novels* were Boccaccio and Matteo Bandello. There had been short fictions before in Cervantes' work. "Meddlesome Curiosity" had been embodied in *Don Quixote de la Mancha* as had "The Captive's Tale"; and there had been short stories in *La Galatea*. The stories in *Exemplary Novels* were written to stand alone, neither to interrupt, however fruitfully, a longer narrative, nor to form part of a cycle. *Novela* in the Spanish of the time meant "deceit" or "happening" and only secondarily, and as a neologism, "short story"; thus the oxymoronic nature to Cervantes and his contemporaries of the title *Exemplary Deceits*, a *concetto* that opens up his purpose and themes to the reader who has this understanding of Golden Age Spanish. The pieces were not written as tales (*contes*) or as anecdotes or as tall tales, but as something akin to our novella. Concerning them, Cervantes wrote: "My intention has been to place in the marketplace of our commonwealth a billiard table [*mesa de trucos*], at which everyone can entertain himself without threat to body or soul, for innocent recreation does good rather than harm." Since moralists in Spain did not like novels, which were characterized as trash fit only for the lower orders, Cervantes called his tales "exemplary." *Exemplary Novels* was an instant commercial success, going through four editions in two months, one a pirated edition from Barcelona and the other a Portuguese forgery.

Amezúa, the modern editor of "Colloquy of the Dogs," places the composition of the story in 1603 or 1604 and "before the spring of 1605." The story opens as Berganza and Cipión, two big watchdogs, find themselves suddenly gifted with the power of speech in the hospital where they serve as the watchdogs of Mahudes, a collector of alms at the Hospital of the Resurrection in Valladolid. The story is written as if it were a play; there are no stage directions, however, and we are given no exposition by the author. The speakers must set the mood, provide the tone, and move the action linguistically rather than structurally. Berganza, who has something in him of the village philosopher, begins speaking and never relinquishes the floor. His earliest memories are of a Seville slaughterhouse from which his first experience of crime and corruption, malfeasance and defalcation, comes: the butchers and their wives and girl friends always take choice cuts of meats for themselves and smuggle them out of the slaughterhouse. One of the butchers trains him to take things to one of his girls, but the other intercepts the dog, takes what he was entrusted with, and beats him; so Berganza runs away and goes to the shepherds outside the city. Thus one of the themes of the story is set, and it becomes a kind of allegory of the condition of those on the bottom of society in Spain—the *conversos, moriscos,* gypsies, thieves, soldiers, whores, and foreigners. Berganza never gets into a scrape that could not be explained if he could speak. It has been suggested that the great works of literature tap into the feelings of the child, especially his feelings of helplessness and his anxieties about the future, and, by resolving the problem set forth in the story, prepare the child to take his place in the world. "Colloquy of the Dogs" certainly captures vividly the feelings of powerlessness and anxiety that those who are weak and ignorant feel.

The dog's second sojourn is with a group of shepherds, who, Berganza soon discovers, have a nice racket worked out: in the middle of the night they cry "Wolf! Wolf!" and the dogs dash up to see a mauled sheep; then they are sent out by their masters to chase the wolf. One night, suspicious, Berganza remains behind and sees the shepherds maul a sheep exactly as a wolf would. When the master of the shepherds comes up later and demands to know what happened, the shepherds blame the lazy dogs for not protecting the flock. The temptation here to see the shepherds as the Inquisitors, the mauled sheep as the *conversos,* and the nonexistent wolves as nonexistent Judaizing is irresistible. In fact, when the Inquisition was beginning, Isabella found it politic to write the Pope that she was not beginning the Inquisition to seize the wealth of the *conversos* (which was probably less than the truth). We know that Cervantes had already taken a shot at the Inquisition in one of his *entremeses.*

Berganza finds a much happier home; in fact the description of it is one of the warmest parts of the tale. He makes himself indispensable to a merchant by becoming his watchdog—his analysis of human psychology is quite amusing—and eventually so ingratiates himself with the family that he accompanies the family's little boy to the Jesuit school. There Berganza does tricks and is fed from the boys' lunches and in general becomes such a clown that the Jesuits send him home; once home, he is chained between the inner and outer doors. He soon finds that his sleep is disturbed and his job compromised by the black maid who must pass by him on her way to see her lover. Usually she scrimps on his food but on the nights she has a rendezvous, she feeds him. He takes the first few bribes, but he is not happy with himself, and one night, without barking, he mauls her severely. After that she offers him a sponge fried in lard, which will kill him, then tries to starve him. He sees how things are going to fall out, so, reluctantly, he escapes through a hole in the wall around the family's compound.

The wall may as well be the limits of society, for now Berganza will live among the marginal people, the outcasts and criminals and atheists and witches of Spain. He has eleven masters, counting Mahudes. Seven of the eleven (seven itself being a cabalistic number) will be the forces spurned or outlawed by society. Berganza meets a constable named Nicolás the Snubnose and is given a brass collar. The metal collar in classical times, certainly in North Africa during Cervantes' captivity, and later in the New World, was the emblem of the slave. After his first trinity of owners, the producers, middlemen, and consumers of meat, Berganza slips into the company of marginal men and wears the emblem of the slave.

The constable and the scrivener make their living walking the constable's rounds and playing the badger game, in cooperation with the whores who are their girls. One night, as they are rousting a Breton caught with the constable's whore, Berganza smells some food in the victim's pants and drags them outside; but this also removes the money the constable had hoped to extort from the victim, and in the ensuing fracas, the Chief of Police has to be called in. The constable's next adventure is defeating six thieves in a swordfight. Then Berganza accompanies the constable to the lair of Monipodio, the *éminence grise* of the thieves of Seville, and discovers that Monipodio had arranged the whole thing. Berganza is now disgusted, and when given a chance later to fall upon his master, he does so, then disappears.

He next falls in with a drummer serving in a company of soldiers marching to take ship. Berganza is taught to perform some tricks, which he finds humiliating, and in consequence of his new talents, he is dubbed the Wise Dog. One night in Montilla, an old witch named Cañizares comes to him and calls him Montiel and takes him to her room where she tells him the story of his birth as she disrobes and rubs on a magic salve that will enable her spirit to fly away to a witches' coven. The famous witch of the age had indeed been from Montilla and was called La Camacha and was burned at the stake by the Inquisition. This woman and Berganza's mother, according to his new patroness, had been La Camacha's disciples.

This is the part of the story that Berganza had wanted to tell first, but he had relented at the insistence of Cipión, something of a traditionalist. Now we learn that the dog's mother, according to the witch, was Montiela, one of the witch's cohorts and fellow disciples. La Camacha made her twin sons be born as puppies and took them off with her, but now Montiel has been "recognized." Cervantes leaves the door open, with his careful ambiguity, to the possibility that she is telling the truth; from this we can make the further inference that the other dog is Cipión, another human in dog's skin and thus equally able to assume that human characteristic, speech.

Berganza reacts adversely to the witch's revelations and tries to kill her. The townspeople believe he is the devil in human form and chase him. Once again, he is on the run, but our feeling that his rendezvous with Cañizares was the purpose of his life is heightened by the fact that the woman is the middle of his eleven masters, that the episode happens almost in the middle of the book, and that we have been warned by the narrator himself that this is the most important part of his story.

The obvious allegory of "The Colloquy of the Dogs" is to Cervantes' life; he would have been called *perro* (dog) himself, as Christian slaves of the Arabs and Turks were. This allegory holds up when we consider that the main nexus between writer and reader is the scene with the witch, for art itself is a kind of sorcery. Another allegory comes to mind when we recall that Protestantism traveled from belief in salvation through faith in the Trinity (the "good" masters are a trinity) to salvation through works—and that in the process it caused wars and an upsurge of witchcraft because people still hungered for the rituals and images of liturgical worship and for the intercession of the myriad saints and the buying of masses and favors from the priests and the orders. The story is also a fable for the critics and an exemplar of how to explore the lower depths without the juridical deadness of the picaroon novel. For whatever reason, this story, with its lively action and constant invention, still stands out as one of the best, most moving, wittiest, and most absorbing short stories ever written; it is a marvel of diction, compression, and depth.

To some, "The Glass Scholar" is a dull story, useful only as a medium for some of Cervantes' apothegms. Others see it as truly outstanding, and still others hail it as the first surrealist short story. All three judgments are correct to a degree.

The plot is simple: an eleven-year-old boy is found sleeping under a tree at an unspecified university by two students, who ask his name. He replies, with the evasiveness we have come to expect of Cervantes characters, that he will not give his real name until he can bring glory to it. Meanwhile, he calls himself Tomás Rodaja (which means *little wheel*). From this and other things, the students assume he is the son of a poor peasant. In those days the servants of students, and this was especially true at Salamanca, could also be enrolled as undergraduates, and soon Rodaja is thus enrolled.

One day, riding back to the university, he is joined on the road by an officer of infantry who extols the delights of army life to him, although Cervantes wryly notes that he leaves out the fleas, hunger, and danger which to the majority are all that constitute military life. The student decides to accompany the army, but not join it, and there follows a travelogue which covers most of the Italian cities and ends in Flanders. Then Rodaja goes back to Salamanca.

At the university, a woman falls in love with him, but he rejects her, and she feeds him a poisoned quince. He sickens immediately and lies in his bed for six months. When he is coherent again, he believes that he is made of glass and that he will shatter if handled too roughly. It terrifies him when his friends embrace him. He says the soul is more efficient in a body of glass than of heavy earth. There is no doubt religious symbolism in his statement, but it is indecipherable. In the winter, Rodaja, ever consistent, sleeps as bottles are packed: in straw up to the neck.

He is finally taken to court for all to gawk at and ask questions of, for he is very good at epigrams ("good painters imitate nature but bad ones vomit it forth"). Finally, he is cured by an Hieronymite friar, possibly because his creator had run out of apothegms. He renames himself Rueda (*wheel*; *vidriera* means glass) and attempts to follow his profession, the law, but ironically, no one wants him now that he is sane and serious; so he enlists in the army and is killed in Flanders. This is a delightful tale, especially if one likes epigrams and apothegms, and almost all of them are good. Moreover, it was and is an audacious story which unites realistic writing with a surrealist premise.

Whether Cervantes used an anecdote from the *Miscelánea* (c. 1590) of Luís de Zapata de Chaves as the basis for his story "Rinconete and Cortadillo" or whether he met the originals in prison on one of his frequent trips there, is difficult to say. The most important thing about the story is that here, as Putnam says, we can find the germ of *Don Quixote de la Mancha*, the "contrast, the humorous incongruity, between the world as it is and the world as it ought to be, which constitutes Cervantes' major theme and forms the basis of his finest art . . . close-to-life realism, which in itself will doubtless suffice for many but which holds a deeper meaning for those who seek it."

Rincón and Cortado are between fourteen and sixteen years old when they meet at the inn of Molinillo on the border of the plains of Alcudia on the road from Castile to Andalusia (there was an inn there and the topography of the countryside around Seville and the city itself is exact). They have no capes or stockings, and their shoes are almost falling off; they are obviously runaways. Each perceives that the other is a criminal.

The younger and smaller one says at first, when the older and larger one questions him, "I do not know the name of my country" and "my land is not my land." (Again, this is the kind of ambiguity Cervantes cherished.) He eventually admits he is Diego Cortado. *Cortado* is the past participle of *cortar* (*to cut*, either a piece of cloth or a deck of cards; it also means to dilute, as in *to cut wine with water*); so even this information is less than revealing. He was born between Salamanca and Medina del Campo, and has been, as it turns out, a cutter for his tailor father as well as a cutpurse (thief). The older boy, Pedro de Rincón (which means *nook* or *corner* in Spanish), is a native of Fuenfrida, today's Fuenfría, and his father sold papal indulgences. One day Rincón stole his father's bag of money and went to Madrid and spent it all. There, after various misadventures, he was caught and flogged and denied entrance to the city for four years. He has occupied himself since then by dealing blackjack. The deck he carries is crooked and will produce an ace whenever he wants it to.

The two boys skin a muleteer with Rincón's crooked deck; and when the man tries to take his money back from them, thinking this will be easy because they are only boys, one pulls a shortsword and the other a yellow-handled cattle knife. They go next to Seville with a caravan, and as thanks to their fellow-travelers, they steal two shirts from one of them and sell it in the flea market for spending money. It is summer, the season for provisioning the outgoing fleet. Porters are needed and the two boys see that this trade will gain them admittance to big houses; they need not pass an examination and they only need two bags for bread and three palm-fiber baskets.

The first day on the job, Cortado steals a student's purse. Another young man, also a thief, notices the two and their real (as opposed to nominal) trade, and tells them they will have to "register" with Monipodio, the prince—or perhaps the prior—of thieves. Their Vergil tells them that Monipodio insists that part of the swag be used to light candles in front of a local icon the thieves hold sacred, to pay officials and to hold masses for the dead parents of the members of the gang. Furthermore, many of them do not steal on Friday or speak to a woman named Mary on Saturday. It is heavy irony of course, but Cervantes also uses this speech to capture the peculiarly Andalusian mixture of brigandage and piety that is one of the presiding ironies of the tale. They go to a house where they meet the "coarsest and most hideous barbarian in the world." He christens them Rinconete and Cortadillo, much in the manner of an abbot giving vocational names to new novices in a religious order. We see the house and its furnishings, the courtyard, the dress of the thieves, whores, and cutthroats who frequent the place; there is even an old moll praying to a cheap print of Our Lady.

This story has no real plot. Sluts beaten by their pimps seek justice from Monipodio, lists of beatings and acid-throwings and cuttings bought from Monipodio are subcontracted, and a young man who wanted a fourteen-stitch cut put in the face of a merchant demands his money back because the thug in charge of the job decided the merchant's face was too small for fourteen, so gave the fourteen to his lackey instead. Monipodio negotiates the case with a gangster's jurisprudential principles, but the legal reasoning employed is as fine as any employed in chancery courts. The atmosphere is part of the very real charm of the piece, but to Cervantes' contemporaries most of this story would have been a shocking, journalistic exposé of the Sevillean underworld. Cervantes may have been interested in showing that this criminal welfare state was far better regulated and more humane than the straight world. Some notice of this could hardly have escaped the contemporary audience.

The day ends and all retire, Cervantes closing his story with the promise that the boys' further adventures in Seville will furnish "edifying" anecdotes—thus making this tale one of postponed exemplariness. It has a far wider importance to us: these boys are the dim creatures of Maxime Gorky's *The Lower Depths* (1902), the fathers of Fyodor Dostoevski's heroes, and the ancestors of the human wrecks scattered along Raymond Chandler's mean streets.

Major publications other than short fiction

NOVELS: *La Galatea*, 1584 (*Galatea: A Pastoral Romance*); *Don Quixote de la Mancha*, 1605; *Los Trabajos de Persiles y Sigismunda*, 1617 (*The Travels of Persiles and Sigismunda*).

PLAYS: *El Trato de Argel*, c. 1585 (*The Commerce of Algiers*); *El Cerco de Numancia*, c. 1585 (*Numantia*).

POETRY: *El Viaje del Parnaso*, 1614 (*The Journey to Parnassus*).

Bibliography

Avalle-Arce, Juan Bautista and Edward C. Reily, eds. *Suma Cervantina*.
Bell, Aubrey F. G. *Cervantes*.
Castro, Americo. *El Pensamiento de Cervantes*.
Duran, Manual. *La ambigudad en el Quixote*.
_____ . *Cervantes*.
Madariaga, Slavador de. *Don Quixote: An Introductory Essay in Psychology*.
Nelson, Lowry, Jr., ed. *Cervantes: A Collection of Critical Essays*, in *Twentieth-Century Views* series.
Predmore, Richard L. *Cervantes*.
Reily, Edward C. *Cervantes' Theory of the Novel*.

John Carr

RAYMOND CHANDLER

Born: Chicago, Illinois; July 23, 1888
Died: La Jolla, California; March 26, 1959

Principal short fiction
Five Murderers, 1944; *Five Sinister Characters*, 1945; *Finger Man and Other Stories*, 1946; *Red Wind*, 1946; *Spanish Blood*, 1946; *Trouble Is My Business*, 1950; *The Simple Art of Murder*, 1950; *Pick-up on Noon Street*, 1952; *Smart-Aleck Kill*, 1953; *Pearls Are a Nuisance*, 1958; *Killer in the Rain*, 1964; *The Smell of Fear*, 1965; *The Midnight Raymond Chandler*, 1971.

Other literary forms
Raymond Chandler is best known for his hard-boiled detective novels featuring Philip Marlowe. Chandler often used material from his short stories to create the novels; and Philip Marlowe's character grew out of the various detectives in the short tales. This archetypal hero has been further popularized through ten major motion pictures. Chandler wrote screenplays for six works by others. His works have been selected for Book-of-the-Month Club Members and his stories and novels have been collected in a number of editions. He also wrote criticism on the art of detective fiction and in his early years conventional poems and essays.

Influence
"The foremost exponent of the tough-guy school of mystery writing" and the best of the *Black Mask* writers in the 1930's, Chandler put his stamp on the popular arts in America. His influence continues through the many reprints and collections (and, more recently, the inclusion of his stories in "serious" anthologies), through his seven novels, and through the ten major films made from his novels. Although his writing goes beyond the single genre of detective fiction, Chandler follows only Dashiell Hammett in being the creator of the mold for the hard-boiled hero. This character type, with roots in the honorable loner from the American West and the moral medieval knight, has become one of the most popular figures in literature in the past fifty years. The many imitations and developments—and even spoofs and parodies—of the type in all media are proof of its popularity.

Story characteristics
Chandler's often cynical stories place the hard-boiled private eye (or a similar character) in the corrupt society of Southern California. The intent of the stories is to make, somehow, a better world against great odds. Violence, murder, theft, blackmail—elements originally called for by the *Black Mask* "formula"—are parts of the stories which explore human behavior and

morality. The author's humor often serves to lighten the somber mood surrounding such subject matter, but the tales remain serious statements.

Biography

Raymond Thornton Chandler, although he was born in Chicago and spent his first seven years in the Middle West, received an English Public School education (Dulwich College) when his mother took him to England after her divorce. He traveled in Europe, spent an unsatisfying few months in the British civil service, and set out to become a writer. After publishing a number of poems and essays, he returned to America in 1912. He worked at various jobs and in 1917 joined the Canadian Army and served in France. After the war, he became a successful oil executive in California and married Cissy Pascal, who was eighteen years his senior. Chandler's dissatisfaction and drinking left him jobless in 1932. He turned to writing again and became the best of the *Black Mask* pulp writers before turning to novels with *The Big Sleep* in 1939. He was a successful and highly paid Hollywood screenwriter throughout the 1940's. Following Cissy's death in 1954, Chandler resumed his rootless life and heavy drinking. He visited England several times. When he died he was president of the Mystery Writers of America and was at work on another Philip Marlowe novel.

Analysis

Joseph T. Shaw, editor of *Black Mask*, the leading pulp detective magazine of the 1930's, remarked upon receiving Raymond Chandler's first story that the author was either a genius or crazy. He must have decided in favor of genius, for he accepted "Blackmailers Don't Shoot" in 1933 and paid Chandler the standard rate of a penny a word, or $180.00.

Chandler reveals in his letters that he taught himself to write for the pulps by reading back issues. He gives full credit to Dashiell Hammett, who wrote stories that commented on contemporary life using the detective story or puzzle framework. Chandler, however, surpasses his mentor in his use of the language. His ability to hear the American vernacular and to transfer it onto the printed page may be his strongest point as a writer. This trait helps to explain Chandler's often aimless sentences and strange word order. His classical education in England made him aware of the finer points of language and of the uses of slang. His characters reveal themselves through their language. Since his fiction describes the interplay between levels or classes in society, the speech of his characters as identifying labels is paramount.

In his early stories, Chandler attempted to master the hard-boiled style of writing while still saying something of value about society and human behavior. "Blackmailers Don't Shoot" is a story about an actress, Rhonda Farr, who is being blackmailed because of a bundle of reckless letters she wrote. The detective character in the story, Mallory, is hired by the actor-turned-gangster recipient of the letters to get them back and to identify the blackmailer. The chase leads Mallory, who is imported to Los Angeles from Chicago for the case, to crooked cops, Rhonda Farr's crooked lawyer, and assorted gangsters. Four men are killed in a short space of time; Rhonda Farr is kidnapped (by the blackmailers) and recovered (by Mallory). The actress turns out to want as much publicity as possible, and she seems only slightly penitent in her reaction to the beatings, killings, and trouble created by her letters. Landrey, the actor-gangster, seems to have created the whole caper in an attempt to recapture the affections of Rhonda Farr. In the aftermath of this plot, two more hoods are killed and one wounded, and Mallory is wounded. He gets a clean slate from the local police, who manage to tie up all the loose ends with ease, including a complete cover-up of the illegal activities of their own men. Mallory decides that he might stay in Los Angeles instead of returning to Chicago.

The action of this story is fast, furious, and somewhat confusing. Mallory uses some deductive reasoning to figure out the details of the case, but he is much more involved in threatening, hitting, and shooting than in deducing. The story exposes the unreasonable desire for publicity in Hollywood, even bad publicity. "You don't know much about this Hollywood racket, do you, darling?" Rhonda Farr chides Mallory. "Publicity has to hurt a bit out here. Otherwise nobody believes it."

The corrupt elements of society are well represented here as well. Practically every character who enters the story has a gun and is willing to use force to have his way over someone else. Chandler wrote that it is the "smell of fear" in the detective tale that ties it to real life. His chief target for criticism seems to be those who, by whatever means, try to rule others unjustly. Since the world of the criminal is built around injustice—toward individuals, society, or its institutions—Chandler found a remarkable wealth of material about which to write.

In the midst of the chaotic world of Los Angeles crime and violence, there is always the good man, the man who tries to bring order. As Chandler wrote later: "Down these mean streets a man must go who is not himself mean, who is neither tarnished nor afraid." Mallory considers himself "the nearest thing to an honest stranger," and he is basically upright. The Chicago police verify that he has "a clean sheet—damn' clean."

Mallory is the direct ancestor, of course, of Philip Marlowe, Chandler's famous private eye. Marlowe did not appear as the central detective character until Chandler began writing novels in 1939. His detective in the earlier short stories—whatever his name—is, however, usually the same man. Chandler probably found it a minor task to change most of the names to Philip Marlowe in later stories and collected printings of the early stories. Thus John Dalmas in "Red Wind" becomes Marlowe in later printings—the only change, incidentally, in the story. It is not true, as some have reported, that all book versions of the stories use the revised Marlowe name. The collection *Red Wind* (World Publishing Company, 1946) keeps the original names used in magazine texts.

Chandler is a moral writer. His detective, even before Marlowe, is a man who sees the truth and works to set things right, often without pay and always alone. He is disappointed in himself and in the world when he is unable to succeed. John Dalmas in "Red Wind" suffers dejection at the breakup of a marriage, even though he knows the man and wife have been equally unfaithful. As a final act of decency, he protects the wife from the knowledge that her dead lover had been "just another four-flusher." Dalmas substitutes a set of obviously fake pearls for the seemingly real pearls given her. Dalmas/Marlowe protects her memory of her lover at considerable expense and trouble to himself. In so doing, he assumes the grief, which we see as he throws the pearls into the Pacific one by one.

An unusual character for Chandler is Ted Malvern in "Guns at Cyrano's." Unlike the typical hard-boiled detective, Malvern is wealthy and essentially idle. He is generous with his wealth, because, as we learn at the story's conclusion, he considers it "dirty money." The money is inherited from his father, who made it

> "out of crooked sewerage and paving contracts, out of gambling concessions, appointment pay-offs, even vice, I daresay. And when it was made and there was nothing to do but sit and look at it, he died and left it to me. It hasn't brought me any fun either. I always hope it's going to, but it never does."

Malvern compensates, in his own hard-boiled fashion, for living on his father's "crooked dough" by consorting with the rougher elements in society and helping to rid the world of at least one crooked politician.

The detective (even when he is not a licensed private investigator) works against tremendous odds to clean up a small corner of the world. He seldom gets paid, he almost never gets the girl, and he knows that the next case will produce just as many seedy and malevolent characters to be dealt with. He does not contemplate his old age or retirement. His violent world is not provided with such sureties. He knows he is alone and that he will probably remain so.

The hard-boiled formula as created by Dashiell Hammett and Raymond Chandler includes an almost automatic confrontation with the police. Thus the detective is the true guardian of morality, between abusive police and equally abusive criminals. He risks arrest and beatings from the former for not revealing his clients' interests, and he risks physical violence and death from the latter for daring to enter the nether world of mobsters and crooks—which he inevitably must do in the course of his work.

His home is not his castle. He lives alone, usually in a spare, if not spartan, apartment. He is likely to find either a pair of unfriendly and incompetent police detectives or a mob of violent gangsters in his living room when he arrives home intent only on a slug of whiskey and much-needed sleep. His office is equally spartan, with no secretary and no fellow workers. He has a waiting room, a desk—with an "office bottle" in one drawer—and a telephone.

Many writers of mystery and detective fiction have been influenced by Raymond Chandler. The violence visited upon Chandler's detective hero may be the source of the almost constant threats, beatings, and incarcerations used by Dick Francis. The security—or lack of it—of the home may help to explain the elaborate system of checks that Travis McGee has installed on his house-boat to see if anyone is or has been aboard. And Robert B. Parker has said that he learned to write detective novels by reading Hammett and Chandler.

Chandler has placed the hard-boiled detective firmly in American literature as a remarkable and enduring character type. The many imitations, exaggerations, and developments upon Philip Marlowe speak well of his profound influence on fiction and the popular arts. Chandler's importance and his craft do not stop there, however; Chandler wanted to be considered a serious writer. He was pleased that the British critics considered him a major writer; and he would no doubt be pleased now to know that he is ever being "discovered" by new generations of American readers and critics. Since the timeliness of the hard-boiled character no longer applies, one must look to other qualities of his writing.

His major themes, alluded to earlier, deserve consideration. His close examination, in both short stories and novels, of society at large reveals a concern for humanity equal to that of Mark Twain. He wrote in almost every work of fiction about human behavior. True, his characters often came from the criminal element, but his works show that the criminal element (or at least the vices of that element) extends into all levels of society, that greed, pride, and violence have no basis in economic or social status. His revelation of Southern California of the 1930's to 1950's offers a view not found in other media of that era.

Chandler's ability to set a scene or mood is also remarkable. "Red Wind" takes its title from the prevailing weather phenomenon present at the time of the story.

> There was a desert wind blowing that night. It was one of those hot dry Santa Anas that come down through the mountain passes and curl your hair and make your nerves jump and your skin itch. On nights like that every booze party ends in a fight. Meek little wives feel the edge of the carving knife and study their husbands' necks. Anything can happen.

Although the wind does not figure in the events of the story, it sets a mood in which the story seems plausible, in spite of several coincidences that the reader may wonder over. As if Chandler realizes this, he seems to joke with the reader:

> "There's a hell of a lot of coincidences in all this business," the big man said.
> "It's the hot wind," I grinned. "Everybody's screwy tonight."

Chandler never lets the reader wonder about a room or a house. The unusual Southern California locations for his scenes seem to be designed as if for a Hollywood set.

> We sat down and looked at each other across a dark floor, on which a few Navajo rugs and a few dark Turkish rugs made a decorating combination with some well-used over-stuffed furniture. There was a fireplace, a small baby grand, a Chinese screen, a tall Chinese lantern on a teakwood pedestal, and gold net curtains against lattice windows. The windows to the south were open. A fruit tree with a white-washed trunk whipped about outside the screen, adding its bit to the noise from across the street.

Chandler felt that such detail helped to build character as well as set the scene. He considered that many readers wanted more than the barest plot filled with action, and his success bears him out.

Chandler's humor is an important element of his work. Perhaps realizing that stories filled with violence and murder need some relief, he frequently allows his narration to entertain the reader. When a man is shot in a bar in "Red Wind," Dalmas relates that "the guy took a week to fall down." In describing the beautiful girl in the story, he tells readers: "She had brown wavy hair under a wide-brimmed straw hat with a velvet band and loose bow. She had wide blue eyes and eyelashes that didn't quite reach her chin." As a car leaves the scene of a murder, Dalmas "got its license number the way I got my first million." He doesn't "like being a witness" because "the pay's too low." The humor presented through the first-person narrator makes him human; he remains a believable, if somewhat exaggerated, character; and he remains a stabilizing force in an otherwise inhuman world. Chandler was aware of the extent of the exaggeration called for by the formula. He wrote "Pearls Are a Nuisance" as a deliberate parody of the type.

Chandler's private eyes invariably find much more action and a more involved plot than the reader suspects, a fact which makes his stories difficult to synopsize. The detective follows one lead to another and ends up walking a narrow path between the mob and the police as new characters appear on the scene. Although the citizen being protected is usually female, Chandler was not afraid to include a woman as the villain. Carol Donovan in "Goldfish" is meaner and tougher than her male rivals, but Carmady (another Marlowe prototype) is equal to the task. Someone else shoots Carol, but only after Carmady has slugged her in the jaw to provide the opportunity.

Chandler is best known as a writer of detective fiction, and he deserves much credit for the phenomenal growth of the genre in popular literature, but his contributions to serious literature and film continue to be recognized by readers and scholars. His revelation of Southern California to the world is unique among his writing peers; his view of human behavior moves his stories into a context encompassing all of the corrupt world of his vision; and his influence will continue to be felt as long as detective stories and crime tales are written.

Major publications other than short fiction
NOVELS: *The Big Sleep*, 1939; *Farewell, My Lovely*, 1940; *The High Window*, 1942; *The Lady in the Lake*, 1943; *The Little Sister*, 1949; *The Long Goodbye*, 1953; *Playback*, 1958.
NONFICTION: *Raymond Chandler Speaking*, 1962; *The Notebooks of Raymond Chandler and English Summer, A Gothic Romance*, 1976.

Bibliography
Bruccoli, Matthew J. *Raymond Chandler: A Descriptive Bibliography*.
Durham, Philip. *Down These Mean Streets a Man Must Go*.
MacShane, Frank. *The Life of Raymond Chandler*.
Pendo, Stephen. *Raymond Chandler on Screen*.

Thomas D. Lane

GEOFFREY CHAUCER

Born: London(?), England; c. 1343
Died: London, England; October 25(?), 1400

Principal works

The Book of the Duchess, 1370; *The House of Fame*, 1372-1380; *The Parliament of Fowls*, 1380; *The Legend of Good Women*, 1380-1386; *Troilus and Crieseyde*, 1382; *The Canterbury Tales*, 1386-1390.

Influence

Geoffrey Chaucer is frequently called the father of English poetry, an appellation made appropriate by his immeasurable influence on writers of the fifteenth century and later, and by the reputation of his work, a reputation which is equaled in British literature only by the reputations of John Milton and William Shakespeare. Chaucer's decision to write in English when French was still the language of influence served to legitimize the vernacular as a literary language and to set a precedent for the use of English by other writers of belles lettres. Drawing judiciously from the traditions of French courtly poetry, from Italian themes and forms, from the native English tradition, and from his own background in Latin and patristic writers, Chaucer produced works of truth and grace that are monuments not only of his time but also of literature in general. Like that of Milton and Shakespeare, his work permeates our literature, our language, and our very culture.

Story characteristics

Chaucer's *The Canterbury Tales*, a compendium of literary genres, contains within its frame story of the pilgrimage a variety of popular story types, including romances, Breton lais, *fabliaux*, tragedies, beast-fables, sermons, exempla, saints' lives, and miracles of the Virgin. Chaucer also uses the dream-vision, another literary form popular in the Middle Ages, as a basis for *The Book of the Duchess*, *The House of Fame*, *The Parliament of Fowls*, and *The Legend of Good Women*, which employ as well such poetic conventions as the world of mythology, the parliament of beasts, and the court of love. Within these poems, Chaucer portrays a multitude of character types that range across the social spectrum from the chivalrous knight, the elegant prioress, and the courtly love heroine to the humble parson, the evil summoner, the lecherous wench, and, of course, the naïve narrator. As these characters' lives are examined through the prism of Chaucer's perspective—a perspective which is penetrating, insightful, and honest, but always sympathetic, tolerant, and loving—some of the truths of the human condition are revealed.

Biography

Household records seem to indicate that as a boy Geoffrey Chaucer served as a page for the Countess of Ulster, wife of Edward III's son Lionel, Duke of Clarence. Chaucer undoubtedly learned French and Latin as a youth, to which languages he later added Italian. Well-versed in both science and pseudoscience, Chaucer was familiar with physics, medicine, astronomy, and alchemy. Spending most of his life in government service, he made many trips abroad on diplomatic missions and served at home in such important capacities as Comptroller of Customs for the Port of London, Justice of the Peace for the County of Kent, and Clerk of the King's Works, a position that made him responsible for the maintenance of certain public structures. He married Philippa de Roet, probably in 1367, and may have had two daughters and two sons, although there is speculation concerning the paternity of some of those children believed to have been Chaucer's. Since Chaucer's career was his service to the monarchy, his poetry was evidently an avocation which did not afford him a living.

Analysis

Geoffrey Chaucer's best-known works are *Troilus and Criseyde* and the unfinished *The Canterbury Tales*, with *The Book of the Duchess*, *The House of Fame*, *The Parliament of Fowls*, and *The Legend of Good Women* positioned in the second rank. In addition to these works and to his translations of *The Consolation of Philosophy* (c. 1380) and *The Romance of the Rose* (c. 1370), there exist a number of shorter and lesser-known poems, some of which merit brief attention.

These lesser-known poems demonstrate Chaucer's abilities in diverse, but typically medieval forms. Perhaps the earliest extant example of Chaucer's work is "An ABC to the Virgin"; this poem, primarily a translation from a thirteenth century French source, is a traditional series of prayers in praise of Mary, the stanzas of which are arranged in alphabetical order according to the first letter of each stanza. Another traditional form Chaucer used is the "complaint," or formal lament. "A Complaint to His Lady" is significant in literary history as the first appearance in English of Dante's terza rima, and "The Complaint unto Pity" is one of the earliest examples of rime royal; this latter poem contains an unusual analogy which represents the personified Pity as being buried in a heart. "The Complaint of Mars" illustrates Chaucer's individuality in treating traditional themes and conventions; although the poem purports to be a Valentine poem, and akin to an aubade, its ironic examination of love's intrinsic variability seems to make it an anti-Valentine poem. Chaucer similarly plays with theme and form in *To Rosemounde*, a ballade in which the conventions of courtly love are exaggerated to the point of grotesquerie; the narrator says, for example, that he is as immersed in love as a fish smothered in pickle sauce. Finally, Chaucer's poem "Gentilesse" is worthy of note for its presentation of a theme, developed in "The Wife of Bath's Tale" and in "The Clerk's Tale," which posits that "gentilesse" depends not on inheritance or social position but on character. In sum, these poems, for most of which dates of composition cannot be assigned, represent a variety of themes and forms with which Chaucer may have been experimenting; they indicate not only his solid grounding in poetic conventions, but also his innovative spirit in using new forms and ideas, and in treating old forms and ideas in new ways.

Of those poems in the second rank, *The Book of the Duchess* was probably the earliest written and is believed to have been composed as a *consolatio* or commemoration of the death of Blanche, Duchess of Lancaster and wife of John of Gaunt, with whom Chaucer was associated. The poem uses the technique of the dream-vision and the device of the fictional narrator as means of objectifying the subject matter, of presenting the consolation at a remove from the narrator and in the person of the bereaved knight himself. The poem thus seems to imply that true consolation can come only from within; the narrator's human sympathy and nature's reassurance can assist in the necessary process of acceptance of and recovery from the loss of a loved one, but that movement from the stasis of deprivation to the action of catharsis and healing can occur only within the mourner's own breast.

The poem is told by a love sick narrator who battles his insomnia by reading the story of Ceyx and Alcyone. Finally falling asleep, he dreams that he awakens in the morning to the sounds of the hunt and, following a dog, comes upon a distinguished young knight dressed in black who laments his lost love. In response to the dreamer's naïve and persistent questions, the knight is eventually prodded into telling of his loss; he describes his lady in love-filled superlatives, reveals that her outer beauty was symbolic of her inner nobility, and acknowledges the great happiness they enjoyed in their mutual love. At the end of this lengthy discourse, when the narrator inquires as to the lady's whereabouts, the knight states simply that she is dead, to which the narrator replies, "Be God, hyt ys routhe!"

The poem thus blends the mythological world, the natural world, and the realm of human sympathy to create a context within which the mourner can come to accept his loss. The dreamer's love sickness causes him to have a natural affinity with the knight, and, by posing as stupid, naïve, and slow-witted, the dreamer obliges the knight to speak and to admit his loss, a reality he must acknowledge if he is to move beyond the paralysis caused by his grief to a position where he is accessible to the consolation that can restore him. This restoration is in part accomplished by the dreamer's "naïve" questions which encourage the knight to remember the joys he experienced with his lady and the love which they shared. The knight is then able to be consoled and comforted by the corrective and curative powers of his own memories.

The poem thus offers a psychologically realistic and sophisticated presentation of the grief process, a process in which the dreamer-narrator plays a crucial role, since it is the dreamer who, through his seemingly obtuse questioning, propels the knight out of the stasis to which his grief has made him succumb; the cathartic act of speaking to the dreamer about his lost love renders the knight open to the healing powers available in human sympathy and the natural world. The poem, even as it is elegiac in its tribute to the lost lover, is in the genre of the *consolatio* as it records the knight's conversion from unconsolable grief to quiet acceptance and assuagement. In establishing the persona of the apparently naïve and bumbling narrator, Chaucer initiates a tradition which not only has come to be recognized as typical of his works, but also has been used repeatedly throughout literature. Probably the earliest English writer to use such a narrative device, Chaucer thereby discovered the rich possibilities for structural irony implicit in the distance between the author and his naïve narrator.

In contrast to the well-executed whole that is *The Book of the Duchess*, *The House of Fame*, believed to have been composed between 1372 and 1380, is an unfinished work; its true nature and Chaucer's intent in the poem continue to elude critics. Beyond the problems posed by any unfinished work is the question of this particular poem's unity, since the connections between the three parts of the poem which Chaucer actually finished are tenuous. In the first book of the poem the narrator dreams of the Temple of Venus where he learns of Dido and Aeneas. The second book details the narrator's journey, in the talons of a golden eagle, to the House of Fame, and the contrast between the eagle's chatty friendliness and volubility and the obviously terrified narrator's monosyllabic responses as they swoop through the air provides much amusement. The third book, describing the House of Fame and its presiding goddess, demonstrates the total irrationality of fame, which the goddess awards according to caprice rather than merit. After visiting the House of Rumor, the narrator notices everyone running to see a man of great authority, at which point the poem breaks off.

Critical opinion differs considerably as to the poem's meaning. Some believe it attempts to assess the worth of fame, or perhaps even the life of the poet, in view of the mutability of human existence; others believe the poem intends to consider the validity of recorded history as opposed to true experience; yet other critics believe the poem attempts to ascertain the nature of poetry and its relationship to love. Although scholars have certainly not as yet settled on the poem's meaning, there is agreement that the flight of the eagle and the narrator in Book II is one of literature's most finely comic passages. Beyond this, it is perhaps wisest to view the poem as an experiment with various themes which even Chaucer himself was apparently disinterested in unifying.

In contrast to *The House of Fame*, *The Parliament of Fowls*, composed around 1380, is a finely crafted and complete work in which Chaucer combines several popular conventions, such as the dream-vision, the parliament of beasts, and the demande-d'amour, to demonstrate three particular manifestations of love: divine love, erotic love, and procreative or natural love. The fictional narrator is here a person who lacks love, who knows of it only through books, and whose very dreams even prove emotionally unsatisfying. The narrator recounts his reading of Africanus Scipio the Younger who dreamed that his ancestor came to him, told him of divine justice and the life hereafter, and urged him to work to the common profit. Having learned of the nature of divine love, the narrator dreams that Scipio comes to him as he sleeps to take him to a park where there are two gardens, one the garden of Venus and the other the garden of Nature. The garden of Venus is clearly the place of erotic or carnal love; it is located away from the sun and consequently is dark, and it has an illicit and corrupt atmosphere. In addition to such figures as Cupid, Lust, Courtesy, and Jealousy, the narrator sees Venus herself, reclining half-naked in an atmosphere which is close and oppressive.

In contrast, the garden of Nature is in sunlight; it is Valentine's Day and the birds have congregated to choose their mates. In addition to the natural surroundings, the presence of Nature herself, presiding over the debate, helps to create an atmosphere of fertility and creativity. The choice of mates is, however, impeded by a quarrel among three male eagles who love a formel. Each eagle has a different claim to press; the first asserts that he has loved her long in silence, the second stresses the length of his devotion, and the third emphasizes his devotion's intensity, pointing out that it is the quality rather than the length of love which matters. Since the lower orders of birds cannot choose mates until the eagles have settled their quarrel, the lesser birds enter the debate, aligning themselves variously either for or against the issues of courtly love which are involved. When the various birds' contributions deteriorate into invective without any positive result, Nature intervenes to settle the matter, but the formel insists upon making her own choice in her own time, that is, at the end of a year. The other birds, their mates chosen, sing a joyful song which ends the dream-vision. When the narrator awakes he continues to read, hoping to dream better.

The poem, then, presents love in its divine, erotic, and procreative forms. Although the narrator sees these various manifestations of love, he is unable to experience them since all are unavailable to him. He is, in some ways, thus akin to the eagles and in contrast to the lower orders of birds who obviously fare well, since at the end of the parliament they are paired with their mates and blissfully depart. The eagles and the formel, however, because of the formel's need to deliberate upon and choose among her courtly lovers, are in a kind of emotional limbo for a year; in effect, they are all denied for a relatively long period love's natural expression. Thus, even as the system of courtliness raises and ennobles love, the system also provides an impediment to the ultimate realization of love in mating. Although there seems to be a movement in the debate from the artificiality of courtly love to the naturalness of pairing off, this movement does not affect the eagles, who remain constrained, in large part because of their commitment to the courtly code. The poem examines, then, not merely the various faces of love but the nature of courtly love in particular and its seemingly undesirable effects upon its adherents.

Like *The House of Fame*, *The Legend of Good Women* is unfinished; although the poem was intended to contain a prologue and a series of nineteen or twenty stories telling of true women and false men, the extant material consists of two versions of the prologue and only nine legends. The poem purports to be a penance for the poet's offenses against the God of Love in writing of the false Criseyde and in translating the antifeminine *Roman de la rose*.

In the prologues, Chaucer uses the techniques of the dream-vision and the court of love to establish a context for his series of tales, which are much akin to saints' lives. In fact, the poem seems to parody the idea of a religion of love; the poet, although he worships the daisy as the God of Love's symbol, commits by his work heresy against the deity and must therefore repent and do penance by writing of women who were saints and martyrs in love's service. The two prologues differ in the degree to which they use Christian conventions to describe the conduct of love; the "G" prologue, believed to be later than the "F" prologue, has lessened the strength of the analogy to Christian worship. The legends, however, are very much in the hagiographic tradition, even to the extent of canonizing women not customarily regarded as "good," such as Cleopatra and Medea. Evidently wearying of his task, however, Chaucer did not complete the poem, perhaps because of the boredom inherent in the limited perspective.

Of Chaucer's completed work, *Troilus and Criseyde* is without question his supreme accomplishment. Justly considered by many to be the first psychological novel, the poem places against the epic background of the Trojan War the tragedy and the romance of Troilus, son of Priam, and Criseyde, daughter of Calchas the soothsayer. Entwined with their lives is that of Pandarus, friend of Troilus and uncle of Criseyde, who brings the lovers together and who, in consequence, earns lasting disapprobation as the first panderer. In analyzing the conjunction of these three characters' lives, the poem considers the relationship of the individual to the society in which he or she lives, and examines the extent to which events in one's life are influenced by external circumstances and by internal character. At a deeper level the poem assesses the ultimate worth of human life, human love, and human values. Yet the poem does not permit reductive or simplistic interpretation; its many thematic strands, and its ambiguities of characterization and narrative voice, combine to present a multidimensional poem which defies definitive analysis.

The poem's thematic complexity depends upon a relatively simple plot.

When callow Troilus is stricken with love for Criseyde, he follows all the courtly rules: he suffers physically, loves her from a distance, and rises to great heights of heroism on the battlefield so as to be worthy of her. When Troilus admits to Pandarus that his misery can only be cured by Criseyde's love, Pandarus is only too happy to exercise his influence over his niece. By means of a subtle mix of avuncular affection, psychological manipulation, and veiled threats, Pandarus leads Criseyde to fall in love with Troilus. The climax of Pandarus' machinations occurs when he arranges for Troilus and Criseyde to consummate their love affair, ostensibly against the stated will of Criseyde and in spite of Troilus' extremely enfeebled condition. Until this point the poem, reflecting largely the conventions of *fabliau*, has been in the control of Pandarus; he generates the action and manipulates the characters much as a rather bawdy and perhaps slightly prurient stage manager. With the love scene, however, the poem's form shifts from that of *fabliau* to that of romance; Pandarus becomes a minor figure and the love between Troilus and Criseyde achieves much greater spiritual significance than either had anticipated.

Although the tenets of courtly love demand that the lovers keep their affair secret, they enjoy for three years a satisfying and enriching relationship which serves greatly to ennoble Troilus; the poem's shape then shifts again, this time from romance to tragedy. Calchas, having foreseen the Trojan defeat and having therefore defected to the Greeks, requests that a captured Trojan be exchanged for his daughter. The distraught lovers discover that the constraints placed upon them by their commitments to various standards and codes of behavior combine with the constraints imposed upon them by society to preclude their preventing the exchange, but Criseyde promises within ten days to steal away from the Greek camp and return to Troilus. Once in the Greek camp, however, Criseyde finds it difficult to escape; moreover, believing that the Greek Diomede has fallen in love with her, she decides to remain in the Greek encampment until the grief-stricken Troilus eventually has to admit that she has, indeed, betrayed him.

At the end of the poem, having been killed by Achilles, Troilus gazes from the eighth sphere upon the fullness of the universe and laughs at those mortals who indulge in earthly endeavor. In his bitter wisdom he condemns all things of the earth, particularly earthly love, which is so inadequate in comparison to heavenly love. This section of the poem, erroneously called by some "the epilogue," has been viewed as Chaucer's retraction of his poem, and as a nullification of what has gone before. Chaucer's poetic vision, however, is much more complex than this interpretation supposes; throughout the poem he has been preparing the reader to accept several paradoxes. One is that even as human beings must celebrate and strive for secular love, which is the nearest thing they have to divine love, they must nonetheless and simultaneously concentrate on the hereafter, since secular love and human connections are, indeed, vastly inferior to divine love. A second paradox is that humans should affirm the worth of human life and human values while at the same time recognizing their mutability and their inferiority to Christian values. The poem also presents courtly love as a paradox since, on the one hand, it is the system which inspires Troilus to strive for and achieve a vastly ennobled character even though, on the other, the system is proven unworthy of his devotion. Criseyde is similarly paradoxical in that the narrator portrays her as deserving of Troilus' love, even though she proves faithless to him.

These paradoxes are presented against a classical background which contributes to the poet's juxtaposition of several oppositions. The world of the classical epic provides the setting for a medieval courtly romance so that, although the characters exist in a pagan environment, they are viewed from the Christian medieval perspective which informs the poem. The poem's epic setting and its romance form, then, like its pagan plot and its Christian point of view, seem thus to be temporally misaligned; this misalignment does not, however, lead to dissonance but instead contributes to the poem's thematic elusion and ambiguity.

The characters, of course, also contribute significantly to the poem's ambiguity. Criseyde, particularly, resists classification and categorization. The ambivalent narrator encourages the reader to see Criseyde in a variety of contradictory postures: as a victim, but also as a survivor, one who takes the main chance; as a weak and socially vulnerable person, but also as a woman who is self-confident and strong; as an idealistic and romantic lover, but also as a careful pragmatist; as a greatly self-deceived character, but also as a self-aware character who at times admits painful truths about herself.

Also ambiguous, but to a lesser degree, is Pandarus, whose characterization vacillates between that of the icily unsentimental cynic and that of the sensitive human being who bemoans his failures to achieve happiness in love and who worries about what history will do to his reputation. He seems to see courtly love as a game, and to disbelieve in the total melding of two lives, but he betrays his own sentimentality when he indicates that he longs to find such love for himself.

Although his mentor seems not to take courtly love seriously, to Troilus it is the center of his life, his very reality. His virtue lies in large part in his absolute commitment to courtly ideals and to Criseyde. The solidity of that commitment, however, prevents Troilus from taking any active steps to stop the exchange, since such action would reveal their love affair, soil Criseyde's reputation, and violate the courtly love code. In this sense, Troilus is trapped by his own nobility and by his idealism, so that his course of action is restrained not only by external forces but also by his own character.

In fact, the poem seems to show that both Troilus and Criseyde are ultimately responsible for what happens to them; the role of fate in their lives is relatively insignificant because their very characters are their fate. As Troilus is governed by his dedication to heroic and courtly ideals, Criseyde is governed by the fact that she is "slydynge of corage." It is her nature to take the easiest way, and because of her nature she is untrue to Troilus.

From the poet's point of view, however, Criseyde's faithlessness does not invalidate for Troilus the experience of her love. Because of his own limited perspective Troilus is himself unable to assess the worth of his life, his love affair, and the values to which he subscribed; the parameters of his vision permit him to see only the inadequacy and imperfection of earthly experience in comparison to the experience of the divine. The poet's perspective, however, is the one which informs the poem, and that perspective is broader, clearer, and more complex, capable of encompassing the poem's various paradoxes and oppositions. In consequence, even though Troilus at the end discounts his earthly experience, the poem has proven its worth to an incontrovertible degree; human life, even though inferior to the afterlife, nevertheless affords the opportunity for experiences which, paradoxically, can transcend their earthly limitations. Ultimately, then, the poem affirms the worth of human life, human love, and human idealism.

Although Chaucer never completed *The Canterbury Tales*, it is his most important work and the one for which he is best known. In its conceptual richness, in its grace and precision of execution, and in its broad presentation of humanity, *The Canterbury Tales* is unequaled. The poem occupied Chaucer for the last one and a half decades of his life, although several of the stories date from an earlier period; it was not until sometime in the middle 1380's, when he conceived the idea of using a framing device within which his stories could be placed, that the work began to assume shape. That shape is the form of a springtime pilgrimage to Canterbury, to see the shrine of Thomas à Becket. The fictional party consists of some thirty pilgrims, along with the narrator and the host from the Tabard Inn; each pilgrim was to tell two stories en route to Canterbury and two on the return trip, making an approximate total of 120 tales. There are extant, however, only the prologue and twenty-four tales, not all of which are completed; moreover, the sources of these extant tales (over eighty manuscript fragments) contain considerable textural variations and arrange the tales in many differing orders. Thus, it is impossible for critics to determine the order which Chaucer envisioned for the tales.

The notion of using the pilgrimage as a frame device was a stroke of narrative brilliance, since the device provides infinite possibilities for dramatic action while it simultaneously unifies a collection of widely disparate stories. In response to the host's request for stories of "mirth" or "doctryne," the pilgrims present an eclectic collection of tales, including romances, *fabliaux*, beast-fables, saints' lives, tragedies, sermons, and exempla. The frame of the pilgrimage also permits the poet to represent a cross section of society, since the members of the party range across the social spectrum from the aristocratic knight to the bourgeois guild members to the honest plowman. Moveover, since the tales are connected by passages of dialogue among the pilgrims as they ride along on their journey, the pilgrimage frame also permits the characters of the storytellers to be developed and additional dramatic action to occur from the pilgrims' interaction. These "links" between the tales thus serve to define a constant fictional world, the pilgrimage, which is in juxtaposition to and seemingly in control of the multiple fictional worlds created in the tales themselves; the fictional world of the pilgrims on their pilgrimage thereby acquires a heightened degree of verisimilitude, especially because the pilgrims' interchanges with one another often help to place them at various recognizable points on the road to Canterbury.

The pilgrimage frame also permits the creation of an exquisitely ironic tension between the fictional narrator and the poet himself. The narrator is Chaucer's usual persona, naïve, rather thick-witted, and easily and wrongly impressed by outward show. This narrator's gullible responses to the various pilgrims are contrasted to the attitude of the poet himself; such use of the fictional narrator permits the poet not only to present two points of view on any and all action, but also to play upon the tension deriving from the collision of those two perspectives. The device of the pilgrimage frame, in sum, allows the poet virtually unlimited freedom in regard to form, content, and tone.

The context of the pilgrimage is established in the poem's prologue, which begins by indicating that concerns both sacred and secular prompt people to go on pilgrimage. Those people are described in a formal series of portraits which reveals that the group is truly composed of "sondry folk" and is a veritable cross section of medieval society. Yet, the skill of the poet is evident in the fact that even as the pilgrims are "types," that is, representative of a body of others like themselves, they are also individuals who are distinguished not simply by the realistic details describing their external appearances but more crucially by the sharply searching analysis which penetrates their external façades to expose the actualities of character that lie beneath.

The tales begin with a group which has come to be seen as Chaucer's variations on the theme of the love-triangle and which consists of "The Knight's Tale," "The Miller's Tale," and "The Reeve's Tale." Like *Troilus and Criseyde*, "The Knight's Tale" superimposes a romance against the background of the classical world as it tells of Palamon and Arcite, knights of Thebes who are captured by Theseus during his battle with Creon and sentenced to life imprisonment in Athens. While imprisoned they fall in love with Emily, over whom they quarrel; since Palamon, who saw and loved her first, thought she was a goddess, Arcite, who saw her second but who loved her as a woman, insists that his is the better claim. Several years later, Arcite having been freed and Palamon having escaped from prison, the knights meet and again quarrel, agreeing to settle the matter with a duel. When Theseus comes upon them he stops the duel and decrees that they must instead meet a year later with their troops to decide the matter in a tournament.

For this tournament Theseus erects a magnificent stadium with temples to Venus, Mars, and Diana. When the stadium is completed and the time for the tournament has arrived, the three members of the love-triangle pray for the assistance of their particular gods: Palomon asks Venus for Emily or for death; Arcite asks Mars for victory; and Emily asks Diana to permit her to remain a virgin or, failing that, to be wedded to the one who most loves her. These various petitions cause a quarrel between Venus and Mars which Saturn resolves by announcing that Palamon shall have his lady even though Mars assists Arcite to victory. Arcite, in consequence, wins the tournament but in the midst of his victory parade his horse rears and he is mortally injured. From his deathbed Arcite summons both Palamon and Emily and commends them to each other, but they continue to grieve during the next several years. Finally, Theseus summons Palamon and Emily to him and tells them that since grief should end and life go on, they are to marry and thus make joy from sorrows.

The poem's plot, then, concerns the resolution of the love-triangle typical of romance. This plot, however, is in the service of a more serious conflict, that between order and chaos. Theseus serves as the civilizing instrument, the means by which order is imposed on the anarchy of human passion. In actuality, by assuming control over the hostility between Palamon and Arcite, Theseus reshapes their primitive emotional conflict into a clearly defined ritual; by distancing it as well in time and space, Theseus forces that conflict into a shape and an expression which is socially acceptable and which poses no threat to the culture's peaceful continuance. Theseus thus makes order and art out of raw emotion and violent instincts.

The love conflict which in "The Knight's Tale" serves to develop this cosmic theme is in "The Miller's Tale" acted out on the smaller scale and in the more limited space of the sheerly natural world, and thus serves no such serious or noble end. Again there is a triangle, but the romantic discord among the aristocratic Palamon, Arcite, and Emily becomes in "The Miller's Tale" the bawdy comedy of the *fabliau* as it arises from the interaction of the young clerk Nicholas and the effeminate dandy Absolon who both desire Alison, the young wife of John, an old and jealous carpenter. At the same time that the amorous Absolon serenades her nightly and sends her gifts in an effort to win her, Alison agrees to give her love to Nicholas as soon as he can create the opportunity. In fact, however, no elaborate stratagem is needed to make possible the encounter Alison and Nicholas both desire. Since Alison's husband is away all day working, and since Nicholas as a student who boards with the couple is at home all day, alone with Alison, there really are no obstacles preventing the lovers from acting on their passions immediately. Alison's insistence, then, that Nicholas devise a plan whereby they can give rein to their passions reflects an important stylistic and thematic connection between the tale and "The Knight's Tale." In the latter tale, Theseus controls the passions of Palamon and Arcite by postponing their encounter and dictating its arena; the distancing in time and space results in a civilized, restrained expression of their passions. In "The Miller's Tale," by contrast, the distancing Alison demands parodies the conventions of romance and courtly love. This distance in actuality simply ennobles base instincts, for Alison and Nicholas inhabit not a courtly world but a natural one, and their intellectual, spiritual, and romantic pretensions constitute only a thin veneer covering their healthy animalism. By using distance as a means of ennobling base instincts, "The Miller's Tale" parodies not only the world and the theme of "The Knight's Tale," but also its poetic treatment.

Nicholas' seduction plan plays upon both the strengths and the weaknesses of the carpenter's character. Telling John that another flood is coming, Nicholas convinces the carpenter that he must hang three barrels from the rafters in which each can remain until the waters rise, when they will cut themselves free to float away. The carpenter's pretensions to spiritual and theological superiority cause him to accept this prophecy unquestioningly, but at the same time his genuine love for his wife causes his first reaction to be fear for her life. When all three on the appointed night have ostensibly entered their barrels, Nicholas and Alison sneak down to spend a night in amorous play.

At this point the plot is entered by Absolon, who comes to Alison's window to serenade her; pleading for a kiss, he finds himself presented with Alison's backside. Bent then on avenging his misdirected kiss, he brings a hot colter and asks for another kiss; presented this time with the backside of Nicholas, Absolon smacks it smartly with the red-hot colter, causing Nicholas to cry out "Water!" which in turn causes the carpenter to cut the rope on his barrel and crash to the ground, injuring both his person and his dignity. Whereas in "The Knight's Tale" the three major characters ultimately obtain what they desire most—Arcite, victory; Palamon, Emily; and Emily, the man who loves her most—"The Miller's Tale" reverses this idea; John, the jealous carpenter, is cuckolded and humiliated in front of the entire town, the fastidious Absolon has kissed Alison's "nether ye," and Nicholas has lost a hand's-breadth of skin from his backside. Only Alison remains unscathed, but then, she must spend her life being married to John.

The poem thus parodies the romance tradition, the idealistic notion that civilized or courtly processes can elevate and ennoble fundamental human passions. Even as it transfers various themes, mechanisms, and perspectives from "The Knight's Tale," "The Miller's Tale" transforms these and reflects them negatively. The generic differences between the two poems, however, demand that content and tone differ. "The Knight's Tale," combining epic and romance, deals seriously with serious considerations, whereas "The Miller's Tale," by virtue of its being a *fabliau*, has as one of its purposes the humorous depiction of human shortcomings.

"The Knight's Tale" and "The Miller's Tale" are differnet tales which have structural similarities; "The Reeve's Tale," which completes the poem's first thematic grouping, shares with "The Miller's Tale" the *fabliau* form but the two differ considerably in tone. The Reeve's story results from his outrage at the Miller's story, which has belittled carpenters; in angry retaliation the Reeve relates the popular *fabliau* concerning the two students who, cheated by a dishonest miller, exact revenge by sleeping with both his wife and his daughter. The plot, which hangs in part upon the device of the misplaced cradle, has as its end the unsophisticated students' triumph over the social-climbing miller. The tone of "The Reeve's Tale," therefore, is bitter and vindictive, told, the Reeve acknowledges, solely to repay the Miller.

Chaucer uses the romance and the *fabliau*, these two forms with which he begins his series of tales, again and again in the course of the poem. Other romances are the unfinished "The Squire's Tale,' which has an Oriental setting; "The Man of Law's Tale," which blends romance and a saint's life in the story of the unfortunate Constance; and "The Wife of Bath's Tale," "The Clerk's Tale," and "The Franklin's Tale," which will be discussed together as "the marriage group." The genre of the *fabliau* is also further represented in "The Shipman's Tale" of the debt repaid by the adulterous monk to his lender's wife, and in "The Friar's Tale" and "The Summoner's Tale," stories which are attacks on each other's professions and which are told to be mutually insulting.

Another popular genre Chaucer employs in his collection is that of the saints' lives, a type used in "The Second Nun's Tale" of St. Cecilia and in "The Prioress's Tale" of the martyred Christian boy slain by Jews. While both tales conventionally concern "miracles of the virgin," the tale of the Prioress is of particular interest because of the nature of the storyteller. Although she is supposed to be a spiritual being, a guardian of other spiritual beings, she is described in the same manner as the heroine of a courtly romance; moreover, although her description points to sensitivity and charity, her moral sensibility is clearly faulty. She worries over a little mouse, but tells a violent tale of religious intolerance. Moreover, the ironies implicit in the engraving on her brooch—"Amor vincit omnia"—are extensive, as are the ironies deriving from the conflicting perspectives of the narrator, who naïvely admires her for all the wrong reasons, and the poet, who clearly sees her as possessed of many shortcomings.

Another popular genre in the Middle Ages was the beast-fable, a form which Chaucer uses brilliantly in "The Nun's Priest's Tale." The story concerns Chauntecleer and Pertelote, a cock and hen owned by a poor widow. When Chauntecleer one night dreams of a fox, he and Pertelote have an extended discussion on the validity of dreams. Believing that dreams are caused by bile or overeating, Pertelote advises the use of a laxative; Chauntecleer, however, holding a different opinion, tells a story wherein a dream is proven prophetic. At this point the fox appears, whom the Nun's Priest likens to such other traitors as Simon and Judas Iscariot. Even as he insists that his antifeminine statements are not his own but the cock's, the Nun's Priest clearly believes that woman's counsel often brings misfortune and points with relish to the fox's sudden appearance as proof of this belief.

The encounter between the fox and the cock reveals the weaknesses of both. Relying hugely on flattery, the fox persuades Chauntecleer to relax his guard, close his eyes, and stretch his neck, providing the fox the perfect opportunity to seize Chauntecleer and race off. As the widow and her household set chase, Chauntecleer advises the fox to tell the pursuers to turn back because he will soon be eating Chauntecleer in spite of them; when the fox opens his mouth to do this, Chauntecleer of course escapes. Although the fox tries to persuade Chauntecleer to come down out of the tree, Chauntecleer wisely declares that he will not again be fooled by flattery and that no one should prosper who closes his eyes when he should watch. The fox, as one might expect, disagrees, declaring that no one should prosper who talks when he should hold his peace.

The poem thus uses the beast-fable's technique of personifying animals to the end of revealing human truths; it also uses the conventions and the rhetoric of epic and courtly romance to talk about the lives of chickens, thus creating a parody of the epic form and a burlesque of the courtly attitude. The poem is also, to a degree, homiletic in treating the dangers inherent in succumbing to flattery; each character suffers as a result of this weakness, the cock by having foolishly permitted himself to be captured, and the fox by having gullibly permitted himself to be hoodwinked by one pretending affinity.

Having begun the discussion of *The Canterbury Tales* with an analysis of the group of tales concerned with the love-triangle, it seems fitting to end the discussion with an analysis of those tales referred to as "the marriage group." "The Wife of Bath's Tale," "The Clerk's Tale," "The Merchant's Tale," and "The Franklin's Tale" bring to that group several perspectives on women and the relation between the sexes. The Wife of Bath, in complete opposition to the traditional view of women, presents one extreme point of view which advocates sensualilty and female authority. An excellent example of what she advocates, the wife is strong and lusty, and insists on dominance in her marriages. In her lengthy prologue to her story she takes issue with patristic doctrine concerning chastity and female inferiority, and uses Scriptural allusions to buttress her opinions. Her prologue thus provides a defense of women and of sensuality.

Her tale, an exemplum illustrating the argument contained in her prologue, concerns a knight who must, in order to save his life, find out what women desire most. Despairing over his inability to get a consensus of opinion, he one day comes upon a "loathly lady" who offers to give him the answer if he in turn will do what she requests. Gratefully agreeing, he learns that women most want "sovereynetee" and "maistrie" over their husbands; he is less pleased, however, to learn that her request is that he marry her. Having kept his promise, the knight on their wedding night is understandably distant from his new wife; when pressed for an explanation, he notes that she is ugly, old, and lowly born. She in turn explains that nobility comes not from wealth or birth, that poverty is virtuous, and that her age and ugliness insure her chastity. She gives the knight a choice: he can have her ugly and old but faithful, or young and pretty but untrue. The knight chooses, however, to transfer this decision and consequently the control of the marriage to her, whereupon she announces that she will be not only young and pretty but also faithful, thus illustrating the good that comes when women are in control.

The Wife's tale, and the wife herself, with her heretical opinions concerning marriage and sexual relations outrage the Clerk, who tells a tale to counter the Wife's; his tale reinforces the doctrine that male dominance on earth conforms to the order of the divine hierarchy. His story treats the patient Griselda, who promises her husband, Walter, to do everything he wishes and never to complain or in any way indicate disagreement. When a daughter is born to them, Walter, who is an Italian marquis, tells Griselda that since the people are complaining about her low birth, he must have the child killed, to which Griselda meekly agrees; Walter, however, sends the child secretly to a relative to be reared. When a son is born, Walter again does the same thing, again to test her obedience, and again Griselda is perfectly submissive. Twelve years later Walter secretly sends for the two children and tells Griselda that since he is divorcing her in order to marry someone else, she must return to her father. Moreover, he insists that she return to her father just as she had left him, that is, naked, since Walter had provided her with clothes. Griselda, with great dignity, requests at least a shift as recompense for the virginity which she had brought to him but which she cannot take away with her. When asked later to come and make arrangements for Walter's new bride, Griselda cheerfully complies, although she does, at this point, give some indication of the great price she has paid for her obedience and her faithfulness to her vow; she asks Walter not to torment his new wife as he did her, the bride-to-be having been tenderly reared and therefore not so well able to withstand such adversity. Walter, finally satisfied as to Griselda's steadfastness, restores her as his wife and reunites her with their children. The Clerk concludes by noting that it is hard to find women like Griselda nowadays.

The tale is one with which critics have long grappled, since it presents seemingly insurmountable interpretive problems. The story can hardly be taken as realistic, even though the Clerk, through his efforts to give Walter psychological motivation, attempts to provide verisimilitude. Although the poem may be intended as allegory, to illustrate that one must be content in adversity, it seems also to have a tropological level of meaning, to illustrate the proper attitude for wives. The narrator's own uncertainty as to whether he tells a tale of real people, a saint's life, or an allegory, contributes to the difficulty one has in assessing the poem's nature and purpose. It is obvious, though, that the Clerk's intended corrective to "The Wife of Bath's Tale" is perfectly accomplished through his tale of the impossibly patient Griselda.

At the end of his tale the Clerk appears to switch directions; he advises that no husband should try what Walter did, and that furthermore wives should be fierce to their husbands, should provoke their jealousy, and should make them weep and wail. The Merchant picks up this notion and echoes the line in the first sentence of his own remarks, which are intended to counter the Clerk's presentation of the saintly wife. The Merchant's own unhappy marriage experience adds a painfully personal coloration to his tale of the old husband and the young wife.

His story of May, Januarie, and the pear tree is well known in the history of the *fabliau*. Immediately after wedding the sixty-year-old Januarie, whose lovemaking she considers not "worth a bene," May meets and falls in love with Damian, who loves her in return. When Januarie becomes temporarily blind, the lovers plot to consummate their love in the pear tree above Januarie's head. Pluto and Proserpina, debating how men and women betray each other, decide to restore Januarie's sight but to give May a facile tongue. Consequently, when Januarie's sight returns and he sees May and Damian making love in the pear tree, May explains that her struggling in a tree with a man was an effort to restore his sight, which is obviously as yet imperfect. Placated, Januarie accepts her explanation and they are reconciled.

The three tales thus present varying views of woman as lascivious termagant, as obedient saint, and as clever deceiver; marriage, accordingly, is seen as a struggle for power and freedom between combatants who are natural adversaries. It remains for Chaucer in "The Franklin's Tale" to attempt a more balanced view, to try to achieve a reconciliation of the oppositions posed in the tales of the wife of Bath, the clerk, and the merchant.

"The Franklin's Tale" is a particular kind of romance called a Breton lai, which conventionally is concentrated, imaginative, and exaggeratedly romantic. While the tale is interesting in its depiction of an integrity which rests upon absolute commitment to the pledged word, the intricacies of the poem's moral issues are ultimately resolved, in a rather disappointing fashion, by something akin to a *deus ex machina*. The tale, nevertheless, has been seen traditionally to function as the reconciliation of the marriage group because of the more balanced relationship portrayed between Arveragus, a knight, and Dorigen, his wife. The couple agree that he will show no sovereignty except for that semblance of it which may be necessary for his dignity, and that their effort will be for freedom, harmony, and mutual respect in marriage, rather than for mastery. In this regard, they represent an ideal example of marriage which is totally antithetical to those of the preceding marriage tales; in Dorigen and Arveragus, Chaucer seems to be exploring the possibility that chivalric ideals and middle-class virtues can be compatible in marriage. Whether the poet really believes this is possible, however, is placed in question by the tale's romance form and by its contrived ending.

While Arveragus is away on knightly endeavors, Dorigen mourns and grieves, worrying particularly about the black rocks which make the coastline hazardous. When Aurelius, who has loved her long, pleads for her attentions, she explains that she will never be unfaithful to her husband but adds, in jest, that if he will remove the rocks she will love him. Two years after Arveragus has come home, Aurelius, made ill by his long-frustrated passion, finds a magician who, for a large fee, creates the illusion that the rocks have vanished. Asked then to fulfill her end of the bargain, the horrified Dorigen contemplates suicide to avoid this dishonor, but her miserably unhappy husband, declaring that "Trouthe is the hyeste thyng that man may kepe," sends Dorigen to fulfill her promise. Pitying them, Aurelius releases her from her promise and is in turn released from his debt by the magician; the tale ends by asking who was the most generous.

Although Dorigen and Arveragus have a marriage based on respect, honesty, and love, and although they share a moral sensibility and agree to the importance of honor to them individually and to their marriage, the artificial resolution of the plot by totally unexpected elements—the decisions of both Aurelius and the magician not to press their just claims—would seem to suggest that the poet himself dared not treat in a realistic fashion the unpleasant and probably disastrous results of the plot which he had created. In effect, he established an ideal marriage situation, set up a test of that marriage's strength, but then decided not to go through with the test. In placing his attempted solution of the marriage problem in the form of a Breton lai, in failing to pursue to the end the very questions he himself raises, and in providing a typical romance ending, the poet seems to indicate that any real solution to the problems pertaining to women and to marriage are not going to be so easily attained.

The Canterbury Tales, then, represents one of the earliest collections of short stories of almost every conceivable type. In addition to being a generic compendium, the poem is also a compendium of characters, since the pilgrims who tell the stories and the people who inhabit the stories together constitute the widest possible representation of character-types. In framing his collection of tales with the pilgrimage, Chaucer permitted himself an eclecticism in form, content, and treatment which was unprecedented in English literature. There are those who would eagerly affirm that the grace of vision which permeates *The Canterbury Tales* makes the work not only one which was unprecedented but also one which has not since been equaled.

Bibliography

Donaldson, E. Talbot. *Speaking of Chaucer*.

Gardner, John Champlin. *The Poetry of Chaucer*.
Muscatine, Charles. *Chaucer and the French Tradition*.
Robertson, Durant Waite, Jr. *A Preface to Chaucer*.
Rowland, Beryl, ed. *A Companion to Chaucer Studies*.

Evelyn Newlyn

JOHN CHEEVER

Born: Quincy, Massachusetts; May 27, 1912

Principal short fiction

The Way Some People Live, 1943; *The Enormous Radio and Other Stories*, 1953; *The Housebreaker of Shady Hill, and Other Stories*, 1958; *Some People, Places, and Things That Will Not Appear In My Next Novel*, 1961; *The Brigadier and the Golf Widow*, 1964; *The World of Apples*, 1973; *The Collected Stories of John Cheever*, 1978.

Other literary forms

John Cheever has published four novels and has written essays for magazines; his story "The Swimmer" was made into a motion picture, and "Children," a dramatization of "Goodbye, My Brother" by A. R. Gurney, was presented at the Manhattan Theatre Club (1976). Adaptations of "The Sorrows of Gin," "O Youth and Beauty," and "The Five-Forty-Eight" were presented on television (1979).

Influence

Heir to the story of symbolic detail and revealing epiphany within an apparently realistic surface and, thus, indebted to Anton Chekhov, Henry James, and James Joyce, Cheever has been the most prolific user of that form which, since 1925, has come to be called "*The New Yorker* story." Breeding fable and parable from grounds which at first link him with a writer of manners such as F. Scott Fitzgerald, he is thought by some to employ a symbolic method similar to Nathaniel Hawthorne's. As an experimenter, he preceded the rage for innovation which began near the end of the 1950's. His prose sometimes suggests poetic cadences linking him with William Butler Yeats and W. H. Auden and, perhaps, with T. S. Eliot and Dylan Thomas. His most affirmative pieces work out the enduring hope of the romantic quester.

Story characteristics

A polished surface suggesting the writer of manners accommodates portraits of recognizable upper-middle-class types which tend to become caricatures of satirical force. A subtle rhetoric of repeated series, rhetorical questions, and catalogs—sometimes holding together the comically incongruous, sometimes weaving images impressionistically—moves toward the startling and the magnificent. Archetypes, narrative interest and pacing, and deft use of the idiom of a class are important techniques for conveying Cheever's sense of modern life in WASP suburbia.

Biography

Educated at Thayer Academy in Milton, Massaschusetts, John Cheever was expelled at the age of seventeen for, he says, "laziness and smoking." After the story about the incident was published in *The New Republic* (October 1, 1930), he wrote for various national magazines. He married Mary Winternitz (March 22, 1941); they have three children (Susan Lily, Benjamin Hale, and Federico). During World War II, he served in the army, including two years in a line-infantry division. He has written television scripts for *Life with Father* (1945-1950) and has taught writing at Barnard College, University of Iowa, Sing Sing Prison, and, most recently, at Boston University, 1974 to 1975. He was made a Guggenheim Fellow in 1951. He has won the Benjamin Franklin Short Story Award (1954), the O. Henry Short Story Award (1955), the National Book Award (1957), the American Academy of Arts and Letters' Howells Medal (1964), the National Book Critics' Circle Award, the Pulitzer Prize, and the Edward McDowell Medal for outstanding contributions to the arts (1979). He is a member of the American Academy of Arts and Letters.

Analysis

John Cheever's stories of life in mid-twentieth century middle-class America depict characters in transit from Sutton Place apartments and the affluent suburbs to houses by lake or seashore and beyond to Italy, where a ruminating writer-narrator makes contact through memory and imagination with these American scenes. We Americans are, Cheever says, despite our rage for permanence, a nomadic lot; and the "short story" is our literature, "the literature of the nomad." On this matter, no one in America could speak with more authority than Cheever, author of more than two hundred short stories and a master of the form.

Cheever's humorous, sometimes satirical portraits of our foibles and absurdities are well served by caricatures of modern men and women caught up in "the tissue of historical, social, and familial forces," none more confining than their belief that the accomplishments of post-World War II America have released them entirely from the sufferings of the past. The more hopeful stories lead to epiphanies about mistaken notions of value and depict characters groping into the past for some enduring symbol, suggesting the human need for still one more joyful integration when the pieces have fallen apart and down the air vent. At best, in the scramble for permanence, the characters become aware of change, decay, and death as mothers of desire and beauty and, sometimes, love.

Cheever has warned readers of the danger inherent in mistaking fiction for autobiography. "Literature," he says, "remains the most intimate and acute means of communication about our deepest apprehensions and intuitions" about "the meaning of life and death." It takes its "splendor" from being "not autobiographical or biographical" but from a "very rich complex of autobiography and biography, of factual and spiritual information." It is more than statistics; it is the "bringing together of disparate elements into something that corresponds to an aesthetic, a sense of fitness." This credo and the stories point to Cheever as one of those heirs to Romanticism who persist in modern literature as if to say to Yeats, "you weren't the last; we, too, seek out 'traditional sanctity and loveliness.' "

The Romantic's faith is a complex one of undulations between the fragmentation and loneliness of the most trying days and the magnificent integrations of the most rewarding ones, which are no less real because they are inseparable from dreams; and Cheever is an American Romantic whose darker visions sometimes demand a mock-heroic edge or even a frenzied outcry regarding lost coherence. In the Romantic's spiritual autobiography, the fiction is the statistic, derivable in no other way and requiring no correspondent support from censuses or psychiatrists. If, like Yeats, Cheever sometimes wears masks of people lost in a "widening gyre," or if, like the earlier modern writers Fitzgerald and Ernest Hemingway, he sometimes shows the planed surfaces of the writer of manners, those apparent anomalies are merely parts of a mature Romanticism that holds on to a kind of faith without being naïve.

Cheever's most memorable pieces are often the title stories of his collections or are placed emphatically first or last, suggesting that the writer is a good critic of his own work. "Goodbye, My Brother," the first story in *The Enormous Radio and Other Stories*, now leads off *The Collected Stories of John Cheever*. Here, as elsewhere, the tensions besetting an upper-middle-class family are national and archetypal ones. The desire for permanence and sustaining rituals and the hope that the darker forces will stay buttoned up and not upset the pretty myths are classical themes; and the puritanical cast of the villain is unquestionably American. The brothers at war, the conflict of "matriarch and changeling," and the wish-fulfillment by violence released and beauty glimpsed indicate that within the linear plot and beneath a realistic surface the fabulous lurks; romance is glimpsed, and not entirely from the slant perspective of the parodist.

A key to the story is the author's use of exaggeration held just this side of disbelief so that finally it produces wonder. The family regulars at the summer cottage inflate the happy hour and evening gambling sessions into rituals which seem to work until the arrival of brother Lawrence. Suffering from an exaggerated case of puritan heritage, he sees only decay and the silliness of the tribe. The presence of his cramped nature impairs the family's ability to maintain its equanimity, although a stepped-up ritual of swimming seems to help. From light and water Cheever catches sustaining glimpses of the awe-inspiring; but the family's cook does not swim, and her exaggerated call to "Eat, eat," as if each meal were the last, is turned to threats of quitting by the "skinny" grump. A Greek might dramatize the need for mediation here, but inspired by Blakean excess, the narrator does not "restrain desire"; rather, he clobbers his brother on the head with a gift from the sea, a piece of wave-worn root. Although back at the cottage he must endure his brother's self-pity, the clobbering seems remarkably satisfying and appropriate. The gods of the sea must think so too, because they send him a vision of Helen and Diana emerging from the sea; "they are naked, unshy, beautiful, and full of grace." His brother's metaphysics no longer impose upon him because he has thrown off guilt, and everything looks beautiful to him.

Cheever is fond of using names to suggest some dignifying or diminishing link with values outside the story proper, often with the past. In addition to its bright goddesses, Helen and Diana, "Goodbye, My Brother" has a stern *Law*rence, a pitiful Ruth, and a whole family of Pommeroys, the Apple Kings. Correspondingly, in Cheever's most frequently anthologized work, "The Country Husband," Francis Weed is out of place in a suburban garden of Dutch colonial houses and ritualized cocktail and dinner parties; his daughter Helen reads *True Romance*; and a Thomas doubts the spiritual validity of Shady Hill which, sounding like a cemetery, is no place to "dream big dreams about the future."

The character's dislocation is urged throughout the story by a preponderance of active details. Riding in a plane that is forced down by a storm near Philadelphia, Francis arrives strangely on time for his usual commuter train from the station in New York; but the sun is shining gloriously, and his tale falls on deaf ears. Later, at home, the ears are even deafer. Frustrated, he proclaims his home a battle ground, and it becomes one. Then Francis has an epiphany that, instead of clarifying, complicates things. At the ritual Friday-night cocktail party, he sees a maid whom he had seen before—at the end of World War II—when she was being publicly chastised for living "with the German commandant during the Occupation." At a crossroads, the villagers had "cut off her hair" and "shaved her skull clean" and had forced her to strip naked. Then, as the cold wind had "made her white skin rough," the villagers had recognized "their common humanity"; the prisoner had become heroic, and "some inviolable grandeur in her nakedness" had lasted "through the ordeal."

This is the second story Francis cannot communicate. He is alone, and the memory mocks his inability to free himself by sharing his emotion. Then the baby-sitter offers a way (or so he thinks); but it turns out to be one more involvement he cannot talk about. When, paradoxically, he spits out a spiteful stream against the young girl's suitor, his soul is in danger. Finally, there is more pity than joy for a man who has to hire a psychiatrist to say "I'm in love," and who accepts a life of therapeutic woodworking instead of skiing in the mountains at one with nature.

Again Cheever creates a magnificent ending. Around the diminished Francis, things widen to include a cat tortured into baby clothes and a king of slipper-eating dogs, as well as a glimpse of "as passionate and handsome a nymph and satyr as you will find on any wall in Venice." The potentiality for imagined happiness is real enough on this night, but with his piece of wood, Francis is not bludgeoning the walls of his confinement. He has descended from the heroic heights, cut down by the story's mock-heroic edge.

In "The Country Husband," there is a sad attempt to endow the airplane and psychiatrist's office with some of the protectiveness of homes; but the homes themselves are painfully open to the disruptive presence of seductive baby-sitters, drunken partiers, and pervasive pressures from atop the social ladder. "The Enormous Radio," a demonic fable, shows that people are what they listen to and that something has the power to intrude within their walls and poison their lives.

From the new and technologically advanced ugliness of the Westcotts' radio come the sounds of ancient discord, and the Westcotts hear the marital conflicts and tinny escape routines of their neighbors in the apartment building. Even worse, Mrs. Westcott becomes hooked on this diet, and her conception of her once happy marriage is severely threatened. Fixing the radio may take the other voices away but not their after-image, the fear that she cannot keep the lid on her own black secrets which the radio's dark view of human nature has coaxed forth. At the end, the Westcotts are fighting almost as fiercely as the worst they have heard; and the radio, although repaired, tolls out the usual disasters of the day with widening horror. The reader is close to the allegory of a parable: civilization, with all of its advances, gives him little that might sustain a dream, and the walls are too thin to keep out invasions by his worst imaginings.

Always the master of rhetorical series and catalogs, used ordinarily for comic incongruity, Cheever here turns these devices to dark purposes. Mrs. Westcott overhears "demonstrations of indigestion, carnal love, abysmal vanity, faith, and despair"; and her husband excoriates her with questions and assertions that unmask her failures and threaten her ability to survive. Increasingly in Cheever's later stories, hard-driving rhetorical repetitions are used to dramatize the frenzy of those who sense the chaos of their world.

Even in the later stories, in which disruption abounds, there is still room for the Romantic's hope, a world for apple kings. In "The World of Apples," it exists for an aging poet and, by implication, for all who accept the validity, vitality, and mystery of memory and imagination. In poet Bascomb's fading years, a malevolent force inside him sends out filthy images, even in the midst of places of reverence in religion and art. At first, nothing works to exorcise the demon; instead of celebrations of the "pure and ardent love" for which his work *The World of Apples* has brought him fame, he becomes a parody of Yeats's wild old wicked man, seeing breasts in hills and, even worse, grinding out scatological epics, dirty limericks, and confessions of various pornographic adventures. Finally, he sets forth on a pilgrimage (parodying

"Sailing to Byzantium") to the shrine of the sacred angel of Monte Giordano.

The trappings of Bascomb's quest are a surrealistic mix of thunder and rain, sleep and dream, religious and secular memories in the "smell of damp country churches, the spare rooms of old houses," and flashes of the "uncleanliness from which he" is trying to escape. He comes upon an archetypal guide, an old man who has reached "an organic peace of mind" such as Bascomb desires. On the next day, however, comic frustration attends the moment he has aimed toward: the priest doubts the value of the Soviet medal Bascomb has brought as a gift. Then a miraculous ray of sunshine lights the medal, the priest is convinced, and Bascomb chants his American Romantic's version of Yeats's prayer: "God bless Walt Whitman. God bless Hart Crane. God bless Dylan Thomas. God bless William Faulkner, Scott Fitzgerald, and especially Ernest Hemingway."

That night, Bascomb does not become a golden bird upon "a golden bough," but in the brassiest of all comic beds, he recovers "a radiance he had known when he was young"; and on the following morning, to the sound of waterfalls, he remembers the "farm in Vermont where he had been raised" and in dreams abounding follows an old man (his father) into "the torrent, bellowing with joy." From the imperfectly understood "substrata of memory" that the writing of poetry exploits, Bascomb, and Cocteau (whom Bascomb credits with the theory), and Wordsworth (whom he might also cite), and Yeats, and Cheever himself have brought forth imaginative integrations of self and soul. Bascomb's version does not move "out of nature," but dreams the poet back into it. The tale is a sometimes embarrassing, sometimes comic, and finally convincing prose statement of the Romantic poet's quest, a form of spiritual autobiography.

Major publications other than short fiction
NOVELS: *The Wapshot Chronicle*, 1957; *The Wapshot Scandal*, 1964; *Bullet Park*, 1969; *Falconer*, 1977.

Bibliography
Burhans, Clinton S. "John Cheever and the Grave of Social Coherence," in *Twentieth Century Literature*. XIV (January, 1969), pp. 187-198.

Chesnick, Eugene. "The Domesticated Stroke of John Cheever," in *New England Quarterly*. XLIV (December, 1971), pp. 531-552.

Hunt, George. "Beyond the Cheeveresque," in *Commonweal*. CVI (January 19, 1979), pp. 20-22.

Moore, Stephen C. "The Hero on the 5:42: John Cheever's Short Fiction," in *Western Humanities Review*. XXX (1976), pp. 147-152.

William P. Keen

ANTON CHEKHOV

Born: Taganrog, Russia; January 17, 1860
Died: Badenweiler, Germany; July 2, 1904

Principal short fiction

Collected Works, 1899-1902 (Volumes I-X); *The Oxford Chekhov*, 1965-1976 (Volumes IV-IX).

Other literary forms

Besides the several hundred short stories that Anton Chekhov wrote during the years 1880 to 1903, he authored seventeen plays: seven full-length dramas and ten one-act plays. Of the full-length plays the best-known are *The Sea Gull* (1896), *The Three Sisters* (1901), and *The Cherry Orchard* (1904). In addition, Chekhov wrote a scholarly work, *Sakhalin Island* (1893) and numerous columns and journalistic articles. Although not intended for publication, his letters, notebooks, and diaries have appeared in print in various forms edited and translated by various scholars.

Influence

Chekhov's influence on the relatively plotless but carefully crafted story that dominated short fiction through the first half of the twentieth century is immense. Katherine Mansfield took Chekhov as her mentor, measuring her stories against what she called the "Chekhov standpoint"; Chekhov's stories, she believed, were true. Although the stories are without beginning or end, Chekhov, she says, touches one point with his pen and then another point and encloses something which has been there forever. Authors such as Chekhov, Mansfield, James Joyce, and Sherwood Anderson turned the short story away from a heavy reliance on plot line and concentrated on everyday people in ordinary circumstances.

Story characteristics

Chekhov's stories rely on precise observation, selective detail (sometimes seemingly irrelevant), brevity, and irony. A reader's interest in the stories is not in what happens, since usually very little does happen, but in how it happens and why it happens. Characters and details are presented without authorial intrusion, and sentences are pared down so that nouns and verbs without adjectival or adverbial qualifications carry the burden of meaning. Short fiction, Chekhov believed, must settle immediately into a reader's brain, and too much detail serves not to clarify but to hinder attention. Chekhov's effort was directed to the reproduction of a fragment of "real life" by means of subtle evocation of tones and moods that connect the particular with the general and so give the fragment a universal significance.

Biography

The grandson of a serf and the son of an unsuccessful grocer, Anton Pavlovich Chekhov began to write in order to help support himself and his family. Turning out short pieces for newspapers and magazines rapidly because remuneration was very small, Chekhov was able to put himself through medical school. By the time he became a doctor, however, receiving a degree from the University of Moscow in 1884, he was well on his way to becoming a successful author; and although he continued to practice medicine in a limited way, most of his energy went into writing the hundreds of short stories on the basis of which he has become known not only as Russia's greatest writer of short fiction but also as one of the short story's most influential practitioners. His total output and achievement is even more amazing considering the fact that he died at the relatively early age of forty-four from tuberculosis contracted when he was a young man.

Analysis

Anton Chekhov's stories range from the lightly humorous to the bitterly ironic, from the wistfully poetic to the starkly tragic. His characters run the gamut from youth to old age and from the excessively rich to the extremely poor. His sympathies, seldom overtly stated but always subtly implied, are with the authentic and the loving, regardless of age or class. His antipathies are always directed to those who live by the lie, who are involved in falsehoods of one kind or another whether through poses, affectations, snobbery, or lack of concern.

"A Trifle from Real Life" and "The Fugitive" are both about children brought into involvement with an adult world of deceit and trickery. The traditional plot line of "A Trifle from Real Life," although slight, is easy to follow. The story begins with a description of Nikolai Ilitch Belayeff, who has come to pay a call on Olga Ivanovna, with whom he has been involved in what he now considers a long and tedious love affair. His smug self-sufficiency is immediately revealed by Chekhov's brief but telling description of Nikolai as "rosy, well fed, and a patron of the race-tracks." Although Chekhov begins the story with a description of Nikolai, it soon becomes apparent that the boy Aliosha, Olga's son, is the story's protagonist. Since Olga is out, Nikolai and Aliosha find themselves together while they await her return. Aliosha is a sturdy little boy of eight, dressed in a velvet suit and long black stockings, but although he is immaculately and picturesquely dressed, he reveals his longing for physical activity by his attempts to mimic the antics of an acrobat he has seen at the circus.

Having nothing better to do, Nikolai addresses the boy, asking if his mother is well. Aliosha's first words in answer to that question, together with his physical movement relevant to his response, focus a reader's attention on the reason for Aliosha's subsequent confession to Nikolai. " 'Not very,' " the boy answers, "shrugging his shoulders. 'Mamma is never really well. She is a woman, you see, and women always have something the matter with them.' " The boy's response, obviously shaped by his father's feelings about women, both foreshadows the revelation that Aliosha has been secretly meeting his father and indicates that the boy is starved for a father's continuing affection. Aliosha's need for his father accounts for his quick and loving responses to Nikolai's advances. The boy touches Nikolai's beard, nestles close to him, and begins to play with his watch chain. When Aliosha inadvertently lets slip the information that his father wears a watch chain, Nikolai pounces on the fact and insists that the boy tell him the secret, "as between friends." The boy, trying to establish a close relationship with Nikolai, asks that the man promise not to tell Olga and then reveals the secret that the servant, Pelagia, takes him and his sister twice weekly to meet with their father at a confectioner's shop.

Having obtained this much information and, more because he is bored with Olga and tired of their affair than out of loving concern, Nikolai pursues the questioning of Aliosha until Aliosha tells that his father blames Nikolai for the breakup of the marriage and the unhappy family situation. Since Nikolai is seeking an excuse for anger, he siezes on the boy's remarks and uses them as a basis for his confrontation with Olga, who comes in at this time. When Aliosha realizes what Nikolai is doing, his face flushes and then grows suddenly pale before it becomes distorted with fear.

> "You gave me your word of honour," the boy moans. But Nikolai motions impatiently, replying, "This is more important then words of honour. This hypocrisy, these lies are intolerable."

Nikolai's promise, a "trifle" to him, means much to Aliosha, and with his trust in Nikolai broken, he comes face to face with deceit for the first time in his life. "He trembled and hiccoughed and cried," Chekhov writes, for "he had never imagined till now that there were things in this world besides pasties and watches and sweet pears, things for which no name could be found in the vocabulary of childhood." Deceit pervades "A Trifle from Real Life," although Chekhov presents it more as undercurrent than as overt movement. Nikolai and Olga have deceived her husband; Aliosha and his sister deceive their mother; Pelagia and Olga's husband deceive Olga and the children; Nikolai deceives Olga. Since the reader can equate deceit with the title of the story, the "trifle" takes on immense and ironic proportions. Aliosha is indeed initiated into the conditions of "real life."

Whereas "A Trifle from Real Life" is about an upper-class boy, "The Fugitive" is about a poor boy, but he, too, like Aliosha, is deceived by an unthinking and uncaring man, a doctor who promises him milk and honey and songbirds but who gives him instead a vision of disease, death, and despair. Seven-year-old Pashka, illiterate, poverty stricken, and sick since Easter with a lesion that has affected the joint of his arm, has arisen long before daybreak to make a trip with his mother through the cold and rain to a hospital. Once there, they wait for two more hours until the doors open and then wait again for their turn to see the doctor. While Pashka is waiting, he can hear the doctor shrilly scolding the ailing peasants, who treat the doctor as the savior his pose declares him to be. When it is Pashka's turn, the doctor first scolds the mother and then declares that Pashka must stay overnight in the hospital. In an effort to seduce Pashka to spend the night willingly without his mother, the doctor promises to show the boy a real fox and take him visiting and to catch songbirds and to buy lollipops.

Once the boy is in the ward, however, the bright promises turn into nightmare visions. All around him the boy sees old age, horrifying disease, and impending death. When one of the sick patients dies during the night he is whisked out of the ward, as Pashka watches and listens, panic-stricken. Then he dashes through the hospital, the patients now becoming grotesque dream images growing bigger and bigger; long-haired monsters with the faces of hags surround him. Finally the boy runs through the nightmare maze of the hospital and finds himself outside, where he stumbles and runs in circles until in back of the clinic buildings he sees graves with white crosses. In terror he calls for his mother. Then out of the spooky darkness Pashka sees a lighted window and, although petrified with fear, he runs toward it, his fear turning into overwhelming joy as he recognizes the doctor. Laughing with happiness, Pashka stretches out his arms to the doctor, when suddenly someone tackles him, and he staggers and falls down, losing consciousness.

It is daylight before he awakes to the doctor's voice that yesterday was bright with promise. "Well, you are a fool, Pashka! Tell me, aren't you a fool? You should get a beating, but there's no one to do it." The doctor's words end the story as suddenly as Pashka had fallen, and just as suddenly the reader knows that the doctor has already administered a beating more terrifying than an actual whipping and that the beating the doctor administers is accomplished unknown to him out of a complete insensitivity and unconcern for the feelings and understandings of a seven-year-old child.

In "The Lament," Chekhov writes not of a child but of an aged cabdriver, Iona Potapov, whose son has recently died and whose grief could be better handled by him if he could find someone to whom he could tell his story. The fares he picks up will not listen to him, a hall porter to whom he tries to talk forces him to move on, and a young cabdriver needs to sleep more than he needs to listen to an old man. Finally Iona is driven to tell his story to his horse, who "munches, listens, and breathes over its master's hand. . . ."

Although short, "The Lament" has a tremendous impact because of the way Chekhov handles details to move the story to its final statement. The opening paragraph sets the scene, introduces the protagonist, and identifies him with his horse and the reader in such a way that the final paragraph which finds the man talking with his horse is both credible and significant. It is twilight; a thick wet snow is falling, covering everything on the city street. Iona is sitting in this cab bent double "as far as a human body can bend double," and he is covered with snow, looking "like a phantom." The horse is also covered with snow. Whereas Iona looks like a ghost, the animal looks like a gingerbread horse "worth a kopek." The horse is no doubt plunged in thought, as "you too" would be if you were snatched from your usual habitat and thrown into this nightmare world "full of monstrous light, unceasing noise, and hurrying people." The dream aura, the snow weighing down horse and man, their isolation in the middle of noise and lights, are details creating a sense of intolerable burden, not only identified with the man and the animal but also forcibly called to the attention of the reader.

Iona's first fare is an officer, not a bad man, but one in a hurry to get to his destination when, as the officer remarks, it looks as though traffic and people "have entered into an agreement" to impede Iona's progress. The officer's words are important on two counts. First, they are a variation on the recurring motif of no one listening; second, they suggest to Iona that here is someone who will listen. Although Iona begins to tell the officer of his son's death, the officer's attention is continually diverted to the traffic, and he does not hear. Iona's second fare is a group of men who offer Iona too little money for the journey they want to take, but Iona is not out on this night to make money but rather to find someone who will listen to him, and he accepts their offer. They, too, are in a hurry and, moreover, they are disagreeable brutes, demanding that Iona use his whip on the horse at the same time that they physically abuse the old man. Nevertheless, Iona tries to tell them of his grief: "My son has died, and I am alive. . . . A wonderful thing, death mistook the door . . . instead of coming to me, it went to my son. . . ."

Once more alone, Iona is surrounded by silence and cold. The crowds hurry by without noticing him or his grief. Finally, after trying to make contact with the hall porter, Iona decides to give up and return his horse to the stable. There he mets a young cabdriver who also cannot listen to him. Unable to be alone with his grief any longer, Iona goes outside and opens his heart to his horse with a full simplicity, human dignity, and tragic potential greater than his appearance would have us believe of him.

In "Dreams," Chekhov abandons the traditional plot line, substituting instead several descriptive paragraphs that enclose a conversation composed mainly of lengthly monologues and ending with a short dramatic scene. Underlying the surface of the story, however, exposition gives way to conflict and complication, which builds to a climax that is quickly followed by a resolution. In the same way that plot structure lies beneath the surface of the narration, the identification of the protagonist is similarly hidden. At first glance it appears that the protagonist is the "tramp" and that the conflict involves his attempt to get to the place of his dreams, but then the tramp convict without a name becomes an Everyman to be identified first with the two soldiers who accompany him and then with any man, any human. As the story progresses, a dismal and surreal picture of life in Russia emerges, symbolized by the road on which the three men travel. No matter how long they walk, they cannot get away from the same spot of ground. "They walk and walk," Chekhov says, "but the ground they walk on is always the same; the wall comes no nearer; the spot remains a spot."

The tramp convict, who refuses to reveal his name, dreams a dream of freedom in Siberia where there is great plenty, where land is available for everyone and the people are rich, where "everything is better." He envisions a river, filled with a great variety of fish, into which the free man "strong of body and valiant of heart" can throw his line and partake of the plentitude the water provides. Yet the actual conditions of his life—imprisonment for a crime he did not commit, a life of penal servitude in densely crowded conditions where "the floor is all filthy and spat over," and constant, hopeless fleeing from the authorities—convey a Kafkaesque projection of life as a nightmare. The dream of escape is just a dream. Freedom is beyond a terrible expanse, further than the man can conceive.

The soldiers share the convict's dream of freedom and participate in the vision the convict reveals. Tramping along with the convict, the three men are yoked together on a walk they will never complete. Although the soldiers participate in the dream, they are jealous of the convict's ability to project his dream pictures, and as if to deny their participation, they ridicule the convict, telling him that he can never get there; the journey will kill him; and "that's a fact." The denial comes close to being a crucifiction with the convict killed by and alongside the two soldiers. The convict rapidly crosses himself. "He is trembling all over, his head is shaking, and he is beginning to writhe like a caterpillar that someone has stepped on."

Two kinds of dreams are operating in this story: the wish-fulfillment dream of escape to Siberia (ironic in itself, since Siberia was used as a prison) and the nightmare projection of "real" life. Set in juxtaposition, these dreams define the human condition. "Dreams" is one of the most complex of Chekhov's stories and one of the most satisfying since understanding comes only by means of a reader's full participation in the story.

For Chekhov, the writer's task was to dramatize the apparently threadbare facts of human existence without preconceived judgments, leaving for the reader the task of deriving meaning. Because as author he stood aloof from his characters and situations, he was often accused of being indifferent and crass. Chekhov himself addresses the question in a letter to a friend, A. A. Souvorin, dated April 1, 1880:

> You abuse me for objectivity, calling it indifference to good and evil, lack of ideals and

ideas, and so on. You would have me when I describe horse-thieves, say: "stealing horses is an evil." But that has been known for ages without my saying so. . . . Of course it would be pleasant to combine art with a sermon, but for me personally it is extremely difficult and almost impossible, owing to the conditions of technique . . . if I introduce subjectivity, the image becomes blurred and the story will not be as compact as all short stories ought to be. When I write, I reckon entirely upon the reader to add for himself the subjective elements that are lacking in the story.

Major publications other than short fiction

PLAYS: *The Sea Gull*, 1896; *Uncle Vanya*, 1899; *The Three Sisters*, 1901; *The Cherry Orchard*, 1904.

NONFICTION: *Stories of Moscow Life*, 1883-1885; *The Case of Rykov and Company*, 1884; *From Siberia*, 1890; *Sakhalin Island*, 1893; *Letters of Anton Tchehov to his Family and Friends*, 1920; *The Note-book of Anton Tchehov*, 1921; *Letters on the Short Story, the Drama and Other Literary Topics*, 1924; *The Personal Papers of Anton Chekhov*, 1948; *Letters of Anton Chekhov*, 1973.

Bibliography

Hingley, Ronald. *A New Life of Anton Chekhov*.
Jackson, Robert Louis, ed. *Chekhov: A Collection of Critical Essays*.
Rayfield, Donald. *Chekhov: The Evolution of His Art*.
Winner, Thomas Gustav. *Chekhov and His Prose*.

Mary Rohrberger

KATE CHOPIN

Born: Saint Louis, Missouri; February 8, 1851
Died: Saint Louis, Missouri; August 22, 1904

Principal short fiction
Bayou Folk, 1894; *A Night in Acadie*, 1897.

Other literary forms
In addition to the short stories which brought her some fame as a writer during her own lifetime, Kate Chopin published two novels, *At Fault* (1890) and *The Awakening* (1899), the latter of which was either ignored or condemned because of its theme of adultery and frank depiction of a woman's sexual urges. Chopin also wrote a few reviews and casual essays and a number of undistinguished poems.

Influence
In her own day Chopin was best known for the short stories which she published in popular magazines such as *Atlantic*, *Century*, *Harper's*, and *Vogue* and in her own collections, especially *Bayou Folk*. Her models included Sarah Orne Jewett, Mary E. Wilkins Freeman, and Guy de Maupassant, but Chopin was usually classed, even for a long time after her death, with other Southern regional writers such as George Washington Cable, Grace King, and Ruth McEnery Stuart. Her work lapsed into obscurity during the first half of this century, but in the 1960's, she was discussed and *The Awakening* was "rediscovered" by critics such as Larzer Ziff and Edmund Wilson. With the collection of her works and a biography by Per Seyersted in 1969 coinciding with the rebirth of the American feminist movement, Chopin's importance has been recognized and her place established as a major American author. It can fairly be said that her influence is just beginning to be felt.

Story characteristics
Many of Chopin's stories are tales of "local color," set among the Cajun and Creole societies of Louisiana; these stories vividly evoke the texture and flavor of life in these societies, but Chopin's purpose is often larger than the simple depiction of a quaint way of life. In these stories as well as others, set in Saint Louis and elsewhere, she consistently presents strong-willed, independent heroines aware of or awakening to their sexuality; suggests the possibility of respect and equality between the sexes; and casts a skeptical eye on the institution of marriage.

Biography
Kate Chopin was born Katherine O'Flaherty in Saint Louis, Missouri, in

1851. Her mother's family was Creole, descended from French settlers, and her father, a successful merchant, was an Irish immigrant. She was educated at the Academy of the Sacred Heart in Saint Louis beginning in 1860, five years after her father's accidental death, and was graduated in 1868. In 1870, she married Oscar Chopin, who took her to live in Louisiana, first in New Orleans and later in Natchitoches Parish, the setting for many of her stories. In 1882 or 1883, Oscar died of swamp fever; Kate Chopin managed her husband's properties for a year and in 1884 returned to Saint Louis. The next year her mother died, and in 1888 Chopin began writing out of a need for personal expression and to help support her family financially. Her stories were generally successful, but *The Awakening*, published in 1899 and now acknowledged as her masterpiece, was condemned by most of those who bothered to review it at all. One reviewer labeled the novel "poison," and it was banned from libraries in Saint Louis and other cities. Chopin herself was blackballed from membership in the Saint Louis Fine Arts Club. After this controversy, Chopin wrote only about a dozen stories and only four of them were published in her life. In 1904, she died of a stroke following a visit to the Saint Louis World's Fair.

Analysis

Until recently, Chopin was known best literarily, if at all, as a "local colorist," primarily for her tales of life in New Orleans and rural Louisiana. Chopin manages in these stories (about two-thirds of her total output) to bring to life subtly the settings and personalities of her characters, usually Creoles (descendants of the original French settlers of Louisiana) or Cajuns (or Acadians, the French colonists who were exiled to Louisiana following the British conquest of Nova Scotia). What makes Chopin especially important for modern readers, however, is her insight into human characters and relationships in the context of their societies whether Creole, Cajun, or Anglo-Saxon—and into the social, emotional, and sexual roles of women within those societies.

Chopin's desire and hope for female independence can be seen in two of her earliest stories, "Wiser Than a God" and "A Point at Issue!" (both 1889). In the first story, the heroine Paula Von Stoltz rejects an offer of marriage in order to begin a successful career as a concert pianist because music is the true sole passion of her life; it is an act which anticipates the actions of Edna Pontellier in *The Awakening*. In the second story, Eleanor Gail and Charles Faraday enter into a marriage based on reason and equality and pursue their individual careers in separate places. This arrangement works very well for some time, but finally each of the two succumbs to jealousy; in spite of this blemish in their relationship, Chopin's humorous tone manages to poke fun at traditional attitudes toward marriage as well.

This questioning though humorous attitude is strongly evident in one of

Chopin's most anthologized and best-known tales, "The Story of an Hour" (1894). Mrs. Mallard, a woman suffering from a heart condition, is told that her husband has been killed in a train accident. She is at first deeply sorrowful, but soon realizes that even though she had loved and will mourn her husband, his death has set her free: "There would be no powerful will bending hers in that blind persistence with which men and women believe they have a right to impose a private will upon a fellow-creature." As Mrs. Mallard descends the stairs, however, the front door is opened by her husband, who had never been on the train. This time her heart gives out and the cause ironically is given by the doctors as "the joy that kills."

It is in her Louisiana stories, however, that Chopin's sympathy for female and indeed human longings emerges most fully, subtly blended with a distinct and evocative sense of locale and folkways. "La Belle Zoraïde" (1893) is presented in the form of a folktale being told by a black servant, Manna-Loulou, to her mistress, Madame Delisle (these two characters also are central to the story "A Lady of Bayou St. John," 1893). The tale itself is the story of a black slave, Zoraïde, who is forbidden by her mistress to marry another slave with whom she has fallen in love because his skin is too black and her mistress intends her for another, more "gentlemanly" servant. In spite of this, and although the slave she loves is sold away, she bears his child and refuses marriage to the other slave. Her mistress falsely tells Zoraïde that her child has been born dead, and the slave descends into madness. Even when her real daughter is finally brought back to her, Zoraïde rejects her, preferring to cling to the bundle of rags which she has fashioned as a surrogate baby. From then on, "She was never known again as la belle Zoraïde, but ever after as Zoraïde la folle, whom no one ever wanted to marry. . . . She lived to be an old woman, whom some people pitied and others laughed at—always clasping her bundle of rags—her 'piti.'" The indirect narration of this story prevents it from slipping into the melodramatic or the maudlin. Chopin's ending, presenting the conversation of Manna-Loulou and Madame Delisle in the Creole dialect, pointedly avoids a concluding moral judgment, an avoidance typical of Chopin's stories. Instead, the reader is brought back to the frame for the tale and concentrated upon the charm of the Creole dialect even while he or she retains pity and sympathy for Zoraïde.

In spite of their Southern locale, Chopin's stories rarely deal with racial relations between whites and blacks. One important exception is "Désirée's Baby" (1892). Désirée Valmondé, who was originally a foundling, marries Armand Aubigny, a plantation owner who is proud of his aristocratic heritage but very much in love with Désirée. He is at first delighted when she bears him a son, but soon begins to grow cold and distant. Désirée, puzzled at first, soon realizes with horror that her child has Negro blood. Armand, whose love for Désirée has been killed by "the unconscious injury she had brought upon his home and his name," turns her out of the house, and she disappears with her child into the bayou, never to be seen again. Later, in a surprise ending reminiscent of Maupassant, Armand is having all reminders of Désirée burned when he discovers a letter from his mother to his father which reveals that his mother had had Negro blood. In this story we see the continuation of Chopin's most central theme, the evil that follows when one human being gains power over another and attempts to make that person conform to preset standards or expectations.

As suggested earlier, Chopin finds that power of one person over another is often manifested in the institution of marriage. Yet, as even her earliest stories suggest, she does not always find that marriage necessarily requires that a wife be dominated by her husband, and she demonstrates that both men and women are capable of emotional and spiritual growth. That possibility for growth is perhaps best seen in the story "Athénaïse" (1895). Athénaïse, an emotionally immature young woman, has married the planter Cazeau, but has found that she is not ready for marriage. She runs back to her family, explaining that she does not hate Cazeau himself: "It's jus' being married that I detes' an' despise. . . . I can't stan' to live with a man; to have him always there; his coats and pantaloons hanging in my room; his ugly bare feet—washing them in my tub, befo' my very eyes, ugh!" When Cazeau arrives to bring her back, however, she finds that she has to go with him. As the couple rides home, they pass an oak tree which Cazeau recalls was where his father had once apprehended a runaway slave: "The whole impression was for some reason hideous, and to dispel it Cazeau spurred his horse to a swift gallop."

Despite Cazeau's attempt to make up and live with Athénaïse at least as friends, she remains bitter and unhappy and finally runs away again, aided by her romantic and rather foolish brother Montéclin. Cazeau, a senstive and proud man, refuses to go after her again as though she too were a runaway slave: "For the companionship of no woman on earth would he again undergo the humiliating sensation of baseness that had overtaken him in passing the old oak-tree in the fallow meadow."

Athénaïse takes refuge in a boarding house in New Orleans where she becomes friendly with Mr. Gouvernail, a newspaper editor. Gouvernail hopes to make Athénaïse his lover, but he refrains from forcing himself on her: "When the time came that she wanted him . . . he felt he would have a right to her. So long as she did not want him, he had no right to her,—no more than her husband had." Gouvernail, though, never gets his chance; Athénaïse has previously been described to us as someone who does not yet know her own mind, and that such knowledge will not come through rational analysis but "as the song to the bird, the perfume and color to the flower." This knowledge does come to her when she discovers that she is pregnant. As she thinks of Cazeau, "the first purely sensuous tremor of her life swept over her. . . . Her whole passionate nature was aroused as if by a miracle." Thus,

Athénaïse returns to reconciliation and happiness with her husband.

Chopin's story illustrates that happiness in a relationship can come only with maturity and with mutual respect. Cazeau realizes that he cannnot force his wife to love him, and Athénaïse finally knows what she wants when she awakens to an awareness of her own sexuality. If Cazeau has to learn to restrain himself, though, Mr. Gouvernail learns the need to take more initiative as well; not having declared his love for Athénaïse he suffers when she goes back home. The tone of the entire story is subtly balanced between poignancy and humor, allowing us to see the characters' flaws while remaining sympathetic with each of them.

The importance of physical passion and of sexual self-awareness which can be found in "Athénaïse" can also be found in many of Chopin's stories and is one of the characteristics which make her writing so far ahead of its time. It is this theme which, as the title suggests, is central to her novel *The Awakening* and which was partly responsible for the scandal which that novel provoked. Chopin's insistence not merely on the fact of women's sexual desires but also on the propriety and healthiness of those desires in some ways anticipates the writings of D. H. Lawrence, but without Lawrence's insistence on the importance of male dominance.

Sexual fulfillment outside of marriage without moral judgments can be found in "The Storm," written in 1898, just before *The Awakening*, but not published until 1969. The story concerns four characters from an earlier tale, "At the 'Cadian Ball" (1892). In that earlier story, a young woman, Clarisse, rides out in the night to the 'Cadian Ball to declare her love for the planter Alcée Laballière. Alcée is at the ball with an old girl friend of his, Calixta, a woman of Spanish descent. Clarisse claims Alcée and Calixta agrees to marry Bobinôt, a man who has been in love with her for some time.

"The Storm" is set several years later. Calixta and Bobinôt have had a child, and Alcée and Clarisse have been happily married. One day, while Bobinôt and his son are out on an errand, a huge storm breaks out. Alcée takes refuge at Calixta's house, and the old passion between the two is rekindled; as the storm breaks about them in mounting intensity, the two make love, Calixta's body "knowing for the first time its birthright." While the storm mirrors the physical passion of the couple, neither it nor the passion itself is destructive. Where one would expect some retribution for this infidelity in a story, the results are only beneficial: Calixta, physically fulfilled, happily welcomes back her returning husband and son; Alcée writes to Clarisse, off visiting relatives, that he does not need her back right away; and Clarisse, enjoying "the first free breath since her marriage," is content to stay where she is for the time. Even today, Chopin's ending seems audacious: "So the storm passed and every one was happy."

Although written almost a century ago, Chopin's stories seem very modern in many ways. Her concern with women's place in society and in marriage, her refusal to mix guilt with sexuality, and her narrative stance of sympathetic detachment make her as relevant to modern readers as her marked ability to convey character and setting simply yet completely. In the little more than a decade in which she produced most of her work, her command of her art grows ever stronger as does her willingness to deal with controversial subjects. It is unfortunate that this career was cut so short by the reaction to *The Awakening* and her early death; but it is fortunate that Chopin left us the writing that she did, and that it has been preserved.

Major publications other than short fiction
NOVELS: *At Fault*, 1890; *The Awakening*, 1899.

Bibliography
Rankin, Daniel S. *Kate Chopin and Her Creole Stories.*
Seyersted, Per. *Kate Chopin: A Critical Biography.*
Wilson, Edmund. *Patriotic Gore: Studies in the Literature of the American Civil War.*
Ziff, Larzer. *The American 1890's: Life and Times of a Lost Generation.*

Donald F. Larsson

CHRÉTIEN DE TROYES

Born: France; c. 1150
Died: France(?); c. 1190

Principal works

Erec et Enide, c. 1164; *Cligès, ou la fausse morte*, c. 1164 (*Cliges: A Romance*); *Lancelot, ou le chevalier à la charrette*, c. 1168 (*Lancelot: Or, The Knight of the Cart*); *Yvain, ou le chevalier au lion*, c. 1170 (*Yvain: Or, The Knight with the Lion*); *Perceval, ou le conte du Graal*, c. 1180 (*Perceval: Or, The Story of the Grail*).

Influence

Chrétien de Troyes is acknowledged as the first writer of Arthurian romance in the vernacular; that is, the first to locate chivalric romance in the court of King Arthur. The narrative structures of chivalric romance of the twelfth and thirteenth centuries duplicate those of Chrétien's work—from the setting forth from Arthur's court to the triumphant establishing of the knight in his own kingdom or a place of honor at court. Chrétien is also the originator of the Arthurian version of the Grail legend, although his is not a fully Christianized version. The legend of the love affair of Lancelot and Guinevere has its origin in Chrétien's *Lancelot*. Without Chrétien's romances, there would have been no "frensshe bookes" for Sir Thomas Malory to recast.

Story characteristics

Chrétien's romances are of approximately three- to six-thousand lines in octosyllabic couplets. Although earlier criticism saw the sequence of adventures as arbitrary, modern analysis has demonstrated the careful gradations of significance to be found in the order of the adventures each protagonist must encounter. Most of the plot-dynamic concerns the balance to be maintained between love and chivalry, since in one or both of these realms the protagonist, a knight of Arthur's court, is immature or unformed. The general structure of the romances, attested by many scholars, involves a rapid progress to a first triumph, a sudden, devastating failure, and a lengthy progress to a triumph that is of greater import than the first. Not all of the stories, such as *Cliges*, conform to this pattern, but all of the romances are in many ways thematically similar. Chrétien makes much use of realistic detail, especially with regard to the human psyche, and he never loses sight of the irony of his characters' situations.

Biography

Although details of Chrétien de Troyes's life are unknown, he names himself in his romances and gives a list of his writings to date in the *Cliges*. His dialect is that of Champagne. There have been many hypotheses concerning his identity, but no significant evidence in support of any of them has been brought forward. That he was attached to the courts of Marie de Champagne and possibly of Phillipe of Flanders may be detected from the texts of *Lancelot* and *Perceval*, respectively. Stylistic traits such as the use of formal rhetorical techniques indicate clerical training, and he may have been in holy orders, although not necessarily higher than the diaconate. If, indeed, he was an inhabitant of Troyes, the site of twice-yearly fairs, he had opportunities for wider general culture than other regions might have provided, and this may account for the variety of his not-too-accurate geographical references. There is, in fact, little beyond the works clearly attributed to Chrétien that can provide evidence, and that only of artistic skill, of this author of at least five influential "courtly" romances.

Analysis

Love, chivalry, *mesure* (moderation or balance), and irony are the primary elements of the romances of Chrétien de Troyes. His protagonist must, to be worthy of love, seek adventures by means of which he can display his prowess in knightly combat; at the same time, he cannot neglect the demands of love for the sake of adventure. Chrétien addresses the former problem in his earliest romance, *Erec and Enide*, his first Arthurian romance. Erec wins Enide as his bride and is so enamored of her that he ceases to enter tourneys or seek adventures. He accidentally hears Enide's soliloquy of concern that he is being mocked for his uxoriousness and commands her to dress in her best garments, to ride before him as he goes out to prove his skill, and to remain silent under all circumstances. Enide, riding ahead, sees ambushes prepared for Erec and breaks his command by warning him. He rebukes her each time and defeats his would-be attackers. The lovers are reconciled after an extended series of adventures; Erec is convinced of his wife's faithfulness and respect and Enide is convinced of his worth.

Erec and Enide demonstrate the pattern of swift rise (the winning of Enide), sudden fall (the blow to Erec's pride), and slow recovery (the adventure sequence) characteristic of many of Chrétien's romances. It is not Erec alone who must be corrected, although his lack of balance, his *démesure*, is greater than Enide's. Enide, whose words alert Erec to his faults, appears also to be submitting to correction as she endures Erec's harshness. She needs to speak and he to hear, but the result of the revelation is Erec's anger and distrust. Although it seems that she is being punished for no reason, earlier circumstances suggest that her concern for Erec's reputation is, in part, concern for her own status, since her marriage to Erec resulted in her being elevated from the daughter of a poor knight to being the wife of the heir to a kingdom. When, commanded to silence, she speaks to protect Erec, and Erec, to preserve them both, must perforce listen; the difference from the initial incident lies in the appropriateness of motivation and response. Once real reconciliation and understanding are achieved, the lovers return to their kingdom, Erec's prowess having been confirmed by his adventures.

The *Yvain* presents the opposite problem from that of *Erec and Enide*: Yvain, a young knight of King Arthur's court, is so involved in knightly adventure that he neglects his duty as a lover, with disastrous results. Yvain leaves Arthur's court in order to be the first to attempt a new adventure—to find a spring whose water will cause a storm when it is poured over a magical rock beside it. The storm summons a knight whom Yvain defeats and pursues into the knight's city. Yvain, trapped in the city, is aided by Lunete, handmaiden to Laudine, the slain defender's widow. Yvain has fallen in love with Laudine and, through Lunete's machinations, the two are wed. Although he is passionately in love with Laudine, he is reminded by Gawain not to neglect adventure. Yvain receives Laudine's permission to seek adventures, but she sets a definite term on that permission—a year—after which her love will turn to hate. Yvain forgets, learns of Laudine's rejection from a messenger before all of the court, leaves the court, and goes mad. He abandons his clothing (signs of his rank), the court (his proper milieu), and his reason in an attempted flight from himself. After a long period of insanity, he is cured and starts on a long series of adventures, in the course of which he is befriended by a lion. All of his adventures necessitate rendering service, the proper use of his skills as a knight. With Lunete's help he conquers the last obstacle, Laudine's determined refusal to forgive him, and the lovers are reconciled.

Chrétien employs the same general structure in *Yvain* as he does in *Erec and Enide*, but the narrative is denser and the characterization more deft. From the beginning, Yvain's youthful self-centeredness and touchy pride prepare the reader for both his lack of understanding of what a lover's fidelity must be and his emotional devastation when his failure is made public. Laudine, whom Lunete manipulates into accepting Yvain as her new husband, is intensely concerned with her reputation—only feudal necessity obviates the potential ugliness of this new courtship—and her own pride is much injured by Yvain's negligence. This same concern with honor plays into Lunete's hands as she entraps Laudine in an oath to do all in her power to reunite the Knight with the Lion with his lady. Lunete's perspicacity contrasts with the prideful blindness of the two lovers, and even the Lion, in a scene of rich comedy and seriousness, demonstrates his faithfulness to Yvain, whom he believes to be dead, by attempting to commit suicide with Yvain's sword.

It is not simply the content of Yvain's adventures but their place in the narrative sequence that is meaningful in the romance. The same Yvain who could not get enough adventure finds himself required by his sworn word to perform two rescues nearly at one time, one of which is rescuing Lunete from the stake to which Laudine has condemned her for the "treason" of having aided Yvain. Yvain learns from his adventures that promises are neither to be made nor to be broken lightly and that he is not to be one such as Chrétien describes at the beginning of the romance, one who hears but does not understand: "for speech is completely wasted if not understood by the heart." At the end, however, Chrétien tempers Yvain's triumph with irony, causing one to wonder how perceptive Yvain really is when one reads of Laudine's less than gracious acquiescense—she has sworn an oath and will not be forsworn even if this means accepting Yvain—and Yvain's delight at their being reunited. In any event, a vital balance has been achieved between love and chivalry, and the Knight with the Lion has progressed in understanding beyond the Yvain of the beginning of the romance.

Although the love conventions Chrétien uses in his romances are usually, and inaccurately, described as those of "courtly love," the protagonists of *Erec and Enide* and *Yvain* are married as are Guillaume and Gratiien his wife in *Guillaume d'Angleterre*. Chrétien's much-contested third romance is the story of a family separated by adversity and rejoined after twenty years, during which both Guillaume and Gratiien have maintained their fidelity and the twin sons of their marriage have remained true to their noble birth despite bourgeois fostering. It is a tale in the romance mode although not strictly within the conventions of medieval romantic, that is courtly, love.

Chrétien does deal with the extramarital passion that characterized the Povençal love lyric in two of his romances, the *Cliges* and the *Lancelot*. In the latter, Chrétien is credited with being the creator of the story of the love between Lancelot and Guinevere, although he claims to have written the story at the behest of his patroness Marie de Champagne, daughter of Eleanor of Aquitaine. However reluctant Chrétien may seem—he turned over completion of the tale to one Godefroi de Leigny—this reluctance did not keep him from creating a complexly structured sequence of adventures each functioning not so much as instructive but as demonstrative of the lover's state. That Chrétien did not complete the romance himself may argue less for reluctance to write a romance of this kind than for the demands of writing the *Yvain*, generally believed to be contemporaneous. All that was significant in the *Lancelot* was completed by Chrétien; only the denouement remained for Godefroi.

In the *Lancelot*, love and reason are set in opposition and love triumphs. Lancelot, in quest of the queen who has been abducted by Meleagant, prince of Gorre, is made to look almost foolish as he venerates a lock of Guinevere's hair as if it were a holy relic, or becomes so involved in a reverie that he is unhorsed when he does not respond to a challenge, yet he never fails in any of his adventures. Those who taunt him for his unavoidable although unknightly ride in a cart when he has no horse cannot touch him with their mockery. Lancelot's reasonable hesitation before riding in the cart leads to his being rejected by Guinevere, but his lover's folly of absolute obedience to Guinevere's commands to "do his worst" at a tournament is accounted to his glory. Chrétien is clear-sighted enough to portray this glorious folly, iron-ically, as folly still, and Guinevere, for all her imperiousness, mourns when a false report of Lancelot's death leads her to believe that her harshness is the true reason for his demise.

Once Lancelot and Guinevere meet in love, Chrétien shifts his emphasis to the conflict between Lancelot and Meleagant; Lancelot, by virtue of knightly prowess, maintains the necessary balance between love and chivalry as he champions Arthur's queen against her abductor's accusation of adultery. Chrétien remains silent with regard to the truth of the accusation against Guinevere, and the tension between truth and protestation remains implicit as he focuses on the contrast between Lancelot and Meleagant as types of the lover: Meleagant, the abductor whose accusation is true, falls before Lancelot, the chivalrous lover, whose protestation is false. Chrétien narrates the story requested of him while making his own ironic observations by means of the dramatic and ironic tensions present in the narrative.

Cliges has been considered by some to be Chrétien's commentary on the Tristan legend. The general structure of the romance, the love story first of the parents and then of their son, Cliges, duplicates that of the Tristan tales. Later, Fenice, lover of Cliges, uses an elaborate stratagem to remain true to Cliges despite her marriage to his uncle, saying that she does wish to be a second Iseult. The lovers Fenice and Cliges are exemplary in their faithfulness to each other, but their derelictions otherwise are glaringly obvious. The romance ends with their being wed, but the closing comments attribute to Fenice's success in deceiving her husband the Eastern practice of using eu-nuchs as harem guards. Chrétien is never blatantly sarcastic, but one senses that the artist relishes giving *his* version of a very popular story.

Chrétien's career of innovation culminates in the unfinished *Perceval*. The romance, which in Chrétien's version is not overtly the Christian spiritual quest it was to become, is built around the theme of the Wasteland whose ruler, the wounded Fisher-King, can only be healed by certain questions asked by the chosen hero. This hero, Perceval, whose character is a compendium of the traits of Chrétien's earlier heroes, is brought up in ignorance and isolation by his mother and is so intent upon observing his conception of knightly decorum in the Fisher-King's presence that, fearing to seem uncouth, he fails to ask the necessary questions. Publicly denounced at Arthur's court, he sets out on a long, uncompleted series of adventures to redress his offense. The romance breaks off in the middle of a series of Gawain's adventures which form a parallel to Perceval's. There is controversy among scholars as to whether the romance would end with Perceval's triumphant return to ask the questions (a denouement used in later retellings of the tale) or with some ending that goes beyond the relatively simple pattern of Chrétien's other romances. The lack of resolution in *Perceval* led to several *Continuations* and one later medieval masterpiece, the *Parzival* of Wolfram von Eschenbach. Almost immediately, Chrétien's story was Christianized; that is, explicit links were made between the Grail and the chalice of the Last Supper and the lance of the Grail-ritual with the lance of the Crucifixion, by Robert de Boron. Later retellings of this version such as the Old French *Quest of the Holy Grail* (1225-1230) linked the grail-quest ever more firmly with the tragic downfall of Arthur's court; these versions led to the grail-story as retold in Middle English by Sir Thomas Malory.

Chrétien's contributions—the quest for adventure, the Lancelot-Guinevere affair, and the Grail-legend—provide the framework, lacking only the downfall of the Arthurian milieu, of the later Arthurian cycle of romances. Conventions that are present, it is true, in other romances of his time are crystallized in his works. It is unfair to his contemporaries and his literary descendants to term them mere imitators, but the medieval romance of chivalry received from Chrétien de Troyes a form ample and flexible enough to accommodate the variations, embellishments, and departures of those who came after him.

Bibliography
Bruce, J. D. *The Evolution of Arthurian Romance*.
Holmes, Urban T. *Chrétien de Troyes: Inventor of the Modern Novel*.
Loomis, Roger S. *The Arthurian Tradition and Chrétien de Troyes*.
Nitze, W. A. and T. P. Cross. *Lancelot and Guenevere: A Study*.

Amelia A. Rutledge

AGATHA CHRISTIE

Born: Torquay, England; September 15, 1890
Died: Wallingford, England; January 12, 1976

Principal short fiction

Poirot Investigates, 1924; *Partners in Crime*, 1929; *The Mysterious Mr. Quin*, 1930; *The Tuesday Club Murders*, 1932; *The Hound of Death and Other Stories*, 1933; *The Listerdale Mystery*, 1934; *Parker Pyne Investigates*, 1934; *The Regatta Mystery and Other Stories*, 1939; *The Labors of Hercules*, 1947; *Witness for the Prosecution*, 1948; *Three Blind Mice and Other Stories*, 1950; *The Under Dog and Other Mysteries*, 1951; *The Adventure of the Christmas Pudding*, 1960; *Double Sin and Other Stories*, 1961; *13 for Luck*, 1961; *Surprise! Surprise!*, 1965; *13 Clues for Miss Marple*, 1966; *The Golden Ball and Other Stories*, 1971; *Hercule Poirot's Early Cases*, 1974.

Other literary forms

Agatha Christie is primarily known for her detective novels and short stories. She wrote plays, an autobiography, and dramatized some of her novels and short stories. Under the name of Mary Westmacott, she wrote six romantic novels. Several of her novels and short stories have been made into films.

Influence

The greatest influences on Christie's work were Arthur Conan Doyle and G. K. Chesterton. She in turn has strongly influenced the development of the detective story. Christie is one of the most popular writers of all time in any language; her books have been translated into more than one hundred languages. She is the second most translated English author (the first is Shakespeare), and she has been outsold only by the Bible and Shakespeare. Her play *The Mousetrap* (1952) has run for more than twenty-five years—the longest continuous run for any play in history.

Story characteristics

Christie's short stories are characterized by their ingenious plots, constructed like puzzles, which the reader is challenged to solve. The settings are often English villages, peopled with stock characters such as lawyers, doctors, vicars, and retired colonels. Another favorite setting is the Middle East. Christie's stories are frequently humorous. The Mr. Quin stories show an interest in the supernatural.

Biography

Agatha Christie was born Agatha Mary Clarissa Miller. She had little formal education, having been educated at home by her mother and by governesses.

As a young girl she wanted to be either a concert pianist or a singer. In 1914, she married Archibald Christie. During World War I she worked as a nurse, then as a dispenser, a job that gave her a good knowledge of poisons. In 1919, her daughter Rosalind was born. After personal problems with her husband who had fallen in love with another woman, Christie disappeared in 1926. She was found suffering from amnesia, and the press wrongly accused her of doing this as a publicity stunt. In 1930, after her divorce from Christie, she met and married Max Mallowan, an archaeologist. Thereafter she often accompanied him on trips to the Middle East. During World War II, she worked again as a dispenser, this time in London, and renewed her knowledge of poisons. She was made Dame of the British Empire in 1971. Dame Agatha died in 1976.

Analysis

Agatha Christie's strength, for which she is famous, was her ingenious plots, which took precedence over either her characterizations or use of language. Her stories are often set in an English village or in the Middle East. Typically, a group of people gather, one of whom is later found dead. Since no outsider could have committed the crime, the murderer is one of the closed group. Unlike some lesser mystery writers, Christie shows her reader the necessary clues, but she often presents the clues so cunningly that the reader does not see their significance until the crime is solved. Although a master of the detective genre, Christie has all the limitations that have been said to be associated with it: the world she portrays is static; the characterizations are thin with no serious attempt being made to develop their personalities in depth; and the criminal, certainly, is a one-dimensional figure—the transgressor. Christie has created several detectives, the most famous of whom are Miss Jane Marple and Hercule Poirot; the others are Parker Pyne, Tommy and Tuppence, Mr. Harley Quin and Mr. Satterthwaite, Ariadne Oliver, and Superintendent Battle.

In her autobiography, Christie says that the Mr. Quin stories are her favorites. Mr. Quin is a mysterious figure who suddenly appears and just as suddenly disappears, always when a crime is about to be committed. He has supernatural knowledge that a crime is to be committed and acts as a catalyst to bring the crime to fruition. He never solves the crime himself, leaving that task to Mr. Satterthwaite after showing him all the clues. "The Face of Helen" is typical of these stories. At the beginning of the story, Mr. Satterthwaite is alone in his box at Covent Garden to hear the opera *Pagliacci* in which a new singer, Yoaschbim, who can sing strange, high notes, is to appear. Christie briefly sketches Satterthwaite's character. He is interested in the arts, belongs to the upper echelons of society, and is gregarious. Suddenly Mr. Quin appears. In the audience they see a beautiful girl who has two rival lovers. After the opera, Mr. Quin leaves saying enigmatically that once again they have seen the drama together. Which drama, *Pagliacci* or the drama of the girl with two lovers, is not immediately clear. Outside, Mr. Satterthwaite rescues the girl, Gillian West, as her two lovers fight over her, and he then takes her home. Later he learns that she is engaged to Charlie Burns, a steady young man, and not to Philip Eastney, the jealous artist. Burns tells of the tragedy and violence that Gillian has unwittingly left in her wake because of her beauty.

When Mr. Satterthwaite visits Gillian, he sees a radio and a beautiful glass beaker with a curious iridescent ball at the end, both of which are wedding presents from Eastney. Eastney has asked Gillian to stay at home on this evening in order to listen to the radio since it is the anniversary of their meeting. Although Mr. Satterthwaite is puzzled by this request since such sentimentality seems out of character for Eastney, nonplused, he goes to a restaurant in the hopes of finding Mr. Quin but finds Eastney there instead. The conversation between the two turns to poisonous gases, to the opera star Yoaschbim, and to Caruso who could shatter glass with his voice.

After leaving the restaurant, Mr. Satterthwaite senses Mr. Quin's invisible presence beside him, and this feeling grows, as does the feeling that a calamity is imminent. Although Mr. Satterthwaite senses that he has all the necessary information to prevent the crime, he cannot piece it together. Suddenly, he grabs a newspaper and discovers that Yoaschbim is to broadcast this evening, and, rushing to Gillian's flat, saves her just as Yoaschbim's high note shatters Eastney's beaker which contains poisonous gas. Thanks to Mr. Satterthwaite and Mr. Quin, the only victim is a cat. When Eastney learns what has happened, he commits suicide. Mr. Quin's appearance has thus alerted Mr. Satterthwaite that a crime was afoot and helped him prevent it.

Agatha Christie got the idea for Miss Marple, her own favorite detective, from the pleasure she took in depicting Dr. Sheppard's sister in *The Murder of Roger Ackroyd* (1926). Miss Sheppard is a spinster with a strong appetite for gossip, whose curiosity compels her to know everything: she is "the complete detective service in the home." Miss Marple, who first appeared in 1930, is like Miss Sheppard. She expects the worst of people, and in this viewpoint, she is often right. She solves her crimes by analogy to occurrences in her village of St. Mary Mead: human nature, in her view, is the same everywhere.

"Miss Marple Tells a Story" is typical of the manner in which she solves cases. She is telling her nephew Raymond, a modern author, and his wife Joan, an abstract painter, about a crime she has solved. She modestly says that she is not as clever as her nephew, but actually she is far shrewder. Her self-deprecation, however, is also mixed with self-pride, pride that she has saved an innocent person and has solved cases that have baffled people more clever than she.

A murder has taken place in the nearby town of Barnchester. Mr. Petherick, a shrewd solicitor, has brought a Mr. Rhodes to see Miss Marple in the hope that she can solve the case. Mrs. Rhodes had retired to bed in the Crown Hotel while Mr. Rhodes worked in the next room on his book. Before going to bed, Mr. Rhodes went to say good night to his wife and found her dead, stabbed through the heart. Their rooms were connected by a door, and each room had a door to the corridor. Mrs. Rhodes's door had been locked and bolted from the inside, the classical closed-door mystery setting. Only the chambermaid had entered, a fact supported by witnesses who could see both doors. Since the chambermaid is innocent, Mr. Rhodes appears to be the murderer. Mrs. Rhodes had said that she had received threatening letters from a woman whose child she had injured in a car accident. Mr. Rhodes, however, had not believed his wife since she had hysterical tendencies and craved excitement. (Just like a young woman in St. Mary Mead, observes Miss Marple.) Although the lawyer briefed to defend Rhodes intends to argue suicide, this is clearly contrary to the facts: Mrs. Rhodes was not a suicidal type, and there were no fingerprints on the dagger.

Without even visiting the scene of the crime, Miss Marple solves the case: clearly, she argues, there were two "maids." The real one came in by Mr. Rhodes's door and left by his wife's, while someone posing as a maid came in by Mrs. Rhodes's door, hid until the real maid was gone, killed Mrs. Rhodes, locked and bolted the door from the inside, and then left by Mr. Rhodes's door. Miss Marple reasons that people do not really notice a maid; they see only the uniform and presume that if a maid goes into a room, it is the same maid they see coming out. Miss Marple deduces that Miss Carruthers (the mother of the child Mrs. Rhodes had injured), a horsey woman staying at the Crown, is the real murderer; she is playing a role since she drops her 'g's when she speaks—an idiomatic speech pattern which nobody under sixty does. Miss Marple thus relies on her common sense and village experience to solve the crime.

Hercule Poirot is the complete opposite of Miss Marple, and unlike her, modesty is not one of his virtues. (During World War I, Belgian refugees were billeted near Torquay, which gave Christie the idea for her detective.) Poirot is eccentric and comical; he has a passion for neatness and symmetry and is inordinately proud of his mustache and his immaculate appearance. His foppish manner, however, is misleading since it disguises a very sharp mind.

"The Adventure of the Egyptian Tomb" is a typical Poirot mystery, and also demonstrates Christie's interest in archaeology. The tomb of King Men-her-Ra has been discovered by Sir John Willard, who dies soon after of heart failure. People start talking about a curse associated with the tomb. This death is followed by two more, that of Mr. Bleibner who had financed the expedition, and by the suicide of his dissipated nephew in New York. Concerned about her son who intends to continue his father's work, Lady Willard asks Poirot for help. Hastings, Poirot's unperceptive Watson, jumps to conclusions as usual; he believes that the nephew, who was hard pressed financially, had visited Egypt, intending to kill his uncle to inherit his money. By mistake, he killed Willard and in despair killed himself saying that he was an outcast and a leper.

The description of Poirot in Egypt is typical of Christie's humor. Poirot is a picture of misery since he has had to travel by sea which he hates. He disembarks in Alexandria, a wraith of his former self. He dislikes Egypt and wages a constant battle against dust and sand; he is also very disturbed that the palm trees are not planted in symmetrical rows. When he and Hastings arrive at the site, they discover that Mr. Schneider of the Metropolitan Museum has died of tetanus. Poirot appears to believe the curse, to the amazement of Hastings, and orders magical signs drawn around his tent to protect him. When Poirot drinks his favorite camomile tea and collapses, Hastings calls Dr. Ames, but Poirot suddenly comes to life: his supposed death was a ruse to catch Dr. Ames who had tried to poison him. Ames commits suicide.

Poirot says that from the start he believed that someone was taking advantage of the curse. Willard had died a natural death. Dr. Ames had taken advantage of the "curse" to kill Bleibner and had persuaded young Bleibner that he was suffering from leprosy, thus driving him to suicide. Schneider was killed because he knew too much. The reason for the murders was money. Young Bleibner had written a will, leaving everything to Ames. Since young Bleibner would inherit Bleibner's considerable wealth, Ames killed Bleibner so that he himself could inherit it. In spite of the heat and sand, Poirot's "little gray cells," as he calls them, functioned well. As usual, Poirot shows calmly that reason can solve any problem.

"Witness for the Prosecution," which has been made into a play, is interesting for its tight plot and its surprising denouement. Mr. Mayherne, a lawyer, is retained to defend Leonard Vole who is accused of murdering a rich old lady, Miss Emily French, whom he knew well. The maid, Janet Mackenzie, asserts that her mistress, Miss French, believed Vole to be single and had hoped to marry him, all of which Vole denies. Vole is apparently surprised to learn that he is the principal beneficiary in Miss French's will, which Mackenzie again swears he knew. Vole claims that he has an alibi, corroborated by his wife Romaine, for the time of the crime. When Mayherne visits her, she points out that the testimony of a devoted wife would not carry much weight. It turns out that Romaine is not really Vole's wife, but his mistress. To Mayherne's consternation, Romaine says she hates Vole and hopes he hangs. She claims that his alibi is false and that he confessed to the murder. The case seems hopeless until Mayherne gets a letter offering to sell information. Following instructions in the letter, he goes to a room in the slums where a slatternly middle-aged woman gives him love letters written by Romaine to another man. The woman desires revenge against Romaine because Romaine had taken her man away, and the man had thrown vitriol in her face, disfiguring her, while Romaine watched laughing. The woman also states that she knows that Romaine was at the cinema rather than at home to see Vole return. Romaine's evidence is a tissue of lies supposedly designed to ruin Vole, and Vole is acquitted. One of Romaine's gestures, however, reminds Mayherne of the middle-aged woman in the slums: Romaine has in fact played the part of the woman, and the love letters are false. When Mayherne asks why she resorted to such means, she reminds him that nobody would believe the testimony of a devoted woman. Surprisingly, she says that she knew Vole was guilty. Her description of his confession was absolutely true but nobody believed her because of the spiteful tone of her testimony and her superb acting. Although the ending is surprising, the reader should have known that Vole was guilty since his behavior towards Miss French was suspect and his testimony left too many questions unanswered.

These stories are typical of the kinds of plots and detectives that Christie uses. Christie has something approaching a moral purpose in writing her stories. In her autobiography she says that it is innocence, not guilt, that matters: "the *innocent* must be protected; they must be able to live at peace and charity with their neighbours." Her pity lies always with the victim, and the more gloriously alive the victim was, the greater her indignation becomes at the murderer. There is never any attempt to "understand" the criminal: the murderer has to be caught and punished (the crime is almost always murder); otherwise the guilt of the unsolved crime falls on all members of the group, on the innocent as well as the guilty. In Christie's stories, justice always wins, upholding her faith in the justness and reasonableness of society.

Major publications other than short fiction

NOVELS: *The Murder of Roger Ackroyd*, 1926; *Giant's Bread*, 1930 (published under the name Mary Westmacott); *Murder on the Orient Express*, 1934; *Unfinished Portrait*, 1943 (Mary Westmacott); *The A.B.C. Murders*, 1935; *Death in the Clouds*, 1935; *Murder in Mesopotamia*, 1936; *Ten Little Indians*, 1939; *Sad Cypress*, 1940; *N or M?*, 1941; *Absent in Spring*, 1944 (Mary Westmacott); *Remembered Death*, 1945; *The Rose and the Yew Tree*, 1947 (Mary Westmacott); *Mrs. McGinty's Dead*, 1951; *A Daughter's a Daughter*, 1952 (Mary Westmacott); *A Pocket Full of Rye*, 1953; *The Burden*, 1956 (Mary Westmacott); *The Clocks*, 1963; *Nemesis*, 1971; *Postern of Fate*, 1973.

PLAYS: *Black Coffee*, 1931; *And Then There Were None*, 1943 (dramatization of an earlier work); *Appointment with Death*, 1945; *Murder on the Nile*, 1946 (dramatization); *The Hollow*, 1951 (dramatization); *The Mousetrap*, 1952 (dramatization); *Witness for the Prosecution*, 1953 (dramatization); *Spider's Web*, 1954; *Go Back for Murder*, 1960 (dramatization).

NONFICTION: *An Autobiography*, 1977.

Bibliography

Grossvogel, David I. *Mystery and Its Fictions: From Oedipus to Agatha Christie.*

Keating, H. R. F. *Agatha Christie: First Lady of Crime.*

Ramsey, G. C. *Agatha Christie: Mistress of Mystery.*

Symons, Julian. *Mortal Consequences: A History from the Detective Story to the Crime Novel.*

Jennifer Michaels

WALTER VAN TILBURG CLARK

Born: East Orland, Maine; August 3, 1909
Died: Reno, Nevada; November 10, 1971

Principal short fiction
The Watchful Gods and Other Stories, 1950.

Other literary forms
In addition to his short stories, Walter Van Tilburg Clark has written three novels—*The Ox-Bow Incident* (1940), *The City of Trembling Leaves* (1945), and *The Track of the Cat* (1949). The first and last of these were made into motion pictures. He also produced an early book of poems.

Influence
Clark's major influence lies in the area of American Western fiction. His novels and stories represent new dimensions in the development of that genre and are themselves some of the best examples of modern Western writing.

Story characteristics
As in his novels, Clark in his short stories presents characters who, although not complete transcendentalists, are searching for the right relationship to the cosmic forces, as well as for their personal identities. His primary setting, the American West, is appropriate enough for his artistic vision, for he has always felt an almost religious kinship with the Rocky Mountains.

Biography
Born on August 3, 1909, in East Orland, Maine, Walter Van Tilburg Clark moved with his family to Nevada in 1917. He received his B. A. and M. A. degrees from the University of Nevada; and, following his marriage in 1933 to Barbara Morse, he began a career of college teaching and creative writing. His first book, *The Ox-Bow Incident*, has remained his most noted. In 1945 he received the O. Henry First Award for "The Wind and the Snow of Winter." Protesting autocratic tendencies of the administration, Clark resigned his teaching position at the University of Nevada in 1953, but eventually returned there to teach creative writing.

Analysis
Walter Van Tilburg Clark once wrote that the primary impulse of the arts has been religious and ritualistic—with the central hope of "propitiating or enlisting Nature, the Gods, God, or whatever name one wishes to give the encompassing and still mysterious whole." Certainly Clark's fiction attests to such a view. In a world in which thought is often confused and fragmented,

Clark advocates for man a stance of intellectual honesty, an acceptance of instinctive values, and a belief in love. The key is human experience. As Max Westbrook so aptly put it in his study of Clark, "Clark's literary credo, then, is based on the capacity of the unconscious mind to discover and to give shape to objective knowledge about the human experience."

"The Buck in the Hills" may be Clark's clearest reflection in his stories of the literary credo mentioned above. Writing more or less in the terse, almost brittle, style of Ernest Hemingway, Clark opens the story with vividly descriptive passages of mountain scenery. The narrator, whose name the reader never learns, has returned to this setting after five years. It is really more than a return for him; it is a pilgrimage to a sacred place. Like Hemingway's heroes, he feels a deep need to replenish his spirit, to reattach himself to things solid and lasting. The clear sky, the strong mountains, and the cold wind all serve as a natural backdrop for the spiritual ritual of his pilgrimage. As he climbs toward the peak of a mountain, he recalls with pleasure an earlier climb with a dark girl "who knew all the flowers, and who, when I bet her she couldn't find more than thirty kinds, found more than fifty." On that day, as on this, the narrator felt a clear sense of the majesty of the mountains and the "big arch of the world we looked at," and he recalls spending two hours another time watching a hawk, "feeling myself lift magnificently when he swooped up toward me on the current up the col, and then balanced and turned above."

When he returns to his campsite by a shallow snow-water lake, he swims, naked, and as he floats in this cleansing ritual, looking up at the first stars showing above the ridge, he sings out "an operatic sounding something." At this point, just when his spiritual rejuvenation is nearly complete, the ritual is broken by the appearance of Tom Williams, one of the two men whom he had accompanied on this trip to the mountains. The plan had been for Williams and the other man, Chet McKenny, to spend a few days hunting, leaving the narrator alone. As he watches Williams approach, the narrator unhappily expects to see McKenny also, a man he dislikes not because of his stupidity, but because of something deeper than that. Williams, however, is alone.

After a while Williams tells the narrator of the experience he has just had with McKenny, whom he calls a "first-rate bastard." During their hunt McKenny had purposely shot a deer in the leg so that he could herd it back to their camp rather than carry it. When they arrived at the camp, he slit the deer's throat, saying, "I never take more than one shot." Sickened by this brutal act, Williams drove off in his car, leaving McKenny to get out of the mountains as best he could. After Williams' story, both men agree that McKenny deserves to be left behind for what he did. In another cleansing ritual, they both take a swim, becoming cheerful later as they sit by their fire drinking beer. The next morning, however, it is snowing, and as they silently head back down the mountain, the narrator feels that there is "something listening behind each tree and rock we passed, and something waiting among the taller trees down slope, blue through the falling snow. They wouldn't stop us, but they didn't like us either. The snow was their ally."

Thus there are two contrasting moods in "The Buck of the Hills": that of harmony and that of dissonance. At the beginning of the story, the narrator has succeeded after five years in reestablishing a right relationship with nature and thus with himself, but at the end, this relationship has been destroyed by the cruel actions of McKenny. The narrator's ritual of acceptance of the primordial in man has been overshadowed by McKenny's ritual of acceptance that man is somehow above nature. Ernest Hemingway's belief that morality is what one feels good after is in one sense reversed here to the idea that immorality is what one feels bad after; certainly the narrator and Williams, on their way down the mountain, feel bad. Man and nature in a right relationship is not a mere romantic notion to Clark. It is reality—indeed, perhaps man's only reality.

In "The Portable Phonograph" Clark ventures, if not into science fiction, at least into a kind of speculative fiction as he sets his story in a world of the future, one marked by the "toothed impress of great tanks" and the "scars of gigantic bombs." It seems a world devoid of human existence; the only visible life is a flock of wild geese flying south to escape the cold of winter. Above the frozen creek in a cave dug into the bank, however, there is human life: four men—survivors of some undescribed armageddon—huddle before a smoldering peat fire in an image of primitive existence. Clark provides little background of these four almost grotesque men. One, the reader learns, is a doctor, probably of philosophy rather than of medicine. One is a young musician, quite ill with a cough. The other two are middle-aged. All are obviously intelligent. The cave is the doctor's, whose name is Jenkins, and he has invited the others to hear him read from one of his four books—the Bible, *Moby Dick*, *The Divine Comedy*, and William Shakespeare. In selfish satisfaction he explains that when he saw what was happening to the world, "I told myself, 'It is the end. I cannot take much; I will take these.' " His justification is his love for the books and his belief that they represent the "soul of what was good in us here."

When Jenkins finishes his reading from *The Tempest*, the others wait expectantly; and the former finally says grudgingly, "You wish to hear the phonograph." This is obviously the moment that they have been waiting for. Jenkins tenderly and almost lovingly brings out his portable phonograph and places it on the dirt-packed floor where the firelight will fall on it. He comments that he has been using thorns as needles, but that in deference to the musician, he will use one of the three steel needles that he has left. Since Jenkins will play only one record a week, there is some discussion as to what they will hear. The musician selects a Debussy nocturne, and as Jenkins places the record on the phonograph, the others all rise to their knees "in an attitude of worship."

As the piercing and singularly sweet sounds of the nocturne flood the cave, the men are captivated. In all but the musician there occur "sequences of tragically heightened recollection"; the musician, clenching the fingers of one hand over his teeth, hears only the music. At the conclusion of the piece, the three guests leave—the musician by himself, the other two together. Jenkins peers anxiously after them, waiting. When he hears the cough of the musician some distance off, he drops his canvas door and hurries to hide his phonograph in a deep hole in the cave wall. Sealing up the hole, he prays and then gets under the covers of his grass bed, feeling with his hand the "comfortable piece of lead pipe."

Structurally a very simple story, "The Portable Phonograph" is rich in its implications. In a devastated world four men represent what Jenkins refers to as "the doddering remnant of a race of mechanical fools." The books that he has saved symbolize the beauty of man's artistic creativity as opposed to the destructiveness of his mechanical creativity. Again, Clark portrays two sides of man, that which aspires to the heights of human spiritual and moral vision and that which drives him on to his own destruction. The cruel and bitter irony is that essentially man's imagination is at once his glory and his undoing. As the men kneel in expectation before the mechanical wonder of the phonograph, they worship it as a symbol of human ingenuity. The music that comes from the record provides for at least three of the men a temporary escape from their grim reality. Thus, man's drive for mechanical accomplishment—the same drive that has destroyed a world—now has also preserved the beauty of his musical accomplishment. This may well be what the musician understands as he lets his head "fall back in agony" while listening to the music. Man is forever blessed to create and doomed to destroy. That is why the piece of lead pipe is such a protective comfort to Jenkins as he closes "his smoke-smarting eyes." In order to protect what is left of art, he must rely on the very methods that have brought about its demise.

In his excellent novel *The Track of the Cat*, Clark takes the reader into the realm of human unconscious as Curt Bridges, the protagonist, is driven to his own death while tracking both a real and an imagined cougar. In the short story "The Indian Well," set in the desert in 1940, Jim Suttler also seeks to kill a cougar, and although the mythological and psychological implications are not developed as fully as they are in the novel, the story is still powerful in its total effect. In what must be one of the best word pictures of the desert and the creatures that inhabit it, Clark devotes a half-dozen pages to the stark drama of life and death that takes place around a desert well; rattlesnakes, road runners, jack rabbits, hawks, lizards, coyotes, and a cow and her calf all play a part.

The story's only character is Jim Suttler, a grizzled old prospector who, with his mule Jenny, still seeks gold in abandoned and long-forgotten mines.

Suttler is a man well-atuned to life in the desert wilderness. Armed with a rifle, an old six-shooter, and primitive mining tools, he is not merely a stereotyped prospector; his red beard and shoulder-length red hair might lead some to see in him a resemblance to Christ, but Suttler is unlike Christ in several ways. Early in the story, Suttler and Jenny arrive at Indian Well. The history of Indian Well is recorded on the walls of the run-down cabin nearby; names and dates go back to the previous century. All had used the well, and all had given vent to some expression, ranging from "God guide us" to "Giv it back to the injuns" to a more familiar libel: "Fifty miles from water, a hundred miles from wood, a million miles from God, and three feet from hell." Before Suttler leaves, he too will leave a message.

Finding some traces of gold in an abandoned mine near the well, Suttler decides to stay for a while to see if he can make it pay off. It is a comfortable time, and both he and Jenny regain some of the weight lost during their recent travels. Two events, however, change the idyllic mood of their stay. The first occurs when Suttler kills a range calf that, along with its mother, has strayed close to the well. While he has some qualms about killing the calf, Suttler, enjoying the sensation of providence, soon puts them out of his mind. Next, a cougar kills Jenny. This event enflames Suttler with the desire for revenge— even if "it takes a year"—so throughout the winter he sits up nights waiting for the cat to return. When he eventually kills it, he skins it and, uncovering Jenny's grave, places the skin over her carcass. His revenge complete, he cleanses himself at the well and leaves as a "starved but revived and volatile spirit." Thus, one more passerby has contributed to the history of Indian Well, and the life around the well goes on.

The basic element in "The Indian Well" is the ironic contrast between the beginning and the ending of the story, just as it is in "The Buck in the Hills." When they come upon Indian Well, Suttler and Jenny enter into a natural world that has its own ordered life and death, and they blend easily into it. Suttler appears to be a man at one with nature, yet at the end of the story, the death that he has inflicted upon the cougar stands as something apart from the ordered world of the well. It is a death that was motivated by the desire for revenge, a very human emotion. The reader might be suspicious when Suttler kills the calf, but he justifies such a killing on the basis of the meat that the calf provides. Killing the cougar, on the other hand, cannot be justified in any external way. The deep satisfaction that it brings to Suttler stands in opposition to any right relationship between man and nature; it is solely a part of Suttler's inner self. When the deed is done, Suttler can blend back into the natural world around him. For that one winter, however, as he lies in wait for the cougar, he exhibits man's all-too-common flaw of putting himself above the natural world. Still, because he knows what he has done and, moreover, accepts it, he is able once more to establish his relationship with the cosmic forces.

In a very real sense, this establishing of a relationship with the cosmic forces is the goal of many of Clark's characters. Caught in the ambiguities of good and evil, of morality and immorality, they struggle to maintain a faith in humanity and to bring moral law into accordance with natural law; for only in that way can man be saved from his own destructive tendencies. Some critics, such as Chester Eisinger, see Clark as being rather pessimistic regarding the success of such a human attempt at unity and attribute to him a desire to retreat from man. If this view is correct, then perhaps the story "Hook" is the best expression of what Clark wants to say. The main character in this story is a hawk who fulfills himself in flight, in battle, and in sex, until he is killed by a dog. His is a life cycle of instinct, and, as he lives it, he can easily enough be seen as an antihuman symbol. If Eisinger's view is wrong, however, then it is possible to see Clark as a writer who seeks not a retreat from man, but an explanation of man. For, like the hawks that appear so often in Clark's stories, man is also a part of nature and because he is, it is possible to see his task as one of defining himself in the context of the natural order of things. Whatever the outcome, Clark's characters do make the attempt.

Major publications other than short fiction
NOVELS: *The Ox-Bow Incident*, 1940; *The City of Trembling Leaves*, 1945; *The Track of the Cat*, 1949.
POETRY: *Ten Women in Gale's House and Shorter Poems*, 1932.

Bibliography
Eisinger, Chester. *Fiction of the Forties*.
Westbrook, Max. *Walter Van Tilburg Clark*.

Wilton Eckley

ARTHUR C. CLARKE

Born: Minehead, Somerset, England; December 16, 1917

Principal short fiction

Expedition to Earth, 1953; *Reach for Tomorrow*, 1956; *Tales from the White Hart*, 1957; *The Other Side of the Sky*, 1958; *Tales of Ten Worlds*, 1962; *The Nine Billion Names of God: Best Short Stories of Arthur C. Clarke*, 1967; *The Wind from the Sun: Stories of the Space Age*, 1972.

Other literary forms

Arthur C. Clarke is best known for novels which chronicle near-future space and sea exploration or suggest transcendence of human form and limitations. He has published an autobiographical novel based on his experience with radar in World War II, and an adaptation of the work he did with director Stanley Kubrick on the motion picture *2001: A Space Odyssey*. A still wider audience knows Clarke as a lecturer and author of nonfiction speculation on space, the sea, and the future (with special attention to communications media). In addition to winning the Hugo Award for the short story "The Star" (1955) and the Nebula Award for the novella "A Meeting with Medusa" (1971), he has won the Hugo, Nebula, Jupiter, and John W. Campbell awards for *Rendezvous with Rama* (1973, novel); the International Fantasy Award for *The Exploration of Space* (1951, nonfiction); and UNESCO's Kalinga Prize for science writing (1961). As of press time, he has won at least the Nebula for *The Fountains of Paradise* (1979, novel).

Influence

Clarke's style and approach are highly idiosyncratic, his low-key, antimelodramatic treatment of events fairly common among British science-fiction writers. His extensive propaganda for space travel helped develop a down-to-earth, matter-of-fact handling of technical and political matters related to space exploration and exploitation. His poetic but low-key domestication of the "alien," with quasimystical overtones, was influential in altering science fiction's negative attitude toward extraterrestrial beings.

Story characteristics

A typical Clarke idea for a story is not fundamentally dramatic, but rather static and panoramic. To reach existing markets, he has adopted a number of strategies, not equally effective. Stories dominated by a "surprise ending" tend to be either jokes or "ghost stories," their buildup of suspense often leading to an anticlimactic conclusion. Elaborate narrative frames focus the reader's attention as much on the teller as on the tale, and sometimes on the audience as well, as in the White Hart series of "tall tales." Perhaps best suited to Clarke's material are the "snapshot" or vignette-style "slice of life"; the first-person retrospective narration, which emphasizes the mental consequences in the present of a series of past events, seen from a distance; and the fable.

Biography

Reared in the country, Arthur Charles Clarke worked as a government auditor (1936-1941) in London, where he became active in the British Interplanetary Society (eventually becoming Chairman, 1946-1947, 1950-1952). A Royal Air Force instructor in the infant technology of radar during World War II, he published the first speculations on "stationary" communications satellites in 1945. After earning his B. Sc. in physics and mathematics at King's College, London (1948), he became assistant editor of *Science Abstracts* (1949-1951) before turning to full-time writing. Introduced in 1953 to scuba diving, he moved to Ceylon (now Sri Lanka), where he has lived since 1956, connected to the West by airlines and electronic communications. Married once (1953-1964) to Marilyn Mayfield, he has no children but maintains a large household in Colombo.

Analysis

Exposed in his childhood to both the pulp magazines of Hugo Gernsback and the English literary tradition of fantasy and science fiction, Arthur C. Clarke has sometimes forged an uneasy alliance between the two in his own stories. The matter-of-fact description of the marvelous of H. G. Wells, the poetic evocation of unknown places of Lord Dunsany, and the immense vistas of space and time of the philosopher Olaf Stapledon lie cheek-by-jowl with artificial suspense devices, awkward sentimentality, schoolboy silliness, and melodramatic manipulation of such hoary motifs as the "stranded astronaut" or the "end of the world" in his less distinguished fiction. At its best, however, Clarke's work shows glimpses of man's rise to interplanetary civilization or evokes the wonder, in suitably subdued tones, of his confrontation with extraterrestrial intelligences.

His 1967 collection of his "favorites," one-fourth of his hundred-odd stories (excluding novels) to date, represents all facets of his career, from the raconteur of tall tales and ghost stories to the fantasist, the sentimentalist, the realist, and the poet of wonder. Most of his best and best-known stories are included, from the haunting rite of passage of a young lunar exile getting his first glimpse of the unapproachably radioactive world of his ancestors (" 'If I Forget Thee, Oh Earth . . . ,' " to such "alien fables" of technological complacency as "Superiority" and "Before Eden." Among them, "Rescue Party," his second professionally published story, looks forward to other tales of human progress and alien contact, but it is unusual in its strong story line and alien viewpoint. Although it makes one of his rare claims for human superiority, a fetish of *Astounding Science Fiction* editor John W. Campbell, Jr., the story's humor, style, and forecasts are vintage Clarke.

"Who was to blame?," it opens, setting the context of a paternalistic "Galactic Federation," sending a ship to rescue a few hundred survivors from Earth before its sun goes nova. With a million years between visits, they had been taken by surprise by man's rise to civilization in two-fifths of that time, signaled by radio waves detected two hundred light years away. With little more than four hours to go, the ship arrives at a deserted planet, sends out two search parties, and barely escapes the cataclysm, burning out its "main generators" in the effort. Directing its course to the receiving point of a communications array on Earth, the mile-long spaceship, now needing rescue itself, approaches rendezvous with an unexpected fleet of ships from the planet. Unprecedented in size, this fleet of "primitive" rockets demonstrates an acceleration of man's technological development so astonishing that the captain, the tentacled Alveron, whose ancient people are "Lords of the Universe," teasingly suggests the vast Federation beware of these upstarts. This "little joke" is followed by the narrator's quiet punch line: "Twenty years afterward, the remark didn't seem funny."

Humor of situation is evident throughout the story, from the concept of "administering" a galaxy to the discovery of the humans' "handicap" of bipedalism from an abandoned portrait of a City Alderman. The incongruity of the rescuers' need for rescue is mirrored by the precision which allows the aliens an unflappable split-second escape but brings them there in the first place too late and with too little to do anything useful, then finds them baffled by relatively primitive communications devices and an automatic subway. Although the story creaks in places—contemporary theory says our sun cannot nova, vacuum tubes are outmoded, helicopters never did become the wave of the future—those details can be sacrificed for the sake of the fable. The primary forecasts of space travel and posturban civilization should not be discounted, at the risk of being as naïve and complacent as the aliens, without even their limited security in their own superiority.

More commonly, Clarke sees alien technology as older and better than man's, as in two stories in which *2001: A Space Odyssey* (1968) is rooted. In "Encounter at Dawn," ancient astronauts "in the last days of the Empire" give tools to primitives a hundred thousand years before Babylon. Fooling the reader at first into thinking future rather than past, Clarke fails to be any more convincing than the later, specious "nonfiction" of Erich von Däniken.

Even more understated, "The Sentinel" is allegedly told by an eyewitness who begins by directing the reader to locate on the Moon the Mare Crisium (Sea of Crises), where the discovery took place. Part of a large 1996 expedition, he recalls fixing breakfast when a glint of light in the mountains caught his eye; staring through a telescope so fascinated him that he burned the sausages. From such homey touches, he led the climb to "Wilson's Folly," a plateau artificially leveled for a twelve-foot crystal pyramid "machine." Its force field gave way, after twenty years of frustrated investigation, to an atomic assault which reduced the mystery to fragments. The rest of the story is speculation, successive stages of Wilson's inferences.

Not a relic of lunar civilization, the artifact, half the age of Earth, was left by visitors: Wilson imagines it saying "I'm a stranger here myself." After its destruction, he "guesses" it must have been a beacon; interrupting its signal has triggered a "fire alarm." Lacking explicit alien intent, the pyramid emblemizes the unknown. Although such a potentially multivalent symbol invites other interpretations, Wilson's is supported by *2001*, in which a *rectangular slab under* the lunar surface signals *after* being exposed to sunlight. The final savage attack on the pyramid also seems significant to the narrator, although the pyramid might have been programmed to self-destruct.

The quasireligious awe, tinged with fear as well as positive expectation, with which Wilson awaits the aliens' return has echoes elsewhere in Clarke. This story, moreover, with its judgment of space travel as a first step toward an incalculable destiny, many readers see as an article of faith in a grand design of a creator god. Such a pattern may lie beneath some of his work, but Clarke has also taken pains to discourage conventional religious interpretations.

His work is dotted with attacks on religious or "mystical" belief and behavior, with one exception: the Scottish-born head of worldwide Buddhism in *The Deep Range* (1957), whose opposition to butchering whales is based partly on the conviction that aliens may judge man on his behavior toward his fellow creatures. Certainly the surprise ending of "The Nine Billion Names of God" is no proof of Clarke's sharing the faith of his Tibetan lamas. Although the story attacks the complacency of Western computer technicians whose efficiency speeds up the counting of all of God's names, the ending ("Overhead, without any fuss, the stars were going out") is that of a joke or a ghost story.

Rather than simply trivializing God, Clarke's award-winning short story "The Star" makes God destructive and merciless. A Jesuit astrophysicist, slightly defensive about his combined callings, the narrator is at the point of quiet desperation. Beginning "It is three thousand light-years to the Vatican," he finds no solace in the crucifix near his computer or the engraving of Loyola, whose order is not all that will end when the expedition makes public its findings.

In a retrospective narration which distances the action, the narrator recounts the ship's approach to the inappropriately named "Phoenix" Nebula, the debris of a supernova which destroyed an interplanetary civilization. Unlike the wandering planet in Wells's story of the same name, this cataclysm did not spare a people and let them find brotherhood. From their remains in a vault on the star's most distant planet, the crew finds evidence that this "disturbingly human" civilization was at its peak when it died. The narrator's colleagues see no room in nature for God's wrath or mercy, and the narrator denies his own right to judge God. He is troubled, however, by the date of the disruption; given its direction and distance, this must have been the "Star of Bethlehem," hanging low in the East before sunrise. Explicitly rejecting keeping the information secret or tampering with the data, he is troubled in his faith because he cannot refuse (or refute) the findings of science.

A masterpiece of compression, poetic in style, somber in tone, and totally devoid of action and dialogue (not even the two lines of "The Sentinel"), "The Star" does not even state its conclusion. The narrator either must conclude that his colleagues are right, or accept a God who would destroy this culture to impress a few humans.

Considerably at variance from these and most of Clarke's short fiction is "A Meeting with Medusa." Appearing four years after his retrospective collection, it is one of his longest stories not given book length, and a sharp improvement over most of his work in the 1960's. Allusive and subtly patterned, both a character study and a tale of adventure, it continues Clarke's interest in "first contact" and alien landscapes, but it also fictionalizes J. D. Bernal's suggestion in *The World, the Flesh, and the Devil* (1929) that space exploration is the proper province of a human mind in a posthuman body.

All but destroyed when a mismanaged robot camera platform sent his dirigible, the *Queen Elizabeth IV*, down in flames, Howard Falcon is restored to life as a cyborg, the physical form of which is not revealed until the last of eight chapters. Seven years later, stronger and more durable, he argues successfully to be sent on an expedition into the atmosphere of Jupiter. After another three years, the actual adventure takes place.

Almost a part of the "raft," *Kon-Tiki*, supported by a hot hydrogen balloon (with emergency ram-jet and rocket motors), the wingless Falcon is nevertheless at a disadvantage when it comes to making contact with native life forms. Expecting at most a kind of plankton, he comes upon creatures whose nearest Earth analogues, in miniature, are varieties of sea life. Manta rays a hundred yards across seem docile browsers of floating wax mountains until their natural enemies appear. Radio-sensitive jellyfish over a mile wide, they repel attacking mantas with electrical discharges that also function for communications. A dirigible pilot once again, Falcon has neither their maneuverability nor their familiarity with local conditions.

Wryly amused at his ambassadorial role, he is understandably reluctant to obey the "Prime Directive" requiring him to avoid attacking intelligent creatures, at the cost of his own life if need be. When tentacles descend around the *Kon-Tiki*, he descends still lower; when the "Medusa" begins to "pat" his craft tentatively with a single tentacle, he cuts loose with his auxiliary engines. The Great Red Spot, blizzards of wax, atmospheric maelstroms, and various other features of the "world of the gods" can wait until another time.

A hero who has reignited man's imagination, Falcon is slipping away from identity with the human race, we now discover, along with our first glimpse of his undercarriage, hydraulic lifts, balloon tires, and seven foot height, if not of his "leathery mask" (now seen in a different light). Like the panicky "superchimp" on the *Queen Elizabeth* whose face he used to see in dreams, he is "between two worlds," the biological and the mechanical. Immortal, it may be, he represents at its extreme the "cosmic loneliness" of Clarke's heroes.

Falcon is at the center of the story, although the predominant interest may be more in what he sees than in what he does. Jupiter is the "hero," at least of the middle sections of the story, in which Clarke combines his undersea experience and astrophysical theory to draw plausible inferences about an unlikely place for "life as we know it." Although he is not an adequate "ambassador" to the Jovians—who could be?—because he is not quite human, Falcon is the best possible explorer. A "new breed," he is for some purposes "more than human," although our bias toward the "handicap" of bipedalism may blind us to it. He is also one more piece of evidence that the "transcendence" of human limitations widespread in Clarke's fiction may be at best a mixed blessing.

Suspenseful yet satiric, adventuresome yet calmly paced, "A Meeting with Medusa" marked a new stage in Clarke's career, looking forward to the still more allusive and complex novels of the 1970's with which he announced the (temporary?) end of his career as a writer of fiction. Yet in its poetic evocation of first contact and its sophisticated variations on transcendence and the "stranded astronaut," it is also a culmination of the shorter fiction which went before.

As a prophet of the space age, Clarke has been largely superceded; his stories of near-future explorations are starting to seem "quaint," like Verne's and Wells's space stories. As a humorist, his popularity is mixed, some readers preferring whimsy, others satire. As a poet of the infinite, however, whose fables judge man from an "alien" point of view, Clarke stands alone.

Major publications other than short fiction

NOVELS: *Prelude to Space*, 1951; *The Sands of Mars*, 1951; *Against the Fall of Night*, 1953; *Childhood's End*, 1953; *Earthlight*, 1955; *The City and the Stars*, 1956; *The Deep Range*, 1957; *A Fall of Moondust*, 1961; *Glide Path*, 1963; *2001: A Space Odyssey*, 1968; *Rendezvous with Rama*, 1973; *Imperial Earth*, 1976; *The Fountains of Paradise*, 1979.

NONFICTION: *Interplanetary Flight*, 1950; *The Exploration of Space*, 1951; *Going into Space*, 1954; *The Exploration of the Moon*, 1954; *The Coast of Coral*, 1956; *The Making of a Moon*, 1957; *The Reefs of Taprobane*, 1957; *Voice Across the Sea*, 1958; *The Challenge of the Spaceship*, 1959; *The Chal-*

lenge of the Sea, 1960; *Profiles of the Future*, 1962; *The Treasure of the Great Reef*, 1964; *Voices from the Sky*, 1965; *The Promise of Space*, 1968; *Report on Planet Three*, 1972; *Beyond Jupiter*, 1972; *The Lost Worlds of 2001*, 1972 (including canceled alternative chapters); *The View from Serendip*, 1977.

Bibliography

Moskowitz, Sam. "Arthur C. Clarke, in *Seekers of Tomorrow: Masters of Modern Science Fiction*.
Olander, Joseph and Martin Harry Greenberg, eds. *Arthur C. Clarke*.
Rabkin, Eric S. *Arthur C. Clarke*.
Samuelson, David N. *Arthur C. Clarke: A Checklist*.
Slusser, George Edgar. *The Space Odysseys of Arthur C. Clarke*.

David N. Samuelson

COLETTE

Born: Saint-Sauveur-en-Puisaye, France; January 28, 1873
Died: Paris, France; August 3, 1954

Principal short fiction

Dialogues de bêtes, 1904 (*Creatures Great and Small*); *Les Vrilles de la vigne,* 1908 (*The Tender Shoot*); *La Paix chez les bêtes,* 1916; *La Femme cachée,* 1924; *Bella-Vista,* 1937; *Chambre d'hôtel,* 1940 (*Chance Acquaintances*); *Gigi,* 1942.

Other literary forms

Besides short stories, Colette wrote novels, plays, stage adaptations, librettos, articles, and what probably needs to be called fictionalized reminiscences. Her *œuvres complètes* (complete works) was published in fifteen volumes in Paris in 1950. As yet, only a small amount of her writings have been translated into English and published in the United States.

Influence

If it is true, as many people say, that Colette's best works, which are read and admired most in France, are her short fictionalized reminiscences, then she can be seen as a forerunner of many contemporary writers in whose work various fictional and nonfictional genres are merged. Lauded in France during her lifetime, she received praise from myriad famous contemporaries, such as Anatole France, Marcel Proust, André Gide, Paul Valéry, François Mauriac, and Jean Cocteau. Her direct and honest treatment of women and of the relationships between women and men opened up areas for discussion not previously given expression by women.

Story characteristics

Colette's short fiction ranges from sketches to parables, from loosely structured reminiscences to tightly developed and highly symbolic short stories. Accordingly, the forms that her stories take vary from the relatively plotless presentation of a single incident to fully developed linear plot lines to truncated plots moving to epiphany. Lengths vary also, from single paragraphs to stories long enough to be classified by some as novellas.

Biography

Written at the insistence of her husband, Sidonie-Gabrielle Claudine, Colette's first four novels were appropriated by him and signed with his pen name, Willy. Later, Colette signed the name Colette Willy to her writings, and still later she used the single name Colette, by which she came to be known and is known today. As soon as she was able to support herself by performing in dance halls, she left her husband, and although she had other liaisons and married again, she supported herself by means of her creative activities for the rest of her life. She became a living legend in France, both a popular author and a performer, praised by her peers. She wrote dozens of short stories and some fifty novels and became the first woman member of the prestigious Goncourt Academy and the second woman in history to be made an officer of the Legion of Honor. At her death in 1954, she was provided a state funeral in the Cour d'honneur of the Palais-Royal.

Analysis

To an American audience, *Gigi* is Colette's most popular work, probably because of an immensely popular musical film made in the 1950's featuring Maurice Chevalier, Louis Jourdan, and Leslie Caron. Although very well done, the movie, for understandable reasons, skims over the real circumstances of Gigi, a girl being groomed to be a high-class prostitute. Gigi lives with her grandmother and mother who, for reasons the grandmother cannot understand, has become a renegade from the grand profession and now makes her living as a music-hall performer. The grandmother's sister, Gigi's grandaunt, acts as a kind of finishing school teacher for Gigi, showing her how to walk, sit, eat, and so forth with social finesse. Fifteen-year-old Gigi surely understands that she is the lamb being groomed carefully for offering as the sacrifice at a price large enough to ensure the future well-being of the whole family. This subject, however, is never mentioned, and Gigi goes about in typically adolescent fashion being by turns innocently charming and recklessly naïve. "At times she looked like Robin Hood, at others like a carved angel, or again like a boy in skirts; but she seldom resembled a nearly grown-up girl."

Into this menage Colette introduces Gaston, a tall, young-looking, and immensely wealthy man. Gaston is comfortable with the family in his visits: "Under their gas-blackened ceiling, these three feminine creatures never asked him for pearls, chinchillas, or solitaire diamonds, and they knew how to converse with tact and due solemnity on scandalous topics traditional and recondite." Gaston, who has had a series of unfortunate relationships with various mistresses, is now attempting to recover from his last affair. "Grandmama" makes him camomile tea, and Gigi, by turns ingenue and tomboy, alternates flirting and arguing with him.

The inevitable happens; Gaston finds himself attracted to Gigi and at last makes an offer to the grandmother and through her to Gigi. Gigi, however, declines the offer; she has, it appears, learned considerably more than her grandmother and grandaunt thought possible. She rejects the notion that "her kind of people" do not marry; she understands that jewels are possible to possess even in a legal arrangement; and she understands that love is not something to be bought. Gigi's grandmother and grandaunt are scandalized by the girl's refusal, and Gaston is frustrated and angered. He leaves in a huff; but as one might expect in a story that is essentially romanticized, he comes back and offers marriage.

The story is a variant of a fairy tale, and a happy-ever-after ending is expected. To expect this, however, does not mean that credibility is not carefully established by characterization, events, and foreshadowing devices. Gigi is a variant of her elders, and she is never shown as the promising initiate for which her grandmother and grandaunt hope. Gigi's mother has already rejected the role, and, indeed, all men. Gaston, already sated, is clearly attracted by Gigi's virginity. In *Gigi*, Colette makes use of a traditional plot line that can be graphed through exposition, complication, climax, and resolution. Pacing is excellent, the omniscient narrator point of view is perfectly appropriate, and alternations between scene and summary are accomplished with great skill. Thus, it is clear that when she desires, Colette can write a short story in the traditional mode.

Colette, however, uses a variety of short fiction forms—from stories written in the modern mode with little or no plot, to stories that are mainly sketches describing a character or situation, to personal reminiscences. "The Patriarch" is relatively plotless, but it is carefully designed, and meaning emerges from the juxtaposition of two parts of the story which at first glance may seem to have no connection with each other. The story is told in the first person by an adult looking back to a time when she was fifteen and a half and half in love with her half-brother Achille, who is some ten years older than she. Achille is extremely handsome, tenderly considerate, a country doctor who works hard, and a kind of surrogate father to the narrator, teaching her how to help him as he treats his patients and makes his rounds.

Achille is also attractive to the village girls who openly try to seduce him. One girl in particular comes to his examining room and, declaring she is pregnant, throws off her clothes and demands that he examine her. The girl is a virgin who has come to Achille to make love, and she leaves "victorious." From this liaison a beautiful child is born. The girl has a baby that she loves, Achille's life is not at all affected, and the whole situation is pictured as a "warm," idyllic episode, as natural as the land.

Seemingly contrasted with this incident is another, telling of Achille's visit to a villager's house to deliver a "very fine child" of his fifteen-year-old daughter. The daughter is described as an antelope, and her somewhat older sisters are also antelopes. One of the sisters is mother to another child who sleeps calmly through the labor. Soon, however, Achille realizes that the father of the daughter is also father to the beautiful grandchildren, and that no one in the house seems disturbed by the situation. The narrator's mother, Sido, is the one who is most disturbed, but she, too, has conflicting feelings. On the one hand, she calls the situation abominable, and on the other, she recalls "ancient patriarchs." The epiphany of the story occurs in the last sentence. The narrator comments: "But she [Sido] suddenly became aware that I was only fifteen and a half and she went no further."

In "The Patriarch," Colette explores human interrelationships on both symbolic and actual levels and accepts vagaries against the social order as having a place, perhaps, in a more natural order. The fifteen-year-old narrator stands in the same symbolic relationship with her older brother as the fifteen-year-old mother with her father.

Although intriguing in its conception and design, "The Sick Child" is more a sketch than a fully developed short story. The narrative concerns a little boy who is near death, and the story takes him through the crisis of his illness and on the way to recovery. What is interesting about the story, however, is the kind of dream projection in which the boy is involved. The hallucinatory visions are more real to the child than his actual existence, and there are times when he prefers his fantasy travels to interaction with his beloved Madam Mamma. As the boy recovers, however, his fantasies diminish until finally he must give them up altogether:

> A time comes when one is forced to concentrate on living. A time comes when one has to renounce dying in full flight. With a wave of his hand, Jean said farewell to his angel-haired reflection. The other returned his greeting from the depths of an earthly night shorn of all marvels, the only night allowed to children whom death lets go and who fall asleep, assenting, cured and disappointed.

As fine as these stories are, however, the kind for which Colette is most praised is typified in "The Rainy Moon," ostensibly little more than an account by Colette of an incident in her past. The story, however, is more than simple incident; it is rather a fully developed and complex short story. The narrator, who seems at the beginning to be merely an observer of the action, is later revealed to be the protagonist of the story whose conflict is mirrored in its action.

Identification between the narrator and the two sisters, Rosita and Delia, is accomplished deftly so that various symbolic doublings take place. In pursuing her relationship with the two sisters, the narrator is seeking to discover insight into her own past and, perhaps, knowledge of her future. The two sisters live in an apartment once occupied by the narrator at a particularly painful period of her life when there had been a break-up of an intense love affair. Rosita, the frustrated typist, is a pallid reflection of the narrator, who is a professional writer. Delia, who likes to work and play with sharp objects, is an alter ego, a projection of all the angry, hostile, and painful feelings of the narrator directed towards men. The two sisters represent extremes; the narrator attempts to find balance, but her search is not successful. Finally, she must withdraw from the situation because she recognizes that it represents the destruction of self.

The basic theme that Colette explores in this story is one to which she returns over and over again. A product of her society, Colette appeared to accept that society's concepts of masculine and feminine roles. Thus, being a sexually active woman meant submission to a master; for a woman to enjoy sexual pleasures, she must subjugate herself, an action which is painful. This condition naturally resulted in hostile relationships between the sexes. The periods between love affairs are "merciful blanks," times that introduce space and order, as between the chapters of a book, "those days in which work and sauntering and friendship played the major part, to the detriment of love. Blessed days, sensitive to the light of the external world."

The title of the story "The Rainy Moon" refers to a particular reflection of the sun, prismlike in its mirrorings, which becomes the major metaphor of the story, tying together the myriad doubling patterns and pointing to the female role in a basically destructive relationship. By the end of the story, the narrator has had enough of her painful probing, but her dreams show the effects of it. She says:

> I realized I was not yet rid of the two enemy sisters nor of another memory. I kept relapsing into a nightmare in which I was now my real self, now identified with Delia. Half-reclining like her on *our* divan-bed, in the dark part of our room, I 'convoked' with a powerful summons, with a thousand repetitions of his name, a man who was not called Eugene. . . .

By means of this nightmare, the narrator realizes that she, like Delia, desires to murder her own sex partners, and she realizes further that she must abandon the sisters "to their stifled, audacious, incantation-ridden lives," and pursue as far as she is able the "merciful blanks."

Major publications other than short fiction

NOVELS: *Claudine à l'école*, 1900 (*Claudine at School*); *Claudine à Paris*, 1901 (*Claudine in Paris*); *La Vagabonde*, 1910 (*The Vagabond*); *Mitsou*, 1919; *Chéri*, 1920; *La Chatte*, 1933; *Julie de Carneilhan*, 1941.

Bibliography
Cottrell, Robert D. *Colette.*
Crosland, Margaret. *Colette: The Difficulty of Loving.*
Davies, Margaret. *Colette.*
Marks, Elaine. *Colette.*

Mary Rohrberger

JOHN COLLIER

Born: London, England; May 3, 1901
Died: Pacific Palisades, California; April 6, 1980

Principal short fiction

Epistle to a Friend, 1931; *No Traveller Returns*, 1931; *Green Thoughts*, 1932; *The Devil and All*, 1934; Variations on a Theme, 1935; *Presenting Moonshine*, 1941; *A Touch of Nutmeg and More Unlikely Stories*, 1943; *Fancies and Good-nights*, 1951; *Pictures in the Fire*, 1958.

Other literary forms

John Collier's novel *His Monkey Wife* (1930) was made into a musical by Collier and Sandy Wilson (author of *The Boy Friend*, 1953), and his dramatic work ranges from *Wet Saturday* (a one-act play) to a "screenplay for the cinema of the mind" of John Milton's *Paradise Lost*. In *Just the Other Day* (1932) he and Ian Lang wrote an informal history of Britain in the 1920's. He also wrote poetry, winning a prize for poetry in 1922.

Influence

Twilight Zone and such television series—more recently the tales of Roald Dahl have been featured—and magazines such as *Fantasy and Science Fiction* have provided ready markets for the sort of thing Collier does superbly, but it cannot be said that he has had many imitators. His light satirical touch is hard to come by; it is refreshing in the world of television and entertainment magazines, but it is also rare. Certainly Edgar Allan Poe (and O. Henry, Saki, and others) have had their effect upon Collier's stories and, to the extent that more recent writers have been able to derive sensational and surrealistic effects from everyday props and situations, they may be said to be writing in the Collier tradition. Collier's stories have instantly recognizable lineaments which were established almost fifty years ago by his first tightly written, evocative, craftsmanlike, and haunting tales. Collier's ABC Stage 67 "Evening Primrose" (music by Stephen Sondheim) made him better known to the public than his movie scripts for such performers as Bette Davis, Katharine Hepburn, and Charlton Heston. He moved right into the new replacements for the novel, films, and television.

Story characteristics

Collier deals in the extraordinary results of asking for trouble and the unpredictable outcome of deliberate or even chance encounters between the diurnal and the diabolical. His subject is often the line between the ordinary and the supernatural or the logical and the psychological. Too often his characters have their dreams fulfilled only to discover that they have been dreaming the wrong things. As in the best of Saki, there is a certain *rightness* about the fate of Collier characters who get into dire straits; also like Saki, Collier knows that the effective story of this kind must be deft and swift. He may not approach Saki's memorable lines, but with a Collier story one never forgets a detail of the plot.

Biography

John Collier, born in London and educated privately, was poetry editor of *Time and Tide* in the 1920's and 1930's, then came to the United States to write screenplays. He then lived in France, London, and California. In the 1950's he published some of his best stories, a novel, and the screen version of *I Am a Camera* (1955). In the 1960's two stories appeared in *The Best from "Fantasy and Science Fiction"*—"Meeting of Relations" in the 1960 volume, "Man Overboard" in the 1961 volume—and he wrote the screenplay for *The War Lord* (1965). Working for the screen he usually had collaborators, but in the demanding art of the short story he needed no assistance. Collier describes his *Fancies and Goodnights* as "a continuing blunder toward an arbitrary, surrealist way of expressing things," but the man who decided early that he wanted to "be a poet" and stuck to the job on an allowance of two pounds a week, supplemented with money earned churning out book reviews and acting as the man in London for a Japanese newspaper, has always been far too determined to be described as blundering.

Analysis

Typical of John Collier's work is the concise and classic story "The Chaser." Like "De Mortuis," another favorite, it has an ending which manages to be that of a horror story as well as a love story. To say that one should not reveal the endings of these stories is to confess that, in the O. Henry style, they have a sting in the tail, but they are more than mere surprise endings. Rather, they are "take-away endings": the reader is asked to finish the story for himself, and is given all the clues he needs to do so.

Characters in Collier short stories who run into the most incredible bad luck (Franklin Fletcher, who encounters a jinn in "Bottle Party," Dr. Carpenter, who makes a "big mistake" in "Back for Christmas," and the stupid man who tries to "refute" a demon) have gone out of their way to get into trouble and deserve what happens. The terrible aunt in Saki's "Shredni Vashtar" is one example of a character similar to Collier's, as is Saki's professor who is killed trying to teach German irregular verbs to an elephant in the Berlin zoo in "Tobermory." Collier's characters never know when a plant will turn on them ("Green Thoughts") or a diabolic messenger will appear ("Halfway to Hell"). One also encounters horribly heartless, practical people in Collier's stories, such as the man who knows exactly what to do in "Sleeping

Beauty" when the maiden wakes up and he realizes that she is not what he wanted.

In every Collier story there are surprises, in details, in symbols, in felicitous descriptions, in deft dialogue, in sinuosities and subtleties of plot, and in the outcome. Most of all, however, there is irony, "an irony so perfectly balanced," says Basil Davenport, "that his horror is hardly ever free of humor, nor his humor of horror." Such stories as "Thus I Refute Beelzy" and "De Mortuis" involve humor, irony, and a trick ending. "De Mortuis" has been described as "a kind of extended joke." The joke, however, is not just on the wife Irene; it is on everybody in the story.

Major publications other than short fiction

NOVELS: *His Monkey Wife: Or, Married to a Chimp*, 1930; *Full Circle: A Tale*, 1933; *Defy the Foul Fiend: Or, The Misadventures of a Heart*, 1934.

PLAY: *Milton's Paradise Lost: Screenplay for Cinema of the Mind*, 1973.

NONFICTION: *Just the Other Day: An Informal History of Britain Since the War*, 1932 (with Ian Lang).

Bibliography

Gawsworth, John. *Ten Contemporaries.*

Leonard R. N. Ashley

WILLIAM CONGREVE

Born: Bardsey Grange, Yorkshire, England; February, 1670
Died: London, England; January 19, 1729

Principal short fiction
Incognita, 1692.

Other literary forms
William Congreve wrote four comedies and one quite financially successful tragedy (*The Mourning Bride*, 1697). He is best known for his last play, *The Way of the World* (1700), although *The Old Bachelor* (1693) was more popular during his lifetime. *The Double-Dealer* (1693) is his darkest comedy, and *Love for Love* (1695) is currently favored by anthologists, who see it as both readable and playable. Congreve also wrote poetry, lyrics which were set by such famous musicians as Henry Purcell and John Eccles, and an opera, *Semele* (1707). He translated works of Ovid, Homer, Juvenal, and Persius and collaborated with William Walsh and Sir John Vanbrugh on a translation of Jean-Baptiste Poquelin Molière's *Monsieur de Pourceaugnac* (1669), known as *Squire Trelooby* (1704).

Influence
The leading literary critic of the seventeenth century, John Dryden, considered Congreve his literary successor, pronouncing him "more capable than any other man" at translating Homer and wittier than Ben Jonson or John Fletcher. Since Dryden, also the period's major dramatist, revised and edited *The Old Bachelor* and offered advice and encouragement to the younger writer until his own death, he is likely the greatest influence on Congreve. A source for *Incognita* was "An Itinerary Contayning a Voyage Made Throughout Italy," by John Raymond. The names of some of the characters and the fairy tale ambience of *Incognita* are similar to those in a comedy by Dryden, *The Assignation: Or, Love in a Nunnery* (1673), but the plot is different. French influences on Congreve include Molière and the novelist Paul Scarron. Among Congreve's strengths are his wit and his love of the sounds of words; as a practioner of these, he was highly admired during the Restoration, and he is still considered one of the most skillful of seventeenth century writers.

Story characteristics
His single piece of short fiction Congreve describes as a "novel," a term then used to describe a short work of the kind ladies liked to read. In its modern reprint version the work itself is only fifty-one pages long. In his Preface, Congreve distinguishes between a romance and a novel in an ex-

tended definition that resembles that of Nathaniel Hawthorne and precedes it by one hundred and sixty years. Having declared his work to be representative of the novel, Congreve then offers his story, which is, however, romantic in every way by virtue of the rank of the principals, the lofty language, and the improbable action.

Biography

Because William Congreve's father was in the army, the family moved several times, one of their longest tours being in Ireland. Congreve attended Kilkenny College (where he met Jonathan Swift), Trinity College in Dublin, and finally the Middle Temple in London. After he wrote *Incognita* and his five plays, Congreve at the age of thirty went into semiretirement as a writer. This action was partially a result of an accusation by the clergyman Jeremy Collier that his work was immoral and profane, and also because he was disappointed in public reaction toward his personal attempts to move toward a more aesthetic art form. Although Congreve never married, he was devoted to at least two women: the actress Anne Bracegirdle, for whom he devised most of his charming, independent, female roles; and Henrietta, the second Duchess of Marlborough, by whom he had a daughter Mary. Congreve was in poor health during his later years, suffering from cataracts and poor eyesight, gout and recurring lameness, and overweight. He died in London in 1729 and was buried in Westminster Abbey.

Analysis

In the Preface to *Incognita*, Congreve tells us that the tale was written "in imitation of dramatic writing, and he boasts that he observes in it the three classic unities of time, place, and action (which he renames contrivance). The story resembles nothing so much as William Shakespeare's *Romeo and Juliet* (c. 1595) without a tragic ending. The two major male characters, Aurelian and his look-alike Hippolito, who have been schoolmates in Siena, arrive in Florence just in time to enter the festivities centering around the upcoming wedding of Donna Catharina, a kinswoman to the great Duke. The young men decide to participate in disguise, lest Aurelian's father restrain their merriment. At the masquerade ball that evening, both young men fall in love, Aurelian with a beautiful young lady who wishes to be known as Incognita, and Hippolito with Leonora, who mistakes him for her cousin Don Lorenzo, whose costume he has bought. On the next day the two young students perform so admirably in the lists that they are granted the honor of the field. Recognizing his son, Don Fabio announces that the wedding of Aurelian and Juliana, which had been previously arranged by the parents, would take place the next day. As Aurelian and Hippolito had exchanged names upon entering Florence, Leonora thinks she is defying custom when she marries Aurelian (who is actually Hippolito). Incognita, who is really Juliana, swoons, runs away in male disguise, and suffers greatly because she feels that because of her love she must disobey her father and marry Hippolito (who proves to be Aurelian, after all). Two family feuds are settled by the marriage, which is approved by both generations after the mistaken identities are revealed.

Walter Allen in *The English Novel* says that "before 'Incognita' prose fiction had been artless in form; indeed, form can hardly be said to have existed at all." He adds that *Incognita* represents in miniature "the formal aspects" of the fiction later associated with Jane Austen, Henry James, and Ivy Compton-Burnett. The civilized, polished, skeptical, and humorous voice of the author gives *Incognita* its unity, but because fiction writing was as yet not a socially acceptable occupation for a gentleman, Congreve abandoned that art form to write drama.

The importance of *Incognita* lies not only in the fact that it is such an early example of short fiction, but also in that its form is so unusual, yet perceptible. It is so dramatic that readers can almost visualize the puckish stage-manager-author standing just offstage and commenting wittily to the audience. The young author indeed intrudes upon this narrative frequently, utilizing the same sophisticated, elegant humor that he is later to allow the protagonists in *The Way of the World*. Congreve includes directions for lighting, sound, and costume, employs theatrical imagery, and permits the tale to fall into an almost visible five-act comedy division. Antecedent action is revealed early, and, at what would surely be the end of Act I, the audience learns that the purchase of Lorenzo's costume for Hippolito is going to cause the visitors some problems.

Just as Congreve the dramatist was later to withhold the introduction of his ladies until Act II, he acquaints us with Leonora and Incognita at the ball only after we have become well acquainted with their two young men. The ball and the tilting (which occur in what would be Acts II and V of a drama) contribute to the symmetry of structure, as both are gatherings of society to which Aurelian and Hippolito are admitted in disguise. The beginning of the tale involves preparations for disguise and offers a balance to the conclusion, when all disguises are removed. Scenes complicated by mistaken identity abound, and after disclosures, discoveries, and recognition, the story ends in a comic celebration with the entire company awaiting the wedding of Aurelian and Juliana. Since *Incognita* begins with the wedding of Catharine and Ferdinand, the symmetry is complete. All "knots" are easily untied, but the spectator-reader will see that the action has not been as probable as Congreve has promised in his Preface. The four major characters remain disguised, literally or figuratively, for most of the narrative's unfolding, affirming its artificiality and emphasizing the difference between appearance and reality, and illusion and life.

Major publications other than short fiction
PLAYS: *The Old Bachelor*, 1693; *The Double-Dealer*, 1693; *Love for Love*, 1695; *The Mourning Bride*, 1697; *The Way of the World*, 1700.

Bibliography

Drougge, Helga. *The Significance of Congreve's Incognita.*
Hodges, John C. *William Congreve, the Man: A Biography from New Sources.*
Novak, Maximillian E. *William Congreve.*
Taylor, Daniel Crane. *William Congreve.*

Sue L. Kimball

EVAN S. CONNELL, JR.

Born: Kansas City, Missouri; August 17, 1924

Principal short fiction
The Anatomy Lesson and Other Stories, 1957; *At the Crossroads*, 1965.

Other literary forms
Evan S. Connell, Jr., has distinguished himself both as a prose writer and as a poet. His best-known works are probably the "Bridge" books, but all of his six novels to date have received critical appreciation. He is also the author of two book-length poems, a feat almost unique in our time. In addition, he has written criticism, edited *Contact*, a prominent literary magazine, and recently completed *A Long Desire* (1979), a nonfiction study of great explorers.

Influence
Connell has long been regarded as among the most important of the "West Coast" writers. His Mr. and Mrs. Bridge short stories and novels have been "cult classics" for years because of their biting, perceptive, satirical dissection of middle-class America, although his other novels and poems have, perhaps, had as great an impact on the writing and intellectual community.

Story characteristics
The economical, Chekhovian short stories of Evan S. Connell, Jr., with their emphasis on character and acute observation of detail and setting, are characteristic of the best realistic short fiction being written today. Typically an "ordinary life" is upset by the introduction of some kind of intrusive element—an odd character, a personal crisis—which forces a reevaluation by the main characters of their lives and situations, all presented in an oblique, understated, impressionistic fashion.

Biography
Evan Shelby Connell, Jr., grew up in the Midwest and began his higher education at Dartmouth until it was interrupted by two years of service as a Naval flight instructor (1943-1945). He completed his education at the University of Kansas, Stanford, Columbia, and San Francisco State, before turning to writing full time. He was a Eugene Saxton Fellow (1953), a Guggenheim Fellow (1963), and he received a Rockefeller Foundation Grant in 1967. From 1959 to 1965, he served as the editor of *Contact*, a "little" magazine published at Sauselito, California. A long-time California resident, he is unmarried and,

when not writing, occupies much of his time with drawing and painting, his "second avocation."

Analysis

Although it is, perhaps, not even a "story" as such, "The Anatomy Lesson," the title piece in his first collection, is probably the best introduction to the techniques and attitudes of the fiction of Evan S. Connell, Jr. This narrative is what its title says it is: an "anatomy lesson" delivered by an artist, Andrew Andraukov, to his beginning drawing class. The students enter, listen to the lecture, then leave; nothing seems to happen in terms of action or plot. Yet in the interplay between the artist and his students, in the clash of attitudes, life styles, and values stated and implied, lies the method and meaning of these early stories.

Before introducing any of the characters in the tales, the author devotes several pages to scene descriptions, a very old-fashioned way to begin a contemporary short story—but few moderns can say so much with setting as Connell. Every detail cited reinforces the shape and themes of the narrative; indeed, the basic conflict is set up before the reader meets any of the characters. The shabby, isolated status of the art building itself designates the "place" of "art" in this modern academic community. The first office described belongs to the department head, Professor A. B. Gidney, whom the reader never meets, and never has to—his office says it all. It is comfortable, complete with teacups, cookies, and a phonograph that plays "operettas and waltzes," and it is always open to students. Art for Gidney, who teaches ceramics, bookbinding, and lettering, is fun and useful, an attitude clearly characteristic of the department and its students. Andraukov's office, on the other hand, is always locked and his studio-classroom is cold, dark, damp, and "shaped like an up-ended coffin." Half-finished creations and artistic debris glut the room. The only music ever heard coming from it are plainsongs or Gregorian chants heard very late at night with the artist singing along "in perfect harmony."

The conflict, of course, is between the idealistic, dedicated, free-spirited, totally honest view of the artist and the shallow, casual, inhibited, artificial complacency of the students. The basic idea in "The Anatomy Lesson" is obvious, perhaps even shopworn and trite, but the directness in presentation, precision in detail, and authenticity in characterization give the story freshness, immediacy, and impact. Andraukov is a vivid, moving character. The pathos of his situation—his commitment to the purity of his art and his teaching coupled with his bitterly ironic awareness of how wasted it all is on the students he faces—is rendered with economy and fidelity. The reader feels for and sympathizes with his need to redeem his time and effort by finding "one student, born with the instinct of compassion, who could learn, who would renounce temporal life for the sake of billions yet unborn, just one who cared less for himself than for others," but, with Andraukov, such a being is more than unlikely in the small, provincial campus that serves as Andraukov's place of exile.

Connell only sketches the students, but the sketches are marvelously deft and accurate. With only a few words he is able to delineate the boorish and arrogant, the sensitive but limited, and the well-meaning but inhibited. The reader also notices that Andraukov's attitudes toward art and life are identical. Both demand total honesty, acceptance, and commitment; the rewards of success in art are a product that realizes one's personal vision; in life, they are a fulfillment of one's potential for experience. While Andraukov knows that few will be able to produce any art of significance, he has hopes that his lessons in living can at least be heeded. With the possible exception of one out-of-place, overaged, bearded man, his students fail at both. Andraukov (and Connell), however, is not unsympathetic even toward the shallow and narrow. He dismisses the sniggering wrestler with contempt, but shows real compassion for the young lady who felt compelled to draw a bathing suit on the nude model. A sympathetic understanding of even the most foolish of his characters is typical of Connell's works.

Thus "The Anatomy Lesson" draws the battle lines that apply in most of Connell's fiction: the mundane, circumscribed, artificial, life-denying world of middle-class routines, values, and experiences are pitted against another more real and free existence suggested in some stories by the artist, in others by a traveler, a mysterious foreigner, a nonconformist, a rebel, or even an exotic animal or bird. Typically in these early stories such a being enters the mundane world of "ordinary" people provoking a crisis that may be of an immediate or visceral kind, but is more likely to be an internal, emotional, and/or spiritual one. In the simpler stories, the intrusive catalyst illuminates and intensifies the shallowness and mediocrity of the ordinary people by comparison; in the better ones, it forces a self-realization, or at least a deep discontent, in the main characters. Thus, in "The Condor and the Guests" the freedom, energy, and beauty of the huge captive bird is juxtaposed against the pettiness and crassness of a small suburbanite clique. In "The Fisherman from Chihuahua" the appearance of a strange, sad, silent Mexican fisherman upsets the cozy world of a Santa Cruz pub owner. When a world traveler named J. D., in "The Walls of Avila," returns to his small Midwestern home-town and attempts to explain his life and experiences to his old school chums, he is frustrated and baffled; they are only disinterested and annoyed.

For all the sympathy and understanding Connell lavishes on his free-spir-ited, creative people, however, his finest short fictions focus on the other side of the coin, on the ordinary people trapped in ordinary lives. The most pathetic and interesting figures are those who lack the drive, imagination, and creativity to be exceptional or unorthodox, but who have just enough insight and sensitivity to realize the limits of their existence and the impossibility of altering it.

"The Beau Monde of Mrs. Bridge" was the first set of sketches of what were later to become Connell's best-known works, the "novels" *Mrs. Bridge* (1959) and, later, its companion piece, *Mr. Bridge* (1969); each work consists of a long series of self-contained, labeled fragments from the lives of the Bridges. The incidents move in a chronological direction, but the narratives lack the sharp crises or climaxes one expects in stories and novels. What appears in both the early short-story version and later in the novels is a meticulously detailed picture of every trivial, pathetic event in the lives of these two people which finally coalesces into a vision of modern middle-class life as a materially comfortable, unremittingly dull, hopelessly trivial existence. Yet one does not simply laugh at Walter and India Bridge. The anxiety, frustration, and even despair beneath the surface of their lives continually threaten to break through. Although the characters are not fully aware of their pain, the reader is, and the dominant feeling stimulated by the Bridge stories is one of modified compassion—"compassion" because of the plight of the pair, "modified" because of the characters' own lack of insight and because of Connell's narrative method which keeps the reader at an objective distance.

No such distance exists in Connell's best short stories, however, because they focus on a character who shares the Bridges' trap, but whose insights and feelings command a sympathetic identification—Karl Muhlbach. Connell introduces Muhlbach in "Arcturus," the best story in *The Anatomy Lesson and Other Stories* volume, fleshes him out in three stories from *At the Cross-roads*—"St. Augustine's Pigeon," "The Mountains of Guatemala," and "Otto and the Magi"—and then makes him the protagonist of two novels (to date), *The Connoisseur* (1974) and *Double Honeymoon* (1976).

"Arcturus" bears the same relationship to the Muhlbach narratives as "A Perfect Day for the Bananafish" does to J. D. Salinger's Glass family saga: it not only introduces the main characters, but it also chronicles the relationships and incidents that underlie all subsequent events. To be sure, the other Muhlbach stories and novels are self-contained, but without the information provided by "Arcturus" the full meanings and implications of Muhlbach's words and actions cannot be appreciated. In its own right "Arcturus" is a masterful story, probably the best of his short fictions and one of the finest examples of the form written in America since World War II.

As usual, Connell offers the "intrusion" into "ordinary" lives that disturbs the complacency and forces new self-examinations and self-realizations. In this story, however, the intruder is death and the realizations to be faced— or avoided—are far deeper and more wrenching than those in any of his other stories. Connell characteristically moves his story with an apparently casual indirection that is, in fact, very tightly structured and precisely developed. In less than fifty pages the author powerfully delineates the critical moments in the lives of four fascinating, complicated individuals, and also sharply sketches in a half-dozen others. "Arcturus" is Connell's most emotionally powerful story, despite the apparently calm surface of the narrative. Indeed, it is the profound tension between the "uneventful" incidents of the story and the intensity of the psychological and emotional conditions of the characters in conflict with one another and, more importantly, with themselves, that gives the narrative its impact.

The Muhlbachs have invited Sandy Kirk, Joyce Muhlbach's old boyfriend whom she has not seen in years, over for dinner. Although it is cold and snowy outside, it is warm and serene indoors. The Muhlbachs mix cocktails while waiting for their late guest; the cook has prepared dinner. The Muhlbach children, Otto and Donna, wait sleepily but expectantly to meet the stranger before going off to bed. In short, the opening scene presents an idyllic picture of domestic felicity, serenity, and safety. Discordant elements creep in, however: the nurse that hovers in the background, the comment that Joyce "begged" Kirk to visit, and the fact that she always has "an odor of medicine" about her. Gradually the reader realizes that Mrs. Muhlbach is dying and that this visit is an attempt to answer some questions while time remains.

The opening of the story is so effective because things are initially being seen through the eyes of the children, or, more precisely, of Otto, whose sleepy confusion and naïveté diverts the reader from the seriousness of the occasion. Once the reader realizes what is going on, the focus shifts to Muhlbach. This careful control and manipulation of viewpoint is one of the primary ingredients that give the story its potency. The narrative seems to move along aimlessly, but each incident fits carefully into an emerging pattern, extending and reinforcing the meanings of the story.

Connell also moves adroitly between carefully presented dramatic scenes and precisely modulated inner reveries. All of the principal male characters—Muhlbach, his son Otto, and Sandy Kirk—have extended musings which crystallize their insights—or lack of them—as the story progresses. Joyce, on the other hand, the focal character in the story, is treated almost entirely from the outside. The story is really about the attempt of these three male characters to come to terms with her pending death, but this is never stated explicitly. As with most good contemporary short stories, it is left to the reader to make the final synthesis and articulate the themes.

Sandy Kirk is a world-traveled man-about-town. In an ironical yet profound deviation from his usual approach, Connell reverses the pattern of his earlier story, "The Walls of Avila"; unlike J. D. in that story, it is the world traveler and *bon vivant*, Sandy Kirk, who is narrow, rigid, and shallow, and Karl Muhlbach, the domesticated, middle-class insurance executive, who exhibits the sensitivity, insight, and capacity for experience. The running contrast between these two men provides the major focus for the story's examination of values and attitudes in the face of mortality.

When Kirk finally has his confrontation with Joyce, his inability to deal with her gives the final shape to the reader's view of him. As the two talk on the couch, "words pour from her nerveless mouth without meaning and Kirk is obviously terrified." Connell wisely refrains from actually dramatizing the conversation; instead, he concentrates on Kirk's reactions, all of which are determined by his selfish, narcissistic ego. Joyce has clearly begged his presence because she needs some kind of emotional response from him—which he fails to provide, a reaction clearly explained by the brief recapitulation of their abortive romance. Kirk resents Joyce's re-intrusion into his life and the unpleasant reality she is forcing upon him; at the same time he resents the fact that she chose Muhlbach and seems happy with the choice. It is as though he felt her to be a piece of property that had been stolen from him and was now being loaned back, in severely damaged condition. Sandy Kirk is a man caught up in a world of his own design, who uses all of the paraphernalia of the "civilized man" to isolate himself from the difficult realities of existence and to feed his own sense of importance. Unprotected by his armor, however, he is helpless; he cannot even drive his car out of the driveway without a push from Muhlbach.

It is Muhlbach, however, who is the most impressive character in the story, although on the surface he appears ordinary and unimpressive. As he demonstrates to Kirk, he is full of surprises. He speaks German, has parents who were born in Zurich, and is even an indirect descendant of Goethe. His jokes may be bad, but his stories are perceptive. His reactions are sensitive and, to Kirk's discomfort, he is solid and in control both of himself and of his environment. Even more disconcerting, he is clearly capable of both giving and receiving love and has an intimacy with Joyce and his children that is evident, but baffling, to Kirk. Muhlbach's character is perhaps best revealed in his complex, poignant relation to his son, Otto. Still a child, Otto is peering over the edge at adulthood and is very apprehensive about it. His need to "grow up" has been accelerated by his mother's condition. Muhlbach realizes all this and tries to ease the transition with a combination of love, advice, and careful guidance. At times he despairs ("surely no one more obstinate and militantly ignorant can lay claim to being human"), while at others he beams with pride, as the time Otto soothed his dying grandfather with a maturity beyond his years.

The title of the story comes from conversations Muhlbach has had with Otto about the stars. Muhlbach has tried to convey some sense of the universe's immensity to his son by describing the constellations, and especially the activity of the star Arcturus, but all he has succeeded in doing is giving his son a sense of the precariousness of the universe. "Are the stars falling down?" has become Otto's standard euphemism for all unexpected, unavoidable catastrophies, both personal and cosmic. His father's reassuring "no" is the only thing that keeps Otto secure; that this answer can so calm the deceptively delicate and vulnerable boy is the final measure of how well Muhlbach has succeeded as a father and a human being.

In the other Muhlbach stories and novels the reader gets to know Muhlbach better, and perhaps affection for him grows, but he never again attains the stature demonstrated in "Arcturus"; in a sense, all the remaining Muhlbach narratives are footnotes to "Arcturus," each describing an attempt by Muhlbach to come to terms with the loss of Joyce. In "St. Augustine's Pigeon" he is at his most self-consciously foolish as he tries to assume the roles of "hip" young man and/or sophisticated roué. In "Otto and the Magi" his attempt to deal with his own isolation and need for solitude by shutting himself up in his recently built "fall-out shelter" provokes a potentially tragic, but ultimately comic reaction, from Otto. In *The Connoisseur*, a very fine novel, Muhlbach tries to fill the void with an obsession for pre-Columbian art. In "The Mountains of Guatemala" Muhlbach is again juxtaposed against supposedly more sophisticated, worldly individuals, only to find that they, too, have their obsessions and oddly childish needs. This brilliant short story, in a slightly altered form, later became the first thirty pages of his most recent novel, *Double Honeymoon*; unfortunately, the power of the story is not maintained through the entire novel. A last view of Muhlbach shows him at his most foolish and, surprisingly, his least perceptive. Yet he is still too alive and interesting to be left alone and one can only hope that his story has not yet run its course.

Major publications other than short fiction

NOVELS: *Mrs. Bridge*, 1958; *The Patriot*, 1960; *The Diary of a Rapist*, 1966; *Mr. Bridge*, 1969; *The Connoisseur*, 1974; *Double Honeymoon*, 1976.

POETRY: *Notes from a Bottle Found on the Beach at Carmel*, 1963; *Points for a Compass Rose*, 1973.

NONFICTION: *A Long Desire*, 1979.

Bibliography

Bensky, L. M. "Meet Evan Connell, Friend of Mr. and Mrs. Bridge," in *The New York Times Book Review*. (April 20, 1969), p. 2.

Blaisdell, Gus. "After Ground Zero: The Writings of Evan S. Connell, Jr.," in *New Mexico Quarterly*. XXXVI (Summer, 1966), pp. 181-207.

Nichols, L. "Mr. Connell," in *The New York Times Book Review*. (April 17, 1966), p. 8.

Keith Neilson

JOSEPH CONRAD
Józef Teodor Konrad Korzeniowski

Born: Berdyczew, Poland; December 3, 1857
Died: Bishopsbourne, England; August 3, 1924

Principal short fiction

Tales of Unrest, 1898; *Heart of Darkness*, 1902; *Youth: A Narrative, and Two Other Stories*, 1902; *Typhoon and Other Stories*, 1903; *A Set of Six*, 1908; *'Twixt Land and Sea*, 1912; *Within the Tides*, 1915; *Tales of Hearsay*, 1925.

Other literary forms

Joseph Conrad is one of the major novelists of the twentieth century. His most important novels include: *The Nigger of the "Narcissus"* (1897), *Lord Jim* (1900), *Nostromo* (1904), *The Secret Agent* (1907), *Under Western Eyes* (1911), *Victory* (1915), and *The Shadow-Line* (1917). Other novels include *Almayer's Folly* (1895), *An Outcast of the Islands* (1896), *Chance* (1914), *The Arrow of Gold* (1919), *The Rescue* (1920), and *The Rover* (1923). He also wrote two volumes of autobiographical prose, *The Mirror of the Sea* (1906) and *A Personal Record* (1912), and two collections of essays, *Notes on Life and Letters* (1921) and the posthumous *Last Essays* (1926).

Influence

Conrad's use of Marlow influenced subsequent writers, including F. Scott Fitzgerald and William Faulkner, to focus on the teller as much as the tale. By showing future writers that reality is in the mind of the beholder, Conrad and Henry James set an example for imperceptive and unreliable narration, and Conrad's emphasis on obsessions, fixations, and dimly acknowledged psychic needs was an important aspect of the development of the modern psychological novel. While he was not the first to abandon traditional chronological order, his juxtaposition of morally relevant incidents in place of chronologically consecutive ones influenced the next generation of modernists.

Story characteristics

The characteristic Conrad tale—"Youth," *Heart of Darkness*, "Falk: A Reminiscence," "The Secret Sharer"—dramatizes a meditative teller coming to terms with his past experience and seeking the values and language with which to understand that experience. In these tales, except for "The Secret Sharer," Conrad is more interested in the retrospective telling as a present tense action than in the past events. In other tales, however—particularly maritime tales such as "Typhoon" and "The End of the Tether"—an omniscient narrator measures a character's conduct under stress, using as a standard

Conrad's conservative maritime values. In the political stories of *A Set of Six*, such as "Il Conde" and "An Informer," Conrad shows an unreliable narrator indicting himself as insensitive and myopic even while believing he is sane and perceptive. Finally, his romances emphasize a melodramatic plot, often with allegorical implications, at the expense of complex characterization. This group includes all the stories in *Within the Tides*, the last volume published in his lifetime, and "Freya of the Seven Isles."

Biography

Joseph Conrad was born in Poland on December 3, 1857, as Józef Teodor Konrad Korzeniowski. His parents were exiled because his father was a political activist; orphaned before he was twelve, Conrad was reared by an uncle. He went to Marseilles in 1874 and began a career as a seaman; he started sailing British ships in 1878 and earned his Master's certificate in 1886. He sailed on his last ship in 1894 and turned to a full-time writing career. After marrying Jessie George in 1896, he had two sons. Although he lived and wrote in England until his death in 1924, his Polish and maritime backgrounds remained important influences.

Analysis

In 1896, after completing *Almayer's Folly* and *An Outcast of the Islands*, Joseph Conrad was plagued by anxiety and self-doubt. He shared with many artists and intellectuals of the 1890's a belief that each man is enclosed in his private world, limited to his own perceptions, and separate and isolated from other men. Conrad believed that man lives in a morally neutral universe where each individual must discover his values. As he writes in a crucial 1895 letter, "No man's light is good to any of his fellows. . . . Another man's truth is only a dismal lie to me." For Conrad, man is cursed not only because he lives within a purposeless cosmos, but also because he is conscious of that position and of his inability to change it.

Conrad's interest in the technical problem of perspective is related to his belief that, because each man perceives and experiences a different reality in an amoral cosmos, he must create his own order from within. Wishing to dramatize how each man must find his own values, Conrad began to shift his focus from the tale to the teller. In a number of early tales, Conrad created one or even two dramatized voices who have a distinct personality and a characteristic speech pattern. "The Lagoon" and "Karain: A Memory" represent two important experiments with an introspective and meditative voice. Each tale presents the perspectives of both a white man and a native to show the similarities that bind their cultures.

In the 1896-1899 period when he not only was confused about his values but also had a serious writing block, Conrad used his fiction to help him define his identity as an author and as a man; he created Marlow to explore himself and to order his world. Marlow is both a fictional character and a surrogate coping with versions of his own psychic turmoil and moral confusion. When Marlow explores his past and tries to define the importance of his past to his present, he is enacting Conrad's quest for values. Indeed, Marlow's words often echo Conrad's letters in the late 1890's, the time when the three major Marlow tales—"Youth," *Heart of Darkness*, and *Lord Jim*—were written. That Marlow does communicate with his audience finally qualifies his despairing view expressed in *Heart of Darkness* that "We live, as we dream—alone."

Marlow's secular meditation in "Youth" represents one method of dealing with the ennui and despair that result from the knowledge that we live in a world which, as he put it in a letter of 1897, is a "remorseless process." By intensely contemplating a significant event in his youth, the older Marlow forgets the passage of time that is taking him toward death. As he recalls his first journey to the East on the *Judea*, he discovers that, despite the voyage's failure, it not only contains great significance for him, but also enables him to recapture the feelings of youthful energy. He begins his narrative with the intention of taking a good-natured, ironical view of a meaningful experience, but gradually his ironic distance dissolves, and he reveals himself as a romantic sentimentalist. As mature Marlow enters enthusiastically into his recollection of youthful adventure, his rhetoric tends to become increasingly hyperbolic and oversimplified, and the distance between older and younger Marlow breaks down.

Underlining the essential irony of Marlow's effort to forestall time, death, and mutability are insistent presences within his narration. The *Judea*'s captain and first mate are unusually old and seem worn out at the voyage's end, while the *Judea* itself is an ancient ship that has to be abandoned because its cargo catches fire. Thus youth is depicted as an inevitable voyage to age, disillusionment, and experience. As in William Shakespeare's Sonnet 73, youth consumes man's vitality and strength and leaves the remnants for old age. Yet the tale shows that man can find temporary solace in his memory of romance and innocence, even though he is inevitably moving toward death. The past feeling of physical and moral strength certainly contributes to Marlow's present emotional life and is part of *his* reality. Here and elsewhere Conrad shows that our subjective life is as real as so-called objective facts.

In *Heart of Darkness*, Conrad used his 1890 Congo journey as his factual source. By reminding his listeners at the outset that the Thames was once also one of the earth's dark places, Marlow anticipates the tale's basic theme, the common humanity of all men. That theme is only affirmed, however, after the tale systematically strips away illusions about civilization's higher morality, illusions that Conrad knew were central to the justification for the colonial presence of European countries in Africa and Asia. The tale dramatizes not only Marlow's efforts to understand Kurtz, but also Marlow's struggle to understand what he regards as the culminating point of his experience—the journey backward in time to the atavistic origins of the human psyche. Kurtz, who as universal genius, potential political leader, poet, and painter seemed to summarize the best of civilization, gradually succumbed to megalomania and savagery. Marlow discovers that the heart of darkness, the potential for evil and barbarism, is within all of us, including himself. His narration emphasizes what Marlow gradually learns about himself and how he becomes sympathetic to a man who not only has participated in barbaric practices and loved a native woman, but also has become a savage chieftain.

Like Kurtz, Marlow had gone to the Congo armed with the belief that European civilization represented progress in the moral evolution of mankind and that the European countries were emissaries of light to the African colonies. As he journeys from Europe to the Congo and then up the Congo to the center of the continent, he becomes disillusioned with the cynicism and exploitation of the European imperialists, whose perspective he originally shared, and begins to sympathize with the victimized natives. Originally, like Kurtz, he believes in conventional Victorian conceptions of integrity, discipline, and the intrinsic value of hard work, but as he sees the mindless shelling of native territory by European gunboats, the neglected machinery lying unused, the objectless blasting of the earth, the natives reduced to slavery, and the cynical materialism of the Trading Company, he begins to abandon these values. The more he becomes disillusioned, the more his journey up the Congo becomes a quest for Kurtz, because the as-yet unseen Kurtz seems an alternative to the malign and hypocritical Europeans he has met. Yet even before he meets Kurtz he realizes that the man who had seemed to epitomize European civilization has lost his moral bearings.

Marlow is tempted by the same forces that destroyed Kurtz. As Marlow follows Kurtz into the jungle, he feels himself responding to the appeal of the jungle, to the appeal of an earlier time and a simpler world. He stalks his prey like a hunter and finds his heart beating in rhythm to the native's drums. He feels the potential for mindless violence within himself. When he confronts Kurtz, however, he overcomes that temptation; the confrontation represents coming to terms with the dark potential within himself. He has, unlike Kurtz, internalized the restraints of civilization. Conrad believed that work itself—whether it is the work at sea that once occupied him or the writing that later occupied him— is central to ordering life in an amoral cosmos. Following Kurtz into the jungle and bringing him back to the ship are necessary tasks not only because, like piloting the steamer, they give purpose to Marlow's action, but also because they represent for Marlow a personal victory over the moral darkness that is epitomized by Kurtz's response to both the Congo and the Europeans.

Marlow needs to believe that Kurtz, the man with whom he has come to identify, has achieved a moral victory. Thus he interprets Kurtz's dying cry

"The horror! The horror!" as a moral affirmation, although these words are at best ambiguous when the rest of his conduct is considered; for example, Marlow has told us that despite Kurtz's eloquence, "there was something wanting in him." Kurtz remains a grotesque symbol of how the human ego can expand infinitely to the point where it tries to will its apotheosis.

When Marlow returns to Europe, he is at first, like Gulliver after returning to the land of the Houyhnhnms, a misanthropic figure. When he visits Kurtz's fiancée, he commits himself to humanistic values by telling her in response to her query that Kurtz's last words were her name; he knows that his lie will sustain her illusion that Kurtz loved her. By doing this, Marlow acknowledges the necessity in a civilized community for both relative morality and compassion.

Conrad wrote a number of important stories in which he examined behavior aboard ship. In such tales as "Typhoon" and "The End of the Tether," he does not dramatize a first-person narrator in the process of discovering the meaning of experience. Rather, an omniscient narrator judges a character's actions by the standards of the British merchant marine—courage, fidelity, integrity, selfless performance of duty; these were standards that Conrad had lived by during his seaman's career and in which he still believed. These stories, as well as "Youth," are characteristic of Conrad's use of a small community onboard ship to examine the dynamics of a group under stress as it makes its way toward its destination. In "Typhoon," Conrad shows the superiority in crisis of MacWhirr, the stolid, dependable, and responsible captain, to Jukes, the imaginative and articulate first mate. Clearly it is Jukes, not MacWhirr, who most resembles Conrad, but Conrad stresses that in times of severe stress, simple courage and diligent performance of duty count for everything and that, in such situations, the more intelligent and imaginative man may be found wanting. (*Lord Jim* and *Under Western Eyes* also explore this perception.) The omniscient voice at first seems to patronize MacWhirr and to sympathize with the ironic and witty Jukes; but when the typhoon strikes, it reveals the inadequacy of Jukes, who becomes virtually paralyzed by fear. It is the quiet leadership, sense of purpose, and integrity of MacWhirr which enable the ship to survive.

In "The End of the Tether," Conrad explores what he believed was the illusion of religious faith. The narrator shows how an aging but formerly heroic figure, Captain Whalley, sacrifices a lifetime of integrity in order to provide for his daughter. By taking command of a steamer even though he is going blind, he risks the safety of the ship and its crew. While Whalley believes his every act is part of God's plan, Conrad shows that he is an all-too-human figure who is guilty of self-deception. Whalley's conception of Divine Justice is a subtle function of his need to feel he deserves his daughter's love and to preserve his self-esteem.

"The Secret Sharer" is one of the great short stories in English; the tale has universal significance because the captain must come to terms with the anxiety and self-doubt that confront all men in the face of major challenges. As the captain reminisces about his first command, the past events take on the immediacy of the present. When the captain assumes command, he feels untested and doubts whether he will be able to fulfill his responsibilities. While the captain is on watch because he is unable to give an order to anyone else, Leggatt mysteriously appears at the ship's ladder. The captain feels an immediate identification with Leggatt on the grounds that they are both young and Conway boys, although he quickly learns in this first meeting that Leggatt, while serving as first mate, has killed an insubordinate crewman, for which he has been put in the brig. The captain's lack of confidence and need for someone who will empathize with his plight create in his mind the illusion that Leggatt is a secret sharer of his life. Almost immediately, the captain affirms complete faith in Leggatt's self-control, sanity, and judgment because he needs to believe that Leggatt is an ideal version of himself. Although he acknowledges that Leggatt was "not a bit like me, really," he adopts Leggatt's perspective to the extent that he actually confuses Leggatt's identity with his own. He accepts Leggatt's insistence that killing the seaman was an act of duty, while the reader understands that Leggatt has not only violated his responsibility by killing the man under him, but also undermined the social fabric of the merchant marine by refusing to stand trial for his action. Nor do we believe that the fastidious captain could ever kill a man in a "fit of temper." Indeed, the two men are, in important ways, opposites. While Leggatt has an unrestrained instinctive self, the captain has the opposite problem: he is like T. S. Eliot's Prufrock and James Joyce's Gabriel Conray, an example of overly self-conscious modern man who is unable to act instinctively because he is paralyzed by self-doubt. Leggatt feels no guilt for his action and, wishing to escape the sanctions of civilized society, he associates himself with Cain, the man cast out by God for killing his brother.

Ironically, to hide Leggatt, the captain is forced by circumstances to act spontaneously and impulsively. The presence of Leggatt forces him to assume command of the ship and eventually to believe in himself. After Archbold, the captain of Leggatt's ship, visits and searches suspiciously for his first mate, the captain accepts Leggatt's insistence that he must depart. They both realize that the captain's career is in jeopardy because he is harboring a criminal. Leggatt's generosity shows that he too has been changed by his experience. We realize that while the captain has been his secret sharer, he has been the captain's. Each uses the other as a buffer to protect himself against loneliness; both desperately seek and find understanding from an empathetic other.

When he abandons Leggatt, the captain takes the ship much closer to land than necessary in order to prove to himself and the crew that he can command the ship. He also wishes to assuage his conscience for casting off his secret sharer to wander among primitive fishing villages. As Leggatt leaves, the captain describes him as "a free man, a proud swimmer striking out for a new destiny"; but for the reader Leggatt is a tragic, lonesome figure, branded not only by the standards of civilization, but also by himself as someone whose behavior has placed himself outside the boundaries of civilization. By contrast, the captain-narrator has lived up to an ideal conception of himself by proving his ability to command.

While recent critics have stressed Conrad's skepticism and even nihilism, a strong humanistic strand runs through Conrad's shorter fiction and his novels. As readers, we feel Conrad's presence within his tales, expressing his sympathy for suffering humanity and struggling to discover the appropriate words and form to render his concerns and values. Ultimately, his dramatization of diverse perspectives derives from his understanding of and sympathy with the pathos and nobility of human life.

Major publications other than short fiction

NOVELS: *The Nigger of the "Narcissus"*, 1897, *Lord Jim*, 1900; *Nostromo*, 1904; *The Secret Agent*, 1907; *Under Western Eyes*, 1911; *Victory*, 1915; *The Shadow-Line*, 1917.

NONFICTION: *The Mirror of the Sea*, 1906; *A Personal Record*, 1912.

Bibliography

Baines, Jocelyn. *Joseph Conrad: A Critical Biography*.
Graver, Lawrence. *Conrad's Short Fiction*.
Guerard, Albert J. *Conrad the Novelist*.
Karl, Frederick R. *Joseph Conrad: The Three Lives*.
Moser, Thomas. *Joseph Conrad: Achievement and Decline*.
Schwarz, Daniel R. *Conrad: "Almayer's Folly" to "Under Western Eyes"*.

Daniel R. Schwarz

ROBERT COOVER

Born: Charles City, Iowa; February 4, 1932

Principal short fiction
Pricksongs & Descants, 1969.

Other literary forms
Robert Coover, primarily a novelist, won the Faulkner Award for his first novel, *The Origin of the Brunists* (1966). His oeuvre includes two other novels and a collection of short plays.

Influence
Except for his most recent novel, *The Public Burning* (1977), which has received some popular acclaim, Coover's work remains largely unknown to the general public; in this sense, he can be considered a "writer's writer." Academic critics place Coover at the forefront of the recent postmodern movement in fiction, metafiction, and antifiction, and his short fictions have enormously influenced the work of young writers now publishing in small literary magazines throughout the country.

Story characteristics
Coover's fictions are postmodern in their self-conscious exploration of the entire range of man's need for fiction-making. A recurrent theme, the clash between rigid, inflexible systems (or fictions) and an openness to revelation, poetic truth, and transformation, emerges as Coover creates contemporary versions of old myths, fairy tales, and folktales. The resultant fictions are dense, complex, and profoundly philosophical. Stylistically, Coover experiments with montage effects, shifts in points of view, allegory, symbols, structural inversions, and spatiotemporal incongruities. None of Coover's fictions belong to the traditional, mimetic mode, which achieves its effects primarily through conventional narrative development.

Biography
Robert Coover attended Southern Illinois University for two years, after which he transferred to Indiana University, where he received his B. A. in 1953. In that same year he joined the Navy and spent three years in Europe, where he would meet his future wife. In 1957, he returned to the United States to enroll at the University of Chicago. Since that time, he has lived approximately half his life in Europe and half in this country. Coover's writing career began in 1961, when he published his first short story. In 1966, he accepted a teaching position at Bard College. He has subsequently, but ir-

regularly, taught writing courses at Wisconsin State, Washington University, the University of Iowa, Princeton, and Columbia. His first novel, *The Origin of the Brunists*, won the Faulkner Award for fiction in 1966. In 1969 Coover received a Rockefeller Foundation Grant; Guggenheim Fellowships followed in 1971 and 1974.

Analysis

Robert Coover's *Pricksongs & Descants* contains twenty short prose pieces the author calls "fictions" rather than "stories." The choice of terms seems appropriate for a number of reasons. First, these fictions deal thematically with the process of fiction-making as an epistemological process and human need. Second, Coover departs radically from the conventional prose stylistics and structural integrities of mainstream American fiction; that is, his fictions do not at all resemble what we have come to regard as a short story. (Coover has little interest in traditional narrative concerns such as plot exigencies, character development, suspense, and chronological necessities.) Third, a growing number of writers since the 1960's—among them Coover, John Barth, Donald Barthelme, Ronald Sukenick, and even Thomas Pynchon—have been experimenting with new, highly self-conscious, open-ended techniques that ignore established aesthetic restrictions and limitations placed upon authors working in the so-called mimetic mode. Robert Scholes has called such works "metafictions"; others have called them, variously, "sur-fiction," "anti-stories," and "disruptive" fiction.

Obviously, one does not read an author like Coover for light entertainment; because his work resists easy accessibility, a Coover text requires numerous readings before it begins to yield to interpretation. It could be argued that Coover's best fictions, among them the extraordinary "prologue" to the volume ("The Door"), require an infinite number of readings. On the other hand, obscurity and novelty do not necessarily assure success. Some of Coover's work, notably his short dramas and a few of the fictions, reflect a period when the theater of the absurd proved immensely, if sometimes harmfully, influential. At its worst, such work now seems pointless, dull, and narcissistic, as though it were frozen in some static, neo-Dadaistic time-warp. It is also evident that literary critics have not yet established a niche for *Pricksongs & Descants* in American letters. While some of the fictions have acquired a limited anthological fame—"A Pedestrian Accident," "The Elevator," and "The Babysitter"—other, better Coover fictions remain virtually unknown.

Reading Coover amounts to an exercise in hermeneutics. Every word, every pause, image, allusion, and symbol, has its significance. As reading becomes interpretation, then, unwittingly or not, the reader-interpreter must perforce enter the text in the role of participatory observer. Coover's textual strategy, therefore, recapitulates Heisenberg's discovery than an observer alters what he observes in the very act of observing; for this reason, his fictions transcend normal narrative and expository engagement. They invite, instead, the neutrally detached reader to take part in perpetual revelatory happenings that challenge his habitual modes of cognition, modes Coover dismisses as defunct and paralyzing—but convenient.

In a fiction such as "The Babysitter," for example, Coover presents the reader with that expository information necessary to establish his (our) text; but he proceeds to destroy this information as the text progresses. By the end, which we can call an "end" only out of deference to conventional typesetting, all that remains is the structure of a banal, contemporary experience— babysitting. What actually happens to this particular babysitter and the other characters associated with her no one can ever finally determine. The "plot" develops ultimately only to annihilate the possibility of "plot" development.

Coover grants a probable matrix of circumstances. One evening a young schoolgirl comes to babysit for a middle-class couple, the Tuckers, who want to go to a party in the neighborhood. The Tuckers have three children, one of whom is still an infant. The babysitter has a boyfriend named Jack, who, in turn, has a friend named Mark. We know the girl arrives at the Tucker house; we know Mr. Tucker and his wife leave for the party; we know Jack and Mark entertain themselves by playing pinball machines at a local drugstore. The rest amounts to either nothing or an indefinite number of simultaneous permutations of these basic "givens." Coover insists that we can never know what really happens on this night because the greater part of what happens does not transpire as plot—that is, on the surface. Much of it takes place in the minds, feelings, and imaginations of the various characters; much of it occurs on the screen of the television in the Tucker living room, a temptation the babysitter cannot resist; much of it occurs as noise and redundancies in numerous telephone conversations that may or may not take place; much of it occurs on the surface of the pinball machine.

If the fiction were analyzed as a traditional story, nothing further needs to happen. A typically commonplace evening begins and ends, and the substance of the evening would belong to what has been called stream-of-consciousness. This is not exactly a new development in fiction, but what distinguishes Coover's metafiction from apparently similar stories in the modernist tradition is the reader's understanding that no one will ever grasp the totality of this situation (or structure). It cannot, after all, contain the responses, or perspectives, of every potential reader in the world—now or in the future. Each individual reader's response fills in textual lacunae, for each reader comes to respond personally to this babysitter, who represents the locus of all sexual activity. In other words, each reader completes the fiction a bit further. Reader participation, therefore, determines narrative development.

"The Babysitter" makes it clear that we cannot contain truth and reality in simulacra of truth and reality (such as fiction); reality, whatever that term

means now, lies elsewhere. Mr. Tucker's possible lust for the babysitter unfolds another narrative universe entirely; the boys' possible rape of the babysitter unfolds another; the babysitter's possible murder of the infant, still
another; and so on. Each new universe unfolds as one in a series of overlapping
contexts, each referring to others before it, each leading to new unfoldings
beyond it. Just as in Kurt Gödel's theory of sets, semiclosed systems always
open up into still more inclusive systems, *ad infinitum*, so Coover's texts
always spill over into still greater texts, texts that do not necessarily exist on
the page or between the lines—but, more likely, in the reader's imagination.

"The Door" illustrates this process quite effectively. Because Coover sub-
titles this fiction "A Prologue of Sorts," its themes and strategies will serve
as keys to Coover's fiction in general. On the surface, "The Door" seems
merely a conjoined retelling of Jack and the Beanstalk, Beauty and the Beast,
and Goldilocks. Four points of view emerge: the narrator's, Jack's, Granny's,
and that of Jack's daughter. Both Jack and Granny live now in a modern,
secular world devoid of mythic truth and beauty, and both remember the
intensity of life in the good old days. Jack recalls his beanstalk climbing as
an experience that made him feel *alive*. Similarly, Granny cannot forget her
terrible mating with The Beast. Jack's present obsession is to spare his only
daughter the mythic terrors, while, at the same time, to teach her their joys;
but he realizes one necessitates the other. He keeps the door to their cottage
tightly closed so that his young daughter may not venture out into the hostile
world on her own. "He'd pretended to her that there were no monsters, no
wolves or witches, but yes, goddam it, there were, there were." Granny,
meanwhile, has prepared to educate the girl: "I'll give her a mystery today,"
she says, "I will if I'm not too late already."

What Granny means is that she, too, senses what the girl senses—that
something momentous is about to happen. The girl feels terror about to
"devour her childhood" and an air "somehow full of spiders." Then, incred-
ibly, she sees the open door. The decision, finally, is her own—not Jack's,
not Granny's. Obviously, the girl has experienced the archetypal transformation from sheltered childhood innocence to hazardous adult experience;
but the narrator adds this: "She realized that though this were a comedy from
which, once entered, you never returned, it nevertheless possessed its own
enticements and conjuring . . . *and more doors*." Suddenly, an amazing series
of identity merges occur. The girl becomes both Jack's mother and lover at
once. Passage through the door alone precipitates such transformations, such
changes. Thus, the door becomes an intensely charged spatiotemporal nexus
between two or more universes (or contexts). Beyond it, on either side, lie
perfect, static, timeless structural constants—the stuff of myth and archetypes.

Coover implies that what happens to the girl about to walk through a door
will happen to the reader who opens "the door" into his book. If they succeed,
the fictions will serve as spatiotemporal nexuses for the reader who would

explore other universes. The psychological equivalent to this exploring is revelation; hence, the fiction itself can be viewed as extended revelations that encompass all of time and space. Only through such revelation can we catch a glimpse of the whole.

Admittedly, these brief commentaries fail to get across the complexity, richness, and density of Coover's finest fictions; the lesser achievements in *Pricksongs & Descants* seem tame in comparison. Consider, for example, a piece called "A Pedestrian Accident." A young man, Paul, has been hit by a truck, and, throughout most of the story, lies smashed under its weight. Various characters—the truck driver, one Mrs. Grundy, a policeman, a doctor—react characteristically to Paul's accident, although none can really help him. In Coover's allegorical world, the fiction implies that people like Paul, who insist upon trying to *understand* reality, suffer the oppression of their own inquisitiveness, while those who merely exist and do not question the *status quo* move about freely. On the other hand—and herein lies the beautiful ambiguity of Coover's work—Paul could just as easily represent those sympathetic souls who attempt to break free of old, stale fictions and lies, only to be crushed finally by the weight of convention itself.

Finally, a very ancient notion appears to inform Coover's fiction at every level. It emerges most definitively in a fiction entitled "Morris in Chains." When Morris, an "insane" old satyr, shepherd, flautist, and poet, confronts Dr. Doris Peloris (M. D., Ph. D., U. D.), who "assumes command," sterile methodology usurps poetic vision once and for all—at least, to the extent that the technicians of mental health literally imprison Morris. Morris, however, singing in his chains, rejoices: "it's the motherin [sic] insane are free!" The insane are those whom no ossified fiction can possibly enslave; and they alone, Coover suggests, are free to imagine new worlds, and, if the occasion or desire arises, to open closed doors.

Major publications other than short fiction

NOVELS: *The Origin of the Brunists*, 1966; *The Universal Baseball Association, Inc. J. Henry Waugh, Prop.*, 1968; *The Water-Pourer*, 1972; *The Public Burning*, 1977.

PLAY: *A Theological Position*, 1972.

Bibliography

Gado, Frank, ed. *First Person: Conversations on Writing and Writing.*
Gass, William. *Fiction and the Figures of Life.*
Harris, Charles. *Contemporary American Novelists of the Absurd.*
Klinkowitz, Jerome. *Literary Disruptions.*
Scholes, Robert. *Fabulation & Metafiction.*
Schulz, Max. *Black Humor Fiction of the Sixties.*

Louis Gallo

A. E. COPPARD

Born: Folkestone, Kent, England; January 4, 1878
Died: Dunmow, England; January 18, 1957

Principal short fiction

Adam and Eve and Pinch Me, 1921; *Clorinda Walks in Heaven*, 1922; *The Black Dog*, 1923; *Fishmonger's Fiddle*, 1925; *The Field of Mustard*, 1926; *Silver Circus*, 1928; *Nixey's Harlequin*, 1931; *Dunky Fitlow*, 1933; *Polly Oliver*, 1935; *Ninepenny Flute*, 1937; *You Never Know, Do You?*, 1939; *Ugly Anna and Other Tales*, 1944; *Fearful Pleasures*, 1946; *Selected Tales from His Twelve Volumes Published Between the Wars*, 1946; *The Dark-Eyed Lady: Fourteen Tales*, 1947; *The Collected Tales of A. E. Coppard*, 1948; *Lucy in Her Pink Jacket*, 1954.

Other literary forms

A. E. Coppard published three slender volumes of poetry, *Hips and Haws* (1922), *Pelagea and Other Poems* (1926), and *Cherry Ripe* (1935), and two collections, *Yokohama Garland* (1926) and *Collected Poems* (1928). In 1957 he published his autobiography, *It's Me, O Lord!*

Influence

In his autobiography Coppard wrote that reading Thomas Hardy's *Life's Little Ironies* (1894) marked "a great day" in his life, and he specified two other books that "took [him] by storm" in his early years: Walt Whitman's *Leaves of Grass* (1855) and *The Shorter Poems* of Robert Graves. Elsewhere he indicated his admiration of unknown authors of folktales and of the stories of Edgar Allan Poe, Henry James, Anton Chekhov, Ivan Turgenev, and James Joyce. His tales are frequently compared with Chekhov's, but the extent of Chekhov's or any other writer's influence on him is unclear. He gained immediate recognition as one of the foremost English short-story writers, and this reputation endured through the 1930's, when his own acclaim and that of the English short story in general experienced a decline from which neither has fully recovered. Coppard's tales have been translated into several languages, broadcast over the radio, and translated into films, notably by *Masterpiece Theatre* for public television. Frank O'Connor called Coppard and D. H. Lawrence the two great masters of the English short story; Rebecca West described him as "the great master of the short story of our times"; and L. A. G. Strong praised him as "the finest English short story writer of all time."

Story characteristics

Coppard wrote lyrical tales of English country folk, highly unified by a tragic atmosphere often associated with the landscape. He also wrote many fantasies or fables, sometimes in the tone of Rasselas. Aside from these, there are many stories in comic tones of marital disruptions and infidelities; of the insensitivity and ineptitude of the clergy and the rich; and of timid characters who shrink from life.

Biography

Alfred Edgar Coppard's remarkable life contributed to his early success. To such an influential editor-writer as Ford Madox Ford, he was a rustic wise man or gypsy, a character out of one of his own dark country stories. Coppard was born into poverty and attended only four years of elementary school in Brighton. His father was a tailor, his mother a housemaid; and when his father died young, Coppard had to help the family survive by taking a series of menial jobs. At age twenty-one, he became a clerk in an engineering firm in Brighton, where he remained for seven years, advancing to cashier. As a teenager and young man he walked the English countryside, absorbing its landscapes and the language of country folk he met in roadside taverns, a favorite setting for many of his later tales. He was a fine athlete and even supplemented his income as a successful professional sprinter. He married in 1906 and a year later took a better position as an accountant for an ironworks in Oxford, a position he held for twelve years. During his years in Oxford he read, often in the Bodleian, associated with students, heard and sometimes met such luminaries as Vachel Lindsay, Aldous Huxley, and William Butler Yeats, and, finally, began to write. He also became involved in Socialist politics, joined the Women's Social and Political Union, and served as an officer in the I.L.P. Finally, in 1919, having published seven or eight tales in journals like the *Manchester Guardian* and a few poems in journals like *The Egoist* (edited by T. S. Eliot), he decided to leave his position at the foundry and become a professional writer. On April 1, 1919, at age forty-one, he moved to a small cottage outside Oxford at Shepherd's Pit, where he lived alone in the woods, becoming aware of "the ignoring docility of the earth" and, finally, publishing his first collection of tales on the second anniversary (All Fool's Day, 1921) of his new career. His first book was well-received and thrust him into prominence as one of the leading English short-story writers. Over the next thirty years his production of tales, poems, and reviews was steady and of high quality. A second marriage to Winifred De Kok in 1931 endured, but his reputation as a short-story writer began to wane in the mid-1930's; his last collection of tales (1954) was not even reviewed by the *Times Literary Supplement*. His *Collected Tales*, however, was a clear success, and the autobiography he completed on the eve of his fatal illness in 1957 is a delight.

Analysis

The unique quality of A. E. Coppard's short fiction derives from his powers as a lyrical writer, his sympathetic understanding of the rural, lower-class folk who organically inhabit the English countryside so memorably evoked in his tales, and his "uncanny perception," as Frank O'Connor remarked, "of a woman's secretiveness and mystery." Coppard's earliest reviewers and critics emphasized the poetic quality of his tales. The title story from *The Field of Mustard* is one of the great stories in English, and it suggests the full range of Coppard's creative genius, including his lyric portrayal of the English countryside and its folk, especially its women, whose language and life-consciousness seem wedded to the landscape.

Like other lyric short stories, "The Field of Mustard" is nearly plotless. It opens with the suggestion that everything has already happened to the main characters, "three sere disvirgined women from Pollock's Cross." What remains for Coppard is to evoke the quality of these lives and the countryside of which they are a part; the tale proceeds as a kind of lyric meditation on life and death in nature. The women have come to "the Black Wood" in order to gather "dead branches" from the living trees, and on their way home, two of them, Dinah Lock and Rose Olliver, become involved in an intimate conversation that reveals the hopelessness of their lives. Rose, wishing she had children but knowing she never will, cannot understand why Dinah is not happy with her four children. Dinah complains that "a family's a torment. I never wanted mine." Dinah's "corpulence dispossesed her of tragedy," and perhaps because she has had the burden as well as the fulfillment of motherhood, she expressed the bitterness of life in what serves almost as a refrain: "Oh God, cradle and grave is all for we." They are old but their hearts are young, and the truth of Dinah's complaint—"that's the cusedness of nature, it makes a mock of you"—is reflected in the world around them: the depleted women are associated with the mustard field and the "sour scent rising faintly from its yellow blooms." Against this natural order, Dinah and Rose wish that "this world was all a garden"; but "the wind blew strongly athwart the yellow field, and the odour of mustard rushed upon the brooding women."

As Dinah and Rose continue their conversation, they complain of their feeble husbands and discover a mutual loss: each had been a lover of Rufus Blackthorn, a local gamekeeper. He was "a pretty man," "handsome," "Black as coal and bold as a fox"; and although "he was good to women," he was "a perfect devil," "deep as the sea." Gradually Coppard's pattern of imagery reveals the source of these women's loss to be the very wellspring of life— their love and sexual vitality. The suggestion is explicit in their lover's name, "Blackthorn," who had brought them most in life yet left them now with "old grief or new rancour." This grim reality is suggested earlier when the women meet an old man in the Black Wood; he shows them a timepiece given him by "a noble Christian man," but is met only with Dinah's profane taunt, "Ah! I suppose he slept wid Jesus?" Outraged, the old man calls Dinah "a great fat thing," shouts an obscenity, and leaving them, puts "his fingers to his nose." Dinah's bitter mockery of Christian love gradually merges with the sour scent of mustard and surfaces transformed in Rose's recollection of how Blackthorn once joked of having slept with a dead man. These women gathered in "the Black Wood" to collect dead wood from the living trees have in effect slept with death. The yellow mustard blooms quiver in the wind, yet they are sour. The same "wind hustled the two women close together," and they touch; but, bereft of their sexual vitality, they are left only with Dinah's earlier observation that "it's such a mercy to have a friend at all" and her repeated appeal, "I like you, Rose, I wish you was a man." The tale ends with the women "quiet and voiceless,"

> in fading light they came to their homes. But how windy, dispossessed, and ravaged roved the darkening world! Clouds were borne frantically across the heavens, as if in a rout of battle, and the lovely earth seemed to sigh in grief at some calamity all unknown to men.

Coppard's lyric tales celebrate the oral tradition. His stories are often tales of tales being told, perhaps in a country tavern (as in "Alas, Poor Bollington!"). In some tales an oral narrator addresses the reader directly, and in others the rural settings, the characters, and the events—often of love ending in violence—draw obviously upon the materials of traditional folk ballads. Coppard himself loved to sing ballads and Elizabethan folk songs, and the main characters in these stories are sometimes singers, or their tales are "balladed about." In many tales, Coppard used rhythmic language, poetically inverted constructions, and repeated expressions that function as refrains in ballads. The most explicit example of a tale intended to resound with balladic qualities is "A Broadsheet Ballad," a tale of two laborers waiting in a tavern for the rain to pass. They begin to talk of a local murder trial, and one is moved by the thought of a hanging: "Hanging's a dreadful thing," he exclaims; and at length, with "almost a sigh," he repeats, "Hanging's a dreadful thing." His sigh serves as the tale's refrain and causes his fellow to tell within the tale a longer tale of a love triangle that ended in a murder and an unjust hanging. Finally, the sigh-refrain and the strange narration coalesce in the laborer's language:

> Ah, when things make a turn against you it's as certain as twelve o'clock, when they take a turn; you get no more chance than a rabbit from a weasel. It's like dropping your matches into a stream, you needn't waste the bending of your back to pick them out— they're no good on, they'll never strike again.

Coppard's lyric mode is perfectly suited to his grand theme: the darkness of love, its fleeting loveliness and inevitable entanglements and treacheries. He writes of triangles, entrapping circumstances, and betrayals in which, as often as not, a lover betrays himself or herself out of foolishness, timidity, or blind adherence to custom. Some of his best tales, like "Dusky Ruth" and

"The Higgler," dwell on the mysterious elusiveness of love, often as this involves an alluring but ungraspable woman. Men and women are drawn together by circumstances and deep undercurrents of unarticulated feeling but are separated before they consummate their love.

Because of its portrayal of unconsummated love, its treatment of the rural poor, and its poetic atmosphere that arises from the countryside itself, "The Higgler" (the first story in *The Collected Tales*) is fully characteristic of Coppard's best work. It is not simply a tale of unconsummated love, for its main character comes to absorb and reflect the eternal forces of conflict in nature. For Coppard this involves more than man's economic struggle to wrest his living from nature; it involves man's conflict with man in war, his conflict with his lover, his conflict with himself, and ultimately, with his own life source, the mother.

Harvey Witlow is the higgler, a man whose business it is to travel the countryside in a horse-drawn wagon, buying produce from small farms. The story opens with the higgler making his way across Shag Moor, a desolate place where "solitude . . . now . . . shivered and looked sinister." Witlow is shrewd and crafty, "but the season was backward, eggs were scarce, trade was bad"; and he stands to lose the meager business he has struggled to establish for himself since returning from the war, as well as his opportunity to marry. "That's what war does for you," he says. "I was better off working for farmers; much; but it's no good chattering about it, it's the trick of life; when you get so far, then you can go and order your funeral." After this dismal beginning, Witlow is presented with an unexpected opportunity to improve his life in every way; but he is destined to outwit himself, as his name suggests, and to know more fully the "trick of life." As the tale develops, then, the reader watches him miss his opportunity and resume his descent into general desolation.

His chance comes when he stops at the farm of a Mrs. Sadgrove. Here the higgler finds plenty of produce as well as the intriguing possibility of a relationship with Mrs. Sadgrove's daughter, Mary, another of Coppards' alluring, secretive women. Mary's quiet beauty attracts Witlow, but he imagines her to be too "well-up" and "highly cultivated" for him. She shows no interest in him, so he is unprepared when, after several trips to the farm and an invitation to dinner, Mrs. Sadgrove tells him of her poor health and her desire that he should wed Mary and take over the farm. The higgler leaves bewildered. Here is his life's opportunity: the farm is prosperous, and he is far more attracted to Mary than to Sophy, the poor girl he eventually marries; besides, Mary will inherit five hundred pounds on her twenty-fifth birthday. It is simply too good to believe, and after consulting with his mother about his opportunity, Witlow grows increasingly suspicious. The reader has already been told that "mothers are inscrutable beings to their sons, always"; and Witlow is confused by his mother's enthusiasm over his opportunity. Even the natural world somehow conspires to frighten him: "Autumn was advancing, and the apples were down, the bracken dying, the furze out of bloom, and the farm on the moor looked more and more lonely . . . ."

So Witlow begins to avoid the Sadgrove farm and suddenly marries Sophy. Within months, his "affairs had again taken a rude turn. Marriage, alas, was not all it might be; his wife and his mother quarrelled unendingly," and his business fails badly. His only chance seems to be to return to the Sadgrove farm, where he might obtain a loan; but he does so reluctantly, for he knows Mrs. Sadgrove to be a hard woman. She exploits her help and "was reputed to be a 'grinder' "; and he has betrayed her confidence. In an increasingly dark atmosphere of loss, therefore Witlow returns across Shag Moor to the Sadgrove farm, where Mary meets him with the news of her mother's death that day. Now a prolonged, eerie, and utterly powerful scene develops as the higgler agrees to help Mary prepare her mother's body, which lies alone upstairs in a state of rigor mortis. He sends Mary away and confronts the dead mother, whose stiff outstretched arm had been impossible for Mary to manage.

Moments later, in their intimacy near the dead mother, Witlow blurts out, "Did you know as she once asked me to marry you?" Finally Mary reveals that her mother had actually opposed the marriage: "The girl bowed her head, lovely in her grief and modesty. 'She was against it, but I made her ask you . . . . I was fond of you—then.' " To his distress and confusion, Mary insists that he leave at once, and he drives "away in deep darkness, the wind howling, his thoughts strange and bitter."

Coppard's vision of life caught in a struggle against itself, of the violence in nature and its mockery of morality, of the deceit among men, and of man's denial of his true nature—all this is marvelously represented in one of his first and finest tales, "Arabesque: the Mouse." It is a psychological horror story of a middle-aged man who sits alone one night reading Russian novels until he thinks he is mad. He is an idealist who was obsessed by the incompatibilities of property and virtue, justice and sin. He looks at a "print by Utamaro of a suckling child caressing its mother's breasts" and his mind drifts to recall his own mother and then a brief experience with a lover. These recollections merge in a compelling pattern of images tht unite finally, and horribly, with an actual experience this night with a mouse. As a child horrified by the sight of some dead larks that had been intended for supper, he sought comfort from his mother and found her sitting by the fire with her bodice open, "squeezing her breasts; long thin streams of milk spurted into the fire with a little plunging noise." Telling him that she was weaning his little sister, she draws him to her breast and presses his face "against the delicate warmth of her bosom." She allows him to do it; "so he discovered the throb of the heart in his mother's breast. Wonderful it was for him to experience it, although she could not explain it to him." They feel his own beat, and his mother assures him his heart is "good if it beats truly. Let it always beat truly, Filip." The child kisses "her bosom in his ecstasy and whisper[s] soothingly: 'Little mother! little mother.' "

The boy forgets the horror of the dead larks bundled by their feet, but the next day his mother is run over by a heavy cart, and before she dies her mutilated hands are amputated. For years the image of his mother's bleeding stumps of arms had haunted his dreams. Into his mind however, now floats the recollection of an experience with a lovely country girl he had met and accompained home. It was "dark, dark . . . , the night an obsidian net"; finally in their intimacy she had unbuttoned his coat, and with her hands on his breast asked, "Oh, how your heart beats! Does it beat truly?" In a "little fury of love" he cried "Little mother, little mother!" and confused the girl. At that moment footsteps and the clack of a bolt cause them to part forever.

The sound of the bolt hurls him into the present, where, frightened, he opens his cupboard to find a mouse sitting on its haunches before a snapped trap. "Its head was bowed, but its beadlike eyes were full of brightness, and it sat blinking, it did not flee." Then to his horror he sees that the trap had caught only the feet, "and the thing crouched there holding out its two bleeding stumps humanly, too stricken to stir." He throws the mouse from his window into the darkness, then sits stunned, "limp with pity too deep for tears" before running down into the street in a vain search for the "little philosopher." Later he drops the tiny feet into the fire, resets the trap, and carefully replaces it. "Arabesque: the Mouse" is a masterwork of interwoven imagery whose unity is caught in such details as the mother's heart beat, the mother's milk streaming with a plunging noise into the fire, the mouse's eyes, and the "obsidian net" of night.

Coppard's characters are sometimes shattered by such thoughts and experiences, but the author never lost his own sense of the natural magnificence and fleeting loveliness in life. It is true that many of his late tales pursue in a more thoughtful and comic manner the natural and psychological forces in life that were simply, but organically and poetically, present in such earlier tales as "The Higgler"; that is, in some of his later stories the reader can too easily see him playing with thoughts about Alfred Adler, Sigmund Freud, and, repeatedly, Charles Darwin (whose prose he admired). Yet the last tale (the title story) of his final volume is one of his best. "Lucy in Her Pink Jacket" is almost a hymn to nature, a song of acceptance in which lovers meet accidentally in a magnificent mountain setting. Their lovemaking is beautiful, natural, and relaxed, and they accept the web of circumstances causing them to part. Coppard's description of his last parting character might serve as our own image of himself: "Stepping out into the bright eager morning it was not long before [he] was whistling softly as he went his way, a sort of thoughtful, plaintive, museful air."

Bibliography
O'Connor, Frank. *The Lonely Voice: A Study of the Short Story.*

Bert Bender

JULIO CORTÁZAR

Born: Brussels, Belgium; August 26, 1914

Principal short fiction

Bestiario, 1951 (*Bestiary*); *Final del juego*, 1956 (*End of the Game*); *Las armas secretas*, 1959 (*Secret Weapons*); *Historias de cronopios y famas*, 1962 (*Cronopios and Famas*); *Cuentos*, 1964; *Todos los fuegos el fuego*, 1966 (*All Fires the Fire*); *El perseguidor y otros cuentos*, 1967 (*The Pursuer and Other Stories*); *Ceremonias*, 1968; *Relatos*, 1970; *La isla a mediodía y otros relatos*, 1971; *Octaedro*, 1973; *Alguien que anda por ahí y atros relatas*, 1977.

Other literary forms

A professional translator for many years of both literature and other types of writing, Julio Cortázar has also published essays, literary criticism, and poems. His novels are well known and notable for their innovative structure, particularly the redoubtable *Rayuela* (1963, *Hopscotch*). Several of Cortázar's books are generically hard to classify: *La vuelta al día en ochenta mundos* (1967, *Around the Day in Eighty Worlds*) and *Ultimo round* (1969) are made up of McLuhanesque miscellanies, anecdotes, reflections, essays, and poems integrally blended with photos, drawings, and engravings. His most famous story, "La babas del diablo" was the basis for a highly acclaimed movie *Blow-Up* by Antonioni. The profits from Cortázar's 1975 comic book *Fantomas contra los vampiros multinacionales* were donated to the Russell Tribunal.

Influence

Cortázar is deeply committed to revolutionary socialism. He believes that his use of the fantastic serves this ideal by requiring what he has termed "reader complicity," a concept roughly equivalent to questions of "deconstruction": the need to see literary discourse not as a closed text but as the productive interpenetration of sociocultural spheres of meaning. In his pursuit of "anti-literature"—the opposite of logical and discursive expression—he has gone far in subverting traditional genres closely bound to the status quo. In this sense he is a revolutionary writer and a truly international figure.

Story characteristics

In Cortázar's fantastic and secretive stories, closely observed routines of daily life become suddenly defamiliarized. Tension is often produced by opposing the phenomenological or "real" world to that of the subconscious, where metamorphoses, time warps, phobias, and bizarre creatures exist freely. The language is startlingly effective in contraposing well-documented, recognizable registers of Buenos Aires Spanish with other highly creative linguistic devices.

Biography

Brought up in Argentina, Julio Cortázar was a teacher until his arrest following an anti-Perón demonstration in 1945. After passing examinations in literature and law in Buenos Aires, he went to France on a scholarship in 1951, becoming a free-lance translator for UNESCO and marrying Argentine Aurora Bernárdez. In the 1950's and 1960's, as his literary prestige increased, he traveled to Italy, the United States and Cuba. He now resides in Paris, where he continues to write.

Analysis

For an author such as Julio Cortázar, who is almost as well known in English and French as he is in Spanish (because of his political commitments, many of his works are banned in Argentina and other Latin American republics, making him less available there than in the United States or France), there is no way to select one truly representative story from among a fairly large *opus*. Therefore, let "Las babas del diablo" ("Blow-Up") serve synecdochically for a group of potentially representative stories—"El perseguidor" ("The Pursuer"), "Las armas secretas" ("Secret Weapons"), "Cartas de mamá" ("Letters from Momma"), "La autopista del sur" ("The Southern Thruway"), "Axolotl." "Las babas del diablo" is certainly one of Cortázar's most famous stories, having served as the basis of Antonioni's film *Blow-Up*. Although the film diverges widely in detail from the story and differs even in substance, the film nevertheless has served the story well in giving it an added recognition among an international audience not enjoyed by Cortázar's other stories.

Essentially, "Las babas del diablo" must be considered in terms of the issue of artistic ideology it proposes, an issue that one finds in large segments of Cortázar's fiction. The narrator is a professional writer-translator who is also an amateur photographer. His disinterested, spontaneous shots of the city— the result of a randomly focused camera—reveal one day a horrifying scene: a young boy being seduced by a woman who apparently serves as bait for a jaded pedophile. The latter, in a masterful touch of observer duplication, observes the entrapment of his prey from a vantage point in a manner similar to a photographer's focus. The reader of the text discovers the photographer discovering in his text (the photograph) the pedophile's contemplation of his own text (the drama of sexual encounter between the child and the man's lure).

What is stunning in the photographer's discovery of what he has captured by chance with camera is not the scene of sexual perversion; rather, it is the realization of how the accident of the photograph has destroyed the presumably well-wrought text of seduction. The narrator perceives a threatening gesture toward himself on the part of the waiting seducer and an expression of anguish on the face of the young boy, as though suddenly sensing that there is more to the encounter with the woman than he had first imagined. The narrator's sense of horror is, of course, not over having spoiled the plan of the two adults, but at having suddenly laid bare an underlying meaning that is both evil in terms of the degrading intent of the seducer and maddeningly inaccessible in the sense that all he is left with is the frozen image—an image suggestive of a human drama that is no longer present before him and that has played itself out in terms that he can never know.

The cultural allusion of the title is to the wisps of spiders' webs that float on the breeze, and it suggests not only the random intrusion of a sign of evil (the implacable entrapment of its victim by the spider, which in turn is made culturally symbolic of the "devil") but also the intangibility of the qualities and forces metaphorized in the allusion.

Although thematically interpretive readings of Cortázar's story may emphasize the issue of intangible reality intruded upon by the photographer's impertinent lens (a point of departure crucial to Antonioni's film), "Las babas del diablo" is more concerned with metaliterary (or metasymbolic) questions concerning literature and photography. Varieties of culturally symbolic discourses are neither neutral nor objective representations of a separable or independent reality. Rather, they serve as much to create and to modify (or distort) what they set out to portray as simply to reproduce it. Thus, the narrator, who, as part of the story's own texture of elusive meaning, speaks of himself alternately in the first and second persons, wonders whether he is not reading his own secret desire for a surprise meaning into the photograph, whether he is guilty of "unreal fabrications." Of course, there is no way of knowing; there is no independent narrator who can furnish the "real" meaning. The reduplicated text, the photograph, is thus suspended between two "readings," one a trivial encounter and the other a sense of pedophilic seduction: the Devil's slobber may only be the Virgin's threads (another cultural metaphor for the same natural phenomenon, "los hilos de la Virgen").

It is in his "second reading" of the photographic text that the narrator realizes the full extent of the scene witnessed by his camera. Understanding the boy to have been a helpless prisoner of the event recorded, the photographer senses himself to be a prisoner of his own artistic event: "And I could do nothing, this time I could do absolutely nothing. . . . I think I screamed, screamed terribly. . . ." The narrator's scream is the emotional correlative of his intellectual shock of recognition: too busy being an artist, being the impartial witness to a separable reality, he has unwittingly contributed to an event of evil corruption. The story of a loss of innocence, "Las babas del diablo" thus represents one significant example of Cortázar's fiction concerning the ideological implications—and limitations—of art.

Major publications other than short fiction
NOVELS: *Los premios*, 1960 (*The Winners*); *Rayuela*, 1963 (*Hopscotch*); *62. Modelo para armar*, 1968 (*62. A Model Kit*); *Libro de Manuel*, 1973 (*A Manual for Manuel*).
POETRY: *Presencia*, 1938 (*Presence* under the pseudonym of Julio Denis); *Los reyes*, 1949 (*The Kings*); *Pameos y meopas*, 1971 (*Pameos and Meopas*).
NONFICTION: *La vuelta al día en ochenta mundos*, 1967 (*Around the Day in Eighty Worlds*); *Buenos Aires, Buenos Aires*, 1968; *Prosa del observatorio*, 1968; *Viaje alrededor de una mesa*, 1970 (*Journey Around a Table*); *La casilla de los Morelli y otros textos*, 1973 (*Morelli's Box*).

Bibliography
Alazraki, Jaime and Ivar Ivask. *The Final Island: The Fiction of Julio Cortázar*.
Foster, David William. *Studies in the Contemporary Spanish-American Short Story*.
Giacoman, Helmy F. *Homenaje a Julio Cortázar*.
Lagmánovich, David, ed. *Estudios sobre los cuentos de Julio Cortázar*.

David W. Foster

NOËL COWARD

Born: Teddington-on-Thames, Middlesex, England; December 16, 1899
Died: Kingston, Jamaica; March 26, 1973

Principal short fiction

To Step Aside: Seven Short Stories, 1939; *Star Quality: Six Stories*, 1951; *The Collected Short Stories*, 1962; *Seven Stories*, 1963; *Pretty Polly Barlow and Other Stories*, 1964; *Bon Voyage and Other Stories*, 1967.

Other literary forms

Bennett Cerf praised Noël Coward as "the man who can do everything" and Coward was certainly that: actor, nightclub performer, and singer; lyricist, composer, and writer of a ballet; raconteur, bon vivant, and autobiographer; wit, poet, and novelist; short-story writer and author of radio and screenplays; revue sketch writer and leading dramatist. Katherine Tappert Willis in the staid *Library Journal Book Review* in 1967 called him the "man who has made headlines for 50 years," even if she missed the chic charm of his lyrics. Coward gave style to a whole generation or two. "Noël Coward," said Irish actor Micheál Mac Liammóir (whom Coward knew from the time the Irish actor had an English name as a boy player), "invented the 20's, just as Oscar Wilde invented the 90's." By the time he reached age twenty-one Coward had already written or had a hand in half a dozen produced plays. By 1924 he had enjoyed immense success with *The Vortex* (which he wrote and in which he played Nicky in London and New York), and that year he wrote *Hay Fever* (1925), *Fallen Angels* (1925), and *Easy Virtue* (1926) and began the immensely glittering career that included everything from some of the greatest West End hits of his time to takeoffs on modern verse under the name of "Hernia Whittlebot" and *A Withered Nosegay: Imaginary Biographies* (1922) and *The Last Bassoon: From the Diaries of Fred Bason* (edited by Coward, 1960).

Influence

Everything Coward did, even his crisp enunciation (said to have been adopted because his mother was hard of hearing), was imitated; but it was chiefly the brittle banter of his drawing-room comedies and not his fiction—his novel has been forgotten and his short stories too much dismissed as light entertainment—that had literary influence. Most of all he contributed style and wit.

Story characteristics

Coward's short stories have largely been denigrated as gossamer, light, sentimental, and anecdotal. They have also been described as moralistic

("Savonarola in a Tuxedo"), cynical, and long-winded. They have nothing of the desire to shock that some (incompetent) critics saw in his plays, such as *Design for Living* (1933); indeed, shocking the public, Coward said, was not only counterproductive for someone who wanted to be a celebrity, a *loved* celebrity, but also an "exceedingly second-rate" ambition. His stories are essentially blithe but moral commentaries on people and situations he encountered in his brilliant career and extensive travels. He is at his best when dealing with the sentimentalities of backstage life. His authorial pose is often that of the character he played in the film *Around the World in Eighty Days*: the script called for someone "superior and ineffably smug," and Coward said it was "type-casting."

Biography

Noël Pierce Coward was born in a suburb of London and went on the stage as a child. He could sing a little, and he became a celebrated performer. His mother had been musical, and he grew up in the "Edwardian era. . .saturated with operetta and musical comedy"; he became a composer and wrote many memorable songs, operettas, musical comedies, and even film scores. Most of all, he had a flair which made him a deft actor in his own and other people's plays; Sir John Gielgud confesses to having begun his career by imitating Coward's mannerisms and delivery. The whole era bore his stamp, in fact, for he epitomized the Bright Young Things after World War I. He had "ferocious chic," brittle charm, and complete professionalism, whether in the West End or in a Las Vegas nightclub. He was "The Master," suave, sophisiticated, witty, and unique.

Coward's life might be summed up in the title of one of his most hilarious songs, "I Went to a Marvelous Party"; he had a wonderful time, and he met everybody from Park Lane to the Fast Lane, many of whom were surprised to discover he was neither shallow nor unapproachable. They were also surprised to find that he was a moralist with a message, despite his offhand assurance that "a professional writer should be animated by no other motive than the desire to write, and by doing so, to earn his living" and his famous estimate of himself as having only "a talent to amuse." What audiences clamored to see, however, was the lighter side of Coward, and like a good performer he always turned the profile they liked best; but occasionally he sneaked in what the Communists used to call "social significance," and they forgave him. The theater and backstage were his life, and his work is at its best when it comes near theater people or those he knew well because he was a theater celebrity. Most Americans now know Coward only through old movies on television (*The Astonished Heart* or *In Which We Serve* or, worse, *Our Man in Havana* and *Bunny Lake Is Missing*), or through irritating (chiefly college or community-theater) productions of his light comedies in which suburban amateurs try for urbanity and achieve only suburbanity.

Analysis

Although the short story was not Noël Coward's forte, his efforts in that genre are marked by his usual impeccable grace, style, and professional polish, and are therefore well worth investigating. Like W. Somerset Maugham, whose stories some of the best of Coward's resemble, Coward often used fact as the basis for fiction; official British residents encountered on far-off Canton Island, became the basis for a story. One wonders if actual events triggered the most hilarious tale in *To Step Aside*, a story called "What Mad Pursuit?" Like the other stories in the volume it hints at Maugham and tries for Katherine Mansfield; *The Boston Transcript* said that in this volume Coward "over-Waughs the Waughs." In any case, the stories are all irresistably entertaining if open to the recurrent charge against Coward that he is "thin." Some of the stories are, to borrow a line from a Coward comedy, "Small talk—small talk—with quite different thoughts going on behind" or mere vignettes touched with sentiment and humor, often with (to quote a line from "Stop Me If You've Heard It") "that particular quality, that subtle balance between grave and gay" that "only really great comedians have."

The same qualities are featured in the long short story which gave the title to the collection *Star Quality*. Other stories in the collection are perfectly realized and contain some of the indomitable spirit that permitted Coward to write cheerfully, "There Are Bad Times Just Around the Corner" and remain as he said "not offensively high-spirited and still unaware that I belong to a dying civilization." Another magnificent Coward story is "Pretty Polly Barlow." In it, plain Polly Barlow gets roped into a world cruise with a selfish and self-indulgent aunt of horrifying proportions. The aunt dies and the young flapper (in the best tradition of the movies) takes off her glasses and, with the help of some fashionable new clothes, launches herself on a life of enjoyment. Of course she *shouldn't*, but we share her delight in what pleasant peccadillos have been thrust upon her. Even *Harper's* called the story "Pleasantly immoral."

There is less cynicism in touching stories such as "Mrs. Capper's Birthday" (her fiftieth, and without her husband Fred) and especially "Me and the Girls," in which the homosexual old song-and-dance man George Banks puts on his last performance with a chorus of nurses and other "hospital personnel" instead of chorines. These subjects which would be saccharine in other writers' hands, Coward infuses with sincerity; a grain or two of salt prevents cloying sweetness.

Major publications other than short fiction

NOVEL: *Pomp and Circumstance*, 1960.

PLAYS: *The Vortex*, 1923; *Hay Fever*, 1925; *Fallen Angels*, 1925; *Easy Virtue*, 1926; *Bitter Sweet*, 1929; *Private Lives*, 1930; *Post-Mortem*, 1931; *Cavalcade*, 1932; *Design for Living*, 1933; *Blithe Spirit*, 1941; *This Happy Breed*, 1943;

Quadrille, 1952; *Nude with Violin*, 1956; *South Sea Bubble*, 1956.

POETRY: *Spangled Unicorn*, 1932; *The Noël Coward Song-Book*, 1953; *The Lyrics of Noël Coward*, 1956; *Not Yet the Dodo and Other Verses*, 1967.

NONFICTION: *Present Indicative*, 1937; *Australia Visited, 1940-1941*, 1941; *Middle East Diary*, 1944.

Bibliography

Braybrooke, Patrick. *The Amazing Mr. Noël Coward.*
Castle, Charles. *Noël.*
Graecen, Robert. *The Art of Noël Coward.*
Lesley, Cole. *The Life of Coward.*
Levin, Milton. *Noël Coward.*
Morley, Sheridan. *A Talent to Amuse: A Biography.*

Leonard R. N. Ashley

JAMES GOULD COZZENS

Born: Chicago, Illinois; August 19, 1903
Died: Stuart, Florida; August 9, 1978

Principal short fiction
Children and Others, 1964.

Other literary forms
Of James Gould Cozzens' fourteen published books, thirteen are novels. Two won special acclaim; *Guard of Honor*, 1948 (Pulitzer Prize for Fiction, 1949) is widely regarded as one of the best American novels of World War II, and *By Love Possessed*, 1957 (Howells Medal of the American Society of Arts and Letters, 1960) was a major best seller. Cozzens' only volume of short fiction, *Children and Others*, contains seventeen of his twenty-nine published stories. It was a Book of the Month Club selection, as were five of his novels.

Influence
Although he did not suffer from lack of exposure during his fifty-five-year career, Cozzens never received the popular recognition accorded a number of his celebrated contemporaries, including Ernest Hemingway, William Faulkner, and F. Scott Fitzgerald. He was among the least read and least taught of major American writers. A man who zealously guarded his privacy, gave very few interviews, and who preferred to stay home and write, Cozzens dramatized, in notably antiromantic fashion, the trials and accomplishments of the responsible man of reason, who makes the best of things, many of them beyond his ability to control or foresee.

Story characteristics
Most of the stories in *Children and Others* display the author's well-known control, insight, and stylistic precision. In depicting his chosen people, middle- and upper-middle-class WASPs, Cozzens avoids the easy dramatic ending, is dispassionate although sympathetic, and develops a common theme, that of often unsuspected human weakness and defect.

Biography
Born in Chicago, James Gould Cozzens grew up on Staten Island, N. Y., attended the Kent School in Connecticut, and then went to Harvard in 1922, where he remained for two years. During the mid-1920's he served as a tutor of American children in Cuba and Europe. In 1927 he married Bernice Baumgarten, a New York literary agent; they had no children. In 1938 Cozzens was briefly a guest editor at *Fortune*. With the outbreak of World War II, he

entered the U.S. Army Air Force, worked on various classified stateside assignments, and was discharged as a major in 1945. Cozzens was a member of the National Institute of Arts and Letters, received two O. Henry Awards for short fiction in 1931 and 1936, the Pulitzer Prize for Fiction in 1949, and the Howells Medal of the American Society of Arts and Letters in 1960.

Analysis

Although most of the stories collected in *Children and Others* were originally published between 1930 and 1937, three of them—including James Gould Cozzens' best, "Eyes to See"—were first published as late as 1964. This fact suggests that his continuing interest in and developing mastery of the short-story form complements and illuminates his career-long devotion to the novel.

Of the five sections into which the collection is divided, the first two, "Child's Play" and "Away at School," containing ten stories between them, are perceptive recollections of childhood experiences. Although Cozzens is rigorously impersonal in his fiction, readers may be pardoned for imagining that one of the children of his title is the young Cozzens. We see a little boy turned in on his own imaginative self, and later a student at Durham (modeled on the Kent School, which Cozzens attended)—precocious, self-conscious, and at times frightened. The third section, "War Between the States," is composed of two Civil War stories. In the late 1930's, Cozzens assembled material for a Civil War novel, but found that he could not write it, and perhaps in the stories we see something of what that novel might have been. Section Four, "Love and Kisses," with four stories, examines the complexity of inexorably changing relations between men and women. The seventeenth, last, and longest story, "Eyes to See," written in 1963, is Cozzens at his distilled best, and hence deserves somewhat more extended consideration than its predecessors.

"Total Stranger," from Part One, which received the O. Henry Memorial Award for the best story of 1936, develops—with typical indirection and understated humor—the process by which a boy begins to see his father in an entirely new light. John is being driven back to his New England prep school by his father, who is distinctly dissatisfied with his son's undistinguished academic performance there, and who does not accept the boy's self-serving explanations and ill-constructed defenses. John has never had trouble getting around his mother; with his father, however, who is authoritative, competent, and always right, it is a different matter.

They stop for the night at a bad but conveniently located hotel and there encounter, by chance, a "total stranger," a Mrs. Prentice. John finds her notably attractive, and shortly discovers that the two adults know each other well from years before. John is curious and confused; Mrs. Prentice seems to know or remember an altogether different man, yet she says to his father,

"Will, you haven't changed a bit!" Words such as "strange," "bewildering," and "astonishment" register the boy's evolving perception of his father and realization, finally, that before he himself had been born, before his father had known his mother, before Mrs. Prentice had met Mr. Prentice, the two of them had been in love. Leaving the next morning, John says, "Somehow it all fitted together. I could feel that."

In literal fact, it is Mrs. Prentice who is to the boy a "total stranger"; metaphorically and more importantly, however, it is his father—or much of his father's life—which John has never before glimpsed. What John sees and hears and intuits of his father and Mrs. Prentice might have evoked alarm, contempt, amusement, or jealousy. That the chance meeting with the stranger in fact strengthens the boy's love and admiration for his father is apparent in the story's last line, in which John confesses that he never did do much better at school, but that "that year and the year following, I would occasionally try to, for I thought it would please my father."

"Farewell to Cuba," a second prize O. Henry Award winner in 1931, is set in Havana and focuses on Martin Gibbs, an American bank employee who is planning to leave the island the next day with Celia after twenty-two years' residence. Cozzens, who lived in Cuba in the 1920's, makes the island atmosphere an almost tangible force in the drama, with its heat, humidity, smells, noise, and the loneliness. Life there has worn Martin out and he is getting old, yet—much as he wants to—he is afraid to leave. He has always been a resident alien, and now, he feels, he is about to desert into the unknown. He wonders both how he can do it, and how he can not do it.

Up in their hot, airless hotel room, Martin tries to comfort Celia. At least they have some money, he tells her. She is haggard, sick, drenched with sweat, and cannot eat. She is trying to rest, perhaps to sleep. Tomorrow, he assures her, they will be gone, heading North. At Celia's urging, and over his protestation that he will stay with her, Martin spends his last night with three old friends—Joe Carriker, a car dealer, George Biehl, a banker, and Homer Loran, a newspaper publisher. He has always had a good time with them, Martin reflects, even though he cannot really see much point in it, since he expects never to see them again, but where else can he go? Through the four friends' conversation Cozzens delineates the life Martin has led for too long. His friends offer advice, warnings, endless drinks, horror stories, even a loan if that will help. Why must he leave? Martin cryptically explains, "As it happens, I'm not alone. That's all."

That is not all, as we discover shortly. Despite initial appearances, Celia is the wife of another man, a very powerful man from whom she has run away. On the stairs up to their room, with his friend George comatose in the lobby below, Martin wonders how his scheme can possibly work—it all seems a terrible mistake. He finds Celia as he left her, quiet on the bed, but there is an empty veronal bottle on the bureau. Celia has taken an overdose; she could not live with her sickness and fear or with her knowledge that Martin had taken ninety thousand dollars from the bank. All that remains is his confession and a call to the police. Martin has come suddenly and inescapably to the end of the road.

By withholding significant information—Celia's true identity, Martin's theft from the bank—Cozzens makes "Farewell to Cuba" in its conclusion a more overtly dramatic story than "Total Stranger," with its benign vision of familial relations. Almost from the beginning of "Farewell to Cuba," however, we have known—or at least strongly suspected—that Martin's escape attempt will fail, that he will not live happily ever after with Celia. How—not whether—he will be thwarted and finally entrapped is the question. Martin, an intelligent, experienced man, does his best. He has planned and schemed for freedom for himself and the woman he loves, and we are never allowed to regard him as a criminal; but in the end, for reasons he could not have anticipated, he is left bereaved, penniless, and facing a long prison sentence.

"Eyes to See," a subtle and ambitious narrative forty-two pages long, is another story of parents and children, love and death, and a boy's coming of age. Cozzens' multiplex development of the first-person retrospective point of view is not only intimately related to but is also a manifestation of theme. The story follows four days in the life of Dick Maitland, age fifteen, son of Dr. and Mrs. Charles Maitland, who on a football Saturday is summoned home from prep school owing to the wholly unexpected death of his mother, who—in the words of the title—he "never had eyes to see," as other than his mother, that is. Plans are made; telegrams, flowers, and family members (expected and unexpected) arrive; the funeral and subsequent gatherings occur; conversations are listened to and overheard; and Dick is sent back to school. The narrator's retrospective reflections on Mrs. Maitland's extramaternal identities shortly expose his more essential concern: those difficult discoveries of self and others that will form the ground of his postadolescent identity.

In Parts One and Two of this thirteen-part story, Cozzens juxtaposes two worlds, the old and the new, waiting to be born, the terrible, paradoxical simultaneous existence with which young Maitland will soon have to grapple. In Part One, bad luck is followed by worse (or is it better?) as Dick's mother dies, her hopeless case aggravated by specialists. In Part Two, at the school football game, bad luck (the star quarterback fumbles) is followed by a successful trick play which brings a touchdown. What these details collectively suggest is that the patterns and assumptions of the protagonist's sheltered, predictable childhood are breaking down. What is good, what is bad, what is usual, all require redefinition.

The new Maitland, as Cozzens first observes in Part Three, feels more than he understands, but not a great deal more. "That which was to be demonstrated lay beyond the then-grasp of my awareness; but only a little beyond."

This is the essence of Cozzens' management of point of view: fully delineating the obliquities and never overtly violating the integrity of the "then-grasp" of his fifteen-year-old protagonist. The adult retrospective narrator easily coexists with his younger self, providing facts, cultural and other history, but, most importantly, reflecting upon and illustrating his younger self's growing but uneven powers of awareness and assimilation.

Two relatives on whom the latter half of the story focuses are Cousin Eben and Cousin Lois, strikingly handsome and beautiful, respectively, nominally son and daughter-in-law of Dick's great-aunt Margaret, who had a generation before scandalized the Maitlands and other respectable people by running off to join the Perfectionists of Oneida (New York) Colony, and whose practice of "complex marriage" (polygamy) places Cousin Eben's ancestry almost beyond young Dick's "then-grasp."

What is within his understanding by the end of the story has much to do with love (or sex) and death, his awareness that "henceforth anything could happen to anyone." From an early point in the story, from his construction of the facts of his mother's biography, the narrator notes his younger self's squeamishness about sex, his refusal of reason's syllogistic instruction that "All children are a result of sexual commerce. A child was begotten on my mother. Therefore. . . ." Before the story ends, young Dick not only receives that fact but vicariously enacts it through the unknowing agency of Cousin Eben and Cousin Lois.

They, who have hitherto embodied mysteries of familial relations and antipathies and, obliquely, parentage, greatly embarrass their priggish young relative, himself now and forever an only child, by having produced three children in three years. As Dick is finally drifting off to sleep on the night of his mother's funeral, various words and phrases rise to consciousness. One is "Theophilus Pell," founder of the Oneida Colony; others are "complex marriage" and "bastard," which Cousin Eben has blithely admitted he is in the eyes of the law. Another is "exceptional children," first heard in Cousin Eben's discussion of the teaching of retarded children. Then Dick hears, shortly visualizes, and—despite prayerful forbearance—is excited to ejaculation by those exotic two in the next room making love: "I also, in extremis, had to give way. . . ."

"Eyes to See," in its lucid though formal prose, its self-assured handling of complex form, and its subtle and moving evocation of adolescent self-discovery, is Cozzens at his best in the short story. Although Cozzens once observed that he stopped writing short fiction when he no longer needed the money, and although he was more at ease and more impressive as a novelist, *Children and Others* is a memorable if uneven collection.

From the beginning of his career in the 1920's, Cozzens' stories and novels evoked sharply conflicting responses. By some critics he was set down as a literary and social conservative, narrow in interests and sympathies, orthodox in technique, increasingly pedantic in style, and too often given to melodrama and pathos. Admirers, equally vigorous, found him unquestionably a major novelist, a master craftsman, and a superb social historian, whose hallmarks were his irony, worldly wisdom, and deadly penetration into individual character and the social environment. Adjudication of such critical extremes must await the passage of time, but Samuel Johnson's dictum—that "Nothing can please many, and please long, but just representation of general nature"— appears to be the aesthetic principle by which Cozzens would be content to be judged.

Major publications other than short fiction

NOVELS: *S. S. San Pedro*, 1931; *The Last Adam*, 1933; *Castaway*, 1934; *Men and Brethren*, 1936; *Ask Me Tomorrow*, 1940; *The Just and the Unjust*, 1942; *Guard of Honor*, 1948; *By Love Possessed*, 1957; *Morning, Noon, and Night*, 1968.

Bibliography

Bracher, Frederick. *The Novels of James Gould Cozzens*.
Bruccoli, Matthew J., ed. *Just Representations: A James Gould Cozzens Reader*.
Hicks, Granville. *James Gould Cozzens*.
Maxwell, D. E. S. *Cozzens*.
Meriwether, James, ed. *James Gould Cozzens: A Checklist*.
Mooney, Harry John. *James Gould Cozzens: Novelist of Intellect*.

Allen Shepherd

STEPHEN CRANE

Born: Newark, New Jersey; November 1, 1871
Died: Badenweiler, Germany; June 5, 1900

Principal short fiction
The Little Regiment, 1896; *The Open Boat and Other Tales of Adventure*, 1898; *The Monster and Other Stories*, 1899; *Whilomville Stories*, 1900; *Wounds in the Rain*, 1900.

Other literary forms
Stephen Crane was both a journalist and a creative writer. His second novel, *The Red Badge of Courage* (1895), remains the best known of his works. He produced five other novels and two volumes of poetry in addition to his short fiction.

Influence
Some critics consider Crane to be a precursor to the Imagist school in poetry. Often ironic, his verse uses concrete imagery with powerful effect—"Mother whose heart hung humble as a button/On the bright splendid shroud of your son. . . ." Some images are so compressed that they must be interpreted by comparison with similar images in his prose.

Crane's fiction is an important part of American literature's shift from Romanticism into realism during the late nineteenth and early twentieth centuries. A friend of William Dean Howells and Hamlin Garland, Crane was even more avant-garde in his focus on the problems and details of ordinary life and in his generous use of conversational and street language. Disturbing friends and outraging critics, Crane set a precedent by exploring serious social problems in novels and sketches of New York street life. His better-accepted *The Red Badge of Courage* broke with conventional idealizations of war by showing an individual soldier's struggle to survive the emotional ravages of combat. Without insisting on direct connections, some modern critics see in Crane's fiction precedents for Ernest Hemingway's use of objective viewpoint, personifications of nature, and approaches to human suffering.

Story characteristics
Crane's sketches and stories are episodic; critics in his day complained that he could not develop a plot. Even quite brief stories may be divided into individual scenes. Conflict may be staged between two traits within a character, between characters, or between a character and the natural or social environment. Characters, often nameless, may have no knowledge of, or only partial knowledge of, their actual predicament. Stories may build philosophical and symbolic patterns at odds with each other, or may establish a theme

and then challenge it. Stories commonly end with a twist or shock which ironically lays open a gap between appearances and realities, thus demanding careful reader engagement. Crane seems to avoid telling the moral of a story, especially when he seems to be doing just that.

Biography

Stephen Crane was the fourteenth child of the Reverend and Mrs. Jonathan Townley Crane. A Methodist minister with family roots in the Revolution, relatives who had fought in the Civil War, and a library reflecting his strong interest in military history, the Reverend Crane steeped his son Stephen in both military and biblical lore; concerned with social welfare, he wrote several religious books decrying the evils and distractions of alcohol, baseball, dancing, gambling, novels, smoking, swearing, sexual impropriety, and theater. Stephen grew up to enjoy all these activities. Widowed in 1880, Stephen's mother wrote for religious periodicals and for newspapers in New York and Philadelphia. Stephen worked for several summers in a news bureau his brother Jonathan managed in Asbury Park, New Jersey. After doing poorly in college, he turned to journalism. As a correspondent, Crane traveled in the West, survived a shipwreck off Florida, and covered wars in Greece and Cuba. From 1897 on, when not on assignment, he lived in England with Cora Taylor, a former madam from Jacksonville, Florida. Crane died of tuberculosis at a sanitarium in Germany in 1900, and was buried in Hillside, New Jersey.

Analysis

Two of Stephen Crane's best stories, "The Open Boat" and "The Blue Hotel," exemplify his use of characters at odds with hostile environments and struggling with—or because of—their perceptions of those environments. The four men adrift in "The Open Boat" struggle against the sea; the correspondent in particular wrestles with his view of himself in relation to the natural universe. Within the winter setting of "The Blue Hotel," the Swede faces a hostile social environment, perceiving every person, word, and deed as a threat typical of the wild and violent West. He steadily forces the real people in the real social milieu to respond according to his perceptions.

The more Crane's characters are aware of their actual situations, the more sympathetic they appear to the reader. A gain in awareness can be a victory of sorts for a character, but is no guarantee of success. Crane's "little man" protagonist of the early sketches often gains knowledge but without significant results. "An Explosion of Seven Babies" shows him beaten for a traveling salesman's fault. When he meets the salesman, the little man kicks the glib peddler in the stomach. He thus displays human willingness to pass trouble along without truly resolving the root problem.

The men of "The Open Boat" are a step beyond mere reaction to an antagonist: they must struggle for three days just to survive. The survivors of the 1897 shipwreck were in fact a cook, Crane the correspondent, the ship's captain, and the oiler, but Crane's fictional use of the reality moves into symbolism. The classical conception of the human being as composed of appetite, reason, will, and the physical body is strongly paralleled. In "The Open Boat," the cook reflects on food, the correspondent ponders philosophical issues, the injured captain makes the decisions, and the oiler is notable for his physical action—rowing, then swimming once the boat capsizes. Contributing to the symbolic caste of these characterizations is Crane's rather typical use of epithets or labels instead of names. Three of the four men are known only by their roles; only the oiler, Billy, is given a greater degree of identity.

The limits of each character's point of view are important in Crane's stories. The survivors' perspectives in "The Open Boat" are limited from the start: "None of them knew the color of the sky. Their eyes glanced level, and were fastened upon the waves that swept toward them." The four are not only confined in a rocking dinghy scarcely able to hold them but also lack perspective. Their understanding of where they are and what help might come is too little, too uncertain for comfort.

The cook and the correspondent, in the first section of the story, dispute the difference between a house of refuge and a lifesaving station. The cook believes one or the other is near the Mosquito Inlet lighthouse. The oiler reminds them "We're not there yet." Nearing shore in Part Three, they must parallel the coast looking for surf low enough for a safe landing. The man they spot on shore gives signals they cannot interpret and, as dusk falls, they know only the wet, the rolling, and the noise of the sea; they row simply to stay afloat. Through the fifth and sixth parts, the correspondent mans the oars. A shark swims near, and the correspondent wishes someone else were awake to keep him company: later he learns the captain had seen the shark, too, but had said nothing. In Part Six he broods about drowning so close to shore. Crane here gives comment on a distressed human's reaction to an indifferent universe: ". . . if there be no tangible thing to hoot he feels, perhaps, the desire to confront a personification and indulge in pleas, bowed to one knee, and with hands supplicant, saying: 'yes, but I love myself.'"

On the third morning, the four turn shoreward, deciding that another day's struggle will only weaken them further. Once the boat overturns, only the oiler swims outright. The captain clings to the boat; the cook, having caught an oar, turns on his back and paddles in; and the correspondent works in, aided by a piece of a lifebelt. A man on the shore, described as having a halo, pulls the survivors from the shallows after they make it through the worst of the surf. Billy the oiler, the man most likely to survive, has drowned, and only after the others are on solid ground do they believe they can understand the experience: "The wind brought the sound of the great sea's voice to the shore, and they felt they could be interpreters."

As does the characterization, the story's structure shows Crane's shaping of reality for concurrent symbolic reading and his tendency to build plots more from conflicting points of view than from especially gripping action. Dividing the already short narrative into seven sections, Crane develops a naturalistic parallel with the Seven Days of Creation in Genesis. Each section includes a trait of the corresponding Creation Day. The First Day features the division of light from darkness: Crane's characters in Part One tell day from night by the color changes in the sea since "None of them knew the color of the sky." The Second Day brings division of the waters above the earth from those below the earth, that is, establishment of a horizon. Part Two closes as the men spot the top of the lighthouse, finding the horizon where before they saw only water. The Third Day of Creation reveals land divided from water by bringing the men close enough to see the shore. Day Four shows lights in the heavens—sun, moon, and stars—and Part Four includes uninterpretable signals from a man on shore; as the coast dissolves in dusk, a single star appears. On the Fifth Day, fish and sea creatures are made: in Part Five, the shark appears near the boat. The creation of humans crowns the Sixth Day, and Crane, in Part Six, comments on the human need to be important not only to the self but also to the universe, strongly suggesting that the human creates God in human image as a reaction to an indifferent universe. On the Seventh Day of the Genesis story, God rests; Part Seven of Crane's story brings the oiler to permanent rest. The others not only rest on solid ground and rest by sleeping, but also rest on the assumption that they can interpret the voice of the sea and find meaning in their ordeal.

The reader, too, may wish to rest on one interpretation or another, but risks missing another of Crane's typical features: irony. The death of the oiler, the physically strongest, is ironic when those who live are an injured man, a fat man, and a man who works more with his mind than with his body. The rescue efforts of the saintly figure are ironic, since the survivors have broached the worst of the surf by themselves and by chance. Ironic, too, is the use of the Genesis Creation motif to pose the view of an indifferent universe and a god-making humanity rather than to extend the traditional concept of the loving God who makes and cares for the human. Most subtly ironic is the potential Crane leaves for the reader to believe that any one point of view embodied in the tale—realistic, naturalistic, or symbolic—is the "right" perspective. All compose a whole. To take a single viewpoint as the truth is to fall in with the characters who feel qualified to read meaning in their experience after the fact.

Whereas "The Open Boat" uses a symbolic motif reflecting Crane's familiarity with scriptural tradition, "The Blue Hotel" focuses more on the interaction of its characters. Symbolic patterns of color, metal references, and so on exist, but are less obtrusive than the scriptural parallels in "The Open

Boat." The harsh winter weather, a hostile natural environment, serves as a backdrop to the human conflict. Also, while Crane uses labels for the Swede, the cowboy, and the Easterner, the reader learns the Easterner's name, and he uses regularly the names of Pat Scully, the hotel keeper, and Johnnie, Pat's son; thus the characters are given a bit more personality.

"The Blue Hotel" is also episodic. Its nine parts give the setting, then the travelers' arrival and their unhappy experiences in Fort Romper, Nebraska. At the hotel the Swede, the cowboy, and the Easterner play cards with Johnnie Scully until the Swede breaks up the game with his odd remarks reflecting a strong fear of being killed—a fear the others cannot understand and find offensive. The third part shows Pat Scully plying the Swede with whiskey to keep him from leaving. In the fourth, the others puzzle over the Swede's behavior until Pat Scully brings him back into the room. In the fifth part, the Swede grows more obnoxious during dinner; playing cards again, he accuses Johnnie of cheating. The two fight outside in the snowstorm in the sixth part, and the Swede leaves the hotel in the seventh. In the eighth episode the Swede plays tough in the local saloon, provoking a fight with the local gambler who knifes him, fulfilling the Swede's conviction that he would die in this wild Western town. The ninth section records a conversation between the Easterner and the cowboy several months after the incident. The Easterner confesses he had seen Johnnie cheating, and he suggests they all were partly responsible for the Swede's death. Irritated, the cowboy explodes in a classic Crane expression of limited perspective: "Well, I didn't do anythin', did I?"

Once more, composite perspectives are in play; but in "The Blue Hotel" they are crucial to both plot and theme. The Swede doggedly holds his distorted view of reality and dies by forcing others to respond to his distortion. The Easterner, by withholding the fact that Johnnie did cheat, falls in with the blind resentment the others have for the Swede. By doing nothing to change either the Swede's or the others' perspectives, the Easterner brings guilt on himself. The cowboy and Johnnie cannot see past their own needs for self-justification, and Pat Scully sees only the need to please his paying customers. Thus the tragedy of "The Blue Hotel" is enacted by characters whose views of reality are too limited to build understanding, understanding which could forestall a needless, deadly conflict.

Two other well-known Crane stories also use conflict of characters' perceptions, but with varied thrusts. "The Bride Comes to Yellow Sky," like "The Blue Hotel," pursues the theme of the difference between the old West and the new West, but in a lighter vein. Sheriff Jack Potter, riding the train back home with his new bride, worries about how the town will react when he suddenly shows up with a wife. The town, meanwhile, waits out another shooting spree of the drunken Scratchy Wilson, who enjoys forcing showdowns with the sheriff. Wilson happens onto Potter, who is trying to sneak his wife home unnoticed. Confronted with a sheriff not only unarmed at the moment, but also married, Scratchy gives up on the wild West image and walks away.

Similarly, "The Monster" depends on characters' perceptions of one another. One of Crane's longer pieces, its twenty-four episodes begin with the friendship between Jimmy Trescott, son of a Whilomville doctor, and Henry Johnson, the black hired man. Johnson rescues Jimmy when Trescott's home burns, but has most of his face burned away when he collapses below a shelf of chemicals in the doctor's laboratory. The grateful Doctor Trescott nurses Johnson back to health and insists on caring for him although the trauma has left him simple-minded and horribly disfigured. Steadily, the townspeople, unable to accept Johnson's appearance and behavior, turn away from the Trescott family. In contrast to the Swede in "The Blue Hotel," Trescott holds a very positive "fixed idea." He still sees Henry Johnson as a human being long after no one else can. Unlike the Easterner in "The Blue Hotel," Dr. Trescott dares to act on the truth he knows. Like the Swede, however, in the end the doctor pays for his inflexibility. The wages of humane loyalty is ostracism—a kind of social death in a small town such as Whilomville.

On first reading a Crane story, one may tend to agree with the early critics who bemoaned a weakness in plotting, but the sensitive reader who notes the outlines of the perceptions or world views of Crane's characters in conflict gains far more than the reader in search of a simple action story. By setting attitudes and opinions in conflict, Crane explores the human sense of self and the relation of the individual to the natural world and to society. Too wide a gap between perceptions and reality can mean isolation or death as in "The Monster" and "The Blue Hotel," can produce humor as in "The Bride Comes to Yellow Sky," or, as in "The Open Boat," may leave the human being with nothing more than his or her own perceptions as means to chart a boundless reality.

Major publications other than short fiction
NOVELS: *Maggie: A Girl of the Streets*, 1893; *The Red Badge of Courage*, 1895; *George's Mother*, 1896; *The Third Violet*, 1897; *Active Service*, 1899; *The O'Ruddy*, 1903 (completed by Robert Barr).
POETRY: *The Black Riders*, 1895; *War Is Kind*, 1899.

Bibliography
Bergon, Frank. *Stephen Crane's Artistry.*
Katz, Joseph, ed. *Stephen Crane in Transition.*
Stallman, Robert W. *Stephen Crane: A Critical Bibliography.*
Stallman, Robert W., ed. *Stephen Crane: An Omnibus.*

Ralph S. Carlson

ROALD DAHL

Born: Llandaff, South Wales; September 13, 1916

Principal short fiction

Over to You, 1946; *Someone Like You*, 1953; *Kiss, Kiss*, 1960; *Twenty-Six Kisses from Roald Dahl*, 1960; *Switch Bitch*, 1974; *Tales of the Unexpected*, 1977.

Other literary forms

In addition to an impressive collection of short fiction, Roald Dahl's works include plays, scripts for films and television, and well-known children's books such as *James and the Giant Peach* (1961) and *Charlie and the Chocolate Factory* (1964). One of his best-known scripts became the James Bond film *You Only Life Twice*. His major television series *Tales of the Unexpected* is aired in Great Britain.

Influence

Dahl's books have been translated into more than fifteen languages and have been best sellers in many countries. Popular in Britain and America, his stories appear in such well-known magazines as *Town and Country*, *The New Yorker*, *Atlantic Monthly*, *Esquire*, and *Playboy*.

Story characteristics

In addition to an early collection of stories about pilots and their experiences in war and peacetime, Dahl has produced a variety of modern Gothic stories which include grotesque fantasies, murder mysteries, and bizarre gamesmanship. Ironic reversals and surprise endings are major devices used to create effects ranging from comedy to terror.

Biography

After graduating from Repton School in 1932, Roald Dahl joined the Shell Oil Company of East Africa and early in his career began working also as a free-lance writer. He served as a Royal Air Force fighter pilot from 1938 to 1945 and held the position of wing commander. He has twice received the Edgar Allan Poe Award given by the Mystery Writers of America and continues to produce a variety of fiction and other works. He is married to the actress Patricia Neal and resides in Great Missenden, Buckinghamshire, England.

Analysis

In stories ranging from the macabre to the hilarious, Roald Dahl has enriched the modern Gothic tale through the indirection and subtlety of a narrative method loaded with surprises for the unsuspecting reader. His most famous works include "Lamb to the Slaughter," "Royal Jelly," "Man from the South," "The Landlady," and "Neck." In situations which include both domestic life and high adventure, Dahl creates suspense and humor of a highly sophisticated nature. Beyond the simple surface of the stories lie the psychological complexities that fascinate his readers. In many of the stories, for example, a hidden sexual theme controls the violence of the plot. Jealousy, hatred, lust, and greed dominate the characters of Dahl's stories.

In one of Dahl's most famous stories, "Lamb to the Slaughter," a woman murders her husband and succeeds in serving the murder weapon, a large leg of lamb (deadly when frozen, delicious when cooked), to the police officers who investigate his death. An ironic *tour de force*, the story is typical of Dahl's ability to develop an effect both chilling and wryly humorous. The story begins as Mrs. Maloney, a highly domestic, apparently devoted wife, awaits her husband's arrival home. His drink is prepared for him, but no dinner is waiting because on Thursdays they always dine out. Six months pregnant, Mrs. Maloney is especially eager to have company in the house since she now remains at home all day. But her husband's behavior when he arrives is much different from the usual friendliness and tenderness she expects. He drinks more than usual and rejects her sympathetic inquiries about his work as a detective. When he bluntly informs her that he is divorcing her, she is stunned and can only think of somehow maintaining their daily routine by preparing supper. Automatically, she descends to the cellar, where she reaches into the freezer and retrieves the first thing she touches, a large leg of lamb. After lugging the heavy package upstairs, she observes her husband standing with his back to her. When he angrily announces that he will go out for supper, she unhesitatingly swings the leg of lamb high in the air and brings it down hard on the back of his head.

Instantly killed, the detective falls to the floor with a crash that brings Mrs. Maloney out of her state of shock, and she begins immediately to fear the consequences for herself and her unborn child. She quickly plans a maneuver which will supply her with an alibi and which prepares the way for Dahl's ironic denouement. She puts the lamb into the oven to cook, tidies her hair, and rehearses an anticipated conversation with the grocer who will sell her the vegetables lacking for her husband's dinner. She manages to chat pleasantly with the grocer, and when she returns home, she unleashes her emotions in an expression of sincere shock and grief at the sight of her husband's crumpled body. Nearly hysterical, she telephones the police, who have all been friends of her husband and who treat her with sympathy and understanding when they arrive. Still, they check her alibi, and finding it satisfactory, they begin to search the house for the murder weapon, which may provide clues to the identity of the murderer. When Mrs. Maloney begs them, as friends deserving hospitality, to eat the meal she cannot bear to eat now, they hesitate but finally agree. While they are devouring the juicy lamb, their dining conversation reflects the irony of their unwitting ignorance: surely, they say, the murder weapon must be somewhere in the house, even right under their noses. In the next room Mrs. Maloney giggles as they finish off the main dish. A simple prose narrative turning on a single major irony, the tale has been transferred to film, and in either medium, it effectively demonstrates the author's characteristically ironic denouement, which has been likened in effect to the appearance of a grinning skull.

Another story which depends upon a pattern of ironies is "Royal Jelly," one of Dahl's famous tales of the grotesque. The plot concerns a baby born to a beekeeper who experiments with the products of his hives. Almost from birth, the beekeeper's new daughter loses weight because she cannot tolerate the formula his wife prepares. When the anxious mother becomes exhausted from worry and sleepless nights, the father calmly takes over the schedule of feedings. Noticing in one of his apiculture journals that bees nurtured on royal jelly, one of the richest food substances known to man, gain many times their birth weight, the concerned father secretly decides to add some royal jelly to the baby's formula.

At first the effect of the new food seems favorable, for the baby begins to eat eagerly and to sleep peacefully between feedings. When the beekeeper adds more and more royal jelly to the formula, the child gains weight and becomes cherublike in appearance. Within a short time, however, the baby demands such huge quantities of the food that the pleased father can no longer hide his secret. His wife is angry when she learns of his casual experimentation with their precious child. In his efforts to reassure her, he makes a still more startling revelation. He himself has been consuming tremendous amounts of the potent substance ever since he read that it helped overcome infertility in men. Their beautiful new baby is the result of his desperate attempt.

For the first time in months the anxious wife looks closely at her husband. To her horror, she finds his appearance much altered. He has not merely gained weight, but the contours of his body seem very strange. His neck has nearly disappeared, and tufts of stiff black body hair point upward to his head. The child in the crib, too, is surprisingly beelike in appearance. Like a queen bee, however, she has begun developing her digestive and reproductive organs at the expense of her tiny limbs. Her belly is swollen and glossy; her arms and legs lie motionless on the sides of the bed. The story concludes with the father's final ironic reference to his daughter as their "little queen." In his concern for her nurture, he has assumed the role of a worker bee; indeed, his capacity for emotional exchange is seriously diminished. The final scene depicts the horror and the helplessness of the mother estranged from her husband and her child by a bizarre turn of nature that she cannot comprehend.

Another of Dahl's most famous tales of the grotesque is "Man from the South," a story of macabre gamesmanship at a fashionable Jamaican resort hotel. The narrator of this story becomes the reluctant referee in a bizarre gambling arrangement between a wealthy, middle-aged South American businessman and a handsome young British soldier. Casually observing the satisfactory regularity with which the soldier's cigarette lighter operates, the South American bets that it will not light ten times in succession. The soldier accepts the bet eagerly, partly in an effort to counteract the boredom of the long summer afternoon and partly to impress an attractive young lady relaxing near the pool. The narrator observes the conversation with only mild interest until he notices the arrogance of the ugly South American, dwarfish yet somehow given to the gestures of a much more powerful man. The stakes he proposes are shocking: the South American offers his Cadillac against the little finger of the soldier's left hand, a situation at first refused by the soldier, then accepted by him in order to avoid losing face. The gamblers, the young lady, and the narrator-referee adjourn from their pool-side setting to an upstairs hotel room, where a maid rather questioningly supplies the objects the South American requests. A cutting board, a sharp meat knife, string, and pegs are provided; the soldier's left hand is tied to the board; the South American places his car keys on the table. All the while the narrator ponders the chilling efficiency with which the older man performs the task.

Despite the anxiety of the narrator and the young lady, the soldier begins nervously to test the lighter. The suspense grows as once, twice, as many as eight times the lighter functions perfectly, but a sudden interruption ends the gambling. The South American's wife enters and begins to shake her husband back and forth so rapidly that he resembles a cigarette lighter himself. Then the woman releases him and apologizes at length for her husband's disgusting gambling practices: he has already taken thirty-seven fingers and lost eleven cars. Moreover, the car he has been using this time belongs to her. In this characteristic reversal, she appears, at least to the narrator and the relieved soldier, a comfortingly normal deliverer and her husband appears the embodiment of the morally grotesque. The narrator relaxes as he watches her walk across the room to retrieve her car keys. Yet his glimpse of her hand on the table provides the final ironic twist. Only a thumb and finger remain on the claw-shaped hand, a grotesque suggestion of what she has won and lost from her husband. A study in the grotesque, the story demonstrates Dahl's surprising reversals and frequent use of an observer-narrator who serves as an intermediate figure between fantasy and reality.

A narrator of the intermediate type also provides the filtering consciousness in the story 'Neck,' which offers another ironic view of the hidden violence of domestic life. Comparable to "Lamb to the Slaughter," the story concerns Sir Basil and his wife, Lady Turton, proprietors of a major British publishing firm. The setting is Wooton House, one of the great stone houses of the

English Renaissance, and it is the atmosphere of wealth, beauty, and ease that attracts the narrator, an ambitious newspaper columnist who visits Sir Basil.

In the manner of relating inner-circle gossip, the journalist begins by describing the wealthy Turton family and Sir Basil's forty peaceful years of bachelor life, marked only by his consuming interest in a collection of paintings and sculpture. After the death of Basil's father, insiders on Fleet Street begin laying bets as to the number of bachelor days remaining to Sir Basil before one of the many ambitious London women succeeds in managing him and his fortune. The insiders are surprised, however, when Natalia, a haughty beauty from the Continent, triumphs over the resentful Englishwomen, and within six years she assumes control of the Turton Press. Having once been seated next to her at a party, the narrator observes that she is a lovely opportunist with the "air of a wild mustang," a rebellious spirit particularly contrary to the mild civility of Sir Basil.

All this information, the narrator insists, is merely background for his experiences at the Turton home, where he discovers an unusually eclectic environment created by the display of modern sculpture in the elegant gardens of the past. Sculptured topiary, pools, fountains, and lovely flowers provide the backdrop for the work of Epstein, Brancusi, and Saint-Gaudens, to name only a few of the artists included in Basil's collection. Certainly the narrator anticipates an enchanting weekend there while he gathers fascinating details about the Turtons for his column. Once in the house, however, he perceives that something is wrong, and he prides himself on his heightened sensitivity, the result of having spent much time in the homes of others.

The almost stereotyped situation of spending the weekend in a great house where mischief seems imminent gives succeeding events the quality of a Gothic burlesque. The journalist's anxiety is multiplied, for example, by the strange behavior of the butler, who requests that he receive in place of tips one-third of the guest's card winnings during the visit. The butler betrays also his dislike for the lady of the house and offers the tip that she almost always overbids her hand, an important detail of characterization which will be fully realized in the climax of the story. First, however, the narrator's suspicions are confirmed when, at dinner with the other guests, he observes a quite obvious triangular love relationship between Lady Turton, Major Haddock, a handsome retired serviceman, and Carmen La Rosa, a wealthy horsewoman visiting the Turtons. Sir Basil seems so distracted by the whole affair that the narrator feels quite embarrassed for him and hopes to leave as soon as possible.

The butler also displays great sympathy for Sir Basil and obvious hatred for Lady Turton, whom the butler regards as a mere usurper and source of pain to his beloved master. The evening concludes most awkwardly when the lady abruptly dismisses the guests, the butler, and even Sir Basil so that she can have a quiet chat alone with Major Haddock. Naturally, the narrator's suspicions mount to tremendous proportions. Indeed, the next morning the household seems more troubled than ever, and Basil behaves so strangely that the concerned narrator suggests they take a stroll around the grounds.

As they discuss the sculptures, Basil's only pleasant distraction, they cannot help noticing in the distance some intruders on the grounds.
Near one of the sculptures done by Henry Moore, a man and woman seem to be behaving flirtatiously. The woman playfully sticks her head and arms through the various openings in the huge statue; her companion laughs uproariously and draws close to her, perhaps to kiss her. As the gentlemen draw nearer, they realize with embarrassment that the pair below are not intruders but Lady Turton and Major Haddock, amusing themselves with Basil's prized collection. Suddenly the lady begins to struggle, however; her head is caught fast in the sculpture, and her partner cannot help her. While she waves her arms frantically, Basil becomes increasingly nonchalant as he slows his pace and resumes casual conversation with the narrator. Certainly Lady Turton has overbid her hand this time.

The climactic scene occurs when Basil and the narrator reach the anxious pair. Natalia furiously demands that Basil cut her free from the sculpture, and the butler soon appears with an ax and saw for his master to use. Basil pauses briefly, however, to admire the sculpture, which is one of his favorites. In the interim, the narrator observes that for some reason the butler seems to want Basil to select the ax, by far the more dangerous of the implements. Then Basil, with startling speed, reaches for the ax and without hesitation prepares to swing at his wife's neck. The terrified narrator shuts his eyes in anticipation of her death. When he opens his eyes, however, the ax appears still upraised, and the lady seems only gurgling with hysteria. Basil, acknowledging that the ax is much too dangerous for this job, exchanges it for the saw. For the narrator, however, the change of implements is insignificant now: in his imagination, the lady's execution has taken place, and after that terrifying moment, nothing will ever be the same. In contrast, Basil's eyes begin to twinkle secretly as he begins sawing through the heavy wood.

Readers are left with a puzzle at the end of the story, for from the description of the lady's head in the last scene, they cannot be absolutely sure that the blow has not landed. For them, as for the narrator, the event is realized in the imagination. Of course, on another level, the lady has only been threatened with a punishment that fits her crime of overreaching. What passes for justice in her case adds to the comic effect generated by the stereotyped situation and such characters as the aspiring journalist, the passionate usurper, the sinister butler, the major named for a fish, and the overweight horsewoman named Carmen. The mild-mannered Basil enjoys a triumph uncommon to most henpecked husbands.

Typical of Dahl, the story "Neck" has several sides: it is an entertaining anecdote offered by an easily impressed narrator, a modern Gothic tale with comic elements, and finally, perhaps, an examination of what constitutes reality. For readers cannot help identifying momentarily with the narrator when he closes his eyes to avoid watching the ax fall; what happens to the lady in the ambiguous final scene is, after all, what readers believe about it. Perhaps a major reason for the success and popularity of Dahl's work and of mystery stories in general is their essentially Romantic attitude, an insistence on a world of possibilities beyond humdrum daily existence. The vision such stories create provocatively mingles the extremes of joy and pain, laughs and shrieks of terror, in offering a singularly pleasing, if brief, sensation of the realities beyond typical human experience.

Chapel Louise Petty